The Applied Theory of Price

The Applied Theory

Donald N. McCloskey

Department of Economics
University of Iowa

# of PRICE

Macmillan Publishing Co., Inc.
New York

Collier Macmillan Publishers
London

To Joanne,
who sees the forest

Copyright © 1982, Macmillan Publishing Co., Inc.

Printed in the United States of America

Macmillan Publishing Co., Inc.
866 Third Avenue, New York, New York 10022

Collier Macmillan Canada, Ltd.

Library of Congress Cataloging in Publication Data

McCloskey, Donald N.
   The applied theory of price.

   Includes bibliographical references and index.
   1. Microeconomics. 2. Prices. 3. Microeconomics—Problems, exercises, etc. 4. Prices—
Problems, exercises, etc. I. Title.
HB172.M39   338.5'21   81–12406

Printing: 3 4 5 6 7 8   Year: 3 4 5 6
ISBN   0-02-379420-8

□ *Preface*

The main novelty in this text on the theory of price derives from its numerous examples and its 1000 or so worked problems. While giving the student the usual outline of the form of economics, it stresses throughout the ways in which an economist uses the form to think about substance.

The motive is clear. A college graduate in engineering can predict that a badly designed bridge will fall down, and why; a college graduate in chemistry can predict that a badly designed compound will blow up, and why. A college graduate in economics should be able to predict that a badly designed tax on gasoline will hurt society, and why. Too often, I think you will agree, he cannot. Our students understand, more or less clearly, the derivation of demand curves from choice-theoretic axioms, the symmetry of consumption and production theory, the role of prices in a market economy, and many other things. But too often they do not know how to apply them and have no idea how to find out. They know the formalities but not the substance of economics.

Whatever the purpose of a course in price theory—whether it is meant to produce informed citizens, perspicacious economic actors, generally educated graduates, useful social engineers, or creative economic scientists—it should give the student more than the formalities. Problem solving does. A lesson on externalities can take the form of an abstract essay: "Define 'externality' and translate it into concise mathematical form." Alternatively, it can take the form of a concrete problem: "Is it true or false that because California is beautiful and has many magnificent public parks it is likely from the economic point of view to be overpopulated?" Like the prospect of being hanged in a fortnight, problems wonderfully concentrate the mind. Students (and, I can say for myself, teachers) do not understand a piece of economics until they have faced and answered problems applying it. Indeed, without this practice they scarcely recognize the economics: a problem is a way of saying "Note well." Textbooks in economics so far have told *about* economics. This one tells about but also tells *how*.

The "about" book is excellent in its place, toward the end of an economic education rather than toward its beginning. After you are knowledgeable about the flesh and blood of economics, the exposure of the logical skeleton comes as a wonderful discovery. Someone who thinks of Jones the consumer, the Ford Motor Company, and the southern textile industry in terms of miscellaneous bits of marginal analysis and is then presented with one of the many books translating and extending Samuelson's *Foundations of Economic Analysis* for the common reader has an experience of intellectual delight. The generation of Samuelson himself, which is responsible for the current texts, was educated originally in an older, more applied economics, and had the delightful experience of discovering its general principles. "Bliss was it in that dawn to be alive,/But to be young [and trained in engineering mathematics] was very heaven!" The attempt to have our students leap directly to heaven, however, has been a mistake. A book in microeconomics these days can contain not a single derivative, or even very many equations, yet communicate the message that the form of economics is its scientific substance. The students learn economic calculus before they learn to reason economically, and their capacity for reasoning is damaged irreparably. The point is not to banish formal training from economics but, rather, to place it at the right stage of the educational process.

The idea of using hundreds of practical problems to transmit a skill is a commonplace in other fields. My college textbook in calculus, and no doubt yours, was jammed with problems, more than half of them answered; the chemistry text was only a little less so. Reading about applications of the theory is a step in the right direction; the completed voyage is to apply the theory oneself.

An economist can hardly maintain—with due respect to Leontief—that economic understanding is produced by a unique recipe calling for large amounts of problem solving in fixed proportions. The production function is doubtless neoclassical to the extent of permitting substitutions. The hypothesis suggested by the experience of other fields, however, is that the ratio of problem solving to other techniques in teaching economics is at present inefficiently low.

The other features of the book are pedagogic implications of this hypothesis. The test of utility in problem solving alters the standard list of topics a little, chiefly in order and emphasis. The treatment of supply and demand is unusually full because supply and demand is unusually useful: the book returns to it repeatedly, each time with new sophistication in using it. The analysis of two-factor production functions has been moved away from the theory of the firm and the industry, where it would only slow down the story, to the theory of marginal productivity and the demand for factors of production, where it *is* the story. The Condorcet–Arrow paradox and similar issues in political economy are treated not as a puzzling addendum but in the middle of a chapter on welfare economics, itself in the middle of the book, as a step in the development of national income as a measure of welfare. Giving measurable utility and risk a full treatment and locating it with ordinal indifference curves early in the book, instead of back in a section of special topics, recognizes its growing importance in economics and its many applications. Consumers' and producers' surpluses get an unusually full treatment as well, because they link the welfare economics of national income, index numbers, and general equilibrium to supply and demand. In all, applied welfare economics is emphasized in the book because it motivates well the behavioral theories, such as marginal productivity. The novelties of mathematical coverage are purposely few: an economic explanation of Lagrangean multipliers, elasticities of excess supply and demand, simple derivations of the Slutsky and related relations among a consumer's elasticities of demand, and a few others. These are included for their uses rather than for their beauty.

When a piece of analysis is not useful, it is not included, whatever the tradition of textbooks has been. Viner's analysis of cost curves, for example, is well-beloved but in its traditional form is not worth the fat chapter usually devoted to it. It appears in this text in a nontraditional form that highlights its usefulness. A younger tradition favors a section on linear programming, but the payoff in economic insight is too small at the level of mathematical and economic sophistication of advanced undergraduates or first-year graduates to warrant the large investment of pages necessary to do it well. Monopolistic competition is treated thoroughly, but only in the locational context in which it has proven its usefulness. The kinky oligopoly demand curve is a poor example of discontinuities in marginal revenue and appears to be wrong besides. Every topic must meet such tests of cost and benefit in making the student into a problem solver.

Certain mechanical features of the book contribute to the teaching by problem and answer. The questions in the text are answered fully, as models for answering the questions that conclude many of the sections. These answers are given in the *Instructor's Manual*, available to adopters, which contains as well a large number of fresh problems. The summaries at the end of each section will help the student to keep sight of the essential formal skeleton to which the problems are attached.

Each point is explained in as many ways as possible—verbally, mathematically, and diagrammatically. The book is unusually full in verbal explanation of the most important points and has double the usual number of diagrams. The diagrams have self-explanatory titles, and points and lines within them are named rather than symbolized. Each diagram has a full explanatory caption (prepared for the most part by John Martin), written to follow the argument but not the wording of the text. The knowledge most worth having in economics is elusive and bears repetition.

The novelty of a problem-solving approach to price theory requires little adjustment in the teacher's routine. The novelty will be in what happens in the student's study, not in the teacher's class. The *Instructor's Manual* contains suggestions for the class. The teacher may wish to reallocate time away from the less useful pieces of price theory and toward the more useful or to lecture a little more on formal principle and a little less on applications, although the many applications in the book may well suggest still more. Above all, the teacher may wish to assign problem sets.

The book fits the standard courses in intermediate price theory. The student is supposed to have had an introductory course in economics, most of which has been forgotten over the summer, and no mathematics beyond high school. Since students of intermediate economics can be expected to be taking a calculus course (in which they will acquire some mathematical sophistication as well as the techniques of differentiation), the mathematical level in the book rises gradually, though calculus stays in the footnotes.

For a single-term course for college juniors who have had the usual basic economics course, and that at a fairly elementary level, the core chapters will be ample, constituting a short book:

Chapter 1. The Budget Line
Chapter 2. The Consumer's Choice
Chapter 5. Trade

A still shorter course, aiming only at a thorough grasp of supply and demand (a noble and sufficient aim, it should be said), might thin out the later chapters in the list. For the year-long course microeconomics for undergraduates that ought to become the standard, the whole book can be worked through methodically.

For very well-prepared college juniors and for MBA students, the whole book can be swallowed in a term without indigestion. I have used it on such audiences for many years with success, finding that in a very selective college even sophomores in their first economics course can digest most of it. We underestimate how much students can learn in three or four months if they are simply required to do so and face up to the requirement: look what the first course in college calculus or chemistry demands and gets from them.

For first-year students of graduate economics, the book is useful as a refresher and foundation. I would like to see this book (or the others like it that will follow, if the principle of entry is true!) put in the hands of every one of them for their first month or so of graduate school. It is my experience, and probably yours, that even in highly selective graduate programs the students are weak in the bread and butter of economic thinking. Let them eat cake in December.

The book is harder than others in some ways, easier in others. The demands on the students' toleration for abstraction are considerably lighter than in other books; the demands on their willingness to think concretely are considerably heavier. But the payoff will be students who see the social world as a thing of opportunity cost, marginal benefit, competition, collusion, equilibrium, search, ownership, maximization, entry, and scarcity; that is, students who think like economists. And that, we can agree, is a fine thing.

☐ *Acknowledgments*

In the summer of 1975 Gilbert Ghez of Roosevelt University and I decided to write this book. After putting in much work, he decided that the opportunity cost of text writing was too high, but his contribution to the final product remains large. My other debts, specific and general, run as follows. At various times Alyce Monroe, Linda Freeman, Tricia Pate, Marye Allen, and Marguerite Knoedel have typed order out of chaos. Anthony English, Charles Place, and Eileen Schlesinger, my editors at Macmillan, have been patient and encouraging far beyond the call of profit, as was at an earlier stage Frank Enenbach of Prentice-Hall. Together they illustrate the paradoxical economic theme that capitalism can be altruistic, or perhaps that altruists can be capitalists. My students at Chicago and Iowa in courses on price theory since 1968 have forced me to think clearly and have laughed at my jokes. John Komlos, Moonie Lavi, Bruce Lehmann, and Fred Lindahl favored me with written comments, but I am uneasily aware that I have lost track of many others whose comments, written and verbal, mattered, too. I want them to tell me so that I can make amends later. Bart Taub, Kevin O'Meara, and especially John Martin made unusual contributions to the book as teaching assistants in recent courses— all three contributed greatly to the stock of problems, and Martin did the captions for many of the diagrams and numerous other editorial tasks with high intelligence and good taste. Carla Oakes copyedited the manuscript. But again I fear that my faulty memory is not recalling every name it should. I shall not forget Gary Hawke of the Victoria University of Wellington for his detailed and encouraging comments. And special thanks to Professor Michael V. Leonesio, of the Univ. of Missouri, St. Louis.

I cannot thank by name but thank here all those who labored anonymously over commentaries to publishers, a task that brings bad pay but that defines our community. The four whose identities I do know—Philip Graves, Jon Nelson, Richard Sutch, and John Vernon—gave Macmillan remarkable value for money and me much good counsel. I thank especially the friends and commentators and editors who have told me I was doing something good. Someone who will exaggerate, even flat-out lie, to raise a man's spirit is friend to a higher truth.

□ *Contents*

The Applied Theory of Price

Introduction

I.1 The Uses of Price Theory

You have just embarked on the study of the theory of price, known also as *microeconomics,* the science of markets.[1] Although its Greek meaning is "small housekeeping," microeconomics is not the little or trivial portion of economics. On the contrary, it comes close to being the whole. It is essential for an understanding beyond the first course. Not all fields of economics are based on microeconomics, but all strive to be: most of the lasting advances in economic thinking over the past century or so have consisted of reducing one or another piece of economic behavior to microeconomics. Without a firm grasp of it, your understanding of foreign trade, economic growth, governmental regulation, socialism, and even depression and inflation will be shallow and confused. Further, microeconomics defines the profession. A grasp of it distinguishes an economist from an historian, sociologist, engineer, or applied mathematician interested in economic matters. Confident skill in price theory defines an economist just as confident skill in diagnosis defines a medical doctor or confident skill in leading others in battle defines a military officer. Other skills are subordinate. When economists say scornfully that so-and-so, a reputed expert on economics, is "not an economist," they do not mean that he is ignorant of the institutions of economic life, or of its history, or of its statistics, or of its mathematical representations; rather, they mean that he is ignorant of the theory of price.

What, then, is this craft or sullen art? Put briefly, it is the understanding of maximization and markets and is one of the great products of the human mind. Although many economists (this one, for example) believe that the theory of price has made economics the most successful of the social sciences, one need not be so arrogant to admire its theoretical beauty and practical power. Invented in the eighteenth century, refined and applied in the nineteenth and twentieth centuries, it is

---

[1] The first of many economic atrocities against English. The other part of economic theory, *macro*economics, is the study of unemployment and the absolute level of prices; microeconomics, by contrast, is the study of employment and of relative prices. These distinctions, though, will mean little to you at present.

the characteristic gift of economics to the study of man. It applies, of course, to the enormous range of ordinary markets for wheat, ditch diggers, insurance, haircuts, heroin, police, guns, Bibles, typewriters, telephones, professors, and preachers. But it also applies to extraordinary markets for education, property rights, political favors, pollution, marriage, discrimination, business skill, charity, public housing, and crime. Price theory, in short, explains much human behavior.

Price theory has been remarkably successful relative to other explanations of human behavior—Marxism, for example, or psychoanalysis. Its central postulate of self-interest, as an instance, appears to be correct. Like fishing without a hook, price theory without self-interest is possible, but it will not catch many fish. A simple hook will suffice: the self-interest need not be a three-pronged monster of ego, but only that mild self-concern typical of people dealing with strangers. And the inferences from the postulate appear to be correct as well.

This is not to say that price theory has the definiteness of chemistry, for example, with its invariant atomic weights and other physical constants. It does, however, say that price theory illuminates and sometimes even predicts human behavior. To put it another way, an economist would win money from a noneconomist in betting on the effects of instituting rent controls in Berkeley, California, of establishing an import tariff on Italian shoes, or of lowering the price for synthetic textiles.

Talking so confidently about the successes of microeconomics may seem peculiar. After all, through the miracle of type and television you may have heard of disagreements among economists—that if all the economists in the world were laid end to end, they would not reach a conclusion or that if ten economists went into a room, they would emerge with eleven different opinions. Ha, ha.

The first lesson in microeconomics is, do not believe everything about the economy or economics that you read in the newspapers. Macroeconomics—the study of unemployment and inflation—is in some ways more difficult and less successful than is microeconomics, and most of the notorious disagreements among economists are about unemployment and inflation, not about markets. Likewise, meteorologists agree on their expectations of weather conditions tomorrow, but disagree on national drought next year or the prospects of a worldwide ice age. The disagreements that remain about markets often turn on disagreements about the moral desirability of some event, not its occurrence. Economists can agree on "positive" economics (i.e., what is), yet disagree on "normative" economics (i.e., what should be). The meteorologists and other nonsocial scientists are spared this additional source of disagreement.

The agreement among economists on microeconomics, positive or normative, is in fact astonishing. If one polled the 20,000 or so members of the American Economic Association on the following questions, to pick a few, most would answer each "yes," whereas noneconomists would answer "no":[2]

[2] A recent survey of opinion among economists found that economists do in fact agree with these or similar propositions. See J. R. Kearl, Clayne L. Pope, Gordon T.

1. If gasoline is taxed to conserve energy, will the quantity consumed go down by a nontrivial amount, despite the protestations of drivers that they cannot do with less than the amount they are now consuming?
2. Is free trade with Japan and Italy, allowing American producers to be driven out of business by unlimited amounts of Japanese televisions and Italian shoes, on the whole a good thing?
3. Would consumers be better off if the Civil Aeronautics Board (regulating airlines) and the Interstate Commerce Commission (regulating surface transport) did not exist?
4. Was the rise in the standard of living of the American worker over the last 50 years chiefly a result of better knowledge and more machines rather than of activity by trade unions?
5. Is the American Medical Association, far from being a benevolent organization set on improving medical care, in fact a monopolistic trade union on the level of the plumbers, longshoremen, and electricians?
6. Does the resting place of the burden of the social security tax depend exclusively on how workers and employers react to a change in wages, and not at all on the legal division of the tax (paid half by workers, half by employers)?
7. Is there an optimal amount, greater than none, of polluted air and water, noisy streets and airports, and ruined countryside?

And so forth. Notice that the economist's answers—all affirmative—are bipartisan, stepping on everyone's toes. Furthermore, they are not mere matters of faith. The economist could persuade the open-minded noneconomist that these economic propositions are true by the same method that an astronomer would use to persuade them that astronomical propositions are true: refined common sense, consistent reasoning, and ascertainable fact.

The economist, however, faces a special obstacle, namely, that the people being persuaded are themselves economic bodies and have elaborate opinions of their own. The Earth's own opinion about the movement of heavenly bodies would probably be that they all move around the Earth itself in circles and (sometimes) epicycles. Untutored economic experience is a bad teacher of economics, just as the unaided eye is a bad teacher of astronomy. Practically everything that you thought you knew about economics before studying it is wrong. Inflation hurts everyone; market competition is chaotic, leaving consumers at the mercy of business; if the penny is eliminated from circulation, merchants will round up to the nearest nickel, contributing to inflation; the draft makes the armed forces cheaper; price controls on natural gas will always help consumers; energy consumption can be predicted on the basis of physical need, without regard to its price; Lake Erie should, of course, be drinkable; a temporary boycott can permanently reduce a high price; a rise in the minimum wage makes workers better off; a tax imposed on employers in Chicago is never a burden on employees; and on and on and on in monotonous confusion.

Whiting, and Larry T. Wimmer, "A Confusion of Economists?" *American Economic Review* 69 (May 1979): 28–37.

The vocabulary of such ersatz economics, the economics of the man in the street (and too often of the journalist), contributes to the confusion: when "sellers outnumber buyers," prices fall from "exorbitant" levels, "gouging" down through "fair" and "just" to "unfair," "cutthroat," and "dumping"; unions and corporations have more "bargaining power" than do their opponents and, hence, "exploit" them; a consumer can "afford" medical care, "needs" housing, and finds food a "basic necessity"; business managers maintain their "profit margins," probably "obscene" or "unwarranted," by "passing along" a higher wage, which causes workers to demand still higher wages, in a "vicious circle"; the protection of the American worker's "living wage" from "unfair competition" by "cheap foreign labor" should be high on the nation's list of "priorities." To understand price theory you must clear your mind of such cant, just as to understand astronomy you must stop thinking of the sun's "rising."

The agreed ideas in price theory use words such as "scarcity," "opportunity cost," "rationality," "competition," "monopoly," "equilibrium," "incidence," "arbitrage," "production functions," "marginal product," and "supply and demand." A widespread but childish presumption to the contrary, however, learning the vocabulary is not learning the science. The essential idea of the science is quite simple. The governing image of ersatz price theory is that of one person cheating another, taking "unfair" advantage; that of <u>real price theory is of many people trying to cheat all the others, but in fact helping them</u>. The unintended consequence of selfish behavior is altruistic; the apparent chaos of competition, unplanned by moral or civil law, leads to orderly social change; direct attempts to help this or that person are thwarted by the logic of economic events. Such are the paradoxes in which economists delight. The key to the paradoxes is that each person's behavior is constrained by all others' behavior. The person is a molecule in a social gas bumping against other molecules, unable to move in a selfish straight line. <u>The theory of price is based on methodological individualism</u>, adding up the bumping molecules.

The theory itself, it should be noted, tells us little about the world; only the facts of the world tell us about the world. One cannot solve great social problems standing at a blackboard. The theory of price merely opens our minds to the facts. Neither an axiomatic system nor a compilation of behavioral constraints, it is a tool for clear thinking.

I.2 How to Learn Price Theory

Price theory combines the pleasures of physics and history: it has the precision (nearly) of the one and the human appeal (nearly) of the other. But it also combines their difficulties. A student of physics may find price theory indefinite; a student of history may find it formalistic. The indefiniteness will just have to be tolerated. Such, alas, is life. The formalities are mathematical and warrant the following notes.

To students with a weak mathematical background: Some slight mathematical competence is useful for economics at any level and essential at the level of this book. It has been said that mathematics is a language, and so it is—the characteristic language of science. The linguistic accomplishment essential here, however, is merely high school geometry and, especially, algebra. But a language is forgotten if it is not used. Many people have forgotten their high school mathematics by the time they come to economics. Fear not. If the logic of similar triangles or of solving for x and y in $y = a + bx$ and $y = c + dx$, not to speak of what α means in X^α or whether log X has anything to do with the lumber industry, is by now hazy in your mind, you will discover that it, like a language learned but forgotten, will come back as you use it in this book. If you are taking simultaneously a calculus course (as you should be if you want to study economics at a more advanced level), all the better.

To students with a strong mathematical background: You start with an advantage over your less mathematically sophisticated colleagues in understanding economics, which in the last 30 years or so has become heavily mathematical. The mathematics in this book, even in the "mathematical" footnotes and appendices, is easy for someone with facility in elementary calculus and trivial for someone with two years of calculus, not to speak of a course in analysis or differential equations. Beware, however, that your advantage does not in the end become a disadvantage. Mathematics is the queen of the sciences, but understanding her is not identical to understanding her subjects. It is easy for a student of economics to overlook this, bemused by marvelous graphs and elegant equations, and to substitute economic mathematics for economic thought. As Alfred Marshall, the great English economist (himself trained thoroughly in the mathematical methods of nineteenth-century physics) said long ago: "The function . . . of analysis and deduction in economics is not to forge a few long chains of reasoning, but to forge rightly many short chains and single connecting links."[3] The best protection against long but weak chains is to ensure that you can answer an economic question verbally in the light of economic reasoning before leaping to a more formal treatment. Most true economic assertions make sense verbally as well as mathematically, and each method is a test of the soundness of the other.

Beyond not being either paralyzed by or swellheaded about the formalities of price theory, the key to success in it is solving problems. Texts, instructions, lectures, and audiovisual aids on hammering a nail or knitting a row are pointless if you do not give the thing a try. The problems and questions in this book, both in the text and after each chapter, are essential reading. Many of them are answered, showing you how to approach the unanswered ones. The following general hints may help:

1. Think about the question concretely, putting yourself into it.
2. Attempt to answer it at first in an exclusively verbal and jargon-free way.

---

[3] Alfred Marshall, *Principles of Economics*, first published in 1920, 8th ed. (New York: Macmillan, 1948, seventh printing 1959), Appendix C, p. 773.

3. Having gotten the basic message verbally, add the formalities of diagrams and mathematics only if these will add worthwhile precision.
4. Be brief and plain speaking; use simple diagrams with no superfluous labeling; do not rederive well-known mathematical truths. Do not, in short, clothe confusion in formalities.

You will probably find that for the first half or so of the book you miss the answers repeatedly. Economic sophistication takes time to acquire. Do not let this depressing experience stop you from reading the problems carefully. They are usually not mere regurgitations of the text but, rather, additions to it worth digesting by themselves.

Price theory cannot be learned in ten easy lessons. Understanding, like most things, is scarce, demanding the sacrifice of many hours of more agreeable occupations. A text on price theory cannot be read like a summer novel. A course in price theory is at least as difficult as a course in, say, chemistry. Yet at the end of all this labor is a great prize: an understanding of the way in which society works.

Part One | DEMAND

The Budget Line

1.1 Scarcity and the Budget Line

A thing is <u>scarce</u> when it is <u>desirable but limited</u>. Oxygen to breath is desirable, but it is not limited and it is therefore not scarce. Garbage is limited, but it is not desirable, and it is therefore not scarce. Food, housing, education, military protection, justice, freedom, books, candy, friendship, children, drinkable water, travel, clothing, and good health are all desirable and limited and therefore scarce. The unpleasant truth from which all economics begins is that scarcity is very common. We cannot, in other words, have much more of the things we want merely by wishing. The fact is unspeakably sad. It is sad that our relative poverty, our inability to have all the automobiles or ice cream sundaes or beautiful poems or true loves that we would like confines us so. It is sad, as economists put it in their monotonous little joke, that there is no free lunch. We are cast out of the Garden of Eden. As the Lord put the point to Adam, "In the sweat of thy face shalt thou eat bread, till thou return unto the ground."

The definition can be put diagrammatically by saying that, along the scale of amounts of desirable things, such as books in your library or food in the world, there comes a stop. You and the world cannot have unlimited amounts of books or food. In Figure 1.1 the area marked unattainable is just that.

The diagrammatic way of putting it makes clear that each book is scarce, though it is not the "last" book that uses up the allotment of books. The reason is that the scale treats all books alike. They can be substituted one for the other. They are, to use a strange word popular among economists, *fungible*. The notion that scarce goods are fungible is astonishingly powerful in applications. The University of Iowa beats the University of Michigan for the Big Ten championship by two points in double overtime, 70 to 68. Whose two points won the game? One's first thought is to look to the last points made. But points are fungible. Any two points can be viewed as the crucial points that make the difference between a score of 68 to 68 and 70 to 68. The free shot that Weisskoff made in the first five minutes of play

Figure 1.1
A Scarce Thing Is Limited

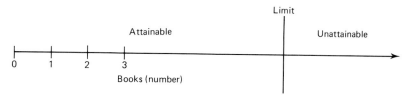

The limit is the most books you can consume because you are not infinitely wealthy.

counts as much as the last. For the purpose of making the score what it is, there is effectively no last, no crucial, point. Consider the following.

Q: Your mother gives you $500 toward a new car. If you were going to buy the car anyway, in what sense is her donation "for" the car?

A: Not at all, or entirely, or partly. The answer is arbitrary because the question is meaningless. You can, if you wish, take the very dollar bills from her gift and pay them to the car dealer. That would be to use them "for" the car. But if you used those dollar bills to pay your grocery bills for a while, using other dollar bills to buy the car, would her gift have been any less "for" the car? No. You are made $500 richer and use the money to buy a car. On the other hand, one could say that some other $500, gotten "earlier," was used to buy the car. Since money is fungible, there is no sensible way in which to draw a line between the mother's money purchases and the nonmother's money purchases.

The applications of the idea of fungibility are limitless. In general, when you hear someone speaking of a certain portion of points or money or motivations as being the reason for a victory or a purchase or a decision, you should suspect that they are ignoring the fungibility of things.

□
Scarcity in Two Dimensions

Because of fungibility, the value of the last increment to a pile of things governs the value of the whole. All the things measured along a single axis (tons of wheat, numbers of books, dollars of income) are taken to be perfect substitutes and are therefore indistinguishable. But wheat is distinguishable from books, of course. The world is not composed of all-purpose little animals that can be eaten, drunk, used for roofing, sewn into cloth, and so forth. The natural extension of the single axis measuring amounts of, say, books is a second axis measuring amounts of all other goods, or some particular good. The expression of scarcity in such a diagram is that the person or the society represented must stay inside some area (see Figure 1.2).

To capture the essence of scarcity, the curve bounding the attainable area need not be smooth, much less straight. Its shape depends on details in the technology of producing books or all other goods with the various resources available. For present purposes the only essential feature of its shape is that it eventually slopes downward; that is, one cannot in a world of scarce resources consume unlimited amounts

**Figure 1.2
Scarcity in Two
Dimensions Means
Staying Inside One's
Budget Line**

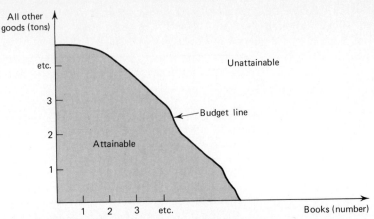

Only the attainable area is attainable. Its edge slopes down. That is, to get more books, one must give up all other goods if one is on the budget line.

of both books and all other goods. Nevertheless, for diagrammatic simplicity in the next few chapters we shall use straight lines. Economists call the lines all manner of names: transformation curve, production possibility curve, books-all other goods trade-off, production frontier, or simply the budget line.

□ A great deal of useful thinking about the world consists simply of close reasoning about the budget lines facing people and societies. The first thing to notice about a budget line between, say, education and other goods is its slope. The decrease in education divided by the increase in other goods along the line ("the rise over the run") measures the cost of increasing the amount of one commodity in terms of sacrificed consumption of the other. It is the cost of one item in terms of the other. It measures, in other words, the *opportunity cost* of one in terms of the other. The economist's way of measuring the cost of, for example, studying economics one more year is not the pain and suffering involved in the year, but the maximum amount of other scarce things sacrificed by choosing the additional year. The cost of assembling another automobile is not the sum of physical toil and mental anguish suffered by workers or the sum of their hours of work, or even really the sum of their paychecks, but the output of other things producible by the workers in some alternative employment of their energies. The alternative employment can be in another job for a wage, in housework, or in leisure.

***Opportunity Cost Is
the Slope of the
Budget Line***

T or F: The cost to a student of a year of college or graduate study is the cost of books, tuition, room, and board.

A: The student sacrifices all that he or she could earn employed full time at the highest wage attainable (including in the wage the amenities of the job), which need bear no relation to the sum given in the question. Therefore, false. Notice that to gain a year of education older students typically sacrifice more than do younger students, because the older students can usually earn higher wages. This is one reason (not a very important one) that the years of education are concentrated in youth.

Opportunity cost, then, is a result of scarcity. Though unpleasant, it is a fact of life. You cannot go to school full time and also work full time. You cannot study economics and also revel to the fullest in the latest album. You cannot go home for Christmas and also go to Fort Lauderdale. To live is to choose, and to choose is to come under the eye of the economist, or of the poet:

> Two roads diverged in a yellow wood,
> And sorry I could not travel both
> And be one traveler, long I stood
> And looked down one as far as I could
> To where it bent in the undergrowth.[1]

☐
The Slope Is the Relative Price

At a rather more mundane level, it is important to realize that the opportunity cost of a thing is simply its price along the budget line, namely, the amount of other things you have to give up to acquire a unit of the thing you are buying.

Q: You go to a bar serving beer at $0.50 a glass and wine at $1.00 a glass. What is the price of wine in terms of beer?

A: Clearly, it is two glasses of beer per glass of wine. One dollar spent on a glass of wine could buy two glasses of beer. Notice that, because the question asks for quantities of beer (in terms of beer) per glass of wine, one divides the given money price of wine (dollars per unit of wine) by the money price of beer:

$$\text{Beers per wine} = \frac{\text{glasses of beer}}{\text{glasses of wine}} = \frac{\$/\text{glass of wine}}{\$/\text{glass of beer}}$$

This is elementary, but mildly confusing at the beginning. The currency used does not matter.

Q: A Victorian novel takes 20 hours to read; the *Classic* comic book recounting the same story, or for that matter a Donald Duck comic book, takes 15 minutes. Considering the time spent, what is the price of novels in terms of comics? (Refer to Figure 1.3.)

A: Again, clearly

$$\frac{\text{Comics}}{\text{Novel}} = \frac{\text{hours/novel}}{\text{hours/comic}} = \frac{20}{1/4} = 80 \text{ comics per novel}$$

[1] From "The Road Not Taken" from *The Poetry of Robert Frost* edited by Edward Connery Lathem. Copyright 1916, © 1969 by Holt, Rinehart and Winston. Copyright 1944 by Robert Frost. Reprinted by permission of Holt, Rinehart and Winston, Publishers. British rights to reprint these lines by permission of Jonathan Cape Limited, London.

or 0.0125 novels per comic. With two weeks of leisure in which to read 10 hours a day, you could consume 7 Victorian novels or 560 comics; alternatively, you could trade off 80 of the 560 comics in order to read 1 novel and $560 - 80 = 480$ comics, or 2 novels and $560 - 80(2) = 400$ comics. In other words, you can consume in two weeks any straight-line combination between 7 novels and 560 comics.

**Figure 1.3
The Budget Line of
Literary Consumption**

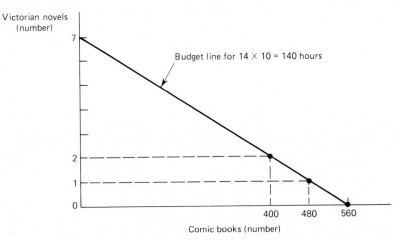

The budget line, drawn for a given number of hours allocated to reading, shows by its slope the rate at which the consumer foregoes reading novels to read comic books.

An economist must develop competence in interpreting varying slopes of budget lines as varying relative prices. Budget line 1984 in Figure 1.4 represents a higher price of books relative to clothes than does 1985. To keep straight which price has changed, imagine sliding 1985 over to 1985′ (read it as "1985 prime"), parallel to 1985 (parallel

**Figure 1.4
Which Relative Price Has
Fallen?**

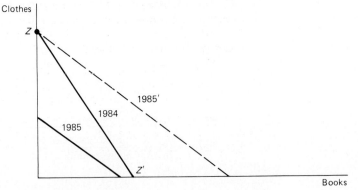

In 1985, more books can be acquired per unit of clothing than in 1984. This is easily seen by pretending through an appropriate shift in the budget line that the maximum quantity of clothing is the same in both years.

THE BUDGET LINE **13**

budget lines have, of course, the same slope and represent, therefore, the same relative price). Starting at the same amount of clothes, Z, you could acquire more books along 1985' than along 1984. Evidently from 1984 to 1985 books became relatively cheaper (and clothes, of course, relatively more expensive.).

Q: Instead of sliding the 1985 line over to Z, slide it over to Z'. Are books still relatively cheaper in 1985 than in 1984? Explain.

A: Yes, they are relatively cheaper. The same amount of books (namely, the amount at Z') buys fewer clothes in 1985 than it did the year before. To say that books buy you fewer clothes is to say that books have cheapened.

Summary

"Scarce" means "desirable but limited in amount." It is natural for economics, the science of scarcity, to assert that scarcity is pervasive. But it is also true. Desirable things are scarce either because they are given and limited (like sunlight in Sweden in December) or because to get them one must use up resources that could be used to produce other things (like a plane ticket from Stockholm to Tahiti). In the latter case scarcity is expressed as a budget line along which the consumer operates. The slope of a budget line measures the relative price of one item in terms of another. In other words, it measures the rate at which one item can be substituted for another. In still other words, it measures the opportunity cost of one item, that is, the amount of the other item sacrificed. As the slope changes, the opportunity cost or relative price changes.

QUESTIONS FOR SECTION 1.1

1. Suppose that bread and housing must be paid for in three ways: money, nontransferable ration coupons, and time spent waiting. To get, for example, a loaf of bread one must pay 10 pence, hand over 3 ration coupons, and stand in line 2 hours.

a. Draw the three budget lines for bread and housing facing Steve Jones. What is the relevant budget constraint along which he can operate?

b. *True or false:* As more bread and less housing are bought, the price of bread relative to housing that Jones faces rises.

2. Malcolm Falkus buys books at a fixed price per book but buys paper at a lower price per ream the more he buys (that is, on paper he gets a quantity discount). Draw the books-paper budget line that Falkus faces.

3. Draw your budget line between consumption now and consumption later (later stands for all future years lumped together). What is the slope (a magic word, one that is used every day)?

True or False

4. When it is desirable, sunlight is scarce.

5. Another way in which to characterize scarce things is to say that they cost something.

6. Children are scarce only because raising them requires *money* expenditure by their parents on food, shelter, and school education.

7. A tax of $3.00 per fifth of liquor will raise the price of Cheapo White Lightning relative to very expensive liquor such as Drambuie, Grand Marnier, and Napoleon brandy.

8. A sales tax of 10% on the before-tax price on automobiles and groceries will leave the price (after taxes) of automobiles relative to groceries unchanged.

9. As more guns are acquired at the sacrifice of butter, the opportunity cost of one additional gun (in terms of butter) falls.

1.2   Income in the Budget Line

Income Is the Height of a Budget Line

☐   In the last section, it was pointed out that the budget line facing a consumer has a slope that measures the cost (the price) of an additional unit of one item relative to the necessary sacrifice of other items. In the present section, it is shown that the budget line also has a position (as well as a slope) that measures the income of the consumer. It is obviously desirable to have a budget line that is positioned higher everywhere, that is, to be richer. It is also desirable to have access to the whole of a higher budget line rather than to only part of it, a truth that applies to the value of gifts in the form of goods as against gifts in money.

T or F: A family receiving charity is equally well off if it receives a monthly check for $100 as if it receives free housing worth $100 a month.

A: False, unless the family would have consumed more than $100 worth of housing of the sort provided by the charity when it had the additional $100 check or unless the housing provided can be resold. The family's budget line is moved from very poor to poor by the $100 check. See Figure 1.5.
   The entire line poor (including the crossed segment) is available to the family. By the gift of charitable housing in the (market) value of $100, however, the budget line is moved from very poor to the uncrossed segment of poor. The crossed segment is not available. Think about that. The area under the budget line—the area available to be chosen—is smaller than it would be if the $100 check were given to the family.

For this reason most economists agree that charity given directly in goods ("in kind") is worse than charity in money, supposing that the purpose of charity is to increase the happiness of the poor by their own lights. Of course, public housing, public food stamps, and public medical care are not in fact meant merely to increase the happiness of the poor by their own lights. Some observers believe their lights are dim. And the purpose may be in fact to increase the happiness not of the poor but of the rich, by assuring the rich that poor people live in housing that is decent, or at any rate distant.
   Do not confuse slopes and positions.

Figure 1.5
Gifts in Kind and
in Money

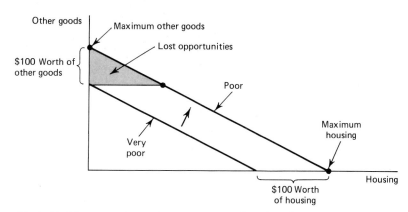

Gifts in kind increase consumption opportunities less than do gifts in money. The area lost opportunities is available to the recipient of $100 in money but not to the recipient of $100 worth of housing.

T or F: Cadillacs are cheaper for a professor than for a poor student.

A: False. A professor's budget line between Cadillacs and food is farther out than that of most students, but both face the same price of Cadillacs relative to food; that is, the slopes of their budget lines are the same, as shown in Figure 1.6.

No one can have unlimited amounts of everything, but a professor with $20,000 can have more of everything than can a student with $2000. When the professor has used fully his large but finite income he, too, faces a trade-off of one thing for another, the opportunity cost of Cadillacs in terms of food. If, as is assumed here, the two face the same prices, the professor's budget line is parallel to the student's.

Figure 1.6
A Price Is a Price

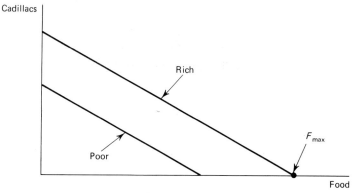

The rich person sacrifices Cadillacs for food at the same rate as the poor person. The difference between the rich person and the poor person is that the rich one has a higher budget line.

The Income Effect

The amounts of a good that consumers buy will change when their incomes and the prices they face change. Between 1947 and 1957 in the United States, the amount of visits to doctors, operations performed, medicine taken, and other medical care consumed increased some 24%. Why? The premise of the theory of the demand for goods is that events such as these are to be explained (if possible) not in terms of the need or whim of consumers but in terms of changes in their incomes and prices. The latter are observable, which is one merit of the theory. From 1947 to 1957, the per capita income of consumers increased in real terms (i.e., after removing general inflation) by 29%; the price of medical care relative to all other items of consumption rose 16%. The budget line changed in position and in slope, as a result of which, the theory asserts, the quantity of medical care changed.

The effect of an increase in income alone (i.e., holding relative prices constant) on the amount of a good consumed is called the *income effect*. It can be positive or negative. If it is positive for, say, medical care (i.e., an increase in income causes an increase in the amount of medical care consumed), medical care is called a *normal good*. Normally one expects consumers to consume more of a good when they become richer. For example, from the evidence for 1947–1957 just given, it appears that medical care is a normal good, since the quantity consumed of medical care increased as income did even though its relative price rose (this by itself, as we shall soon see, would cause the quantity to decrease).

If the income effect is negative, the good is called an *inferior good*. "Inferior" here is merely a technical word: it does not mean that the good in question is a bad, garbage to be disdained by consumers with refined tastes; it means simply that, as a consumer's income rises, the consumer substitutes away from the good. Consider Cynthia Morris, a poverty-stricken carnivore who consumes only hamburger and the best steak at given prices. In Figure 1.7 she is initially at point *A*. She then receives a large inheritance from a rich aunt; that is, her budget line moves out parallel to the old one (parallel, of course, because the prices do not change). She will move from *A* to some point on her new budget line. If she moves to point *B* after the rise in her income, she has reduced her consumption of hamburger and has increased her consumption of steak; in other words, hamburger is for her an inferior good and steak a normal good.

T or F: Not all goods can be inferior.

A: True. Look at Figure 1.7. If both were inferior, the consumer would have moved after an increase in income to a point such as *D*. This behavior would violate the premise that more is preferred to less, because she would have preferred (chosen) less of both commodities even though (by virtue of her increased income) she could have consumed more of both.

T or F: If one good is inferior to a consumer, the other goods consumed by her must be, considered as a group, normal.

A: True. Take hamburger as the one good and steak as all other goods, applying the same reasoning as before.

Notice that the hamburger-steak example involves two varieties of the same commodity, namely, meat. As the consumer gets richer, she consumes more of the better variety of meat and less of the worse. A bad variety of a thing is often inferior, technically speaking, even when the thing as a whole is normal. It would not be surprising to find that, within food, hominy grits and bacon ends are inferior (sirloin steak being normal); or that, within transportation, bus and subway rides are inferior (auto trips being normal—a difficulty that enthusiasts for public transportation face); or that, within clothing, homemade cotton underwear and wooden shoes are inferior (factory-made shirts being normal). Broadly defined, goods (food, transportation, clothing) tend to be normal.

**Figure 1.7
Inferior and Normal
Goods**

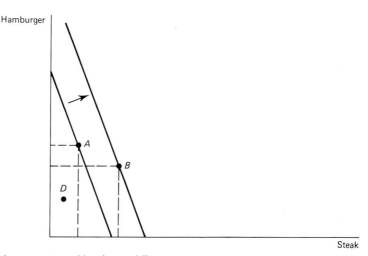

If consumption of hamburger falls as income increases, consumption of steak must rise if the consumer is to stay on the budget line. Thus at least one good must be normal.

☐
***The Simple
Mathematics of
Budget Lines***

All this can be summarized in a little easy and essential high school algebra. Suppose that a consumer is allocating money between candy and all other goods. Call the income of the consumer Y dollars (Y is one of many conventional symbols in economics for income). Signify prices by P's and quantities by Q's, with subscripts attached of C for candy and A for all other goods. The consumer spends all his or her income by definition, for savings is one of the other goods. Evidently, then, the sum of all the prices times quantities of the goods (i.e., the sum of what the consumer spends on each good) will equal income: $P_C Q_C + P_A Q_A = Y$. This is one equation for the budget line. Alternatively, if you wanted to express it as a relationship between Q_C on the vertical axis and Q_A on the horizontal, you could solve it for the variable Q_C, to get in a couple of steps the equation

$$Q_c = \frac{Y}{P_c} - \frac{P_A}{P_c}\left(Q_A\right)$$

If the consumer is on the budget line, the amounts of candy and all other goods satisfy this equation in one of its forms. That is, the consumer is free to choose only one of the two quantities Q_c or Q_A. The quantity Y/P_c is an intercept, as they say in high school algebra. When Q_A is zero, Q_c takes on the value of the intercept. When Q_A is something greater than zero, the amount Q_c is reduced to some degree, the degree depending on the slope of the budget line, namely, $-P_A/P_c$. The slope is the relative price, or opportunity cost.

The theory of consumption, which is the subject of this and the next few chapters, asks how the consumer reacts to changes in the intercept and slope of the budget line. In other words, it asks what is the income effect, discussed here, and what is the relative price effect, discussed in the next chapter. To put it still another way, the theory asks what happens to a consumer when the budget line changes in some way.

Summary

The position, as distinct from the slope, of the budget line measures income. The more limited the income, the tighter the budget constraint and the closer to the corner the budget line. Algebraically, for two commodities bought in quantities Q_c and Q_A at money prices P_c and P_A with money income Y, the budget line is all points for which $Y = P_c Q_c + P_A Q_A$.

The theory of consumption asserts that changes in the quantities of a good consumed are caused by changes in incomes and prices facing consumers. An increase in income, prices held constant, is represented by an outward, parallel shift of the budget line. The effect of an increase in income is called, naturally, the income effect. If it is positive the good in question is *normal;* if it is negative the good is *inferior.* Inferior varieties of a good tend to be inferior in this technical sense as well.

PROBLEMS FOR SECTION 1.2

1. From 1947 to 1957, real per capita income in the United States increased 29%, yet per capita consumption of clothing did not change. Because of the introduction of synthetic fabrics, the price of clothing fell 14% relative to other goods. *True or false:* On this evidence, clothing is an inferior good.

2. When food and all other goods sell for money *and* for ration coupons (each coupon equaling one point and the two goods selling for different numbers of points), the consumer faces two budget constraints. That is, Morris faces two if she cannot trade ration points for money. But she faces only one if she can trade ration points for money. Prove this last assertion and interpret the budget constraint you get verbally, graphically, and algebraically, using the following notation: F = amount of food, A = amount of all other good (notice that Q is not used: it is often a convenience to use the letter of the item for its quantity), P_A = price of all other goods, P_F = price of food, Y = money income actually spent, Y^* = money income with which a consumer is endowed, c_A = coupon points per unit of all other goods, c_F = coupon points per unit of food, C =

coupon point income actually spent, $C^* =$ income of coupon points with which the consumer is endowed. What is the full price of A in terms of F? What is the full income of the consumer?

1.3 Prices in the Budget Line: The Law of Demand

The income effect is simple. The price effect—the substitution of one good for another holding income constant—is somewhat less simple and much more useful. The effect is embodied in the *law of demand*: more is demanded of a thing when its relative price falls. Because the price of a hand calculator falls from $300 to $10, the number sold increases manyfold (and slide rules vanish from the shelves of university bookstores). Because the price of gasoline rises, the quantity demanded falls (despite the declaration of drivers that they need G gallons per week and can survive on no less). Because the price of divorce falls, the number increases; because the price of children rises, fewer are conceived. All this happens in the face of assertions that the amounts consumed of calculators and gasoline, not to speak of divorces and children, are determined not by price but by fashion, social pressure, advertising, impulse, whim, habit, or need.

Let us be clear. First, the law of demand does not apply to comparisons between different goods. To say that more toothpaste is demanded than perfume because toothpaste is cheaper is to say nothing, certainly not the law of demand. "More" does not mean anything in such a context. Is a tube of toothpaste more or less than a bottle of perfume, or more or less than a motorcycle or a pin?

A second and more subtle confusion is between relative prices (of which the law speaks) and absolute—money—prices (of which it does not). Consider the following.

T or F: A consumer buys housing and all other goods. A doubling of all the prices the consumer faces, including the price of his or her labor (wage), will have no effect on the amounts of housing and all other goods that he or she consumes.

A: True, by the simple logic of budget lines. Consider the representation of the consumer's initial position in Figure 1.8.

Only if the budget line changes in some way will the consumer have any interest in moving from the point chosen initially, Z. Does the budget line change if all prices and income double? No. The slope of the budget line (P_H/P_A) does not change, because both P_H and P_A have doubled (or trebled or risen 10%: clearly the proportion in which both rise does not matter, as long as it is the same for both). Does this position of the budget line change? No. H_{max}, for example, is still the point at which the budget line intersects the H axis, because both Y (income) and P_H have doubled.

Properly understood, the law of demand is difficult to disbelieve. Consider a consumer of food and all other goods consuming initially bundle 0 along the solid budget line in Figure 1.9. The relative price of food rises, and the consumer, Morris, is to have constant real income: her

Figure 1.8
A Proportional Change in
Prices and Money Income
Has No Effect on Amounts
Consumed (for a budget
line $Y = P_A Q_A + P_H Q_H$)

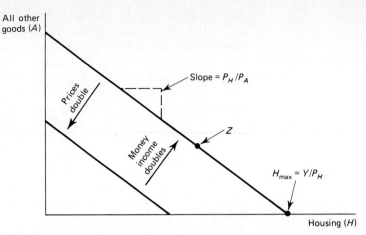

An equiproportional increase in money income Y and money prices P_H and P_A leaves relative price and real income unchanged and, therefore, has no effect on behavior.

new budget line is the dashed one, pivoting around 0. The question is, to which point will she move on the new dashed budget line—point 1 or point 2?

At first it is not obvious. At 1 she has more of all other goods and less of food; at 2 less of all other goods and more of food. But the introduction of a simple and innocuous postulate implies that she will always move to point 1, not 2; that is, if the relative price of food increases, real income held constant, the amount of food consumed will decrease (and the amount of all other goods will increase). This is, of course, the law of demand. The postulate, first formulated in 1938 by Paul Samuelson, is that the consumer is consistent, in the following sense. If the consumer is presented with an opportunity to

Figure 1.9
A Proof of the Law of
Demand

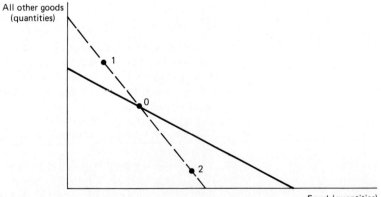

A rise in the price of food will not cause the consumer to abandon 0 for 2, because the consumer has shown by the original choice of 0 that 0 is preferred to 2. Thus a rise in the price of food will not cause the consumer to reduce food consumption.

buy some bundle, call it 2, yet chooses in fact to buy another bundle, call it 0, then the consumer will never choose to buy 2 in circumstances in which 0 can also be purchased. This is called the *Weak Axiom of Revealed Preference* (WARP). That it is innocuous is plain enough. It says that, if a consumer reveals by her behavior that bundle 0 is preferred to bundle 2, she will never act later as though in fact 2 was preferred to 0. If consumers' preferences changed in this way, it would clearly be difficult to frame a theory of consumer behavior, and it would be impossible if one had no insight into why preferences changed. To use an analogy that we will see in the next chapter is less remote than it sounds, if mountains and valleys moved around the landscape, it would be difficult to draw contour maps.

Look back at Figure 1.9. When Morris faced the solid budget line, before the rise in the price of food, she could have chosen to consume bundle 2, for bundle 2 is inside the line: bundle 2 is in the attainable area. But she in fact chose 0. That is, bundle 0 is "revealed preferred" to bundle 2. When the consumer faces the dashed budget line, she is also able to consume bundles 0 and 2. If she in fact chose to consume 2, she is violating the WARP, for in that case she reveals by her behavior that she in fact prefers 2 to 0. Indeed, if she chose any point along the dashed budget line to the right of 0, she would be violating it. When the WARP holds, therefore, if the relative price of food rises (real income held constant), Morris will assume a position along the other segment, such as 1. Points such as 1 cannot violate the WARP because they were not available initially. Along the solid budget line bundle 0 is not revealed preferred to 1 because with that budget line Morris is not able to consume 1 when she chooses in fact to consume bundle 0. A consumer satisfying the WARP, in short, will always move to the left of 0 when the relative price of food rises. She will consume less food. This, to repeat, is the law of demand.

☐
The Law of Demand Applied
A most perceptive philosopher once remarked that "not for nothing do we call the laws of nature 'laws': the more they prohibit, the more they say." What the law of demand prohibits—a rise rather than a fall in the quantity demanded of some thing when its price goes up—does not seem at first glance to be much of an insight into the laws of social behavior. At second glance, however, it is the hammer in the economist's box of tools. It reveals its full power only when applied to groups of consumers, that is, to markets, the subject of most of the rest of this book.

For the present you can get some idea of its significance by adopting the notion of the typical consumer and his behavior.

T or F: Simultaneous increases in the surface mail rate from 10 cents to 12 cents and the air mail rate from 13 cents to 15 cents will leave unaltered the proportions in which the two types of mail are consumed.

A: One's first instinct might be to suppose that, because both types have increased in price by the same amount, the consumption of both types would be reduced by the same amount. But the law of demand concerns relative prices, not absolute prices, and the relative price of air mail has fallen. More, therefore, will be consumed relative to surface mail, even though—again by the law of demand—fewer mail services considered as one commodity will be consumed. Therefore, false.

This is a good place to introduce a piece of diagrammatic reasoning that will be extremely important later. The top panel in Figure 1.10 is the same as in earlier diagrams, plotting consumption of surface mail against consumption of air mail. The bottom panel plots the demand curve, that is, the relationship between the price of air mail relative to surface mail (measured on the vertical axis) and the quantity of air mail consumed. Notice that the horizontal axes of the two diagrams both measure the quantity of air mail.

For every diagram of the top type (in Figure 1.10), there is a diagram of the bottom type. For each budget line (having a certain slope = P_A/P_S), there corresponds a price (P_A/P_S) along the demand curve.

Figure 1.10
The Relationship Between Budget Lines (a) and the Demand Curve (b)

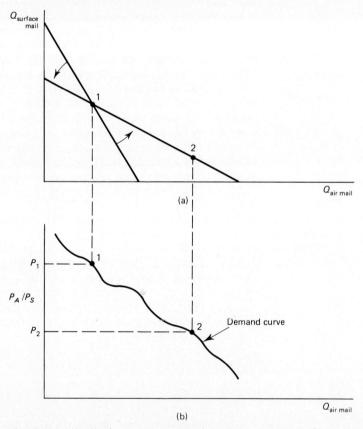

The slope of the budget line (top) corresponds to a price (bottom). As the budget line swings toward the horizontal, the relative price of air mail falls and a larger quantity is demanded.

The law of demand in the top panel is that a rotation in the budget line causing air mail to cheapen will cause consumers to take up a position in which they consume more air mail. The law of demand in the bottom panel is that the demand curve for air mail slopes downward.

Now consider the following problem.

Q: During Prohibition in the United States, much to the dismay of Eliot Ness and the Women's Christian Temperance Union, alcoholic beverages continued to be produced and sold, despite the threat of confiscation, fine, or jail. *True or false:* One would expect the average quality of alcoholic beverages to be lower than before Prohibition.

A: False. One might well expect it to be higher. If the fines and the probability of being apprehended were the same per bottle whether the stuff is Sterno or Napoleon brandy, the relative price of Napoleon brandy would have fallen during Prohibition. If the only penalty were confiscation, there would be no effect, assuming again that the probability of apprehension were the same, since the penalty would be proportional to the value of the good consumed.

The applications of the law of demand are not confined to postage stamps and the other minutiae of life.

T or F: One would expect voter participation on election day to be higher in densely populated urban areas than in sparsely populated rural areas.

A: True, for polling places in sparsely populated areas would be on average farther from the voters, and the cost of going to the polling place therefore higher. By the law of demand, at the higher price of voting less would be demanded.

Comment

The operative phrase in the question is "One would expect." The law of demand provides in this case merely a working hypothesis, the violation of which would occasion mild surprise and a search for an explanation. It is perfectly possible, for example, that the value of time is lower in the countryside or that rural citizens are markedly more public spirited than are their urban compatriots and march to the polls in droves. The experiment is not controlled perfectly in the way that is imagined in the law of demand. Yet this fact does not make the law useless. In the case of higher public spirit, for example, if rural voters in fact turn out more heavily on election day, their public spirit (or whatever else it is that moves them) is so strong that it is offsetting the price effect. If the sensitivity of participation to distance from the polling place were known in other contexts, the higher participation of rural citizens would measure the strength of their public spirit. That jumbo jets fly is not a violation of the law of gravity; it is simply an indication of the force of their lift working against gravity—and a way of measuring the force.

T or F: The price of higher education relative to most other goods has increased in the last 40 years. But the percentage of college-age people going to college has also increased. These observations contradict the law of demand.

A: False. Many other things have changed in the last 40 years, most notably the average real incomes of potential buyers of higher education. As their incomes have risen, they have bought more of it (education is a normal good), even though the relative price of a college degree has risen. Once again, the law of demand, like the law of gravity, is a statement about what will happen in the absence of countervailing forces. Doubtless without the rise in the relative price of a college degree, still more would be demanded.

Summary

The law of demand holds real income constant, but it can (if the issue demands it) hold money income constant nearly as well. When the budget share of the item in question is small, the two analyses are virtually identical. The law can be stated with a demand curve as well as with budget lines: the demand curve slopes downward, in which form the law will be applied repeatedly elsewhere in the book.

PROBLEMS FOR SECTION 1.3

1. Mr. Roderick Floud consumes only food and clothing, initially in these monthly amounts and at these prices: food: 60 pounds at $1 per pound; clothing: 20 yards at $2 per yard.

First, some trivial preparations:

a. What is Floud's money income in dollars?

b. What is the share of food in his total money expenditure (= income)?

c. What is the share in (b) multiplied by -10%, a 10% fall?

Second, the substantive question:

d. Floud's real income in terms of his initial bundle is Y, his money income, divided by P_F (60 pounds) + P_C (20 yards), a price index with weights on the (varying) prices P_F and P_C equal to the initial amounts of the two goods (60 pounds and 20 yards). When P_F and P_C are at their initial values (namely, $P_F =$ $1 per pound and $P_C =$ $2 per yard), this quotient is 1.0 (satisfy yourself that this is true). Suppose that P_F alone changes, rising by 10% from $1.00 to $1.10. If money income is held constant, what happens to the quotient? Calculate it with the new value of P_F. What is the percentage change in the quotient?

Third, the interpretation:

e. Notice that the answer to (d) is the same as the answer to (c). What general rule do you suppose holds for small price changes among the percentage change in a price, the share of the item in total expenditure, and the percentage change in real income?

2. A student of economics went one night to Jimmy's Bar where beer and whiskies both cost $1.00 and drank six beers and four whiskies. The next night, on the eve of the final examination, the student went to the Eagle Bar where beers cost $0.50 and whiskies $1.50 and drank two beers and six whiskies. *True or false:* The student was too irrational to pass the final examination.

3. In 1958 underground coal miners in Italy spent 803,000 lire on their purchases and underground coal miners in Germany spent 7330 marks. The Italian bundle would have cost 6270 marks in Germany; the German bundle would have cost 1,139,000 lire in Italy. *True or false:* With these data one cannot reject the hypothesis that Italian and German coal miners have the same tastes.

4. Consider the following data on purchases of coal miners in France and the Netherlands:

Value of Purchases by Coal Miners at Local and Foreign Prices (local currency units, in thousands)

At Prices in	Bundles (quantities) in	
	France	Netherlands
France	919	990
Netherlands	6.84	6.56

True or false: According to these data the French bundle is superior.

5. What are the rankings of bundles in the following data? Is the WARP ever violated? What do you conclude about appealing to differences in national tastes to explain differences in consumption bundles?

Value of Consumption at Local and Foreign Prices for Underground Coal Miners, Married with Two Children, for Six Localities in the European Coal and Steel Community, in 1958 (local currency, in thousands)

At Prices in	Value of Bundles Bought in					
	Germany	Belgium	France	Italy	Netherlands	Saar
Germany	7.33	9.85	8.99	6.27	9.19	8.43
Belgium	88	107.8	101.8	70.6	104.1	100.4
France	828	1031	980	625	990	925
Italy	1139	1462	1246	803	1387	1278
Netherlands	5.59	7.14	6.84	4.87	6.56	6.35
Saar	835	1082	959	649	1023	935

6. Bloomingdale's is an expensive and fashionable department store in New York; Woolworth's is an inexpensive and unfashionable one. *True or false:* A rise in the cost of parking in New York would favor Bloomingdale's.

2 The Consumer's Choice

2.1 The Hill of Happiness

The one matter left vague so far is how exactly a consumer chooses a particular point on various budget lines, that is, how exactly the consumer's demand curve is positioned. The device economists use to think about this matter is the *indifference curve*, which is directly useful for a good many problems in itself and indirectly useful in underpinning the demand curve and the logic of exchange.

☐

The Consumer Has Tastes and Tastes Are Hills

At the most general level, it is clear that consumers choose a point of rest on their budget lines in accord with their tastes. The earlier discussion has already made two assumptions about consumers' tastes: that more is preferred to less and that consumers are consistent. Sets of indifference curves characterize tastes in more detail. Consider a contemplative farmer, Richard Zecher, who consumes only corn (food for his body) and books (food for his mind). Figure 2.1 portrays Zecher's budget line between the two, C_{max} being his income expressed in corn (i.e., the amount of corn he could consume if he ate all he made, exchanging none of it for books).

It is clear that a farmer who valued the life of the mind highly relative to the life of the body would take up a position such as A and that a farmer with the opposite tastes would take up a position such as A'. In general a farmer would assume the position on the budget line that maximized his happiness. There are serious problems with talking about "happiness," problems discussed in later chapters. But for now imagine a hill of happiness rising out of the page, the altitude of which measures for any combination of books and corn the happiness achieved by that combination. Evidently, at the origin the altitude is zero; that is, with no corn and no books, the farmer's happiness is zero. Evidently, too, as more of both corn and books are consumed, moving out a line such as Z, his happiness increases, for it is a fine thing to have both much corn and many books. That is, as he moves out along Z he crosses successively higher contour lines of equal happiness—exactly like the contour lines of equal altitude on the map of a physical hill. Were it not for the scarcity of his re-

26

Figure 2.1
The Choice of a Position
Is a Matter of Taste

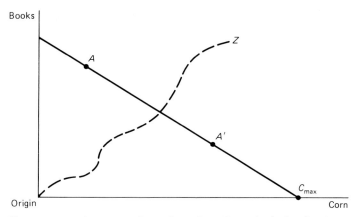

The consumer chooses a point such as *A* or *A'* on the budget line in accordance with his or her tastes. Moving out from the origin, along line *Z*, the consumer's happiness is increasing.

sources, the farmer would move to the point of saturation in Figure 2.2 (the peak of the hill). Beyond saturation, at a point such as *P*, he has both too many books (they are stacked in the barn, and he trips over them and cannot find the ones he wishes to read) and too much corn (it lies in heaps on the ground, rotting and stinking, for he cannot eat it fast enough). At this point corn and books are not goods, but bads, garbage that he will throw away in the amounts that will bring him back to saturation. At point *P'*, corn is garbage but books are not: if neither were scarce he would throw away corn but acquire more books to arrive at saturation.

Figure 2.2
Tastes Are a Hill

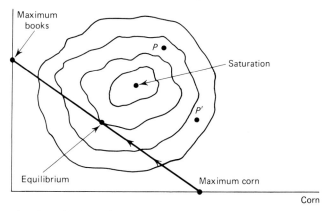

In a world where books and corn are free, the consumer chooses saturation. Scarcity implies a budget constraint that makes saturation unattainable. The rational consumer chooses a point that puts him on the highest attainable contour, which is the contour as close as possible to saturation.

*Equilibrium Is at a
Point of Tangency*

But corn and books, alas, *are* scarce, and Zecher the farmer is confined to choosing points inside his budget line, maximum books to maximum corn in the diagram. Where will he move? To the highest contour line attainable inside or on the budget line, namely, to equilibrium, where a contour line just touches (is tangent to) his budget line. One can view him as starting at, say, maximum corn and traveling up along his budget line crossing contour lines of higher and higher happiness until he reaches equilibrium, at which point further travel would have him crossing successively *lower* contour lines. So he stops at equilibrium. This is not the best position he can imagine (saturation is), but it is the best position he can attain given his income and the rate at which he can get books in exchange for corn. This is how consumers choose points of equilibrium on their budget lines. Contour lines on the hill of happiness are a characterization of tastes, and these tastes guide the consumer to the best attainable combination of goods.

*The Uses of
Saturation*

The point of saturation (the peak of the hill) is not itself relevant to many economic problems. To repeat, scarcity is pervasive. It is, however, a useful diagrammatic device for keeping clear the shapes of indifference curves.

Q: Draw sets of indifference curves between food and housing for C. K. Harley (on the whole, a food lover) and Paul David (on the whole, a housing lover).

A: Harley's indifference contours are crowded toward the food axis, David's toward the housing axis. To use the saturation points, Harley's idea of heaven is point saturation for Harley in Figure 2.3; David's is saturation for David. Drawing roughly circular contour lines around the points gives the two sets (solid lines for Harley, dashed for David).

**Figure 2.3
Using Points of Saturation
to Envision Sets of
Indifference Contours**

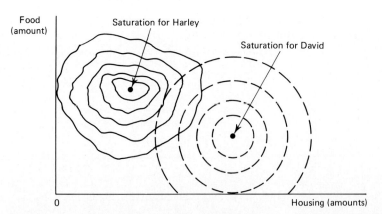

A food lover requires more food and less housing for saturation than does a housing lover. The indifference curves near the food lover's saturation point are in regions of more food and less housing than are those of the housing lover.

Figure 2.4
The Position of the
Indifference Contours (a)
Affects the Position of the
Demand Curve (b)

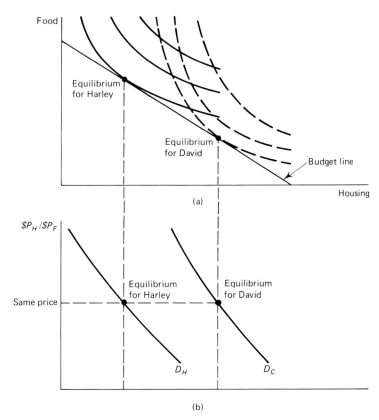

The food lover's indifference contours are crowded toward the food axis as compared with those of the housing lover. The food lover will demand less housing than will the housing lover if both face the same prices and have the same income.

If both food and housing have positive prices and if neither Harley nor David can attain their saturation point (all of which is to say that food and housing are scarce for both), then the relevant parts of the two contour maps are the parts sloping downward on the origin side of the saturation points, such as the maps in the top portion of Figure 2.4.

If Harley and David have the same income and face the same prices (i.e., if they have the same budget line), Harley will choose equilibrium for Harley and David the equilibrium for David; in the same circumstances, naturally, the housing lover (David) chooses more housing (equilibrium for David has more housing and less food than does equilibrium for Harley). Now look at the bottom portion of the diagram, recalling the correspondence discussed briefly in the last chapter between diagrams of budget lines (with quantities of, say, food and housing on the two axes) and diagrams of demand curves (with the quantity of one good, say, housing on the horizontal axis and its price relative to the other good, say, food on the other axis). Supposing some price to be the relative price of housing in terms of food, equal to the slope of the budget line in the top portion, in the bottom portion Harley chooses on his demand curve equilibrium for Harley and David chooses equilibrium for David. In other words, the diagram formalizes the obvious: a housing lover's demand curve for housing is farther out than is a food lover's when the two people find themselves facing the same constraints of income and price; at the same income and relative price, a housing lover (David relative to Harley) demands more housing.

☐

The Uses of the Hill: The Case of Bads

The notion of a hill of happiness can be used to think not only about private choice but also about social choice, such as the choice to have more or less goods in exchange for more or less bads.

Q: 1. Draw a set of indifference curves between automobile rides and air pollution for a society (unanimous in its opinion and collective in its decisions) that likes automobile rides but dislikes air pollution. (Hint: Use the saturation point; where is it located?)

 2. Presuming that the society must sacrifice some rides if it wishes to get *less* pollution, draw the budget line facing the society. (Hint: In a budget line for two goods—as distinct from a good and a bad—one must reduce M to get *more* N; i.e., the budget line slopes *downward*.)

 3. What is the optimal amount of pollution?

A: 1. The saturation point is obviously somewhere on the rides axis, because putting it off the axis would say that heaven had some rather than zero air pollution. Drawing indifference contours around the point yields upward-sloping indifference curves, as shown in Figure 2.5.

 2. The budget line also slopes upward, because along it a rise in the number of rides results in more, not less, pollution. The attainable area is shaded. Mathematically, the budget line between two *goods*, M and N, is derived by solving the budget constraint, $Y = P_M(M) + P_N N$, for, say, M:

$$M = \frac{Y}{P_M} - \frac{P_N}{P_M}(N)$$

The slope of this line is negative. The budget constraint between a good (rides) and a bad (air pollution) is $Y = P_R R - P_A A$. Air pollution has a negative price, $-P_A$, because the less that is spent to *eliminate* it (as opposed to *acquiring* it) the more of income, Y, can be spent on rides. That is, expenditure on rides is $P_R R = Y + P_A A$ (i.e., with more A, $P_R R$ can be higher). The budget line is therefore

$$R = \frac{Y}{P_R} + \frac{P_A}{P_R}(A)$$

and its slope is positive.

 3. The optimal amount of pollution is A_E, the amount corresponding to the tangency point of the budget line and the indifference contours. The idea of an "optimal amount of pollution" strikes noneconomists as absurd. But if pollution is costly to remove, the idea is not absurd, sad to say. The abatement of pollution is a good thing; in view of the costs of doing it, its utter elimination is not.

Figure 2.5
The Choice Between a Bad
That Is Costly to Remove
and a Good

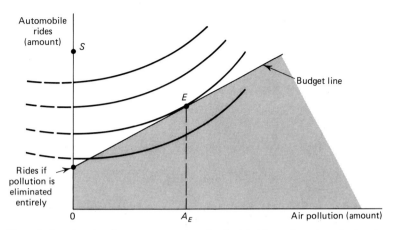

The rule for choosing between a good and a bad is identical to the rule for choosing between two goods. Given the budget line, choose the highest indifference curve that the budget line touches.

Summary

The income and prices that consumers face limit their choices, but within these limits the exact amounts of goods (or bads) they choose are a matter of taste. A consumer's taste for two goods such as guitar lessons and beer can be described as a hill of happiness. The consumer chooses the highest contour in the beer-lessons plane that he can reach on his budget line, that is, the point at which a contour line is tangent to the budget line. These points of rest are also points on demand curves. This apparatus of thought is applicable to any choice, such as the public choice between schools and highways, defense and courts, or automobile rides and air pollution.

APPENDIX TO SECTION 2.1

Mathematically speaking, the farmer's problem, as formalized by the economist observing him, is to choose the amounts of books, B, and corn, C, to maximize his *utility function* (a function of B and C) subject to the constraint that the combinations of B and C chosen satisfy (i.e., lie on) his budget constraint (money income, say, $Y = P_B B + P_C C$, supposing that his expenditures on books and corn exhaust his income). To solve this problem one needs to know the utility function. A simple case is $U = BC$; that is, the level of utility (happiness) of the farmer is the product of the amount of books and the amount of corn he consumes. With 10 books and 3 bushels of corn, his utility would be 30 units; with 2 books and 20 bushels of corn, 40 units; and so forth.

□
Brute Force
Solutions

For any particular values for Y, P_B, and P_C in the budget constraint, the problem can be solved graphically. Plot the budget constraint on a graph of B and C; plot a utility contour on the graph for one chosen value of U (say, $U = 10$), then for another, and another, and another; keep plotting the utility function until you find one that is just tangent to the budget line; then read off the equilibrium values of B and C. An alternative algebraic method of trial and error would be to choose a pair of B's and C's that is on the budget line by choosing at random a value of C and inserting it into $(Y/P_B) - (P_C/P_B)(C) = B$ to get the corresponding value of B; from the utility function $BC = U$ calculate the utility for this pair; then increase C a little, recalculate the B from the budget line, recalculate U, and see whether U rises or falls; if it rises, continue increasing C; if it falls, decrease C in the next trial. And so on, until either you have discovered the maximum attainable U or the battery in your calculator has gone dead.

An Elegant Solution with Calculus

☐ For such a simple utility function, however, first-term calculus solves the problem quicker and gives more insight into the solution. The budget constraint must be satisfied always. To ensure that it is, solve it for one of the goods, for example, books, and substitute this expression for B into the utility function:

$$U = \left[\frac{Y}{P_B} - \frac{P_C}{P_B}(C)\right](C) = \frac{Y}{P_B}(C) - \frac{P_C}{P_B}(C^2)$$

Geometrically, this substitution amounts to slicing the three-dimensional surface of utility along the budget line. The equation for U now shows how utility rises and falls as the amount of corn is varied along the budget slice. Because it now embodies the way in which B depends on C along the budget constraint, the utility function has been made into a function of C alone. Y, P_B, and P_C are given numbers, and C alone is variable. To maximize U, set its derivative with respect to C at zero:

$$\frac{dU}{dC} = \frac{d}{dC}\left[\frac{Y}{P_B}(C) - \frac{P_C}{P_B}(C^2)\right] = \frac{Y}{P_B} - 2\left[\frac{P_C}{P_B}(C)\right] = 0$$

The optimal C, given Y, P_B, and P_C, is simply the solution of the last equality:

$$C = \frac{1}{2}\left(\frac{Y}{P_C}\right)$$

This, incidentally, is the demand curve for C, though a very strange one for any actual good. The optimal B can be derived in the same way, and naturally, because the utility function here is symmetrical, the form is similar to the expression for C, $B = \frac{1}{2}(Y/P_B)$; or by substituting the expression for C back into the budget constraint

$$B = \frac{Y}{P_B} - \frac{P_C}{P_B}(C) = \frac{Y}{P_B} - \frac{P_C}{P_B}\left[\frac{1}{2}\left(\frac{Y}{P_C}\right)\right] = \left(\frac{Y}{P_B} - \frac{1}{2}\left(\frac{Y}{P_B}\right)\right) = \frac{1}{2}\left(\frac{Y}{P_B}\right)$$

If income were $100, the price of books $2 per book, and the price of corn $1 per bushel, the equilibrium combination would be

$$B = \frac{1}{2}\left(\frac{\$100}{\$2}\right) = 25 \text{ books}$$

$$C = \frac{1}{2}\left(\frac{\$100}{\$1}\right) = 50 \text{ bushels}$$

To summarize, then, the geometry of choosing the best bundle along the budget line—that is, choosing the one point at which the budget line is tangent to a contour line, can be put mathematically as follows. Choose the bundle to maximize the utility function subject to the constraint that expenditure equals income. First-term calculus suffices to solve the problem—at any rate if the utility function is a simple one and if only two goods are involved.

QUESTIONS FOR SECTION 2.1

1. Do animals obey economic laws? Describe an experiment to discover whether rats obey the law of demand and other pieces of consumer behavior, using the following ideas. Rats like food and water; each good can be given a price in right- or left-lever pushes; income can be N pushes a day. Relate the laboratory conditions to the theory of consumption item by item.

True or False

2. Because more is preferred to less, the hill of happiness has no overhanging cliffs. (Hint: Draw the contours for an overhang.)

3. If consumers are consistent and more is preferred to less, then indifference contours on the hill of happiness cannot cross. (Hint: Draw two contours that do cross; compare points with more of both goods on the two, showing that the conclusion violates consistency.)

4. The demand curves for B and C derived in the appendix satisfy the law of demand.

5. The utility functions $U = \alpha + \beta(BC)$, where $\alpha + \beta$ are constraints and β is positive, or $U = (BC)^2$ or $U = \ln(BC)$ give exactly the same demand curves as does $U = BC$.

2.2 The Shape of Indifference Curves

☐
Complements

The shape of contours on the hill of happiness—or, in duller language, the shape of indifference curves—is sometimes apparent from the definition of the goods.

Q: Draw the utility contours between left and right shoes.

A: Such goods are called *perfect complements*, as shown in Figure 2.6.

You are better off with 10 pairs of shoes (point *A*) than with 3 pairs (point *B*), but 3 pairs plus 7 left shoes (point *C*) is no better than 3 pairs alone; that is, it is on the same contour. Parallel assertions are true of other goods one commonly thinks of as complementary, such as bread and butter, housing and furniture, autos and gasoline, and the like (although doubtless in these and similar cases the corner in the contours is not perfectly sharp). Mathematically, the utility

Figure 2.6
The Pricing of
Complements Does Not
Matter to Consumers

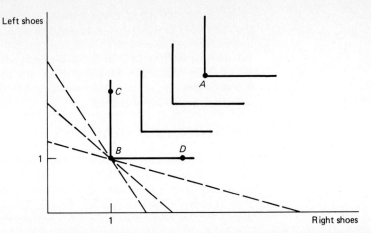

If goods are <u>perfect complements</u>, then increasing the quantity of one without increasing the minimum quantity of both will not increase utility ($B \rightarrow C$, $B \rightarrow D$). Increasing the quantity of both goods *will* increase utility ($B \rightarrow A$). An income-compensated change in prices causes no substitution effects when goods are consumed in fixed proportions.

function between perfect complements L and R is $U = \min [\alpha L, \beta R]$, which for $\alpha = \beta$ says what the diagram says; that is, utility (happiness) is determined by the minimum of the number of left or right shoes (supposing them to be pairable). Increasing the number of one type alone fills the closet floor but does not increase utility.

As long as the price of a pair of shoes does not change, it clearly does not matter to a consumer how each shoe is priced. At $15.00 a pair the consumer will think it odd but unobjectionable if a lunatic shoe-seller sells left shoes at $14.99 and right shoes at $0.01. The buyer of one pair makes the same sacrifice of income to acquire a pair, which is to say diagrammatically that the budget lines for the various relative prices of left and right shoes (all adding up to $15.00) run through the same bundle, as in Figure 2.6. Shoe-sellers often display left shoes in unsupervised street stalls, pricing them, as it were, at the low cost of stealing them. But to step out with any grace you must step in and pay up.

The pricing of complements is not always so innocent. Computer cards (IBM cards in particular) are complements with the services of an electronic computer (an IBM computer in particular). It might appear that it does not matter whether International Business Machines takes its just reward in high prices for cards or high prices for the computer itself. As the discussion in Chapter 18 will show, however, a high price for cards is a way of extracting more money from heavier users.

☐

Substitutes

At the other extreme are substitutes. One consumes bread *and* butter (complements) but butter *or* margarine (substitutes).

Q: Draw Dudley Baines's indifference curves between odd- and even-numbered bottles of 1967 Château Latour.

A: As Figure 2.7 shows, if the relative price of even bottles in terms of odd falls below 1.0 (as along the dashed budget line), Baines will buy only even-numbered bottles. Because there are many such Baineses who would drive a low price for one type back up, the prices of the two types must stay equal. This holds for less perfect substitutes. The prices of domestic and foreign goods, for example, move together, as do those of butter and margarine, felt-tipped pens and ball-points, or one book on price theory and another.

If the price of even relative to odd bottles of Château Latour is exactly 1.0 (it is, of course), Baines does not care which he buys. The budget line lies on an indifference curve, and any point on the budget line is as desirable as any other. The indifference curves for perfect substitutes are straight lines; that is, the utility function has the same form as a budget line, $U = \alpha X + \beta Y$. For odd, X, and even, Y, bottles, it is clear that $\alpha = \beta$, which can be interpreted as saying that X and Y make equal contributions to happiness. In less trivial cases, α and β can be different, and the slope of the indifference curves therefore different from 1.0.

☐
The Usual Shape Is Convexity

The usual shape of indifference contours for consumers as a group, however, is *convex* to the origin, that is, bowed toward the origin (the opposite of convex is *concave*, which you can remember by noting that curves with a hollow—a cave—open toward the origin are con-*cave*).

The convexity of indifference curves can be expressed in several different ways—another example of the terminological proliferation

Figure 2.7
Perfect Substitutes Have Straight-Line Indifference Curves

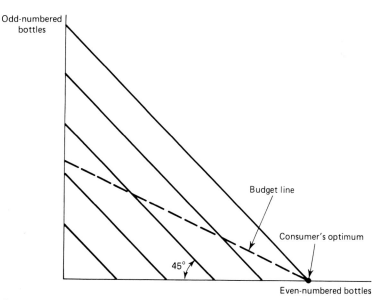

If goods are perfect substitutes, it is optimal for the consumer facing constant prices to specialize in the cheaper one of them.

that afflicts economics as it does other products of the intellect. The slope of an indifference curve between food and clothing is called the *marginal rate of indifferent substitution* between food and clothing or, somewhat more vividly, the *marginal valuation* of food in terms of clothing. It is the minimum amount of clothing that a consumer would accept in exchange for giving up a unit of food—the minimum amount being, of course, the amount that just barely keeps the consumer on the same indifference curve (see Figure 2.8).

If the consumer got more or less than ΔC in exchange for ΔF, the consumer would arrive at a point such as better or worse (than the initial point start). Convexity can be expressed so: moving along any given indifference curve in the direction of increasing food and decreasing clothing will decrease the marginal valuation of food. This way of putting it is plausible for the same reason that the law of demand is plausible. In fact, it *is* the law of demand. The more food you have relative to clothing, the less you will value the prospect of still more food.

Summary

The usual shape of indifference curves is bending in (convex) to the origin. The limiting cases for two goods are perfect complementarity—corners—and perfect substitutability—lines. For complements such as furniture and housing, a change in the relative price at a given real income has no effect on the amounts consumed; for substitutes such as Italian-made shoes and American-made shoes, a change in the relative price has a large effect. These limiting cases, and even cases beyond the limits (nonconvexity), do occur. But generally, people neither consume goods in rigid proportions nor specialize in consuming one good. To repeat the usual case in alternative language, the marginal rate of substitution usually declines, and the point of rest is usually interior.

Figure 2.8
The Slope Is the Marginal Rate of Substitution Is the Marginal Valuation Is the Minimum Acceptable Exchange

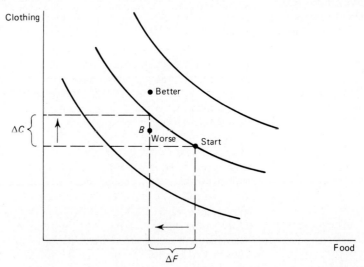

Convexity of indifference curves implies that $\Delta C / \Delta F$ rises (ignoring the negative sign) as the consumer moves in the direction of more clothing along a given indifference curve.

QUESTIONS FOR SECTION 2.2

True or False

1. If Hal Gemery's utility contours between clocks and peanut butter are all straight lines and he faces fixed relative prices, he will never change the commodity (clocks or peanut butter) in which he specializes as his income increases.

2. The corners of indifference contours for complements need not lie on a straight ray through the origin.

3. A consumer with con*cave* indifference contours between heroin and bread will specialize in consuming heroin or bread.

4. If the bread price of heroin increases instead of staying constant as more heroin is consumed (a situation that is, in fact, said to characterize the market for heroin), the corner solution is not inevitable even with concave indifference curves.

5. Corner solutions are possible with convex indifference curves.

6. Portions of indifference contours may well be shaped perversely (rising marginal valuations), but for a consumer with a straight budget line, such portions will never be points of rest.

2.3 The Uses of Indifference Contours

Like crossword puzzles and mathematical games, the study of the shapes of indifference curves has a certain arid charm. The next chapter will continue the fun and games. But it is as well to show immediately here (as the rest of the book will show repeatedly) that indifference curves are not mere toys; on the contrary, they illuminate real behavior.

This would be obvious if economists had actually measured indifference curves. If they could look up in a "Handbook of Hills of Happiness" the typical shapes of curves between food and all other goods, as engineers can look up the breaking point under stress of a certain kind of steel, then they would have no trouble predicting exactly how consumers will react to a rise in the price of food or to a fall in income. There is no such handbook. Economics, like other social sciences and unlike physics and chemistry, cannot very easily fill in the blanks in its theories with laboratory experiments. Like astronomy or meteorology, it must take its experiments as the world gives them, with the additional handicap that, unlike astronomy and meteorology, which are applied physics and chemistry, it cannot draw on a rich array of laboratory results (economic psychology is underdeveloped). Statistical methods in economics—*econometrics*—has since the 1930s filled in some of the blanks. Yet a lamentable tendency to apply these methods only to recent experience has narrowed work on the facts, and the next chapter offers some further, theoretical, reasons why the handbook of facts does not exist.

Subsidies of Income and of Price

Still, economists can go a long way with a crude notion of the shapes of indifference curves, the crude notion, to be specific, that they are convex. To return to a point made earlier, for example, it is the mere convexity of indifference curves that makes a subsidy in cash more valuable than a subsidy in kind (see Question 1 at the end of this section).

A similar point applies to subsidies that reduce prices, such as those that are given to customers of the U.S. Postal Service or the telephone company in Baroda, Michigan or Fairfield, Vermont in the form of rates lower than the cost of mail or calls there (paid for by rates above costs in Los Angeles or New York, or by government subsidies). The dashed budget line in Figure 2.9 is the budget line representing the full cost of sending and receiving letters in Fairfield; the solid line is the budget line after the subsidy.

The subsidy is S if the citizens of Fairfield buy M^* mail and achieve the indifference curve I^*. They would be even better off, however, if the subsidy, S, extracted from New Yorkers was simply given to the Fairfieldians directly as income (all other goods) without the artificial reduction in the relative price of mail. The Fairfieldians would move out the cross-hatched line to E^{**} tangent to a higher indifference curve, I^{**}. The cross-hatched line constructed in this way (parallel to the unsubsidized price line) always intersects the old indifference curve at the old equilibrium, E^*, which means that there is always a superior point such as E^{**}. In short, it can be shown in a simple diagram of indifference curves and budget lines that for the same hurt to New Yorkers, S, Fairfieldians would be made better off by paying the full cost of mails and telephones and receiving the subsidy as income.

Figure 2.9
A Subsidy to Income Is Always Better Than a Subsidy to a Price

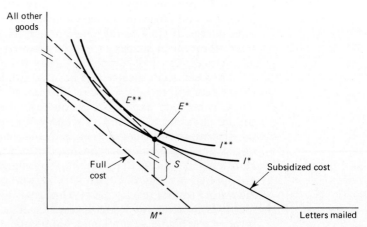

A subsidized postal rate that results in the government's spending $\$S$ is inferior to a direct transfer of $\$S$, because the former enables consumers to reach indifference curve I^* and the latter I^{**}.

Gifts That Foreclose
Other Opportunities

☐   It is not always so that subsidies to a price or gifts in goods increase the amounts consumed. This too can be demonstrated with indifference curves. Consider a good provided free that makes it impossible to buy still more of the good, such as education. If Joseph Reid goes full time to a free public school or college, he cannot simultaneously go full time to an expensive private school or college.

Q: 1. Draw the budget line between education and all other goods facing Reid. (Hint: It is not a line alone, but a line and a point outside the line.) Assume that public education is a standardized amount, E^*, and that the alternative, private education, can be purchased in varying amounts.
  2. Draw an indifference curve that would imply that Reid would not accept the offer of free public education.
  3. Draw an indifference curve implying that Reid would accept it and would therefore consume *more* education than he would without the offer.
  4. Draw an indifference curve implying that Reid would accept it but would therefore consume *less* education than he would without the offer.
  5. When would you expect an offer of a standardized amount of public education to reduce rather than raise the educational attainment of the population?

A: Reid can either accept the offer of free public education, getting E^* education and devoting all his income to all other goods, or he can refuse the offer, giving up some all other goods to get some private education. In other words, his budget *line*—the collection of attainable points—is the line private education *or* (not *and*) the point public education (at which he consumes the bundle AOG_{max}, E^*). See Figure 2.10.

Figure 2.10
Free Education Can
Reduce the Amount
Consumed

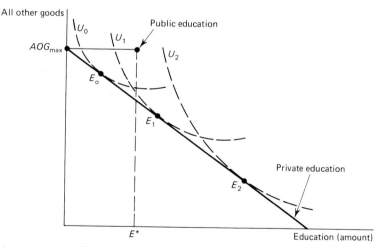

A consumer initially at E_0, with preferences given by indifference curve U_0, accepts the offer of E^* units of free public education and thereby increases his or her consumption of education. A consumer at E_1, with preferences given by U_1, accepts the offer and thereby consumes less education. A consumer at E_2 rejects the offer. If there are enough consumers at E_1, and if E_1 is far enough to the right of E^*, the amount of education consumed will fall.

If the indifference curve tangent to private education resembles U_2, then the offer of the alternative public education would have no effect, since the point public education is on a lower indifference curve. This is the case of education-loving students, for whom the standardized quantity of public education, E^*, is too low to be tempting. If the indifference curve resembles U_0, then the offer increases the amount of education consumed, since public education is now on a higher indifference curve, and in accepting the offer students consume more (E^* is more than E_0). This is the case of all-other-goods-loving students, for whom the standardized quantity of public education exceeds the amount they would consume privately.

If the indifference curve resembles U_1, however, the offer *decreases* the amount consumed, since public education is on a higher indifference curve, but in accepting the offer students consume less than they would without the offer (E^* is less than E_1). This is the case of education-liking-but-not-loving students for whom the standardized quantity of public education is literally acceptable, but less than they would consume privately. Evidently, if much of the population is in this last category, consuming before the offer larger amounts of education per student than is to be provided free, then the offer can reduce the educational attainment of the population. The population is happier with the offer (at any rate if one ignores the hurt from the taxes necessary to make it), but happily ignorant. Figure 2.10 exhibits how the government may fail if it is attempting to increase the amount of education consumed.[1]

☐
Hazardous Product Warning: The Society Must Stay on Its Budget Line

A warning is in order. The arguments about how a subsidy of one or another sort affects consumers are fine if one is interested only in how the particular group of consumers is affected and if the group is not a large one in society as a whole. The cross subsidies from New Yorkers to Fairfieldians fit the mold; the subsidy to all public education does not.

To provide the point public education in the diagram shown in Figure 2.10, the economy must tax itself. That is, the society as a whole cannot in reality provide itself with a point such as public education outside its original budget line. And the budget line typical of the society as a whole must be the budget line in the diagram. Unless a tiny group is being subsidized disproportionately by the rest of society (as is the case, for example, with state-supported higher education), an analysis that simply assumes that the point public education is available is incomplete and may be radically misleading.[2]

---

[1] The logic of the argument is not controversial, but the facts are. Two people who believe the facts warrant taking the argument seriously are Sam Peltzman, "The Effect of Subsidies-in-Kind on Private Expenditures: The Case of Higher Education," *Journal of Political Economy* 81 (January 1973): 1–27, who applies it to college education in the United States; and E. G. West, "Educational Slowdown and Public Intervention in 19th-Century England," *Explorations in Economic History* 12 (January 1975): 61–87, who applies it to primary schooling in England after the introduction of state education in the 1870s.

[2] The point is made in Milton Friedman, *Price Theory* (Chicago: Aldine, 1976), pp. 65–75, and works cited there. It was first made by Friedman and others in the late

Summary

Economists have usually only a vague idea of the shape of indifference curves between bread and meat or education and all other goods. Vague though it is, the idea of convexity is enough to cast light on many social questions. The key to answering such questions is often close thinking about the budget lines involved: a nonordinary budget line dropped onto ordinary indifference curves may yield definite results. Definite though they are, however, the results must accord with the society's true budget line.

QUESTIONS FOR SECTION 2.3

True or False

1. To keep the poor at the same level of happiness, a scheme of direct money payments to the poor (the so-called "negative income tax," for example) would have to have money payments to the poor below the money value of the food, housing, medical care, and so forth given to them directly under present welfare programs.

2. If education and all other goods are perfect complements, then an offer of free public education will never reduce the amount consumed.

2.4 Measurable Utility

☐
The Relation Between Total and Marginal Utility

There is an old-fashioned way of looking at indifference curves and the consumer's choice that has been declared dead many times but refuses to stay in its coffin. It is called *marginal utility*. Suppose that Richard Zecher's hill of happiness lying between the books and corn axes has altitudes measured in joys (a unit of happiness). One could slice the hill at, say, 25 books and look at the profile of the slice. The profile would be Zecher's total happiness or utility in joys achieved from 25 books and varying amounts of corn (the middle panel of Figure 2.11).

The lower panel is Zecher's marginal utility of one more bushel of corn given various amounts of corn already in hand: an expressive but obsolete piece of jargon calls it the schedule of the *final degree of utility*. In other words, it is a plot of the increments to his total utility when the amount of corn he has increases a bushel at a time. In still other words it is the slope of his total utility curve (look at the cases for 20 and 50 bushels), the first example of dozens in this book of drawing *marginal curves* (i.e., curves that are slopes of other curves).[3]

1940s, in response to widespread misuse of the newly popular method of indifference curves.

  [3] You might, incidentally, be able to persuade yourself of the true assertion that the shaded area under the marginal utility curve from 0 to 20 bushels is equal to the total utility at 20 bushels: the sum of the increments to utility from the bushel 1, 2, . . ., 20 (which is the area) is clearly the total utility achieved up to bushel 20. If you can do so, congratulations, for you have grasped the fundamental theorem of the calculus. If you cannot, do not despair: the point will come up again in many other contexts until it is clear.

**Figure 2.11
The Relations Among
Indifference Curves (a),
Total Utility Curves (b),
and Marginal Utility
Curves (c)**

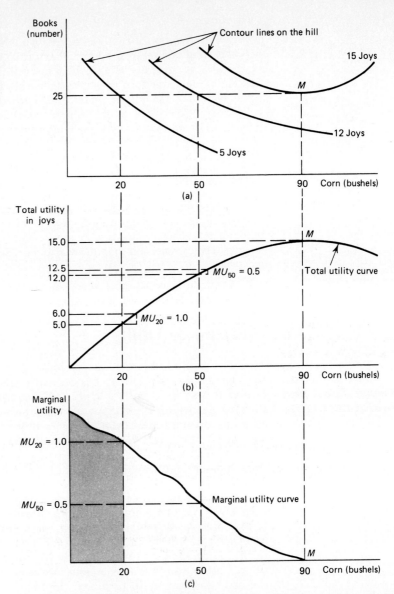

As bushels of corn consumed increases, the number of books remaining constant, the consumer moves to higher (farther from the origin) indifference curves yielding higher (numerically greater) utility (top). Total utility is thus a function of bushels of corn (middle); so is marginal utility, which is the rate of change of total utility relative to the rate of change of bushels of corn (bottom).

*The Rule of Rational
Life*

The point of these diagrams is that they provide a description of the consumer's choice alternative to the language of tangencies of indifference curves with budget lines. In fact, marginal utility was the first description, the leading idea in the "marginalist revolution" in economics during the 1870s. Since that time economists have never ceased to talk of margins, for the good reason that the rule of rational life is: *Pursue an activity until the marginal benefit is equal to the marginal cost of pursuing it further.* The marginal benefit of talking this way is to this day still above its marginal cost.

Zecher, with 19 bushels of corn, is deciding whether to pursue his corn-consuming activity a little further (i.e., considering whether to buy another bushel (number 20). The marginal benefit from another bushel is the marginal utility of bushel 20, $MU_{C=20}$. The marginal cost—that is, what he has to sacrifice to get the bushel—clearly has something to do with the money price of the bushel, $\$P_{corn}$. Dollars and joys, however, are not directly comparable. To measure the marginal cost in units comparable with the marginal utility, one must multiply the dollar price by the utility sacrificed elsewhere (in consuming other things, such as books) per dollar spent on corn. This multiplier can be called the marginal utility of income, MU_{income}, the amount utility falls when a dollar of income is taken away (by spending it on corn). Figure 2.12 sets Zecher's marginal utility of corn against the price times the marginal utility of income.

**Figure 2.12
How a Consumer Uses
Marginal Utility to Make
a Choice**

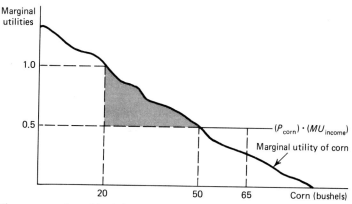

The consumption of bushel 50 of corn yields a certain amount of utility. The income used to purchase bushel 50 would yield the same amount of utility if it were spent on other goods instead of on corn. Therefore 50 bushels is optimal.

Notice that the marginal utility of corn declines as more is consumed.

As Tom Nall ate his seventy-fourth tortilla in a sitting at Marciano's Mexican Restaurant in Dallas on October 16, 1973, he undoubtedly reflected that the first tasted better. Had his purpose been pleasure in the food rather than winning the second world championship in tortilla eating, he would have stopped eating sooner. Likewise, Zecher does as well as he can when he arranges his affairs to set equal the marginal utility of an extra bushel of corn and the marginal cost of the bushel. That is, he buys 50 bushels. At 20 bushels he would do well to buy more, because what he gains in utility from more corn is greater than what he loses elsewhere;[4] at 65 bushels, for parallel reasons, he would do well to buy less.

☐

The Equations of Marginal Utility

The form of the rule of rational life is in this case $MU_{corn} = P_{corn} \times MU_{income}$. Unless it is a very peculiar good, the marginal utility of corn (and of other things, such as tortillas) diminishes after some point as more is purchased and consumed, enabling Zecher to achieve equilibrium at 50 bushels. In other words, the marginal utility of corn is a function of (depends on) the amount of corn consumed and is in fact after some point a diminishing function. It is also in general a function of the amount of other goods consumed, such as books: a choice of 10 rather than 25 books in the first panel of Figure 2.11 would have resulted in a different slice of total utility and a different curve of marginal utility. Therefore, the theory is not complete unless it also tells how the number of books is determined. The number is determined as corn is, by the marginal utility equation; that is, MU_B $(C, B) = P_B \times MU_Y$, in which the C and B in parentheses remind one that marginal utilities are functions of the amount of goods consumed. Nor is the theory complete unless it keeps Zecher on his budget line—he cannot spend more than his money income, Y, and will not spend less, that is, $Y = P_C C + P_B B$. The marginal utility theory of the consumer's choice is therefore completed by three equations:

1. $MU_C (C, B) = P_C \times MU_Y$ Best choice of C

2. $MU_B (C, B) = P_B \times MU_Y$ Best choice of B

3. $Y = P_C C + P_B B$ All income spent on C and B

These are to be solved for three unknowns, the amounts of corn and books purchased and the marginal utility of income. All three will usually vary as income, Y, and prices, P_C and P_B, vary. Any particular choice of income and price determines the three.

☐

Marginal Utility Theory Is the Same as Indifference Curve Theory

At first glance all this appears to be radically different from the theory of consumers' choices that has them seeking tangencies between their budget lines and one of their indifference contours. At second glance, however, the two theories are the same. Look at the three equations just given. Eliminating MU_Y by substitution leads to one equation in place of the first two:

$$\frac{MU_C}{P_C} = \frac{MU_B}{P_B}$$

It is illuminating to express this equation in a different notation, by writing out MU_C as $\Delta U/\Delta C$—the change in utility per unit of change in corn consumed:

$$\frac{\Delta U}{P_C(\Delta C)} = \frac{\Delta U}{P_B(\Delta B)}$$

[4] In terms of the previous footnote, he could gain the shaded area in utility (units of joys) by increasing his consumption from 20 to 50 bushels.

In other words, to be satisfied with his choice of corn and books, the consumer must get equal increments to utility per additional dollar spent on each (since $P_C(\Delta C)$, for example, is the number of dollars spent on ΔC), a persuasive way of putting the behavior of an optimizing consumer. Now begin thinking again of budget lines and tangencies. Think of Zecher as moving along his budget line, reducing his books in exchange for increasing his corn. From this perspective the equation just given says that, when the consumer has achieved equilibrium, the utility lost from fewer books is exactly balanced (not over- or underbalanced) by the utility gained from more corn. That is, total utility is now constant. That is, the two ΔU's are equal. One can rearrange the equation and cancel the ΔU's:

$$\left.\frac{\Delta B}{\Delta C}\right|_{U_{\text{constant}}} = -\frac{P_C}{P_B}$$

The vertical bar signifies a side condition and the negative sign appears because more corn implies (along the budget line) fewer books. The equation now says that Zecher sets his marginal valuation of corn equal to the slope of the budget line ($-P_C/P_B$). As was just demonstrated, the marginal valuation is related to the slope of an indifference curve, *an* indifference curve because utility is held constant. But arranging matters so that these slopes are equal is the tangency condition for an optimum in the more usual theory. Adding the condition that consumers spend all their income will complete the theory, identical in content to the marginal utility theory.

Once the identity of the two theories is recognized, the marginal utility variant, with its cumbersome expression, loses much of its initial attractiveness. It is more direct to say "Zecher chooses the highest indifference curve he can reach" than to say "Zecher equalizes the marginal utilities per dollar of expenditure on each good, subject to his budget constraint," much less to say "Zecher, subject to his budget constraint, sets the marginal utility from a good equal to the product of the good's price and the marginal utility of income." Life is too short for pointless mental gymnastics. It is testimony to this tendency to uselessness in the theory of marginal utility that it can be used to obscure for examination purposes simple points in the theory of indifference curves:

T or F: If Max Hartwell consumes only bread and water and if the marginal utilities of each depend only on the ratios in which the two are consumed, then neither is inferior to him, technically speaking.

A: True. Along any ray through the origin in Figure 2.13, the marginal utilities of bread and water are constant, because along a given ray the ratio in which the two are consumed is constant. Since the marginal utilities along the ray are constant, so too are their ratios. But the ratio of marginal utilities is the slope of an indifference curve, as was just shown

$$\frac{MU_B}{MU_W} = \frac{\Delta U/\Delta B}{\Delta U/\Delta W} = \left.\frac{\Delta W}{\Delta B}\right|_{U_{\text{constant}}}$$

Therefore the slopes of all indifference curves along any given ray are the same, as shown in Figure 2.13. In other words, a rise in Hartwell's income (prices being constant) will cause him to increase each good in the same proportion, as he does, for example, for E_0 to E_1. Both goods increase with income. Neither is inferior.

Summary

The theory of marginal utility is the oldest theory of the role of tastes in consumption. It amounts to an application of the rule of rational life: pursue an activity (such as consuming corn, producing steel, seeking high public office, waging war, or learning economics) until the marginal benefit of pursuing it a little further has fallen to the point of being equal to its marginal cost. To do less or more is to forego some happiness. Attractive as this formulation is, it is clumsier in expression than the theory of indifference curves and identical in content.

**Figure 2.13
A Condition for the
Expansion Path to Be a Ray**

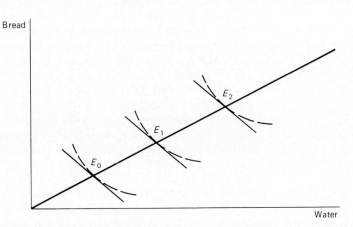

If marginal utilities, and hence marginal rates of substitution, depend only on the ratio of the two goods consumed, then the consumer does not alter the ratio of goods consumed when his or her income increases.

APPENDIX TO SECTION 2.4

The Mathematics of Marginal Utility: Lagrangean Multipliers

A Symmetrical Way of Stating the Consumer's Maximizing Problem

☐ Paradoxically, the indirect language of marginal utility is nonetheless sometimes an advantage. Recall that the appendix to Section 2.1 showed how first-term calculus solves the consumer's problem. The present section shows how second-term calculus solves the problem by a neater method, known as the method of the *Lagrangean multiplier*. In economic applications the method might better be called the *method of the marginal utility of income*.

The consumer's problem is to choose, say, books and corn to maximize a utility function, say, $U(B, C)$, subject to a budget constraint, $Y = P_B(B) + P_C(C)$. In Chapter 1 the budget constraint was substituted into the utility function, yielding an ugly and asymmetrical thing to be maximized (were B, for example, eliminated by substitution)

$$U\left(\frac{Y - P_C C}{P_B}, C\right)$$

Now it was just shown that the theory of marginal utilities is the same as the theory of indifference curves. In view of this fact, it must be true that the problem to which the three solution equations of the theory of marginal utility correspond is a correct formulation of the consumer's maximizing problem. Look at the three equations again:

$$MU_B = P_B \times MU_Y$$

$$MU_C = P_C \times MU_Y$$

$$Y = P_B B + P_C C$$

The terms P_B, P_C, and Y are all fixed and are given to the consumer. Marginal utilities are derivatives, indeed, partial derivatives (slopes of slices of hills). Call MU_Y λ (the Greek "L," in honor of Lagrange, the mathematician who invented the method). Now ask, what maximizing problem would give the three equations as the necessary conditions for a solution? A little experimentation will make clear that it is maximize with respect to B, C, and λ the expression $U(B, C) + \lambda(Y - P_B B - P_C C)$, because taking partial derivatives with respect to B, C, and λ and setting them equal to zero leads to the three equations. Thus,

1. $\dfrac{\partial(\text{the expression})}{\partial B} = \dfrac{\partial U(B, C)}{\partial B} - \lambda P_B$ is to $= 0$

2. $\dfrac{\partial(\text{the expression})}{\partial C} = \dfrac{\partial U(B, C)}{\partial C} - \lambda P_C$ is to $= 0$

3. $\dfrac{\partial(\text{the expression})}{\partial \lambda} = Y - P_B(B) - P_C C$ is to $= 0$

These three equations are the equations of the marginal utility theory. The nicely symmetrical expression from which the three equations are derived is called the _Lagrangean._ It consists of the utility function (whatever it may be: BC or $(BC)^{1/3}$ or whatever) plus the Lagrangean multiplier (i.e., the marginal utility of income) multiplied by the budget constraint when the constraint is expressed as an equation to be set equal to zero, that is, when all income is spent $Y - P_B B - P_C C = 0$.

☐

The Lagrangean Multiplier Is the Price of Income

The chief virtue of the method of Lagrangean multipliers is that it keeps the economics in plain view instead of burying it under algebra. A Lagrangean multiplier can be interpreted as the marginal opportunity cost of violating a budget constraint, that is, underspending or (attempted) overspending of the available money income. Some choice of B and C yields the maximum utility that Barbara Solow can attain (call it $U^M = 10.77$ joys, for example) for the income that she has and the prices that she faces. If she is sloppy about making her choices, she will choose some bundle, say, B^A, C^A, that entails underspending her income—by $Y - P_B(B)^A - P_C(C)^A$. The utility she sacrifices by being so foolish is clearly the amount of income she underspends multiplied by the marginal utility of income, λ. This is what it means to say that λ is also the marginal opportunity cost of underspending. If her marginal utility of income is, for example, 0.072 joys per dollar of income and she underspends by 12 dollars, she is sacrificing 0.86 joys of utility, or about 8% of her total happiness.

Another way of looking at the Lagrangean multiplier will seem odd but will illuminate its economic meaning. Suppose for a moment that Solow valued having unspent income left in her bank account, in the amount $Y - P_B B - P_C C$, whatever it might be. The λ (the marginal utility of income) can then be interpreted as the utility value she puts on each unspent dollar. It is the utility price of spending a dollar rather than leaving it unspent; since it is not literally a price she faces in a market, it is called a *shadow price*. The Lagrangean expression $U(B, C) + \lambda(Y - P_B B - P_C C)$ will be the total utility she gets, both from consumption, $U(B, C)$, and from storing money, $\lambda(Y - P_B B - P_C C)$. Given a value for λ, choosing B and C to maximize the Lagrangean will maximize her total utility. The Lagrangean, in other words, has a direct economic interpretation.

Now the supposition that she in fact values unspent income was to be made only "for a moment." Actually she wants to have zero unspent income. But suppose that she is a disorganized person who cannot keep close track of her bank account. If she set λ in her mind at the right level, she could buy, say, corn out to the point at which $MU_C = \lambda P_C$ and let the bank account take care of itself. For the right choice of λ (i.e., the equilibrium value of λ), her choices of B and C would exactly exhaust her income. If she chose λ too high—that is, if she overvalued unspent income in the bank—she would leave too much income in the bank, namely, some income: she wants it to be zero. If she chose λ too low—that is, if she undervalued unspent income—she would have too little unspent income, namely, negative income. In other words, she would spend more than her income, or she would try to do so until her banker and the sheriff caught up with her.

In other words, Solow can use the Lagrangean multiplier, which is the marginal utility of unspent income, to decentralize her decisions. It summarizes in one number the tightness of her budget constraint and leads her as by an invisible hand to spend only as much as she has.

The same logic can be applied to the internal affairs of businesses (in which a dollar earned in the Benton Harbor branch has clearly the same value as a dollar earned in the Wassau branch) or governments. Decentralization has a contrived air in a consuming unit, but it is natural in a producing unit, as we shall see. In any case, the Lagrangean multiplier is not merely a mathematical trick. It is a price.

Summary

The theory of marginal utility has the merit of leading naturally to the method of the Lagrangean multiplier. The multiplier is interpretable as the marginal utility of a dollar of income, the opportunity cost of a dollar of underspending, the value put on a dollar left unspent, the utility price a consumer would pay to increase his or her income by a dollar, or the price charged for a resource used by the branches of a decentralized enterprise. All are the same. The method is applicable to maximization under a constraint.

QUESTIONS FOR SECTION 2.4

1. Larry Westphal produces in one hour 5 fish or 1 bushel of wheat, fish and wheat being his only objects of desire. Set up his Lagrangean problem. What is the interpretation of the Lagrangean multiplier?

True or False

2. The marginal utility of garbage is negative.

3. If the marginal utility of heroin increases as more is consumed, an addict would set the marginal utility of a shot of heroin equal to its price multiplied by the marginal utility of income.

4. In taking an exam, Atack, a rational student, allocates his time to the various questions so as to equalize his marginal point utility per minute on all questions.

5. The marginal utility of food to Zecher depends only on the amount of food (and not on the amount of housing) and the marginal utility declines as more food is consumed; likewise for housing. Therefore, both food and housing are normal goods. (Hint: Express the first two equations of the marginal utility theory in the alternative form $MU_F/MU_H = P_F/P_H$. Notice that P_F/P_H is fixed. If all of an increase in income is spent on F, can the equality be maintained?)

6. Margaret Comi, a consumer of housing and food with a so-called *Cobb–Douglas utility function,* that is, $U = H^\alpha F^\beta$, will increase her amounts of housing and food (prices held constant) in proportion to increase in her income, Y, and will spend the same shares of her income on housing and food regardless of their prices or her income.

3

The Measurement of Utility and the Economics of Risk

3.1 Paradise Lost: Nonmeasurable Utility

□

*The Measurement of
Utility Is Difficult*

The talk of "marginal utility" and "contour lines on a hill of utility" began to make economists uncomfortable almost as soon as it started. How is one to measure utility? To put it another way, how could one devise an experiment to determine whether or not Frenkel gets more utility from the third hot dog than from the fourth? Such questions are answerable for height or temperature. For example, having agreed that a certain platinum-iridium bar at the International Bureau of Weights and Measures near Paris is to be called "1 meter," Frenkel's height in meters is measurable; having agreed that the height of a column of mercury at the freezing point of water under certain specified conditions is to be called "32° Fahrenheit" and the boiling point "212°," his body temperature is measurable. The question is not so obviously answerable for his utility of hot dogs. The volume of his squeals of delight as successive hot dogs are presented to him is not much of an answer. Neither is his own testimony, for in that case his observation of his own behavior ("Ah yes, the third hot dog gives me 10 joys, the fourth only 8 joys") is being substituted for the scientist's, and tomorrow he may testify differently, or confess that he lied today. The objectivity and invariance of measurement so treasured in science is spoiled by Frenkel's participation in the measurement. The entire theory appears to depend on unmeasurable quantities.

□

*The Measurement of
Utility Is Pointless*

For nearly 50 years some of the best minds in economics, from Pareto in his *Manuele di economia politica* (1906) to Houthakker in his "Revealed Preference and the Utility Function" (*Economica*, 1950), labored to free economists from the embarrassment of speaking quantitatively about things they could not quantify. The labor was successful, although it is unclear that the result was worth the opportunity cost of alternative employment for these minds. The result is easily explained. So long as two hills of happiness between housing and food have the same contours dropped onto the housing-food plane, each will yield the same equilibrium point for given budget lines. In other words, it does not matter whether three successively higher contour

50

lines are labeled, on the one hand, 10 joys, 20 joys, and 30 joys or, on the other, 65.3 joys, 65.4 joys, and 6,598,135 joys. If the consumer is able to move from the second to the third utility contour, it does not matter whether the move transports the consumer to ecstacy or merely to a bit more of the pathetically small happiness attainable in this veil of tears. The consumer will in either case make the move. The jargon is that indifference curves need only be _ordinal_ (a certain curve is the first, another the second, and so on) not _cardinal_ (a certain curve yields 10 joys, another 20 joys, and so on) to describe the observable behavior resulting from tastes.

□ **The Theory of Consumption Can Get Along Without Measurable Utility** The _indifference curve_ is, then, an appropriate phrase. It speaks of combinations of food and housing among which a consumer is unable to choose, not of the amount of happiness the consumer derives from the combinations. Conceivably one could map the indifference curves of a consumer by an elaborate questionnaire, asking the consumer to rank many different bundles of, say, housing and all other goods. Economists, however, are more suspicious of questionnaires than are other social scientists, so suspicious that they seldom invoke even imaginary questionnaires, preferring to infer preferences from imaginary behavior. In the most neutral language, indeed, indifference curves are called _behavior lines_. The experiment from which one could infer behavior lines is an exercise in revealed preference, exhibited in Figure 3.1. Recall that one combination of housing and all other goods presented to Cynthia Morris is "revealed preferred" to another if the second combination is inside the budget line when she buys the first (she could have bought the second combination rather than the first, but did not). Present a consumer with budget line α and watch her choose point A on it. Now find a budget line β with a slope greater than α for which the consumer will choose a point such as B, also on the α budget line. Now find a budget line γ with a slope greater than α for which the consumer will choose a point such as C, also on the β budget line. By revealed preference, A is the best of the three points

Figure 3.1
Revealed Preference Can Yield Indifference Curves

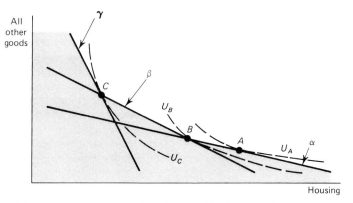

Indifference curve U_A is found by finding all budget lines that contain no points that are revealed preferred to U_A.

(see the dashed indifference curves); indeed, it is superior to the entire shaded area below the budget lines for which the three points are in fact chosen.

By parallel reasoning one can construct an upper shaded area of points better than A. And by putting B very close to A, C close to B, D close to C, and so forth, one can reduce the unshaded area to a line, at least locally. The line will separate points superior to A from those inferior to A. It will be an indifference curve (the U_A curve). The experiment (which, it must be pointed out, has never been performed on anyone but college students in the grip of professors of economics or psychology) yields behavior lines (or indifference curves or whatever one wants to call them) without mentioning the dreaded word "utility."

As the inventor of indifference curves put it in 1881, "We cannot *count* the golden sands of life; we cannot *number* the 'innumerable smile' of seas of love; but we seem to be capable of observing that there is here a *greater*, there a *less*, multitude of pleasure-units, mass of happiness; and that is enough."[1]

Summary

From the 1870s on, economists hoped that experimental psychology, with its new techniques for measuring stimuli, would provide them with a way to measure happiness. They gradually lost hope, but made the best of a bad situation by noticing that none of their uses of contour lines on the hill of happiness depended on the measurability of their altitudes. Measurable marginal or total utility was a fifth wheel in the theory of the consumer's choice. The problem remained that the shape of the contour lines themselves appeared to depend on asking consumers to rank bundles. Asking consumers whether they are happier with one bundle than with another is only less subjective than asking them how much happier they are. In the 1930s and 1940s, however, even this element of subjectivity was expunged from the theory, by demonstrating that the observed behavior of consumers (not their testimony) sufficed (albeit under ideal circumstances) to draw up their indifference curves.

APPENDIX TO SECTION 3.1

The mathematics of the ordinality of indifference curves depends only on the chain (or the function of a function) rule of the calculus. Take Morris's utility function to be any function, $U(H, F)$. The condition for equilibrium, signifying partial derivatives with subscripts, is $U_H/U_F = P_H/P_F$. Now suppose that $U(H, F)$ is transformed by inserting it into a function G, such as $G(U) = U^2$ for positive U, that always rises and has no flat places (i.e., it is monotonically increasing).

[1] Francis Ysidro Edgeworth (1845–1926), *Mathematical Psychics: An Essay on the Application of Mathematics to the Moral Sciences* (London, 1881), pp. 8–9, his italics. Edgeworth, fellow of All Souls College, first editor of the *Economic Journal*, the product of a marriage of an Anglo-Irish landowner to a Spanish refugee, invented much of the diagrammatic machinery of economics. To quote him as an ordinalist (although that is what the sentence appears to mean) gives an inaccurate picture of his views. Like most of the leaders of the marginalist revolution, he believed utility to be measurable.

The hill is stretched to higher altitudes, and the higher a place on the hill is initially the more it is stretched. The "new" equilibrium for the new utility function will be, applying the chain rule, $(G_U \times U_H)/(G_U \times U_F) = P_H/P_F$. Clearly, if G_U is never zero (i.e., if G has no flat places), G_U cancels, and the same condition as before holds. The equilibrium is not new; it is the same. Clearly, therefore, any assignment of utilities to various contours that retains their order (as does a monotonically increasing reassignment) will do as well as any other. That is, HF, $(HF)^2$, $\log HF$, $\alpha + \beta(HF)$, and so forth all have the same indifference contours in the H, F plane.

3.2   Paradise Regained: Measurable Utility

□

The Utility of Different Prospects

In 1944 the goddess of knowledge played a great joke on economists. At the very moment they were growing confident by the preceding reasoning that (thank God) their theories of the consumer's choice did not require measurable marginal utility, it pleased this goddess to give them a method of measuring it.[2] The method uses gambling. Just as subjecting John Martin to various budget lines induces him to reveal the order in which he ranks bundles of goods, subjecting him to various gambles can induce him to reveal the utility levels he attaches to bundles of goods.

Suppose that Martin buys a 7-room house at Cairo, Illinois on a low-lying bank of the Mississippi. He consumes each year in addition to the 7 rooms of housing some other goods, say, 200 pounds of hamburger. The gamble he faces each year is that the Mississippi will flood and his house will be destroyed. In the event of this unlucky chance, he will consume, let us say, 2 rooms of housing (a mobile home) and 120 pounds of hamburger: the flood reduces his income (strictly speaking, his wealth), and he therefore consumes less. He has so far two bundles, lucky and unlucky. Suppose that he also has available a third bundle, namely, buying insurance on the house each year that will make him a little poorer but safe. The insurance, unless it is provided in the form of flood relief by the government, is not free to Martin, so paying it will shrink his annual budget line below the lucky budget line of no flood. Suppose that in this safe situation he consumes 180 pounds of hamburger and 6 rooms (cutting his hamburger consumption and renting out room 7 to pay the insurance company). His three possible budget lines and the three bundles they lead to are portrayed in Figure 3.2.

Notice that Martin follows the arrows if he does not buy the insurance and the flood comes. The house is destroyed, but he does not sit mournfully in the rubble with 0 rooms: he uses some of his hamburger (all other goods) to buy 2 rooms. Notice, too, that unless the

[2] Her agents were John von Neumann and Oskar Morgenstern, *Theory of Games and Economic Behavior* (Princeton, N.J.: Princeton University Press, 1944), Chapter 3. The book is one of the classics of economics. There is no new thing under the sun, and von Neumann and Morgenstern were anticipated in this by two mathematicians, Frank Ramsey in 1931 and, for a special case, Daniel Bernoulli in 1738.

Figure 3.2
The Choice Between
Insurance and a Gamble

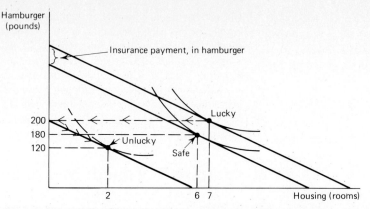

The consumer can buy insurance that guarantees the budget line safe or can take the gamble with the river, which will leave either budget line lucky or budget line unlucky.

insurance (paid in hamburger) costs more than the house, the safe budget line lies between the lucky and unlucky budget lines.

□
Introducing
Probabilities of
Prospects

So far there is nothing novel in the analysis. The indifference curves in the diagram are merely ordinal, merely rankings that might be revealed by subjecting Martin to an experiment in shifting budget lines. But suppose that he is told (and believes) that there is a 1 in 20 chance each year that the Mississippi will flood and a 19 in 20 chance that it will not. If he does not buy the insurance, then it is reasonable to say that he has revealed a preference for this gamble over the safe bundle. In other words, descending into a vocabulary of cardinal, measurable utility, were the three utility numbers (in joys) attached to the three possible bundles called U_{lucky} joys, U_{unlucky} joys, U_{safe} joys, he could be said to have revealed that the utility he gets on average from the gamble, that is, $\frac{19}{20}(U_{\text{lucky}}$ joys$) + \frac{1}{20}(U_{\text{unlucky}}$ joys$)$, is for him a greater number than is U_{safe} joys. This is the crucial step in the argument. Martin is assumed to behave like a smart professional gambler, who takes a gamble for money only when he thinks that the money he will end up with on average (the phrase "on average" meaning weighting the lucky and unlucky dollars by their chances of happening) is greater than the money he started with (and can have safe for sure by simply not taking the gamble). The difference is that Martin gambles for joys instead of dollars.[3]

[3] The assumption that Martin—or anyone—gambles for joys as a wise gambler gambles for money is still controversial, more than 30 years after it was first proposed. The essence of one objection is that people may love or hate gambling itself. If Martin hates gambling, he may refuse the gamble (i.e., buy the insurance) even though the average utility of taking the gamble is higher than the utility of the safe bundle. The essence of another objection is that people do not calculate as closely as the theory demands, that they are ignorant of the facts, or that they are governed by habit. Such objections could be made (and have been, frequently) of all economic theory, and do not appear to have special force in the present context.

Figure 3.3
One's Choice Between
Safe Bundles and Gambles
Reveals One's Utility

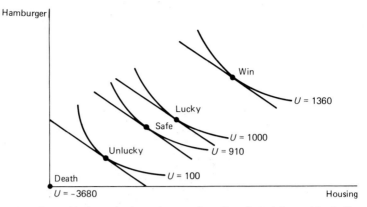

If the utilities of lucky and safe are known, the utility of win is learned by finding a gamble that includes win. If the utilities of safe and lucky are known, the utility of win can be learned. A gamble that offers win or safe is found that is as desired as the prospect of not gambling and remaining at lucky. Then the equation $P_{win} U_{win} + P_{safe} U_{safe} = U_{lucky}$ can be solved for U_{win}.

The Utility of the
Prospects Can Be
Derived from the
Experiment

Now suppose that the announced risk of the flood is raised above 1 year in 20. Were the risk very high, say, 1 year in 2, he would buy the insurance, revealing that he preferred the safe bundle to the gamble. Suppose that 1 flood every 10 years is the level of risk that makes him just indifferent between buying the insurance and taking the gamble. Therefore the average utility in joys from the gamble must be equal to the utility in joys from the safe bundle: $\frac{9}{10}(U_{lucky}$ joys) + $\frac{1}{10}(U_{unlucky}$ joys) = U_{safe} joys.

If one knew the number of joys from the lucky and unlucky bundles, one could put a number on the safe bundle. Go ahead. Set U_{lucky} at, say, 1000 joys and $U_{unlucky}$ at, say, 100 joys. The U_{safe} is then $\frac{9}{10}(1000) + \frac{1}{10}(100) = 910$ joys. This number is "the" utility of the safe bundle in much the same sense as "the" temperature today in Iowa City is 50° Fahrenheit. A scale of temperature requires two arbitrary numbers to set it (32°F freezes water, 212°F boils it), because two numbers are required to fix how much a single degree is. Likewise, the scale of utility requires two arbitrary numbers to set it (U_{lucky} = 1000 joys, $U_{unlucky}$ = 100 joys). Once the scale of joys is set, any bundle Martin consumes can be placed on the scale by subjecting him to choices between gambles linked to the initial points.

The Army Corps of Engineers builds a levee that eliminates gambling with floods. A local sport offers him a 1 in 5 chance at 50 additional pounds of hamburger (that Martin would use to move out to point win in Figure 3.3) in exchange for the hamburger formerly used to pay the insurance if he loses (in which case he would end at point safe).

Were he just indifferent between risking the insurance money this way and staying at a third bundle, lucky, win would be worth the solution of

$$\frac{1}{5} U_{\text{win}} + \frac{4}{5} U_{\text{safe}} = U_{\text{lucky}}$$

or

$$\frac{1}{5} U_{\text{win}} + \frac{4}{5} (910) = 1000$$

or

$$U_{\text{win}} = 1360 \text{ joys}$$

as in the diagram. And by the meaning of an indifference curve, all the bundles on the indifference curve running through win would have this same utility, 1360 joys. Again, suppose the Corps' levee broke, leaving Martin at unlucky, a desperate man. He might contemplate some other dangerous activity, such as attempting to jump a motorcycle across the Mississippi for money. Suppose that success in this attempt would give him the bundle win, that failure would give him the bundle death, and that he was just indifferent between making the attempt on the one hand and staying at unlucky on the other when the chance of success was 3 in 4. Then death would be worth the solution of

$$\frac{1}{4} U_{\text{death}} + \frac{3}{4} U_{\text{win}} = U_{\text{unlucky}}$$

or

$$\frac{1}{4} U_{\text{death}} + \frac{3}{4} (1360) = 100$$

or

$$U_{\text{death}} = -3680 \text{ joys}$$

as in the diagram. In like fashion one could attach a utility number to every conceivable indifference curve. If you know the probabilities Martin attaches to various events, then, his utility is in one sense measurable.

Summary

An experiment in alternative budget lines suffices to give indifference curves a rank; an experiment in alternative gambles suffices to give them numbers. The numbers measure utility in nearly the same sense as temperature is measurable.

QUESTIONS FOR SECTION 3.2

1. Derek Van Hoorn contemplates buying 100 shares of Nachtschwärmer Home Improvement Company at $1 a share. He believes that there is a 1 in 4 chance that he will gain $400 and a 3 in 4 chance that he will lose the $100 entirely. He finds himself unable to decide between buying the shares and doing nothing. *True or false:* His marginal utility of income around his present income is declining.

2. Suppose that you knew somehow that Van Hoorn gets 35 joys from the $100 lower income, 36.25 joys from his present income, and 40 joys from the $400 higher income. Suppose further that Van Hoorn loves playing the stock market, to the extent of getting 2 joys from the thrill of buying any Nachtschwärmer stock and participating in its ups and downs.

a. If Van Hoorn believes that there is a little over a 1 in 20 chance of the Nachtschwärmer investment's earning him the $400 gain (and a little below a 19 in 20 chance of it earning him the $100 loss), what choice will you observe him making between his present income and the gamble?

b. If you knew as before that the $100 lower income was worth 35 joys to Van Hoorn and the $400 higher income worth 40 joys but did *not* know that his present income was worth 36.25 joys or that the joys he got from gambling was 2 joys, what number would you put on Van Hoorn's utility from his present income?

c. What do you conclude about the necessity for the method of measuring utility of assuming no love or hate of gambling?

3. Marilyn Coopersmith, an executive in a publishing firm, will gain $100,000 for the firm if an economics book she publishes is (very) successful; she will lose $25,000 for the firm if the book is unsuccessful. *True or false:* If Coopersmith will not publish any book that she believes has less than a 1 in 5 chance of success but will publish one with more than a 1 in 5 chance (that is, in such cases she preserves the firm's present income, *Y*, instead of risking some of it in the book), then her marginal utility of income for the firm is constant.

True or False

4. If rooms of housing sell for 50 pounds of hamburger per room, Martin's marginal utility of income declines from unlucky and safe compared with safe and lucky.

3.3 Imperfections in Paradise?

☐
Utility Is Not Measurable Absolutely

There are, however, several different senses of measurability, and there are three senses in which the method of gambling does *not* measure utility. The first is trivial. Because the unit of marginal or total utility depends on the scale chosen (just as one chooses a meter to be a meter or a degree Fahrenheit to be a degree Fahrenheit) and no scale is uniquely suitable, the unit in which marginal or total utility is measured has no absolute significance. The utility of lucky could be set at 1 joy or at 10,000 joys, multiplying all the other utilities by 0.001 or 10, without affecting any conclusions drawn.

The second is somewhat less trivial, but not much less. Although one *marginal* utility for Martin can be said to be three times another, one *total* utility cannot be said to be three times another. Each degree of temperature in the centigrade (or Celsius) scale, in which the freezing and boiling points of water are 0° and 100° instead of 32° and 212°, corresponds to 1.8° in the Fahrenheit scale. Neither scale is "correct," for the choice of what numbers to attach to the freezing and boiling points of water is arbitrary, just as choosing to call the utility of Martin's lucky bundle 1000 joys and that of his unlucky bundle 100 joys is arbitrary. Another choice results in another scale. A temperature of 212°F is 212/32 = 6.63 "times as hot" as 32°F only in the Fahrenheit scale; in the Celsius scale it is 100/0 (i.e., undefined nonsense) times as hot.[4] It is therefore meaningless to say that the winter of 1977 was "twice as cold as normal." On the other hand, it is meaningful to say that the increment of temperature (the marginal temperature) from 60°F to 212°F is 5.43 times the increment from 32°F to 60°F, because no matter what scale is used, the statement is true. Thus 60°F is 15.56°C, and $(212 - 60)/(60 - 32) = 152/28 = 5.43$ gives the same result as $(100 - 15.56)/(15.56 - 0) = 5.43$. In similar fashion, as you can show by replicating the calculations for a scale of $U_{\text{lucky}} = 2000$ $U_{\text{unlucky}} = 1000$, it is meaningless to say that Martin gets $910/1000 = 0.91$ times more utility from safe as from unlucky, but it is meaningful to say that his additional (i.e., marginal) utility derived by moving from unlucky to safe is $(910 - 100)/(1000 - 910) = 9.0$ times the additional utility derived by moving from safe to lucky. As long as marginal utility is measurable on some scale, it is no great loss to be unable to measure total utility, since it plays no role in the economist's model of the consumer.

□
Utility Is Not
Comparable
Between People

The third and final sense in which the gambling theory leaves utility unmeasurable is more serious. It is that utilities, whether total or marginal, cannot be compared between Martin and, say, Keavy. To assert that Martin (a poor man) gets more joys from an additional dollar of income than does Keavy (a rich man) is, regrettably, meaningless. What is regrettable about it is that, were such an assertion possible, we could redistribute income from Keavy to Martin with confidence that the world's happiness was being increased. What is meaningless about it, in one usage of the word by philosophers, is that no conceivable experiment could convince someone who disbelieved it that Keavy's dollar contained more happiness than did Martin's.[5]

---

[4] Once absolute zero is found (−460°F or −273°C) as it was by physicists in the nineteenth century, such statements take on meaning. Starting each scale from its absolute zero, the boiling point of water on the Fahrenheit scale is $(212 + 460)/(32 + 460) = 1.366$ times its freezing point and the same on the Celsius scale: $(100 + 273)/(0 + 273) = 1.366$. But there is no obvious way to measure absolute zero on a utility scale. Death will not usually suffice, because most people can imagine fates worse than mere death: their own deaths compounded by the deaths of their families, for example, or terrible and worthless lives. For the undignified egomaniac that economists sometimes assume typifies mankind, however, death may be zero.

[5] "No conceivable experiment" is perhaps a little strong, for a philosopher, John Rawls, in *A Theory of Justice* (Cambridge, Mass.: Harvard University Press, 1971), and a number of economists have in fact conceived one. They have extended in a most ingenious way the notion of revealing preferences by gambling to social as well as private choices. The gamble they propose is to imagine yourself before you knew who you were going to be (the daughter of a millionaire in Texas or the son of a porter in Hong Kong) choosing how you would wish society to be organized. The lucky event in this lottery would be to become the millionaire's daughter, the unlucky event to become the porter's son. Rawls believes that you would choose to make the society you were about to

**Figure 3.4
The Uneasy Case for
Progressive Taxation**

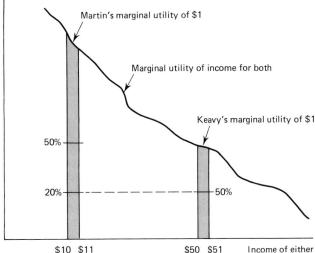

If marginal utility of income were measurable and comparable among individuals (it is, in fact, neither) and were diminishing, then a tax that equalized marginal sacrifice would be progressive with respect to income.

Q: The incomes of Martin (who is poor) and Keavy (who is rich) are to be taxed. Suppose that their marginal utilities of income fall as their incomes rise. *True or false:* If it is thought to be just that both make equal marginal sacrifices of utility in paying income tax, then it can be demonstrated scientifically that the tax should be progressive; that is, the rich Keavy should be charged a higher percentage tax on a dollar of extra income than the poor Martin.

A: False, because science cannot compare the utilities felt by the two from an extra dollar. By contrast, this argument for progressive taxation assumes that Keavy and Martin have the same commensurate curves of marginal utility (see Figure 3.4).

Martin's utility from an extra dollar is the tall column in the diagram, Keavy's is the shorter one. Were the tax on the dollar proportional instead of progressive, for example, 50% for both men (see the two points marked 50%), the $0.50 taken from Martin would be more valuable than the $0.50 taken from Keavy (a poor man's sacrifice of utility would be larger than a rich man's). To bring the marginal sacrifices into equality, Martin's additional dollar must be taxed at a lower rate (20% in Figure 3.4) than Keavy's (50%). That is, income taxes should be progressive. But the elaboration of the argument is idle,

---

enter more equal in income, to reduce the risk in the lottery. If this were true, it would solve implicitly the problem of comparing utilities. But it is uncertain whether it is true. See, for example, Robert Nozick, *Anarchy, State and Utopia* (New York: Basic Books, 1974), especially Chapter 7, Section II.

because we do not know whether or not Keavy has the same curve of marginal utility as Martin.

As the economist Henry C. Simons remarked in 1938, at the time the weaknesses in the argument were becoming clear,

One derives practical implications from the criterion of equality, or proportionality, of sacrifice precisely in proportion to one's knowledge of something which no one has ever known, or ever will know, anything about. Perhaps this goes far toward explaining the popularity of these doctrines among academic writers.[6]

The case for progressive taxation must rest directly on a moral premise that more equality of incomes is desirable, not indirectly on a pseudo-scientific comparison of happinesses. Such are the limits of measurable utility.

Summary

The analogy between measuring utility and measuring temperature (at any rate before absolute zero had been located) is quite exact. Neither the units nor the proportions between levels of utility or temperature are immutable; what is immutable is the proportion between differences. Marginal utility is not measurable uniquely any more than is the increase in temperature (the "marginal temperature") between a cold and a hot day (an increase of 60°F can be expressed as an increase of 33.3°C). But the rate of decline of marginal utility *is* measurable uniquely, just as a rise in temperature of 60°F is half a rise of 120°F (33.3°C and 66.6°C). The analogy breaks down in only one important feature: you can make interpersonal comparisons of rates of rise of marginal temperature, but you cannot make interpersonal comparisons of rates of decline of marginal utility.

QUESTIONS FOR SECTION 3.3

True or False

1. If Martin's utility of lucky is set at 100 joys and of unlucky at 10 joys (instead of 1000 and 100), then his utility of death is −368 joys.

2. If Martin's utility of lucky is set at 1000 joys (as before) but his utility of unlucky at 500 joys (instead of 100), then his utility of win is 1200 joys (instead of 1360).

3. Accepting interpersonal comparisons of identical curves of the marginal utility of income, if the sum over Mrs. Rich and Mrs. Poor of utility lost from income taxation is to be as small as possible, then only Rich should be taxed (unless the government wants so much tax revenue that Rich's income is driven down to Poor's).

[6] *Personal Income Taxation* (Chicago: University of Chicago Press, 1938), portion reprinted in R. W. Houghton, ed., *Public Finance: Selected Readings* (London: Penguin, 1970, p. 21). For an excellent, nontechnical discussion of the issue, see Walter J. Blum and Harry Kalven, Jr., *The Uneasy Case for Progressive Taxation* (Chicago: University of Chicago Press, 1953), and subsequent editions.

3.4 Living in Paradise: The Uses of Measurable Utility

The Utility of Income

☐ It is not immediately obvious that whether or not a personal index of utility can be measured is important for explaining human behavior. Economics has long been an academic pursuit, and therefore the issues about which it has revolved have often had, naturally enough, an academic tone. The measurement of utility is merely one of many issues whose practical import seems small—whether or not cost determines price or whether or not an economy will under certain ideal conditions work optimally.

What has been fruitful about these debates is not usually their conclusions (if any) but the tools for understanding behavior invented along the way. The premier tool is the curve of the utility of income. Just as the marginal utility of food is the slope of a clean slice of the hill of happiness for a given quantity of all other goods, the marginal utility of income is the slope at an irregular slice along the best path (for given prices) up the hill. In the top panel of Figure 3.5, the slice is the dashed expansion path. The bottom panel plots against income the utility of income (income measured in all other goods). The resulting curve is the way in which the slice would appear if you looked at it along the budget lines standing on the all other goods axis.[7]

Whatever one might think of its status in a world of certainty, the shape of the curve has meaning in a world of uncertainty. It does measure something, for utility is measurable, at least for a single person. And it neatly summarizes the person's condition in various circumstances, allowing the analysis to collapse all commodities into one (*income*) with an associated utility. The idea is a very useful one.

Increasing Marginal Utility Implies Accepting Unfair Gambles

☐ Consider, for example, the situation of Linda Zecher, a gambler playing in a casino in Las Vegas.[8] Zecher knows that the games are unfair, in the technical sense that on average she will lose. The State of Nevada and the casinos take a certain percentage of the amounts wagered and give back to the gamblers only what is left (from 95% in blackjack, more if the gambler has a good memory, down to 70 or 60% in slot machines). Yet Zecher plays. Why? An obvious and true answer is that she likes the thrill of playing. Another is that she miscalculates the odds or believes that Lady Luck is smiling on her. But there is another possibility that would be the only possibility for a cold-blooded person with a sure grasp of the odds who nonetheless gambles.

Q: Zecher faces a 50:50 chance of gaining $10 or losing $10. *True or false:* If her marginal utility of income is increasing, she will prefer the gamble to keeping her present income.

---

[7] Notice that the curve will shift if relative prices shift. For the analysis to be simple, the gambles contemplated must be gambles that do not themselves shift relative prices.

[8] The first, decisive step in translating the von Neumann–Morgenstern theory into a tool for understanding behavior was taken by the economist Milton Friedman and the statistician L. J. Savage in their paper, "The Utility Analysis of Choices Involving Risk," *Journal of Political Economy* 56 (August 1948): 279–304. The following draws heavily on this paper.

A: True. The gamble is a fair one. That is, on average she neither gains nor loses income by taking it. In Figure 3.6 Zecher's utility of income is upward curving, the gamble is the line between lose and win, and with 50:50 odds Zecher expects to arrive on average at the point average halfway along the line (i.e., at the income she started with, measured along the horizontal axis).

Zecher will accept the gamble because the average utility she derives from it (namely, the utility of average, measured along the vertical axis) is greater than the utility derived from holding on to her present, riskless income, *Y.* Another way of putting it is to say that, because Zecher's marginal utility of income is rising (the slope of total utility is rising), the $10 increase in income is valued more than is the $10 decrease, and if the two are equally probable she expects to gain utility

Figure 3.5
How the Utility of Income Is Connected with Budget Lines (a) and Utility Contours (b)

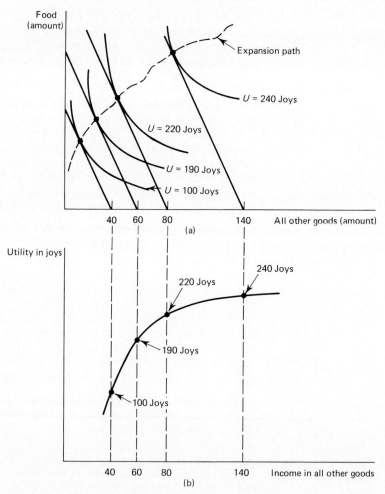

The utility of a given income in all other goods is equal to the utility associated with the highest isoutility contour attainable by a consumer with that income.

Figure 3.6
Increasing Marginal Utility
of Income Implies a
Preference for Risk and
Accepting Unfair Gambles

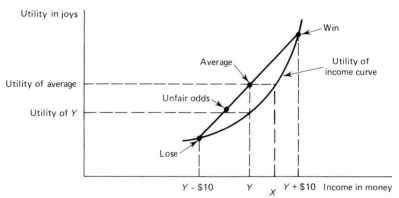

A risk-preferring person may find the prospect of increasing her income by $10 sufficiently attractive, relative to the prospect of losing $10, to accept a gamble that will leave her, on average, with a lower income than if the gamble had not been taken.

on balance by taking the gamble. In fact, she would accept worse odds than 50:50 and still take the gamble. Odds that placed her at unfair odds in the diagram (unfair because they lead to an income on average below her present income) give Zecher's utility a little above the utility of her present, riskless income. She would therefore accept them. She plays the tables at Las Vegas although the odds are unfair.

So a person with an upward-curving utility of income (i.e., a rising marginal utility of income) prefers fair (and even some unfair) gambles to a secure income. Equivalently, were the present, riskless income at X in Figure 3.6 instead of Y, the person would be willing to pay $X - Y$ dollars to get into a casino that offered an uneven chance of ending up at a new, lower income, Y, which explains why casinos are able to charge big admission fees to poker games held on their premises. A person who will pay to gamble is said to exhibit a preference for risk.[9]

Risk Aversion and
Unfair Insurance

Similarly, a person who will pay *not* to gamble is said to exhibit an aversion to risk, and the marginal utility of income is declining.

Q: Joe Reid pays $400 a year for automobile insurance that covers him against suits for damages if he kills somebody with his car. He reckons (correctly) that during the year there is a 1 in 1000 chance that he will kill somebody and be sued for $100,000. *True or false:* Reid is irrational to buy the insurance.

[9] A preference for risk in this sense is not the same as a love of gambling. The distinction is between liking the results of gambling and liking the act of gambling. If you find the distinction elusive, you are not alone—many economists agree with you. The question is whether or not acts of gambling themselves enter the utility function. As was shown in Question 2 at the end of Section 3.2, the method of gambling breaks down if gambling itself is a good or a bad. The distinction, however, is meaningful, in the sense that one can imagine an experiment to test whether or not acts of gambling enter the utility function. If our gambler in Las Vegas would be willing to pay to get into the fair game more than she could possibly earn by winning, that is, earnings $= (Y + \$10) - Y = \$10$, then it is clear that she likes the act of gambling, not merely its results. The hypothesis that she likes only its results is falsifiable.

A: False. The insurance he buys is, to be sure, unfair, again in the technical sense that he pays more for the insurance ($400) than the income he would expect to lose on average from taking the gamble: $-100,000 \, (1/1000) + 0 \, (99/1000) = \$100$. But if his marginal utility of income is declining, as in Figure 3.7, he is in fact willing to pay as much as $800 to avoid having to take the gamble (to make the argument clear, Figure 3.7 is purposely not drawn to the correct scale).

His position without an accident is win, but he faces the risk of lose, and on average will end up at average. The insurance company offers to give him a riskless income of $Y - \$400$. Because his marginal utility of income is declining, this amount of riskless income yields him more utility than does average. He therefore buys the $400 insurance, quite rationally.

Comment

Notice that the insurance company, insuring thousands of Joe Reids, will pay $100 a year in claims to the average Joe while collecting $400 a year from each. Its profits (which are practically riskless if the number of Joes is large) will be $300 times the number of Joes. But if the insurance companies compete with each other by tempting each others' clients away with lower insurance premiums, the companies will drive the premium down to $100 plus the administrative costs of insuring the clients. That is, the insurance will become fair, the Joes will be even better off than they were accepting the $400 offer (they will be at fair insurance rather than at insured at $400), and insurance companies will earn the normal profit of enterprise. That insurance was not fair on average would imply that insurance companies were to some degree protected from the full rigors of competition—by collusion to stop price cutting, for example, or, more innocently but with the same result, by the ignorance of their customers that cheaper prices exist.

Figure 3.7
Decreasing Marginal
Utility of Income Implies
an Aversion to Risk and
Accepting Unfair
Insurance

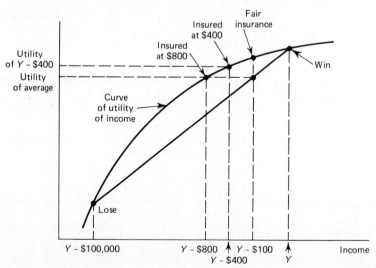

Someone with diminishing marginal utility of income finds the prospective loss of $100,000 so unattractive that he buys insurance against the loss, even at premiums so high that he pays the insurance company more than it will, on average, pay him.

*Crime and
Punishment*

The applications of the utility-of-income curve are not merely to gambling in casinos or insuring against rare disasters. All life is a gamble, and insurance is ubiquitous. Consider, for example, a life of crime.[10]

Burglary (breaking and entering) is a good case, for it is a passionless, premeditated, and nonviolent crime that few would claim is beyond the reach of economic analysis. Suppose that burglars were risk averse. This means that their marginal utility of income is declining and that they will only take gambles that raise their income on average (and not even all of these). It does not mean they will take no gambles. The gamble they take per burglary in the United States is about a 1 in 10 chance of being caught, convicted, and sent to prison for about two years on the one hand and a 9 in 10 chance of getting away with whatever they can steal and sell on the other. Since it is sad but true that people exist who will accept such odds, apparently the situation of the typical burglar is as portrayed in Figure 3.8.

**Figure 3.8
Why Burglars Burgle**

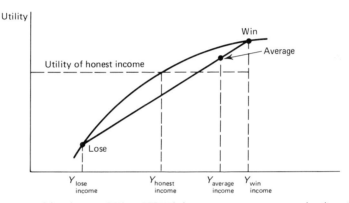

A rational burglar commits a crime if doing so increases expected utility. A risk-averse burglar will only commit a crime if the expected income from crime is greater than from the foregone noncriminal activity.

The burglar's income in prison is Y_{lose}, the money equivalent of such misery; his income if he is not caught is Y_{win}. His average utility from the gamble exceeds the utility of the income, Y_{honest}, he could earn in legal employment: that is why he is a burglar. His average income (distinct from his average utility) is also greater in burgling. To put it another way, in this case crime pays (it always pays in a utility sense if any criminals exist) for the same reason that being a human cannonball or a coal miner or a test pilot pays. Burglary is risky relative to, for example, working at a filling station, and a risk-averse and dishonest person will move from working at the filling station during the day to breaking into it during the night only if the odds of success are better than fair.

Each of the standard proposals for reducing burglary fits the diagram.

[10] What follows draws on an article by Gary S. Becker, "Crime and Punishment: An Economic Approach," *Journal of Political Economy* 76 (March–April 1968): 169–217, reprinted in William Breit and Harold M. Hochman, *Readings in Microeconomics*, 2nd ed. (New York: Holt, Rinehart, 1971), pp. 339–369.

The object is to place the point average below the utility of honest income, making crime not pay in a utility sense. One approach is to improve the economic lot of potential criminals, by reducing unemployment, for example, or by improving the welfare system. This amounts to raising Y_{honest} enough that the utility from it exceeds the utility of average. Another approach is to reduce the level of win, by not leaving $50,000 worth of diamonds on the dresser table or by making it more difficult to fence stolen television sets. Another approach is to move average down the gambling line, increasing the risk of getting caught by spending more on discrete burglar alarms and indiscrete police officers. Another is to make his "income" in jail, Y_{lose}, lower, by giving longer sentences (spending more on prisons) or making prison more unpleasant (spending less on prisons). And still another is to change his utility function, making him more risk averse (in which case he will demand more favorable odds before embarking on a life of crime) or making him feel that crime is evil (in which case he will dislike the act of taking a criminal gamble and will not in this sphere conform to the model of gambling with utilities), by giving him religion or psychiatry.

☐
Other Risk-Averse Behavior: Diversification

Risk aversion (concave utility of income) rather than risk preference is normally assumed to characterize human behavior, for the good reason that it explains much human behavior (the behavior, for example, of economists).

T or F: A person with a doctoral degree in economics employed by General Motors earns 40% more than one employed by the University of Michigan. Part of the difference can be explained by noting the greater security of academic employment and by supposing that the academicians are relatively risk averse.

A: True, obviously. Were economists risk preferrers, it would be false; that is, they would pay to gamble on employment by General Motors. But they are in fact risk averters and pay (in a lower salary) to avoid a gamble. There are, of course, compensations besides security that contribute to the charm and therefore to the low salaries of academic life: being abused in student riots, grading examinations, serving on committees with verbose colleagues, and so forth.

The assumption that aversion toward risk is the normal attitude leads to another, related diagram equally useful for thinking about risky choices. If Peter Hill, a cattle rancher in Montana, is risk averse, he must be compensated in higher average income for taking a risk. He feels that risk is a bad, and only by giving him more of a good (higher average income) will he accept more of it. Figure 3.9 portrays as dashed lines the contours on Hill's hill of happiness between average income and variability around that average.[11] If Hill were risk preferring,

[11] You should be able to convince at least your intuition that there is a connection between these contours and the utility-of-income curve. If the left side of your brain, too, wants satisfaction, it will first have to learn some statistics.

Figure 3.9
Risk as a Bad

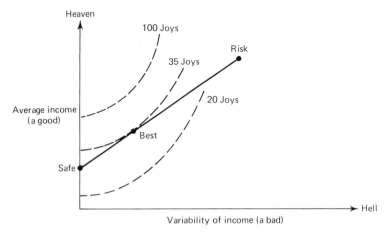

An optimizing consumer may not choose a perfectly safe income if his or her average income can be increased by accepting some variability of income. If safety is costly, less than the maximum possible amount of safety is, in general, chosen.

the contours would slope downward instead of upward; if he were risk neutral (with a straight line for a utility-of-income curve), the contours would be straight, horizontal lines running out of the average income axis.

The usefulness of the diagram derives from the following reasoning. Suppose that, if Hill puts all his wealth into savings accounts at the First National Bank of Bozeman, he achieves point safe on the average income axis (with zero unreliability); and if he puts it all into cattle, he achieves point risk, with a higher average income but also a more variable income. At safe, he earns, say, $10,000 a year every year for sure; at risk, he earns on average, say, $30,000, but in some years nothing at all and in other years, say, $60,000.

_T or F:_ Hill chooses point best; that is, he holds part of his wealth in savings accounts and part in cattle.

_A:_ True. By varying the amounts he puts in the two assets, he can move anywhere along the safe-risk line.[12] If he puts half his wealth in each asset, for example, he achieves an average income of $\frac{1}{2}(\$10,000) + \frac{1}{2}(\$30,000) = \$20,000$ and a variability of income on the upside of $\frac{1}{2}(\$60,000) + \frac{1}{2}(\$10,000) = \$35,000$ and on the downside of $\frac{1}{2}(\$10,000) + \frac{1}{2}(0) = \$5000$. Both the average and the variability are halfway between safe and risk. That is, he is on a straight line between them, his budget line. The best point on or below the budget line is best.

[12] If safe had any variability, the line would in general no longer be straight but, rather, curved. And if the income from safe moved inversely with the income from risk, the curve would have the opposite curvature as the indifference curves. The reason is simple. When he is holding two assets whose incomes tend to move inversely, their variations will on average offset each other. The 50:50 mix, for example, will give the same average income as will the straight line, but because of the offsetting, the same average income will be associated with lower variability.

This is the moral of the tale. Hill does not in general put all his wealth into one investment but, rather, holds a mixture of safe bank accounts and risky cattle, the better to achieve the best combination of risk and return. With a different attitude toward risk, he would hold a different bundle. Similarly, Margaret Green might own a high school education, a bank account, and a piece of swamp in Florida, with various amounts of her wealth tied up in each asset. And General Electric, likewise, owns on behalf of its stockholders a diverse portfolio of land, patents, and factories. The diagram, which can be elaborated in various ways, exhibits the behavior of risk-averse people, namely, people who do not put all their eggs into one basket.

Summary

Spain searched for Eastern spices and found Western gold. In like fashion, the search for measurable utility—an apparently pointless academic expedition—found something better. The utility-of-income curve and related curves can describe behavior toward risk: gambling, insurance, and other choices among risky activities. Life is a lottery, and in the last quarter century or so, economists have been pleased to introduce this unlucky fact of life into their thinking. The new thinking is applicable to the economics of gambling, insurance, crime, capital punishment, investment, knowledge, technical change, war, unemployment, occupational choice, agriculture, and enterprise—that is, to much of the theory of price.

QUESTIONS FOR SECTION 3.4

1. Consider Richard Sylla deciding how much of a $100 fund he is going to invest in two assets, money balances (amounts in the cookie jar or in his checking account, which are perfectly secure but yield no interest rate) and bonds (which yield an interest rate but are not perfectly secure). Sylla is risk averse.

a. Describe for a given average interest rate on bonds how he chooses the proportion to invest in money balances.

b. What happens to the proportion if the average interest rate on bonds falls but the variability of the interest rate stays the same?

True or False

2. It is impossible to imagine a utility-of-income curve that would imply simultaneously taking unfair gambles for large but improbable gains and taking unfair insurance against large but improbable losses. (Hint: Draw one that is concave for low incomes and convex for high incomes.)

3. It costs John 1 cent worth of time and trouble to fasten his seat belt on each trip in his car; putting on the seat belt reduces the probability of dying in a crash from 1 in 2 million on each trip to zero; and John's utility curve of income is a straight line. Therefore, if John were just indifferent between fastening the seat belt and not fastening it, he would be willing to be shot one year from now for $20,000.

4. If criminals were risk preferring, crime would not pay.

5. A risk-averse burglar will prefer a harsh but improbable punishment to a mild but more probable punishment if his average income from the two gambles is the same.

6. A risk averter will never specialize in holding a risky asset.

7. A risk averter minimizes risk.

Indifference Curves and Demand

4.1 The Law of Demand Derived Completely

Indifference curves, then, apply to choices among both certain and uncertain bundles. But the chief use of indifference curves is less direct, namely, to provide an alternative way of looking at demand curves. Showing that you can look at the law of demand in either of two related diagrams does not on the face of it seem a good way of spending scarce mental energy. Once again, however, an apparently pointless academic game yields large returns.

☐
All or Nothing Consider Robert Fogel, a pioneer farmer living at Ogden, Utah in 1869 near the about-to-be-completed Union Pacific Railway. Fogel buys transportation for himself and his crops by giving up some of his income of all other goods. At the price of transport in terms of all other goods that he faced before the railway (i.e., high price in the panels of Figure 4.1), he purchased 10 ton-miles of transport, arriving at the point start. Now the railway opens, selling transport at a lower price than the teamsters and mule-drivers of Ogden whom he patronized before. What happens to Fogel's purchases of transport? The answer depends on the nature of the offer the railway makes. It could require that if Fogel buys any transport he must buy at least 45 ton-miles, an "all-or-nothing" offer as marked at 45 in the top panel of Figure 4.1. As the diagram is drawn, Fogel is just indifferent between accepting the offer from the railway or continuing to buy at the high price from the nonrailway transporters. The point all or nothing is on the same indifference curve as start.

☐
***Free Purchase or
Entry Fee*** Although it does highlight the desirability of thinking closely about the nature of the offer, the all-or-nothing offer is here a mere curiosity. The true business at hand depends on the distinction between two other offers. The railway could allow Fogel to purchase at the low price any amount he wanted, the usual offer in a market. In the top panel of Figure 4.1, he arrives at finish, on the highest attainable indifference curve. In the bottom panel the railway makes him another offer: it charges him a fee to buy (now along the heavy budget line)

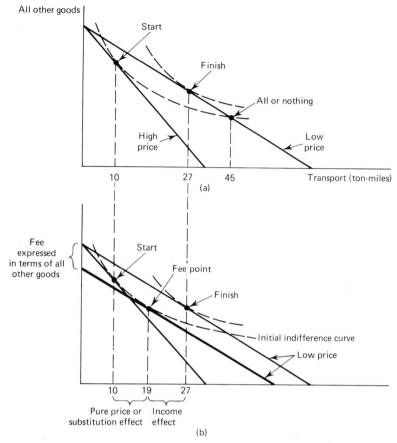

Figure 4.1
The Indifference Curves
for All or Nothing and for
Free Purchase (a) and for
an Entry Fee (b)

The consumer is offered a lower price and free choice of quantity, choosing to increase consumption from 10 to 27 ton-miles. The increase consists of two logically distinct parts: from 10 to 19 in response to the change in price alone, holding real income constant, and from 19 to 27 in response to the price-induced change in real income.

any amount he wants at the new, low price. The case illustrated is the largest fee it could charge and still interest him in the offer, that is, the fee (bracketed on the all other goods axis) that at the low price leaves him barely above the start indifference curve. He arrives at fee point.

Without the fee, made virtually richer by the fall in price, Fogel buys 27 ton-miles of transport; with the fee, made literally poorer by the fee in exactly the amount, he is made virtually richer by the fall in price: he buys only 19 ton-miles. The fee can be thought of as the income benefit expressed in all other goods he gets from the fall in price (income he would willingly give up rather than forego the fall in price). Finish is to the right of fee point because transport is assumed here to be a normal good. Were the fee given back to him he would become richer than at fee point and would buy more transport. The additional amount he would buy (27 − 19 = 8 ton-miles) is the income effect of the fall in price. The additional amount he buys even though the fee is extracted ($19 - 10 = 9$ ton-miles) is the substitution or pure price effect.

In other words, the way in which a consumer facing the usual offer of a free purchase reacts to a fall in price splits naturally into two parts. On the transport axis, the substitution effect is the move from 10 to 19 ton-miles, the income effect being the move from 19 to 27 ton-miles. Inside the diagram, the substitution effect is the move from start to fee point, the income effect being the move from fee point to finish. The sequence of moves does not actually take place. True, if the railway first made Fogel the offer with the fee and afterward, in a fit of generosity, gave the fee back to him, he would move first to fee point and afterward to finish. But this is not the important point. The point is that the increase in transport bought after a fall in price depends on two features of the consumer's indifference map, namely, how sensitive he is at a given real income to changes in price, the substitution effect (i.e., how great is the curvature of an indifference curve), and how sensitive he is at a given price to changes in real income, the income effect (i.e., how much more transport he buys as he moves up to a higher indifference curve).

□
The Offer Curve Is an Alternative Representation of the Demand Curve

Bearing these notions in mind, consider how Fogel would react to a succession of offers of low prices, such as low, lower, lowest in the top panel of Figure 4.2. With a free choice of how much to buy, he would take up the points indicated, and were these points (and other intermediate ones) connected up, they would form a curve, called, naturally enough, the *offer curve*. The bottom panel plots the slopes of the successive budget lines against the quantities of transport to which they lead (as in Chapter 1), giving the solid demand curve.

The ordinary demand curve, then, is merely an alternative representation (with one of the axes redefined) of the offer curve. By contrast, with the maximum fee charged at each low price, Fogel would move along the initial indifference curve, I_0. The dashed demand curve plots the succession of slopes of this indifference curve. Such a demand curve is called _income compensated_ because it compensates for (i.e., takes away) the income effect—in this case the income effect of prices falling from high (notice that the two demand curves coincide at high price). It is the demand curve holding real income constant. The indifference curve through point initial is here taken as the standard for judging changes in real income. But any indifference curve could be the standard. In other words, corresponding to each indifference curve there is an income-compensated demand curve derived by imagining Fogel to be charged fees (or for higher prices to be given subsidies) that keep him on the indifference curve. His free choice demand curve (derivable from his offer curve) connects up such entry fee demand curves (derivable from his indifference curves), as shown in Figure 4.3.

In this diagram as in the indifference curve diagram, the effect of a fall in the price of transport from, say, low to lower can be broken into two parts, as the arrows in the diagram and on the transport axis show:

**Figure 4.2
Offer Curves (a)
Correspond to Demand
Curves (b)**

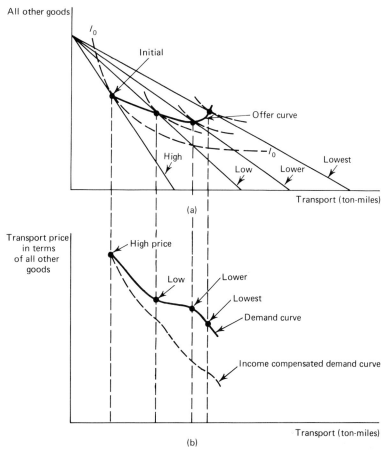

The offer curve is a set of tangency points between the consumer's indifference contours and all possible (straight) budget lines drawn for a given endowment of all other goods. To construct the demand curve from the offer curve, read quantity off the horizontal axis and plot this as a function of price, as given by the slope of the budget line. If the budget lines are drawn so as to hold the consumer on a given indifference contour, rather than at a given endowment point of all other goods, then income-compensated offer and demand curves can be drawn.

moving down along the dashed income-compensated demand curve that runs through low, the substitution effect; then moving out along a fixed price (namely, lower) to the new, higher compensated demand curve running through lower, the income effect.

☐
***The Uses of
Compensated and
Uncompensated
Demand***

The payoff to this mind-boggling set of correspondences between diagrams of indifference curves and diagrams of demand curve will become apparent in later chapters. Put briefly, it allows one to move easily from speaking of particular markets for transport or food or housing to speaking of their general effects on the society's income or happiness.

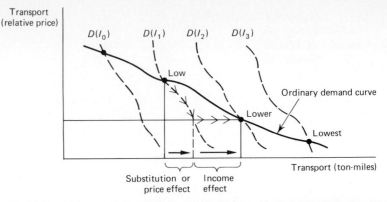

The income-compensated demand curve $D(I_1)$ shows only the pure substitution effect of a fall in price because it holds the consumer on indifference curve I_1. However, an uncompensated fall in price, which includes an income effect, moves the consumer to a new, higher indifference curve, I_2. Therefore each point on the ordinary demand curve corresponds to a different indifference curve and therefore lies on a different compensated demand curve.

In the present case, for example, the maximum fee that Fogel would pay to be permitted to buy cheap transport from the railway (i.e., the income of the income effect) is a measure of the benefit he derives from the opening of the railway. If you knew the shape of his demand curve and of the demand curve of other typical buyers of transport in the nineteenth century (farmer Fishlow in Illinois, for example), you could estimate the social benefit derived from the introduction of railways. This has in fact been done, arriving at the surprising conclusion that the social benefit was small.[1] The same techniques, described in Chapter 10 in more detail, are applicable to projects of any sort: a subway in San Francisco, a pipeline in Alaska, a shopping center in Cleveland.

In the present chapter the only payoff to the logic of income and substitution effects is in the production of examination questions of diabolical difficulty.

T or F: If transport is a normal good for Fogel, his ordinary demand curve for transport has a lower slope than do any of his income-compensated curves.

A: True. Look at Figure 4.3. The rightward march of the income-compensated demand curves—$D(I_0)$, $D(I_1)$, $D(I_2)$, $D(I_3)$—expresses the normality of transport. At a given price relative to all other goods Fogel consumes more transport if his income allows him to reach a higher indifference curve. He will always move to a compensated curve with a higher index—from $D(I_0)$ to $D(I_1)$, say, or from $D(I_1)$ to $D(I_3)$—when the price falls, for a falling price always makes him for all practical purposes richer. Since normality implies that

[1] R. W. Fogel, *Railroads and American Economic Growth* (Baltimore: Johns Hopkins, 1964); and Albert Fishlow, *American Railroads and the Transformation of the Antebellum Economy* (Cambridge, Mass.: Harvard University Press, 1965).

compensated curves with higher indexes are more rightward, a fall in price is associated with a rightward move in the amount consumed. Not so difficult after all.

The logic involved is clearer if you consider the opposite case.

T or F: If transport is an inferior good for Fogel, his ordinary demand curve has a *higher* slope than do any of his income-compensated curves.

A: True. Higher indexes now march leftward, and the virtual enrichment from a fall in price now causes him to buy less, not more.

The income effect of a fall in price from, say, low to lower is now negative. It offsets to some degree the substitution effect, resulting in a smaller increase in transport bought than would occur if Fogel were fixed by fee to the indifference curve he had attained at the low price.

☐
Giffen Goods

As was shown in an elementary way in Chapter 1, the substitution effect of a fall in price is always positive. It is conceivable that food or starchy foods or potatoes or Irish potatoes in 1846 could be so inferior that the negative income effect would overwhelm the positive substitution effect. The English economist Alfred Marshall awarded (incorrectly) the credit for realizing that this was conceivable to Sir Robert Giffen. In the *Giffen paradox*, a demand curve would have a perverse, upward slope (as shown in Figure 4.4).

The law of demand, then, can be put as follows: there are no Giffen goods. George Stigler has offered a characteristically economic bit of reasoning on the empirical success of this proposition:

If an economist were to *demonstrate* its failure . . . he would be assured of immortality, professionally speaking, and rapid promotion. Since most economists would not dislike either reward, we may assume that the total absence of exceptions is not from lack of trying to find them.[2]

☐
The Peculiar Economics of Need, Priority, and Other Pathologies in Demand

If you know something definite about the shape of indifference curves (such as that the income effect is strongly negative, as in the Giffen paradox), you can, of course, say something definite about the shape of the corresponding demand curve. A particular class of shapes lies behind the economic thinking of the man in the street. They turn on the word "need," a word that economists find much more difficult to use than do statesmen, journalists, and other people innocent of economics. Perfectly ordinary sentences, which might occur in any political speech or newspaper editorial, leave many economists unhappy: "We *need* natural gas, a *basic commodity* that we *cannot do without.* Providing this *necessity* at a price people can *afford* should be high on our national *priorities.*" The nub of the issue is the shape of indifference curves and the corresponding demand curve.

[2] George Stigler, *The Theory of Price,* 3rd ed. (New York: Macmillan, 1966), p. 24, his emphasis.

Figure 4.4
The Giffen Paradox as an
Exercise in Drawing an
Offer Curve (a)
Corresponding to a
Demand Curve (b)

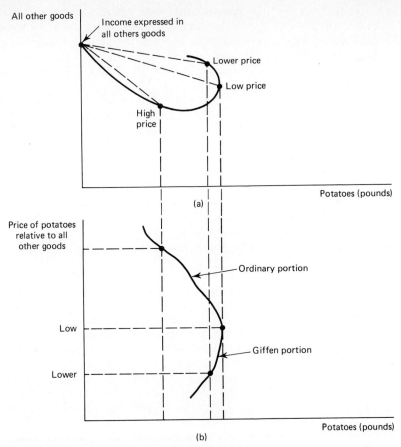

The Giffen paradox is illustrated by drawing an offer curve with a backward-bending segment. This segment corresponds to the positively sloped, or Giffen, portion of the demand curve.

***

Q: Draw Gary Hawke's indifference curves between food and all other goods and his demand curve for food (given an income in all other goods) if Hawke needs 1 pound or more of food a day to survive.

A: The indifference curves are all outside the shadow of the valley of death (see Figure 4.5). Outside the valley, Hawke has an ordinary demand curve; inside it (i.e., at a price of food such as death price so high that he literally cannot "afford" to buy 1 pound), he is dead and, needless to say, has no demand curve.

This is one interpretation of "need": some minimum amount below which utility is zero or at some unpleasant minimum. The mental experiment that people perform when they assert that food or steel or health care are "basic" is to imagine life without them, below the

Figure 4.5
Need as a Minimum:
Indifference (a) and
Demand (b) Curves

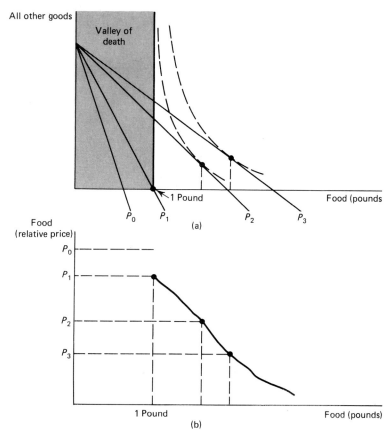

(a)

(b)

A person who "needs," in the economist's sense, 1 pound of food will never voluntarily consume less. If the price of 1 pound is greater than one's income, one will (involuntarily) die; otherwise one will consume at least 1 pound.

---

need point. If you ask a noneconomist whether health care or rock music is the more appropriate object for veneration, regulation, and subsidy, he will answer, "health care." If asked why, he will answer, "because it is a basic need." But the needfulness of health care is irrelevant to social choices beyond the need point. Most social choices are choices between more or less health or rock music, not between some or none. The mental experiment behind the notion of "basic needs" is usually the wrong one.

A slightly different meaning of need lies behind the word "priority" (which, despite its air of technical sophistication, is never used in economics).

Q: Larry Neal values only food until he has consumed 2 pounds; beyond this point he values only shelter. Draw his indifference curves between food and shelter.

A: When 2 pounds of food is unattainable (outside a budget line such as poor), he consumes only food; when it is attainable, he consumes 2 pounds of food and spends all his remaining income on shelter (see Figure 4.6). In other words, food has a higher priority than does shelter. First he buys food, and only when he can buy all the food he needs (namely, 2 pounds) does he buy shelter. Although the generalization cannot be drawn in two dimensions, the idea can be generalized to a list of successive needs, such as food (1), shelter (2), clothing (3), . . ., electric can opener (350). It is influential in psychology, where it is called the "hierarchy of needs": in ascending order, physiological, safety, social, ego, and self-fulfillment needs. It is not influential in economics, where it is called *lexicographic preferences* (if you look up "lexicographic" in the dictionary, you will first look at the "L's"; then second, having met that need, the "E's"; then third the "X's," and so forth). Such preferences violate common economic observation. It is not true that the poor live by bread alone, nor, equivalently, is it true that the demand curves of all commodities become perfectly vertical at low prices or high incomes (i.e., after the need for something can be satisfied). And even were it true that the preferences of each consumer were lexicographic, if consumers did not all have the same preferences, consumers as a group would behave as though they had ordinary preferences. In short, economists do not believe it is useful to speak of "priorities" and suspect that this word, as is true for the phrase "basic need," is merely a verbal club with which to batter people who do not value the B-1 bomber, clean air, monopolies of doctors, or the welfare of the poor as highly as does the speaker. Interpreted literally, these words of noneconomic economics entail implausible or irrelevant shapes of indifference and demand curves.

Summary

A demand curve in a diagram of the price faced and quantity bought of transport corresponds to an offer curve in a diagram of quantities of transport

**Figure 4.6
Lexicographic Preferences**

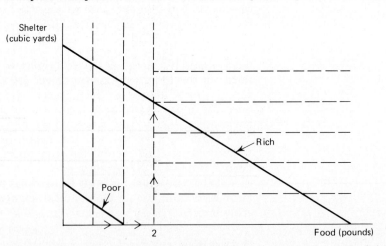

The consumer derives satisfaction from the first 2 pounds of food consumed, but not from subsequent pounds. The consumer derives satisfaction from shelter only if at least 2 pounds of food are being consumed.

and all other goods. The distinction between an offer of a free choice and an offer of a fee with the choice produces the distinction between income and substitution effects. A compensated demand curve contains only the substitution effect, an ordinary demand curve both the substitution and the income effects.

The distinction between the income and substitution effects of a fall in price is applicable to the pathologies of demand curves: demand curves that slope upward rather than downward (the Giffen case) or demand curves that are vertical (at the point of fulfilled needs). The pathologies are factually unimportant and are useful chiefly as mind-expanding exercises in the connection between indifference and demand curves.

QUESTIONS FOR SECTION 4.1

1. Movie theaters typically offer candy bars in large sizes only. Lloyd Guptill would like 2 ounces of candy at 10 cents an ounce but must buy 8 ounces at 40 cents. *True or false:* This is an example of an all-or-nothing offer.

2. Universities typically discourage part-time students, either by charging them higher prices per course or by insisting that all students be enrolled in a degree program. *True or false:* This is an example of an all-or-nothing offer.

3. The Woodlawn Bar and Tap, popularly known as Jimmy's, can serve each drink at a cost to Jimmy of 25 cents.

a. Draw the budget line and indifference curves of a patron if he faced the 25 cent (zero profit) price. How much would he buy?

b. Pick any point inside the budget line of (a). If the patron chooses this point, what would be Jimmy's profit (expressed in all other goods) from the patron's patronage? (Hint: It is a certain vertical distance.)

c. Now draw the indifference curve running through the patron's endowment of all other goods. Can Jimmy force the patron to a point below this curve? What point along it maximizes Jimmy's profit? (Hint: A vertical distance between any two curves reaches a maximum when the slopes of the two curves are equal along a vertical line, that is, when the curves are vertically parallel.)

d. Describe on the one hand a cover charge and price per drink and on the other a required minimum number of drinks and price per drink that would leave the patron at the point described in (c).

e. What would happen to these schemes if Jimmy's faced competition from other bars?

4. A heavy smoker climbs the walls if he has too few cigarettes a day and coughs convulsively if he has too many. Draw his demand curve for cigarettes.

5. Betsy White can trade off hours of leisure for tons of all other goods (namely, food, housing, and so forth) by selling the hour of leisure at the going wage per hour. She is endowed, of course, with 24 hours of leisure. Draw White's offer curve for leisure by pivoting her leisure-all other goods budget line around the point of 24 hours of leisure. Draw the corresponding demand curve for leisure. Note that the supply curve of hours of labor is simply 24 hours minus the demand curve for leisure. Does the supply curve ever bend backward; that is, does the number of hours supplied ever fall when the wage rises?

True or False

6. The standard eight-hour day is an example of an all-or-nothing offer.

7. If Eric Jones's indifference curves have the usual shape (i.e., a convex shape), then his demand curve for books necessarily has a convex shape.

8. If housing and all other goods are perfect complements, then the income-compensated demand curves for housing are vertical straight lines.

Part Two | EXCHANGE

5

Trade

5.1 Supply and Demand

In the ordinary way of speaking, an American buying fifteenth-century Italian paintings abroad is a demander. At $5000 per painting John James might demand ten. But he is in fact simultaneously a supplier, for he supplies the foreigner with $50,000, that is, with $50,000 worth of American goods. The money throws a veil over the essence of the transaction, a swap of ten paintings for some computers or wheat or whatever bundle of American goods the foreigner buys with the American money. That the American buyer of the paintings is not literally a maker of computers or a grower of wheat is irrelevant, for in his job of oil drilling or museum curating he has acquired the power (the money) to purchase the goods the foreigner demands. The giving of money makes it unnecessary for James to lug around wheat and computers in his trips to foreign art dealers. But in all essential respects, that is what money allows him to do. Buying and selling, to repeat, are swaps of one good for another, thinly veiled behind money.

This argument has been implied in the discussions of demand so far. Because it is true, for example, that consumers have been said to trade (supply) all other goods (not money) for food, consumers have been endowed with incomes in all other goods (not money), and the price of food relevant to its demand curve has been expressed relative to all other goods (not money). Figure 5.1 makes it explicit, showing to the left of the usual diagram James's supply curve of all other goods (the arrows on the axes help keep clear which direction is a high price or quantity).

At some low relative price of all other goods (a high relative price of paintings), James supplies zero all other goods; that is, he demands zero paintings. At a high relative price of all other goods, the position portrayed inside the diagram, he does supply some all other goods; that is, he demands some paintings (ten in fact). Corresponding to the demand curve for paintings there is a supply curve of all other goods. The supply curve slopes upward, not downward, as you can see by turning the book counterclockwise on its side. The supply curve and the demand curve are merely alternative ways of looking at the

82

**Figure 5.1
A Demand for *X* Is a
Supply of All Other Goods**

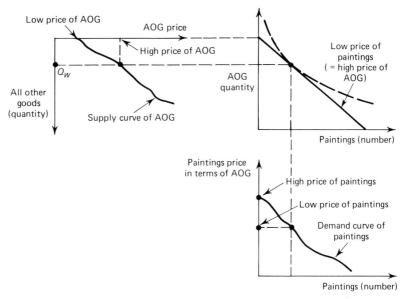

At a price above the low price of all other goods, the consumer will trade some of his endowment of all other goods for paintings and will be a supplier of all other goods and a demander of paintings.

---

same act of exchange by James. Since $50,000 is $50,000 no matter how you look at it, the dollar price of the paintings multiplied by the number James demands is equal to the dollar price of, say, wheat multiplied by the tons he (indirectly) supplies. That is, $(\$P_P)Q_P = (\$P_W)Q_W$. This is just James's budget constraint. The shaded rectangle under the demand curve for paintings is the wheat value of the paintings demanded at the relative price of paintings $\$P_P/\$P_W$, that is, $(\$P_P/\$P_W)Q_P$, which is to say that it is the quantity supplied of wheat (Q_W in the diagram) at the relative price of wheat $\$P_W/\$P_P$. In other words, each point on the demand curve is also a point on the supply curve. Having drawn one you have implicitly drawn the other.

It is a sad commentary on the failure of economists to educate lawmakers that this simple idea is applicable to great issues of policy.

T or F: If international trade were limited to trade in goods and services (not also in gifts, IOUs, and money balances), it would be impossible for a country to succeed in a policy of increasing its exports and reducing its imports.

A: Under such circumstances, the United States could not supply wheat to the world without simultaneously demanding shoes, small cars, and the other things with which the world pays for the wheat. Therefore, true. The point, again, is that exchange involves the budget constraint, namely, that the value of the goods you provide to someone else in an exchange must be equal to the value of the goods you receive from that person. When applied to whole economics, the point is known as one version of *Say's law*.[1]

In fact, you can go further, allowing for trade in money as well as in goods.

Q: The United States has had a balance-of-payments deficit with Japan. That is, overall, the value of American wheat and so forth exported has been less than the value of Japanese autos and so forth imported into the United States, and the Japanese have cheerfully accepted American dollars (after subtracting out American IOUs) to make up the difference. The deficit has alarmed American policy makers. *True or false:* Their alarm is misplaced, for Americans as a whole are made better off by the deficit: the Japanese accept green pieces of paper in exchange for autos, television sets, and other objects of American desire.

A: The correct answer is contrary to what you may have gathered from the evening news. Dollar bills cost American society the trivial cost of printing them. If the Japanese lust after them to the extent of offering real goods to get them at the value printed on their faces, fine. The willingness of the Japanese to give $1 worth of goods for a piece of paper costing less than a cent to produce allows Americans to consume outside their real budget line between autos and wheat.[2] The veil of money makes an exceptionally good bargain look like an alarmingly bad one. In short, true.

□
A Demander at One Price Might Be a Supplier at Another

For a person or a country, then, the budget constraint connects the demand for one good with the supply of all others. Furthermore, a person with an initial endowment of, say, food and machinery will at some prices be a supplier of machinery and at some prices a demander. Betsy White is happy with her endowment only if she faces a price, labeled self-sufficient price in Figure 5.2, that offers her no better indifference curve. That is, only at one price is Betsy satisfied (in view of its price) with the machinery she begins with.

At a lower price, such as demand price, she demands more than she has initially; at a higher price, supply price, she demands less, which is to say that at the high price of machinery she willingly gives up some machinery (supplies it) to acquire more food. The portion of her demand to hold machinery above self-sufficient is a supply curve, if read from right to left starting at endowment of machinery. The upshot is that the analysis of demand over which we have labored is

[1] After Jean-Baptiste Say (1767–1832), the first French academic economist, immensely popular in his time for the sterile lucidity and system he brought to economics (in contrast to the fruitful chaos in contemporary British economics).

[2] That is, it allows them to violate Say's law, while obeying *Walras's law*, namely, that the summed monetary value of the goods and *money* you provide to someone else must be equal to the monetary value of the goods and money you receive from that person. M. E. Leon Walras (1834–1910; pronounced "vall-*rah*," not like the well-known aquatic mammal) was a French academic economist, immensely popular after his time for the sterile lucidity and system he brought to economics (in contrast to the fruitful chaos in contemporary British economics).

Figure 5.2
At a High Price a
Demander (a) May
Become a Supplier (b)

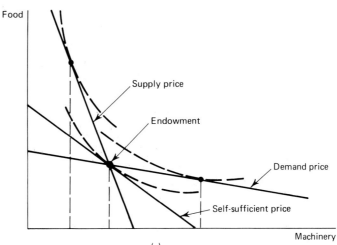

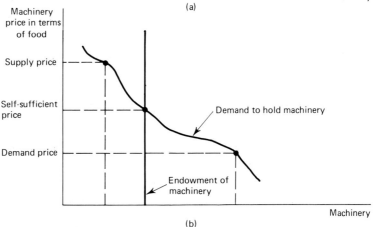

An economic agent will be a net demander of machinery if the price of machinery is lower than the agent's self-sufficiency price. If the price of machinery is higher than this price, the agent will be a net supplier of machinery.

also an analysis of supply.[3] Just as Betsy's demand curve for machinery gives the amounts at various prices a person will demand from sellers, her supply curve of machinery—which is an upward continuation of her demand curve when she has an initial endowment of machinery to sell—gives the amounts at various prices she will supply to buyers.

Q: A peasant grows 125 bushels of grain and 50 pounds of wool. *True or false:* He will buy some more grain if his marginal valuation of grain at

---

[3] The earlier diagrams yielded only demand curves (and not, as here, supply curves as well) because the endowment was always placed on the vertical axis instead of inside the diagrams. The endowment was the income in all other goods. An endowment on the food axis in the present diagram would signify a zero initial amount of machinery. You cannot supply what you do not have.

125 bushels is higher than the market price of grain, and he will sell some of his own grain if his marginal valuation is lower than the price.

A: True. <u>The marginal valuation</u> (relative to wool) <u>is the slope of his indifference curve. If the</u> (relative) <u>price is equal to this slope at 125 bushels, he remains self-sufficient. At a higher price, he is a supplier, at a lower price a demander.</u> Self-sufficiency is a matter of prices.

Summary

The inquiry into consumer budget lines and tastes has arrived at exchange, that is, at supply and demand. A consumer's demand curve is also the consumer's supply curve, in two senses. First, to demand something Betsy White must supply something else. That she usually supplies money obscures the nature of the exchange: goods for goods, with money as merely a convenient intermediate step. Second, a consumer demanding a car at one price will at another price supply it. White must, of course, have a car to supply if she is to supply it. Her supply-demand curve is simply her initial endowment of cars minus her demand for cars. If she demands many cars relative to her endowment (the price is low, she is rich, or her endowment is small), then she will have an "excess demand" for cars; if she demands few, then she will have an "excess supply."

PROBLEM FOR SECTION 5.1

Rondo Cameron has and consumes oats and books in Lochielside, Scotland. Because transportation costs to and from the market town are high, the relative price he faces for oats is high if he buys oats and low if he sells oats. Describe his situation, supposing the cost of transporting books to be trivial. What will happen if the cost of transporting oats falls?

5.2   Exchange Between Two People

☐

Exchange Is Mutually Beneficial

A perfectly ordinary but widely applicable thought about an exchange is that both parties to it must be made better off. Force, fraud, or mistake aside, an exchange that happens must be one that is as economists put it *mutually beneficial.* Otherwise it would not happen. It takes two to tango, and if either partner is made worse off, he or she will sit out the dance.

Ordinary and obvious though this first principle of exchange is, it is commonly misunderstood. The starving farmer taking a loan from the moneylender is commonly said to have "no choice" but to take the loan at an "exorbitant" interest rate from the moneylender, who is "exploiting" the farmer and making him a "virtual slave to indebtedness." Most economists choke on these words. The farmer does have a choice, albeit a dismal one: starve. He *is* made better off by the loan. In certain technical senses to be described in Chapter 24, he may well be "exploited" by the moneylender, but not in the sense of being made worse off by the "exorbitant" interest rate or his "virtual slavery" than he would be if the moneylender did not make the loan and left the farmer to starve. The economist's phrase "mutually advantageous exchange" has a cheerful sound, but in fact it promises only that exchange makes people better off, not that it makes them best off in the best of all possible worlds.

Q: John Pynchon was the richest man in seventeenth-century Springfield, Massachusetts. He made loans to the townsfolk, many of whom died in debt to him or lost to him their pitiful scraps of land. *True or false:* Pynchon was evidently exploiting the townsfolk.

A: False. He and the townsfolk were engaging in mutually advantageous exchange of present for future goods. That the townsfolk died in debt to him is evidence that they could get present goods in exchange for unfulfilled promises of future goods, escaping debtless to a better world. As it happens, Pynchon charged interest rates well below the prevailing rates elsewhere on the frontier. Were interest rates the appropriate standard, one could say that the townsfolk were exploiting him. But in return for his liberality on this score, he got deference and political power (supplementing the political power granted to him by the Massachusetts General Court). The loans were mutually advantageous. Miserable as the townsfolk were, their voluntary choice to take the loans indicates that they believed the loans made them better off.

The Beneficiality of Exchange Exhibited by Indifference Curves

Exchange, then, is beneficial. Getting beyond this first principle requires indifference curves. What appears to be the simplest market group is two people trading with each other. Some time ago West Germany and the Soviet Union concluded a deal whereby a certain amount of Soviet natural gas was exchanged for a certain amount of West German steel pipes. The question is, how were the "certain amounts" arrived at? Consider the German indifference curves between gas and pipes (shown in Figure 5.3).

The Germans start at point endowment, with a certain number of pipes and no natural gas. Needless to say, they would like the Soviets

Figure 5.3
No One Will Accept a Deal That Leaves Him or Her on a Lower Indifference Curve Than the One on Which He or She Started

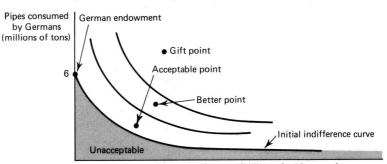

The Germans are willing to exchange pipes for gas on terms that leave the Germans at any point above their initial indifference curve and are unwilling to make deals that leave them at points below this curve.

to offer their natural gas at a very low price in terms of pipe, allowing the Germans to move, for example, to better point; indeed, they would like the Soviets to offer it at a zero price, or still better a negative price, making a gift of not only some gas but also some steel pipes of their own (acquired from the Japanese, say), leaving the Germans at a point such as gift point or beyond. If necessary, however, the Germans would accept any exchange that improved their welfare, that is, any exchange that put them on a higher indifference curve than the initial indifference curve. Any point outside the shaded area is such an exchange. The Soviets, undoubtedly with a different set of indifference curves, would behave in a similar way. The Soviets start with some gas but no pipes. Again, they would like the other party to sell its goods at a low, zero, or negative price. So, too, some shaded area is unacceptable to them. If a mutually advantageous deal is possible, it must fall within the acceptable area for *both* the Germans and the Soviets.

□
The Edgeworth Box

What is needed is a device for exhibiting the acceptable areas simultaneously, exhibiting the two consuming molecules bumping together and constraining each other's behavior. Such a device would show where the consumer's constraint (budget line) comes from. The device is called an _Edgeworth box,_ after the same F. Y. Edgeworth who a century ago invented indifference curves. It is evident that any actual exchange reduces the natural gas the Soviets have by the same amount that it increases the amount the Germans have; likewise for steel pipes. This is what is meant by an exchange. Furthermore, there is a fixed total amount of gas to be distributed among the two and a fixed total amount of pipes. Therefore, if one tipped the Soviet pipes-gas axis and its indifference curves upside down and placed it on the German axis, forming a rectangle with the German endowment of pipes as its height and the Soviet endowment of gas as its length, any point within the rectangle would represent a distribution of gas and pipes after a deal between the Germans and the Soviets (see Figure 5.4).

Any point outside the rectangle represents a deal unattainable with the initial endowments. In the outside gift case an amount of gas ends up heating German homes in excess of what the Soviets have to offer. The acceptable points—the deals that increase the utility of both parties—are within the lens-shaped, unshaded area. For example, an exchange of 2 million tons of German pipes for 1 billion cubic meters of gas leaves the two at the both better point. Notice the little dashed indifference curves through the point: both are better than the utilities of the initial, pre-exchange distribution of pipes and gas; that is, after the exchange, both are on higher indifference curves, one curve looked at from the German, the other from the Soviet origin. By contrast, the distribution represented by the Soviets' worse point does indeed make the Soviets worse off, for it is on a lower Soviet indifference curve than they started on before exchange. The Soviets would balk at such a deal, and it would not come off.

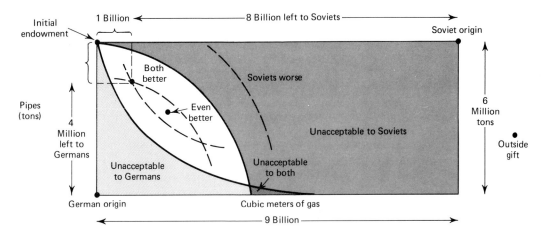

Figure 5.4
The Edgeworth Box
Represents Exchange

A deal between the Germans and the Soviets must take both sides to higher indifference curves than their initial ones if the deal is to be mutually acceptable. The only points that are acceptable to both sides are those inside the lens formed by the indifference curves passing through initial endowment. At the point both better, the Soviets value the marginal quantity of gas less than do the Germans; the same holds for the Germans and pipes. A lens of mutually acceptable points remains, so further trade is possible, to even better, for example. Trade is finished when there are no more lenses out of the point arrived at.

This peculiar diagram represents the ordinary thought discussed earlier: exchange must be mutually beneficial if it is to take place voluntarily, and voluntary exchanges are mutually beneficial. Deal making stops when the deal made leaves no lens-shaped area of further benefit to both parties. The Germans and Soviets might conclude a deal to move from the point initial endowment to both better.

At both better, however, there is still available a lens-shaped area of further benefit, and both parties will want to move to a point such as even better inside the lens; that is, they will want to exchange more. They will stop only when no lens exists or when their indifference curves are tangent or when their marginal valuations of the goods are equal or when no further dealing is mutually beneficial: four ways of saying the same thing.

☐ Consider the following:

There Is No One
Best Point

T or F: For a given lens of advantageous exchange between the Germans and the Soviets, there are not one but many exchanges that will leave them unwilling to exchange further.

A: True. Look at the lens in Figure 5.5. Any point of tangency between a Soviet and a German indifference curve will leave no lens of further exchange beneficial to both. But there are many such points (in fact, infinitely many, along the heavy line), three of which are shown in the figure.

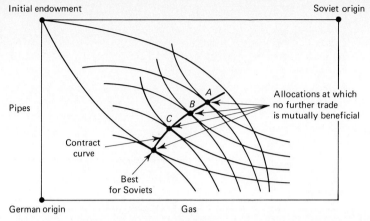

Points on the contract curve are "efficient" in the sense that at these points neither party can be made better off without making the other party worse off. Because German and Soviet indifference curves are tangent to each other at point C, a move in any direction, such as to the southeast, makes one party, in this case the Soviets, worse off. Any point on the contract curve can be reached by a deal that is beneficial to both sides. The point actually reached by the Germans and the Soviets will depend on their bargaining abilities.

If they move to any of these points, they will not both wish to make further deals. The collection of all such points is known as the *contract curve,* the notion being that the Germans and Soviets would both be willing to enter a contract to move from a point off to a point on the contract curve.

Moving to the contract curve inside the lens, then, makes both parties better off. But note the following.

T or F: Once the Germans and Soviets have taken up a position on the contract curve, the Soviets cannot be made better off without making the Germans worse off.

A: True. Look again at the diagram. If they arrive at point A, the Soviets would like to move to point B or, better still, to point C. Moves along the contract curve in this direction—away from the Soviet origin—obviously make the Soviets better off. But they make the Germans worse off, that is, drive them to lower indifference curves than at A. Such a move reduces the German holdings of both gas and pipes, which is clearly disadvantageous. Consequently, the Germans will not agree voluntarily to move from A to B or C. The Soviets might try to force the Germans to do so by trying to bully them with words or bombs. But, force aside, the move will not occur.

Any point on the contract curve, in other words, is a point of rest in exchange. To put it in economic jargon, any point on the contract curve is *Pareto optimal* or *efficient.* A deal is efficient if it leaves the Soviets unable to make themselves better off without making the Germans worse off. The idea of efficiency is the main idea in economic thinking about society's happiness, and it will come up again and again later in the book.

*Where Do Two
People Bargaining
End up?*

For the moment, however, we are concerned not with how people achieve happiness but with how they behave. Consider what has been said so far about their behavior. If the Soviets and Germans conclude a bargain free from force, it is clear that they have moved to a point inside a lens-shaped area. If they are skillful bargainers, furthermore, they will conclude a bargain somewhere on the contract curve, because any bargain off it leaves a further bargain that makes both better off. This much we suppose they know about bargaining behavior. We do not know, however, *where* on the contract curve skillful bargaining between two parties will lead. That is, we do not know how many pipes the Germans will give up in exchange for gas. Exceptionally subtle bargaining on the part of the Soviets, with skillful use, for example, of threats to break off bargaining entirely, might lead to a point such as best for Soviets in the diagram, at which Soviet welfare is as high as it can be subject to the constraint that the Germans are no worse off than when they started (if they were worse off, one can assume that they would not accept the deal). But economists have not discovered very much about what constitutes exceptionally subtle bargaining.[4] There are profound reasons why this is so.

For example, if some bargaining technique were known to be useful when employed by the Soviets—such as threatening to abandon bargaining altogether in a week if the Germans do not accede by then to the terms demanded—the Germans would come to understand this, the Germans would use it themselves, and its usefulness to the Soviets would vanish. In general, any knowledge that the analyst of the situation acquires can be expected to be acquired by the participants, who will alter their strategies in view of the knowledge, making the knowledge obsolete. The Soviet bargainers make a "last" offer. The German bargainers know that the offer is insincere (that there are quotation marks around "last") and ignore it, making their own "last" offer. But the Soviets know that the Germans know that the Soviets' "last" offer is insincere and prepare a "real" last offer. But the Germans know that the Soviets know that the Germans know that the Soviets' "last" offer is to be replaced by their "real" last offer, itself insincere. And so forth.

The conclusion, then, is that bargaining between two people can end up anywhere on the contract curve—or even, if the bargainers are clumsy, off the contract curve. Lamentable though it is that economists cannot predict exactly how bargainers will behave, it is not surprising. Look at common experience. Within limits, the amount you will pay Dario Comi for a secondhand Chevy depends on your narrative skill in telling him about your poverty or your distaste for Chevrolets or the superior offer that George Dunsmore has made to you. Within limits, the frequency with which you can bluff the other players in a poker game with a busted straight depends on how much the others know about your personality, your history as a poker player, and your

[4] They do have something to say about it. See, for example, Thomas C. Schelling, *The Strategy of Conflict* (Cambridge, Mass.: Harvard University Press, 1960), and other works in the "theory of games," for which see Chapter 21, "Competition Among the Few."

mood at the moment. Within limits, the success with which a congress-woman can change a military procurement bill to make her district better off depends in part on how well she can conceal her intention to vote for the bill anyway. Poor-mouthing, bluffing, and empty threats are not very well understood.

Summary

What would seem to be the simplest case of exchange—bargaining between two people in isolation—is in fact the most complex. The Edgeworth box brings indifference curves to the task of illustrating its complexity. <u>For an exchange to take place, clearly, the exchange must make both parties better off</u>. That is, there must exist in the Edgeworth box a lens-shaped area of mutual advantage. Or, to put it another way, at the pre-exchange allocation of money and cars or pipes and gas, the supplier's marginal valuation of the thing that he or she is supplying must be less than the demander's. An exchange that puts the bargainers on the contract curve leaves them with tangent indifference curves by definition; that is, it eliminates the lens shape. Such a position is called "efficient." Along the contract curve one bargainer cannot be made better off without making the other worse off: no further exchanges are possible that are advantageous to both. But where the bargainers will end up on the contract curve, or even whether they will end up on it at all, is indeterminate. Within limits, the trading of cars or votes exceeds the predictive power of economics. The next section, however, will show that more bargainers narrow the limits.

APPENDIX TO SECTION 5.2

The calculus of contract curves is not difficult. Call the German utility from a bundle of gas, G, and pipes, P, the function $U(G, P)$. If the Germans have the bundle G and P, then the Soviets have what is left over, namely, 9 billion cubic meters minus G and 6 million tons minus P. Call the Soviet utility function $V(9$ billion $- G$, 6 million $- P)$. Now the contract curve is simply the collection of bundles for which the slopes of the German and Soviet indifference curves are equal. In other words, it is the solution for the amount of gas, G, as a function of pipes, P, derived from solving the following equation for G in terms of P (subscripts signify partial derivatives):

$$\text{Slope of German indifference curves for given } G, P = \frac{U_G(G, P)}{U_P(G, P)}$$

$$= \frac{V_G(9 \text{ billion} - G, 6 \text{ million} - P)}{V_P(9 \text{ billion} - G, 6 \text{ million} - P)}$$

$$\equiv \text{slope of Soviet indifference curves for the same } G, P$$

A particular choice of the functions U and V gives a particular contract curve. For example, suppose that U was GP and that V was $(9 \text{ billion} - G)$ (6 million $- P)$. That is, Germans and Soviets have the same utility function (recall that Soviet consumption is a residual from German). Take derivatives and insert them into the equation for equal slopes:

$$\frac{U_G}{U_P} = \frac{P}{G} = \frac{6 \text{ million} - P}{9 \text{ billion} - G} = \frac{V_G}{V_P}$$

from which

$$P \text{ (in millions} \atop \text{of tons)} = \left(\frac{6 \text{ million tons}}{9 \text{ billion cubic meters}} \right) G \text{ (in billions} \atop \text{of cubic meters)}$$

As a check, notice that canceling the units on the right-hand side produces the units on the left-hand side (namely, million of tons of pipe).

The contract curve for the present choice of utility functions, then, is a straight line between the Soviet and German origins in the Edgeworth box. You can understand why this special result is in the present case a natural one if you notice, first, that these particular utility contours of the two have an unchanging slope for a given ratio of gas to pipes and, second, that the two utility functions are the same. The slopes are the same along the contract curve; therefore, in this special case, the Soviets and Germans consume gas and pipes in the same ratio along the contract curve; that is, the contract curve runs as a straight line between the origins.

Recall that steadily increasing functions of a utility function give the same indifference map.

_T or F:_ If the German utility function were $56.3 + (GP)^{5/7}$ instead of GP in the problem just given, the contract curve would be different.

_A:_ False. The contract curve is a matter of tangencies between sets of indifference curves, and indifference curves are a matter of shape, not height. Since the new utility function is a monotonic transformation of the old function, the shapes of the utility contours do not change. Therefore the contract curve does not change.

In general if the utility functions do not have the property of equal slopes for equal ratios of consumption (called _homogeneity_) or are not identical for the two parties, then the contract curve is not a straight line. For example, the utility function G^2P, like GP, is homogeneous, because its slope (the ratio of its derivative with respect to G and with respect to P) is $2P/G$, which is clearly unchanged if G and P remain in the same ratio. Suppose that G^2P were the German utility function and that $(\gamma - G)(\pi - P)$ were the Soviet's, where γ and π are the total endowments of gas and pipes. Inserting the derivatives into the condition of equal slopes gives

$$\frac{2GP}{G^2} = \frac{\pi - P}{\gamma - G}$$

Solving for G gives

$$G = \frac{2P\gamma}{\pi + P}$$

This is not a straight line between the origins. If it were, then P set at $\frac{1}{2}\pi$ would yield a $G = \frac{1}{2}\gamma$; in fact it yields

$$\frac{2\gamma\left(\frac{1}{2}\pi\right)}{\pi + \frac{1}{2}\pi} = \frac{2}{3}\gamma$$

QUESTIONS FOR SECTION 5.2

True or False

1. If the Soviets put a very high marginal valuation on the last cubic meter of the 9 billion cubic meters of gas they had initially, exchange might not take place.

2. If the Germans and Soviets each had equal initial endowments of gas and pipes, they would not trade.

3. The greater the difference in two traders' initial endowments, the larger the gains from trade.

4. A contract curve represents the greatest happiness for the greatest number.

5. A law prohibiting people from buying medical treatment from quacks (as defined by the American Medical Association) keeps patients and quacks off the contract curve.

6. A point outside an Edgeworth box is a gift from the rest of the world.

5.3 Trade Among Many People: Behavior

□
Why You Do Not Bargain Every Day

Fortunately for someone trying to understand and predict it, most economic behavior is not bargaining between two people. The reason is simple: there are many people. What prevents you from haggling with the storekeeper about the price at which he will sell you a quart of milk? The answer is that both you and the storekeeper can go to someone else to make the exchange. If you do not like the price he offers, you can go to another store; if he does not like the price you offer, he can wait for another customer to come in. Only when the alternative stores or customers are known to offer worse deals or are expensive to contact can a quart of milk and the dollars to buy it become objects of bargaining. A bunch of flowers sold during the week at the North End market at a fixed price becomes at 11:55 Saturday night (the market is closed on Sunday) an object of bargaining between the last customer and the last flower vendor. During the week, competition for the flowers and for the money determines their price, competition among many buyers and sellers of the same item. In such circumstances (the other circumstances, competition among the few, are the subject of Chapter 21), each seller or buyer takes the price obtainable as given, for with many sellers and buyers no one of them can alter the market price by threatening to refuse the bargain. If you individually refrain from buying a loaf of bread, the price does not change perceptibly, for another of the millions of consumers of bread steps into your place and buys it. We are, in short, back to one consumer facing given income and prices.

One Man, One Toilet

This is one of the most important bits of reasoning in economics. It bears restatement. One buyer of bread among a hundred or a million cannot perceptibly affect the terms on which he or she buys bread. The buyer is, as the jargon has it, a *price taker,* and quite sensibly so. The price may vary from time to time, but not because of variations in the amounts the buyer individually buys. It would be irrational for the buyer to think otherwise. If all people flushed their toilets at once, the city water mains would burst. But a man bearing a grudge against the city would be insane to chortle in gleeful anticipation of a mass flushing as he flushed his toilet. One man, one toilet: that is the limit of his influence over the water supply, as is his one vote over an election or his one decision to not buy a loaf of bread over the price of bread.

Therefore all the apparatus constructed earlier of a consumer facing prices and income "given" to him or her (i.e., over which the consumer individually has no influence) applies to exchange in populous markets. And it is intuitively clear why the analysis of such a situation of price taking will lead to definite conclusions while the analysis of two-person bargaining over the price leads nowhere. The essence of the complexity in two-person bargaining is that my offer affects thine which affects mine, and so on to mental exhaustion. Price taking cuts the story short at the first words: I buy a pound of bread at the going market price without reflecting on how my act will change the price at which the storekeeper will offer the bread, because it will not in fact change his offer.

How the Market Achieves Equilibrium

A radical simplification in the theory of exchange is permitted by price taking. It eliminates bargaining. One can still, however, look at the behavior of the market in an Edgeworth box, and a great deal can now be gotten out of it. Each farmer has an endowment of wheat to sell for other goods (money) and each consumer an endowment of money to sell for wheat. Thousands of farmers and consumers (literally their agents) meet in Chicago to exchange their little bundles of wheat and money. The Edgeworth box for this situation is shown in Figure 5.6.

The tiny box in the lower left-hand corner is the Edgeworth box for an exchange between the farmer Gale Johnson and the wheat eater Margaret Reid. The whole box is the Edgeworth box for exchanges between thousands of Johnsons and Reids, that is, for the whole market. Each Reid is unable to influence the money price of wheat she faces in the market and therefore takes the price as given. When the price varies, she varies her consumption of wheat, as do all the other Reids. The wheat-consuming Reids, in other words, move along the heavy consumers' offer curve just as does a single consumer in the analysis

Figure 5.6
Price Taking Implies
Market Offer Curves

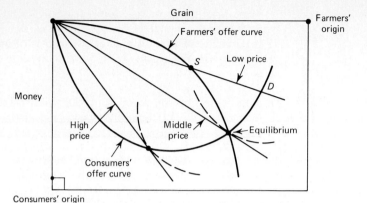

The market offer curves reveal that middle price line is tangent to the indifference curves of both farmers and consumers at point *E,* so farmers wish to sell the same quantity that consumers wish to buy. At low price, consumers demand a larger quantity of wheat than farmers offer to sell.

of demand in the last chapter.[5] Some portions of two of the Reids' indifference curves tangent to the high price and to the middle price are shown as dashed lines to jar your memory of how such offer curves are constructed. The heavy farmers' offer curve is similarly constructed from the farmers' indifference curves. Of course, since the Edgeworth box flips the farmers' indifference curves, their offer curve has the opposite curvature. At the crossing point of the two curves, equilibrium, the middle price induces farmers to sell exactly as much wheat as consumers are induced to demand at that price. That is, equilibrium is the only point on the two curves for which the offer made by farmers as a group is consistent with the offer made by consumers as a group. At any price other than middle price, the offers will be inconsistent.

Low price, for example, induces farmers to supply wheat only out to point *S,* whereas it induces consumers to demand at point *D.* Quite naturally, in other words, a low price of wheat causes suppliers to supply less than demanders demand. Equally naturally, the price will tend to rise. With demanders banging on his door and telephoning him day and night in a search for more wheat at the low price, it will be in the self-interest of each supplier of wheat to withhold his wheat until the price rises; likewise, it will be in the self-interest of each unsatisfied demander to raise the amount of money he offers, enticing wheat supplies away from other demanders. The self-interest of both, then, pushes the price up, and continues to do so until middle

[5] To be perfectly candid, it should be admitted that the argument here is fallacious, although not enough to seriously mislead you if you continue reading through the next chapter. The fallacy is the implicit assumption here that the Reid indifference curves can be added up into indifference curves for all Reids, known technically as *community indifference curves.* Only under very stringent conditions can this easy-sounding feat be accomplished. But so clear do community indifference curves make certain arguments in economics—like the present one in the text—that you will find economists using them for exposition without comment.

price—the price of equilibrium—is achieved.[6] And a similar story applies to high price: it is not sustainable, and it tends to fall to middle price. At middle price demanders do not wish to buy more wheat than is supplied by suppliers; suppliers do not wish to sell more wheat than is demanded by demanders. The market price is determined; the self-interest of thousands of price-taking suppliers and demanders has led to the end of the story (background music to crescendo, fade to credits, house lights up), blessed Equilibrium.

☐
The Equilibrium Is No One's Plot

The determination of market price by the self-interest of large numbers of price-taking suppliers and demanders is routinely misunderstood by the man in the street. A failure of the Brazilian coffee crop and the consequent rise in the price of coffee leaves people muttering about a conspiracy by the Brazilian government. A rise in the price of natural gas or meat leads their representatives in Congress to open hearings into "price-gouging" by big oil companies or big meat wholesalers. The implicit model of price determination used in such analysis is a bargaining model, with one malevolent mind determining the quantity supplied and the price, altering the price at its pleasure. Accurate as the model is for some markets (see Chapter 17), it is inaccurate for most to which it is applied. The point to understand about markets of price takers (i.e., with many participants none of whom has a noticeable influence on the price faced) is that no participant intends the price to be what it is. However high the price of meat, suppliers would like it to be higher; however low the price, demanders would like it to be lower. The equilibrium price is the unintended consequence of the self-interested exchange. Suppliers charge as high a price as they can, what the market will bear; if you as a demander are irritated by this lack of charity, feel free to call it "price gouging" or charging an "exorbitant" price. But keep in mind that you as a consumer offer

---

[6] To be perfectly candid once again, it should be admitted that another assumption has slipped into the argument, the assumption known as *recontracting*. The notion is that farmers and consumers make tentative contracts to exchange at low price, but recontract when it is discovered that low price does not produce equilibrium. The contracts become binding and the exchange is actually made only when the price has no tendency to change (i.e., at middle price). The purpose of this artificial assumption (which does apply, though, to certain well-organized commodity markets) is to eliminate exchanges at nonequilibrium prices. The point is that, were these to take place, the endowments of the parties would be, in effect, altered. They would move first to some intermediate position short of equilibrium, such as *S*, and then trade from that position. The diagram would be pointlessly complicated, because then offer curves would have to be redrawn out of *S*, and redrawn again out of the next intermediate position, and so forth. In applications, the defense of the simplifying assumption of recontracting can run along various lines. Recontracting may literally exist (as in the well-organized markets just mentioned). Equivalently, the goods may be auctioned off (an auction ends when the price has no tendency to change). For most markets the defense has to be that the gains and losses of trading at nonequilibrium prices average out. Some wheat will be exchanged for money at a higher than equilibrium price, some at a lower than equilibrium price. The defense is not always persuasive. If for some reason much wheat, for example, is bought at a very high price (the market falsely anticipating a harvest failure, say), wheat consumers may be so impoverished by the transaction that the equilibrium price ultimately achieved is very different from what it would have been with recontracting.

as low a price as you can, what the market will bear: in the supplier's eyes you are "exploiting" the supplier or paying an "unfair price." These words imply intent and therefore moral responsibility. To repeat, however, no single price taker is responsible for the going price.

Summary

One person's decision to buy or not to buy a bushel of wheat, a house, or a suit of clothes has a trivial influence on the going price of wheat, housing, or clothing. Having no influence, the person behaves as a "price taker," taking the market price as given and making the best choice possible in view of it. In other words, the person is the isolated consumer of earlier chapters facing a given budget line. Adding up the offer curves of each isolated demander and supplier results in *market offer curves* (demand and supply curves). The intersection of the curves determines the equilibrium price and quantity toward which self-interest will drive the market. This process is blind: no participant conspires to make it happen, but it does.

QUESTIONS FOR SECTION 5.3

1. Claudia Goldin and Peter Temin are candidates for the Senate in what is expected to be one of the closest races in American history. A million people are expected to vote, yet a swing of only a thousand votes one way or another is expected to make the majority. If each arrangement of the thousand votes is equally probable, it follows that the probability of an exact tie—the only circumstance in which an individual vote counts—is expected to be 1 chance in 2000. You value a Goldin victory at $100. That is, if some political magician could guarantee Ms. Goldin's victory for a fee (he cannot, of course), you would be willing to pay him $100. Set aside any pleasure you get from fulfilling your patriotic duty. *True or false:* If it costs you more than 5 cents in time and trouble to go to the polls and vote, it would be irrational for you to do so.

2. Under common law, the "enclosure" of an English village before the eighteenth century required the consent of every one of the 40 or 50 owners of rights in the village ("enclosure" entailed chiefly the gathering of scattered plots of land into consolidated holdings). During the eighteenth century the English Parliament developed another method of enclosure, which could take the place of the common law method and which required only a vote by a majority of the 40 or 50 owners to enclose, not unanimous consent.
a. Under common law method, what would happen if one owner refused to enter the bargain? What could the recalcitrant owner demand of those who wanted the enclosure to go forward? Who else would have an incentive to make this demand?
b. Under the new parliamentary method, what happens to the power of one owner to block an enclosure? Why? Would you expect enclosure to become more common after the new method was introduced?

3. When the Bally Corporation decided to build a casino in Atlantic City it announced that it would pay $100,000 to each owner of a house lot on the proposed site. Even though the assessed value of the houses was less than $15,000, some homeowners still held out for more. Why?

True or False

4. Rich employers are in a better bargaining position than are poor workers.

5.4 Trade Among Many People: Happiness

Adam Smith's Theorem

☐ It is now possible to prove a central and celebrated theorem in economics: that the exchange brought about by the pursuit of self-interest in a market of price takers is efficient; that, in other words, the equilibrium of supply and demand leads suppliers and demanders into a position in which one cannot be made better off without making another worse off. The proof wraps the arguments of this and the preceding chapter into one lovely diagram (Figure 5.7). The top panel shows the offer curve of farmers and consumers of wheat, the bottom the demand and supply curves corresponding to the offer curves.

**Figure 5.7
Exchange Among Price
Takers Is Efficient: The
Offer Curves Intersect at
a Point of Mutual
Tangency (a) so That
Supply Equals Demand (b)**

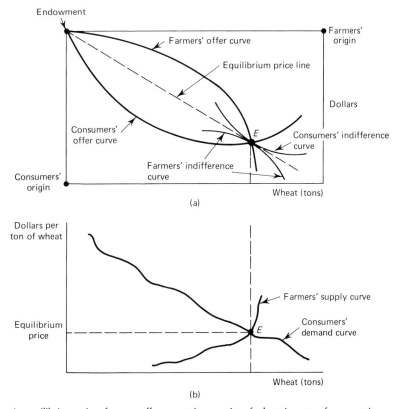

At equilibrium price, farmers offer a certain quantity of wheat in return for a certain amount of money. Consumers offer an identical amount of money in return for an identical amount of wheat. Thus quantity supplied equals quantity demanded at the equilibrium (average) price.

It has just been shown why *E* (in either panel) is the equilibrium exchange and why therefore the slope of the dashed equilibrium price line (in the top panel) is the equilibrium price. Look closely at the point *E* in the top, Edgeworth box panel. By the way in which offer curves are constructed, a farmer's indifference curve (drawn in lightly) touches the equilibrium price line at *E*; likewise, a consumer's indifference curve (also drawn in lightly) touches the equilibrium price line at *E*. That is, at *E* the two indifference curves, touching the same price line at the same point, touch each other. But exchanges at points of tangency between two indifference curves are on the contract curve (not drawn). That is, the point *E* is on the contract curve; it is efficient. Q.E.D.

The theorem, proven in this form at the end of the nineteenth century and reproven repeatedly in more subtle forms down to the present, was made a leading theme in economics in 1776 by Adam Smith. *Smith's theorem* is a paradox of selfishness. The least admirable of human motives leads in a market of small sellers and buyers to an admirable result, the exhaustion of mutually advantageous exchanges. That is, selfishness leads onto the contract curve, and we have seen that a move from a point off the curve to certain of the points on it is unambiguously desirable. Supply and demand selects one of these desirable points. Splendid.

☐
That Supply Equals Demand Is Efficient Does Not Imply That It Is Good

Recall, however, that the contract curve consists of infinitely many such points. There is nothing morally sacred about the point selected by supply and demand. The moral choice between points on the contract curve is a choice between one person's happiness and another's, much harder than the choice between making both happier (moving to the curve) and leaving both with the happiness they have (staying off the curve).

Q: Make a plausible case in a diagram that, by altering within the initial lens of mutually advantageous exchange the endowments of wheat and money in the hands of farmers and consumers, a market of price takers can arrive at any point on the portion of the contract curve inside the lens.

A: In Figure 5.8 the heavy offer curves running out the initial endowment have, as they should, the same direction of curvature as do the initial indifference curves defining the lens but more of this curvature. They meet at unimpeded equilibrium. By altering the endowment to ceiling supply, one generates another pair of offer curves (dashed), meeting at another point, called here morally better for reasons that will be clear in a moment. Both points are the result of price-taking markets, and both are on the contract curve (drawn as a light line), but at morally better farmers are worse off and consumers better off than at unimpeded equilibrium. It is intuitively clear from the diagram that an endowment can be found that leads to any given point on the contract curve.

In other words, changes in the distribution of goods change the offer curves (supply and demand curves) and change the final distribu-

**Figure 5.8
Changes in Initial
Endowments Change the
Offer Curves.
Redistribution and Free
Markets Can Improve
upon Unimpeded Markets**

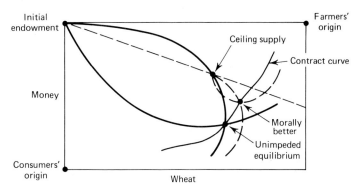

Any point on the contract curve can be reached by a series of exchanges that exhausts the possibilities for mutually beneficial exchange. A price ceiling gets consumers to the morally better point but leaves society at ceiling supply, which is inefficient. A redistribution that makes ceiling supply the endowment point guarantees morally better to consumers and permits farmers and consumers to further improve their happiness by free trade to the contract curve.

tion of goods to which they lead. Unless the present distribution of goods among people is thought to be morally best, there is no case that economics can make, unassisted by moral judgments, that leaving the present market to work unimpeded is the best policy. This is what it means to say that the point on the contract curve selected by supply and demand is not morally sacred.

☐
***The Economist's
Presumption in
Favor of Letting the
Market Work***

Yet Smith's theorem began a long love affair between economists and the market. As a general proposition, love knows no reason, but economists do have a reason for their love of the market. Suppose it were determined that the unimpeded equilibrium in the market for wheat was socially undesirable, that in a better world the wheat consumers should be made better off and the farmers worse off. There are two ways of achieving this, the noneconomist's and the economist's way. The noneconomist's way is to interfere with the market directly, setting, for example, a price ceiling on wheat that will benefit consumers. The economist's way is to change the initial endowment in favor of the consumer by taxing or subsidizing income, letting the market work unimpeded thereafter. In Figure 5.8 the dashed straight line representing the price ceiling leads farmers to supply wheat out to ceiling supply, which may indeed put consumers on a higher indifference curve than unimpeded equilibrium (the lower amount of wheat consumers get may be more than outweighed by the smaller amount of money they have to give up to get it).

Economists argue, however, that the point ceiling supply can be improved upon by making it, for example, the initial endowment and then letting both parties trade out to the morally better point on the contract curve. At morally better both will be better off than at ceiling supply. That is, the society should reshuffle the endowments of wheat and money instead of interfering with the market directly. Any distribution of happiness achieved by interfering with the wheat market can be improved upon by interfering instead with the distribution of income and then letting the market work.

This is the reasoning behind, for example, what has been called the "negative income tax": replace the present labyrinth of subsidies to housing, food, and medical care for the poor with money payments to the poor. As James Tobin, one of the inventors of the negative income tax, put it,

While concerned laymen who observe people with shabby housing or too little to eat instinctively want to provide them with decent housing and adequate food, economists instinctively want to provide them with more cash income. Then they can buy the housing and food if they want to, and if they choose not to, the presumption is that they have a better use for the money.[7]

The best way in which to enrich the poor, in other words, is to enrich them, not to tinker with the markets in which they operate. If the employees and stockholders of Zenith Television are considered to be appropriate objects of public charity, the charity should take the form of money gifts to them, not quotas to protect them (at the expense of consumers) against Japanese competition. If farmers are considered to be an especially desirable group for the nation to subsidize, the subsidy should again take the form of money gifts, not (again at the expense of consumers) price supports, officially sanctioned marketing boards, acreage allotments, and payments for nonproduction.

The argument is not conclusive. As Tobin remarks, it "rarely satisfies the intelligent egalitarian layman . . . [because he knows] that there are pragmatic limits on the redistributive use of taxation and cash transfers."[8] To be sure, one of the "pragmatic limits" is precisely the explicitness with which redistribution of income puts the social question: there would undoubtedly be more opposition to a subsidy to Zenith Television if it appeared as a line on the income tax form ("Zenith Subsidy: Add $3 to calculated tax") than if it appeared, as it does, as a small item in the financial section of the newspaper ("Zenith Hits Unfair Sony Practices, Calls for Quota"). But the main point is that the taxes required to get the money for the subsidy are themselves interferences in a market, the market for the taxed good (income or cigarettes or whatever).

This is one among many sophisticated objections to the economist's love for the market that will be discussed in more detail in later chapters. At any rate the flaws in the unsophisticated objections are by now clear. That people are poor, for example, is not a decisive objection to permitting the market to operate unimpeded: their poverty can sometimes be alleviated directly, leaving the market to achieve the additional benefits of efficiency. Smith's theorem, in short, is not easily dismissed.

[7] "On Limiting the Domain of Inequality," *Journal of Law and Economics* 13 (October 1970): 263–277, reprinted in E. S. Phelps, ed., *Economic Justice* (Harmondsworth, England: Penguin Education, 1973), p. 449.

[8] Tobin, in Phelps, ed., p. 449.

Summary

Smith's theorem asserts that a selfish price taker competing with others "intends only his own gain, and he is in this, as in many other cases, led by an invisible hand to promote an end which was no part of his intention,"[9] namely, a better price for his customers and an efficient exchange. Capitalism is altruistic, not in intent but in result. Smith's theorem, however, does not guarantee social bliss. The point on the contract curve that the intersection of supply and demand selects is not necessarily the best point. Yet the economist can argue, if he argues with care, that questions of efficiency—whether society should be on the contract curve—can be treated separately from questions of equity—where society should be on the contract curve.

PROBLEMS FOR SECTION 5.4

1. The United States imposes an effective quota on its imports of Italian shoes. *True or false:* By comparison with the free trade point, the quota makes both Americans and Italians worse off.

2. The guns for today's war can be paid for by two methods. On the one hand, the government can force its citizens to give up resources today by taxing them. On the other, it can entice them to give up resources today by offering them an interest rate if they will loan the government the resources, to be paid off tomorrow. To pay off the loan tomorrow it will have to tax its citizens tomorrow. *True or false:* In a sense the method of borrowing to pay for the war transfers the burden from today's generation to tomorrow's.

---

[9] Adam Smith, *The Wealth of Nations*, first published in 1776 (Chicago: University of Chicago Press, 1976), Book IV, Chapter II, p. 477.

<table>
<tr><td>

6

</td><td>

Using Market Supply and Demand

</td></tr>
</table>

6.1 The Uses of Equilibrium

Inferring Price Movement from Supply and Demand

Economists study markets; supply and demand curves apply to markets of price takers; price taking is the common lot of human beings; therefore, the notion of *supply and demand curves* is the most useful instrument in economic analysis. Happily, it is also the easiest, or at any rate easier than the notion of an Edgeworth box and its offer curves. To think clearly about the happiness people get from markets, the Edgeworth box is essential; to think clearly about how people behave in markets, however, usually all that is necessary is the diagram of supply and demand. Demand curves slope downward; supply curves upward. For many problems, that is all the economist knows on earth, and all ye need to know.

An astonishing range of economic problems reduces to the simple assertion that the *market must clear*, that is, that the price adjusts to make quantities supplied and demanded equal. The problem of predicting what will happen to the market price and quantity when supply or demand curves move is one example (see Figure 6.1).

Q: More gasoline and tomatoes are sold in the summer than in the winter. Yet the price of gasoline is higher and the price of tomatoes lower in the summer than in the winter. Why?

A: The "yet" is misleading. There is nothing unexpected about the way in which the prices move. Generally speaking, the supply curve of gasoline does not vary from season to season, because the technique of making gasoline from crude oil does not vary. Likewise, the demand curve for tomatoes does not vary from season to season, because the tastes and incomes of tomato eaters do not vary. But as people take to the road in the summer to visit Aunt Louise or to prevent Aunt Louise from visiting them, the demand curve for gasoline moves out, and as Northern gardeners harvest their crops, the supply curve of tomatoes moves out. This is shown in Figure 6.1.

The prices must adjust to clear the market, that is, to make equal the quantities demanded and supplied. At the low winter price of gasoline in the face of the summer demand the market would not clear:

104

Figure 6.1
How Movements in the
Price and Quantity
Depend on Which Curve
Moves. When Demand Is
Out and Supply Is
Unchanged (a); When
Supply Is Out and
Demand Is Unchanged (b)

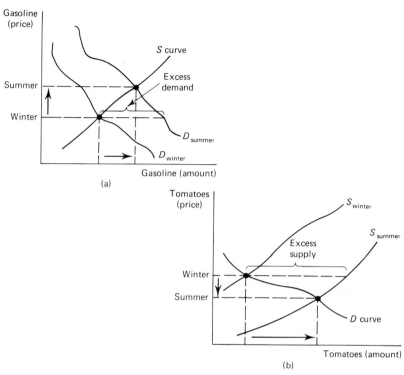

When the demand schedule shifts outward and the supply schedule remains fixed, price and quantity rise. When the supply schedule shifts outward and the demand schedule remains fixed, price falls and quantity rises.

there would be excess demand, which would force the price up. At the high winter price of tomatoes there would be excess supply, which would force the price down. As the diagram says, the movements in price depend on which curve moves—supply or demand.

☐ The argument can be run in reverse, inferring what has happened to supply and demand curves from how price and quantity behave (see Figure 6.2).

Inferring Supply
and Demand from
Price Movements

Q: In the last few years both the quantity and the relative price of medical care have increased. Therefore the demand curve has moved out faster than the supply curve.

A: True. You observe the two points in the left panel of Figure 6.2. If the market is in equilibrium, these are points of market clearing, that is, of intersection of supply and demand curves. The two points are explained in the right-hand panel. Notice that the demand curve has moved out faster than has the supply curve (compare the short and long arrows out of the old equilibrium, once). You would not be surprised to learn that something important happened on the demand side of the market, namely, Medicare for the elderly, inducing the elderly to buy more.

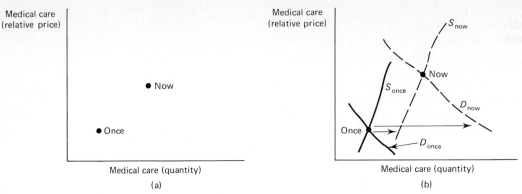

**Figure 6.2
Changes in Price and
Quantity: What You
Observe (a) and How
You Explain the
Observations (b)**

Price and quantity are greater now than once. The cause must be an outward shift in the demand curve. If the supply curve also shifted out, the shift must have been less than the shift in the demand curve.

☐
***The Market Must
Clear***

The following remarkable assertion depends only on recognizing that a fixed quantity supplied is the equivalent of a perfectly vertical supply curve and that the market must clear.[1]

> ***Q:*** In years of bad harvests in England a century ago, the rich would buy up grain and sell to the poor all they desired at half the market price. *True or false:* Contrary to its appearance and intent, the plan did not benefit the poor at all, but benefited instead the holders of grain (other rich men, grain dealers, etc.).

> ***A:*** True. Before the intervention of the charitable rich, the grain dealers sell the available supply of grain to the poor at the equilibrium price the market will bear (see Figure 6.3).

> As shown, after the intervention the grain dealers still sell the same supply to the poor, who must still be induced to consume only the available supply. The sole difference in the situation is that now the grain passes through the hands of the rich, who mark it down to half the price they paid. Since the final price to the poor cannot change (it must be equilibrium price if the poor are to have only the available supply), competition among the rich for the grain to sell to their poor will cause the price the rich pay to exactly double, to double price in the diagram. The plan enriches holders of grain (who get double price) and has no effect on the poor (who still pay equilibrium price). Another way in which to see the truth in the argument is to imagine

---

[1] Due to Mountiford Longfield (1802–1884), an Irish economist who anticipated early in the nineteenth century most of the developments in economics late in the nineteenth century. George Stigler uses the example in "The Politics of Political Economists," in G. J. Stigler, *Essays in the History of Economics* (Chicago: University of Chicago Press, 1964), p. 60.

Figure 6.3
Scarce Goods Must
Somehow Be Allocated

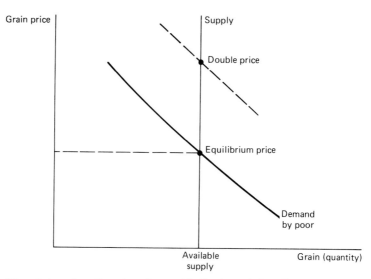

Attempts to reduce the price of a good in fixed supply by selling it at a lower price will fail. The price after lowering must be high enough to choke off demand to exactly the same extent as before the attempt to lower the price. That is, the price must be the same, implying that the market price will rise exactly enough to frustrate the attempt to help buyers.

in the diagram a demand curve by the charitable rich (a portion of which is drawn as a dashed line through double price). The rich will pay a price double whatever the poor will pay; the poor will pay equilibrium price for what is available. Therefore, the demand by the rich derives from the demand by the poor, the willingness to pay being exactly double the poor's. The quantity to be sold determines the poor's willingness to pay, which determines the rich's willingness to pay (namely, double). The rich fail in their attempt to benefit the poor because any attempt to sell the grain to the poor at less than equilibrium price causes the poor to demand more than is available, which causes their agents, the rich, to demand more than is available, which causes the price paid by the rich to rise.

☐
The Law of One Price

Another way of putting the elementary but powerful proposition that a market must clear is the *law of one price*. In equilibrium, all participants in a market for, say, standardized units of housing must be paying or getting the same price. If the law of one price is violated, there are further deals to be made, further reshuffling of suppliers and demanders. The market has not yet cleared.

The practical significance of the law of one price is that when it is true the *location* of a shift in supply or demand does not matter. It is exceptionally easy to fall into fallacies in this connection.

Q: Cotton cloth is cheap to transport and many countries produce it. Between 1913 and 1927 British exports of cotton cloth fell from 7.1 billion to 4.2 billion linear yards. In 1913 the chief market for British cloth had been India, taking 3.2 billion of the 7.1 billion. By 1927, however, India had developed its own cotton cloth industry and took only 1.8 billion yards of British cloth. *True or false:* If India had not developed its own industry, British exports of cotton cloth would have fallen half as fast as they in fact did between 1913 and 1927.

A: False. Put away your pocket calculator and ignore the arithmetic, for it is only relevant (and tenuously so even then) if India and Britain were the only consumers and producers in their markets for cotton cloth. But they were not. Both were in a single world market. The outward movement of the Indian supply curve (this is what it means to say that it developed its own industry) would push back the demand curve facing *all* exporters of cloth and would drive down the world price. This, in turn, would reduce the amount exporters, such as Britain, would want to supply. But the fall in the Indian demand would not reduce yard for yard the demand facing Britain, as is implied by the arithmetic. That Britain in an arithmetical sense "depended" on Indian imports reflects minor advantages of political connection and of special treatment in India for British exports. Aside from these minor advantages, British exporters faced a world market (a world price). The location of the demand did not matter.

Summary

The equilibrium point of a market can be described as the price at which the quantity supplied is equal to the quantity demanded or, equivalently, as the quantity at which the price suppliers will accept is equal to the price demanders will accept. It is the intersection of the curves of supply and demand. To use the analysis of supply and demand, you must rivet your attention on this equilibrium point. The supposition that the point is achieved is remarkably powerful, explaining why prices vary, why observed prices and quantities reveal whether supply or demand varied more, why amounts supplied must be limited if the price is to be high or the price high if the amount is limited, and why the source of supply or demand does not matter in a market obeying the law of one price.

QUESTIONS FOR SECTION 6.1

1. The price of meat (sugar, coffee, toilet paper, or whatever) is now exorbitant. *True or false:* A good scheme for solving the problem is for consumers to boycott meat (sugar, coffee, toilet paper, or whatever) driving down its price; when its price is low, consumers can resume their higher purchases.

2. If Britain has a fixed exchange rate (i.e., the number of U.S. dollars per British pound is fixed), then inflation abroad can be imported. Since Britain imports wheat and autos, a rise in the world price of wheat or autos will raise British prices. It is usually asserted that the strength of this effect depends on the ratio of imports to national expenditure, that the effect will be stronger in Britain (where imports divided by income equal 0.26) than in America (where it is only 0.06).

But America and Britain import roughly the same list of commodities. What is different is merely the share of total British consumption of, say, autos provided by imports. *True or false:* The law of one price suggests that the strength of imported inflation would be the same in both countries.

3. In 1907 the British iron industry accounted for three quarters of world exports of pig iron but only one sixth of world production. Which figure is the best summary measure of Britain's "importance" in the market for pig iron?

True or False

4. The two observed points in Figure 6.2 are consistent with any number of supply and demand curves running through them.

5. If the Organization of Petroleum Exporting Countries wishes to hold the price of oil above its equilibrium level, it must hold the amounts its members supply below their equilibrium levels.

6. The banning of American exports of wheat to South Africa will cause more people in Zaire (another wheat-importing country) to starve.

6.2 Adding up Supply and Demand

☐
How to Add up Individual Demands and Supplies

Equilibrium and the law of one price clear up an earlier embarrassment in market demand. Recall that in the last chapter the market demand curve was derived from market indifference curves, using the fiction of the representative consumer. We no longer need the fiction.

Suppose that there are many demanders of housing in Iowa City. Each demander is a price taker (because there are many), and at any given market price each will want to buy a certain quantity of housing according to his or her demand curve—a demand curve derived from the demander's individual indifference curves and free from the embarrassing ambiguities of market (or "community") indifference curves. If the law of one price holds, then at any given market price the quantity demanded by the market (i.e., by all demanders) will be the sum of all the individual quantities. The market demand curve, in other words, is the horizontal sum—the sum at various given prices—of the demand curves of all demanders. Were there only two demanders, Ransom and Sutch, the market demand curve for housing in Iowa City would be constructed as shown in Figure 6.4 (two demanders here violate for the sake of simplicity the condition that there be many).

Notice the kink in the market demand at the price ($1500) below which Ransom begins to demand housing. Notice too the slashes that identify in the style of high school geometry horizontal segments of equal length (in the case portrayed, at a price of $500).

The same construction gives the supply curve of housing. Add up at each price the quantities supplied in Iowa City by four landlords, DeCanio, Higgs, Reid, and Wright. Mathematically, the procedure is to express the individual quantities demanded and supplied as functions of the price of housing and then add up the functions. The demand function would be, speaking in generalities, $D(P)_{\text{Ransom}} + D(P)_{\text{Sutch}}$

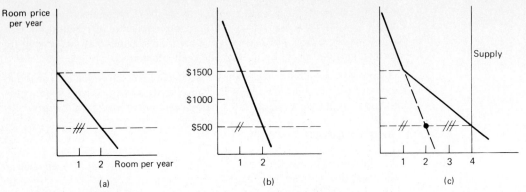

Figure 6.4
Market Demand Is the
Horizontal Sum of
Individual Demands:
Compare Ransom's
Demand (a), Sutch's
Demand (b) and Demand
for Both (Market) (c)

The quantity demanded by the market at any price equals the quantity demanded by Ransom plus the quantity demanded by Sutch. Thus the market demand curve equals the horizontal sum of the individual demand curves.

and the supply function $S(P)_{\text{DeCanio}} + S(P)_{\text{Higgs}} + S(P)_{\text{Reid}} + S(P)_{\text{Wright}}$. To be specific, Ransom's demand curve for rooms might be $Q_R = 3.0 - 0.002P$. This equation says that Ransom will buy, for example, no rooms at a price of $1500 per room [$3.0 - 0.002(1500) = 0$] and 3 rooms at a price of zero. Likewise, Sutch's demand might be $Q_S = 2.5 - 0.001P$. The market demand curve would therefore be the sum of these two, $Q_R + Q_S = 3.0 - 0.002P + 2.5 - 0.001P = 5.5 - 0.003P$, which is in fact the equation for the line below the kink in the diagram. Against this demand curve might be set a fixed supply of one room from each of the four suppliers. A fixed supply is insensitive to price; that is, the amount supplied is not a function of the price. The supply curve, therefore, is a vertical line at four rooms, as in the diagram. The equilibrium price is the price that makes the two demanders satisfied to consume exactly four rooms in total:

$$\text{Quantity supplied} = 4 = \text{quantity demanded} = 5.5 - 0.003P$$

The price is the solution to this equation, $500, as (again) in the diagram.

The equilibrium price could be put back into the two individual demand curves to find out how much Ransom and Sutch each demand in equilibrium. Ransom, for example, demands $2.5 - 0.001(500) = 2.0$ rooms per year. The diagram mimics the algebra exactly. The individual demand and supply curves are added up into market supply and demand curves, the intersection of the two determines the equilibrium price and quantity for the entire market, and the equilibrium price can then be run back to the individual supply and demand curves to determine the allocation of quantities among demanders and suppliers.

□
*Why Price Taking
Is Necessary*

The law of one price is obviously necessary for the adding up of the curves: "adding up" must be in some definite direction, for example, horizontally, at one price. Price taking is also necessary: if quantities are to be added at a given price the price must be given.

T or F: A group of demanders who are not price takers do not have an aggregate demand curve.

A: True. The market does not give them a fixed price. That is, the price they get depends on the amount they demand (each one faces a rising supply curve, not a flat, horizontal price). A demand curve, however, *is* a schedule of amounts purchased at various *given* prices. Not taking price as given, these "price-searching" demanders do not have such schedules. The analysis of supply and demand applies only to price takers.

A great deal more than mere theoretical tidiness comes out of the idea of adding up individual supply and demand curves. It is the heart of applied economics.

□
*Uses of Adding up:
The Keynes Problem*

The general technique for handling questions involving supply and demand is simplicity itself: (1) Identify all the suppliers and demanders in the market, grouping them into categories enlightening for the purpose at hand. (2) Write down in one form or another the condition for equilibrium (i.e., summed supply equals summed demand, drawing the corresponding diagram). (3) Answer the question.

Being the greatest economist of the twentieth century is no protection against missing one or all of these steps.[2]

Q: In 1924 J. M. Keynes, a well-known economist of the day, argued that the Colonial Act of 1900, which *permitted* British trusts (holding funds of charities, trade unions, and the like) to invest abroad (before 1900 they had been required by law to invest in Britain), had hurt Britain. The effect of the act, he said, was "to starve home developments by diverting savings abroad and, consequently, to burden home borrowers with a higher rate of interest than they would need to pay otherwise." Accepting for the purposes of argument that a rise in the interest rate *is* a Bad Thing, was Keynes correct? You may wish to know that both before and after the act there

---

[2] John Maynard Keynes (his father, John Neville, was also an economist), 1883–1946, First Bursar of King's College, editor of the *Economic Journal*, advisor to the British Treasury, patron of the arts, first Baron of Tilton, architect of half a century of economic thinking and economic policy, was, to use his own description of Ricardo, "the greatest mind that found economics worthy of its powers" [this in R. F. Harrod's, *The Life of John Maynard Keynes* (New York: Harcourt Brace, 1951), p. 467]. "Keynes" rhymes with "brains." The argument and quotation in the question come from his "Foreign Investment and National Advantage," *Nation and Athenaeum* 35 (1924): 586.

were others (private investors, banks, and so forth) besides the trusts making investments at home.

A: Keynes was wrong. Consider the situation after the trusts are permitted to invest where they please. The nontrust British investors must be included in the market. The equilibrium rate of interest (the price in this market) occurs when the supply of loanable funds from the trusts plus the supply of funds from the nontrusts (both British) equals the demand from British users of funds plus the excess demand of foreign users of funds. That is,

$$S_{\text{trusts}} + S_{\text{nontrusts}} = D_{\text{British}} + D_{\text{foreign}}$$

The diagram corresponding to this equation adds horizontally the supply and demand curves of the usual shape (see Figure 6.5).

The heavy curves are the summed supply and demand curves that determine equilibrium. Notice that, as the diagram is shown, at the equilibrium interest rate, i_E, the British quantity demanded of funds, Q_B, is greater than is the quantity supplied by the trusts, Q_T. Now suppose (to run the history backward) that the trusts are *required* by law to invest in Britain. What happens? Nothing of consequence. Since the trusts can place all their funds in Britain at the existing interest rate without oversupplying the British market (Q_B is greater than Q_T), nothing happens to the equilibrium interest rate when they obey the law and bring their funds home. Some of the nontrusts formerly in Britain now move to foreign loans, trading places with the trusts. But no gap between British and foreign interest rates can develop. The nontrusts still investing in Britain are free to move to foreign loans and would do so if such a gap developed, raising British interest rates and lowering foreign interest rates until the gap disappeared. The presence or absence of the act, therefore, has no important effect, and no effect at all on British interest rates, contrary to Keynes's assertion. Only if the trusts supplied more funds than British demand would

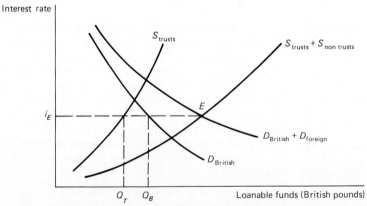

A law requiring the trusts to supply only the British demand would be ineffective if the trusts in any case supplied less than the total British demand: the law would not push funds into any channel in which they were not already flowing.

absorb at the equilibrium interest rate would the presence or absence of the act matter. That is, only if the diagram were redrawn to make Q_T larger than Q_B would Keynes be correct. But Q_T greater than Q_B contradicts the observation that nontrusts supplied some British demand before the act.

☐
Other Uses of Summing Supplies and Demands

The choice of the equation and diagram that best suits the problem at hand is an acquired skill. For example, when the geographical separateness of two sets of demanders and suppliers is important, the curves can be separated. The American television market is separated from the Japanese (America imports as well as produces televisions). The equilibrium condition is that the televisions supplied by the Japanese in excess of Japanese demand find a home in America fulfilling demand in excess of American supply, $S_J - D_J = D_A - S_A$, which is merely a rearrangement of the assertion that world (i.e., Japanese and American) demand equals world supply, $D_A + D_J = S_A + S_J$. The diagram corresponding to the rearranged equation is shown in Figure 6.6.

Figure 6.6
Excess Supply in One Market Equals Excess Demand in Another

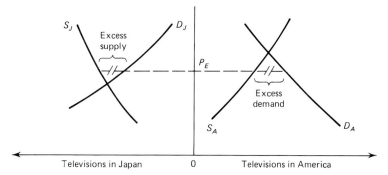

If televisions move costlessly between the United States and Japan, the same price will prevail in both markets. This price will equate total supply and total demand. Thus excess supply in one market must be matched by excess demand in the other.

The American and Japanese diagrams share a price axis because the markets have the same price (they do not in fact, but that is unimportant here). To accommodate the shared axis, the Japanese curves run in the opposite direction. In equilibrium the excess supply from Japan equals the excess demand in America; that is, at P_E Japanese exports equal American imports, as indicated by the slashed segments.

T or F: If an effective quota is imposed on American imports of televisions from Japan, then the American price will rise and the Japanese price will fall. American consumers of televisions will be hurt; Japanese consumers will be benefited.

A: True. To have any effect the quota must be less than the current quantity of American imports. The segments excess demand in the American half of the figure and excess supply in the Japanese half will have to become equal to the quota, and smaller than they are initially. This is only possible if American excess demand is choked off by a higher American price and Japanese excess supply choked off by a lower Japanese price. (Look at the diagram: only under these circumstances will a smaller segment fit between both curves.) A gap will form between the high American price and the low Japanese price.

☐

Why Price Taking Is a Consequence of Summing

An alternative arrangement of the equilibrium condition is appropriate when one wishes to look at the situation of a single participant or group of participants. Consider, for example, the situation of Peter Lindert, one consumer of bread among 200,000,000. The supply curve of bread facing him is the total supply (suppose it to be fixed at 10 billion loaves per year) minus the summed demand curves of the other 199,999,999 consumers. This assertion is, again, merely a rearrangement of the assertion that total supply equals total demands. $S_{\text{total}} = D_{\text{Lindert}} + D_{\text{others}}$ can be written as $D_{\text{Lindert}} = S_{\text{total}} - D_{\text{others}}$, the right-hand side being the supply curve facing Lindert. A supply curve of bread is a schedule of the amounts of bread one can acquire by offering the market various prices. Suppose that Lindert offers 0.10 cents over the market price for loaves of bread. If he buys up anything the market offers him at this new price, the price will rise by 0.10 cents. Suppose that such a rise causes each other consumer to reduce his annual consumption of bread by a quarter of a loaf. Therefore if Lindert persists in buying all the market offers him at the new price, he will be able to buy $\frac{1}{4}(199,999,999) = 20$ million more loaves of bread. That is, the logic of adding and subtracting supply and demand curves implies that Lindert faces a virtually horizontal supply curve. Consuming now, say, 50 loaves a year at 40 cents each, he can if he wishes consume the colossal quantity of 20,000,050 loaves by raising the price he offers very slightly, to 40.1 cents each.

The same point applies to less extreme cases. One apartment renter among 1000 or 1 automobile buyer among 10,000 faces a supply curve so nearly horizontal that nothing is gained by keeping in mind its slight upward slope. One demander among many faces a given price at which he or she can buy virtually all that he or she wishes without affecting the price. By similar logic, one supplier among many is also a price taker. In other words, the logic of supply and demand, which assumes price taking, itself justifies the assumption in the case of large numbers of participants in a market. All this comes from manipulating the obvious assertion, "the sum of all supplies must equal the sum of all demands."

Summary

The summing of supply and demand curves is essentially an application of the law of one price in conditions of price taking (i.e., in conditions of many suppliers and demanders participating in a market). Each arrangement of the condition for equilibrium—supply equals demand—has a corresponding diagram. The diagrams are among the most useful tools of the economist's craft. They make it clear, for example, why the initial allocation of a good does not matter for its final allocation, precisely where large numbers of participants fit into the theory of supply and demand, and how the theory is used.

QUESTIONS FOR SECTION 6.2

1. Devise a diagram that embodies a constant price differential (due to, say, transport costs) between the price of the television exporter (Japan) and the television importer (America).

2. Helen Louise Stueland has a demand curve for stocks of clothing: the lower the price, the larger her wardrobe. Draw a diagram exhibiting how she determines each year how much new clothing to buy in view of her existing stock, supposing that half the stock wears out each year.

True or False

3. The ownership of housing in Iowa City before trade begins does not affect the ownership after trade.

4. A high television tariff (a tax on televisions shipped from Japan to America) could stop Japanese exports to America entirely.

5. The proof of a horizontal supply curve of bread facing a single demander would break down if bread were not assumed to be in fixed supply.

6.3 Extensions of Supply and Demand

☐

Substitutes and Complements Require Two Diagrams

Supply and demand is the economist's first and best tool, a Swiss army knife of possibilities from basic blade to folding scissors. It can be applied, for example, to related markets, such as the markets for cotton and wool cloth or the markets for cotton cloth and the buttons, needles, and sewing services to make it into clothing. These markets are related through their demand functions. The demand function for cotton cloth contains, of course, the price of cotton cloth, entering with a little superscript minus sign attached to it to signify that the quantity demanded goes down when the price goes up: $Q^{\text{demand}}_{\text{cotton cloth}} = f(P^{-}_{\text{cotton cloth}})$. The negative sign is represented by the downward slope of an ordinary demand curve. A fuller statement of the demand function for cotton cloth would include among other things the price of substitutes (wool cloth, P_W) and complements (sewing services, P_S): $Q^D_C = f(P^{-}_C, P^{+}_W, P^{-}_S)$. Notice the signs of the superscript. These tell how the ordinary demand curve shifts in or out in response to changes in the prices of substitutes and complements. The definitions of "substitute" and "complement" given in Chapter 2 depended on the shape of indifference curves; the definition here, more direct and useful, depends on the sign of the effect of price on quantity demanded. (As you might expect, the two definitions are connected.) More expensive wool causes substitutions in favor of cotton cloth; more expensive sewing services, on the other hand, causes the price of clothing to rise and the quantity demanded of clothing and (therefore) cotton cloth to fall.

Q: The supply curve of cotton cloth moves out. *True or false:* The less sensitive to price is the quantity supplied of wool cloth, the smaller will be the increase in the quantity demanded of cotton cloth.

A: The assertion translates the Figure 6.7 into words.

EXCHANGE

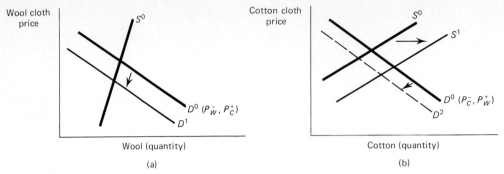

Wool cloth price — Wool (quantity) — (a)

Cotton cloth price — Cotton (quantity) — (b)

Figure 6.7
One Way to Think About Related Markets: Markets for Wool (a) and Cotton (b) Cloth

An outward shift in the supply schedule of cotton causes a fall in the price of cotton. Because cotton and wool are substitutes, a fall in the price of one causes a downward shift in the demand schedule for the other. Thus the original shift in supply causes a downward shift in the demand schedule for both goods.

The heavy curves are the supply and demand curves before the disturbance. After the supply curve of cotton cloth moves out to S^1, the price of cotton cloth drops. Since cotton is a substitute for wool in the production of clothing (signified in the initial demand curve for wool by the plus sign attached to P_C), the fall in the price of cotton pushes in the demand curve for wool, as indicated by the light demand curve D^1. Because the supply curve of wool slopes upward—instead of being flat—the price of wool will therefore be driven down. And because wool is a substitute for cotton, the fall in the wool price will in turn push the demand curve for cotton downward to D^2, making smaller (as required by the assertion) the increase in the quantity demanded of cotton cloth. Notice that the feedback from the market for wool to the market for cotton would be cut if the supply curve of wool were flat, that is, if the quantity supplied of wool were very sensitive to its price. In that case the price of wool would be pegged by its flat supply curve, and the rise in demand would be unable to affect the price. The flatter the supply curve, in other words, the smaller the fall in the price of wool and the smaller the consequent fall in the quantity demanded of cotton cloth, as asserted.

Joint Supply Requires Vertical Summation

☐ A demand curve is a schedule of the amount people are willing to buy at a given price. At $10 a head, Nicholas von Tunzelmann is willing to buy 40 sheep, buying (that is) out to the point at which the things he gets from an additional sheep are worth just $10 to him. But looked at the other way, the demand curve is also a schedule of the price that people are willing to pay at a given quantity. At 40 sheep, von Tunzelmann is willing to pay $10 for another one. Recall the earlier jargon: the price along a demand curve for sheep is the marginal valuation of a sheep at various quantities.

Suppose, then, that a sheep provides two things in rigidly fixed proportions: mutton (sheep's meat) and wool. And suppose that, having

5 sheeps' worth of wool and mutton, von Tunzelmann values the wool from an additional sheep at $15 and the mutton from the same sheep (slaughtered when its wool gives out) at $20. What is von Tunzelmann's demand price at 5 sheep? It is $15 + $20 = $35, the sum of the separate values; that is, he is willing to pay $35 for an additional sheep. If he has a larger number of sheep—say, 40—he is willing to pay only a smaller amount for the wool and mutton of still another sheep, since at 40 sheep he is already well clothed and fed. That is, his demand curves for wool and mutton slope downward and therefore so does his demand curve for sheep, which is the *vertical* sum of the wool and mutton curves in Figure 6.8.

In other words, when things like wool and mutton, movies and air-conditioned comfort, lumber and wood shavings, vocational training and general education, or my protection from conquest and thine are jointly supplied, the demand curve for the whole thing (sheep, movies in hot weather, timber, college, or national defense) is the *vertical* sum of the separate demand curves. The contrast between vertical and horizontal sums can be brought out by noting that the demand curve for sheep by Nicholas and Carol von Tunzelmann together is the *horizontal* sum of their separate demand curves for sheep, each of which is the *vertical* sum of their individual demands for sheeps' worths of mutton and of wool. The order in which the horizontal or vertical summation is performed does not matter. Carol's demand for mutton at various prices could be summed horizontally with Nicholas's and then their willingness to pay for a given sheep's worth of wool and mutton summed vertically, or the vertical sum could precede the horizontal. Either gives the same result. Furthermore, the demanders of wool and mutton need not be the same people. As long as they bought the same sheep, Nicholas could demand only mutton, Carol only wool. Their demand curve for sheep would still be the vertical sum of the

Figure 6.8
The Demand for Sheep Is the Vertical Sum of the Demand for the Corresponding Wool and Mutton

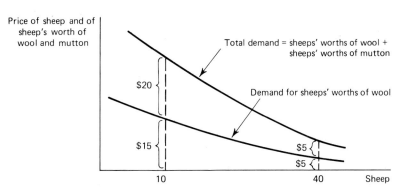

The amount a consumer is willing to pay for a sheep, which supplies mutton and wool in given quantities, is equal to the amount the consumer would pay for the mutton plus the amount he or she would pay for the wool.

**Figure 6.9
The Separate Demand
Prices Must Add up to the
Supply Price**

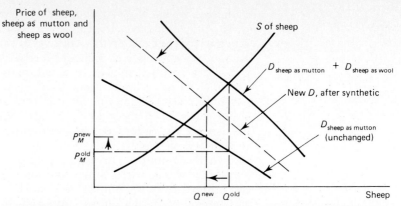

A wool substitute reduces consumers' willingness to pay for wool, lowering the demand curve for sheep. Fewer sheep are now brought to market, and the price of mutton rises as the marginal unit of mutton now goes to a more valued use.

demands for sheep as mutton and sheep as wool. The critical point is simply that a single sheep provides double pleasure.

Facing the market's vertical sum of demands is an ordinary supply curve of sheep. Just as the equilibrium price implies an equilibrium distribution of the total quantity among demand curves summed horizontally, so too the equilibrium quantity implies an equilibrium distribution of the total price among demand curves summed vertically. That is, the prices at which wool and mutton sell separately are determined. This equilibrium has remarkable consequences.

T or F: The invention of a synthetic substitute for wool will raise the price of mutton.

A: The willingness to pay for wool will fall when the substitute arrives. The demand curve for sheep as wool will fall, reducing the desirability of raising sheep and reducing the quantity supplied. The price of sheep as mutton will have to rise to induce consumers to consume the smaller quantity of sheep. Therefore, true. Figure 6.9 makes the same point as the words without giving the impression that (as it were) wool is being pulled over one's eyes.

The total demand price falls, which reduces the quantity supplied. At the lower quantity the price of sheep as mutton is higher.

☐
Uses of Joint Supply

The idea of vertical addition is easily generalized. For example, the characteristics supplied jointly by a single product can be more than two. The price of a typical automobile, for example, is the sum of the values attached to its horsepower, weight, length, standard equipment, and so forth.[3] Again, one can generalize the idea to joint demand, in parallel with joint supply.

[3] See Zvi Griliches, "Hedonic Price Indexes for Automobiles: An Econometric Analysis of Quality Change," *Government Price Statistics, Hearings,* U.S. Congress, Joint Economic Committee, January 24, 1961 (Washington, D.C.: G.P.O., 1961), pp. 173–196,

Figure 6.10
Joint Demand for Houses
and Furniture

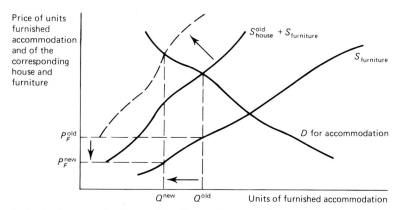

A rise in the cost of a house shifts the supply curve of a house plus furniture inward. The price paid for furniture now falls because a lower quantity of furniture is now supplied.

T or F: A rise in the cost of houses will lower the price of furniture.

A: True. The whole product—call it furnished accommodation—becomes more expensive and the quantity demanded will fall. Since houses and furniture are demanded jointly, the quantity demanded of furniture will fall. Therefore its supply price will fall (see Figure 6.10).

The applications of joint supply or demand are many. To take an unlikely looking and dismal example, consider the following.

Q: The price of slaves in the United States before the Civil War, it is said, consisted of not only the return to the business use of slaves (in house or field) but also a return to the prestige value of slaves. In other words, a slaveowner's social position is said to have depended on the number of slaves he owned, independent of the income he extracted from them. Supposing the national supply curve of slaves to be vertical at the number of slaves that existed (it was: slave importation was ended in 1807), show, first, that the price of slaves would be bid up above their business-only value. If you were told that in fact slaves sold for their business-only value, not higher, what would you conclude about the importance of prestige in the demand for slaves?

A: Because business value and prestige value are supplied jointly by the same slave, the two demand curves are summed vertically (see Figure 6.11).

The price P is the business-only value, that is, what the slave would sell for if his or her only value was to work in the owner's field or household. The higher price P^* adds on the feelings of feudal dignity and political power that slaveowners are alleged to have enjoyed as

reprinted in Arnold Zellner, ed., *Readings in Economic Statistics and Econometrics* (Boston: Little, Brown, 1968).

**Figure 6.11
Prestige Value Bids
Up the Price**

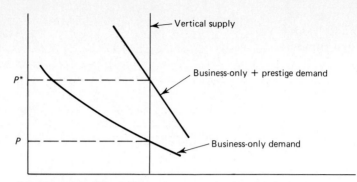

Slaveowners would be willing to pay more for slaves if slaves were a source of prestige as well as income.

---

well. But the allegation is false, for slaves did sell at the business-only price. Prestige was apparently not an important factor in the demand for slaves. The broader significance of the point is that slave-owners would appear to have been capitalistic and calculating in their attitude toward slaves—not, as both critics and apologists of the system have sometimes argued, feudal and uncalculating.[4]

A final and important application of joint supply is to what are called *public goods*. These are supplied to all consumers when they are supplied to any, the usual example being national defense. If $50 billion is spent on defense, that defense is provided to each resident of the country, whether or not the resident paid anything for it or wishes to pay anything for it. Henry David Thoreau spent a night in the Concord jail because he did not wish to pay taxes to protect peace-loving Americans against wicked and aggressive Mexicans; nonetheless he got the protection. Television signals or knowledge of economics are available to anyone with a television set or a library card. A fire station provides protection to all the houses in its neighborhood simul-taneously. All these are supplied jointly to all consumers. A rational government imbued with utilitarian ethics deciding how much to spend on fire protection would sum the demands of all consumers vertically, as though selling sheep. The socially desirable amount is the amount at which the marginal cost of fire protection is equal to the summed values of the marginal benefit. And likewise for knowledge or national defense.

Summary

The idea of related markets, like that of equilibrium and of adding up supply and demand curves, is simple: write down as a set of simultaneous equations

---

[4] The argument and its extensions are controversial. It was first made by A. H. Conrad and J. R. Meyer, "The Economics of Slavery in the Antebellum South," *Journal of Political Economy* 66 (April 1958): 95–130; it was recently remade by Robert W. Fogel and Stanley L. Engerman, *Time on the Cross: The Economics of American Negro Slavery* (Boston: Little, Brown, 1974), pp. 70–73, and *Evidence and Methods—A Supplement* (Boston: Little, Brown, 1974), pp. 62 ff. An attempt to unmake it is P. A. David and P. Temin, "Capitalist Masters, Bourgeois Slaves," *Journal of Interdisciplinary History* 5 (Winter 1975): 445–457.

the supply and demand curves in all the closely related markets. The idea has uses in analyzing oil and coal; cotton and wool; gasoline and automobiles; or trains, buses, and airplanes. The idea that a demand curve is a curve of willingness to pay leads naturally to the notion that it is the vertical sum of the willingness to pay for each characteristic of the good. A sheep provides wool and mutton, each with its own demand. So too a supply curve is a vertical sum of the willingness to accept of each input into the good. A knife consists of a blade and handle, each with its own supply.[5] These ideas are applicable to all manner of cases, from slavery to national defense. The rule of application is nicely symmetrical. If two things are demanded jointly in product Z, add up at given Z worths their supply curve; if two things are supplied jointly in product X, add up at given X worths their demand curves.

QUESTIONS FOR SECTION 6.3

1. Suppose that instead of valuing slaves for both business and prestige simultaneously slaveowners divided into two distinct classes, one (Cavalier Fops) valuing slaves *exclusively* for prestige, the other (Grasping Capitalists) *exclusively* for business. What now is the appropriate demand curve? If you take measurements of the business value of slaves from businesslike (and record-keeping) plantations, what relation will you find between the business value and the market price of slaves? Will this finding shed light on the prevalence of Cavalier Foppishness among slaveholders?

2. In England (and in other places) before the twentieth century, the ownership of land brought prestige and power. A successful London merchant would abandon trade for a landed estate, his son would ride to hounds, and his grandson would sit in Parliament. Investments in land earned a money return of 2% annually when comparably secure investments elsewhere earned 5%. Why?

True or False

3. In the example of cotton and wool cloth in the text, the lower demand curve for cotton does not end the story; a lower demand curve implies a lower price, which lowers still further the demand curve for the substitute, wool; this in turn lowers the demand curve for cotton again; and so on in a vicious cricle.

4. By symmetry with the parallel assertion about substitutes (cotton and wool cloth), the less sensitive to price is the quantity supplied of sewing services (a complement to cotton cloth), the larger will be the increase in the quantity demanded of cotton cloth coming from an outward move in its supply curve.

5. If the supply of sheep is perfectly vertical, then the invention of a synthetic substitute for wool will have no effect on the price of mutton.

6. A rise in the demand for beef will reduce the price of dog food, soap, shoes, and leather jackets.

[5] Incidentally, the wool-mutton and blade-handle examples are both inventions of Alfred Marshall, *Principles of Economics*, first published in 1920, 8th ed. (New York: Macmillan, 1948, seventh printing 1959), Book V, Chapter VI. Marshall (1842–1924), a mathematical physicist by training, was the guru of British economics from the 1880s on. He perfected the analysis of supply and demand, completing the marginalist revolution.

7. If an additional year of schooling increases the student's future income, properly measured, in excess of the costs of tuition and foregone employment, but the student finds the additional year excruciatingly unpleasant, then the student will quit school prematurely from the point of view of maximum money income.

8. The prestige value of slaves can enter the utility function of slaveowners (along with the business value of slaves) yet play no part in determining the market price of slaves.

7 Measuring Supply and Demand

7.1 Elasticities of Supply and Demand: The Essential Ideas

Average and Marginal Propensities to Consume

☐ The argument so far has been qualitative, not quantitative. That is, the scale of diagrams and the exact shape of curves have not mattered. The farther a family lives from the center of New York, the cheaper is its housing space and the more will it consume. The more unlikely is a fire, the less will a householder pay for insurance. The higher is the price of wheat, the more will a Kansas farmer supply. The higher is a Californian's income, the more will she consume of a normal good, such as drinkable wine. These all say more or less, but not how much more or less. It is now time to pay attention to how much.

Diagrams, if taken literally, embody quantitative opinions. For example, drawing the solid rather than the dashed curve in Figure 7.1 expresses an opinion that income has much rather than little influence on wine consumption (ignore the light tangent lines for a moment). The rise in wine consumption for a given rise in income is large along the one curve, small along the other.

The qualitative assertion that a higher income induces higher wine consumption does not distinguish between these two quantitative opinions; it says that there is some sensitivity of wine to income, but not the extent. The extent is measured by a slope of the wine-income line (i.e., by the slope of a line tangent to it). The sensitivity at the point of $5000 of income along the solid curve, for example, is measured by the rise over the run of the tangent line, that is, by 50 bottles divided by $4000, or 0.013 bottles per dollar. This *marginal propensity to consume* wine (to use other words) is lower along the dashed line. At the same $5000 of income, for example, it is nearly zero; that is, the wine-income curve is at this point nearly flat. On the other hand, at $5000 the *average propensity to consume* wine is higher along the dashed line. The average is the slope of a ray from the origin out to the point at which the average is being measured, and high average has a higher slope than does low average. Symbolically, if income is I and wine W, the average propensity is W/I and the marginal $\Delta W/\Delta I$ (the change in wine divided by the change in income). At

Figure 7.1
The Slope of the
Wine-Income Function
Measures the Sensitivity
of Wine to Income

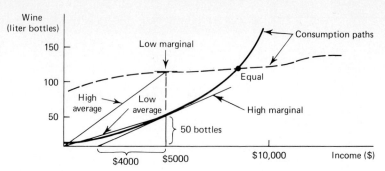

The marginal propensity to consume wine at an income of $5000 is equal to the slope of a line tangent to the consumption path at $5000. The average propensity to consume at $5000 is equal to the slope of a line segment connecting the origin and the consumption path at $5000.

$5000 the dashed-line consumer drinks a lot of wine (high average) but is insensitive in his or her wine drinking to rises in income (low marginal).

T or F: At point equal in the diagram, both consumers have the same average and marginal propensities to consume wine.

A: False. They have the same average but not the same marginal propensity. That is, the ray from the origin to equal is the same for both curves, but the slope of the solid curve at equal is higher.

Similar thinking applies to problems with more social significance.

T or F: If the rich have a higher average propensity to save than do the poor, then a redistribution of income away from the poor and toward the rich will raise total saving.

A: False. What matters is the marginal, not the average, propensity to save. A dollar taken from the poor reduces their savings according to their marginal propensity to save out of the dollar; giving the dollar to the rich increases their savings according to their marginal propensity. The average propensity is irrelevant, as can be seen in Figure 7.2 The average propensity to save of the person with rich income is higher than that of poor (look at the slopes of the dashed rays from the origin), yet the reshuffling of the dollar has no effect at all because the marginal propensity is constant (look at the equal rise and fall of savings on the vertical axis).

Consider the argument that increasing inequality of income increased savings in eighteenth-century England:

It is generally recognized that more saving takes place in communities in which the distribution of wealth is uneven than in those in which it approaches more closely to modern conceptions of what is just . . . the rise of new institutions, including that of the National Debt, intensified the disparities that had been handed down from earlier generations. . . . In this way, increasingly,

Figure 7.2
The Average Describes,
the Marginal Predicts

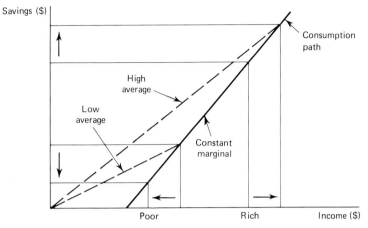

A consumption path for which the marginal propensity is constant over a certain range of income may yield a falling average propensity to consume over the same range. The effect of a redistribution of income on total savings is determined by the marginal, not the average, propensities.

wealth came into the hands of those whose propensity was to save, rather than to spend.[1]

The argument is wrong. The observation that the rich save more than do the poor as a proportion of their incomes is not sufficient to make the case. The marginal not the average propensity to save predicts behavior.

☐
The Income
Elasticity
The average and marginal propensities suffice for making comparisons within the world of wine drinkers or savers. A major objective of speaking quantitatively, however, is to bring to bear our intuitions about wine drinking compared with, say, bread eating, that is, to compare different products. One intuition, for example, is that bread eating is less sensitive to income than is wine drinking. Bread is, in the vernacular, a necessity, wine a luxury (at least outside of France and its spiritual colonies). But "less" sensitive is meaningless if the measure is the marginal propensity: 0.013 liter bottles per dollar is neither more nor less than 1 loaf of bread per dollar. The difference in units makes it nonsensical to speak of moreness or lessness. Another way in which to exhibit the ambiguity is to note that the marginal propensity depends on the choice of units, itself arbitrary. If one measured wine in quarts (1 liter = 1.057 quarts) and income in $5 units ($5 = 1 fin), the slope of the wine-income function would change from 0.0130 liter bottles per dollar to 0.0027 quart bottles per fin. What is wanted is some way of altering the marginal propensity to spend on wine that rids it of this ambiguity. The alteration is to divide it by the average propensity. The average propensity is measured in the same units (liters

[1] T. S. Ashton, *The Industrial Revolution 1760–1830* (London: Oxford University Press, 1948), pp. 7–8.

per dollar, quarts per fin, etc.) and is therefore made large or small by the choice of units in the same way as is the marginal propensity. Dividing the marginal by the average corrects, so to speak, for the arbitrary choice of units.

The result is the economist's well-beloved measure of the sensitivity of one variable to another, the *elasticity* of (in the present case) wine consumption with respect to income:

$$\frac{\text{Marginal propensity}}{\text{Average propensity}} = \frac{\Delta W/\Delta I}{W/I}$$

$$\equiv \text{elasticity of } W \text{ with respect to } I$$

Because the units of W and I, as you can see, cancel in the division, the elasticity has no units. It is simply a number, such as 1.0 or -3.6, with no units of weight, volume, money, or whatever attached. That this is the case is clear if the definition is rearranged a little:

$$\text{Elasticity of } W \text{ with respect to } I = \frac{\Delta W/W}{\Delta I/I}$$

This alternative definition reads "elasticity is the proportionate change in wine consumption, $\Delta W/W$, divided by the proportionate change in income, $\Delta I/I$, that causes the change in wine consumption." The proportionate change in wine consumption is unaffected by the units in which the wine is measured: a rise in W from 10 liters to 11 liters is the same as a rise from 10.57 quarts to 11.63 quarts, namely, a 10% rise. A proportionate (or percentage) rise is unitless, and therefore so too is the ratio of two proportionate rises.

Elasticity, then, is a unitless measure of sensitivity. The elasticity of wine with respect to income is denoted by η_{WI}, the subscripts reading "of W with respect to I." The definition in its various incarnations is

$$\eta_{WI} \equiv \frac{\text{marginal}}{\text{average}} = \frac{\Delta W/\Delta I}{W/I} = \frac{dW/dI}{W/I} = \frac{\Delta W/W}{\Delta I/I}$$

$$= \frac{d \log W}{d \log I} = \frac{\text{rate of change of } W}{\text{rate of change of } I}$$

A curve plotting the amount purchased of, say, food against income is called an *Engel curve*.

Figure 7.3 illustrates some elasticities of Engel curves for food. Notice especially the three simple cases: (1) the elasticity of food with respect to income equal to zero, with food purchases utterly insensitive to income and the Engel curve flat; (2) the elasticity equal to 1.0, with food proportional to income and the Engel curve any ray through the origin; and (3) the elasticity to infinity, with food purchases jumping from zero a little below I^* to some large amount a little above I^* and the Engel curve vertical. The more curved curves can be thought of as combinations of these three. An extreme version of the curve market $\eta > 1$ would approach the shape of $\eta = \infty$, which is one way of recognizing that its elasticity is indeed greater than 1.0. Another way is to notice that at point point the curve is rising faster than a

Figure 7.3
How Various Income
Elasticities Look

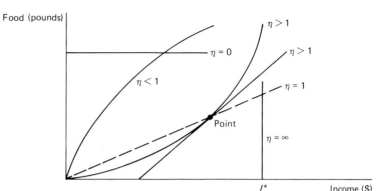

The more sensitive is food consumption to changes in income, the higher the income elasticity of food.

ray through the origin; that is, the percentage change in food is greater than the percentage change in income (the two changes being equal along a ray).

Notice that, if the vertical food axis is multiplied by the price of food, the Engel curve represents how money expenditure on food depends on income (total money expenditure).

T or F: That the share of food expenditure in total expenditure has fallen as income has risen over the last century and a half in the United States indicates that (setting aside changes in the price of food relative to other goods) the income elasticity of demand for food is less than 1.0.

A: True. If food expenditure rose by the same percentage as did income, then the elasticity would be 1.0. But the falling share means that in fact food expenditure rose by a *lower* percentage than did income, which implies in turn that the elasticity is less than 1.0, which was to be demonstrated. The significance of income elasticities is apparent in the low ones over the last 50 years: nonautomotive travel, for example, had a low income elasticity, with the consequent bankrupting of rail passenger travel; rented housing also had a low income elasticity, condemning city centers densely populated with such housing to decay.

☐
The Price Elasticity   An elasticity can be defined for any dependent variable with respect to any independent variable. Food consumption depends on price as well as on income in a demand curve and on price alone in a supply curve. The definitions of income elasticity of Engel curves translate directly to the price elasticity of supply curves with only the modification necessary to allow for the convention of putting the independent variable (price) on the vertical instead of the horizontal axis (as is income in an Engel curve). Thus, a straight ray through the origin is a supply curve with a price elasticity of 1.0; a line horizontal at some price has infinite price elasticity; a vertical line zero elasticity; and so forth.

The price elasticity of demand is a little less simple because it is naturally negative. As the price of housing goes up by $100(\Delta P/P)\%$ the quantity demanded goes down by $100(\Delta Q/Q)\%$, the elasticity being $\Delta Q/Q \div \Delta P/P$. If the percentage rise in price were the same as the percentage fall in quantity, the elasticity would be -1.0 and the total expenditure on housing (i.e., PQ) would remain unchanged. That is, a 1% rise in price that causes a 1% fall in quantity leaves price multiplied by quantity at whatever it was before: $10 times 100 ft^2 = $11 times 90.91 ft^2$. Just as the special significance of an income elasticity of 1.0 arises from its implication of a constant share in total expenditure for the item, so does the special significance of a price elasticity of -1.0 arise from its implication of constant money expenditure on the item. The *unit* (-1.0) elasticity is a border between rising expenditure as the price rises (elasticity less than -1.0 in absolute terms, e.g., -0.55 or zero) and falling expenditure as the price rises (elasticity greater than -1.0 in absolute terms, e.g., -3.5 or $-\infty$). The point point in Figure 7.4 can be seen to be one of *in*elastic demand (i.e., elasticity less than 1.0 in absolute terms) in three ways. First, notice that the area of rectangles fitted under the demand curve are revenues (price times quantity). The rise in price from P to P^* obviously causes the rectangle of total expenditure to rise, which implies inelastic demand; that is, the subrectangle marked with a minus sign is evidently smaller than the one marked with a plus sign, making the loss of revenue from the lower quantity less than the rise in revenue from the higher price.

Second, notice the construction with the tangent at point. The height P (price) multiplied by the slope of the tangent, $\Delta Q/\Delta P$, gives the horizontal segment marked off on the housing axis $P \times \Delta Q/\Delta P$. This distance divided by the segment marked as Q (which is what it is) gives $P \times \Delta Q/Q \times \Delta P$, which is the price elasticity at point. Because the segment Q is here larger than the other segment, the elasticity is

Figure 7.4
Three Ways of Reckoning
the Elasticity of a
Demand Curve

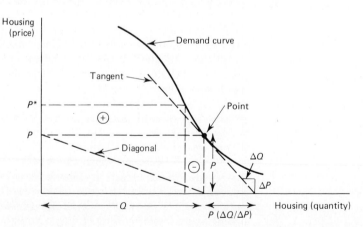

That demand is inelastic at point is demonstrated by any of these: (1) area plus is greater than area minus; (2) tangent is steeper than diagonal; (3) line segment $P(\Delta Q/\Delta P)$ is smaller than line segment Q.

less than 1.0 (in absolute terms). Third, notice that the definition of the price elasticity can be written in the marginal/average form as $\Delta Q/\Delta P \div Q/P$. The slope of the diagonal is evidently Q/P (slope here being looked at from the price axis), which is in the case portrayed of greater slope than the tangent (which has the slope $\Delta Q/\Delta P$). The elasticity is therefore in absolute terms less than 1.0.

☐
Uses of Price Elasticity

The classification of goods into low and high price elasticity follows from the notion that elasticity measures sensitivity. If the amount demanded of a good is very sensitive to price, as it would be (for example) if it had good substitutes, then the elasticity of its demand curve is high. Cigarettes as a whole have a low price elasticity, but individual brands—holding constant the price of substitute brands—have high elasticities. The simpler applications of this idea revolve around price elasticities greater than or less than 1.0 (dropping henceforth the tiresome but important qualification "in absolute terms").

Q: Headline: "Detroit Buses in Red, Seek Fare Hike, No Schedule Change." What are the managers of the Detroit bus company assuming about the elasticity of demand for bus trips?

A: They are assuming that it is less than 1.0, for only in this case will the fare increase raise money revenues. Since costs do not change ("No Schedule Change"), the bus company can concentrate exclusively on the revenue side, making it big. The direction in which to change fares to make it big depends on the elasticity.

Likewise, farmers cheer or groan at a harvest blight depending on whether the demand curve facing farmers with the same misfortune is inelastic (less than 1.0) or elastic (greater than 1.0). Since farmers in medieval Europe faced a local market in which the demand for grain was inelastic, they were overcompensated for harvest blight by the rise in price. With improved transportation over wider weather regions in early modern times, they lost this advantage, because high prices no longer accompanied low crops.

The price elasticity need not be the same everywhere along a demand curve. The straight-line demand curve contains all the possibilities, from 0 to ∞ elasticity, the elasticity of 1.0 (remember: −1.0) occurring halfway along it. Any of the three diagrammatic ways of exhibiting elasticities suffices to show this. The method of diagonals of the price-quantity rectangle, for example, arrives at the results given in Figure 7.5.

Notice that the diagonal corresponding to the midpoint is necessarily parallel to the demand curve itself, implying by the diagonal method that the elasticity is 1.0. At higher prices the demand curve has, viewed from the price axis, a higher slope than does the diagonal, implying that $\Delta Q/\Delta P$ is greater than Q/P and that, therefore, the elasticity is greater than 1.0.

If you compare the rectangles in the diagram, you can convince yourself that the midpoint, $\eta = 1.0$, is the point of largest revenue.

Figure 7.5
The Elasticity of a Straight-Line Demand Curve Is 1.0 at the Midpoint

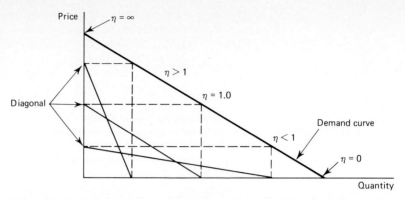

Demand is elastic (inelastic) above (below) the midpoint of a linear demand curve, because the slope of the demand curve is less (greater) than the slope of the diagonal. At the midpoint, demand is neither elastic nor inelastic; that is, it is unit elastic.

T or F: The owner of the only bridge across a river facing a straight-line demand curve for trips will charge as high a price as possible for each trip, supposing the trips themselves cost the owner nothing.

A: False. The owner has no costs, so revenues are profits. Therefore the owner sets the price at the point of unit elasticity, which will maximize revenue (= price times quantity), not at "as high a price as possible." The man in the street thinks of a monopolist as pursuing a "high profit margin." A self-interested monopolist, however, pursues high profits in total, not high profits per trip or per telephone call or per office visit. The idea of price elasticity keeps this in view.

Elasticities, then, are a vocabulary of quantification. Table 7.1 gives the jargon for income, I, and price elasticities, P, of demand for housing, H.

Table 7.1
Impressive Jargon for Elasticities

	Income Elasticities			Price Elasticities (defined positive)		
Good Is		η_{HI} Is	As Income Rises the Share of H in Total Expenditure	Demand Curve Is	η_{HP} Is	As Price Rises the Expenditure $(P \times H)$ on H
Normal good { Luxury		> 1	Rises	Perfectly elastic	= ∞ }	Falls
Unit elasticity		= 1	Remains constant	Elastic	> 1 }	Remains constant
Necessity		Between 1 and 0 }		Unit elasticity	= 1	
Inferior good		< 0 }	Falls	Inelastic	< 1	
				Perfectly inelastic	= 0 }	Rises
				Example of Giffen paradox	< 0 }	

Summary

Elasticity means "sensitivity." The elasticity of rented housing consumption with respect to real income is the percentage change in rented housing divided by the percentage change in real income causing that change in rented housing; alternatively, it is the marginal propensity to spend on rented housing divided by the average along an Engel curve. The price elasticity of demand is defined similarly (although its natural negative sign is frequently suppressed). The uses of both income and price elasticities often turn on whether they are larger or smaller than 1.0.

QUESTIONS FOR SECTION 7.1

True or False

1. If people are granted copying money in fixed amounts and if no one without a grant can use the machines, then the price elasticity of demand for copying facing the machines will be 1.0.

2. The partial destruction by earthquake of a city's housing will reduce money expenditure on housing.

3. The demand curves facing sellers of Kent cigarettes, an hour of unskilled labor, and a 1979 Ford Mustang serial number 368590 are all highly elastic.

4. The supply curves facing Gerry Gunderson, ordinary consumer, are perfectly inelastic.

7.2 Constant Elasticities

Exponents Are Elasticities

A demand curve in the form of a straight line, such as $Q = 50 - 0.5P$, has varying elasticity at various different points—1.0 at the midpoint, higher at higher prices, lower at lower. Since little else is known about a demand curve than what roughly its elasticity might be, one will often want to assume that the elasticity is not varying but constant. The general form of a demand function with a constant price elasticity is $Q_{demand} = DP^{-\eta}$, in which D is a constant serving to position the demand curve and the exponent η is the (absolute value of the) elasticity of quantity demanded with respect to price. It is not instantly obvious that constant elasticity implies this exponential form.[2] The

---

[2] It can be proven with second-year calculus; see, for example, R. G. D. Allen, *Mathematical Analysis for Economists* (London: Macmillan & Co., 1960), p. 418. And first-year calculus suffices to show the converse, that is, that the exponential form implies constant elasticity, as follows. The definition of elasticity in its derivative form is $P\,dQ/Q\,dP$. For the demand function $Q = DP^{-\eta}$, the derivative with respect to P, dQ/dP, is $^{-\eta}DP^{-\eta-1}$. Multiply this by P and divide it by Q to arrive at an expression for the elasticity:

$$\frac{P\,dQ}{Q\,dP} = \left(\frac{P}{Q}\right)(-\eta DP^{-\eta-1}) = \left(\frac{P}{DP^{-\eta}}\right)(-\eta DP^{-\eta-1})$$

Notice that, when the expression for Q is inserted, everything cancels out except $-\eta$. That is, the elasticity is the constant $-\eta$. Q.E.D.

special case of unit elasticity will make it plausible: when $\eta = 1.0$, $Q = DP^{-1} = D/P$, or $QP = D$; that is, with unit and constant elasticity the total expenditure for any price is a constant, D, which is the assertion just proven in a problem. Another particular case worked out in detail makes it still more plausible. For example, if the demand curve for gallons of gasoline per week is $Q = 7.75P^{-0.5}$, how much does gasoline consumption fall if the price of \$1.60 a gallon is raised 10%? The otherwise useless square root key on your pocket calculator comes into play: $7.75/1.60^{0.5} = 6.13$ gallons a week at \$1.60 a gallon becomes $7.75/1.76^{0.5} = 5.84$ gallons at \$1.76 a gallon. That is, a 10% rise in price has caused a (roughly) 5% fall in quantity because $(6.13 - 5.84)/6.13 = 0.05$ roughly, just as the elasticity of -0.5 would imply: 5% is 0.5 of 10%.

A more complete demand curve for, say, apartments in Boston would include terms for consumers' income, Y, and for the price of substitutes such as houses, P_H:

$$Q_A = 65.3P_A^{-2.0}P_H^{1.2}Y^{0.8}$$

You should get into the habit of interpreting the exponents in multiplicative functions of this sort as elasticities.

T or F: If the demand function for apartments is indeed $65.3P_A^{-2.0}P_H^{1.2}Y^{0.8}$, then a 10% rise in income and all prices will have no effect on the quantity demanded of apartments.

A: True. The exponents are elasticities (i.e., percentage changes in the quantity demanded of apartments for each percentage change in the variables). Thus, a 10% rise in P_A causes a $(-2.0)(10\%) = 20\%$ fall in Q_A; a 10% rise in P_H causes a $(1.2)(10\%) = 12\%$ rise in Q_A; and a 10% rise in Y causes a $(0.8)(10\%) = 8\%$ rise in Q_A. The 20% fall just offsets the $12\% + 8\% = 20\%$ rise. Notice that the result is familiar. The demand function here satisfies as it should the condition that a doubling of money income and all prices—which does not alter the budget line—must not alter the consumer's equilibrium.

Exponents in multiplicative functions, then, are elasticities. Conversely, constant elasticities can always be expressed in multiplicative form.

T or F: Jeffrey Williamson, with an income of \$5000 per year, spends 10% of his income on saving, for which his income elasticity of demand is 2; therefore, if his income rises to \$6000 per year, he will spend 12% of his income on saving.

A: True. An answer requiring nothing more than arithmetic is as follows. He spends 10% of his income, or 500 units of savings at \$1 a unit, initially. His income goes up by $(\$1000/\$5500) = 18\%$, taking the midpoint between \$5000 and \$6000 as the base (this choice of base is arbitrary: \$5000 or \$6000 would be good, too). His income elasticity is 2, so the percentage increase in his consumption of saving will be $2(18\%) = 36\%$. So he will now consume $(1.36)(500) = 680$ units of saving. Taking the midpoint again, he will devote $\$680/\$5500 = 12.36\%$ of his income to saving, which is 12%, near enough.

Comment

To come to the conclusion that the assertion is false because the result of such a calculation is not 12% exactly is to let arithmetic dominate reason. Depending on the (arbitrary) choice of base for the calculations of the percentage rates of change, one can arrive at a variety of results centered around 12%.

Alternative Solution

A neater solution exploits the implicit assumption that the income elasticity is constant, that is, that Williamson's consumption of saving is $S = kY^2$, a multiplicative form. The scaling constant, k, can be determined by solving for it when $S = \$500$ and $Y = \$5000$ (the initial values). In these units $k = 0.00004$, so $S = (0.00002)Y^2$, and the result that the new S will be $720 (exactly 12% of 6000) can be inferred by setting $Y = \$6000$ and solving for S.

The Rate of Change of a Constant Elasticity Expression Is Linear

An important point about constant elasticity functions such as $Q_A = DP_A^{-2.0}P_H^{1.2}Y^{0.8}$ or $S = kY^2$ is that they are linear in logarithms. That is, if you take the logarithm of both sides of the saving function, say, you get $\log S = \log k + 2 \log Y$. If you know that on logarithmic graph paper a plot of something growing at a constant percentage rate is a straight line, it will come as no surprise that the "rate of growth transformation" of $S = kY^2$ has the same linear form, namely, $S^* = k^* + 2Y^*$, in which an asterisk (*) signifies "rate of change of." Another way of seeing that this is true is to divide the last expression by Y^*, holding k constant (i.e., setting the rate of change k equal to zero). The result on the left-hand side is S^*/Y^*, which is the definition of the income elasticity of saving with respect to income. The result on the right-hand side is 2, which you know to be the income elasticity. Therefore the original equation of rates of change was a true one.

The point is that constant elasticity functions can be linearized by taking rates of change, making them very useful because expressible in the simplest mathematical form. For example, a popular choice of a functional form for the demand for money to hold is

$$M_d = \frac{kPy^\alpha}{i^\beta}$$

because it is easy to express it in a linear form suitable for statistical manipulation:

$$M_d^* = P^* + \alpha y^* - \beta i^*$$

where y is real income, P the price level, and i the interest rate. The numbers α and β are elasticities of the quantity of money demanded with respect to real income and the interest rate (e.g., $\alpha = M_d^*/y^*$ holding P and i constant).

The applications of these ideas to real problems depend on a number of simple but important facts about rates of changes, some of which have been used already. The algebra to prove them, exhibited in the appendix to this section, is routine. All are unambiguously accurate only for small rates of change, for 10% changes but not for 100% changes.

As you can see in the appendix to this section the ambiguities arise from the arbitrariness of choice of base for rates of change: a change from 100 to 110 is 10% (10/100) or 9.1% (10/110) or some intermediate figure depending on whether 100 or 110 or some intermediate figure is taken as the base. The facts are, illustrating them with variables for which they might be significant, $(P^{-\eta})^* = -\eta P^*$ for η constant; $(PQ)^* = P^* + Q^*$; $(C/Q)^* = C^* - Q^*$; and, finally,

$$(q_1 + q_2)^* = \left(\frac{q_1}{q_1 \pm q_2}\right) q_1^* \pm \left(\frac{q_2}{q_1 \pm q_2}\right) q_2^*$$

The last fact serves to establish the obvious proposition that the elasticity of the market demand curve at any price is equal to a weighted average of the elasticities of demand of the individual demanders. Begin with the truth that the total quantity demanded at any price is the sum of the demands by, say, the two individuals in the market: $Q = q_1 + q_2$. The rate of change of this sum will be, then

$$Q^* = \left(\frac{q_1}{Q}\right) q_1^* + \left(\frac{q_2}{Q}\right) q_2^*$$

Now price elasticities have the form Q^*/P^*. In the search for an expression in elasticities, therefore, divide both sides by P^* (the percentage change in the one market facing each individual) to get

$$\frac{Q^*}{P^*} = \left(\frac{q_1}{Q}\right) \frac{q_1^*}{P^*} + \left(\frac{q_2}{Q}\right) \frac{q_2^*}{P^*}$$

If the individual rates of change, q_1^* and q_2^*, are interpreted as the rates of change caused by the change in price, then the equation is

$$\eta_{QP} = \left(\frac{q_1}{Q}\right) \eta_{q_1 P} + \left(\frac{q_2}{Q}\right) \eta_{q_2 P}$$

That is, as asserted, the elasticity is a weighted average.

Q: The elasticity of the demand for slaves in southern cities was fairly high, that is, 0.86 (there were good substitutes for slaves in city occupations); the total elasticity of demand for slaves, in city and countryside together, was 0.08; 96% of slaves lived in the countryside. *True or false:* Therefore, the elasticity of demand for slaves in the countryside was very low, that is, 0.05 (there were no good substitutes for slaves in country occupations).

A: True. City and country can be viewed as two demanders. According to the formula just derived the elasticity is η in

$$0.08 = (0.96)(\eta) + (0.04)(0.86)$$

Solving gives $\eta = 0.05$.[3]

Simple though it is, then, the formula gives useful meaning to the "importance" of a particular demander. But think before applying it.

T or F: If the elasticity of demand for each of several brands of cigarettes taken separately is 10, then the elasticity of demand for the several brands taken as a group is also 10.

A: False. It is cruel to deceive you, but the deception makes the point that common sense must dominate mathematical formalism. The formula just given refers to the demand *of* demanders of cigarettes, not, as in this equation, the demand *facing* suppliers of one brand. Plainly, if the price of Marlboros rises with other prices constant (which is what the elasticity of demand for Marlboros "taken separately" must mean), people will substitute other cigarettes (whose price has not changed) for Marlboros. On the other hand, if the prices of all cigarettes move up simultaneously (which is what is relevant for the "elasticity of demand for the several brands taken as a group"), there will be less or no interbrand substitution. Evidently, this latter elasticity of demand must be much smaller than 10 (say, 0.10).

☐
The Elasticity of Demand Facing One Seller

The formula relevant to this last problem and to others like it is less simple than the first. By way of introduction, consider the situation of a single large firm in the market for, say, coal, and suppose that you wish to know the elasticity of demand facing the firm. One reason for wishing to know it, for example, is that the elasticity is a reasonable measure of the firm's *market power*: if the elasticity is very high, the firm has little power to raise the price it faces; if it is very low, the firm has much power. In one sense, any firm has the power to raise its price. The owner of a coal mine is free to raise the price the firm charges the wholesaler to $1000 a ton, although the owner will find that the quantity the mine sells at such a price is zero. The point is that a small firm with little market power cannot raise the price it charges without losing all its business. In other words, the "power" is to face a less than complete fall in quantity demanded when raising the price, that is, to face a less than perfectly elastic demand curve.

The question is, then, what is the elasticity of demand facing a single coal-selling firm? As does much clear thinking in economics, the answer begins with a simple equilibrium condition, namely, that the quantity demanded from the firm equals the total quantity demanded in the market minus the amount supplies by other firms:

$$q_i = Q_D - Q_S$$

Applying the formula for the rate of change of a sum or difference, the rate of change of this is

$$q_i^* = \left(\frac{Q_D}{q_i}\right)Q_D^* - \left(\frac{Q_S}{q_i}\right)Q_S^*$$

[3] See Claudia D. Goldin, *Urban Slavery in the American South 1820–1860: A Quantitative History* (Chicago: University of Chicago Press, 1976), p. 101.

Now suppose that the firm in question—Peabody Coal, say—raises the price of coal. The other firms could behave in either of two ways: either keep their own price unchanged or match Peabody's price. If they keep the price unchanged, Peabody will lose all its business (nobody will buy coal at $16 a ton from Peabody when they can get it for $15 elsewhere), and without recourse to the formula, it is obvious that the elasticity facing Peabody is infinite. If the other firms match Peabody's price, however, Peabody will lose some but not necessarily all its business, and the formula comes into play. Since the other firms must in fact get a higher price to be enticed to serve Peabody's former customers, the price-matching behavior is the natural one. The new, higher price of coal established on Peabody's initiative decreases the quantity demanded by consumers and increases the quantity supplied by other producers. How much? By the amount of the elasticities of demand, $\eta = Q_D^*/P^*$, and of supply, $\epsilon = Q_S^*/P^*$. Dividing the formula just derived for the rate of change of Peabody's quantity demanded, q_i^*, by the rate of change of the price, P^*, therefore, leads to

$$\eta^i = \left(\frac{Q_D}{q_i}\right)\eta - \left(\frac{Q_S}{q_i}\right)\epsilon$$

If the elasticity of demand—which is naturally negative—is defined to be positive, then the formula is

$$\eta^i = \left(\frac{Q_D}{q_i}\right)\eta + \left(\frac{Q_S}{q_i}\right)\epsilon$$

The formula expresses an important and familiar economic idea, namely, that for given market elasticities (η and ϵ) the elasticity of demand facing one supplier is higher the higher is the output of other suppliers relative to the one in question.

T or F: If Peabody Coal supplies 20% of the coal purchased, if the elasticity of supply of other coal sellers is 1.0, and if the elasticity of demand for coal is 0.5, then Peabody Coal faces an elasticity of demand of 6.5.

A: True. Look at the formula, inserting the numbers given:

$$\eta^i = \left(\frac{1.0}{0.2}\right)(0.5) + \left(\frac{0.8}{0.2}\right)(1.0) = 6.5$$

In the absence of a conspiracy among coal suppliers (or steel or oil or automobile suppliers), this arithmetic is reason for being skeptical of assertions that even quite large companies can "administer" prices. Peabody Coal might by itself raise prices 10%, but it would have to be willing to suffer a consequent loss of $(10)(6.5) = 65\%$ of its business.

☐ **Writing down Elasticities of Excess Supply or Demand**

The general task in such problems is to find unknown elasticities from known ones and market shares. The technique of solution takes rates of change of the equilibrium condition that supply equal demand. You will find it useful to learn how to leap directly from the equilibrium condition to the elasticity equation, that is, from $q_i = Q_D - Q_S$ to

$\eta^i = (Q_D/q_i)\eta + (Q_S/q_i)\epsilon$. When you have made the leap, check the place you have landed by making sure that the signs in the equation make sense, as they do in the coal problem. If the elasticity of demand is defined positively, the equation says that rises in the elasticity of both demand and supply raise the elasticity facing the residual supplier, which is as it should be, because these raised elasticities both signify a raised amount of demand left to Peabody Coal at a higher price. This, in turn, is in accord with the diagrams of excess supply and demand (see Chapter 9).

Q: The elasticity of demand for grain is generally thought to be low among poor peasants, say, 0.25 numerically. The elasticity of total supply of grain from poor peasants is also thought to be low, say, 0.10. The peasants are said to be set in their ways, responding weakly to the incentive of price. Furthermore, the peasants are often only slightly involved in the outside market, exporting only 5%, for example, of their total supply. *True or false:* If all this is true, a 1% increase in the price of grain will result nonetheless in a nearly 7% increase in the amount exported, making the peasants look, to the careless eye, as very responsive to the incentive of price.

A: True. The supply to the rest of the world by the peasants must equal the supply in total produced by the peasants minus the demand by them for their own grain. Skipping to the figures,

$$\epsilon_{\text{to rest of the world}} = \frac{20}{1}(0.10) + \frac{19}{1}(0.25) = 6.75$$

In this sense the peasants are indeed responsive to price, but not in their underlying attitudes.

Such are the practical uses of elasticities of excess supply and demand. A theoretical use can cap the argument. It is that small demanders and suppliers face given prices of supply and demand. Richard Weisskoff, a single buyer of an apartment in Cambridge, for example, might take 1% of the whole supply in a month. The elasticity of supply he faces, therefore, can be derived from the identity $S_{\text{to Weisskoff}} = S_{\text{total}} - D_{\text{others}}$. It is $\epsilon_W = (100/1)\epsilon_T + (99/1)\eta_O$. The elasticities of supply and demand could be very low—0.05 and 0.2, say—yet still lead to a very high elasticity facing Weisskoff: $(100)(0.05) + 99(0.2) = 24.8$. In other words, if Weisskoff raised his offer per room as little as 1% he would be supplied with about 25% more rooms that he could buy, if he wanted them, at 1% above the old price. If he lowered his offer 1%, he would be supplied with 25% fewer rooms. He faces a virtually flat supply curve, a given price. This is the algebraic version of the geometry of price taking. A single small buyer among many other buyers and a single small seller among many other sellers face a price over which they have no influence. The smaller the share, the closer is the supply or demand curve facing the buyer or seller to being utterly flat.

Summary

Constant elasticity is the simplest assumption consistent with a little knowledge about the shape of a curve. Its mathematical form is especially simple: for example, $Q = SP^\epsilon$, which could be a supply curve with price elasticity ϵ and location S. Such forms are easy to manipulate, because their logarithms or rates of change are linear: for example, the rate of change Q^* equals $S^* + \epsilon P^*$. The algebra of rates of change—and in particular the rate of change of a sum—leads to a way of connecting known and unknown elasticities. The technique is to write down the equilibrium condition in quantities (quantity supplied equals quantity demanded), take the rate of change of this expression, and divide by the (marketwide) rate of change of price. Since a price elasticity is a rate of change of a quantity divided by the rate of change of the price causing the change in quantity, the resulting equation is in elasticities. The technique is widely applicable to problems of excess supply and demand, such as, at the most general level, the problem of the elasticity of supply facing a single demander with a small share of the market. The elasticity of supply facing the demander is higher the smaller is his or her share, providing an algebraic proof of the geometry of price taking.

APPENDIX TO SECTION 7.2

The Algebra of Rates of Change

The rate of change of Q is the change in Q divided by Q in some base period, taken here (arbitrarily) to be its initial value. When Q rises from 100 to 110, the $\Delta Q/Q$ (signified by Q^*) is $10/100 = 10\%$ instead of $10/110 = 9.1\%$. The method of deriving the truths about rates of change of exponential, multiplicative, and summed expressions is illustrated best with the rate of change of PQ:

$$(PQ)^* = \frac{\Delta(PQ)}{PQ} = \frac{(P+\Delta P)(Q+\Delta Q) - PQ}{PQ}$$

$$= \frac{PQ + P\Delta Q + Q\Delta P + \Delta P\Delta Q - PQ}{PQ}$$

$$= \frac{P\Delta Q}{PQ} + \frac{Q\Delta P}{PQ} + \frac{P\Delta Q}{PQ}$$

$$= \frac{\Delta Q}{Q} + \frac{\Delta P}{P} + \left(\frac{\Delta P}{P}\right)\left(\frac{\Delta Q}{Q}\right) = P^* + Q^* + P^*Q^*$$

$$\cong P^* + Q^*$$

when P^* and Q^* are small, because when they are small their product, P^*Q^*, is very small. Thus, the rate of change reduces multiplication to addition (and division to subtraction). In the same way, it reduces exponents to multiplication, and addition to weighted averaging. For example, the exponential expression Q^η has a rate of change

$$(Q^\eta)^* = \frac{(Q+\Delta Q)^\eta - Q^\eta}{Q} = \left(\frac{Q+\Delta Q}{Q}\right)^\eta - 1$$

$$= (1 + Q^*)^\eta - 1$$

The expression $(1 + Q^*)^\eta$ is similar to the expression for the value of a dollar placed at compound interest at $i\%$ for N years, $(1 + i)^N$. For small rates, compound interest is about the same as simple interest, which is $1 + Ni$. That is, for small rates of change, Q^*, the expression $(1 + Q^*)^\eta - 1$ approximately equals $1 + \eta Q^* - 1 = \eta Q^*$. That is, for small Q^*, $(Q^\eta)^* = \eta Q^*$, as was to be shown.

Deriving the rate of change of a sum (or difference) is even simpler:

$$(q_1 + q_2)^* = \frac{(q_1 + \Delta q_1 + q_2 + \Delta q_2) - (q_1 + q_2)}{q_1 + q_2}$$

$$= \frac{\Delta q_1 + \Delta q_2}{q_1 + q_2} = \frac{\Delta q_1}{q_1 + q_2} + \frac{\Delta q_2}{q_1 + q_2}$$

Dividing top and bottom of the first term in this last expression by q_1 and similarly for the second term gives

$$(q_1 + q_2)^* = \left(\frac{q_1}{q_1 + q_2}\right)\left(\frac{\Delta q_1}{q_1}\right) + \left(\frac{q_2}{q_1 + q_2}\right)\left(\frac{\Delta q_2}{q_2}\right)$$

$$= \left(\frac{q_1}{q_1 + q_2}\right)q_1^* + \left(\frac{q_2}{q_1 + q_2}\right)q_2^*$$

which was to be demonstrated. Notice that this result, unlike the others, is exact, whatever the size of q_1^* and q_2^*.

Notice, too, that all the results are derivable with the calculus, using in particular the idea of total differentials. Thus, for the exponential function Q^η,

$$\text{Rate of change} = \frac{dQ^\eta}{Q^\eta} = \eta\frac{Q^{\eta-1}\,dQ}{Q^\eta} = \eta\frac{dQ}{Q} = \eta Q^*$$

The more primitive method of Δ's is worth retaining, though, because it keeps the exact results for large changes (instead of infinitessimal changes, dQ) in view when they are needed.

QUESTIONS FOR SECTION 7.2

1. Suppose that you wanted to find how much of the 15% or so per year growth of cotton cloth production in the United States 1815 to 1833 was attributable to technological change (the coming of the power loom and the factory) and how much to demand (the rise of population and incomes and the transport improvements that made the demand of the West available to the factories of the East). The problem is evidently one of supply and demand. Suppose that the demand curve can be represented as $Q = DP^{-\eta}$, in which a rising D represents an outward-moving demand. The supply curve can be represented as $P = (1/T)Q^{1/\epsilon}$, in which a rising T represents a falling price at which cloth producers would offer a given quantity—this being one natural way of measuring technological change. (The peculiar inversion of the elasticity, ϵ, is merely a ploy to make ϵ be the elasticity of supply, even though here the price and not the quantity is taken to be the dependent variable.) Suppose, finally, that the elasticity of demand is about 2.5, the elasticity of supply about 20, the rate of change of demand, D^*, about 10% per year, and the rate of change of technology 2.5% per year. Solve the problem by stating the demand and supply functions in rate-of-change form, then solving the resulting linear equations for Q^*.

2. The balance of payments is the annual net flow of money out of (deficit) or into (surplus) a country. In other words, according to the "monetary approach to the balance of payments," a country's balance of payments is conveniently viewed simply as the excess supply of money (deficit) or the excess demand for money (surplus) by citizens of the country during a year. Suppose that there are two countries in the world, the United States of Great Britain (USGB) and the Federal Republic of Nippon (FRN), having the same form of their demand curves for money, namely,

$$M_D^i = k_i P y_i^\epsilon$$

where i names the country, M_D^i is the quantity of money demanded, k_i is a constant pertaining to the ith country, P is the world price level (assumed to be the same as each country's price level by the working of arbitrage in commodity markets), y_i is the ith country's real income, and ϵ is the income elasticity of the demand for money.

a. If the world's supply of money is fixed and the world starts from an equilibrium distribution of the supply, show that if the USGB grows slower than the FRN (but both are growing some), P will fall, the USGB will have a persistent deficit in its balance of payments, and the FRN will have a persistent surplus.

b. Show that, if the conditions of (a) hold, except that each year the USGB produces new money (the only new money produced in the world) in an amount that raises the world stock faster than the rate of growth of the demand for money, then there will be world inflation, and the surpluses and deficits in the annual balance of payments in the USGB and the FRN will be larger than in (a).

3. "Wherever American slavery touched urban conditions, it was in deep trouble. The free atmosphere and cosmopolitan exposure of cities made slaves increasingly difficult to control, and the economic life of the cities, with their growing factories staffed largely by white immigrant laborers, became increasingly poorly suited to the institution."

The keystone of the evidence for this view (developed by the author) is that between 1820 and 1860 the total slave population grew by 180%, while the slave population of the ten largest southern cities grew by only 90%.

a. Write down the total demand curve (city and country combined) for slaves in terms of the price, P, the shift terms in urban, D_u, and rural, D_r, areas, and the elasticity of demand in urban, η_u, and rural, η_r, areas. If the total quantity of slaves, Q, was inelastically supplied (as it was), write down the equilibrium condition.

b. Explain why the availability of white immigrant labor in the cities and the lack of substitutes for slave labor in the countryside (free men would not tolerate the gang labor so efficient in cotton production) suggests that in absolute values the urban elasticity, η_u, was greater than the rural elasticity, η_r.

c. The hypothesis that cities were increasingly hostile to slavery can be interpreted as the assertion that the rate of change of D_u was less than that of D_r. Show that, if the slave price were rising, the same observation of slower growth of slave population in the cities than in the countryside could be explained by $\eta_u > \eta_r$ and that, if the price were falling, this pattern of elasticities would imply a faster growth of the population in the cities.

d. If the relative decline of urban slavery could be explained by the rates of

Table 7.2
Changes in Slaves and
Prices, St. Louis,
1820–1860

Dates Compared (census years)	Rate of Change of Slave Labor Force in St. Louis	Rate of Change of Slave Prices in St. Louis
1820–1830	+55%	−3%
1830–1840	−41	+32
1840–1850	+79	−25
1850–1860	−47	+84

Source: Claudia A. Goldin, *Urban Slavery in the American South 1820–1860: A Quantitative History* (Chicago: University of Chicago Press, 1976), Table 25, p. 83, and Table 23, p. 70.

change of D_u and D_r, one would expect the decline to be the same from one decade to the next. It was not. The urban slave population oscillated violently. Show that the data in Table 7.2 for St. Louis (duplicated less dramatically in other slave cities) are consistent with the alternative explanation of the relative decline of slavery in the cities, namely, $\eta_u > \eta_r$ in absolute values.

4. The supply curve of slaves in the American South from 1830 to 1860 was perfectly inelastic to price (the slave trade from Africa had been closed) but was moving out at 2.3% per year (the growth rate of the slave population). The elasticity of demand for slaves was very low, around 0.08. The price of slaves rose about 2.7% per year. *True or false:* If all these assertions are true, then the demand curve for slaves 1830–1860 was growing a little faster than was the supply curve (but only a little faster).

True or False

5. The only supply curve with a constant elasticity of 1.0 is a straight line through the origin at a 45° angle.

6. If Brazil supplies a third of the world's demand for coffee and if the elasticity of demand for coffee is 0.1, then the elasticity of demand facing Brazil is at least 0.3.

7. If the United States consumes a fifth of the world's oil production and if the elasticities of world supply and of non-American demand are both around 0.3, then the elasticity of the supply curve facing American consumers is 2.7.

8. If the price elasticity of demand for coal is 2.0 and the price elasticity of demand for all fossil fuels (coal, oil, natural gas) is 1.0, then the price elasticity of demand for noncoal fossil fuels must be less than unity.

9. If steel is produced only in Pittsburgh, if the price of steel at Pittsburgh is not affected by the quantity of steel demanded (horizontal supply curve), and if railway services are used in fixed proportion to the quantity of steel shipped to all markets as a whole, then the elasticity of demand for railway services in the shipping of steel with respect to the price of the railway services is equal to the elasticity of demand for steel multiplied by the ratio of costs of railway services used to ship steel to the final market price of steel. (Hint: Work through step by step the effects of a 1% increase in the price of transport on the demand for transport and thence on the demand for transport itself.)

10. If the cost of transporting ships is a negligible percentage of their price and if the output of Japanese shipyards is growing faster than the output of German shipyards, then the German supply curve is moving out faster than the Japanese.

11. For a certain product in a certain locale, the lower the ratio of the elasticity of demand to the elasticity of supply (ignoring signs), the higher the ratio of local consumption to local production. Illustrate the truth or falsity of this proposition with automobiles, housing, and wheat in both the producing and consuming locales.

12. Other things equal, one would expect the elasticity of supply of food to the world market to be *lower* in a region with mostly subsistence farmers (who eat a lot of their own food) than in a region with mostly commercial farmers (who do not).

13. The elasticity of demand for sheep always lies between the elasticity of demand for wool and for mutton.

7.3 Relations Among the Consumer's Elasticities of Demand

☐
All a Consumer's Elasticities

The talk of elasticities has so far been about groups of consumers moving outward, as it were, from the individual consumer. This long concluding section talks about the individual consumer's elasticities moving inward. The central point is very simple. The theory of consumption connects Alexander Gerschenkron's consumption of food, Q_F, and all other goods Q_A, to the two money prices, P_F and P_A, and the money income, Y, that he faces. He will have, therefore, six different elasticities of demand with respect to the things (P_F, P_A, and Y) that he is affected by: two *own-price elasticities* connecting Q_F to P_F and Q_A to P_A; two *cross-price* or simply *cross elasticities* connecting, in cross-over fashion, Q_F to P_A and Q_A to P_F (notice the differing subscripts); and two *income elasticities* connecting Q_F and Q_A to Y. In other words, the theory of consumption says that Gerschenkron has a demand function for food, $Q_F = D_F P_F^{\epsilon_{FF}} P_A^{\epsilon_{FA}} Y^{\epsilon_{FY}}$ in constant elasticity form, and for all other goods, $Q_A = D_A P_A^{\epsilon_{AA}} P_F^{\epsilon_{AF}} Y^{\epsilon_{AY}}$. The six elasticities in these equations (the six exponents) describe his behavior. The central point is that the various elasticities are connected to one another. If you know some of them, you know something about the others.

☐
The Income Elasticity Condition

The simplest proposition is that the sum of the income elasticities of each good weighted by its share in expenditure is 1.0. The proposition is familiar from earlier chapters. It is verbally plausible: as income increases the amount bought of goods in general increases in proportion, suggesting that the goods in particular making up goods in general must also increase in proportion, typically. Equal and proportionate increases are elasticities of 1.0. It is also geometrically plausible. In Figure 7.6 the expansion paths have elasticities above 1.0 for one good and below 1.0 for the other, suggesting that typically the elasticities will average 1.0. And the proposition is mathematically true. Look at

Figure 7.6
The Weighted Average of
Income Elasticities Is 1.0

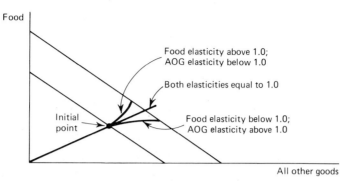

For a given percentage increase in income (equal to the percentage increase in the food or all other goods intercept of the budget line), an equiproportional increase in food and consumption of all other goods follows the path of a straight line drawn from the origin; in this case both food and all other goods have income elasticities equal to 1.0. If food consumption increases at a greater rate than income, consumption of all other goods must increase more slowly than income. In this case food has an income elasticity greater than 1.0, all other goods less than 1.0.

the budget constraint, namely, that expenditure on food and all other goods must sum to income:

$$P_F F + P_A A = Y$$

By the rate-of-change arithmetic developed earlier, then

$$\frac{P_F F}{Y}(P_F^* + F^*) + \frac{P_A A}{Y}(P_a^* + A^*) = Y^*$$

The experiment contemplated in an income elasticity is a change in income, Y^*, with no change in prices (P_F^* and P_A^* are zero). Dividing by Y^*, therefore, the equation is

$$\frac{P_F F}{Y}\left(\frac{F^*}{Y^*}\right) + \frac{P_A A}{Y}\left(\frac{A^*}{Y^*}\right) = 1$$

But this is merely another notation for

  1. Income elasticity condition: $S_F \epsilon_{FY} + S_A \epsilon_{AY} = 1$

which was to be proven.

T or F: Poor people have little use for extra income because most of their expenditure is on food; and food, we know, has a low income elasticity of demand.

A: False. As low as may be the income elasticity of food, the income elasticity of all other goods must be large enough (in view of its share) to yield an average of 1.0. They use the income on all other goods instead of on food, but it gets used.

☐ The next proposition is less obvious, although proven in the same
The Price Elasticity simple way. For the two goods food and all other goods, it is
Condition

  2. Price elasticity condition: $S_A(1 + \epsilon_{AA}) + S_F \epsilon_{FA} = 0$

The ϵ_{FA} is the elasticity of food demanded with respect to the price of all other goods; that is, it is the "cross-price" elasticity mentioned. The proof starts, as before, with the rate of change of the budget constraint:

$$S_F(P_F^* + F^*) + S_A(P_A^* + A^*) = Y^*$$

Notice that both elasticities in the proposition to be proven are with respect to the price of all other goods, P_A. The other prices, P_F, and income, Y, are being held constant. Set their rates of change therefore at zero in the equation just given, to get

$$S_F(F^*) + S_A(P_A^* + A^*) = 0$$

Divide through by P_A^*, in search of the price elasticity (which here and elsewhere in this section carries its natural sign: it is not defined positive).

$$S_F\left(\frac{F^*}{P_A^*}\right) + S_A\left(1 + \frac{A^*}{P_A^*}\right) = 0$$

This again is merely another notation for the proposition to be proven:

$$S_F \epsilon_{FA} + S_A(1 + \epsilon_{AA}) = 0$$

It is useful more in proofs of other propositions than in itself.

T or F: If the cross elasticities of demand for food and all other goods are both zero, then the own-price elasticities, ϵ_{AA} and ϵ_{FF}, have a weighted average of -1.0.

A: True. According to the price elasticity condition, if ϵ_{FA} is zero, then $S_A(1 + \epsilon_{AA}) = 0$ likewise for the other price elasticity. Adding and rearranging these two equations in ϵ_{AA} and ϵ_{FF} gives $S_A(1 + \epsilon_{AA}) + S_F(1 + \epsilon_{FF}) = 0$, or $S_A\epsilon_{AA} + S_F\epsilon_{FF} = -S_A - S_F = -1.0$, which was to be shown.

The generalization to three or more goods is obvious from the mathematics.

Q: Roy Astley has three objects of desire, food, clothing, and all other goods, spending equal amounts on each. A rise in food prices of 1% causes a 2% rise in his demand for clothing and a 1% fall in his demand for all other goods. What is his elasticity of demand for food?

A: Write the equation for three goods, food being the varying price:

$$S_F(1 + \epsilon_{FF}) + S_C \epsilon_{CF} + S_A \epsilon_{AF} = 0$$

Substitute the information given:

$$\frac{1}{3}(1 + \epsilon_{FF}) + \frac{1}{3}(+2) + \frac{1}{3}(-1) = 0$$

which yields $\epsilon_{FF} = -2.0$.

Notice that these first two propositions—the *income* and the *price elasticity conditions*—depend for their truth only on the budget constraint. If all income is spent, they are true. They are as true for groups of consumers, therefore, as they are for single consumers, because groups also operate along a budget constraint. By contrast the third proposition is strictly true only for a single consumer. It is

3. Homogeneity condition: $\epsilon_{FF} + \epsilon_{FC} + \epsilon_{FA} + \epsilon_{FY} = 0$

which is to say that the elasticities of the quantity demanded of food with respect to all prices and income sum to zero. The proposition is familiar in another form; that is, a doubling of all prices and incomes does not change the consumption of any good. In fact, that is how it is proven. Imagine the effect of a doubling of income and of all three prices on a consumer's demand for good 1. It will be the sum of 100% multiplied by each elasticity: $(100\%)(\epsilon_{11}) + (100\%)(\epsilon_{12}) + (100\%)(\epsilon_{13}) + (100\%)(\epsilon_{1Y})$. But by the familiar diagrammatic reasoning, the sum must be zero, for the impact on the budget line of such changes is zero altogether. Dividing both sides by 100% leaves $\epsilon_{11} + \epsilon_{12} + \epsilon_{13} + \epsilon_{1Y} = 0$, as was to be proven.[4]

The *homogeneity condition* is empirically falsifiable, but it is not a bold hypothesis. It says simply that the consumer has an equilibrium point on a budget line. She has indifference contours (of arbitrary shape) that lead her to pick one point along a budget line; she does not, in other words, change her consumption unless her budget line changes; or, in still other words, she does not suffer from "money illusion" (i.e., the illusion that changes in money prices and incomes warrant consideration beyond their effects on the budget line). Putting it this way makes it clear why the homogeneity condition need not hold true for a group. The aggregate budget line facing Laura and John may not change, yet an internal change in the distributions of income between them may lead them as a group to come to rest at a different point on the aggregate budget line. The theory of a single consumer prohibits such an event, which on the individual level would be a case of split personality, the left hand not caring what the right was doing.

The homogeneity condition, like the other conditions, is useful in drawing out the implications of what you think you know and in checking the knowledge for consistency.

Q: An econometrician decides that Eric Gustafson's demand function for housing is $Q_H = 3(6P_H^{-2}P_0^1Y^2)$, in which P_0 is the price of *all* other goods, and Y is money income. *True or false:* Something is wrong.

[4] The word "homogeneity" comes from a piece of mathematical jargon. A function $Z = F(X, Y)$ is said to be "homogeneous of degree α" if multiplying X and Y by a proportion λ causes z to change by a proportion λ^α (note the exponent). The function $z = XY$, for example, is homogeneous of degree 2, because $F(\lambda X, \lambda Y) = (\lambda X)(\lambda Y) = \lambda^2 XY = \lambda^2 Z$; $Z = X^{1/2}Y^{1/2}$ is homogeneous of degree 1. The homogeneity condition on demand functions is that they be homogeneous of degree *zero* in money income and prices. That is $D(\lambda P_1, \lambda P_2, \lambda Y)$ should give the same quantity demanded as $D(P_1, P_2, Y)$. A demand function, such as $Q = DP_1^{-2}P_2^{-1}Y^{+1}$ is homogeneous of degree zero in prices and incomes, because $D(\lambda P_1)^{-2}(\lambda P_2)(\lambda Y)$ gives the same result (canceling λ's) as the original function.

A: True. The demand equation, which allegedly contains *all* the relevant goods, does not satisfy the condition that such inclusive demand equations should satisfy, namely, the homogeneity condition. The exponents in the constant elasticity form are the elasticities, and $\epsilon_{HH} + \epsilon_{HO} + \epsilon_{HY}$ should equal zero. But in fact it equals $-2 + 1 + 2 = +1$.

Consider what has been said so far. To take a sufficiently general case, the behavior of a person consuming three goods is described by the array of 15 variables in Figure 7.7. The encirclements represent relations among variables. The three horizontal encirclements, for example, are the three homogeneity conditions; the first three vertical ones are the price elasticity conditions; the last vertical one around the column of income elasticities is the income elasticity condition. The condition that the shares add to 1.0 is not an independent condition but merely a definition of shares.[5] The third share, in other words, might as well be written as the residual from the other two. As a matter of high school algebra, then, among 15 variables there are 7 independent equations, leaving 8 variables to be set arbitrarily (arbitrarily, that is, within whatever limits the 7 equations might impose). Once these 8 are chosen all the other variables follow.

Q: You know a good deal about the demand for good 1 and good 3, but nothing about good 2, the only other good consumed. Find the values of the remaining variables presented here, using the array given as a guide:

$$\frac{1}{4} \qquad -1.0 \qquad \epsilon_{12} \qquad +1.0 \qquad +1.5$$

$$\frac{1}{4} \qquad \epsilon_{21} \qquad \epsilon_{22} \qquad \epsilon_{23} \qquad \epsilon_{2Y}$$

$$S_3 \qquad \epsilon_{31} \qquad +1.0 \qquad -0.5 \qquad +1.0$$

A: The remaining item in the top row, ϵ_{12}, must be by the homogeneity condition -1.5 (to satisfy $-1.0 + \epsilon_{12} + 1.0 + 1.5 = 0$). Likewise, in the bottom row ϵ_{31} also $= -1.5$. With the top and bottom rows filled out, it only remains to apply the income and price elasticity conditions to get the middle row. The remaining income elasticity, for example, is ϵ_{2Y} in $\frac{1}{4}(1.5)$

[5] It can be shown, in fact, that the condition $S_1 + S_2 + S_3 = 1$ is derivable by substitution from the other seven equations. It is not independent. For two goods, 1 and 2, the proof is as follows. First, write out the two price elasticity conditions:

$$S_1(1 + \epsilon_{11}) + S_2(\epsilon_{21}) = 0$$
$$S_2(1 + \epsilon_{22}) + S_1(\epsilon_{12}) = 0$$

Second, eliminate the ϵ_{21} and ϵ_{12} terms from these by substituting the expressions from the two homogeneity conditions:

$$S_1(1 + \epsilon_{11}) + S_2(-\epsilon_{22} - \epsilon_{2Y}) = 0$$
$$S_2(1 + \epsilon_{22}) + S_1(-\epsilon_{11} - \epsilon_{1Y}) = 0$$

Third, add the two equations, canceling the terms in ϵ_{11} and ϵ_{22} and using the income elasticity condition to give

$$S_1 + S_2 - 1 = 0$$

The condition that the sum of shares equals 1.0, therefore, is implied by the other conditions.

$+ \frac{1}{4}(\epsilon_{2Y}) + \frac{1}{2}(1.0) = 1$, or $\epsilon_{2Y} = 0.5$. The own-price elasticity is ϵ_{22} in $\frac{1}{4}(1 + \epsilon_{22}) + \frac{1}{4}(-1.5) + \frac{1}{2}(1.0) = 0$, or $\epsilon_{22} = -1.5$. The other two elasticities, likewise, are $\epsilon_{21} = 3.0$ and $\epsilon_{23} = -2.0$, both by the price elasticity condition, and the full array is

$$
\begin{array}{ccccc}
\dfrac{1}{4} & -1.0 & -1.5 & +1.0 & +1.5 \\[2mm]
\dfrac{1}{4} & +3.0 & -1.5 & -2.0 & +0.5 \\[2mm]
\dfrac{1}{2} & -1.5 & +1.0 & -0.5 & +1.0
\end{array}
$$

The homogeneity condition serves as a check on the new middle row: $3.0 - 1.5 - 2.0 + 0.5 = 0$ as required. Great fun.

Figure 7.7
All Demand Elasticities
and All Constraints

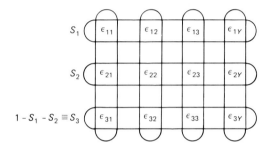

☐
The Symmetry
Condition

An alternative proposition can take the place of some of these equations. It is, for any two goods, 1 and 2.

4. Symmetry condition: $S_1(\epsilon_{12} + S_2\epsilon_{1Y}) = S_2(\epsilon_{21} + S_1\epsilon_{2Y})$

It says, to give the usual story, that there is a relationship between the price elasticity of tea with respect to coffee and of coffee with respect to tea. In this form it is not very enlightening; to tell the truth, in no form is it very enlightening. For the moment the only point to grasp is that it is not an independent constraint additional to the ones already given but is derivable from them.[6]

---

[6] The proof is a little tedious. Start by multiplying out the condition

$$S_1\epsilon_{12} + S_1S_2\epsilon_{1Y} = S_2\epsilon_{21} + S_1S_2\epsilon_{2Y}$$

By the price elasticity condition the third term, $S_2\epsilon_{21}$, is equal to $-S_1(1 + \epsilon_{11})$. By the homogeneity condition the ϵ_{11} in this expression is equal to $-\epsilon_{12} - \epsilon_{1Y}$. Making these substitutions (both affecting the third term alone) gives

$$S_1\epsilon_{12} + S_1S_2\epsilon_{1Y} = S_1\epsilon_{12} + S_1\epsilon_{1Y} - S_1 + S_1S_2\epsilon_{2Y}$$

Cancel the term $S_1\epsilon_{12}$ on both sides and divide both sides by S_1:

$$S_2\epsilon_{1Y} = \epsilon_{1Y} - 1 + S_2\epsilon_{2Y}$$

By the income elasticity condition the last term, $S_2\epsilon_{2Y}$, equals $1 - S_1\epsilon_{1Y}$. Making this substitution and canceling the two 1's gives

$$S_2\epsilon_{1Y} = \epsilon_{1Y} - S_1\epsilon_{1Y}$$

Dividing through by ϵ_{1Y} gives $S_2 = 1 - S_1$, which is true. The original equation, therefore, is true and is derivable from the other conditions.

□
The Slutsky
Equation

The final exhibit in this museum of the algebra of elasticities is the most famous. It is the *Slutsky equation*.[7] The equation gives mathematical expression to the diagrammatic difference between substitution and income effects. Recall that the total change in quantity from a fall in price can be split diagrammatically into a substitution effect—the movement along the initial indifference curve out to the slope of the new, lower price—and an income effect—the parallel shift of the budget line that would then put the consumer on the new, higher indifference curve. The Slutsky equation asserts that the ordinary price elasticity, ϵ_{11}, is composed of a pure substitution elasticity, ϵ'_{11} (note the prime), and an income effect involving the income elasticity, $S_1\epsilon_{1Y}$ (the share multiplied by the income elasticity).

5. Slutsky equation: $\epsilon_{11} = \epsilon'_{11} - S_1\epsilon_{1Y}$

Bear in mind that here and elsewhere in this section own-price elasticities have their natural negative sign. The equation says, then, that the income effect normally adds to the elasticity, making it a larger negative number.

The corresponding diagram (Figure 7.8) might portray Cynthia Floud consuming 100 pounds of hamburger at point initial. The price then falls 10% (purposely exaggerated in the diagram to make the argument clear). Floud's total increase in hamburger consumption of 30 pounds to point final can be split into 20 pounds of substitution effect and 10 pounds of income effect. That is,

$$\underset{\text{Total}}{\frac{+30\%}{-10\%}} = -3 = \underset{\text{Substitution}}{\frac{+20\%}{-10\%}} + \underset{\text{Income}}{\frac{+10\%}{-10\%}}$$

The compensated elasticity ϵ'_{11}, which is the only new element, is a measure of the curvature of the indifference curve, that is, the sensitivity of the equilibrium position along a given indifference curve to changes in the slope of the budget line. It is negative when, as they are, the indifference curves are convex, ranging from $-\infty$ (perfect substitutes) to zero (perfect complements).

Q: Floud spends 1% of her income on hamburger, has an income elasticity of demand for hamburger of 0.5, and has a compensated elasticity of -1.00. What is her elasticity of demand for hamburger?

A: From the Slutsky equation, it is $\epsilon_{11} = -1.00 - (.01)(0.5) = -1.005$.

[7] After Eugen Slutsky, a Russian economist and statistician who published the seminal paper on the subject in 1915. It is translated in American Economic Association, *Readings in Price Theory* (Homewood, Ill.: Irwin, 1952). Its notation makes it difficult for all but the mathematically sophisticated. The modern version of the argument was given by J. R. Hicks in an appendix to his *Value and Capital* (Oxford: Oxford University Press, 1939) and in an elasticity form more congruent with the present elementary treatment as his *Théorie Mathématique de la Valeur* (Paris: Hermann et Cie, 1937).

Figure 7.8
The Total Elasticity Is the
Sum of a Substitution
Elasticity and an Income
Effect Elasticity

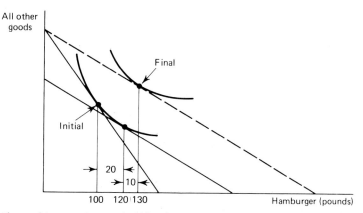

The total increase in pounds of hamburger consumed that is caused by a fall in the price of hamburger can be separated into a pure price (substitution) effect on quantity and an income effect on quantity. Rendering these quantity changes independent of units yields the Slutsky equation of elasticities.

Comment

Notice that, when the share is very small, as here, the ordinary, uncompensated elasticity is very close to the compensated elasticity. The difference between the two is $S_1\epsilon_{1Y}$, which is very small when S_1 is very small. The compensated elasticity is the elasticity holding real income constant; the ordinary elasticity is the elasticity holding money income constant. In other words, as was argued diagrammatically in Chapter 2, for goods that are small shares of expenditure, it does not matter whether one holds money or real income constant: they give virtually identical elasticities.

The proof of the Slutsky equation is quite simple. What needs to be proven is, rearranging the equation, that $\epsilon'_{11} = \epsilon_{11} + S_1\epsilon_{1Y}$. One needs to show, to put it in words, that the compensated elasticity is the sum of the ordinary elasticity and the income effect elasticity. What one means by the "compensated" elasticity is the effect of a 1% fall in price after having removed from the whole effect the effect of the virtual enrichment from the lower price. The whole effect is by definition ϵ_{11}. A 1% fall in price causes an ϵ_{11}% rise in quantity demanded, so the term ϵ_{11} is naturally negative. It only remains to show that the term $S_1\epsilon_{1Y}$ (naturally positive and therefore removing part of the whole, negative effect) does represent "the effect of the virtual enrichment from the lower price." What virtual rise in income does a 1% fall in the price of good 1 cause? Clearly, a S_1% rise. If Floud spends $40 out of every $100 of income on housing, a 1% fall in the price of housing will free 0.4% of his income for expenditure on housing and other goods; that is, the enrichment is $(S_1)(1\%)$. This enrichment has the effect of increasing consumption of good 1 by the enrichment multiplied by the income elasticity of good 1, $S_1\epsilon_{1Y}$. In short, the compensated elasticity, ϵ'_{11} (naturally negative), will be $\epsilon_{11} + S_1\epsilon_{1Y'}$ as asserted.

☐
Extensions and Uses of the Slutsky Equation

The Slutsky equation, then, says that any price elasticity can be written as the sum of a pure substitution effect and an income effect. *Any* price elasticity can—not only ϵ_{11}, but also (obviously) ϵ_{22} and (less obviously) ϵ_{12} and ϵ_{21}. A world of two goods, 1 and 2, has four Slutsky equations:

$$\text{Two own price:} \quad \epsilon_{11} = \epsilon'_{11} - S_1\epsilon_{1Y}$$
$$\epsilon_{22} = \epsilon'_{22} - S_2\epsilon_{2Y}$$
$$\text{Two cross price:} \quad \epsilon_{12} = \epsilon'_{12} - S_2\epsilon_{1Y}$$
$$\epsilon_{21} = \epsilon'_{21} - S_1\epsilon_{2Y}$$

In writing down the cross-price equations, notice that the share, S_2, in the income term measures the virtual change in income from the change in the changing price and therefore carries the subscript of the changing price (the price of good 2 in ϵ_{12}, for example), and that the income elasticity, ϵ_{1Y}, measures the change in quantity demanded from this virtual change in income and therefore carries the subscript of the changing quantity (the quantity of good in ϵ_{12}).

The idea of a compensated elasticity makes possible prettier looking statements of the various conditions on elasticities:

Price elasticity: Replace $S_1(1 + \epsilon_{11}) + S_2(\epsilon_{21}) = 0$
                 with $S_1\epsilon'_{11} + S_2\epsilon'_{21} = 0$

Homogeneity: Replace $\epsilon_{11} + \epsilon_{12} + \epsilon_{1Y} = 0$
               with $\epsilon_{11} + \epsilon'_{12} = 0$

And, the most dramatic simplification,

Symmetry: Replace $S_1(\epsilon_{12} + S_2\epsilon_{1Y}) = S_2(\epsilon_{21} + S_1\epsilon_{2Y})$
               with $S_1\epsilon'_{12} = S_2\epsilon'_{21}$

Beyond prettiness, the Slutsky equation applies whenever one can make distinctions between income and substitution effects.

T or F: A demand curve for housing holding real income constant is always less elastic than is the corresponding demand curve holding money constant.

A: False, though it is only false if housing is inferior (has a negative income elasticity). The Slutsky equation for housing is $\epsilon_{HH} = \epsilon'_{HH} - S_H\epsilon_{HY}$. If housing is normal, the term $S_H\epsilon_{HY}$ increases the elasticity (i.e., makes it more negative) relative to ϵ'_{HH}, which is itself the elasticity "holding real income constant." But if housing is inferior, the term decreases the elasticity. The argument, by the way, is the mathematical version of Sections 7.1 and 7.2.

Or, more substantively, consider the following.

T or F: Because food is a larger share of the budget in a poor than in a rich country, one would expect the elasticity of demand for food to be higher in the poor country.

A: True. The talk of elasticities and shares suggests to the alert mind the Slutsky equation; that is, $\epsilon_{FF} = \epsilon'_{FF} - S_F\epsilon_{FY}$, in which a share affects an elasticity. The higher the share (given a positive income elasticity), the higher (absolutely) the price elasticity, as asserted. The reasoning depends, of course, on the elasticities ϵ'_{FF} and ϵ_{FY} being the same in both countries. There is no reason to suppose otherwise.

The Content of the Theory of Consumption

The sense in the Slutsky equation depends clearly on the existence of indifference contours. It makes no sense to speak of a compensated move along an indifference contour if the contour does not exist. For groups as distinct from individuals, of course, the contour need not exist. A group of automobile buyers facing in the aggregate unchanged prices and income may experience internal redistributions of income that change the amounts of Chevys and Cadillacs they buy. The group might not behave as though it had stable indifference contours, picking off a unique point on a given budget line. In other words, the Slutsky equation, like the homogeneity condition (and the symmetry condition, derived with its aid), need not apply to groups. Economists unanimously assume, however, that it does, and they almost unanimously assume that the homogeneity and related conditions do as well. The assumption amounts to a plausible-sounding but by no means self-evident hypothesis about the world: a group behaves like an individual, namely, both have stable indifference contours.

The uses of the Slutsky equation and many of the other conditions on elasticities of demand depend, therefore, on a hypothesis about group behavior that is foreign to the individualistic vocabulary of economics. The hypothesis can be put, however, in a less distasteful form. The variations in the money or real income of a group that are contemplated in the definitions of income and price elasticities do not alter the distribution of income inside the group enough to spoil the parallel with individual behavior. The result can be put in a table of increasingly stringent assumptions about behavior (see Table 7.3).

These are not on their face, to repeat, very bold hypotheses. No great leap of faith is required to believe even the most stringent of the conditions, the law of demand. Yet, as we have seen again and again in previous chapters, even the less stringent conditions are rich

Table 7.3 What the Pure Theory of the Consumer Says About Elasticities of a Group's Demand

Conditions	Behavior of the Group Sufficient to Lead to the Conditions
Income and price elasticity	Operates along a budget constraint; that is, no goods are left out of the budget constraint.
Homogeneity, symmetry, Slutsky	Operates along a budget constraint *and* has indifference contours (of arbitrary shape, but unchanging).
Compensated elasticity negative, $\epsilon'_{11} < 0$	All of the above, *and* indifference contours convex
Law of demand: Uncompensated elasticity negative, $\epsilon_{11} < 0$	All of the above, *and* no Giffen goods.

in applications. The mere idea of a budget constraint or the mere idea of convex indifference curves are astonishingly applicable. The theory of demand, in short, has an abstract and sterile appearance, but concrete and fruitful uses. We turn now to the appearance and uses of the other half of economics, the theory of supply.

Summary

If one knows some of a consumer's elasticities of demand, one knows something about the other elasticities of demand. The income elasticities weighted by shares, for example, must sum to 1.0, and the own-price elasticity (plus 1.0) and the cross-price elasticities weighted by shares must sum to zero. These are the income and the price elasticity conditions, consequences of the mere existence of a budget constraint. The homogeneity condition is a consequence of the mere existence, in addition, of indifference contours. It says that doubling all prices and incomes will have no effect on the point chosen along the (unchanging) budget line. Since there are many ways of doubling the combined income of John and Laura (all to John, all to Laura, some to both), each of which affects the point chosen differently, the homogeneity condition is not as easy to believe of a group as it is of a single person. The Slutsky equation—which separates the whole elasticity of demand into a substitution effect, ϵ'_{11}, and an income effect, $S_1\epsilon_{1Y}$—has the same difficulty: it applies to any consumer with indifference contours, but it may not apply to a group within which the distribution of income can change. The income distribution is usually assumed to be invariant enough to ignore, in which case the Slutsky equation provides a convenient expression for the rest of consumption theory. The convexity of indifference curves is expressed by the negativity of the compensated elasticity, ϵ'_{11}; the absence of Giffen goods is expressed by the negativity of the uncompensated elasticity, ϵ_{11}, otherwise known as the law of demand.

QUESTIONS FOR SECTION 7.3

1. Fill in the question marks:

	Food	Clothing	All Other Goods
Shares	$\frac{1}{2}$	$\frac{1}{3}$	?
Income elasticities	?	.2	1.6

2. Food is a "gross substitute" for all other goods if the cross elasticity of demand for food with respect to the price of all other goods is positive; that is, a rise in the price of all other goods makes food more attractive. Show that, if food is to be a gross substitute for all other goods, then the own-price elasticity of demand for all other goods must be greater in absolute value than 1.0.

3. Show that, if food is a gross substitute for all other goods, it is *not* necessarily true that all other goods is a gross substitute for food, that is, that $\epsilon_{FA} > 0$ does not imply $\epsilon_{AF} > 0$. (Hint: Notice that the assertion is that ϵ_{AF} and ϵ_{FA} may have different signs; that is, the product, $\epsilon_{AF}(\epsilon_{FA})$, may be negative. Write the expression for ϵ_{AF} and ϵ_{FA} from the price elasticity condition in this form and consider its sign.)

4. The own-price elasticity of Piers Plowman's demand for food is low, about -0.2; the income elasticity of demand for food is also low, about 0.25; and the share of food in total expenditure is high, about 0.5. What do you know about all other goods?

5. For a demand function for Gustafson's housing, the homogeneity condition can be written as (dropping the extra H subscript in each elasticity) $\epsilon_0 = -\epsilon_H - \epsilon_Y$. In words, the cross elasticity of the demand for housing with respect to the price of other goods is equal to the negative of the (naturally negative) own-price elasticity, ϵ_H, minus the (naturally positive) income elasticity.

a. Show that, if the condition holds, the demand function can be written as a function of the relative price of housing and of real income alone, that is, in constant elasticity form as

$$Q_H = D\left(\frac{P_H}{P_0}\right)^{\epsilon_H}\left(\frac{Y}{P_0}\right)^{\epsilon_Y}$$

b. Show that, if the condition does not hold, so that $\epsilon_0 = -\epsilon_H - \epsilon_Y + c$ (c being some number measuring how badly it fails to hold), then the demand function will have an extra term, P_0^c. Interpret this as money illusion.

6. Good 1 is a *net* substitute for good 2 if ϵ'_{12} (*compensated* cross-price elasticity) is positive. Use the homogeneity condition and convexity, $\epsilon'_{11} < 0$, to show that any one good must be a net substitute for all other goods taken as a whole.

True or False

7. If William Dowling's demand for antiques has an income elasticity of 2.5 and he spends half his income on antiques, then his demand for all other goods has a negative income elasticity.

8. If the income elasticity of demand for food is 0.4 and that of all other goods 1.20, then the share of food in total expenditure is $\frac{1}{4}$.

9. A service with a low income elasticity, such as religious guidance, will have a lower price elasticity than will a service with a high income elasticity, such as nightclub entertainment.

10. If all goods were perfect complements with each other the simple, unweighted sum of their own-price elasticities would be -1.0.

11. If gin is a net complement to tonic, then tonic is a net complement to gin.

12. If X is a net complement to Y and Y is a net complement to Z, then X is a net complement to Z. (Hints: Think of a concrete example, using the normal meanings of "complement" and "substitute," and study the homogeneity conditions for the special case of a three-goods world.)

13. The elasticity of demand for housing with respect to the price of food is equal to the elasticity of demand for food with respect to the price of housing.

Part Three | PRODUCTION AND WELFARE

8 Production Possibilities

8.1 Production and Specialization

Look to the True Opportunity Cost

☐ The theory of demand, just completed, asks how people behave given a budget line; the theory of supply, now begun, asks how the budget line came to be given. In the theory of demand, the premise of no free lunches is imposed from the outside; in the theory of supply, it is the result. The central idea in the theory of supply is opportunity cost, namely, that supplying one thing costs not supplying another thing. Opportunity cost is merely a restatement of scarcity or, in other words, of the budget line. But a close attention to opportunity cost characterizes the most economic of economic arguments. Few noneconomists, for example, would take the following proposition seriously:

T or F: From the social point of view, and given equal power to deter crime, fines are better than prison sentences.

A: True. Fines merely transfer money from the criminal to the state (or to the victim). They do not reduce the society's ability to consume. Prison sentences, by contrast, do reduce the society's ability to consume: the guards, the prison walls, and the time of the prisoners themselves are diverted from employments in which they could be making other things. A guard on a prison wall could be employed as a farmer or a traffic cop. He would be so employed under a system of fines, and society would be getting his output. Social output would be higher. Note, by the way, that fines are not necessarily less severe or less crime deterring than is prison. A $15,000 fine might deter the same amount of armed robbery as a two-year sentence in prison. If it does not, it can be raised to $20,000 or $30,000 or whatever.

The Specialization Theorem: Make the Opportunity Cost Smallest

☐ The most important application of opportunity cost is the *specialization theorem*, namely, that production of all goods can be larger if people are permitted to specialize in production and to trade their products. Free trade, as was shown earlier, leads to a best point of consumption inside a given Edgeworth box; the specialization theorem asserts that free trade leads also to the largest possible Edgeworth box. A federated United States, a European Common Market, a world without import tariffs, or an economy without ghettos, segregation, apartheid, passports, entry restrictions, or other barriers to trade will produce more.

The reason is simple. If a baker cannot trade with a carpenter, the baker must build his own house. Each room the baker builds will have a high opportunity cost in loaves foregone. The baker's hour produces many loaves but few rooms, and to build a room is therefore to sacrifice many loaves of bread. The carpenter's bread baking, likewise, will have a high opportunity cost in rooms unbuilt. If they can trade, however, each can specialize in what each one does best—to use the jargon, in his *comparative advantage*. Comparative advantage matters because the decision to specialize depends on what one does best compared with the other things one could do. The carpenter may be in fact a better baker than the baker, but so long as his hour of baking has a higher cost in foregone housing than does the baker's, the carpenter will continue to specialize in carpentry. After each has produced his own good in the best way, that is, at the lowest cost in output (of other things) foregone, they can each consume both goods by trading for the other.

For people, the argument is called the *division of labor*; for nations, it is called *specialization by comparative advantage*. It applies to all levels of society, from the family to international trade. If a family is to produce the largest output, its members must specialize by comparative advantage. John is undoubtedly quicker at chopping a pile of wood than is little Bobby, his son, but if the opportunity cost of John's chopping is starting the furnace and replacing a tire on the car, while the opportunity cost of Bobby's is only playing marbles and sweeping the back stairs, it is best to assign Bobby to the woodpile. This division of labor will produce the chopped wood with the least valued sacrifice of other goods (started furnaces, played marbles, etc.).

□
Proof of the Theorem in the Case of Foreign Trade

A diagram makes the argument clear, showing along the way how to connect individual and social opportunity costs. To take an historically important example, consider the possible combinations of food and manufactures that the Old World and the New World could produce in the nineteenth century each by itself (see Figure 8.1).

The possible combinations are bordered by as it were a social budget line, called, you remember, the production possibility curve. Its slope is here constant (a straight-line production possibility curve), representing constant marginal opportunity cost. The Old World, for example, sacrifices as indicated the same amount of food for each additional unit of manufactures produced. The labor and land and so forth of the Old World can move from farm to factory without rising costs in food foregone.

Were trade prohibited between the Old and New Worlds, each would pick by the usual indifference contours some point such as E or E' along each curve, at which both are producing (in order to consume) both goods. Were trade allowed, however, the two worlds would be in effect merged into one. The production possibility curve for the merged world is constructed as follows. Think of producing successively

**Figure 8.1
The Production Possibility
Curves of the Old (a) and
New (b) Worlds**

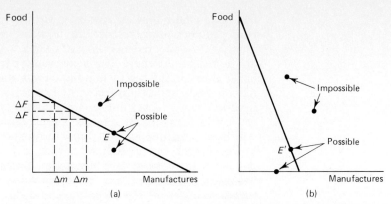

The Old World produces manufactures at a lower opportunity cost in terms of food than does the New World. The cost is given by the slope of the production possibility curve.

larger amounts of manufactures as cheaply as possible in food foregone. The early production, clearly, will be located entirely in the Old World, because the production there will have the lowest cost in food foregone. Only when the Old World is completely specialized in manufactures will the production of still more manufacturers require the New World to produce some. Moving to the right along the manufactures axis, in other words, first the Old World's and then finally the New's production possibility curve is used to produce manufactures (see Figure 8.2).

**Figure 8.2
Specialization Is More
Efficient than
Nonspecialization**

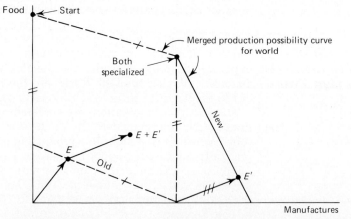

The production possibility curves of the Old and New Worlds are added to give the production possibilities for the world as a whole. If both sides produce both food and manufactures, a point of, for example, $E + E'$ is reached. This point is inefficient because it is not on the production possibility curve. A point E', for example, which is efficient, can be reached only if the Old World specializes in manufactures. Alternatively, the New World might specialize in food.

When no manufactures are produced anywhere, the merged world is at start, both places producing only food. As the capacity of the Old World to produce manufactures is used up, the world moves along the dashed line (along which the New World still produces only food); after the capacity is used up, the world moves along the solid line. The outmost line, dashed and solid, is the world's production possibility curve with trade.

Now the proof of the specialization theorem is simple. Notice in the diagram the points E and E'. These are the points of production (and consumption) before trade. The point $E + E'$ adds the two bundles together and is inside the world's production possibility curve. All such sums of nonspecialized points are inside the curve. Specialization and the trade that permits specialization, in short, yields more goods than does self-sufficiency. Prohibiting trade always reduces total income; opening trade increases it.

□

Specialization Implies the Conventional Bulge for the Production Possibility Curve

Figure 8.3 A Bulging Production Possibility Curve Implies Upward-Sloping Supply Curves

The specialization theorem is in one sense obvious. Obviously, removing a restriction by opening trade cannot hurt the world. It is restrictions, after all, that hurt, and removing them must help. Removing restrictions is at the least nonhurtful.

The theorem is one way of deriving a convex (i.e., bulging outward) shape for production possibility curves. Just as two straight-line production possibility curves in the New and Old Worlds resulted in a (kinked) bulge in the world's curve, so also in a single economy many straight-line production possibility curves of Smith, Johnson, Brown, Williams, Miller, Jones, Davis, Anderson, Wilson, and Taylor would

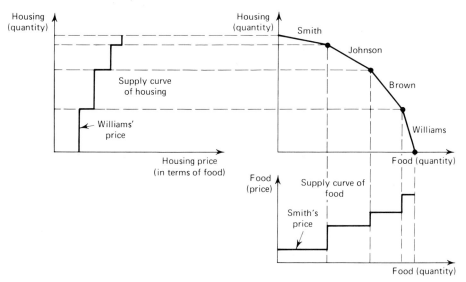

The concave production possibility curve indicates that, as more food is produced, the cost of food in terms of housing increases. This implies an upward-sloping supply curve for food. The same is true of the production of housing.

result in a bulged curve for the nation. The bulge is significant because it is an alternative picture of a feature of supply assumed so far with little comment (i.e., its upward slope). Figure 8.3 exhibits the case for an economy of Smith, Johnson, Brown, and Williams producing food and housing. The production possibility curve for the economy between food and housing is in the upper right-hand panel. The other two panels are plots of the slopes of the curves (one way or the other); that is, they are the marginal opportunity costs, or the supply curves. From the idea of opportunity cost, then, comes an upward-sloping curve of supply.

Summary

The theory of demand produced an upward-sloping supply curve of food only as an excess supply, subtracting a small own demand for food from a large initial supply. The initial supply was given and unproducible. Eating food, therefore, has socially speaking no opportunity cost in, say, housing foregone. The theory of supply, by contrast, allows production. Producing food, therefore, has an opportunity cost in housing: for the society as a whole as well as for single consumers, more food means less housing. Opportunity cost is a characteristically economic idea, and it motivates the economist's distaste for prisons relative to fines or for subsidies masquerading as production. It is the nub of the specialization theorem, namely, that a division of labor by comparative advantage raises a nation's production possibilities. And the specialization theorem, in turn, is the nub of supply, namely, that at higher relative prices for, say, baked goods, more labor and machinery are brought into the production of bread. The fresh recruits of labor and machinery are, to be sure, less suited to specialization in baking than are the earlier. But that is the point. Only the higher relative price permits the higher opportunity cost of the relatively ill-suited labor and machinery to be incurred. Only at higher relative prices is more output forthcoming. As the production possibility curve bulges outward, the supply curve slopes upward.

QUESTIONS FOR SECTION 8.1

1. When every few years or so a big company cannot meet its debts, there arises a clamor for subsidies. The Secretary of Transportation is worried at the thought of Penn-Central's bankruptcy; the Secretary of Defense is alarmed at the thought of Boeing's; the Minister for Industry is appalled at the thought of Chrysler–U.K.'s; the President is shocked at the thought of Chrysler–U.S.A.'s. "The bankruptcy of Big Company X," the cry goes, "would be an intolerable disaster for the nation. Imagine life without X! We must intervene at once with $N million." Evaluate the clamor. Does bankruptcy entail a cost to the society as a whole?

2. Show that, if the New and Old Worlds had the same slopes for their production possibility curves, then the point $E + E'$ representing production before trade would be on—not below—the world's production possibility curve.

3. Suppose initially that three countries—Japan, Britain, and America—were self-sufficient, producing each along a straight-line of production possibility curve. The maximum tons of food and numbers of machines each could produce by devoting all of its resources to producing one or the other good were as follows:

Maximum Possible Amount of	Japan	Britain	America
Food (millions of tons)	6	15	30
Machines (millions)	20	20	30

a. What will be the price of a machine expressed in tons of food in each country? Which is the low-cost producer of machines?

b. To take an especially simple case, if consumers in all three countries demanded food and machines in fixed proportions, 1 ton of food with 1 machine, what would be the world's production (= consumption) of the two goods? (Hint: The expansion path would be the ray $F = M$ for each country; the point of consumption would therefore be the intersection of $F = M$ and the equations for the production possibility curves.)

c. Sketch at an approximately correct scale the world's production possibility curve if the three countries open themselves to free trade. If the world has the $F = M$ preferences, as given, on which country's segment will production and consumption fall? Describe the pattern of specialization.

d. After free trade and specialization, how much will the world consume and produce of each good? Compare these amounts with those in (b) and draw the moral of the tale.

4. A production possibility curve between food and all other goods is analogous to an indifference curve between the two. The production possibility curve characterizes technology, the indifference curve tastes. Experiments in revealed preference are interpretable as assertions that one can or cannot draw an ordinary indifference curve. *True or false:* If two combinations of food and all other goods violate the weak axiom of revealed preference, then from one combination to the next it is conceivable that technology has stayed the same, but inconceivable that tastes have; if the combinations satisfy the axiom, then it is conceivable that tastes have stayed the same, but inconceivable that technology has.

5. After 1859 Japan was opened to trade with the West (earlier it had had limited trade with Holland). That is, Japan was suddenly presented with the world's relative price of, say, food in terms of all other goods. Supposing Japan in 1859 to be so small as to have no effect over world prices and to have a straight-line production possibility curve between the two goods, describe in diagrams the impact on Japan of the opening of trade. In what conditions would the opening of trade have no effect?

True or False

6. The $100 cost of journeying from New York to Washington is in all economic respects identical to a $100 tax. Were it in fact costless to make the trip, a tax equal to the actual $100 cost would have the same economic effects as the cost itself.

7. From the point of view of social output (if not necessarily of social morality), it is better for members of Congress and government bureaucrats to be bribed directly in cash than to be influenced indirectly by hordes of lawyers and advertisers armed with elaborate offices, researchers, and business luncheons.

8. On grounds of efficiency we should not acquire a president by election: the office should be for sale to the highest bidder.

8.2 The Production Function Also Leads to the Production Possibility Curve

□
The Production Function Is Similar to the Hill of Happiness

The fundamental idea in the theory of supply is, to repeat, the idea of opportunity cost or its diagrammatic representations, the production possibility curve and the upward-sloping supply curve. One way of arriving at an outward-bulging production possibility curve (and therefore an upward-sloping supply curve) is the specialization theorem. The other way—underneath it all, the same way—is the *production function.*

The word "function" is here used in its mathematical sense of a one-to-one correspondence between maximum output (what is produced) and inputs (the producers). In plain lanaguage, the production function of, say, food is the book of recipes for making food from the ingredients available. Just as various combinations of housing and all other goods "produce" happiness according to the *utility function,* so too various combinations of farmland, tractors, laborers, fertilizer, grocery space, transportation, and so forth produce food according to the *production function.* Look at the corner of the room, at the floor. The corner itself can be the origin. The vertical axis goes from floor to ceiling, measuring food production as a height above the floor. The intersection of the floor with the left and right walls (as you look at them now) are the two other axes, measuring amounts of farmland and farm labor (more than two inputs require more than three dimensions). Imagine a hill of food production rising out of the corner. Someone climbing the hill would start at a low (or zero) altitude in the corner and would cross higher and higher contour lines of food altitude as she climbed up the hill, moving out over the middle of the room. The production function, in other words, is analogous to an ordinary hill and, recalling utility functions, to the hill of happiness.

The analogies between utility and production functions are exact, the main difference being that the utility from a bundle of goods is not measurable in any unambiguous way, while the output from a bundle of inputs is measurable quite easily: the output of food can be touched, inspected, tested, and weighed as utility or joys or happiness cannot. The recipe for French bread contains four material ingredients (flour, salt, yeast, and water), one piece of capital equipment (the oven), and one laborer (an inspired baker). Combining these in such-and-such proportions has a measurable result, one loaf. But combining the loaf with cheese and wine in a lunch on the grass produces ecstasy of an unmeasurable sort, having no natural units and incomparable between two people. To an extent unmatched in utility theory, therefore, economists have actually measured production functions.

Substitutability Is Common in Production as in Consumption

What they have found in the measurements is in accord with common sense, namely, that there is more than one recipe for food, and more than one blueprint for housing, and more than one way in which to make goods out of the resources available to the economy. The opposite idea is a production function with fixed proportions, that is, one and only one recipe, called a *Leontief production function* in honor of the economist who made the most fruitful use of it. The hill of production in this case has a ridge. In chemical processes the recipes are often fixed, as in the making of water (H_2O) from two atoms of hydrogen and one of oxygen (see Figure 8.4).

Given 2 atoms of oxygen, more than 4 of hydrogen does not produce more water. The excess hydrogen is simply unemployed, because all of it that is needed to produce 2 molecules of water is 4 (not 5 or 10 or 8). The production of 2 molecules of water *requires* 4 atoms of hydrogen and 2 of oxygen. The words "needed" and "requires" suggest that the situation does not involve choices and is therefore not economic. Just so. Corners in utility contours represent the antieconomic idea of "need" in consumption; likewise, corners in production contours represent need in production. The basic hypothesis in the theory of consumption is that consumers can satisfy themselves with various bundles of goods, not only with the one bundle they "need"; likewise, the basic hypothesis in the theory of production is that producers can make bread, houses, automobiles, or whatever with various bundles of resources, not only with the unique recipe. The contour lines for most products are not corners, but smooth.

Or, to put it another way, there's more than one way to skin a cat. You can skin the cat in a machine-intensive way by dropping it into an automatic cat-skinning machine, starting the motor, and press-

Figure 8.4
In Production Functions with Fixed Proportions the Contour Lines of Output Have Corners

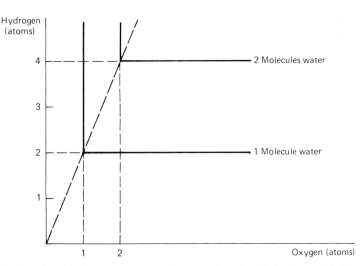

If the ratio of hydrogen to oxygen is greater than 2 to 1, hydrogen is being wasted; if less, oxygen.

Figure 8.5
There Is More than
One Way in Which to
Skin a Cat

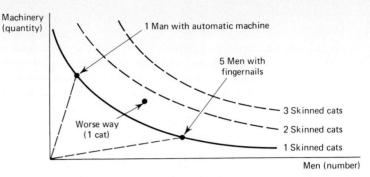

Isoquants display the technically efficient means of producing. Technical efficiency requires that the combination of inputs used to produce a given quantity of output is such that the quantity of one input cannot be reduced, holding the other inputs constant, without reducing the quantity of output.

ing the button. Or you can skin it in a labor-intensive (and machine-light) way by giving it to a team of bloodthirsty men with long fingernails. The various ways of skinning one cat are represented by the contour lines of altitude 1 skinned cat on the hill of production (see Figure 8.5).

Note the contrast in shape with Figure 8.5. The curve (contrasted to the corner) says that there are many ways in which a cat can be skinned. The point worse way is technically speaking an inefficient way to skin one cat.[1]

The Uses of Substitutability

☐ The mere idea of substitutability in production, like the mere idea of substitutability in consumption (the law of demand), is powerful and important. Consumers can gratify given tastes in many ways; producers, similarly, can use given technological knowledge in many ways. The idea applies to the production of anything—grain in India, education in America, steel in Britain, industrial output in Russia, all output in Brazil. A recurrent example is the enemy's output of soldiers and equipment in the field.

Q: Criticize from the point of view of the economics of production the following argument in favor of "strategic bombing," that is, bombing of the enemy's sources of supply at home. "The enemy needs railways (or ball-bearings or oil) to wage modern war; therefore, we can cheaply disarm him, with little risk to our own forces, by bombing from a great height his rail yards (or ball-bearing factories or oil refineries)."

A: The argument supposes that the enemy (successively in this context from the 1930s to the 1970s the Ethiopians, the Loyalists, the Germans, the North

---

[1] The *unit isoquant* (i.e., the contour for one cat) represents the ways that use the least machines or people to do the trick.

Koreans, and the North Vietnamese) *needs* railways, that is, that one man in the field *requires* so many miles of operating track and that bombing the track will make it impossible to sustain the man in the field. But the economic presumption—not always true, but always worth considering—is that on the contrary there are many ways of sustaining a man in the field. To be sure, placing a ton of TNT on the first way of doing it will raise the cost of sustaining the man, because the second way (marshalling repair crews to fix the track quickly, rerouting the trains, carrying the equipment on people's backs down the Ho Chi Minh Trail, or whatever) is more expensive. That is why it is the second, not the first, way. But "more expensive" is not "impossible." Although the evidence is in some cases controversial, strategic bombing has in fact seldom had the effects claimed for it. Because there is more than one way in which to skin a cat, the "essential" part of the enemy's war machine destroyed by the bombing was seldom been truly essential.

Similarly, the economist is suspicious of the engineer's declarations that San Francisco "needs" a rail system of public transport, or that farmers in the San Joaquin Valley "need" a million gallons of water, or that America "needs" X million barrels of oil. He has seen alternatives, such as buses and cabs in Hong Kong, water conservation in Kansas, and smaller cars and colder houses in Europe. A world of unique recipes for each thing would be simpler, but it is not the world as it is.

□
Substitutability Implies That the Production Possibility Curve Is a Curve, Not a Point

Such is the direct, practical use of the idea of a production function. It will come up later again and again: as utility functions are to demand, production functions are to supply. The indirect, theoretical use, however, is the chief business here, the use in illuminating the allocation of resources. Suppose that the United States in 1944 produced two goods, guns and butter, by allocating two resources (or *factors of production*), labor and land, between the two production functions. All the labor and land could be allocated to guns, producing the highest possible level of guns and zero butter, or all of it could be allocated to butter, or various possible combinations in between. Think of the parallel between utility in joys as a function of inputs of food and all other goods and production in guns as a function of inputs of labor and land. The thought suggests that, just as an Edgeworth box can represent the allocation of two goods between the utility of John and of Harry, so too it can represent the allocation of two factors between the production of guns and of butter (see Figure 8.6).

At point inefficient, for example, lots of labor is allocated to butter production and lots of land to guns, the rest of each factor going to the other product. The analogy with consumption theory suggests further that the line of tangencies between the two sets of contours has especially desirable properties. So it does. Starting from an allocation on the line (the contract curve, you recall), a central planner of the economy would not get more guns without sacrificing butter. From

**Figure 8.6
An Edgeworth Box for
Production**

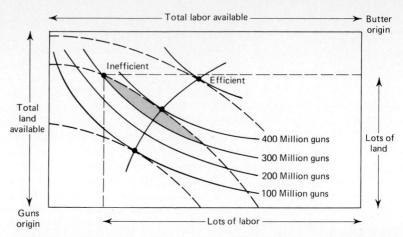

At the point inefficient, the output of guns could be increased to 400 million without reducing the output of butter. This is done by reallocating land and labor to gun production in such a manner that the economy moves along the butter isoquant from the 300 million to the 400 million gun isoquant.

point inefficient, on the other hand, he could get more guns *and* more butter by shifting the allocation to any point inside the shaded lens shape. All of which is to say—and this is the payoff—that combinations of guns and butter along the contract curve are points on the economy's production possibility curve, that is, efficient points, at which production of both guns and butter cannot be increased.

**Figure 8.7
Points on the Contract
Curve Correspond to
Points on the Production
Possibility Curve**

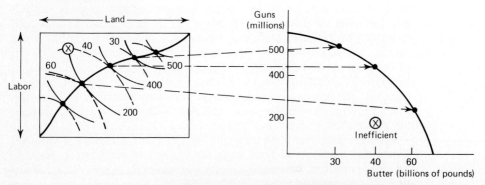

At points of tangency between gun isoquants and butter isoquants, more of one good cannot be produced without sacrificing some of the other. Therefore the levels of guns and butter produced at these points are at the frontier of the production possibility region.

Figure 8.7 shows the correspondence between the contract curve (for production) and the production possibility curve. The point inefficient is just that: off the contract curve in the Edgeworth box and (therefore) inside the production possibility curve.

Summary

From the marriage of the idea of a production function and the idea of factors of production (as in the preceding section from the marriage of the idea of specialization and of diversity of natural gifts) has come the production possibility curve. No other child could be expected, because the fixed endowments of factors and the fixed production functions that allow one to draw the Edgeworth box for production are merely two kinds of scarcity—a scarcity of resources to make things and a scarcity of (a limit on) the knowledge of how to use resources to make things. And scarcity is the idea underlying the production possibility curve.

PROBLEMS FOR SECTION 8.2

1. Grain could move from Chicago to New York by two routes, water (by way of the Great Lakes and the Erie Canal or down the Mississippi to New Orleans and thence by ship to New York) and rail. By the end of the nineteenth century about 70% of the grain in fact went by rail. *True or false:* Had the railway never been invented, the United States would have lost an amount equal to the value of the transport of grain provided by the railway.

2. Visualize the contour maps in Figure 8.8 (isoquants = equal quantities) in three dimensions and describe them as hills of production.

**Figure 8.8
Alternative Shapes of
Isoquants**

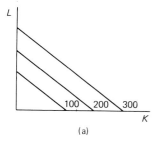 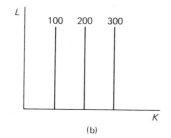 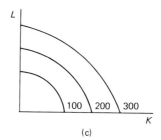

3. A company, industry, or whole economy facing a budget line of L and K would choose the highest contour attainable within the budget line. In view of this, and using the analogous argument in consumption theory, show why the typical shape of output contours is none of the shapes in the previous problem but rather that shown in Figure 8.9.

**Figure 8.9
No Specialization in Using
Factors**

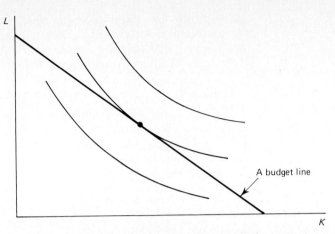

Isoquants that are convex to the origin will cause a firm that purchases inputs at constant prices to employ both L and K production.

---

4. According to the "need" theory of economics, a continuously depleting resource should rise continuously in relative price, driving the economy to disaster. Oil needed for tractors, which are needed to make flour, which is needed for bread, which is needed to sustain life, should rise continually in price as it depletes. Yet in fact the price of such resources often levels off or falls after an initial rise. The price of Greenland whale bone, for example, rose from £250 per ton in 1835 to about £2800 around 1900, but then fell to £2500 by 1910; the price of whale oil rose from its base of £40 per ton after 1835 but had fallen to £25 by 1910. With cat skinning in mind, why?

5. Consider an Edgeworth box in which labor and land are fully employed and are divided, say, 50:50 between guns and butter. How would you represent less than full employment of labor? Is more output attainable from putting the unemployed to work? How would you represent unemployment in the corresponding production possibility curve? What is the result in this diagram of putting the unemployed to work? Is there a free lunch?

6. Use the Edgeworth box for production to show that, if food and all other goods both use land and labor in rigidly fixed proportions (the proportions being different for the two goods and lying on opposite sides of the proportional endowment of land and labor in the nation as a whole), then only one allocation of land and labor to the two goods (i.e., only one point in the box) will fully employ both land and labor.

8.3   The Law of Upward-Sloping Supply

*Diminishing
Returns Implies
That the Production
Possibility Curve
Bulges Outward*

☐   It must still be shown that the idea of a production function leads not only to a production possibility curve but also to a production possibility curve that bulges outward. Not only are guns scarce, in other words, but as more are made, they become relative to butter more scarce: the supply curve of guns slopes upward. The specialization theorem had no difficulty showing this, since only at high prices will people and other resources with comparatively less advantage in it be drawn into gun specialization. The production function can show, however, that the argument is not quite conclusive, that is, that it is possible for supply curves to slope downward.

Possible but not usual. The usual condition of gun or butter production is that, as more resources are devoted to their production, output goes up less than proportionately. That is, less and less suitable resources flow into, say, gun production, which shows, by the way, that the specialization theorem and the production function are at root the same argument. The first gun produced uses a little urban land (the best location for the factory) and a little mining land (the best source of ore for steel). But the last gun produced must use resources much better suited to producing butter, such as farmland remote from the city and bereft of mineral wealth. Likewise for butter. America in 1944 producing only butter would be using arsenals as barns and machinists as milkmaids.

The usual condition is known as *diminishing returns to scale;* the unusual condition would be *increasing returns to scale.* That is, in the unusual case as all the inputs were doubled the production of, say, guns would be more than double. The easiest way to understand this terminology is to take the special case of a production function for output with only one input, called input.

T or F: "Diminishing returns" means that as input increases output falls.

A: False. It means that output rises less than proportionately with input, as does the solid production function in Figure 8.10. The dashed function marked constant returns is just that: it exhibits, as would any ray through the origin, proportional increases in output and input. Along the function marked increasing returns, by contrast, a doubling, say, of input causes a more than doubling of output, from early to late.

It is easy to show for this special case of a single input that diminishing returns in all industries will yield a production possibility curve with a conventional, outward bulge. Start on the left of Figure 8.11 with input into guns measured from left to right and input into butter

Figure 8.10
The Varieties of Returns to Scale in the Case of One Input

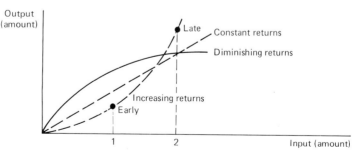

Constant returns to scale implies that the ratio of output to input is the same for all rates of input. Diminishing returns implies that the ratio falls as the rate of input increases; increasing returns, that it increases.

**Figure 8.11
Diminishing Returns (a)
Implies an Outward
Bulge (b)**

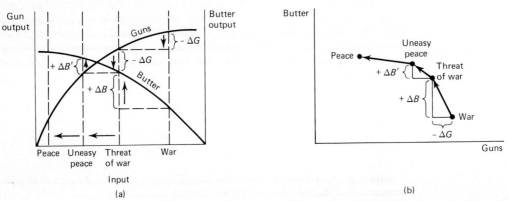

(a)

(b)

Each unit of input added to gun production increases gun output less than did the previous unit. Each unit of input removed from butter production reduces butter output more than did the previous unit. Both factors cause the cost of guns in terms of butter to rise as more guns are produced.

measured from right to left. A particular allocation of input, say, the allocation marked war, will give outputs shown by the gun and butter curves. Notice that both curves exhibit diminishing returns to scale.

Now pick another point, such as threat of war, and plot the changes

**Figure 8.12
Increasing Returns (a) Can
Cause an Inward Bulge (b)**

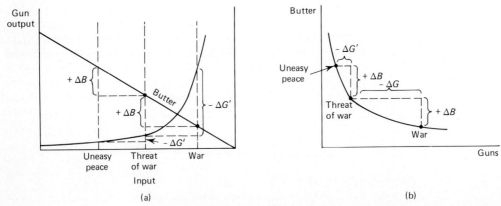

(a)

(b)

Each unit of input added to gun production increases gun output more than did the previous unit. Each unit of input removed from butter production reduces butter output by the same amount as did the previous unit. Therefore the cost of guns in terms of butter falls as more guns are produced.

in gun ($-\Delta G$) and butter ($+\Delta B$) production in the right-hand panel of the diagram. Now go farther, picking a point such as uneasy peace that gives the same fall in gun production as before. Because of diminishing returns it will necessarily be so—and is plain in the left panel of the diagram—that the accompanying rise in butter production ($+\Delta B'$) will be smaller than before. The consequence in the right panel is that the slope of the production possibility curve falls as fewer guns are produced. In other words, because both production functions exhibit diminishing returns to scale, the production possibility curve bulges out.

☐

Increasing Returns Can Reverse the Bulge, But Need Not

A similar argument can show that increasing returns in one of the industries might cause the production possibility curve to have a perverse inward bulge. Again, three points suffice. Since butter production is here assumed to have constant returns, equal spacing along the input axis will give equal rises in butter output (see Figure 8.12).

The marginal opportunity cost of guns falls instead of rises, as more are produced; the supply curve is downward, not upward, sloping. The result carries over to the more general case of two (or N) inputs, labor and land.

☐

Constant Returns and Two Inputs Implies an Outward Bulge

To repeat, however, the usual condition of production is diminishing or, at best, constant returns to scale with a resulting production possibility curve that bulges outward. The outward bulge can be shown to be still more certain in the case of two or more inputs, as follows. Suppose that both guns and butter had, taking the extreme, *constant returns to scale* and that the economy was initially producing only butter. Suppose now that the central planners wished to cut butter production by half in order to increase gun production. One simple (though clumsy) way in which to achieve this is to order half of each one of the resources to move to producing guns—half the milkmaids (to assemble shells), half the dairy cattle (to haul barrels), half the land (to test the guns). What is clumsy about the halving order is that it sets to gun making the least as well as the best suited resources. The output of butter achieved by such a needlessly clumsy order would be exactly half the maximum producible, since all the inputs to butter in the all-butter case are being cut exactly in half and since by assumption the production function for butter has constant returns to scale. For the same reason, the output of guns achieved by the order would be exactly half the maximum. In short, the simple but clumsy order would put the economy at clumsy in Figure 8.13

Were the central planners more intelligent, they would release from butter the resources less suited to butter production instead of simply half the milkmaids, half the machinists, half the farmland, half the gunsmiths, and so forth. The machinists and gunsmiths would be the first to go, yielding more guns for the butter sacrificed. The point clumsy, in other words, can be improved upon, which is to say that there is a better attainable point beyond the straight line. The same is true at other points on the straight line, corresponding to reductions

Figure 8.13
The True Production
Possibility Curve Is Always
Outside a Straight Line

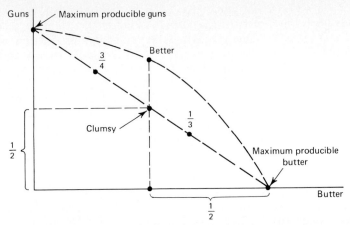

Random allocation of resources to production of guns and of butter, without regard to the productivity of the resources in the two uses, leaves society inside the production possibility curve.

of one third or three fourths or whatever in butter production. The true production possibility curve, in other words, is the same as the straight line at its end points and is beyond the straight line at the intermediate points. As was to be proven, the production possibility curve bulges outward.

Therefore, constant returns to scale implies that the supply curve of any one good—guns, say—slopes upward, for the marginal supply price is simply the opportunity cost (in terms of butter) of an additional gun, and the outward bulge implies that this opportunity cost increases as more guns are made. Guns become more scarce.

Summary

The law of supply—that supply curves slope upward—plays the same role on the production side of the economy as does the law of demand—that demand curves slope downward—plays on the consumption side. The merely logical connection between supply curves and production possibility curves can be summarized in Figure 8.14. The upward-sloping segments of the supply curve correspond to outward-bulging segments of the production possibility curve. As a matter of logic, again, constant (or diminishing) returns to scale imply an outward bulge; increasing returns can (though need not) imply a perverse inward bulge. The factual assertion, disputed by some economists but accepted by most, is that constant returns predominate in real economies and therefore that real economies face upward-sloping, not downward-sloping, supply curves. Whether they do or not is of more than academic interest. Downward-sloping supply curves would provide a rationale for certain interventions in the economy, tariffs, for example, that protected "infant industries," that is, those that could grow to maturity if allowed to exploit their economies of scale.

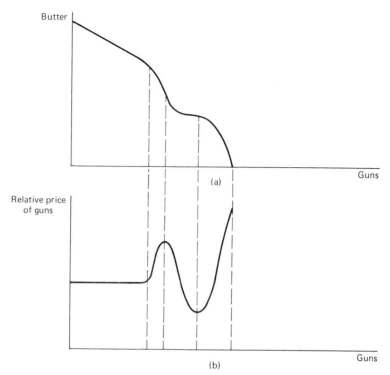

A straight-line production possibility curve corresponds to a perfectly elastic supply curve. A concave production possibility curve corresponds to a falling supply curve; a convex production possibility curve, to a rising supply curve.

With the conventional bulge, on the other hand, the presumption is that self-interest unassisted by sages will achieve national efficiency.

QUESTIONS FOR SECTION 8.3

1. Divide the economy into number 2 pencils and all other goods. *True or false:* Since number 2 pencils take a trivial percentage of the nation's resources, the production function of all other goods will exhibit virtually constant returns to scale over the range of outputs caused by expansions or contractions of the pencil industry.

2. Canada produces food and manufactures, facing an unalterable world price for one in terms of the other. Show that, if Canada's production possibility curve is outward bulging, Canada maximizes the value of its production (valued at world prices) when each of its many farmers and manufacturers produces to equalize the slope of the production possibility curve with the world price.

3. Show that, if increasing returns in manufactures are strong enough to make the production possibility curve bulge inward over part of its length, then equalizing the slopes might not maximize the value of Canadian production.

True or False

4. The more sharply diminishing are returns to scale in food, the more bulged is the production possibility curve.

5. Increasing returns to scale in the production of guns is sufficient by itself, regardless of the nature of returns in butter, to make the production possibility curve between guns and butter bulge inward.

6. With one input (labor) and constant returns to scale in wine and cloth, the production possibility curve of England is a straight line.

7. The production possibility curve in its various possible shapes is analogous to a budget line facing a single person, with fixed prices or quantity discounts or quantity penalties.

8. If wine and cloth have constant returns to scale in their use of two inputs, labor and land, but if they always use the two inputs in the same proportion (2 acres per ton, say), then the production possibility curve will be a straight line.

9. By an argument similar to that in Question 1, the resources used in all other goods that will be released (in minute amounts) when the output of pencils increases will have no special suitability in producing all other goods.

10. In view of the answer to Question 9, the production possibility curve between number 2 pencils and all other goods will be bulging outward straight, or bulging inward, depending on whether the production function in the number 2 pencil industry exhibits diminishing, constant, or increasing returns.

8.4 How an Economy Works in the Large

☐

Adding the Law of Supply (the Outward Bulge) to the Law of Demand

Guns become more expensive, then, as more are made. Furthermore, as more are made, they become less valuable. The armies are well supplied, the hunters are armed to the teeth, and an extra gun has a lower marginal valuation than did earlier increments to the supply. Corresponding to the supply curve obeying the law of supply (upward sloping), then, is a demand curve obeying the law of demand (downward sloping).

The impulse to put the supply and demand in the same diagram and to watch where they cross is irresistable. The supply curve is the marginal cost (i.e., the slope of the community's production possibility curve); the demand curve is the marginal valuation (i.e., the slope along the production possibility curve of the community's indifference curves). That is, the top panel in Figure 8.15 leads to the bottom panel.

The marginal valuation constituting the demand curve must be measured along the production possibility curve because only along the curve are resources fully employed. The marginal valuations come from whatever marginal valuation the amount and distribution of income casts up at the point in question on the production possibility curve.

**Figure 8.15
Production Possibilities
and Indifference Curves
(a) Lead to Supply and
Demand (b)**

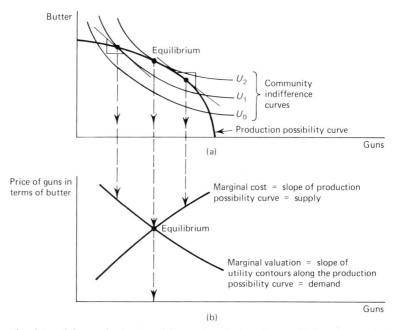

(a)

(b)

The slope of the production possibility curve tells the price at which a given quantity will be supplied. The slope of the indifference curve at a point that lies on the production possibility curve tells the price at which a given quantity will be demanded.

*The Equilibrium Is
Efficient*

☐ Now look at point equilibrium. Equilibrium in the top panel is the point of the highest community indifference curve (or the highest indifference curve of the typical consumer) attainable within the production possibility curve. At that point the community is doing as well as it can. The point is also, to put it a second way, the one of equal slopes of indifference and production possibility curves. This second way of saying that point equilibrium is a good thing is represented by the other point equilibrium in the bottom panel: supply (the slope of the production possibility curve) is equal to demand (the slope of the indifference curve along the production possibility curve).

Allowing for production, in other words, leaves unaltered the conclusion of earlier chapters: when markets work well (much of the rest of the book examines their failures to work well), they lead to efficiency, as by an invisible hand. The selfish interests of the butter producer lead him and his colleagues to sell butter at its true opportunity cost in terms of guns. The selfish interests of the butter consumer, likewise, leads him to buy at its marginal valuation. Marginal valuation is equal to marginal cost, and the opportunities for mutually advantageous exchange between producers and consumers, as between different consumers, are exhausted. The economy is driven by self-interest to be efficient both in consumption and in production.

☐
The Uses of the Economywide Diagram

The connection between this moderately happy result and heaven on earth (which it is not) is the subject of the next chapter. In the meantime, the model itself is applicable directly to questions of how economies behave.[2]

Q: It is said that two decades of weather favorable to British agriculture before the middle of the eighteenth century affected the output of nonagricultural goods, especially manufactures. But it is not clear how. One historian has argued that good harvests cheapened food, therefore enriching city dwellers, and therefore increasing the demand for manufactures—and advancing the Industrial Revolution. Another has argued that good harvests cheapened food, therefore impoverishing farmers (the demand for food was inelastic, implying that a lower price gave lower total expenditures on food), and therefore decreasing the demand for manufactures—and retarding the Industrial Revolution. Arbitrate this dispute.

A: One decrease plus one increase equals zero. Both are partly correct, but both are taking a part of the nation (each a different part) as the whole. City dwellers were enriched, farmers impoverished. But the enrichment of one *is* the impoverishment of the other, offsetting in total effect: to the extent that one is made better off (paying less), the other is made worse off (receiving less). These analyses of the effects of good harvests, in other words, concern the shifting of Britain's left hand to its right. What is required is an analysis of the effect of her increased output overall (arising from the good harvests), not shifts in distribution.

Q: Good weather, like technological improvement, raises the production function of agriculture: at each bundle of inputs the resulting output is higher than it was before.
  1. How does it affect the production possibility curve between agriculture and all other goods?
  2. How does it affect the corresponding supply curves of agriculture and all other goods?

A: 1. The simplest way in which to answer (1) is to look at the two ends of the production possibility curve. At all agriculture the economy devotes all its resources to agriculture, and the higher productivity in agriculture has its maximum effect (see Figure 8.16). At all AOG, on the other hand, the higher productivity in agriculture has no effect, because there is no agriculture to be affected:

> "Shall we be trotting home again?"
> But answer came there none—
> And this was scarcely odd, because
> They'd eaten every one.

A 20% rise, say, in the output reaped from given inputs would have a larger absolute effect the larger was agricultural output initially. Therefore, the final curve is a horizontal stretching of the initial curve.

[2] The example is taken from Richard Ippolito, "The Effect of the 'Agricultural Depression' on Industrial Demand in England, 1730–1750," *Economica* n.s. 42 (August 1975): 298–312.

2. The answer to (2) depends on the effect of the stretching on the slope of the production possibility curve. Such smooth stretching—as opposed to rough stretching, which could leave the final curve in some irregular shape—affects the supply curves of agriculture and all other goods as follows (turn the book clockwise on its side to see the left panel). Refer to Figure 8.17. The lower supply of all other goods (i.e., the higher supply price for a given amount) is an inevitable result of the cheapening of agriculture. To put it another way, the new, higher productivity of resources in agriculture implies that employing them in all other goods has a higher marginal opportunity cost.

Figure 8.16
An Improvement in
Agriculture Pushes the
Production Possibility
Curve Outward

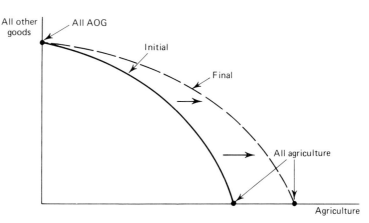

An increase of factor productivity in agriculture permits more agricultural products, in total, to be produced for any given amount of all other goods produced. The resulting shift in the production possibility curve can be equiproportional along the agriculture axis, as shown, or can be irregular.

Figure 8.17
Improvement in
Agriculture (a) Raises the
Supply of Agriculture (b)
and Lowers the Supply of
All Other Goods (c)

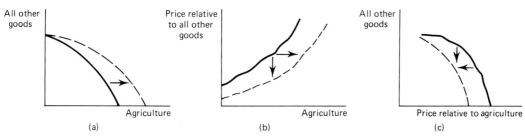

The outward shift in the production possibility curve along the agriculture axis affects supply curves as follows: more agricultural goods are forthcoming at any given price; fewer all other goods are produced at that price.

Return, then, to the historical question: what *was* the effect of good harvests on the demand for British manufactures and the Industrial Revolution? Suppose that manufactures are equivalent to all other goods. The effect of the good harvests on the whole demand curve is plain. Good harvests plainly make the nation richer, which means that, if manufactures are normal goods, the income effect will be positive and the demand curve will move outward. The effect on the quantity demanded in equilibrium, however, is ambiguous. The demand curve has moved outward, but the supply curve has moved inward, since manufactures have now a higher opportunity cost. In other words, the income effect works to increase the amount of manufactures demanded while the substitution (or price) effect works to decrease it. The supply and demand curves move in opposite directions (see Figure 8.18).

The net effect pictured here is a small rise. But the effect could easily be a fall or a larger rise. The answer to the historical question depends on the relative strengths of the income and substitution effect. And in any event the substitution effect serves to moderate the income effect. It can be shown, in fact, that the net effect was trivially small. Looking at the good harvests from the national perspective reveals that they had little effect on the coming of the Industrial Revolution.

Such are the uses of supply and demand applied to entire economies. You will sometimes hear it said that supply and demand are ideas applicable only to little markets for shoes, ships, and sealing wax in isolation. The jargon is that the model of supply and demand is a *partial equilibrium* rather than a *general equilibrium* one. General is not always better than partial equilibrium because the costs of complexity may exceed the benefits of accuracy and completeness. The main point here, however, is that the model of supply and demand can be given a very general interpretation, as a portrayal not merely of local events in the market for, say, shoes, but of the national links between shoes (or consumer goods or manufactures) on the one hand and all other goods on the other.

**Figure 8.18
The Ambiguous Effect of
Bigger Harvests**

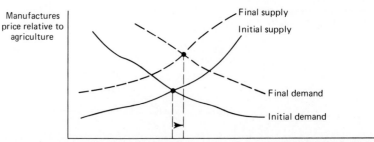

When the demand schedule shifts outward due to an increase in income and the supply schedule shifts inward due to in improvement in factor productivity in the other good, the effect on the quantity of manufactures is ambiguous.

Summary

The maximization of communal utility subject to the constraint of a production possibility curve is the same as equalizing supply and demand. In other words, even when people produce goods as well as exchange them, the point of equality of supply and demand is efficient. Supply and demand have economywide interpretations, the one as the slope of the economy's production possibility curve, the other as the slopes of utility contours along the production possibility curve. Supply and demand, in other words, apply to the entire economy as to single markets.

QUESTIONS FOR SECTION 8.4

1. Interpret the price-taking consumer's choice of equilibrium along a straight budget line as a choice of making the supply of, say, milk equal to (the consumer's) demand, in the style of Figure 8.4.

2. In rich countries over the last century, the birth rate has fallen. Children can be viewed as an item of consumption in which technological change has been small relative to that in all other goods over the last century. Show that, if the income elasticity of demand for children is small (say, zero, to take the simple extreme), then the small rate of technological change in child-rearing implies a fall in the number of children.

3. Suppose that Britain in 1750 faced a given international price of agricultural relative to manufactured goods. At the given price it could buy or sell any amount without altering the price. Exhibit in a production possibility diagram how Britain would choose its point of production and its (different) point of consumption. Identify exports and imports.

True or False

4. If the British economy in the eighteenth century were open to trade (see Question 3), it is more likely that good harvests would have raised manufacturing output.

<table>
<tr><td>

9

</td><td>

The Economics of Welfare and Politics

</td></tr>
</table>

9.1 The Economics of Ethics

☐
Why Bother with Happiness?

People are not satisfied with merely understanding how the economy operates; they want also to judge the operation morally, to say whether it is good or bad and to convince Bud McGrath next door of its goodness or badness. The invention of a type of wheat that is so short and stout that it can bear a very large number of grains without breaking will have certain predictable effects. Big farmers who are willing to buy the fertilizer necessary to get the larger number of grains will in the first instance make more money out of the invention than small farmers; the price of wheat will fall; India and Mexico, formerly importers as well as producers of wheat, will become exporters; and so forth.

Economists could if they wished confine their work to making such predictions of outcomes, leaving to moral philosophers or politicians or those in the street the task of judging the outcomes good or bad. There is a case to be made for evading in this way the responsibility for offering moral judgments as an economist, because (the case goes) an economist has no special wisdom about morality. Two reasonable people could agree on all the predictions of the outcomes of the "green revolution" in wheat yet disagree on whether the revolution was, on balance, a good or a bad thing. In this view, the economist refusing to go beyond prediction merely recognizes his or her comparative advantage. Economic argument and evidence could convince reasonable people of the truth of the "positive" (i.e., "what is") predictions, but economic argument and evidence cannot, it is said, end a "normative" (i.e., "what should be") disagreement. As Lionel Robbins put it in 1932,

If we disagree about means, then scientific analysis can often help us to resolve our differences, [but] if we disagree about ends it is a case of thy blood or mine—or live and let live according to the importance of the difference. . . . [For example] if we disagree about the morality of taking interest (and we understand what we are talking about), then there is no room for argument.[1]

[1] Lionel Robbins, *An Essay on The Nature and Significance of Economic Science* (London: Macmillan & Co., 1932), p. 134, sentences reordered. Quoted in A. K. Sen, *Collective Choice and Social Welfare* (San Francisco: Holden-Day, 1970), pp. 62–63, which is useful a (though advanced) discussion of the point.

180

Robbins and a long generation of economists after him, however, went much too far in distinguishing arguments about ends from arguments about means. For one thing, although arguments about what the end should be may ultimately be less easy to decide than are arguments about what the means in fact are, this is irrelevant to deciding the arguments at a stage short of the ultimate. For another, the materials for scientific argument are on close inspection similar to those for moral or aesthetic argument. That murder is evil and Michaelangelo's *David* is beautiful are no more or less true than that the law of demand is reasonable and that 5% is a good level at which to perform tests of statistical significance. Science is shot through with aesthetic and social judgments; morality is shot through with facts and logic.

□

Laissez-faire

The economist's brand of moral philosophy is called *welfare economics.* The central controversy in welfare economics concerns *laissez-faire*, a French idiom meaning "let things drift" or "refrain from interference," which has come to mean the policy of removing the government from economic affairs: no Federal Communications Commission, no health inspectors, no minimum wage, no antitrust laws. Because there would be little point to expressing a moral opinion about economic policy if no government was contemplating an intervention to implement the opinion (violating *laissez-faire*), much of welfare economics consists of arguments for and against *laissez-faire*.

The argument in its favor is by now a familiar one. Start with the premise that envy is not to be indulged, that the childish instinct to throw the candy down the sewer if not all can have it is to be resisted. The goal is to make each person as happy as possible without hurting other people. It would seem at first that such a goal would require the close attention of the prince, rushing about with his inspectors and police to make sure that laws ordering happiness (such as minimum wages and protective tariffs) and prohibiting hurt (such as factory safety regulations and laws against price gouging) were obeyed. Wonder of wonders, however, if people are merely permitted to exchange and if the exchanges take place under certain favorable conditions, the goal will be achieved with *laissez-faire*, without the prince's lifting a finger. As has been shown repeatedly in earlier chapters, at the conclusion of trade the distribution of goods will be efficient; that is, all mutually advantageous exchanges will have taken place. To revert to earlier language, people will be on the contract curve, along which no one can be made better off without making someone else worse off. Unexpectedly, then, the invisible hand will achieve with ease what the prince and all his guards, counselors, sheriffs, and servants could achieve only with difficulty.

□

Laissez-faire Arrives on the Utility Possibility Curve

The technical way of putting this is to say that well-functioning markets will put society on the *utility possibility curve*—a curve that is to the Edgeworth box in which two goods are allocated between Crusoe and Friday (the only two people in the society) as the production possibility curve is to the other Edgeworth box in which two inputs

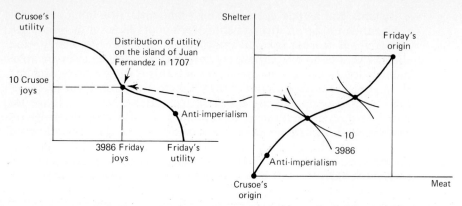

Figure 9.1
Laissez-faire **in a Perfect World Achieves Some Point on the Utility Possibility Curve**

The utility possibility curve shows the efficient combinations of Crusoe's and Friday's utilities. The points on the curve are efficient as they are derived from the contract curve; along the contract curve, the utility of one party cannot be increased without decreasing the utility of the other. This property of the contract curve also gives the utility possibility curve its negative slope.

are allocated between guns and butter (the only two products in the society). This is shown in Figure 9.1.

The curve slopes downward like the production possibility curve, but unlike it has no particular direction of bulge: along the contract curve Crusoe cannot become better off without Friday's becoming worse off, but because the measure of utility can vary from person to person, the axes can be stretched to achieve any bulge.[2]

A particular endowment of goods and bargaining skill will lead to a particular point on the contract curve and—what is the same thing—a particular point on the utility possibility curve. Any point on the curve is efficient, in the technical sense of making one person as happy as is possible without reducing the happiness of the other. As usual, then there are infinitely many social arrangements that are efficient, that is, infinitely many different points on the curve.

One could stop here, declaring good any society that achieved by free exchange some point on the utility possibility curve. Any point off it can be improved upon by mutually advantageous exchange; any point on it cannot. Such a society would not necessarily be noble or equal or just. But, to repeat the most modest claim, it would be efficient; or, to state the claim that is sometimes made, it would be free.

[2] Strictly speaking, the curve can slope upward too. If Crusoe, for instance, values Friday's utility, then a move along the contract curve ostensibly making Friday better off at the expense of Crusoe might in fact make Friday and Crusoe better off. Or Friday may be so badly fed that his work for Crusoe suffers, in which case both could be made better off by giving Friday more food. Compare J. de V. Graaff, *Theoretical Welfare Economics* (Cambridge: Cambridge University Press, 1957), pp. 59–63, for this and other finer points.

Another initial endowment of goods and power between Crusoe and Friday would lead to another point, on the curve, point anti-imperalism, say, with Crusoe worse off and Friday better off. The ethic of *laissez-faire* does not rank the two points. In its fullest form, it merely requires that the process of attaining a distribution of utility be mutually agreeable (peaceful, uncoercive, voluntary), not that any particular distribution be attained.[3] If Crusoe were a superb basketball player, for example, and Friday an avid fan, there would be nothing unfair by this standard about Crusoe's earning a million a year by charging admission to Friday (and Friday's fellow fans) to see him make slam dunks. The final distribution of income and even of utility (could it be measured and compared between people) might be grossly unequal, yet *laissez-faire* would not permit a redistribution of incomes that had themselves been achieved by just means. Justice in this view lies not in the distribution of income but in how the distribution is achieved.

Utilitarianism Chooses a Point on the Utility Possibility Curve

Over the past century and a half, however, an increasingly popular ethic alternative to *laissez-faire* has wished to go beyond life, liberty, and the pursuit of happiness. The ethic is that of *utilitarianism,* the doctrine that there is a social good achievable by balancing one person's happiness against another's. In other words, utilitarianism declares that the various distributions of utility between Crusoe and Friday can be ranked. Frequent talk of "the general will," "national interest," and "what's good for America" makes the declaration sound trivial, but on the contrary it is a controversial and significant moral step. The significance is that as soon as one takes it—as soon as one accepts the idea that Crusoe's utility can be weighed against Friday's and the two added up to get a number for social utility (which is to be made as large as possible)—then the positions achieved by free exchange no longer have a special moral claim. The government might now be justified in seizing a rich person's property to improve the lot of the poor; or for that matter, seizing the poor person's property to improve the lot of the politically powerful and rich. That Friday and his fellow fans freely chose to accept Crusoe's offer of a year of slam dunks in exchange for a million dollars is no longer very important. What is important is that Crusoe ends up rich and Friday poor, which is good or bad depending on how one values Crusoe's utility against Friday's.

The diagram of utilitarianism adds contours of a social indifference curve to the diagram of the utility possibility curve, valuing Crusoe's utility against Friday's (see Figure 9.2). The best point is bliss, the highest attainable contour within or on the utility possibility curve. The point *laissez-faire* would only by a wildly improbable accident correspond to bliss.

Social indifference curves are a representation of feelings about society (to which we will turn in a moment). It is difficult to have scientific

---

[3] As given, for example, in Robert Nozick, *Anarchy, State and Utopia* (New York: Basic Books, 1974), from which the athletic example following is drawn.

Figure 9.2
The Idea of Utilitarianism
Can Be Represented by
Social Indifference Curves

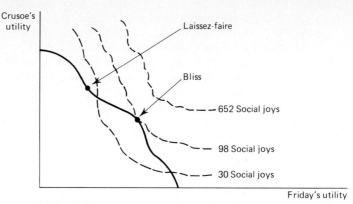

Utilitarianism seeks to maximize social joys, a function of individual joys. The optimum distribution of utility is located at the tangency between the social joys indifference curve and the budget constraint for the distribution of joys to individuals.

convictions about the size of unmeasurable and (in any case) incommensurate things, such as Crusoe's and Friday's level of happiness. The difficulty can be sidestepped by measuring money incomes instead of utility on the axes of the diagram, in which case one can compare different attitudes toward social utility.[4]

☐
***Shapes of Social
Indifference Curves***

With this amendment, the analogies with the theory of a single consumer's of utility are exact. The case of perfect complementarity, for example, is the social indifference curve for an egalitarian: any of Crusoe's income in excess of Friday's income is worthless, contributing nothing to social utility (see Figure 9.3).

Society's move from the position poor to the position inequal rich has no effect on social utility by this standard. As the leading modern proponent of such indifference curves put it, society is "perfectly just when the prospects of the least fortunate are as great as they can be."[5] At inequal rich they are not; a move to the perfect equality of equal rich improves the prospects of the least fortunate (Friday) and makes the increase in income socially useful.

The egalitarian curve is from one perspective generous: it is a generous millionaire who wishes to give away his millions. From another perspective it is envious: it is an envious pauper who begrudges every dollar of someone else's enrichment. The opposite indifference curves—either nongenerous or nonenvious depending on the perspective—are analo-

---

[4] The replacement of utility by income and the giving of moral weight to income depending on who earns it involves a logical flaw. Put briefly, it is that larger income for Professor North is not always better for him. If he gets the larger income by working much harder, then his net happiness may in fact fall. "Net happiness" (i.e., utility measured in dollars) must be on the axes, not income. This devastating criticism has not prevented people from using moral weights on income.
[5] John Rawls, "Distributive Justice," in P. Laslett and W. G. Runciman, eds., *Philosophy, Politics and Society*, 3rd ser., 1967, reprinted in Edmund S. Phelps, *Economic Justice* (Harmondsworth, England: Penguin, 1973), p. 328.

**Figure 9.3
Egalitarian Social
Indifference Curves Have
Corners at the Line of
Equality**

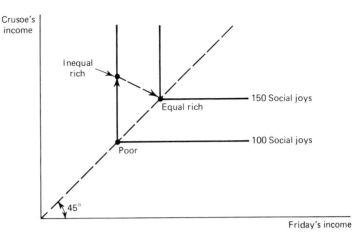

Perfect egalitarianism views the level of social utility as determined by the income of the poorest member of society.

gous in the theory of consumption to perfect substitutability. A dollar of Crusoe's income is exactly equal in social worth to a dollar of Friday's (see Figure 9.4). Point better is better than point worse because total income in dollars is higher, even though the move impoverishes Crusoe. That is, such indifference curves say that things are better when income is higher regardless of who gets it.

☐ **Laissez-faire
Demands More than
a Dollar-Is-a-Dollar**

At first glance, the dollar-is-a-dollar curve appears to be identical to *laissez-faire*, for if markets work perfectly *laissez-faire* will also lead to maximum income. All the resources in the society could be owned by slothful idiots uninterested in running the economy in a productive fashion but would come to be managed by whoever could use them

**Figure 9.4
In Social Indifference
Curves Blind to Inequality,
a Dollar Is a Dollar
Whoever Earns It**

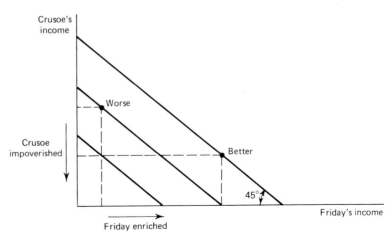

A utilitarian who views the level of social utility as being a function only of society's total wealth will regard Crusoe's and Friday's incomes as perfect substitutes.

the most efficiently. Valuing resources the most is achieving the most income. Therefore *laissez-faire*, like the dollar-is-a-dollar curve, recommends maximum income.

Laissez-faire, however, requires further that income be achieved by free exchange, not by theft or taxation. By contrast, the dollar-is-a-dollar indifference curves would register a social gain even if higher income were achieved by forcing people into collective farms and tractor factories by threats of violence. The very idea of social indifference curves, to repeat, is hostile to *laissez-faire*, because such curves value end states, not methods of achieving them. *Laissez-faire* concerns itself with how people behave (lawfully, uncoercively, etc.), not with how they end up (poor, unequal, etc.).

☐
Typical Curves

The social indifference curves that most people nowadays carry in their heads is described as follows.

Q: Draw typical indifference curves between incomes of Friday and of Crusoe for an observer who to some degree values equality (but is not a perfect egalitarian) and who also to some degree values high social income (but is not a perfect inegalitarian).

A: See Figure 9.5. Because the observer presumably does not care whether it is Friday or Crusoe who gets the higher income, the curves are symmetrical around the 45° line. A move equal to inequal rich now *is* socially useful; but so too is the subsequent move to equal rich. For any symmetrical inward-bulging set of indifference curves, both are true. Both equality and enrichment have value.

Figure 9.5
Common Shapes of Social
Indifference Curves
Represent Common
Opinion

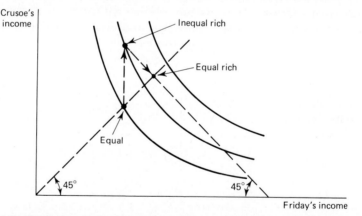

A social utility function in which both equality and total social wealth are goods is represented by indifference contours that are curved and, typically, convex to the origin.

Summary

"Welfare" economics is the economist's contribution to moral philosophy. The economist could if he wished abstain from offering an opinion on the happiness of society, just as an engineer abstains from offering an opinion on the desirability of a bridge that she is asked to build. The economist's opinion, it is often claimed, is merely an opinion, a matter of taste. Yet "normative" (what-should-be) economics, like art criticism or ethics, makes the taster more wise about tastes. For example, a taste for *laissez-faire* (i.e., "leave alone," do not use the government to interfere) implies that one favors allowing people to trade to an efficient point (a point on the utility possibility curve, getting the most utility possible for Crusoe given that Friday is not to be hurt). Such a taste makes no choices between one efficient point and another. Indeed, it forbids the government from intervening to make such choices.

An alternative taste is embodied in social indifference curves, that is, a characterization of how one feels about Crusoe's utility relative to Friday's (and Saturday's and Sunday's and so forth). The assertion that comparisons like this should be made is called utilitarianism. It includes a wide range of opinion on the social good, from egalitarianism to a dollar-is-a-dollar-regardless-of-who-earns-it. The analogy with the contrasting shapes of individual indifference curves for complements and substitutes is exact. But the more fundamental contrast is between *laissez-faire* and utilitarianism, between economic morality based on entitlement (the justice of how a distribution was achieved) and economic morality based on end states (the justice of what a distribution looks like, however achieved).

QUESTIONS FOR SECTION 9.1

1. Suppose that John D. Rockefeller achieved his immense wealth by providing good service at a low price not (as you may have heard) by underselling the competition, and then raising prices to monopoly levels. Suppose that he passed on his wealth to his children and grandchildren by legal and ethical means. Fabulously wealthy as they are, should the present Rockefellers be made less wealthy?

True of False

2. An end-state theory of justice could imply that it was morally admissable to compel Crusoe to perform slam dunks for Friday and his friends or to force Crusoe to pay taxes for the support of Friday.

9.2 National Income and Its Ambiguities

The Problem of Valuing a Shifting Bundle of Goods

□ Social indifference curves asserting that a dollar-is-a-dollar-no-matter-who-earns-it are the simplest imaginable ones and therefore play a special role. They achieve simplicity by merely sidestepping the hard ethical problem in economics, namely, that economies are made up of more than one person. They amount to reducing the measurement of society's happiness to the happiness of the typical person.

Consider, therefore, the question of whether David Galenson is better off in 1984 than in 1983, given the knowledge of the bundles of goods he consumes each year. If his utility function for food, housing, automobiles, books, and so forth were known, then one could simply insert the two bundles into the function and read off which gave more joys. But in practical terms his utility function is not known; only his observed bundles and the market prices he faces are known. If his consumption of every single good has increased between 1983 and 1984—gasoline, hot dogs, pencils, and everything else—the question of whether he is better off in 1984 is not very challenging. Obviously he is better off. But if his consumption of some goods has increased and of others decreased, the question is not so simple. Refer to Figure 9.6.

In terms of food, his real income has decreased from 1983 to 1984 (the amount of food has decreased); in terms of all other goods, it has increased. Simply adding together the tons or the numbers of foods and all other goods to solve the problem of weighting the increase in the one against the decrease in the other would be silly. Two oranges plus one living room couch equal nothing in particular. Yet this is how such problems are commonly solved in other contexts, such as that of measuring the amount of crime: the FBI's "index crimes" are all crimes of a serious nature and the number of them (one murder = one auto theft) divided by the number of people is "index crimes per capita."

□
**The Solution:
Relative Prices**

Economists have the advantage over other observers of society that the world sets in front of their noses a more attractive way of weighting one things with another to form an aggregate (of crime or power or, in this soluble case, income): namely, the relative price of the two. The solution is attractive because prices do measure the marginal value consumers put on, say, one unit more of food relative to all other

**Figure 9.6
Ambiguity and Its
Resolution**

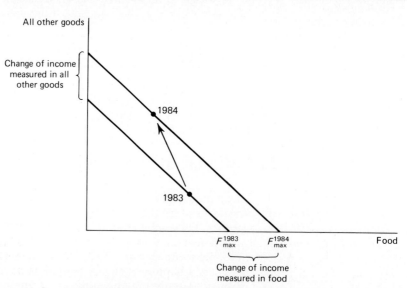

More of some goods and less of others may make the consumer better off, but need not. If prices are unchanging, however, a knowledge of prices and consumption bundles is sufficient to determine in which year the consumer is better off.

goods, because consumers are on their budget lines. Weighting goods by their prices can be viewed, in fact, as a crude (very crude) approximation to a utility function. And in any event it permits the two goods to be expressed in one intelligible unit.

If the relative price of food and all other goods has not changed between 1983 and 1984, one can simply express the bundle in terms of one of the goods, say, food, by adding the amount of food consumed to the product of the price of all other goods in terms of food and the amount of all other goods consumed, as was done in Figure 9.6. In the case pictured, income has increased over the year. The 1984 bundles is (revealed) preferred to the 1983 bundle, and real income therefore has increased. Indeed, one can say how much real income has increased, namely, by the distance bracketed on the food axis (or, in terms of all other goods—which can be translated back into food by multiplying by the price—the distance bracketed on the all other goods axis).

In the simple case of one person, then, the answer to the question "Can you detect an increase in happiness?" is "yes." The logic is that of revealed preference. The more difficult question of the *amount* in joys that happiness has increased is not, however, solved by this measure of the amount in dollars. That Galenson has 30% more dollars or the goods they buy in 1984 than in 1983 does not mean he is 30% happier, rising from, say, 100 to 130 joys. But the weighting of goods consumed by their prices does at least measure whether and by how much the budget line has moved outward.

□

Applications of the Measurement of Real Income

The idea of measuring the rise or fall of the budget line of the nation as though it were the budget line of a single person is a powerful one.

Q: Suppose that an economy produces and consumes two goods, energy intensive and all others. The sages of the community determine that too much energy intensive is being produced and order its production cut. Illustrate how income declines in a diagram of the community's production possibility curve and indifference curves.

A: The community starts at start (though see the comment following and refer to Figure 9.7). It finishes at finish, the edict requiring that energy intensive fall by this extent. Measured in the starting prices the finishing income is the lower dashed line. The decline in income must be expressed in one or the other good: measured in all other is one alternative. Saving energy is bad.

Comment

The implied criticism of the policy of cutting the output of the energy-intensive good is valid if the start is at start. But if the economy is indeed producing too much energy-intensive goods by the economy's criterion of a divergence between supply price and demand price—as at point distorted, perhaps because energy is underpriced (as a result, say, of another, earlier edict)—then an edict cutting the output of the energy-intensive good can be good for the economy.

Figure 9.7
Adding a Constraint Hurts
a Community

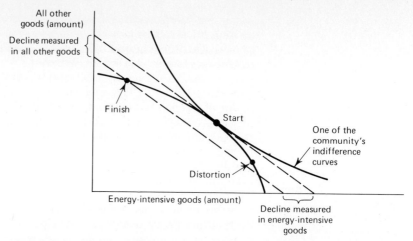

Constraining an economy initially at start to consume finish or less of energy-intensive goods causes a decline in national income measured in prices as they were at start.

The arithmetic of national income is the arithmetic of budget lines. The budget line is lower or higher depending on whether the sum of expenditures at some set of prices is lower or higher. In the United States over the past century, for example, the production per person of petroleum, paper, and rubber increased, while that of whale oil, hemp, and homemade tables decreased. To determine whether or not national income per person increased on balance, one must add up at the beginning and at the end the value of all goods at some constant set of prices. The outward movement of parallel (same-price) budget lines in a diagram (a many-dimensional one for many products) corresponds to a higher value of consumption possibilities, or income. The American sum expressed in 1975 prices rose from about $830 in 1840 (a real income per head roughly comparable with present-day Mexico) to about $7000 in 1975. Although output of buggy whips and flintlocks declined, the average budget line as a whole moved out by a factor of about 8.4.

☐ It can be said to "move out" across countries as well as across time.

An Application to
Comparisons
Between Two
Countries

Q: In the first decade of the twentieth century, the average working-class family in England and in America consumed bread, beef, and pork in the amounts per week given in Table 9.1. Americans, in other words, consumed more meat but less bread than did Englishmen. Suppose (contrary to fact) that bread, beef, and pork were the only goods consumed. Prices in England were 1.25 pence per pound for bread, 6.75 pence per pound for beef, and 8 pence per pound for pork. Which bundle—American or English—was best? By how much?

A: The weekly "income" (so to speak) of Englishmen is the amount they spend on the three goods; that is, 1.25 pence per lb × 22 lb + 6.75 pence per lb × 4.5 lb + 8 pence per lb × 0.5 lb = 27.5 + 30.38 + 4 pence =

61.9 pence. Similarly, the weekly income of Americans *in English prices* would be the American bundle evaluated at English prices; that is, $(1.25)(8.25) + (6.75)(6.75) + (8)(2.25) = 73.9$ pence. The American income is higher than the English income since 73.9 pence is higher than 61.9 pence: the American family consumed 12 pence worth more per week of bread, beef, and pork taken together. To put it another way, the relatively high American consumption of meat more than offsets (in view of the value that consumers put on meat relative to bread) the relatively high English consumption of bread. On balance, Americans ate $73.9/61.9 - 1 = 19\%$ more.

Table 9.1
Weekly Consumption of
Bread, Beef, and Pork by
an Average Working-Class
Family in England and
America c. 1900–1910 (in
pounds)

	Bread (bakery)	Beef	Pork
England	22.0	4.5	0.5
America	8.25	6.75	2.25

Source: Great Britain Board of Trade, *Report of an Inquiry . . . into Working Class . . . Retail Prices,* Cd. 5609, British Parliamentary Papers 1911, vol. 88, pp. lxvi–lxvii.

Notice that simply adding up pounds of meat and bread would be foolish—the equivalent of adding a murder to a car theft to get crime. By the pound "price" (one pound of sirloin equals in value one pound of grass), Englishmen are better off by $(22 + 4.5 + 0.5)/(8.25 + 6.75 + 2.25) = 27/17.24 = 1.57$, or 57%, and they could be made even better off by substituting still more bread for beef in hamburgers.

To be sure, there are prices alternative to the market price that make some sense (if not cents), for example, calories. For some purposes of comparison such as comparing body weights or the work a person can do, the caloric "prices" of 1250 per pound for bread, 1600 for beef, and 1800 for pork are relevant. For comparing the ability to satisfy desires, however, the prevailing relative prices are the only relevant ones.

☐
The Index Number
Problem

A very serious problem in all of this, however, is that prevailing relative prices change from one year to the next. To return to Galenson's consuming food and all other goods in 1983 and 1984, the question is, "Which relative prices does one choose to weigh the goods, 1983 or 1984?" There is no answer. Or to put it another way, one is free to choose either price. And relative prices might change so much that using one year's prices would not give even the same direction for the change in real income as would using the other. If the price of food rises enough between 1983 and 1984, for example, valuing the two bundles at the two different relative prices gives two measures of real income, one rising and the other falling (see Figure 9.8).

The distance A is the rise in income (expressed in real terms, in this case physical amounts of food) and B is the fall. Notice that the ambiguity comes out in revealed preference: at the prices actually observed in the years (the solid lines) neither the 1984 nor the 1983

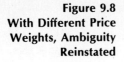

**Figure 9.8
With Different Price
Weights, Ambiguity
Reinstated**

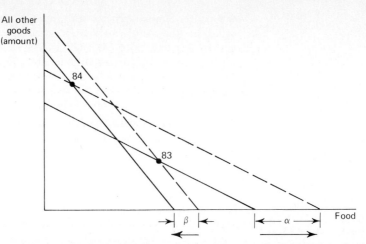

Income has either risen or fallen from 1983 to 1984, depending on whether 1983 or 1984 prices are used to measure income.

bundle is revealed preferred to the other. The ambiguity is *the index number problem.*

The problem is that an assertion made from one point of view (from the point of view of 1984 prices real income fell between 1983 and 1984) may be false from another point of view (namely, the prices of 1983). It is most serious when prices change greatly, as when comparisons of real income are being made over long stretches of time or between two very different countries. The English-American comparison, for example, used English prices to evaluate the bundles of bread, beef, and pork. The American bundle was 19% larger by this standard. But suppose that one had used American instead of English prices to evaluate the bundles in the two countries. Bakery bread, as it happens, was much more expensive relative to meat in America than it was in England, which would improve the relative position of the bread-rich English bundle. Indeed, it turns out that from the American point of view the English bundle was *better*, not (as indicated) worse, than the American bundle. The calculations are, using the amounts in Table 9.1 and the American prices (2.79 pence per pound for bread, 7.00 pence for beef, 6.50 pence for pork),

$$\begin{aligned}
\text{Value of English bundle} &= (2.79 \text{ pence})(22 \text{ lb of bread}) \\
&\quad + (7.00 \text{ pence})(4.5 \text{ lb of beef}) \\
&\quad + (6.50)(0.5 \text{ lb of pork}) \\
&= 96.13 \text{ pence}
\end{aligned}$$

$$\begin{aligned}
\text{Value of American bundle} &= (2.79 \text{ pence})(8.25 \text{ lb of bread}) \\
&\quad + (7.00 \text{ pence})(6.75 \text{ lb of beef}) \\
&\quad + (6.50)(2.25 \text{ lb of pork}) \\
&= 84.89 \text{ pence}
\end{aligned}$$

By this reckoning the English bundle is 13% (i.e., 96.13/84.89 − 1) *better* than the American, not 19% *worse.*

Taking a different point of view reverses the direction of superiority. And whether or not the superiority is reversed, it is in any case a different magnitude when different prices are used. Nothing could be more obvious yet more important. The index number problem is a numerical version of moral relativity, that different valuations produce different judgments of good and bad.

Laspeyres Uses Early, Paasche Late Weights

□ The index number problem can be given an expression in some jargon that will prove useful later on. An index of Galenson's income is said to be a *Laspeyres index* if it weights the quantities of food and all other goods by *early* prices (i.e., those of 1983 rather than 1984); it is said to be a *Paasche index* if, by contrast, it uses *late* prices (i.e., 1984). The jargon of Laspeyres and Paasche commemorates two pioneers of index numbers. Laspeyres is pronounced as though it were spelled in English "la spairce" (the second word rhymes with "scarce"); Paasche rhymes with "squash"; you can keep in mind which is which by noticing the "L" comes before "P" in the alphabet and that the Laspeyres index uses weights that come before Paasche's.

The usefulness of the jargon is that, in making the simplest of all comparisons, between two bundles, one must choose either early prices or late prices, and it is nice to have distinct tags for each.[6] Most indexes you will read about in the newspapers are in fact Laspeyres early weighted indexes because it would be inconvenient to change the point of view as each year became the late year. For example, real national income (or "real GNP" or "real income" or "income in constant dollars") is at present measured in the United States in the prices of 1972. A comparison of real income per head now and in 1972 would be a Laspeyres comparison: it views products from the relative prices of 1972, not of today.

Laspeyres and Paasche indexes differ and neither can be said to be the *correct index*. Indeed, "correct" in this context has a Laspeyres and Paasche ambiguity of its very own. The notion of a correct index of, say, Galenson's income between 1983 and 1984 requires indifference curves running through the bundles consumed in the two years. The percentage increase in income is then the difference between the two indifference curves, divided by the level. Using the prices of 1983 in Figure 9.9, for example, the rise in real income is the vertical distance *A*—the distance between the 1983 budget line and a budget line that at the 1983 prices would just permit Galenson to achieve the happiness he actually achieved in 1984. The percentage change is A/B (notice that α/β measured horizontally is in the same ratio; you can measure the change in income along either the food or the all other good axis).

But one might just as well use the prices prevailing in 1984 as the standard for constructing the tangency, using a Paasche instead of a Laspeyres measure of the distance between the two indifference curves, in which case the vertical distance Z would be the rise in real income.

---

[6] Mature reflection may suggest to you that in this case as in others the only merit of learning the jargon is that economists use it (rather than the simpler "early weighted" and "late weighted"). Such cynicism is a common accompaniment of maturity.

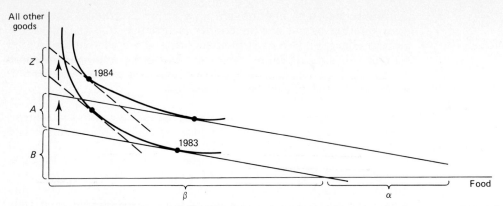

**Figure 9.9
The "Correct" Measure of
a Rise in Income Is
Ambiguous**

The increase in the consumer's welfare from 1983 to 1984 consists of the consumer's moving from a lower to a higher indifference curve. But trying to express this move in terms of an amount of all other goods leads to different amounts, depending on the prices used.

**Figure 9.10
The True Change in
Income Lies Between the
Laspeyres and the Paasche
Measures**

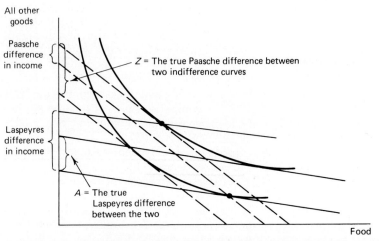

The Laspeyres and Paasche measures of differences in income between the two bundles bound the Laspeyres and Paasche measures of differences between the two indifference curves on which the bundles lie.

To put it another way, the "correct" indexes are measured from the budget lines of pure income effects, but there are as many definitions of the income effect as there are relative prices at which to compare two indifference curves.

☐
***Laspeyres and
Paasche Are Bounds
on the Truth***

In any case, Figure 9.10 shows that the ordinary Laspeyres and Paasche indexes of income lie on either side of these (two or more) "correct" measures. If you have calculated Laspeyres and Paasche indexes of the percentage change in Galenson's income between 1983 and 1984, you know at least that the "correct" measure is somewhere between the two. The Laspeyres difference in income is, you see, necessarily larger than the distance A; likewise, the Paasche difference is necessarily smaller than distance Z. So the Laspeyres index is an upper bound on the true change in income and the Paasche is a lower bound.[7]

Summary

Talk of America's well-being involves treating America as one person. National income does. It is the sum of all expenditures by Americans on bread, rent, car insurance, movies, shoes, schooling, roads, haircuts, and so forth. To compare two different years or two different places, the prices used to evaluate each thing must be chosen to be the same (i.e., 1975 prices chosen to evaluate income in both 1975 and 1840, or British prices chosen to evaluate both British and American expenditures). Comparing two bundles, therefore, involves comparing two parallel (same-price) budget lines: the higher one is the larger the sum. National income is simply the nation's budget.

But the choice of weights that must be made to add up quantities or prices into "real national income" or "the general price level" is arbitrary. It can be early or late weights (Laspeyres comes before Paasche in alphabetical order) or some entirely new set of weights. But the choice must be made: God or Nature or Daddy does not make it. The index number problem, in other words, is insoluble. You must adopt a point of view to look at something. It is childish to suppose that the looking is uninfluenced by the point of view.

QUESTIONS FOR SECTION 9.2

1. The production of grain (wheat, corn, rice) in the world in the early 1970s was about 1 billion metric tons selling at $170 per metric ton: the production of all other goods was 3200 billion units selling at $1 per unit. *True or false:* Since world income expressed in metric tons of grain was 19.8 billion metric tons of grain, the world could in fact have produced that much grain if it wanted to.

2. Comment on this headline in the *Chicago Tribune* for July 11, 1979: "Murder up 17%, rape 20%, but total crime off 4% here."

3. Bread, beef, and pork have natural units—pounds or loaves or whatever. But the method of comparing budget lines (i.e, index numbers) applies also to whole classes of commodities, such as manufactures, that have no natural units. Between 1859 and 1874 in the United States, manufacturing output increased by 40% per capita, while agricultural output decreased by 8%.[8] If the quantity

---

[7] This bounding of truth, strictly speaking, depends on prior knowledge that the Laspeyres index of the growth of income is larger than the Paasche. Normally it is.

[8] These and the statistics following are taken from Robert Gallman, "Commodity Output 1839–1899," in National Bureau of Economic Research, *Trends in the American Economy in the Nineteenth Century* (Princeton, N.J.: Princeton University Press, 1960), pp. 46–48, 54, 56.

of manufactured goods in 1859 is expressed as 100 manufacturing units selling at $1 per unit and the quantity of agricultural good as 168 agricultural units selling at $1 per unit, how large was the percentage increase of all commodity output (manufacturers plus agriculture) from 1859 to 1874?

4. The median income of families in the United States was $7000 in 1965 and $13,700 in 1975. The consumer price index went from 94.5 in 1965 (the year 1967 is defined to be 100) to 161.2 in 1975. What was the real percentage change in median income?

True or False

5. Opening trade increase national income.

6. If John Stuart's salary rises from 1985 to 1986 in the same proportion as does a Laspeyres index of his cost of living, then according to revealed preference he is better off after the rise.

9.3 The Economics of Politics

☐
Voting Is No Guide to the General Will

If everyone were a utilitarian and had precisely the same social utility function, say, "maximize national income" or "maximize the prospects of the least fortunate," then choices of government policies would reduce to mere calculation. The Council of Economic Advisors or the Lord High Economist would calculate the economic impact of a quota on Japanese steel (as against no quota), a deregulation of airlines (as against continuing the Civil Aeronautics Board), closing of the Naval Supply Station at Norfolk, Virginia (as against keeping it open), or a 5 cent rise in cigarette taxes (as against no rise) and then insert the implied change in the distribution of happiness among Tom, Dick, and Harriet into the social utility function. The council would then choose the alternative giving the greater social happiness, to the unanimous applause of the citizens.

But for better or for worse, no country has such unanimity. In other words, treating America as one person for purposes of measuring national income is not obviously acceptable. John and Laura may each have a social utility function, but they may not have the same function. Opinions about the social good differ. People disagree. Politics exist.

An enthusiast for social engineering might reply that this very politics will solve the problem of disagreement, because voting on the deregulation of airlines or the closing of the Norfolk Naval Supply Station reveals the general will. The reply sounds persuasive, but it is wrong. The arguments showing that it is wrong were discovered two centuries ago by a French philosopher, the Marquis de Condorcet, who pointed out that majority voting does not always lead to a decision, and when it leads to a decision does not always properly reflect the opinion of the voters.[9]

[9] See Keith M. Baker, ed., *Condorcet: Selected Writings* (Indianapolis, Ind.: Bobbs-Merrill, 1976), pp. 52–53; and K. J. Arrow, "Values and Collective Decision-Making," in P. Laslett and W. G. Runicman, eds., *Philosophy, Politics and Society*, vol. 3 (1967),

It is indeed not very surprising that a collection of people with varying tastes and interests cannot always agree. What is surprising is the gullibility with which people swallow the idea of the general will, identified as the simple majority or the vote of two thirds of the Senate or the edicts of a man on a white horse. Cavaliers and roundheads, democrats and fascists cannot be expected to agree. John Adams estimated that fully a third of the people in the American colonies during the Revolution were loyal to the British crown.

□

Market Solutions: The Theory of Dollar Voting

Economists as economists (thought not perhaps as democrats), then, are skeptical of the moral claims of majority rule. Someone will be outvoted, and there is no reason to give the minority's dissatisfaction with the outcome less moral weight than the majority's satisfaction. A decision to jail all communists would have pleased most Americans during the 1950s, yet would have displeased supporters of the Bill of Rights, not to mention the communists themselves. A decision to soak the rich is ever popular, but it ignores the rights of the rich to their riches. The decision during World War II to put 120,000 Japanese-Americans in concentration camps was acceptable to voters (of non-Japanese descent), Congress, the Secretary of War, President Roosevelt, and even the Supreme Court, but such a weight of opinion against the Japanese-Americans is no guide to justice.

The economist's usual guide is unanimity. If literally everyone agrees that a new road should be built from the main highway to Great Durnford, then it should be built. If everyone has a veto over the taxing and spending by the village government to build the road, then the case is similar to a free trade between two people, because the people affected, like the two people trading, can enter or not enter the deal voluntarily. A new road or other project is desirable if it makes someone (or many) better off without making others worse off, that is, if the project is efficient.[10] And in such a case, setting aside mere spite, everyone would agree to let the project go forward.

Unanimity is an absurdly strict test of a project's worth if no side payments, bribes, or vote trading are allowed. The new road could be a social bonanza, bringing a previously isolated village into contact with the wide world, enriching and enlightening everyone in the village—except the mule skinner, whose pack train was previously the only way out of the village and who is impoverished by the new road. He by himself can veto the road if unanimity is required, denying others the great benefits.

The solution, however, is simple. Allow the rest of the village to buy off the mule skinner. If the rest of the village gains from the road enough to share some of the gain with the mule skinner (enough

---

reprinted in Phelps, ed., *Economic Justice.* The best elementary treatment of the subject and the others mentioned in this section is Dennis C. Mueller, *Public Choice* (London: Cambridge University Press, 1979).

[10] Or in fancier language, *Pareto efficient* or *Pareto optimal.* The only point of the fanciness is to commemorate the role of the Italian sociologist and economist Vilfredo Pareto (1848–1923) in framing the idea clearly.

to make him happy with the outcome) and yet still has some net gain left over, then the project is mutually advantageous and should go forward. Likewise, a rule of unanimity—or, for that matter, even a strict rule of majority—would paralyze Congress if its members were somehow forbidden to trade votes. But with vote trading allowed, Congress is able to pass hundreds of bills a year, for better or for worse. The practice has bad-sounding names: vote trading, graft, vote buying, bribery, venality, log-rolling (you help roll my log, I'll help roll yours). But in fact the results can be good, selling a bill to the highest bidder and using the money collected to compensate the losers in the bidding. Voting without vote trading enriches the winners at the expense of the losers; voting with vote trading compensates the losers at the expense of the winners.

Bargaining in good faith under a rule of unanimity, then, makes politics into a market. It solves the problem of discerning the general will: the general will is whatever money can buy. It suggests that, if democracy (the rule of the people) is to be fair to minorities, it must become plutocracy (the rule of the rich), with the losers in elections by dollar votes being compensated by the plutocrats. Obnoxious as the argument may seem when put boldly, it does at least in the style of all such market arguments ensure the largest happiness from a given distribution of money (power), and it has some merit, furthermore, as a description of real politics (or, rather, *realpolitik*). The payment to losers need not be coin of the realm. Farmers wanting the votes of a shipbuilding district for a farm subsidy may bribe the senator or representative involved by promising to vote for a Navy contract to build two submarines in American yards. Indeed, the payments need not be selfish. If the people to be bribed, the shipbuilders, are for some unselfish reason filled with enthusiasm for the Salvation Army, the bribe may be a money contribution or spiritual support for the Army. Like ordinary exchange, with which it is now comparable in every detail, the political exchange need not be direct to achieve efficiency.

☐
The Vertical Addition of Marginal Valuations

The argument can be made more explicit by introducing the curves of marginal willingness to pay for roads on the part of the citizens of Durnford. An eight-lane superhighway is at one extreme of road quality, the blazing of a mere track through the forest at another, and the citizens have marginal valuations of road quality in between. For the mule skinner the marginal valuation may be negative; for the rest of the citizens it is positive but diminishing as more is acquired. Suppose that the road is a commonly consumed good in the sense that no one can be excluded from benefiting from it once it is built. National defense, public parks, police protection, and knowledge are similar goods. The society is unable or refuses to charge admission person by person to these services. Each person in the community gets the one level of service decided by the community as a whole.

Q: What, therefore, is the whole society's marginal valuation of road quality?

A: It is the vertical sum of all the individual curves of marginal valuation. In other words, a commonly consumed good is a good that jointly supplies services to each member of the community. Its demand curve is determined by vertical, not horizontal, addition.

Q: What is the efficient level of road quality?

A: It is the amount at which the marginal cost of road quality rises up to meet the diminishing marginal valuation of quality by the community as a whole, the point efficient in Figure 9.11.

Figure 9.11
The Best Road Is the One
Whose Marginal Cost Is
Equal to Its Marginal
Social Benefit

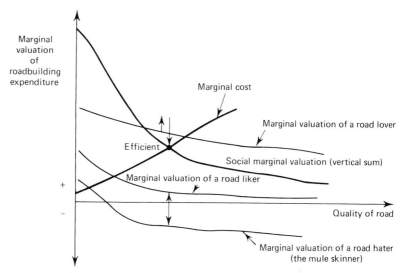

The social marginal valuation is represented by the *vertical* sum of the marginal valuations of three citizens, a road lover, a road liker, and a road hater. The point efficient is the one the society should attain if it accepts marginal valuation as a morally relevant measure of intensity of feeling.

If citizens were able to cast dollar votes, in short, the right amount of road would get built. <u>If politics is transformed into a market, it works like a market: efficiently.</u>

□
Flaws in the
Practice of Dollar
Votes: Extortion

Very well, if citizens would give and accept honest graft under a constitution requiring the unanimous consent of the governed for every public act, then no one would be coerced by the majority or cheated by the minority. Supposing for a moment that the original distribution of dollar votes were thought to be good (or that it could be made good by redistribution), then the voluntary reshuffling of dollar votes in compensation for losses would also be good.

As a description of politics in democratic countries this picture is useful, within limits. Citizens with very strong feelings about the military draft or tuitions at public universities can and do band together into pressure groups to bid for the attention of Congress in perfectly honest but expensive ways, casting dollar votes as though political votes were literally for sale. The flaws in the picture as a description are political convictions and the costs of banding together, costs that may be low for a group of American television manufacturers seeking a tariff but high for the much larger group of American buyers of televisions hurt by the tariff. In the absence of such flaws one could affirm that whatever public policy is undertaken is in fact the one preferred, on balance, by the people casting dollar votes.

But the charming picture of winners compensating losers in the economic game has flaws even as a prescription of how society should look. The nature of the flaws is suggested by the rarity of its central element, unanimous consent. Criminal trials by jury, certain club memberships, and a few other social decisions are made unanimously. All other decisions require something less than everyone's consent, from a two-thirds majority in the Senate to ratify a treaty down to Idi Amin's solitary consent to exterminate his enemies. Why? In Idi Amin's and like cases, the answer is brute force. Idi wishes it to be so. But even in free countries, the usual procedure is to coerce by outvoting the few (or many) opponents of a treaty or a police action or a tax. This is odd. Surely, one would suppose, well-wishers of humankind would urge that unanimous consent be required before a superhighway is built through a city neighborhood or before income taxes are imposed to pay for national defense. But the reason the well-wishers do not so urge is clear from the examples. One cantankerous householder (and therefore all householders) could stop a highway, claiming that her love for her house in its present location was worth $6 million to her. The point is familiar from the chapter on exchange. Since one's vote is essential, a rule of unanimity puts each person in the position of bargaining with the rest of the community. Unanimity encourages extortion.

Flaws When Commonly Consumed Goods Are Present: Lying

□

Furthermore, even if the procedure were not literal unanimity but merely dollar contributions for a commonly consumed good, there would be the problem of lying. A taxpayer paying voluntarily (supposedly in accord with his or her marginal valuation of the commonly consumed good) has an incentive like anyone in a bargaining situation to lie about that marginal valuation, putting it too high when the pollster comes to the door and too low when the tax collector comes to the door. The bargainer in the market stall does not tell you that he would actually be willing to sell the antique picture for $10; he tells you instead that, if he sells it for anything less than $50, his poor old mother will go without bread.

Competition with other sellers for customers—that is, the prospect of losing your dollars if he does not sell for the low price—is what in the end forces him to admit his true willingness to accept the low payment and brings the society to the correct amount of paintings sold. Likewise, the householder overstates how much he would be willing to accept to allow his house to be demolished for a road and the taxpayer understates how much he would be willing to pay for national defense. In these cases, however, there is no competition driving the householder or taxpayer to tell the truth. On the contrary, if the householder overstates the value of his house, he gets the large amount; if the taxpayer understates the value of national defense, other taxpayers nonetheless pay and he gets a free ride on the backs of his fellows. In the absence of some system to induce people to reveal truthfully their valuation of commonly consumed goods in the way that ordinary markets induce them to reveal truthfully their valuation of private goods, the existence of commonly consumed goods spoils the elegant theory of dollar votes as a prescription for social happiness.

☐
The Fundamental Flaw: The Smell of the Income Distribution

The most fundamental objection to using willingness to pay as a criterion of social choice, however, goes well beyond these practical difficulties. The objection is that your willingness to pay or to accept payment depends on how rich you are. John Kennan's willingness to accept a bribe in exchange for allowing the city to build a road through his front yard depends on Kennan's original income. If he is poor, he will presumably accept little, on the grounds that his marginal evaluation of the amenity of a nice front lawn is small when he would rather spend most of his pitiful income on food. If he is rich, he will only accept a large amount. The marginal valuations are dependent on the initial distribution of income.

One is driven back to judgments that unanimity was supposed to avoid, judgments about the ethical value to be put on John's income versus Tom's or Forrest's. A dollar is no longer a dollar, and total national income is no longer an uncontroversial way of testing society's happiness. Who gets what slice of the pie now matters, even if the whole pie becomes bigger. The introduction of the power loom into textiles in Britain in the early nineteenth century increased national income a great deal, but it ruined the livelihoods of the handloom weavers. True though it is that cheaper cloth made many people happier, there is no morally uncontroversial way of asserting that their happiness outweighed the misery of the weavers.

Economists sometimes try to skirt the issue by observing that the gainers from cheaper cloth could fully compensate the losers from less demand for hand weaving. Out of the proceeds of efficiency could come a fund for fairness, following the logic of dollar votes under a rule of unanimity. The important difference, however, is that it is hypothetical. *If* winners *could* bribe losers, then winning should go forward without restraint. In such a scheme the winners do not actually have to offer the compensation; they merely have it to offer should they wish. But the world is not obviously a better place if the rich *could* out of their new riches keep the poor from getting poorer *but do not*. Without some explicit judgment on the morality of the distribution of income, in short, measures of its size are only partial guides to policy.

The counterargument is that higher average national income is after all good on average. Taking the good with the bad, a person contemplating entering a high-income society or a low-income society would prefer the high-income society. Having no knowledge of Betsy Hoffman's ultimate position—making her choice behind ''a veil of ignorance,'' as this method of constitutional decision making is called—she would expect to do better on average as an American than as an Ethiopian.

The argument helps in framing rules of the game, not in determining the actual distribution of income between John and Forrest or weavers and clothiers. It asserts that in the long run a society with the rule "maximize income per head" will do better for the average person than will one with the rule, say, "keep incomes equal." In a sense, then, there is a democratic justification for the economist's fascination with income per head, a democracy among the unborn.

Only in a sense, however, for the present distribution of income continues to haunt the argument. The present distribution of income in society determines the demand curves, which determine the prices with which one evaluates the changes in national income. The very prices one uses to weigh together goods in national income smell of the distribution of the society's income. If the rich love large automobiles and distant beaches while the poor love beans and corrugated iron, and if the rich are very rich, then large automobiles and distant beaches will have high prices. The "society" will value highly things that a more equal society would value less. The problem is the index number problem in another guise. To evaluate a rise in national income using today's prices is to build in an opinion that today's distribution of income is an appropriate point of view.

□
The Moral

The hard truth about counting society's blessings, then, is that there is no perfectly satisfactory way in which to do so. It is nevertheless worth doing, if only to provide magnitudes against which to balance the uncountable. The staff of the Senate committee counts the cost of the proposed dam; that the senator decides that its high cost to the nation is small when compared with the uncountable enrichment of the good construction workers and ranchers of his state does not make the calculation of the cost irrelevant, merely less than decisive. The distant nation of Santa Americana experiences a doubling of per capita income, as counted; that the doubling leaves millions living in squalid huts in the chief city's garbage dump countably worse off than before and uncountable powerless besides does not make the calculation irrelevant, merely less than complete.

Summary

Despite their modesty on these points, economists have a great deal to say about social morality. Most of what they have to say is that there are no infallible guides to the social good. Voting is certainly no guide. And unless one accepts a utilitarian ethic that permits one person to be used as a means to another's end, the only guide can be unanimity, this being the only assurance that no one is hurt. At first the theory of dollar votes seems a promising extension of the rule of unanimity. It is in fact the moral premise that underlies much practical economic thinking, such as that exhibited in the next chapter. But it, too, is flawed. It depends on a premise that the original distribution of dollar votes is morally acceptable.

For this and other reasons, you should be skeptical of national income as an all-purpose measure of national happiness: it ignores the distribution of income and it treats the status quo (with its distribution) as special. Your skepticism need not paralyze all thought. The measure is not worthless merely because it is partial. The weather is not the only cause of a good or bad day, yet we all want to know the weather report. Average income is not the only cause of a good or bad society, yet we all want to know the nation's income.

QUESTIONS FOR SECTION 9.3

1. Three furniture moving companies, Ripoff by Regulation, ICC Incognito, and Highwayman, have pooled their business to make profits as a monopoly. They now sit down to divide up the spoils. A majority of three can determine how the spoils are divided. *True or false:* If there is no limit (set by an agenda, say) on the bargaining permitted, the majorities for one or another division will be cyclic; that is, the companies will not be able to agree on how to divide up the spoils.

2. In the United States, education through high school is supplied by local governments, with majority voting on the amount to be spent per pupil, collected through taxes.

a. Suppose a certain community has three social classes, U(upper), M(middle), and L(lower), each of which acts as a single person having different tastes for expenditure per pupil (depending on the average number of children in school for each social class, the importance of education to the social class, etc.). Suppose that U values educational expenditures most, M next, and L least. Show the three demand curves for expenditure per pupil. How do you construct the marginal *social* willingness-to-pay (demand) curve for expenditure per pupil from these three separate demand curves, recognizing that all members of the community must consume the same amount of expenditure per pupil (all the children go to the same school)? Draw this social curve, along with the three separate class curves, all on the same graph.

b. If the marginal cost of additional expenditure per pupil is constant, what is the socially optimal output of expenditure per pupil? Explain why. Draw this point on the graph of (a).

c. If the marginal cost is shared *equally* in taxes among the three classes, at what points will each class begin to vote against more expenditure per pupil? In general, will majority rule (2 out of 3 in this case, generally, 51%) produce the socially optimal expenditure? Explain.

d. Show how manipulating the burden of the school tax among the three classes could, given majority voting, yield the socially optimal output.

3. Suppose that two people, Harold Hawk and Donald Dove, are willing to announce truthfully the money value each puts on numbers of bombs used for the defense of their nation (of which they are the only citizens).

a. With 100 bombs in the arsenal, another bomb has a marginal valuation of $10 to Hawk, and $4 to Dove. What is the whole nation's marginal valuation of a bomb?

b. With 200 bombs another bomb has a marginal valuation of $5 to Hawk and zero to Dove. What now is the whole nation's marginal valuation?

c. If bombs for the nation's arsenal can be produced by sacrificing other commodities valued at a constant marginal cost of $10 per bomb, will 100 be too few and 200 too many bombs? Why or why not? Draw a diagram with marginal cost and marginal valuation that illustrates the socially correct number of bombs.

d. Show that, if bombs cost $10 each at the margin, then the only division of the marginal tax burden to pay for the last bomb that both Hawk and Dove will accept is a division according to their marginal valuations of the bomb.

True or False

4. Giving bribes to traffic police is socially speaking more efficient than is taking the consequences of a traffic ticket (i.e., having to go to court, pay a fine and court costs).

5. According to Question 4, therefore, we should encourage the police to accept and the public to offer bribes.

10

Consumers' Surplus

10.1 Consumers' Surplus: The Elements

Value-in-Use Is Higher than Value-in-Exchange

National income is a way, flawed though it may be, of measuring happiness in money. So too is *consumers' surplus.* In fact, as will be shown in the next section a properly measured change in consumers' surplus is the same thing as a properly measured change in national income. The root definition of "consumers' surplus," however, sounds very far from such mundane terms as national income. It is the money value of the willingness of consumers to pay in excess of what the market price requires them to pay. As George Stigler put it, "When a reflective man buys a crowbar to open a treasure chest, he may well remark to himself that if necessary he would have been willing to pay tenfold the price. . . . Marshall gave the odd name of 'consumer's surplus' to these fugitive sentiments."[1] The crowbar costs $5 but the man would have been willing to pay up to the entire value of the opened chest—$50 or $500 or $50,000. The excess—$45 or $495 or $49,995—is a measure of the man's gain from trade. The difference is between the money amounts of value-in-use and value-in-exchange, and in this terminology it has long been understood: *value-in-use* minus *value-in-exchange* equals *consumers' surplus,* which for voluntary exchange is always positive. The value-in-use always exceeds the value-in-exchange, simply because the most you would pay must always exceed what you actually pay, or else you would not pay. You buy a house for $40,000. Unless you are just indifferent between buying and not buying, the value-in-use of the house is larger than $40,000; if it were only, say, $10,000, you would not pay the $40,000 value-in-exchange to get it.

Q: The Chicago Fire of 1871 destroyed half the cubic contents of the city's buildings. The value of the surviving buildings after the fire probably exceeded the value of all buildings before. *True or false:* We see here the madness of economics, and of economies, which witness a rise in value despite a great calamity.

[1] George Stigler, *The Theory of Price,* 3rd ed. (New York: Macmillan, 1966), p. 78.

205

A: False. We see rather the ambiguity of the word "value." The value-in-exchange, which is what is meant in the second sentence, may go up, to be sure. But because the fire leaves fewer usable buildings the value-in-use, which is what is meant in the third, always goes down, in accord with good sense. The maximum amount that someone would pay for a house like the one at 1206 S. DeKoven St., say, $500, is unchanged by the fire. The market price might rise from $100 to $250, closer to the maximum amount, but the maximum itself is still $500.

Figure 10.1
A Fall in Supply Reduces
the Value-in-Use

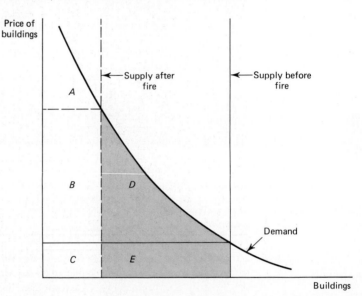

The decrease in the supply of building services increases value-in-exchange by *B − E* and value-in-use by *D + E*. Value-in-use falls unambiguously; value-in-exchange may increase or decrease.

The distinction between value-in-use and value-in-exchange is useful. It positively explodes in usefulness, however, when it is attached to a demand curve.[2] The problem on the Chicago Fire can illustrate the point. Interpret the demand curve for buildings as a curve of marginal valuation, that is, *marginal* willingness to pay. That is, its height is how much consumers will pay for each successive increment in buildings. The area under the demand curve, therefore, is the *total* willingness to pay, because adding up all the marginal willingness out to the amount of buildings will exhaust all the willingness. But the total

[2] The idea of doing so is commonly attributed to Alfred Marshall, but it is more accurately attributed to a French engineer, Jules Dupuit, "On the Measurement of the Utility of Public Works," first published in 1844, reprinted in K. J. Arrow and T. Scitovsky, eds., *Readings in Welfare Economics* (Homewood, Ill.: Irwin, 1969), reinvented for the English-speaking world by another engineer, Fleeming Jenkin, "On the Principles Which Regulate the Incidence of Taxes," first published in 1871–1872, reprinted in R. A. Musgrave and C. S. Shoup, eds., *Readings in the Economics of Taxation* (Homewood, Ill.: Irwin, 1959). That engineers invented it testifies to its use in evaluating engineering projects such as roads and dams.

willingness to pay is the same as the value-in-use: the total amount consumers will pay if all their willingness is extracted building by building is evidently the maximum they would be willing to pay in a lump sum to get the buildings. Or so at least we can assume until the argument is made more rigorous later. Now look at Figure 10.1.

   The value-in-exchange before the fire is $C + E$, the value-in-exchange after is $C + B$, and because the demand curve is inelastic it has risen. But the total value-in-use before is the whole area $A + B + C + D + E$; after, it is only $A + B + C$, a fall by the shaded area $D + E$. In short, the diagram captures the verbal argument that the maximum people would pay does not rise and that the burning of half the buildings does reduce (by the shaded area) the "value" enjoyed in this sense. Indeed, the diagram makes the verbal argument much clearer. The triangular area $A + B + D$ is the consumers' surplus from the buildings before the fire; the area $C + E$ is the income of building owners. The fire causes consumers' surplus to fall to merely triangle A, with some of the loss, B, reappearing as income to building owners and some, D, disappearing entirely.

☐
Consumers' Surplus Is Useful for Reckoning the Benefit of Public Projects

The idea that an area under a demand curve is a money measure of total happiness is astonishingly fruitful. The first fruit is a rule for constructing toll-free bridges, dams, post offices, railway lines, highways, and other public edifices for which there is no charge. Since there is no charge, there is no revenue by which to judge the usefulness of the edifice. Unlike a flower stand or an auto factory, the market does not toss up a measure of usefulness.

Q: Suppose that the city fathers of Boston and Cambridge contemplate building a bridge, the Lars Anderson Bridge, to link their fair cities across the Charles River. Suppose, too, that the clientele for the bridge for its life divides into three parts: 500,000 Harvard students, who each would be willing to pay $10 for a career of crossings (in view of the alternative routes); 1,000,000 townies, who would be willing to pay $5 each; and all the rest of the people, who would be willing to pay nothing and would require in fact some slight payment to go out of their way to cross it.
   1. What is the demand curve for lifetime permits to cross? If no price is charged for the permits, what is the number of people who will cross?
   2. How much would they be willing to pay, if necessary, to do so? What, then, is the total value of the bridge?
   3. If the bridge costs in sacrificed opportunities elsewhere $9,999,999 to build, should it be built? What if it costs $10,000,001?

A: 1. The demand curve is a stairway. At 500,000 the Harvard stair is used up and the marginal valuation falls down to $5 (see Figure 10.2). If the price is zero (no toll), exactly 1,500,000 Harvard students and townies cross.
   2. Each of the 500,000 $10 people would pay $10, which yields $5,000,000 from all of them; each of the 1,000,000 $5 people would pay $5, which yields another $5,000,000, for a total of $10,000,000 in willingness to pay, that is, in value-in-use (the value-in-exchange is zero if the toll is zero).
   3. If the bridge costs less than the money value of the satisfaction it brings

(i.e., willingness to pay), then it should be built. Otherwise, as when it costs a dollar more than $10,000,000, it should not. A society that indulged in such projects would fill in the Great Lakes for ski resorts or level the Rockies for farmland.

Figure 10.2
The Total Value-in-Use of a Bridge Is the Area Under Its Demand Curve

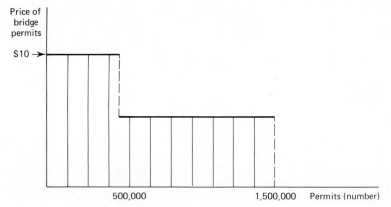

The social value of the bridge equals the sum of the amounts that individuals are willing to pay for bridge permits equals the area under the demand curve for permits.

□
Consumers' Surplus Is Useful for Deciding How to Charge for the Project

The method of value-in-use, then, is a guide to whether Mars landings, aqueducts, radar systems, and the like should occur at all. Of course, in many cases it would require the aid of a clairvoyant to know the demand curve to evaluate the projects. But the method gives general guidance to how they should be paid for.

Q: Suppose another crosser at 10 P.M. adds nothing to the cost of the Golden Gate Bridge in either replacement costs of the bridge itself or in inconvenience to others by crowding. Suppose that the cost of the bridge divided by the number of crossings that will occur over the life of the bridge is 50 cents. *True or false:* Therefore the toll at 10 P.M. should be 50 cents.

A: False. It should be zero, which is the additional cost of the crossing. The social purpose of prices is not to punish people, or even to achieve the apparent equity of making the beneficiaries of the bridge pay for it. The purpose is efficiency, that is, to induce people to use the bridge in a way that will maximize the value-in-use gotten from it and from the alternative uses of resources. For this purpose the relevant fact is that Molly McClelland as the extra crosser costs no sacrificed opportunities elsewhere. So McClelland should cross free. If her crossing wore off 8 cents worth of paint and bridge surface, it would be desirable to make her face this cost in an 8 cent toll, to induce her to forego the crossing unless it were worth in use at least the 8 cents of sacrificed opportunities it cost. But, if not, the cost of the Golden Gate Bridge incurred in the past is utterly irrelevant to this matter of *marginal* cost. By the assumption of the question the marginal cost is zero, and so should be the toll. The toll of 50 cents reduces society's happiness by the shaded triangle of willingness to pay (see Figure 10.3).

Figure 10.3
The Best Toll on a Bridge
Is Zero

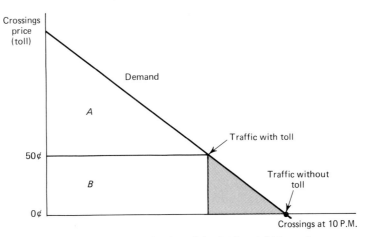

A zero toll maximizes the social value of the bridge. A higher toll causes a social loss, because it induces individuals to forego a quantity of crossings that would have rendered the crossers a positive benefit and would have cost society nothing.

With a 50 cent toll the *A* area still accrues to crossers as consumers' surplus (the excess of value-in-use, *A* + *B*, over value-in-exchange, *B*). The *B* area is the part of willingness to pay extracted from crossers and given to whoever owns the bridge. From the social point of view the crossings that still take place with a 50 cent toll cause happiness in the value of *A* + *B*. But the distribution of income is changed by the toll, shifting *B*'s worth of purchasing power from crossers to owners. The critical point is that the shaded triangle is sheer waste. Crossings not worth at least 50 cents do not take place, even though these crossings have some value and no opportunity cost. "The *distribution* of wealth among members of the community is affected by the mode of payment adopted for the bridge, but not the total wealth, except that it is diminished by tolls. . . . This is such plain common sense that toll bridges have now largely disappeared from civilized communities."[3]

☐
Producers' Surplus
Is Analogous, the
Producers' Gain
from Trade

Consumers' surplus, then, is the consumers' net gain from trade, namely, a triangle equal to their gross gain (the trapezoid of value-in-use) minus their cost (the rectangle of value-in-exchange). Consumers imply producers. A *producers' surplus*, therefore, ought to exist that resembles consumers' surplus. In fact it does, and like consumers'

---

[3] Harold Hotelling, "The General Welfare in Relation to Problems of Taxation and of Railway and Utility Rates," first published in 1938, reprinted in Musgrave and Shoup, eds., p. 158. He added: "But New York City's bridge [sic] and tunnels across the Hudson are still operated on a toll basis, because of the pressure of real estate interests anxious to shift the tax burden to wayfarers, and the possibility of collecting considerable sums from persons who do not vote in the city." Today 6 out of 19 roads off the island of Manhattan charge tolls, and all the roads to New Jersey do. Yet New York does not fall below San Francisco in civilization: all four of the bridges across San Francisco Bay charge tolls. As we shall see in the next chapter, however, assigning degrees of civilization is not quite so easy when it is realized that the taxation to pay for the bridges (if tolls are to be zero) itself creates triangles of net social loss under the demand curves for the taxed goods. It is a choice between two evils.

surplus is the producers' net gain from trade. Consider, for example, American exports of wheat.

Q: When the crop is poor and wheat is expensive in America, it seems reasonable to restrict American exports. After all, our own citizens should be fed first, shouldn't they?

A: False. Our own citizens will be best off when the trade in grain is free. The supply curve of wheat to the rest of the world slopes upward in Figure 10.4 because more wheat is producible only at the expense of ever more costly resources in shipping, growing, and the like; and because more wheat from a given production is suppliable to the rest of the world only at the expense of ever more valuable uses in consumption at home. That is, the supply curve is the marginal (opportunity) cost.

The shaded area, *C*, under the marginal cost is therefore the whole cost of supplying the equilibrium quantity, for it is the summation of all the successive increments to cost. The rectangle *C* + *S* is the revenue from selling the equilibrium quantity to the rest of the world at the world price. The unshaded triangular area, *S*, then, is the surplus of producers' revenues over costs. In a word, it is America's profit. In another, it is America's *economic rent.* In still another, it is America's producers' surplus, and it reaches a maximum when trade is free and the equilibrium quantity is sold. At a lower quantity the value of wheat is lower in America than in the rest of the world. Americans could do better in terms of their own valuation of wheat and all other goods by selling more wheat at the high world price. The all other goods they get more than outweigh in value to them the wheat they give over to the rest of the world.

Figure 10.4
Free Trade Maximizes
Producers' Surplus

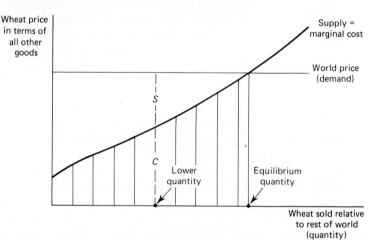

A quota on wheat exports prevents Americans from trading wheat for goods that Americans value more than wheat and thereby reduces producers' surplus.

The Two Surpluses
Together Show That
Free Trade Is Good

A generalization of the argument makes the familiar point that free trade is best and even shows how it might not be. Should there be a free market for motorcycles in Columbus, Ohio? Well, suppose that competition would drive the market to equilibrium in Figure 10.5.

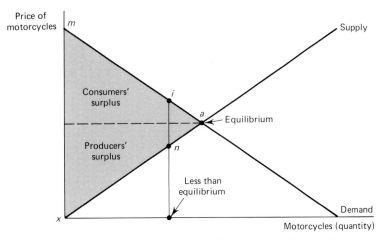

The point equilibrium, which will be reached by the free market, maximizes the sum of consumers' and producers' surplus. The quantity less than equilibrium would only be observed as a result of interference with the market. The social loss at less than equilibrium, relative to the optimum, is the triangle *ina*.

The sum of consumers' and producers' surplus is a measure of the entire gain from trade, the gain of student motorcyclists at Ohio State University plus the gain of Columbus motorcycle sellers. Equilibrium maximizes it. This fact is obvious for quantities less than equilibrium, because the big, shaded triangular area (bounded by the three points *m, a, x*) is chopped down to a trapezoidal area (*m, i, n, x*) of smaller extent. It requires a little proof for larger quantities. Suppose, just to be definite, that the market deal takes place at a point on the demand curve (not along the supply curve or along neither). What needs to be proven is that, at more than equilibrium compared with equilibrium in Figure 10.6, the undoubted gain by student motorcyclists of a large quantity and low price is more than offset by the consequent loss by motorcycle sellers.

The increase in consumers' surplus in the move from equilibrium to more than equilibrium is the horizontal trapezoid *A + B + C*. Is the decrease in producers' surplus larger, as it should be if more than equilibrium is on balance bad for society? Yes. The area *A + B* is the fall in revenue to producers on the old quantity of motorcycles. The old quantity still costs its old cost, but its revenue is less by *A + B* since the market price is lower. So surely producers' surplus (revenue minus cost) has fallen by *A + B*, for a start. Now the more quantity sells for revenue *R* but costs the vertical trapezoid *R + C + L* to produce. This unhappy fact is a result of the costliness of motorcycles. The result is an additional loss of producers' surplus of the little trapezoid *C + L*, the loss on producing and selling more quantity. So the whole loss to producers of moving to more than equilibrium is (*A + B*) + (*C + L*), which exceeds the gain to consumers (*A + B + C*) by the shaded triangle of *social* loss, *L*. Only at equilibrium is the social loss zero. And in view of the accounting by triangles, only

**Figure 10.6
Too Many Motorcycles
Hurts Producers More
than It Helps Consumers**

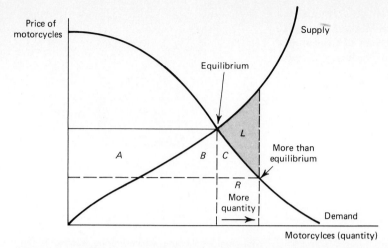

If more than equilibrium motorcycles are exchanged, the cost of supplying more quantity, as shown by the area under the supply curve, exceeds the benefit to buyers of more quantity, as shown by the area under the demand curve. A triangle L of social loss is the result.

there is the sum of consumers' and producers' surplus maximized, which was to be demonstrated. Equilibrium, in other words, is efficient.

Notice that, in the way of efficiency, equilibrium is not best for either consumers by themselves or producers by themselves. Consumers, for example, could do better if they could compel producers to give away the motorcycles; and short of such robbery they could do better, even if they had to stay on the producers' supply curve, by restricting their own purchases a little.[4] Equilibrium is best for "society," that is, for consumers and producers together on balance, not taking more from one pocket of "society" than is put into another. The quotation marks around "society" concede that the notion of a measurable social good sweeps a great mess under the rug, as the last chapter showed.

☐
***The Feasible Area of
Exchange Is the
Triangle of Surplus***

There is another way of exhibiting consumers' surplus and its uses.[5] The landlords of New Orleans, say, have a supply curve of rental housing upward sloping because more houses are expensive to build and because the landlords themselves can be enticed to live elsewhere at a high enough price. But the supply curve is a schedule of the *minimum* acceptable price for any quantity, such as small. Landlords would be pleased to get more than the price bearly acceptable to suppliers for the quantity small (see Figure 10.7).

So it is with other quantities along the supply curve. The whole vertically shaded region *above* the supply curve, in other words, is

[4] As will be shown in Chapter 17 on monopoly and in a question at the end of this section.
[5] The idea is Milton Friedman's in his *Price Theory* (Chicago: Aldine, 1976), Chapter 2.

Figure 10.7
Competitive Equilibrium
Exhausts the
Opportunities for
Mutually Advantageous
Exchange

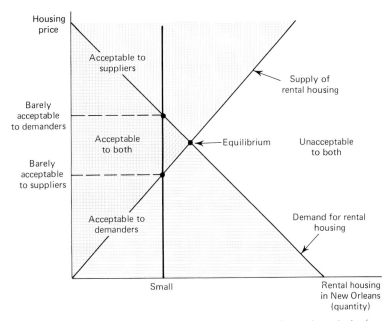

At equilibrium, the marginal landlord is willing to rent a house for exactly the amount that the marginal renter is willing to pay. A quantity smaller than equilibrium will leave mutually beneficial deals unmade; a quantity larger than equilibrium cannot be reached by purely voluntary actions of landlords and renters.

the region of deals acceptable to landlords. Tenants likewise would be pleased to get the quantity small at any price *less* than the price bearly acceptable to demanders, and the whole *horizontally* shaded region *below* the demand curve in the diagram is the region of deals acceptable to tenants. Putting the two areas together yields the cross-hatched area of possible deals compared with no deals (zero housing rented) that make both landlords and tenants better off. The cross-hatched area, in other words, is the area of mutually advantageous deals, and these are exhausted at the corner marked equilibrium. At equilibrium the mutually advantageous deals have been exhausted and to have larger quantities rented by landlords to tenants would make one or both worse off; at small the deals have not been exhausted, and to have larger quantities rented would make both better off.

Interference in Free Trade

The connection between consumers' surplus and this way of looking at curves of supply and demand is that the areas of mutual benefit are the same money measures as consumers' surplus. The shaded triangle in Figure 10.7 is a money measure of the inefficiency of staying at small.

Q: Suppose that the market for rental housing in New Orleans is in equilibrium initially and that at the equilibrium money price the government imposes rent control (i.e., making it illegal to offer or accept a rental above the initial price). Now suppose that the demand curve of tenants rises, perhaps because the population of New Orleans or the money income of tenants has risen. Describe the social loss from the rent control, assuming that it is enforced.

A: The old demand curve, which determined the old price, is the dashed line in Figure 10.8. Because the government forbids rentals above the old price, a landlord has no incentive to surrender more housing, and tenants are unable to express in money offers to the landlords their new and larger willingness to pay for housing. The shaded area is the money measure of inefficiency, that is, the loss to everyone—tenants as well as landlords—from making new deals impossible. Or, to put it another way, the shaded area is the sum of consumers' and producers' surplus foregone.

**Figure 10.8
Why Most Economists
Disapprove of Rent
Control**

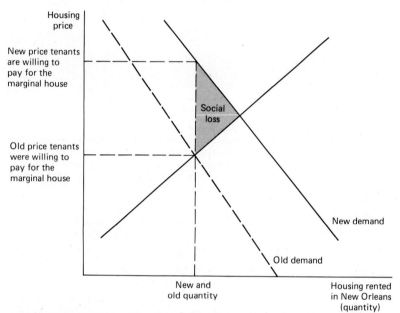

With a price ceiling of old price, suppliers will supply no more than new and old quantity. If demand shifts to new demand, society loses the value it would have derived from the increase in supply that would have occurred in an uncontrolled market.

Summary

Consumers' surplus is the excess of value-in-use (accruing to the consumers) over value-in-exchange; likewise, producers' surplus is the excess of value-in-exchange (accruing to the producers) over value-in-use elsewhere, as for example in use by the suppliers themselves. The expression "consumers' surplus" is sometimes used to stand for both surpluses. The two are the gains from trade to all the parties, that is, money values of the happiness gained over not trading money for houses or motorcycles or bridges. The sum of the two surpluses is the total social gain from trade and is maximized when the quantity traded is that of supply equal to demand. The idea is unremarkable. What is remarkable is its wide applicability to social questions, from free trade in housing and grain to the desirability of building bridges.

QUESTIONS FOR SECTION 10.1

1. "Some very capable engineers wanted to know what was the utility of the French roads, and starting from the datum that the prices paid by society for their use amounted to 500 million (francs) per annum . . . they said that since society consents to pay 500 million for these transport facilities, their utility is 500 million."[6] Are the engineers capable in economics?

2. The cost of electricity from a dam is very largely the cost of constructing the dam. Once constructed, the costs of opening and closing the sluice gates, repairing the generators, checking the security of the dam, and so forth are essentially trivial. If the demand does not crowd the capacity of the dam, the opportunity cost of an additional kilowatt-hour of electricity produced is essentially zero. Suppose that the cost of a dam is $30 million, that the demand curve for electricity over the life of the dam (expressed in the form of price dependent on quantity measured in 100,000 millions of kilowatt-hours) is price in dollars per kilowatt-hour = $0.04 − 4Q, and the dam can supply with no crowding all the electricity demanded of it. Should the dam be built? Measure Q in units of 100,000 millions. Price is measured in dollars per kilowatt hour.

3. Show with consumers' and producers' surplus that for a point both above the demand curve and below the supply curve for motorcycles (i.e., at a quantity other than equilibrium) the gain for one group to equilibrium is more than offset by the loss to another. Assume that demand plus supply curves properly measure all social benefits and costs. (Notice that the version of the problem worked in the text assumed that the deals took place along the demand curve. The present version complicates your analytical life by considering a deal off the demand curve and the supply curve, in which neither consumers nor producers are pleased.)

4. Consumers can do better than equilibrium if they can somewhat restrict their purchases from producers, driving down the purchase price enough to offset the loss of value-in-use from smaller purchases.

5. A motorcycle costs society and its owner the sacrificed alternatives of the steel, labor, and so forth that has gone into making it. But it also costs the sacrificed alternative of peace and quiet in the neighborhood. Unless Nick Lash is exceptionally public spirited, he will not, when he buys a motorcycle, include the cost of noise in the cost he reckons when deciding whether to buy. Show with areas of consumers' and producers' surplus how many motorcycles people will buy, how this number differs from the social optimum, and how much society as a whole (the aggregate of students, sellers, and the new, third party of people who sleep) is hurt by the difference. Think in terms of two marginal costs of various amounts of motorcycles, a *marginal private cost* (which the buyer faces) and a *marginal social cost* (which is higher at each amount by the value of sacrificed peace and quiet the neighborhood faces).

6. Show that, if motorcyclists foolishly underestimate the probability of killing themselves on the motorcycles, and would value motorcycles less from an informed perspective, then too many motorcycles will be produced. Identify the social loss.

[6] From Dupuit (1844) in Arrow and Scitorsky, eds., *Readings in Welfare Economics*, p. 256.

True or False

7. It does not matter for the portrayal of the market equilibrium or of the loss relative to the optimum from receiving it whether the cost of noise pollution from motorcycles is viewed as an addition to society's supply curve or as a subtraction from society's demand curve.

8. In the matter of loud motorcycles in Columbus, the hurt to sleepers exceeds the gains to producers and consumers from moving from the optimum point (viewed from supply, say) to the market point.

9. So long as the socially correct quantity of housing is somehow demanded and supplied (perhaps by compulsion), it does not matter at all for the maximization of the sum of consumers' and producers' surplus how the supply is priced.

10.2 Further Uses of Consumers' Surplus: Middlemen and Other Exchanges

☐

Middlemen Are Merely Transporters of Goods Across Time

Consumers' surplus is a fine tool for examining the goodness or badness of all manner of markets. Middlemen in commodity markets, for example, have always attracted suspicion. It is said that one who makes a living buying wheat or copper or hog bellies at low prices in one month and selling them at high prices in the next month (and sometimes in the next minute) is not making anything or doing anything. In the language of medieval regulation the person is said to be a "regrater"; in the language of ersatz economics the person is said to be a "profiteer." At one time or another, tulip bulbs, British government bonds, canals, sugar, coffee, cotton, export goods, building sites, land confiscated from nobles during the French Revolution, public lands, copper, foreign money, gold, buildings, commodity futures, stock options, and the ownership of English country banks, of the British East India Company, of foreign mines, of railroads, of joint-stock banks, of discount houses, of new corporations, and of old corporations have been objects of buying low and selling high.[7] An air of disrepute hangs about these markets. But it is not justified.

T or F: If the crop of coffee will certainly fail in 1987, the middleman's purchase of 1986 coffee to sell at an obscene profit in 1987 is socially desirable.

A: True. The middleman is a mere transporter of coffee. Coffee in 1987 will be more expensive than in 1986 if Teresa Baker does not transport coffee, and therefore she can make money doing so. In trying to make money out of buying low and selling high, to put it another way, the speculator plays the same role as someone trying to make money out of a difference in automo-

---

[7] The list is from Charles P. Kindleberger's *Manias, Panics, and Crashes: A History of Financial Crises* (New York: Basic Books, 1978), pp. 39–40. The book is a good one and a good antidote to the views on arbitrage, speculation, and the like expressed in the pages that follow.

bile prices between California and Illinois or a difference in wheat prices between Canada and China. For the same reason that ordinary trade across space is desirable, so too is trade across time. The pound of coffee withdrawn from consumption to be stored in 1986 is worth only, say, $2 a pound, emerging from the storehouse in the year of crop failure (1987) worth, say, $5 a pound. Since the demand curve in both years is the same (the consumers are roughly the same people), values such as these can be read off one curve for both years (see Figure 10.9).

Baker induces coffee drinkers in the good year to give up a little coffee that they themselves will value higher in the bad year. She induces them to do what they would want to do for themselves if they had the good information and good storage facilities she has. Value has been created by mere waiting, the difference between the tall and short columns of willingness to pay being the net gain in value.

Figure 10.9
Buying and Holding for
Profit

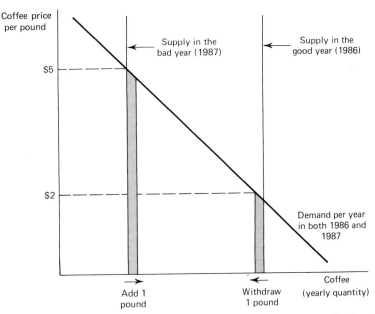

The middleman in coffee increases net social surplus by withdrawing coffee from lower-valued uses (consumption in the good year) and storing it for higher-valued uses (consumption in the bad year).

As Baker and her competitors continue to _arbitrage_ the present and future price (that is, to _buy in the low-price market in order to sell in the high-price market_), the prices and quantities converge. If arbitrage and storage have no costs, and if the future is certain, the process stops only when prices in the two years are equal, that is, only when quantities are equal, as at quantities arbitraged in Figure 10.10.

The larger shaded area $(E + F + G)$ is the gain to society from having more coffee in the bad year, and the smaller area $(H + I)$ is

Figure 10.10
Society as a Whole Desires
Stable Output

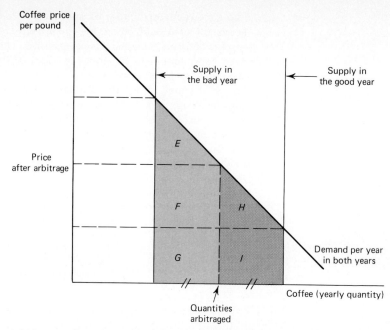

Arbitrage equalizes prices and quantities in the bad and the good years, if costs associated with storing coffee are zero. Society gains areas *E, F,* and *G* from arbitrage and loses areas *H* and *I.*

---

the loss to society from having less coffee in the good year. Since the larger area is indeed larger, if the demand curve slopes downward there is always a net gain from the middlemen. For the straight-line demand curve the gain is area *F.* In general it is *E* + *F* − *H* (since *G* and *I* are equal and cancel).

Another way of putting the point is to say that society as a whole gains from the stabilization of output. Who exactly gets the gain is irrelevant to the question of whether society as a whole gains. A monopoly of middlemen, for example, might be able to extract for itself all the net gain, by taking every dime of excess willingness to pay. But middlemen are people, too. They are part of the "society" that gains: who gains is a matter of distribution, not efficiency; of the ownership of national income, not its size. Usually the middlemen do not get all the gain, for they compete with each other in offering cheap good-year coffee to consumers in the bad year. In the extreme they get none of the gain, being paid only enough to bring them out of other occupations and into being middlemen. But whoever gets the gain, it exists. National income rises. Trade is productive, whether over space or over time, and the middleman who carries out the trade deserves two cheers and our heartfelt gratitude.

Such an analysis of arbitrage requires two comments:

1. The future is uncertain. Our gratitude would sour if the middlemen were wrong. If the harvest were in fact very good instead of very bad,

the stored coffee released in the good year would merely reduce the price further, causing a social loss relative to no storage rather than a social gain. The storage and resale would amount to transport from a region of scarcity and high prices to a region of abundance and low prices, the opposite of the desirable flow. Middlemen cannot always be right. Sometimes they will expect next year's crop to be bad, when in fact it will be good, leaving them (and society) with still more coffee in a year of abundance. Wrong arbitrage is bad. That middlemen are sometimes wrong, however, is not an argument for outlawing them. Unless someone else—God, the Department of Agriculture, or whoever—can do better, and supposing that the predictions are not usually wrong, a case can be made for leaving the middlemen alone to put their money where their mouths are. Unlike their critics, after all, they do back their predictions with their money. If they make money, then their predictions were on average right, and society is on average better off. If they lose money, then their predictions were on average wrong, and society is on average worse off. Exactly contrary to the teachings of ersatz economics, you see, the more profitable the arbitrage, the greater the good the arbitragers do for society. Profitability on average is the guarantee of goodness on average.[8]

2. Consumers alone would prefer to stop the middlemen. The details of the distribution of the gains are veiled when the analysis uses only vertical areas of willingness to pay, as it has so far. There is another way of looking at the question, using horizontal areas, that lifts the veil. It comes to the same result if done correctly. If done incorrectly, as it frequently is, however, it leads to strange results.

T or F: For a straight-line demand curve, the larger the amount of coffee already being consumed, the larger the gain to getting it cheaper and the larger, therefore, the increased consumers' surplus.

A: True. For example, consumers of the supply in the bad year in Figure 10.11 get only area $B + E$ in increased consumers' surplus if they are allowed to buy from the good year at the lower price after storage and sale: before they paid $B + C + D$ for coffee giving them $B + C + D + A$ in satisfaction, which left A in consumers' surplus; after they pay $C + F + D + G$ for coffee giving them $C + D + G + A + B + E$ in satisfaction, which leaves $A + B + E$. The difference—and net gain—is $B + E$.

In contrast, by the same reasoning a move from paying for quantities equalized at the high price to paying for supply in the good year at the lower price gives the consumers the much larger area $C + F + H$ in increased consumers' surplus. That is, the more they consume the more they like it to be cheap.

[8] The diagram used is, in truth, ill suited to speaking of goodness or rightness or anything else "on average." It contains no uncertainty about the future crop. The middlemen in such a case are perfectly certain in a good year that next year will be bad. They are in fact mere storers and transporters, not "speculators," for what speculation is there in a certainty? A small amendment to the diagram given as a problem, however, brings in uncertainty. The amendment is due to Bart Taub.

**Figure 10.11
Horizontally Measured
Consumers' Surplus Is the
Gain to Consumers Alone**

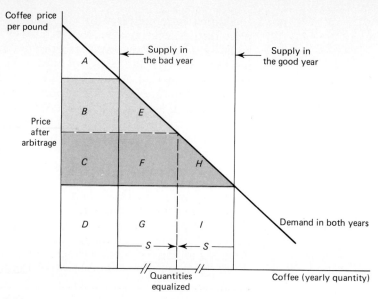

Arbitrage causes price to fall in the bad year and to rise in the good year. Consumers gain $B + E$ in the bad year and lose $C + F + H$ in the good year.

The strange implication of this argument goes as follows.

T or F: Far from wanting a smooth path of consumption, consumers will sometimes prefer to buy all the output in one year and none in the other.

A: True, which may explain the hostility of consumers to middlemen, arbitragers, speculators, and other movers of goods from low to high prices. With identical straight-line demand curves in two years, for example, the consumers get the most consumers' surplus when all the supply is shifted to one year, driving down the price in the year. The supply of 1986 shifted to 1987 causes the area hurt, but is more than offset by the area benefit (see Figure 10.12). The consumers by themselves would like to see coffee moved from a year of scarcity to one of abundance.

☐   But would anyone else like it to be so moved? No, they would not. Buying the amount indicated at high price and selling it at low price gives the emphasized area of loss. No one would engage in such a silly deal voluntarily. In other words, consumers will not be able to find suckers with whom to make the deal of cheapening cheap coffee still more by buying expensive coffee and dumping it on the cheap market. As Paul Samuelson has put it, the experiment would require an "outside Santa Claus."[9]

***A Solution to the
Apparent Paradox***

[9] Paul Samuelson, "The Consumer Does Benefit from Feasible Price Stability," *Quarterly Journal of Economics* 86 (August 1972): 476–493. His article is a correction of an influential article by F. W. Waugh in 1944 that made the error of leaving out the suppliers. See also B. F. Massell, "Price Stabilization and Welfare," *Quarterly Journal of Economics* 83 (May 1969): 284–298.

**Figure 10.12
Consumers Can Prefer
Unstable Prices**

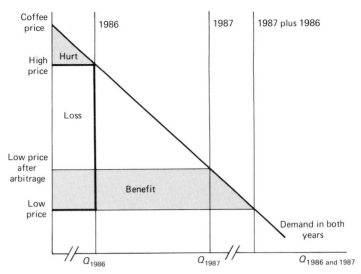

If all the coffee were sold in 1987 at low price, consumers would gain area benefit and lose area hurt. Consumers would gain if arbitrage did not occur, but arbitragers would lose area loss.

The key to the correct result is to include all members of society—a Christmas with mutual gift giving but without a white-bearded visitor in a sleigh. Someone owns the coffee. The gains or losses to people as consumers of coffee are matched by gains or losses to people as owners of stocks of coffee. The gains and losses include not only those on coffee stored and resold but also those on coffee held. If arbitrage causes the price of coffee to fall below what it would have been in 1987, the owners of a given amount of 1987 coffee are made worse off by having less command over resources than they would have had.

Figure 10.11 can be seen to contain such areas of gain and loss if looked at closely (see Figure 10.13, which reproduces it). Consumers in the good and bad years gain and lose the "horizontal" areas $B + E$ and $C + F + H$. To collapse the rest of society into one group, suppose that the original owners of coffee are the middlemen. Owners of coffee in the bad year lose through the storage and resale of good-year coffee the area B, that is, the reduced value of the existing coffee. Likewise, owners of coffee in the good year gain the area $C + F$, that is, the increased value of the coffee owned and consumed in the good year. They also gain the profit on storing the quantity stored and selling it at the price after storage and sale. The area is the two triangles $H + J$ or equivalently (since what is stored in the good years equals what is sold in the bad) the rectangle F. The complete analysis, then, adds up in both years all the gains (+) and losses (−) for both consumers and owners, as shown in Table 10.1.

The important point is that the net gain, $E + F - H$, is exactly the same as the net gain calculated earlier by attending to vertical areas of willingness to pay. The horizontal consumers' surplus amounts

Figure 10.13
The Gains and Losses to Owners

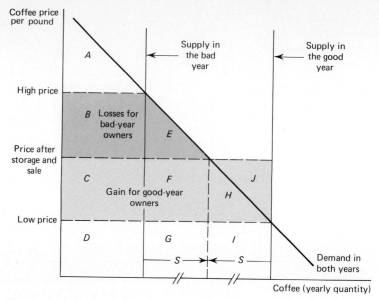

Owners, assumed also to be middlemen, lose area *B* by selling the bad-year harvest at less than high price and gain *C + F + H + J* by selling the good-year harvest at a price higher than low price.

to the same thing as the vertical consumers' surplus. The vertical analysis is appropriate when the question is one of income as a whole, the horizontal when the question is one of the distribution of income among various participants in the market. The method of vertical areas ignores the distribution of the gain but is simpler and more sure; the method of horizontal areas exhibits who benefits but is more complicated and easier to get wrong. Take your choice.

Other Sorts of Trade

The examples so far have involved trade across time. All the principles of using consumers' surplus vertically and horizontally can be illustrated for literal trade across space.

Table 10.1
The Balance of Gains and Losses[1]

To	Areas	Description
Bad-year consumers	$+B + E$	Consumers' surplus gained
Good-year consumers	$-C - F - H$	Consumers' surplus lost
Bad-year owners	$-B$	Inventory value lost
Good-year owners	$+C + F$	Inventory value gained
Plus	$+H + J = +F$	Profit on stored and resold coffee
Society as a whole[2]	$+E + F - H$	Net social gain from storage and resale

[1] Gains (+) and losses (−) from storage and resale.
[2] Add up all of the above.

Figure 10.14
Forbidding Exports Helps
Consumers but Hurts
Producers More

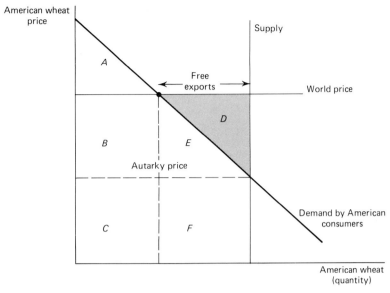

Consumers gain areas $B + E$ from autarky, but producers lose $B + E + D$. Alternatively, exports gain society $D + E + F$ in payments from foreigners but cost $E + F$ in opportunity cost of foregone consumption. Either way, free trade increases Americans' wealth by area D.

Q: A popular policy in times of unusual scarcity is to forbid exports. Thus, if wheat prices rise after a bad world harvest and American harvest, American consumers will clamor for restrictions on exports of American wheat to China or the Soviet Union. Suppose that the world price is given. Using both the horizontal and vertical approach to consumers' surplus, describe diagrammatically the effects of forbidding exports:

1. The loss the Americans as a whole.
2. The gain to American consumers.
3. The loss to the owners of the American wheat crop (after the harvest: ignore costs of production).
4. Compare (1), (2), and (3).

A: Figure 10.14 portrays a world price high enough to cause free exports if they were permitted. The perfectly inelastic supply curve expresses the costlessness of the wheat crop after it has been produced. Part (1) is best answered with vertical areas, for it treats the nation as one enterprise. The nation as a whole earns from the amount free exports the value in all other goods of the rectangle $D + E + F$ but would be willing to pay to use that quantity for its own consumption only the trapezoid $E + F$. The net social loss from forbidding exports, forcing all the supply onto the American consumers, is therefore the shaded area D. Part (2) is a question about the gain to one segment of society, and is best answered with horizontal areas. At the autarky price, consumers get $B + E$ more consumers' surplus. No wonder they clamor for restrictions. If the world price were lower, presumably the clamor would be lower as well. Part (3) is simply a matter of rectangles of revenue: at the world price the owners of the fixed supply get $C + F + (B + E + D)$; at the autarky price they get only $C + F$. They lose $B + E + D$ on balance. But according to (2), the $B + E$ portion of the loss is a gain to consumers. So—to answer (4)—the loss to American owners over and above what American consumers gain is the shaded area D. The vertical and horizontal methods yield the same result.

Summary

You are now equipped with a powerful tool, consumers' surplus. It can be used two ways, vertically and horizontally, but either way yields the same answer if the question is the same. The horizontal way emphasizes the distribution of gains and losses; the vertical emphasizes their size. The key to using the tool correctly is to include all the people you intend in the analysis. An analysis of middlemen that ignores owners of the coffee or copper or wheat, for example, will arrive at the result that middlemen are bad. But the correct analysis shows that middlemen—like other traders between times and latitudes—are on the whole good. Consumers do feel that middlemen are bad for them, and they are perfectly justified in the feeling. But consumers are not the whole of society; or, to put it another way, people play many roles, only one of which is the role of consumer. The whole of society includes people in their roles as owners. If you shift a stone from your left hand to your right, your left hand is relieved, but you as a whole are not. Staring fixedly at one hand or at one party to a transaction is a mistake if the question is about the whole body or body politic. A question about wholes requires an analysis of wholes. Consumers' surplus is the economist's way of adding up whole groups of consumers, owners, producers, and people in general.

QUESTIONS FOR SECTION 10.2

1. True speculation would involve uncertainty about the crop. This problem shows how to allow for uncertainty. Suppose that there are only two sorts of years for the coffee harvest, good and bad, the one twice as large as the other. Suppose now that you are in a good year and are deciding whether or not to store 10% of the crop in the hope that next year will be bad. Suppose that coffee can be stored only one year, at which point it must be sold. Suppose further that there is a 50:50 chance that next year will be bad. And suppose finally that the demand for coffee is the same straight line in all years.

a. You buy and store and sell next year 10% of this (good) year's crop, paying and getting money along the demand curve. Illustrate in a diagram how much you as a middleman make if next year is bad.

b. What do you make if contrary to your hope next year is good?

c. Answer (a) and (b) for the case of buying the next 10% of this (good) year's crop.

d. If you and your many competitors are neutral toward risk, at what point do you all stop buying up this year's crop to store and sell next year? Compare the result with that of perfect certainty about the future (i.e., the result of the earlier exposition).

2. The chance of next year's crop being bad was 50% in the last problem. If the chance were 25%, what would happen to the optimal amount stored?

True or False

3. If the demand curve for coffee is approximately a straight line, then the social gain from costless storing of coffee in anticipation of a perfectly foreseen bad crop is approximately half the difference between the unarbitraged quantities multiplied by half the difference between the unarbitraged prices.

4. If an anticipated fall of 10% in the wheat crop would cause a 20% increase in price along a straight-line demand curve without storage, allowing (free) storage to occur will increase world income by $(10\%)(20\%) = 2\%$ of the value of the wheat crop.

5. Consumers by themselves prefer instability in prices, even though society as a whole prefers stability in supplies (and therefore in prices).

6. If middlemen buy and sell all the coffee stored in accurate anticipation of a harvest failure at the price after arbitrage, then their profits are zero and the social gain is also zero.

7. If demand curves for a storable commodity are not straight lines, consumers might benefit (even strictly as consumers) from shifting output from a good year to a bad year.

8. For nonstraight, nonidentical demand curves in the good and bad years, middlemen will shift output from good to bad until prices are equalized.

10.3 A Change in Consumers' and Producers' Surplus Is the Same as a Change in National Income

☐

Surplus as a Tool in Cost-Benefit Analysis

Consumers' surplus measures the benefit side of costly projects. The railways of the nineteenth century, for example, were so beneficial and costly that many observers have believed they were the chief stimulus to economic growth. Railways were spectacular machines, built by giants and run by heroes, and it is therefore not astonishing that they have been thought to be epoch making. Stripped of their glamor, however, they were merely a cheaper way of moving some sorts of freight and passengers than the canals, rivers, and highways with which they competed. As a result of the coming of railways, in other words, the opportunity cost of transport per ton-mile or passenger mile fell.[10] One can think of the society, then, moving down the demand curve for transport, as in Figure 10.15.

The benefit from the coming of the railways is simply the horizontal area $B + D$, that is, the increase in consumers' surplus. Recall that areas in such a diagram are measured in units of all other goods. Before railways, the acquisition of $A + B + C$ in willingness to pay required the sacrifice of the rectangle $B + C$ of all other goods in opportunity

---

[10] This thought and its elaboration is due to Robert W. Fogel, *Railroads and American Economic Growth* (Baltimore: Johns Hopkins, 1964); Albert Fishlow, *American Railroads and the Transformation of the Ante-Bellum Economy* (Cambridge, Mass.: Harvard University Press, 1965); and dozens of similar studies in the economic history of transportation published since then.

Figure 10.15
The Iron Horse Is a Fall in the Cost of Transport, and the Fall in Cost Is a Rise in Income

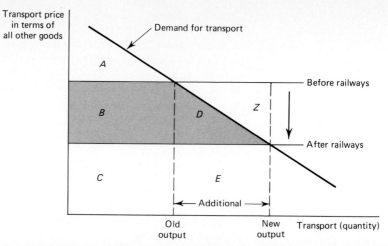

The social benefit of railways, areas $B + D$, is the net gain in consumers' surplus owing to the fall in the cost of transport. It is intermediate between B, which is the fall in price times the old output, and $B + D + Z$, which is the fall in price times the new output.

cost. After railways, the acquisition of the larger area $A + B + C + D + E$ required the shorter but broader rectangle $C + E$ of all other goods in cost. The net gain in consumers' surplus over opportunity cost is the shaded trapezoid $B + D$. To put the matter another way, consumers of transport got the old quantity at a cheaper price in opportunity cost by the amount B, and furthermore they got additional transport at the low bargain price after railways (for a benefit of D). The total benefit to society was the opportunity cost saving on the old output (namely, B) plus the advantage of buying additional transport at a price below its value in use (namely, D).

☐
The Change in Surplus Is the Change in Income

The argument so far has been mere embellishment of the idea that the sum of consumers' and producers' surplus measures the benefit from a new device such as the railway. Another way of measuring benefit is national income, and the similarity of vocabulary between surpluses and national income suggests a similarity in substance. As a matter of fact *national income goes up after the railway by exactly the same amount as does the sum of consumers' and producers' surplus.* That national income goes up by some amount is no surprise, since railways are a better way of transporting and transport is part of the bundle of things called "national income." But that it goes up by the amount of the shaded area of consumers' and producers' surplus in a diagram of demand and supply is a great surprise and requires proof, as follows.

Return to Figure 10.15. The rectangle B is the portion of the benefit coming from cost saving. Since the relative price is expressed in amounts of all other goods per amount of transport, the area is the additional amount of wheat, houses, iron, education, and all other goods the society can have if it can provide the old output at the low, after railways price. In other words, B is one measure of the increment to national income. It is merely one of many measures of income because it chooses one of many solutions to the index number problem. The opposite solution is to look at the cost saving from the point of view of the larger new output. The rectangle area $D + Z$ added to the rectangle B is the cost saving on the new (as opposed to old) output. If the new output had to be produced by before railway techniques, it would cost in foregone amounts of all other goods the whole rectangle $B + D + Z$. The two areas of cost saving (that is, B by itself and B plus D plus Z) are alternative measures of the increase in national income. But note well that the two shaded areas of increased income *bracket* the area of net consumers' surplus (the horizontal trapezoid $B + D$). Therefore, to perform the final twist, the area of net consumers' surplus is a compromise measure of the increase in national income, falling between the two alternative measures. In other words, to the accuracy allowed by the index number problem, the rise in consumers' (and producers') surplus *is* the increase in national income.

The two areas of cost savings, in fact, can be shown to be precisely the Laspeyres (early prices weighting output) and Paasche (late prices) measures of the change in national income resulting from a fall in transport costs. Take the Paasche as an example.

Q: Using the diagram of production possibilities between transport and all other goods (Figure 10.16), show that the area B (in the earlier diagrams) is the Paasche measure expressed in all other goods of the rise in national income.

A: To establish such correspondences one requires an up-and-down diagram familiar from earlier chapters. The steps are numbered. Put the diagram of supply and demand on top of the diagram of production possibilities (note that the lines are straight, to capture the constancy of opportunity cost).

The dashed line (marked 10) in the bottom panel is drawn parallel to the new, farther-out curve of production possibilities. The vertical distance marked C will therefore be the same as the area C in the top panel: the distance C is the old output multiplied by the new price of transport in terms of all other goods (in other words, the run multiplied by the rise over the run equals the rise, because the runs cancel out). By identical reasoning (the old output multiplied by the old price), the vertical distance marked $C + B$ is exactly the same as the area $C + B$ in the top panel. It follows that the differences between the two are equal. The emphasized vertical line B in the bottom panel is equivalent to the shaded area B in the top. B is B. But B in the bottom is the Paasche measure expressed in all other goods of the rise in national income, since it is the difference measured in prices after railways between the value of the before and the value of the after bundles of transport and all other goods. The area B in the top panel, then, is the Paasche rise in national income.

A similar proof applies to the other, Laspeyres, rise. The benefit from railways measured as consumers' surplus lies between the two measures of national income.

Figure 10.16
Laspeyres (a) and Paasche
(b) Measure of National
Income Are Upper and
Lower Bounds on the
Benefit in Consumers'
Surplus

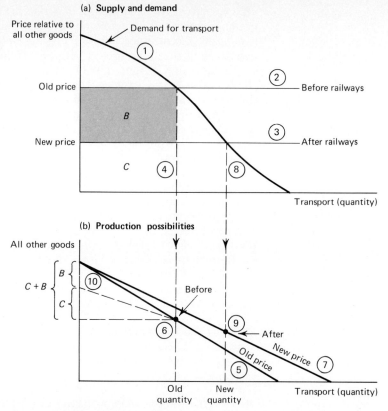

The Paasche measure of the gain in income due to a fall in price is area *B*, which equals the fall in price times the old output.

T or F: If American transport of crops was 1 billion units in 1890, if the price of carrying it without the railways would have been $0.50 more per unit than it actually was, and if American national income was $12 billion in 1890, then the increase in national income from the cheaper carrying of crops was 4.2% at most.

A: True. The statistics give the dimensions of the rectangle of cost savings on the after railway quantity of transport (that is, the large rectangle $B + D + Z$ in earlier diagrams). The area of the rectangle is 1 billion units of transport times $0.50 more cost per unit of transport equals $0.50 billion in more cost of transport without the railway. In other words, $0.50 billion was the cost saving from having the railway, or $0.50 billion ÷ $12 billion = 4.2% of 1890 national income. The increase is "at most" 4.2% because the rectangle is the larger, upper bound (the rectangle using the before railway quantity is the smaller, lower bound). With such methods, Robert Fogel was able to assert that in American economic growth during the nineteenth century railways were far from indispensible.

What makes the calculation simple is that you do not need to know the shape of the demand curve; to get an upper bound, all you need to know is the one point on it actually achieved in 1890. By assuming, so to speak, that the demand curve for transport was perfectly inelastic, you get an upper bound on the true rise in consumers' surplus. The question arises, "If you know the demand curve can you refine the estimate of the benefit?" Yes, you can, but the refined measures are ambiguous, and it is doubtful that the refinement gains much in the end. The bounding of the surplus by two measures of national income is the crudest but most important truth.

☐

Surplus Has the Same Difficulties as Income

The change in consumers' surplus, then, is the same as the change in income. It is not a more precise method demanding more stringent assumptions for its validity. One will hear it said that consumers' surplus requires the "constancy of the marginal utility of income" or some other more or less improbable-sounding condition to be true. This is false. Consumers' surplus is a true measure of social happiness to the exact extent as national income is.[11]

National income, of course, is a doubtful measure of social happiness. At the technical level, both national income and consumer's surplus must face the index number problem. At the moral level, unless a change in national income has been generated by a just society with just rules for making alterations in its affairs, a rise in national income—whether it is called a rise in income or a rise in consumers' surplus—is not morally decisive. But if the criticisms of national income apply also to consumers' surplus, so too do the replies: that a rise in the sum of producers' and consumers' surplus (to use the more comprehensive term) is morally defensible as the sort of change one might want to encourage from behind a prenatal veil of ignorance of where exactly in society one would end up when born; and that morally defensible or not, the rise and fall in the surplus is a statistic one would in any case like to know, the better to balance it against other considerations.

Summary

The change in consumers' and producers' surplus is a measure of the benefit from some innovation, such as the railway. The measure turns out to be, in fact, a compromise estimate of the change in national income caused by the innovation, lying somewhere between the Paasche and the Laspeyres measures of the change in national income. In other words, the change in the surplus *is* the change in income. It is not a more elaborate or questionable measure. It is questionable to the same degree as national income is questionable. And this is scarcely odd, because the two are the same.

---

[11] Compare A. C. Harberger, "Three Basic Postulates for Applied Welfare Economics," *Journal of Economic Literature* 9 (September 1971): 785–797.

QUESTIONS FOR SECTION 10.3

1. The total social benefit from a railway can be divided up among separate demanders and suppliers. It is clear that each of, say, two demand curves, one for the West and the other for the East, could be faced separately with the same fall in transport costs. Can they be faced with it together, in one diagram of western and eastern demands added together?

2. Prove that the Laspeyres measure of the rise in national income from the invention of railways is the cost saving on the after railway amount of transport.

True or False

3. Even if the supply curves of transport were upward sloping before and after the railways, the area of social benefit would have the same definition as with flat supply curves, namely, the area bounded by the axes, the demand curves and the lower and higher supply curves.

4. If the demand curve is a straight line, then the benefit from railways measured in consumers' surplus is exactly halfway between the Laspeyres and Paasche measures of the rise in national income caused by the railways.

Part Four

PRODUCTION AND MARKETS

11 The Firm

11.1 Whether and Why Firms Exist

The Firm Is an Agent for Other People

☐ A dark place in the picture of the economy drawn so far is that between single people and the whole economy. "The economy" or "the society" is said to choose between guns and butter; "a consumer" is said to buy butter from "a farmer." But in countries without central planning, there is no general will choosing guns or butter; and in countries with any complexity to their economies, there is little direct exchange between eaters and farmers. You do not trade, really, with the Iowa farmer Richard Zecher: millions of people are involved directly or indirectly to supply you with this or that grain of corn.

Between the economy and the individual stands the business enterprise or government agency or charitable institution: in a word—the economist's usual word—the "firm." The United States has 1 profit-pursuing business (usually a tiny proprietorship) for every 15 people. Federal, state, and local governments employ in countless agencies a fifth of the nonfarm labor force. Some 2700 institutions of higher learning enroll 8 million students. Each of about 7000 hospitals employs on average 400 workers. Only 7% of workers work for themselves: the rest receive a check as employees of some firm. The present chapter casts light on this hitherto dark firm.

But do not let the light blind you to the irrelevance for many purposes of the farmers, manufacturers, wholesalers, retailers, regulators, carriers, bankers, educators, and so forth put between you and Zecher. The firm is a mere intermediary; in the vernacular, a "middleman." Daniel decides to save some money for a rainy day, putting it in (loaning it to) the Hyde Park Bank and Trust. The bank loans some money to Margaret to buy equipment for her new law offices. Underneath it all, Daniel is loaning money to Margaret, even though we speak of "the bank" as making the loan. Likewise, Jacob Metzer grows an orange, sells it to a buyer in Haifa, who ships it to a wholesaler in New Zealand, who sends it by lorry to a supermarket chain, where it is bought by Lynn Jones. Underneath it all, Metzer is selling to Jones, even though we speak of "the kibbutz" or "the supermarket" making the sale. Again, Larry Westphal works nights at the plant that makes the engine for

232

the Oldsmobile sold to railway executive Steven Weiss. Underneath it all, Westphal is working for Weiss and Weiss for Westphal, trading hours of assembly work for hours of railway execution, even though we speak of Westphal working "for Oldsmobile" and Weiss "for the Milwaukee Road."

Looking at a firm without realizing that its personnel are agents of other people is a fruitful source of error.

T or F: In making rental apartment buildings into condominiums (i.e., apartments to be bought outright rather than rented) money-hungry bankers, realtors, and developers benefit no one but themselves.

A: False. These people, so detestably money hungry (unlike the former renters) do benefit themselves, but they also benefit the present owners of the buildings and the future buyers of the apartments. If they did not do so, they would not make money and their money hunger would go unsatisfied. They buy the buildings from the present owners without coercion: they resell them (improved or not) to the future owners without coercion. Both must feel that the deal is doing them a favor. The present and future owners may for some reason be less worthy of our concern than the present renters, but they are not nobody.

☐
The Wheel of Wealth

In other words, deals take place at one point on a *wheel of wealth*, but an economist must look around it. On the bottom of the wheel are households, to which everyone belongs; on the top are firms of various sorts (universities, grocery stores, government agencies, banks), which someone owns. Money payments go around the wheel in one direction, goods and services in another, as shown in Figure 11.1. Only the households really exist: the firms are merely legal fictions. The households own the firms, work "for" them, buy "from" them. Underneath it all, households are dealing with each other. To repeat an earlier formulation, "we has met the enemy and he is us."

Another use of the wheel of wealth depends on its balance. Since <u>firms are merely accounting devices to organize transactions among households</u>, <u>what firms pay to workers, landowners, and capitalists must equal what firms get from customers</u> (who are those same workers, landowners, and capitalists). A seller's income is the same as the buyer's outgo. The seller in this case, however, is the buyer. The resulting balance of the wheel of wealth, with $6000 per head of expenditures by American consumers equal exactly to their earnings of $6000 per head, is merely a restatement that income equals outgo.

The consequences are important. For example, contrary to a widely held opinion, inflation does *not* hurt everybody. The inflation in the prices of meat at the grocery store, automobiles in the showroom, and shelter from the landlord is met penny for penny by an inflation of incomes of butchers, farmers, grocers, auto factory workers, and landlords, among others. The inflation of outgoings that we face is offset by an inflation of incomes. We "is" the enemy, simply because we are buying from and selling to ourselves. In moral terms the hurt of

Figure 11.1
The Wheel of Wealth

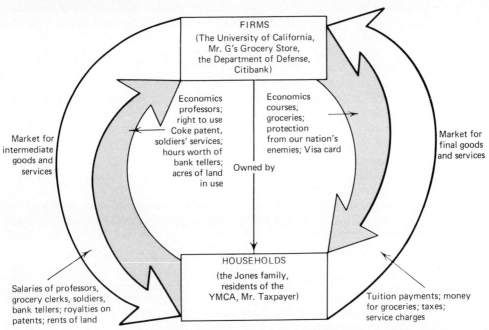

FIRMS
(The University of California,
Mr. G's Grocery Store,
the Department of Defense,
Citibank)

Economics
professors;
right to use
Coke patent,
soldiers' services;
hours worth of
bank tellers;
acres of land
in use

Economics
courses;
groceries;
protection
from our nation's
enemies; Visa card

Owned by

Market for
intermediate
goods and
services

Market for
final goods
and services

HOUSEHOLDS
(the Jones family,
residents of the
YMCA, Mr. Taxpayer)

Salaries of professors,
grocery clerks, soldiers,
bank tellers; royalties on
patents; rents of land

Tuition payments; money
for groceries; taxes;
service charges

Households earn income by supplying services to firms, which demand the services of households to produce goods that households demand. The process, although circular, is one of exchanges that are mutually beneficial.

inflation to the old woman on an fixed income in money is not balanced by the land speculator's benefit; but in money terms the two cancel. And wage earners, on average, have no legitimate complaint.

One must follow around the wheel the consequences of a shock. For example, a rise in meat prices that is a *demand pull* (consumers demand more) may look like a *cost push* if the rise is not traced to its source. Suppose that meat consumers demand more, perhaps because they have become richer, but the grocer does not at first raise prices to match. Meat supplies on the grocer's shelves will run out unusually fast; the butcher will order unusually large amounts from the supplier, who will order in turn unusually large amounts from the packer and, finally, the farmer. The farmer will only supply more meat at a higher price. The higher price will now be passed around the wheel of wealth through packer, wholesaler, and grocer. Each will believe, quite reasonably, that the rise in price came from "costs." No one, least of all the consumers and their outraged representatives, will realize that the rise came from the demands of consumers themselves. Firms hide the underlying transactions. The economist must look around the wheel of wealth to the households of farmers and meat consumers transacting with each other.

*Why Firms Exist:
They Are a Cheaper
Way to Do
Something*

☐ Economists habitually look below the surface of an institution to the relations among people that they insist are "underlying." If the habit is carried too far, however, it leads to the fallacious conviction that institutions are pointless, mere layers of middlemen clogging the market economy. The man in the street's version of the fallacy is as follows.

T or F: Because it can buy directly from the manufacturer, eliminating middlemen's profits, a large discount store can sell exactly the same air conditioner at a lower price than can a small neighborhood store.

A: In spirit, false. The middleman performs services (shipping, stocking, guaranteeing) that the discount store must either perform itself or not perform at all. If it performs them itself, then it earns the usual reward for the services in the price; if it does not perform them, then it is offering less of an air conditioner. An air conditioner without a guarantee, without service, without delivery is not the same as one with these things.

The existence of a firm suggests that it does what it does cheaper than some alternative institution. The discount store probably sells "no-frills" (i.e., no-service) air conditioners cheaper than does the local store; and both stores probably sell all sorts of air conditioners cheaper than the average unassisted consumer would be able to get them herself, directly from the manufacturer or, still more directly, from the makers of the steel and copper and plastic that go into the air conditioner.

One alternative to a firm, then, is self-help; but the more important alternative is a market. A market, as we have seen repeatedly, induces people to specialize and cooperate unconsciously; a firm also induces them to specialize and cooperate, but consciously. Firms in the midst of markets are "islands of conscious power in the ocean of unconscious co-operation like lumps of butter coagulating in a pail of buttermilk."[1] In economies in which workers may move to another firm at will, the conscious power of the manager of the firm over the workers is not complete. But within the limits of the contract to which the worker and manager have agreed, the manager is a little dictator, the boss.

The alternative would be a market in which, say, checkers and baggers at a grocery store contracted with the manager to do the checking and bagging for a fee, with the manager required to keep her nose out of their business. The butcher, likewise, could be an independent businessman, as could be the stockmen and bookkeepers. The grocery store could become literally a marketplace, like the central market in many European towns. That the alternative is not adopted suggests that in this case "the operation of a market costs something and by forming an organisation and allowing some authority (an 'entrepreneur') to direct the resources, certain marketing costs are saved."[2] In

---

[1] Dennis H. Robertson, *Control of Industry* (New York: Harcourt, 1923), p. 85, quoted in Ronald H. Coase, "The Nature of the Firm," *Economica* n.s. 4 (November 1937): 386–405, reprinted in G. J. Stigler and K. E. Boulding, eds., for the American Economic Association, *Readings in Price Theory* (Homewood, Ill.: Irwin, 1952). The view on the nature of the firm expressed here are Coase's.

[2] Coase, "The Nature of the Firm," p. 338.

other words, the costs of locating people to trade with on the spot (Is there a butcher in the house?) or of agreeing on a price for the particular service (What am I bid for an hour's worth of hamburger grinding today?) may make it worthwhile to hire employees by the month and order them about inside a grocery firm.

Summary

The firm is a clump of consciousness standing between households in the unconscious order of a market economy. Although usually confined to profit-seeking enterprises, the word "firm" and the economic reasoning that accompanies it is in fact also applicable to hospitals, charities, cooperatives, post offices, the Navy, Ohio State University, and the Memphis Fire Department. A firm does not exist independently of the people who own, work for, sell to, and buy from it. Households dealing with a firm are implicitly dealing with other households. The wheel of wealth exhibits the payments that housholds make for things from firms and the payments firms make in turn for services from households. One must look around the wheel to understand why taxing "business" is a tax on households or why a "bank" loan is really a loan from one houshold to another. Underneath it all (as economists say), Metzer deals with Jones, Zecher deals with Gordon.

But to say that the existence of the U.S. government or the local grocery store "does not matter" because "we own it" is an exaggeration. Of course it matters. The grocery store organized consciously does (presumably) a cheaper job of selling groceries than would a more traditional market organized by exchange. By contrast, a retailing industry organized by exchange into separate grocery, clothing, furniture, appliance, record, book, magazine stores does (presumably) a cheaper job of selling consumer goods than would an all-purpose local store organized by command. The presumption—by no means always true, but always worth considering—is that the firms that exist do the job best.

QUESTIONS FOR SECTION 11.1

1. Draw wheels of wealth for societies with
a. Households buying food from grocers, wholesalers, packers, farmers.
b. Households' savings deposited in banks loaned to business.
c. Households and firms buying importables from and selling exportables to the rest of the world.
d. Households paying taxes to the government and receiving government services.

2. What is wrong with the bumper sticker "Tax Corporations, Not People"?

3. Only bookstores, not individuals, can advertise for books in *The Clique,* the magazine of the secondhand book trade in Britain. One Mr. S. Murray-Smith complained in a letter to the *Times Literary Supplement* (June 18, 1971) that

What this in effect means is that the customer has to buy his book through two bookshops, rather than one: [the retail shop] . . . and the shop that sells to the first shop. He presumably has to pay two profit margins.

What is wrong with Mr. Murray-Smith's argument?

True or False

4. The nation's product can be measured not only by adding up the value of the goods and services produced for households but also by adding up the incomes of households as workers, landlords, and capitalists.

11.2 The Profit Motive

☐
What Does the Firm Maximize?

The theory of the firm asks why firms choose a certain scale of activity. Why, for example, does a farmer in Illinois produce 30,000 rather than 60,000 or 10,000 bushels of corn? The usual answer is that 30,000 bushels is the most the farmer can produce, the notion being that firms produce as much as they can. But the notion is surely false. The farmer could produce more by doing more—applying more fertilizer, working longer hours, hiring extra help—or produce less by doing less.

Likewise, as a mere matter of engineering, General Motors *could* produce more automobiles; the Army Corps of Engineers *could* build more dams than it does; the college of the University of Chicago *could* have 25,000 rather than 2500 students. Firms choose not to produce all they could. A farmer could run a farm in the intensely cultivated fashion of a city garden, getting 200 bushels an acre; he chooses in fact to run it like a farm, getting 100 bushels an acre. Why?

The answer obviously must depend on the farmer's motivations, that is, on his utility function, that is, on what he likes. He could like having lots of land, as the lord of a large domain; he could like the soil and its riches, cultivating deep; he could like to follow in his father's footsteps; he could like leisure; he could like independence; and last but not least, he could like having the things that can be bought with money. The making of money for what it can buy is the most powerful description of why people engage in producing for sale things or services, although other descriptions are possible and could form the basis of alternative theories of the business firm. They do in social sciences other than economics. Most governmental firms, for example, appear to be run for the nonpecuniary benefit of certain groups in the polity or of bureaucrats and politicians, not for making money—although, to be sure, the newspapers are filled with scandals consisting of cases in which they were directly; and indirectly the power exercised in government bestows goods and services. The motivations of governmental firms is the leading subject of political science. The motivation of other firms (by the economist's widest definition)—churches, armies, neighborhood clubs—is the leading subject of sociology. Economists, however, believe that the money motive is dominant for business firms and well worth mentioning, at the least, for other firms. In short, the farmer produces 30,000 bushels because at 30,000 he makes the most money.

Money-Making Is a Means to Other Ends

There is nothing very surprising about the assertion that an Illinois farmer farms for money. Nonetheless, the widespread feeling that money-making is nasty makes people uncomfortable with the assertion. Surely it demeans the nobility and dignity of humankind, they say, to attribute to it these base motives. "The age of chivalry is gone. That of sophisters, economists, and calculators, has succeeded; and the glory of Europe is extinguished forever." The distaste for money-making, indeed, is characteristically (and paradoxically) European.[3]

No member of European civilization or its offshoots much likes the idea that his dear old Uncle McClelland farming by Cayuga Lake in upstate New York resembles the purest definition of "economic man." It is some comfort to note that although "economic man is incapable of sympathy, benevolence or love. . . . he is also incapable of envy, malevolence or hatred. In short, he is splendidly neutral to others." Even the money-grubbing subspecies of *homo economicus* has this quality of neutrality.[4]

In any case it is a mistake, though common, to confuse the normative issue of the goodness or badness of money-making with the positive issue of its prevalence. In view of the confusion, the testimony of the money-makers often misleads on the matter of prevalence. You will hear a truck driver declaring that he does not work for money but for his family; or a lawyer that she does not work for money but for the good opinion of her colleagues; or an owner of a shoe factory that he does not work for money but for his own independence and for the well-being of his workers. The declarations can be honest and even true, yet can all be consistent with the pursuit of money. Money buys these things. Even when it is not the plain motive, then, money-making pops up.

Q: The hired manager of a large company, it is said, has little incentive to do what is best for the owners of the company. He wants power, prestige, a high salary, and other things for himself, motives quite different from maximizing the owner's profits. Therefore, the "separation of ownership from control" so common in the modern world is said to leave money-making (for the owners) a poor description of the working of the economy. *True or false:* If the manager gets power, prestige, high salary, and whatever else he likes by pleasing the owners, then the reasoning is false.

A: True. The business page of the newspaper is filled with reports of takeover bids and of the comings and goings of managers. Such events are examples of a market incentive to please owners. Even the allegedly passive owner of a few shares of stock in a large company worries about its value and

---

[3] Eastern civilizations are candidly materialistic, contrary to a widely held belief among Westerners that they are holier than we are. Contrast, for instance, the modest request in the Lord's Prayer for "our daily bread" to the prayer to Durga, the Mother Goddess of Hinduism: "Give me longevity, fame, good Fortune, O Goddess, give me sons, wealth, and all things desirable" [Nirad C. Chaudhuri, *A Passage to England* (London: Macmillan & Co., 1959), p. 178; see also his Chapter V, "Money and the Englishman"].

[4] David Collard, *Altruism and Economy: A Study of Non-Selfish Economics* (New York: Oxford, 1978), p. 6.

when he thinks the management of the company is bad he sells out (probably too late). When many passive owners do so, the fall in stock values makes it likely that there will be a takeover or merger by another company. In effect if not in law the owners hire and fire managers. However remote from the owners a manager seems in the organization chart of the company, the manager is forced by the market to be close to them in goals—making money for the owners.[5]

**Figure 11.2
How to Succeed in
Business Without Really
Trying**

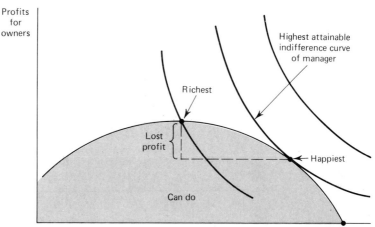

The owner of a firm usually cannot exercise perfect control over the firm's managers but can exercise partial control by tying the manager's salary or tenure to the firm's profits. A manager who likes to have a large number of subordinates will, if subject to this partial control, hire more employees than the profit-maximizing number but will not dissipate all the firm's profits in indulging her own tastes.

**The Agency Problem
Modifies the Profit
Motive**

☐ You should not take the argument just given as a conclusive proof that a manager of, say, Imperial Chemical Industries never works for personal aggrandizement and always works in the interests of its stockholders. Separation of ownership from control might be a serious flaw in modern capitalism. The question is answerable only by fact, not by mere logic. But the logic guides the search. One could ask how frequently in fact bad sales managers lost their jobs; or whether in fact a vice president's lust for power proved to be inconsistent with enriching the owners. Figure 11.2 embodies the logic.[6]

[5] This is the usual line of argument against the first generation of economic thinking on ownership versus control, a first generation represented by Thorstein Veblen, and by Adolf Berle, and Gardiner Means in *The Modern Corporation and Private Property* (New York: Commerce Clearing House, 1932) and, of late, J. K. Galbraith in *The New Industrial State* (Boston: Houghton, 1967).

[6] The analysis is that of Oliver E. Williamson, *The Economics of Discretionary Behavior: Managerial Objectives in a Theory of the Firm* (Englewood Cliffs, N.J.: Prentice-Hall, 1964), as summarized in Armen Alchian, "The Basis of Some Recent Advances in the Theory of Management of the Firm," *Journal of Industrial Economics* 14 (November 1965): 30–41, reprinted in William Breit and Harold Hochman, eds., *Readings in Microeconomics*, 2nd ed. (New York: Holt, 1971). Alchian's article is a good introduction to the second generation of economic thinking on ownership versus control.

Suppose that a manager, Teresa Baker, values the profits of the owners to some degree (or else she will get fired, replaced in a takeover, or passed over for promotion) but also values having large numbers of employees subordinate to her. She has, then, indifference contours in the profit-employees plane. When the number of employees is below the profit-maximizing level of richest, the manager's goal of moving up her hill of happiness is consistent with the owner's goal of higher profits; but when the number is larger the goals are inconsistent. The possibilities are represented by the can-do region in Figure 11.2.

The manager is happiest by moving to happiest, which gives her more of the pleasures of a large staff at the expense of lost profits for the owners. If the owners could at no cost detect and punish the manager for failing in this way to be a good agent, they could force her to run the firm at richest for them. The "agency problem" in economic life is precisely that the detection and punishment is costly. It is costly to stop managers from pleasing themselves instead of the owners, just as it is costly to stop government bureaucrats from pleasing themselves instead of taxpayers or to stop professors from pleasing themselves instead of students and other patrons of learning.[7]

☐
The Uses of the Hypothesis of Profit Maximization

Money-making, then, is not the only motive even in market economies. Especially in parts of the economy sheltered from the test of profit, the managers or workers can indulge tastes for a quiet life, comfortable offices, socially responsible behavior, socially reprehensible behavior, leisurely schedules, and people whom they like on the job. An amusing example from the sheltered parts is the former Department of Health, Education, and Welfare, which was found to discriminate against women (indulging a taste for working with men?), at any rate according to the peculiar standards the department itself applied to universities accused of such discrimination.[8] The matter of discrimination in the labor market will come up again. For the present it is enough to acknowledge the possibility of other motives in the activities of firms and then pass firmly (so to speak) to the fact, namely, that as a very good approximation firms maximize money profits alone.

T or F: The garment industry is fiercely competitive, and since prejudices are expensive to indulge, the garment industry is less likely than a sleepy monopoly to discriminate in hiring against Jews and blacks.

[7] Although such reasoning is widely accepted by economists, it is incomplete, as will become clear in Chapter 25 on labor supply. It speaks as though paying a manager partly in numbers of subordinates were an accident of the technology of detecting and punishing the manager's failures to maximize profits. In doing so it overlooks the supply of managers: if the manager can get employment in other industries in which total pay (both money and many subordinates, attractive secretaries, plush carpets, fancy bathrooms, and other perquisites of the executive suite) gives the same satisfaction as does happiest in the diagram, then the owners in the industry cannot do better than to let the manager stay at happiest. Otherwise the manager will leave. To put it another way, the cheapest way to entice a manager to do good for owners may be to pay him or her partly in nonmoney coin, and it may be the cheapest way even when it is easy to detect and punish movements away from richest.

[8] George J. Borjas, "Discrimination in HEW: Is the Doctor Sick or Are the Patients Healthy?" *Journal of Law and Economics* 21 (April 1978): 97–110.

A: True to the extent that the "fierce" competition forces the bulk of the firms in the industry to minimize money costs. One does not minimize costs by turning away every Jewish stockboy or black cutter who seeks employment on Seventh Avenue when they are skilled and inexpensive relative to the preferred group. The money motive is here the friend of the worker. And in fact the ethnic composition of the garment industry has undergone several transformations over the last century.

The question has this answer, in truth, by mere assumption: namely, the assumption that the firm's utility is simply money alone, not a function of money and the quiet life and the pleasures of command and the satisfaction of prejudice and so forth. But the assumption appears to be factually powerful. People do not rush into obviously unprofitable businesses; a rise in the price of wheat does induce farmers to grow more; money invested in various different industries does earn roughly similar returns in each. The facts do not always speak clearly, but they suggest that the simple utility function $U = \$$ is promising.

Many of the disagreements economists have with other observers of society turn out to be disagreements about whether or not things other than dollars significantly affect the utility of firms. The test of whether or not they do is simple. Could the firm make more money by behaving differently? In terms of Figure 11.2, the question is whether the firm is at happiest or a richest. Consider the following example.

Q: Historians have long believed that British managers in the late nineteenth century valued leisure and tradition excessively, neglecting innovations that would have been profitable in money. A leading example is alleged to be the neglect of cheap iron ore in Lincolnshire for making iron. The Lincolnshire ore in 1900 was half a shilling per ton cheaper than were the traditional ores. On the other hand, coke (a treated coal used in ironmaking) was 2 shillings more expensive per ton in Lincolnshire. If a ton of iron required 3.3 tons of ore and 1.5 tons of coke, could British ironmasters have made more money by using the Lincolnshire ore? Do leisure and tradition appear to have been important reasons for the neglect of Lincolnshire ore?

A: The difference in the cost of iron between Lincolnshire and the traditional locations is the lower cost of ore weighted by the ore required plus the higher costs of coke weighted by the coke required (−0.5 shilling)(3.5 tons ore/ton iron) + (2.0 shillings)(1.5 tons coke/ton iron) or 1.35 shillings per ton of iron in total. That is, the Lincolnshire location was more expensive, not cheaper, than the traditional locations (albeit only slightly so, for iron sold at about 40 shillings a ton). There is no need to call on any motive beyond money-making to explain the "neglect" of Lincolnshire in 1900: it was a worse place to make iron.[9] What is important here is the simplicity of the method for uncovering motives other than money-making: find out whether the location or technique actually chosen was the best for making money.

[9] See D. N. McCloskey, *Economic Maturity and Entrepreneurial Decline: British Iron and Steel 1870–1913* (Cambridge, Mass.: Harvard University Press, 1973), especially Chapter 4.

The second-guessing of decisions to see whether they were money-making is a common activity of economists, especially when they face historians or government officials or others doubtful of the single- and simple-minded rationality of their subjects. The discovery reported earlier that American slaves were held for business not prestige provides one example. The repeated findings of cold-blooded profit making in the decisions of allegedly irrational peasants in poor countries provide many others.[10] Money-making is more common than most people would like to believe. The economists must defer to the facts, of course, as they do in the case of the typical large landowner in eighteenth-century England. That his investment in a large estate earned only 2% in money when equally secure investments elsewhere were earning 5% implies that the landlord earned the value of 3% in nonmonetary prestige and power from his estate. Yet even in such cases, you see, the simple logic of money-making proves useful, for it allows one to measure in money terms the value of nonmonetary motives. Nonmonetary motives leave measurable footprints in the snow of making money.

Summary

The question of why the owner of a firm does what he does is a question of what his utility function is and what constraints he faces. The constraints are the subject of the next section. The simplest and most powerful choice for the utility function of most business firms is money profit. Only a miser or a coin collector values the coin for itself; but the coin can buy power, prestige, comfort, safety—things most people value. Managers of firms may choose to pursue power and prestige directly, at the sacrifice of maximum money profits, just as they may indulge a taste for workers of a certain race or a taste for an easy life. If they do so, the simplicity of the theory is spoiled, though the simplest theory still provides a standard against which to measure how much they value nonpecuniary rewards.

11.3   Marginal Cost: Why the Firm Produces What It Produces

A Firm Follows the Rule of Rational Life

☐ Money-making, then, is the economist's first, best explanation of buying, hiring, manufacturing, transporting, stocking, advertising, and selling by the business firm. This is part of the answer to the question posed by the theory of the firm: a firm does these things because it wants to make money. The rest of the answer tells why it does them in the amounts it does, why exactly the farmer produces 30,000 rather than 60,000 bushels. The answer is an application of the same principle applied earlier to consumers, the rule of rational life. The rule is, you recall, to pursue an activity until its marginal benefit is equal to its marginal cost. The marginal benefit of an Illinois farmer's growing another bushel of grain is the price the farmer gets for the bushel; the marginal cost is by definition the change in the farmer's total

---

[10] See Samuel Popkin, *The Rational Peasant* (Berkeley: University of California Press, 1979), especially Chapter 1.

costs caused by growing the additional bushel. The farmer produces 30,000 bushels, then, because at 30,000 the marginal cost is equal to the marginal benefit. Diagrammatically, at 30,000 bushels the farmer's marginal cost and marginal benefit curves cross (see Figure 11.3).

The diagrammatic reasoning in detail is as follows. A familiar truth about marginal curves is that the cost of producing the first unit (given that the farm is in existence) is the area 1 in the middle panel of Figure 11.3; the cost of the second is 2, of the third 3, and so forth, the whole cost being therefore the sum of all these areas. That is, the area under the *marginal cost* out to the quantity produced in, the diagram is the whole cost of that output (except for land rents, license fees, repayment of loans, and other fixed costs that do not vary with output). The rectangular area under the *marginal revenue* curve is the whole revenue, that is, price times quantity produced. Therefore the shaded area profit is just that (except for fixed costs): it is the whole revenue minus the whole cost. Producing too small or too large leaves a positive area of profit foregone (although there is still some profit) or a negative area of loss incurred (offsetting to some degree the area of profit).

The simplest way in which to see that just right is just right is to note that anywhere else a change in quantity produced can make more money. At too small the marginal revenue from more output is more than the marginal cost: a larger quantity will make money. At too large the marginal revenue is less than the marginal cost: a smaller quantity will save money, costs falling by marginal costs and revenues

Figure 11.3
Marginal Revenue Equals
Marginal Cost and Makes
the Most Profit

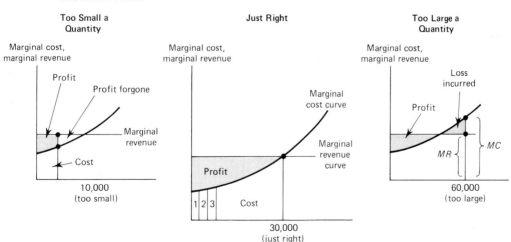

The firm that produces too small an output sacrifices potential profit because the marginal revenue of unit 10,000 is below its marginal cost. At too large, profit is sacrificed because marginal revenue is below marginal cost. Only at just right are profits maximized.

by only marginal revenues if output is cut below 60,000 bushels. The area of profit, in other words, is at a maximum—with no profits foregone or losses incurred—at just right.[11]

☐
Average Cost Is Irrelevant to the Rule

An important point to understand here is that marginal cost (the change in cost from another bushel) is not the same as average cost (all cost dividend by the number of all bushels). Whatever its attractions to lawyers, regulators, and journalists, to an economist the idea of average cost is nearly useless. Its only use, as one of several ways of expressing the desirability of going into business, will be described later. But it is no guide to how much to produce. The fallacy in using it as such a guide is the fallacy of profit margins, a piece of ersatz economics that is in fact antimarginal.

Q: In the year 1884 the Montsou Mining Company raised 250,000 tons of coal, sold it all at 3,000,000 francs, and paid only 2,000,000 francs for miners, steam engines, pit props, and so forth. *True or false:* With such a profit margin the owner would be foolish not to expand production still further, because he makes 33 centimes on each franc's worth of coal he brings out of the mines.

A: False. To be sure, the price of coal was 12 francs per ton (3,000,000/250,000) and the average cost of a ton only 8 francs (2,000,000/250,000). But this average cost over all output is irrelevant to the question of the effect of a small increment of decrement. That is, the company does *not* earn 12 francs revenue minus 8 francs cost on additional tons, only on all earlier tons. The cost of getting an additional ton to add to the 250,000 could well have been exactly 12 francs, in which case to try to get more would be unprofitable. Marginal units at lower outputs had cost less, but squeezing the last ton out meant pushing against the capacity of the machinery, hiring another and less energetic person, digging deeper into a thinner seam of coal. The marginal not the average cost measures the cost relevant to a comparison with marginal revenue. Rational life is a matter of margins.

☐
Why Firms Do Not Maximize the Profit Margin

The logic of profit margins would in fact lead business managers into earning none. If any enterprise making a profit margin (or even a "healthy" profit margin) were expanded, it would arrive after its expansion at an output that would offset in losses incurred the profits available from stopping at just right, because only at such a point would all the profit margin and the accompanying "incentive" to expand be gone. The detailed reasoning is as follows. The necessary relation

[11] The first-term calculus of all this is very simple. Suppose that cost is a function, $C(q)$, of the quantity produced and revenue another function, $R(q)$. Then the profit function is, obviously, $R(q) - C(q)$. It reaches a maximum (the top of the hill) when its derivative with respect to q (the slope of the hill) is zero, when $dR(q)/dq - dC(q)/dq = 0$, that is, when $dR(q)/dq = dC(q)/dq$. But the left-hand side of this, $dR(q)/dq$, is merely the mathematical expression for marginal revenue (the change in revenue per change in q), which is in the simple case discussed in the text simply the price; and the right-hand side, $dC(q)/dq$, is simply the marginal cost. At just right, then, marginal revenue equals marginal cost, and profit is maximized.

Figure 11.4
Average Nonfixed Cost Is
Half a Straight-Line
Marginal Cost

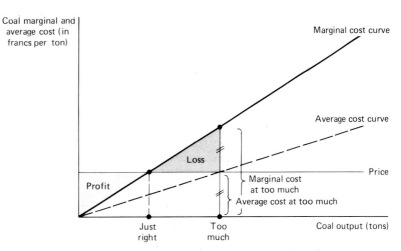

A rising marginal cost curve lies above the average cost curve. A firm that increases output beyond the point just right until average cost equals price is sacrificing the area profit by producing too much output. Such a firm earns zero profits.

for a firm with no fixed costs between a straight-line curve of marginal cost and the corresponding average cost curve can be shown to be that the average curve cuts in half the marginal cost of each output (or, equivalently, the marginal cost of some output is double its average cost), as given in Figure 11.4.

The assertion, in other words, is that at any quantity, say, too much, the average cost at too much is half of the marginal cost at too much. The geometry here is important, and the simple proof is therefore worth giving, as follows. At too much the total cost is the area under the marginal cost curve. For average cost to be total cost divided by output (which is what it is), the position of the corresponding point of average cost must be such that the triangle marked profit just equals the triangle marked loss. Only in this case will the rectangular area of average cost multiplied by quantity equal the total cost, as it must by definition. Notice that this relation among the triangles must hold true even when the marginal cost is not a straight line, but a curve, the "triangles" in this case having one curved side. The relation serves as a check on any diagram involving average and marginal magnitudes. In the straight-line case, the equality of the triangles profit and loss is achieved only when average cost is half of marginal cost, for only then are the two the same shape (with the same lengths of sides and the same sizes of angles) and therefore the same area. Such is the relation between average and marginal.[12] This being the case, it is easy

---

[12] The second-term calculus of all this is simple, though less simple than the geometry given in the text. Suppose the curve of marginal cost is $MC = \alpha + \beta q$, that is, a straight line. What is to be shown is that such a marginal cost implies an average (nonfixed) cost with a slope of $\frac{1}{2}\beta$ will cut in half the marginal cost at any quantity measured from where the marginal cost starts on the cost axis). Well, the marginal cost is by

(Continued)

246   PRODUCTION AND MARKETS

to see that producing out to the point of a zero profit margin is foolish. If the price is price, then the quantity just right maximizes the area of profit. An output of too much exactly eats up the profit with a loss. An economics of profit margins is irrational.

Why Firms Do Not Maximize the Average Profit

A related fallacy is that firms maximize average profit; that is, they seek the highest profit per unit of sale as against higher total profit at some larger output. Cautious firms are sometimes said to act this way. But the point of maximum average (per unit) profit is not, of course, the point of maximum total profit. The simplest way to convince yourself that it is not is to reflect that maximizing anything other than total profit will not in general achieve maximum profit. The fastest pitch is not the most accurate; the best term paper is not the longest; the simplest way of convincing yourself is not the most conclusive. There is no good reason why a firm would maximize average instead of total profit, and at least one good reason why it would maximize the latter: maximizing total profit maximizes total profit.

Why Firms Do Not Maximize Short-Run Profits

Another and more important fallacy in the ersatz alternatives to the theory of the firm is that of short- *versus* long-run profits. You will often hear it said that "the market (as opposed to the government or the Sierra Club)—maximizes short-run rather than long-run profits." The phrase occurs often in discussions of conservation. The lumber barons of Michigan and Wisconsin in the late nineteenth century, for example, are alleged to have cut trees at a yearly rate too fast for long-run profits, though just right for short-run profits. The distinction between the two sorts of profits, however, is at best unhelpful. A dollar is a dollar. Aside from a discount to compensate people for waiting so long for it (discussed in Chapter 26), a dollar of long-run profits in 1899 is the same as a dollar of short-run profits in 1882. Both dollars have the same effect of raising by a dollar the owner's wealth, and it is wealth that a rational owner tries to maximize.

Another way of saying the same thing is that maximizing total profit summed over all future years will maximize the price that people will be willing to pay to buy out the firm. The price of the right of ownership in the firm is simply the summed stream of future profits, because if it were less or more, people would rush to buy up the firm or rush to sell out the firm. Unless the lumber barons did not own the rights to future profits, as would be the case if the forest was not their private

---

definition the first derivative of the total cost with respect to q. Therefore, the total cost is the integral of (the area under) the marginal cost:

$$\text{Total cost} = \int_0^q (\alpha + \beta q)\, dq = \alpha q + \tfrac{1}{2}\beta q^2 + K$$

where K is mathematically speaking a constant of integration and economically speaking the fixed (i.e., constant with respect to q) cost of the firm. If this fixed cost is assumed to be zero, as it is here, the average cost curve (which is the total cost divided by q) is simply $(\alpha q + \tfrac{1}{2}\beta q^2)/q = \alpha + \tfrac{1}{2}\beta q$. This was to be shown: the slope of the average cost curve, $\tfrac{1}{2}\beta$, is half that of the marginal cost, β.

property, the rate of cutting would maximize long-run profit (i.e., maximize the present value of the woods). A lumber baron who cuts so fast that the land was eroded, say, and grew no more trees will find that the value of his forest is lowered, since no one wants to pay very much for the rights to a moonscape of eroded land. If he holds the forest for a long time, he has an incentive to exploit it properly; likewise, if he plans to sell it in six months he has the identical incentive, for buyers will not pay as much for an overexploited forest.

☐
Profit Maximization Is Not Attained Exactly

The ersatz theory of the firm, then, must give way to the genuine theory, which asserts that a <u>firm maximizes profit</u> (or better, as we have just seen, the discounted stream of profits: wealth) <u>and does so by choosing the output that brings marginal cost up to price.</u> The maximization of profit or the equalization of marginal cost and price need not be perfect to 11 digits of accuracy for the theory to be useful. The ratio of the diameter to the circumference of a circle is not actually 3, or even 3.14; it is actually 3.1415926536 . . . ad infinitum. But the use of 3 or 3.14 rather than 3.1415926536 is for most uses an unimportant mistake. A map of Baltimore on a scale of 1 inch for every 2 miles is not actually a full representation of the city, for it is insufficiently detailed to name even South Baltimore, much less 1524 Hollins Street or H. L. Mencken's writing table. Any map less than the whole of Baltimore itself leaves something out and is "inaccurate" or "unrealistic." But Baltimore itself is a little cumbersome to unfold in the car while attempting to bypass Baltimore. For this and many other purposes, the approximation works fine.

The consequence of a failure of price to equal marginal cost exactly is, of course, that profit is not at a maximum exactly. By adjusting output to yield a more exact fit of marginal cost to price, the firm could make more money, just as by adjusting one's consumption of housing and other goods to every slight variation in the prices and income one faces one could be happier. But such adjustments of output or consumption are themselves costly. Indeed, <u>the profit gained by doing a better job of profit maximizing is available to pay the manager who does the better job.</u>

Suppose, for example, that the price facing Bethlehem Steel fluctuates unpredictably from high to low. A stupid or cautious manager might produce always at small output, sacrificing when the price was in fact high, the shaded area of more profit (see Figure 11.5). That area—which could be millions of dollars for a large company like Bethlehem—is available to pay a brighter or bolder manager. If half the time when the price was high, for example, the bright manager realized it and reacted to it, then the company would be richer by half the area.

T or F: One would expect big companies in volatile industries to pay their top executives more than little companies in routine industries.

A: True, because bad decisions are more costly and good decisions more valuable for a big company in a volatile industry (e.g., Bethelehem Steel in the steel industry as against Dr. X in the psychoanalysis industry). Notice that the prestige of the company or the dignity of rank need have nothing to do with it.[13]

The Economics of Rules of Thumb

☐ The alternatives to the usual theory of the firm were described as nonprofit-maximizing descriptions of the motivation of owners or managers. The present reasoning suggests another description: maximizing sales or profit margins or short-run profits might be merely rules of thumb that conserve the scarce resource of managerial intelligence. The rules are simpler to implement than "equalize over the long-run marginal cost to price." If they diverge too much from the strictly correct rule, then they are abandoned. Tom Thumb would miss much if he used his thumb's breath as an inch rule in carpentry and would change his rule of thumb. On the other hand, a company that aims at high sales (not profits) over the next three years (not the long run) may be rational enough if high sales approximate maximum profit

**Figure 11.5
The Reward to Better
Managers Can Be the
Additional Profits They
Earn**

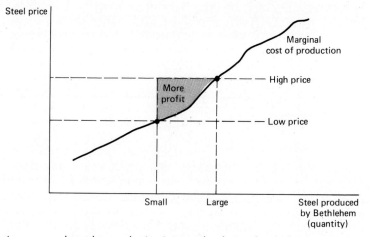

A manager who orders production increased to large when high price prevails earns area more profit for the firm. A rational firm will pay such a manager up to, but no more than, the additional profit earned for the firm.

and if a dollar in the fourth and later years is worth little in view of the rate of interest and the uncertainties of life. A firm in a market has an incentive to pull itself together if such rules of thumb are very poor approximations to maximizing profit. A firm outside a market has less incentive, the leading case in point being the behavior of firms in centrally planned economies such as that of the Soviet Union. With the best intentions but without a profit motive, a manager told to maximize, say, tonnage of paper clips or glass will tend to produce large paper clips and thick glass. In the event, it is said, managers in

[13] Compare Thomas Mayer, "The Distribution of Ability and Earnings," *Review of Economics and Statistics* 42 (May 1960): 189–195.

Russia produce 5-pound paper clips and 6-inch-thick plate glass.[14] The closeness of the approximation to maximizing profits depends on the incentives to make it close.

Summary

Why does a farmer produce and sell 30,000 bushels of corn? Because that production and sale makes the farmer as rich as possible—or so says the simplest theory of the firm. The alternative theories can be arranged in order of increasing production, from less to more than the output of a profit maximizer. Table 11.1 exhibits the order and the sort of manager who would be associated with each output.

Table 11.1 What Various Theories of the Motivation of the Firm Imply About the Scale of Production

What Is Maximized	Output	Who Might Choose to Maximize in This Way
Marginal profit	Zero	A lunatic
Average profit	Low output	The French family firm in cases of high fixed costs (see end-of-section problem)
Wealth (total profit over the long run)	Profit-maximizing output	A selfless manager with full information or an owner-manager
Utility of manager	High output	A selfish manager who values a large staff
Output or revenue subject to some limit on losses	High output	A manager without full information following a rule of thumb; a manager in a command economy (Soviet Union, General Motors)
Output	Infinite	Another lunatic

The maximization of profit has great merit among these alternatives. It is a true description of the motives of many firms. It is defensible as an approximation forced on the firm by the market. And it is readily testable against the facts. For these reasons the economist's theory of the firm puts great emphasis on the equalization of marginal cost and price, using it as a standard of comparison even when it is false.

[14] See Alec Nove, *The Soviet Economic System* (London: Allen & Unwin, 1977), pp. 94–96. The Soviet humor magazine *Krokodil* once published a "a cartoon showing an enormous nail hanging in a large workshop. 'The month's plan fulfilled,' said the director, pointing to the nail" (p. 94).

PROBLEM FOR SECTION 11.3

French managers in the eighteenth century, it is said, were less rationally motivated than were their British counterparts. In France, and indeed elsewhere on the Continent, the owner of a little family bakery or jewelry shop had a "preference for the greatest possible profit per unit of sale, as against higher total profit at some larger output."[15] *True or false:* If the marginal and average cost of producing bread or necklaces were rising, then by any definition of "profit per unit of sale" (average or marginal), a firm maximizing it would produce only one loaf of bread or one necklace per year.

11.4   Equimarginality: How the Firm Produces What It Produces at Minimum Cost

The idea that profit is at a maximum when marginal benefit is equal to marginal cost is applicable, then, to the foreign policy of the firm, that is, to the policy of how much to produce and sell. It is also applicable to the domestic policy of the firm, that is, the policy of how to produce a given amount cheapest. The pursuit of minimum costs, we shall see, leads the firm to balance the marginal benefit against the marginal cost of reorganizing its activities.

☐
The Inventory Problem

For example, an electric utility tries to balance the storage cost of holding large coal inventories against the cost of reordering coal frequently; a grocer balances the spoilage, capacity, and interest costs of holding large food inventories against the cost of reordering; and so forth across the range of firms. To bring the point home, so to speak, consider your own inventory problem.[16]

Q: You could buy your food in enormous ten-cart loads every two months or in tiny loads through the express counter every day or something in between. To do one you would need a warehouse at home; to do the other you would need hours of free time. What is the optimal load? The answer depends on what load makes the sum of the two kinds of inventory costs—the carrying costs (the warehousing costs) and the reordering costs (the shopping costs)—as low as possible:

1. Suppose that you go to the food store only when your cupboard is bare. In other words, you get a load of groceries in amount L pounds and consume it steadily and entirely before going back to the store for another load of L. What, therefore, is your average amount of food on hand? This is your average inventory of food. If it costs $\$c$ per pound per year to store the food (in shelf space, in the opportunity cost of tied up money, in deterioration of fresh foods), what is the yearly dollar cost of storing the aver-

---

[15] David Landes, *The Unbound Prometheus: Technological Change and Industrial Development in Western Europe from 1750 to the Present* (Cambridge: Cambridge University Press, 1969), p. 132.

[16] The analysis that follows is given more fully in William Baumol, *Economic Theory and Operations Analysis*, 2nd ed. (Englewood Cliffs, N.J.: Prentice-Hall, 1956), Chapter 1.

age inventory? Draw a diagram of this yearly carrying cost against the load amounts *L*.

2. If you consume *Q* pounds over a whole year and always buy food in loads of *L* pounds, how many trips to the store do you make in a year? If each trip costs $r in time, trouble, and expense, what is the yearly trip cost of eating the amount Q? On the same diagram as in (1), draw a diagram of this yearly reordering cost against the load amounts *L*.

3. Now add vertically the reordering costs to the carrying cost, showing at what load, *L*, the minimum total cost occurs. Why must the minimum occur at the point at which the slopes of the two separate curves—in (1) and in (2)—are equal?

4. Write down the total cost in an equation, "total cost is" (some algebraic expression). If you have had first-year calculus, find the minimum of the expression. Note the similarity of the minimum condition to the geometric condition mentioned in (3). Now solve the minimum condition for *L*. That is, display the algebraic equation that tells what the best (lowest cost) *L* will be for various values of *Q, c,* and *r*. If your household size doubles (you get married), will your best inventories double?

☐

The Problem Translated into Pictures

A: 1. The average amount of food on hand taking one day with another is clearly half of the load you bring home, *L*. Your inventory is saw-toothed (see Figure 11.6), which means that the dashed line halfway up *L* is the average, as asserted. If the assertion is not immediately clear, think of taking area *A* and putting it in the space of area *B*: if *A* exactly fills up the space *B*, then the excess over the average in the first days of the month is exactly offset by the deficit below the average in the final days of the month. Choosing the dashed line to make this so, in other words, gives you a dashed line that is the average. With the eating curve a straight line, you can see that the dashed line that makes area *A* equal to area *B* must be halfway to the whole initial amount, *L*. The average food on hand, then, is *L*/2 in, say, pounds. If the food costs $c per year per pound to store, the carrying cost per year of a policy of buying food in loads of size *L* will be $\frac{1}{2}L(\$c)$. The cost rises as *L* does, in a straight line marked carrying cost in Figure 11.7.

**Figure 11.6
Average Inventories Are
Half the New Load
Brought Home**

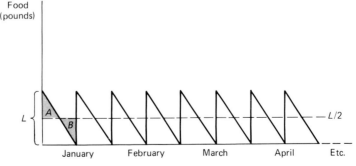

If food is consumed at a constant rate and a new stock is bought as soon as the old is exhausted, the graph of food on hand is a sawtooth. The average amount of food on hand is *L*/2.

**Figure 11.7
Carrying Costs Rise and
Reordering Costs Fall as
the Loads Bought Rise**

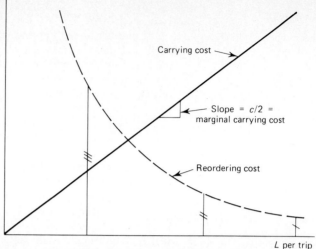

If the consumer buys more food on each trip, this increases average amount of food on hand and thereby increases inventory carrying cost. But a larger quantity purchased per trip reduces the number of trips and reduces reordering cost.

---

2. Evidently, Q pounds in L-pound loads will require making Q/L trips (e.g., 100 pounds in 5-pound loads requires 20 trips). So the reordering cost is $(Q/L)(\$r)$, the dashed line graphed in Figure 11.7. Note that it falls as L rises.

☐
***The Geometric
Solution***

3. The two costs added together—one cost rising and the other falling—produce a U-shaped curve with a minimum as marked in Figure 11.8 (note the examples of vertical distances, as on Figure 11.7). At L_{low} the falling cost of reordering if L rises a little offsets the rising cost of carrying, which implies that *total* cost (the two summed) is still falling. The case is the same in the opposite sense on the other side of the lowest-cost L. Only at the lowest cost is the increment in one cost equal to the decrement in the other, yielding no change in total costs. The rule is that of rational life: set marginal costs equal in all directions. And if one views the fall in reordering cost as a benefit, the rule appears in exactly its familiar form: set marginal cost equal to marginal benefit.

☐
***The Algebraic
Solution***

4. The total cost is $cL/2 + rQ/L$. Using calculus, it reaches a minimum with respect to L when its derivative with respect to L is zero, that is, when

$$\frac{d}{dL}\left(\frac{cL}{2} + \frac{rQ}{L}\right) = \frac{c}{2} - \frac{rQ}{L^2} = 0$$

The term $c/2$ is the slope of the curve of carrying cost; the term rQ/L^2 is (calculus tells you) the negative of the slope of the curve of reordering cost. The condition for a minimum, in other words, sets these slopes equal,

**Figure 11.8
The Equality of Marginal
Costs Determines the
Minimum Point of Total
Costs**

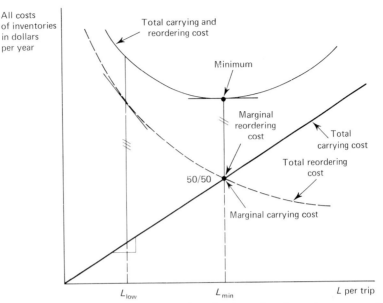

At L_{min}, the marginal carrying cost, equal to the slope of total carrying cost, equals the marginal reordering cost, except for sign. Therefore the sum of the two marginals is zero, as shown by the slope of total carrying and reordering cost, and the point chosen is a minimum.

just as the geometry of (3) alleged. Solving for L the condition gives in steps

$$\frac{c}{2} = \frac{rQ}{L^2}$$

or

$$L^2 = \frac{2rQ}{c}$$

or

$$L = \sqrt{\frac{2rQ}{c}}$$

The result is remarkably definite, although its qualitative message is not surprising. It says that one wants big loads, L, and therefore high average inventories, $L/2$, when the cost of keeping groceries at home, c, is small, when the cost of making a trip to the store, r, is large, and when one eats a lot of food, Q large. An elderly widow with time on her hands living in a small apartment will buy small loads. A divorced father with three children living in a big house with a freezer will buy large loads. If the father remarries, acquiring three more children in the bargain, the already large load does not double, for the elasticity (exponent) on Q is $\frac{1}{2}$, not 1.

☐

***The Inventory
Problem as the Rule
of Rational Life***

The general lesson of the problem is that the <u>minimization of costs</u> <u>from two perfectly complementary activities entails an equalization</u> <u>of the two marginal costs.</u> It does not hold for three or four types of cost all dependent on output, because in general there is no single output that would bring the slopes of three (or more) total cost curves into equality. If the marginal heating cost of running a hospital at some output were equal to the marginal cleaning cost, it would only be an accident that at that same output the marginal doctoring cost happened also to be equal to either of the others. What is true is that if all costs are divided in two—marginal heating cost, say, and marginal all other cost—then one could use the principle of equimarginality to locate the minimum cost.[17] And, again, if all costs were divided into rising (marginal) costs and falling (marginal) costs, the principle would be a dear old friend: set marginal cost equal to marginal benefit, in pursuit of the rational life.

☐

***The Two-Plant
Problem***

A more easily generalized case is that of the <u>minimization of cost</u> <u>from two or more perfectly *substitutable* activities.</u> An example is the Brooks Shoe Company, producing shoes from many plants and trying to decide how to assign production among the plants. Here the principle of equimarginality—the rule of rational life thinly disguised—holds without complication, for here the marginal costs are compared horizontally instead of vertically. The analogy is with vertical addition of demand curves for public goods such as national defense and horizontal addition for private goods such as housing. Just as the optimal allocation of housing among Higgs, DeCanio, Reid, and Wright leads to equal values of marginal benefits to each, so too the optimal (lowest-cost) allocation of tasks to different plants leads to equal marginal costs.

The simplest case is the firm with two plants, though the case is generalizable to any number of plants. How much should each plant produce to minimize the overall cost of producing a given output? The University of Maryland, for instance, can within limits assign students to its College Park campus or to its Baltimore County campus. Each student added to a campus brings with him or her increased costs of housing, classrooms, teachers, administration, libraries, and so forth. Each student subtracted takes away costs. Clearly the lowest all state cost is achieved when the numbers of students on each campus are such that no reshuffling brings lower cost, that is, when moving one student from College Park to Baltimore County raises costs at Baltimore County by the same amount it lowers costs at College Park. Dashed vertical lines in Figure 11.9 represent various alternative allocations of the total number of students to the two campuses. Notice

---

[17] The calculus is illuminating. Suppose that there are three types of cost, represented by functions $A(.)$, $B(.)$, and $C(.)$, all dependent on output, q. The total cost is $A(q) + B(q) + C(q)$, which is minimized where the derivative of A is equal not to the derivatives of B or C by themselves but to their sum. Signifying derivatives with primes, the condition for a minimum is $A'(q) + B'(q) + C'(q) = 0$, which implies $A'(q) = -[B'(q) + C'(q)]$. Clearly, if B and C were put together and called D, the last equation would display equimarginality: $A'(q) = -D'(q)$

**Figure 11.9
Equality of Marginal Costs
Achieves the Minimum
Total Cost**

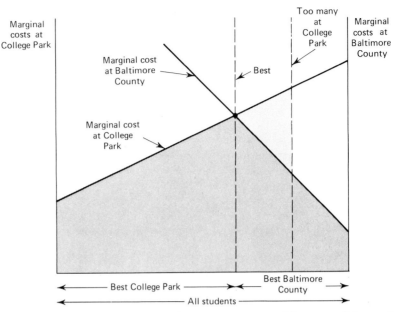

A given number of students is allocated to two campuses at minimum cost if the marginal cost of a student is the same at both campuses. The lightly shaded area, equal to the difference between the cost actually incurred and the least cost method, shows the costs of a misallocation.

that in the familiar style of such allocation diagrams, the enrollment at Baltimore County is measure backward, from right to left, and that its cost curve therefore rises backward as well.

For the allocation represented by the right line, too many at College Park, the marginal costs are *not* equal, which implies that costs can be made lower by reshuffling, in this case from College Park to Baltimore County. The allocation best achieves the lowest total cost, namely, the lowest heavily shaded area under the two marginal cost curves. Any other allocation will result in a light shaded triangle of additional cost such as that for two many at College Park.

☐ Notice that it is marginal, not average, cost that is to be equalized.

**The Irrelevance of
Average Cost to the
Two-Plant Problem**

T or F: A given output of ammunition is produced in the best way if the output is divided up among ammunition factories so that the average cost per bullet is the same in each.

A: Only by accident would the average costs (below marginal costs if marginal costs are rising) be equal at the truly best way (i.e., the way that equalizes marginal cost). What matters is whether a little reallocation can reduce total cost, which depends on the little rises and falls in total cost caused by little reallocations. But these little rises and falls *are* marginal costs. If an extra bullet from the Enfield Arsenal costs $1.00 and from the Watertown Arsenal only $0.50, it is clear that the last bullet ought to be produced in

Watertown, not Enfield, even if Enfield's cost per bullet for the sum of previous bullets is much less than Watertown's. Therefore, false.

The cost per bullet averaged over all previous bullets is of course much easier for a firm to measure than is marginal cost. You will sometimes find people justifying using a comparison of average rather than marginal costs for this reason. It is true that marginal cost will be measured with more error. If the true marginal cost of a bullet were $1.00 when total costs were $100,000, even a tiny percentage error in the cost estimate after the rise in output would cause a large mismeasurement of marginal cost. The firm would have to perform a larger experiment than raising output by just one bullet to get a reliable estimate of marginal cost. Or it would have to engage in an extremely subtle measurement of all the myriad ways in which rising output causes total cost to rise. By contrast, average cost is easy to measure accurately: divide current costs (no experiments here) by current output. That it is easier to look for a lost wallet under the lamp post, however, is irrelevant if the wallet was lost in the dark 50 feet away. Average cost is simply irrelevant. However crudely measured, marginal not average cost guides allocation.

☐
The Don't-Do-It-All-Yourself Principle

Another application of the same idea is to the question of the desirability of self-sufficiency, as when American Motors wonders whether or not it should make its own crankshafts.

T or F: If it wants to maximize profits, American Motors should have a policy of making all its own crankshafts (a rising marginal cost per shaft) rather than buying some of them from Nippon Crankshaft (at a constant price).

A: "Having a policy" would mean that American Motors would buy American regardless of how cheaply Nippon sold the shafts. But to put it generally, it can never be better to add such a constraint to one's behavior. To put it precisely, American Motors minimizes the cost of any given output by setting the amounts of its two sources of supply (itself and Nippon) so that the marginal cost of crankshafts is equal from both. And since Nippon's offer is a constant price for any amount bought, the Nippon price fixes the marginal cost (see Figure 11.10). Therefore, false.
  The similarity between this allocation diagram and the last one reflects the similarity in the economic arguments. If American wanted a lot of crankshafts, it would make the American amount itself and buy the rest from Nippon, such that marginal costs of crankshafts (like marginal costs of students at the University of Maryland) were equal. Self-sufficiency, doing-it-itself, would cost it the extra shaded area. The lightly shaded area of total cost is minimized, given that a lot of crankshafts are to be produced, by letting Nippon do some of it. The policy of self-sufficiency among companies as among nations is no way to maximize profits. Therefore, false: American should not do it all itself.

Nippon would do all of it if its price were everywhere below American's marginal cost. The Nippon price would be this low if there were

Figure 11.10
Self-sufficiency Will Not
Equalize Marginal Costs

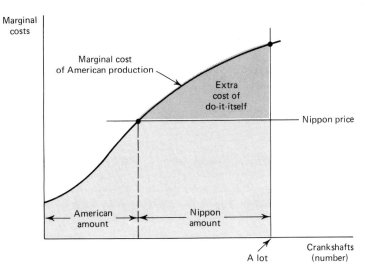

American Motors minimizes total costs by purchasing crankshafts from Nippon, because at quantities above American amount Nippon's price is below American's marginal cost.

economies of scale in the production of crankshafts (that is, marginal cost falling) that Nippon could exploit because of the large extent of the market for crankshafts.[18] Even if American Motors also had access to the technology with economies of scale, it might pay American (and Ford and General Motors and Toyota and others) to abandon its own, low-volume production of crankshafts in favor of adding its business to the already extensive market of Nippon Crankshaft. American and Nippon would be dividing up the labor of making a car, Nippon specializing in making crankshafts and American in assembling and selling them (with a few thousand other parts attached). The principle involved was enunciated by Adam Smith two centuries ago, namely, "that the division of labour is limited by the extent of the market."[19] It is an answer to the question posed in earlier chapters of why firms are constituted as they are, that is, why they buy some things and make others themselves, why they choose the marketplace for one task and the command economy inside their walls for another.

Summary

The marginal cost of different activities can guide the firm to the allocation that minimizes total cost. A steel firm with four different plants and hundreds of alternative suppliers (external and internal) of coal, ore, repairs, transport, accounting, metallurgical analysis, and so forth will do best to equalize the marginal cost of each. For minimum cost the marginal cost of steel from the

[18] The definition of economies of scale is to some degree arbitrary. Here it is falling marginal cost. More usually it is falling average cost.
[19] *The Wealth of Nations* (1776), title of Chapter III. The analysis here relies on George Stigler's essay of the same title, *Journal of Political Economy* 49 (June 1951): 185–193, reprinted in many places, for example, William Breit and Harold Hochman, eds., *Readings in Microeconomics*, 2nd ed. (New York: Holt, 1971).

Gary, South Chicago, Pittsburgh, and Birmingham plants must all be equal. And the marginal opportunity cost of, say, coal from the company's own inventories on hand must be equal to the marginal cost of bringing more from the company's mines and also equal to the marginal cost of purchasing the coal from another company. At some low price externally relative to a high price internally, the steel company will buy all its coal from a coal company. That is, it will divide the labor, such division being limited by the extent of the coal company's market. In this way do economic cells divide and multiply.

QUESTIONS FOR SECTION 11.4

1. Dannon Yogurt could deliver to grocery stores daily or monthly; it could as a result have very fresh or very spoilt yogurt. *True or false:* Dannon makes the most profit by delivering infrequently.

2. You can choose between keeping all your notes for all your classes in one enormous notebook or keeping notes for each class (or each week or each hour) in many separate notebooks. Formulate your choice of the optimal size of notebook as an inventory problem.

3. You have a choice of keeping your income (Y per month arriving on the first of the month) as a temporary inventory of money (think of cash, although the argument works for checks also) or as a temporary investment in an interest-earning asset, say, bonds. Suppose to simplify the argument that you are paid in bonds earning i per month. Suppose, too, that you spend all your income, implying that all your income must go through the cash form sometime. The question is, what is the best plan for making bonds into cash in regularly spaced loads of L each? At one extreme you could take all your income as cash at the beginning of the month in one big load, minimizing reordering costs (call it r times the number of loads, Y/L) but maximizing the opportunity cost in interest foregone (namely, all of it). At the other extreme you could leave your money as long as possible in bonds, minimizing the opportunity foregone (i.e., the average inventory of cash, $L/2$, times the monthly interest rate, i) but maximizing the reordering costs. By analogy with inventories of food, write down the formula for the optimal size of load, L, and the average inventory of cash ("money balances," or $L/2$). If there was a general price rise doubling both Y and r (the only dollar magnitudes in the formula, for i is a percentage per month), what would happen to money balances? If you think of r as being proportional to the general price level, what is the elasticity of the demand for *real* balances (correcting $L/2$ by dividing it by the price index r) with respect to *real* income, Y/r? With respect to the interest rate?

4. Show minimum cost for two plants on an allocation diagram with *total* cost curves. (Hint: Use curves with progressively steeper costs—i.e., rising marginal cost; remember that each plant's total cost curve is added to the other to get *total* total cost.) Prove the equivalence of this point to the point of equality of marginal costs. Where is the point of equality of average costs?

5. Suppose that Houston Power and Light Company has two power plants, one a steam plant with rising marginal costs of a kilowatt of electricity produced and the other an atomic plant with falling marginal costs. *True or false:* It should concentrate all production in the atomic plant if it wishes to produce a given output at the lowest cost.

True or False

6. A given output of wheat will be produced at least cost if the output is divided among farms in such a way that the average cost of production is exactly the same on all farms.

Cost Curves of the Firm

12.1 Production and Input Supply: Why Marginal Cost Is as It Is

Output Depends on Input

☐ For some questions, then, it is enough to know about the firm's marginal cost curve. But for others one wants to look behind the curve to its causes. Its causes are, put briefly, the constraints imposed on the firm by the state of markets and of knowledge. The firm combines costly ingredients according to the best recipes it knows to produce a given output at minimum cost. A steel company produces outputs of bars, angles, sheets, rails, structural shapes, and so forth with inputs of coal, iron ore, ingot buggy operators, marketing managers, insurance, limestone, blast furnaces, soaking pit crane operators, computers, file clerks, rolling mills, and thousands of other distinct entities, whether purchased from other people or owned by the steel firm itself. The set of recipes located in big books and cunning hands for combining the inputs is called the *production function*—an idea that was used earlier and will be used later still again. A firm might have dozens of outputs and inputs. For present purposes, however, one output and one input will do, adding up steel sheets and cold rolled bars into one output, in amount Q, and adding up soaking pit crane operators and rolling mills into one input, in amount I. The simplification directs attention away from the message of a many-input production function that there is more than one way to skin a cat and toward the even more fundamental message that output depends on input. That is, some function F connects output to input; thus, $Q = F(I)$. An especially convenient function, for example, might be a constant elasticity one, such as $Q = 5I^{0.8}$.

Diminishing Returns Is, for One Thing, a Fact Directly Observed

☐ A feature this particular function shares in the relevant range with other functions that might satisfactorily describe a firm's recipes is concavity, namely, the shape marked acceptable in Figure 12.1. What is acceptable about it is that it exhibits diminishing marginal returns to scale, which is to say that, as the firm attempts to produce more output by pushing in more input, each additional dose of input pro-

Figure 12.1
Eventually Diminishing
Marginal Returns to Scale
Are Necessary

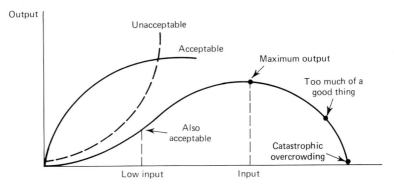

An empirical law of production is that, at sufficiently high levels of input, the marginal product of input will be falling; at these levels, the increase in output per unit of input is lower, the greater the input. Marginal product can be falling at all rates of input greater than zero, as shown by acceptable, or can be increasing at rates less than low input, and negative at rates higher than maximum output, as shown by also acceptable. But marginal product cannot be everywhere increasing.

duces less. The slope diminishes. Unlike the man in the street, economists do not believe that bigger is always better. Early in the application of fertilizer, labor, machinery, and so forth to a given plot of land (or all these and land to a given farmer), there may well be economies of scale in producing corn. But eventually the input defining the firm—the plot of land or the farmer himself—is overwhelmed by the additional inputs. The 50 tractors crowded onto the 2 acres of Mr. Craft's farm smash into each other and explode; the fertilizer left in tons on each square yard buries the young corn plants to a depth of 6 feet; the thousands of laborers become a mob and take to sleeping, fighting, and card playing on company time, then turn to Crafts's house and burn it down for sport. The point of catastrophic overcrowding in Figure 12.1, needless to say, will never be reached by a rational firm; indeed, it will never reach beyond maximum output. Less colorful stories apply to the earlier, observable segments of the curve, but the moral is the same. Along acceptable, marginal returns diminish continually; along also acceptable, they at first increase, then diminish. The critical point is that the functions do not end like unacceptable, upward curving. The reasons are two, the first being fact: in circumstances in which they can be measured well—chiefly farming—production functions of firms do not exhibit continuously increasing returns to scale.

☐
How to Reason from
the Shape of the
Production
Function to the
Shape of the Cost
Functions

The second reason the slope declines becomes clear as the argument goes forward. Suppose the all-purpose input has a fixed per unit price of *w* (for wage, the price of the input that is most often the subject of thought). The price is one of the constraints facing the firm. If the firm were a large enough demander of the input, it would face an entire somewhat inelastic supply curve, with the price, *w*, rising to some degree as the firm bought more. But here it is assumed that the firm is small in its factor markets and faces therefore a price, *w*, over which it by itself has no influence.

With the fixity of *w* settled, one can leap with ease from the production function to the cost curve, as in Figure 12.2. The left panel has the production function laid on its side, with the shape like also acceptable in Figure 12.1. Look at it with the arrow pointing up, and you will see that it merely reverses the direction in which input is measured. If *w* is fixed, the total cost is simply *wI* (i.e., the input price times the input amount), which means that the vertical axis can be stretched by the factor *w* to represent costs, an operation that clearly will leave the general shape of the curve unaltered. The result is the total cost curve in the second panel of the figure. The third (right) and final panel simply plots the slope of the total cost curve against quantity: the slope is the rise in total cost per unit of a rise in quantity; that is, the slope is marginal cost.

The diagram contains or implies everything you will ever need to know about cost curves. Notice the way in which the little tangencies along the total cost curve follow as they should the falling and rising shape of the marginal cost curve. Notice, too, that the average cost is the slope of a ray from the origin to the total cost curve, because such a slope measures total cost divided by output, and that therefore when the ray reaches a minimum in slope at lowest average cost on the total cost curve (middle panel) it is also identical to the *slope* of the curve. That is, marginal cost is equal to average cost once, slicing up through the average cost at its minimum point, an amusing and surprising fact that is useful for drawing self-consistent diagrams of average and marginal cost.

**Figure 12.2
The Shape of the
Production Function (a)
Determines the Shape of
the Total (b) and Marginal
(Average) (c) Cost Curves**

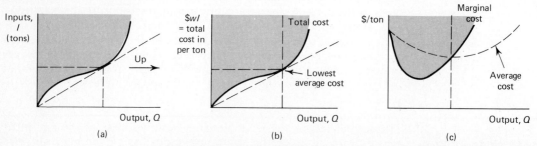

(a)   (b)   (c)

If inputs are available at a constant price, the total cost curve and the production function are identical except for scale. The slope of the total cost curve at a given quantity is marginal cost at that quantity. The slope of a line through the origin intersecting the total cost curve at a given quantity tells average cost at that quantity.

Other Things Equal, Diminishing Returns Imply Rising Marginal Cost

The most important result, however, is the mere upward slope of the curve of marginal cost. The upward slope comes directly from the diminishing returns to scale. Put verbally, the lower increments to output forthcoming from additional units of input mean that given increments to output will require larger and larger doses of inputs (i.e., higher and higher costs). With marginal cost rising, the firm will arrive at a particular finite output if it applies the rule (of rational life) "to maximize profit set output such that marginal cost equals marginal revenue."

T or F: If on the contrary the production function implied higher increments to output from additional units of input, the firm will expand without limit.

A: With increasing returns to scale (and a fixed factor price, w) the marginal cost curve slopes downward. A competitive firm would be minimizing, not maximizing, profit if it stopped at the output that equalizes marginal revenue and marginal cost (see Figure 12.3). The firm makes a positive marginal profit on each quantity sold beyond the point MC equals MB and will therefore continue moving to the right indefinitely. Therefore it would expand indefinitely. Therefore, true.

Again, consider the following.

T or F: Although increasing returns to the scale of a perfectly competitive firm is not consistent with equilibrium, constant returns is.

A: By the reasoning just given, constant returns implies a flat marginal cost curve—by contrast with the rising one of decreasing returns and the falling one of increasing returns. If a flat demand curve—a price given to a perfectly competitive firm—is the marginal benefit, then there are three possibilities, none of which is attractive (see Figure 12.4). Therefore, false.

**Figure 12.3
Why Marginal Cost Must
Slope Upward**

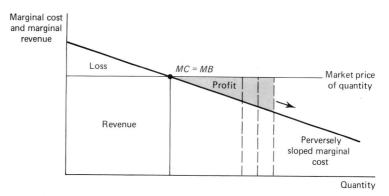

A firm facing a horizontal demand curve cannot have a marginal cost curve that is everywhere falling and that lies, in part, below the demand curve. If all these conditions held, the optimal size of the firm would be infinitely large.

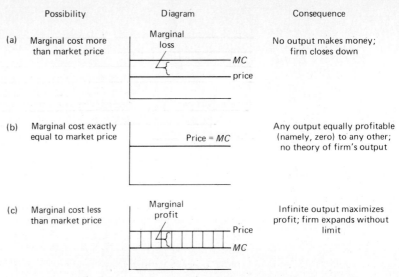

**Figure 12.4
Constant Returns Is
Inconsistent with an
Equilibrium Scale for the
Firm**

A firm facing a horizontal demand curve and having a horizontal marginal cost curve would produce either nothing or an infinite quantity or would be indifferent to the amount it produced. Therefore the conditions stated are inconsistent.

☐
*Transport Costs
Might Not Be Equal*

Such considerations demonstrate that a flat marginal cost is inconsistent with a *price-taking* firm—a firm that is so small in its market that it faces a flat demand curve. But a firm that is big in its market, and that faces therefore a downward-sloping demand curve (because it faces such a big part of the entire demand curve), could rationally stop at a finite size though its marginal cost of production were flat. The reason, to be elaborated in Chapter 17 on monopoly, is that selling too much could carry the firm so far down the demand curve that the fall in price would overbalance the rise in quantity. A monopolist, in other words, faces diminishing returns in selling that can play the same role of limiting the scale of the firm as do diminishing returns in production or (as we shall see in a moment) in buying inputs.

Another and parallel case of a single firm's facing a downward-sloping demand curve is that of a firm that can get more customers only from farther afield, with higher costs therefore of delivering the product. Costs may be constant or even declining as output rises *at the plant but the cost of delivery from the plant leads to a finite equilibrium.* Big hardware stores, for example, are better, since they can stock a wider range of hardware and assure that each visit by a customer is more certain to yield the kind of paint, nails, or tools the customer wants. Should Chicago therefore have one big store? No. It has in fact over 400, because a local store is convenient; the trip to the One Big Store would be expensive.

Q: A careful study of economies of scale in the generation of electricity by privately owned American utilities in 1955 concluded that they were very strong: in the form $Q = I^\alpha$, the α was 2 or higher for the firm (any α

greater than 1, recall, is an unacceptable elasticity in Figure 12.1).[1] Yet there were over 400 privately owned electrical utilities in the United States in 1955. Why?

A: Transporting electricity is expensive, and the farther it is transported the more expensive it is. Therefore a flat or downward-sloping marginal cost at the plant is consistent with a rising marginal cost at the place of use. Other *natural monopolies* limited by transport costs are said to include grocery stores, schools, drugstores, banks, and the like.

☐
*Diminishing
Returns Can Limit
the Size of the Firm*

Unless it is offset by transport costs, then, a flat or downward-sloping marginal cost curve for a competitive firm is a great theoretical nuisance. For many firms the costs of transport are insignificant. Clothing manufacturers on Seventh Avenue or automobile dealers in Los Angeles or wheat farmers in Kansas are not isolated from each other's competition by economically significant distances, yet they are finite in size. To have a theory of such finite firms actually observed in the world, one is forced to abandon the common notion that firms always reap endless economies of scale or even the less common notion that costs are constant.[2] The argument is one of survival, in the style of biology since Darwin. A firm that is "fit" in the size it has chosen will survive by being profitable. Unfit species will vanish. If sizes of firms in the retail women's clothing trade cluster around one size (of firm—or, for that matter, of dress), we seek reasons for the apparent optimality of the size. We use the results of selection to guide what would otherwise be an impossibly difficult inquiry into the cost curves of firms.[3] If there were no presumption that the sizes and other characteristics of firms that survive are in fact the least cost characteristics, economic studies would be as crippled as would be ecological studies that could make no presumption that the cowardice of wolves in the hunt or the falling of leaves in autumn are in fact valuable for the survival of wolves or of broadleaf plants.[4]

Chapter 14 will exploit the argument from survival to its limit. For the present the argument serves merely to buttress the belief that marginal cost curves rise. It is the second reason for the upward curvature:

[1] The facts, the question, and the answer are taken from Marc Nerlove, "Returns to Scale in Electricity Supply," in C. F. Christ et al., eds., *Measurement in Economics* (Stanford, Calif.: Stanford University Press, 1963), reprinted in Arnold Zellner, ed., *Readings in Economic Statistics and Econometrics* (Boston: Little, Brown, 1968).

[2] The various attempts to actually observe the cost curves of firms, however, show with embarrassing frequency that cost curves do appear to be flat. The observations can often be rationalized as mismeasurements; compare Milton Friedman, in National Bureau of Economic Research, *Business Concentration and Price Policy* (Princeton, N.J.: Princeton University Press, 1955, pp. 230–238. The best case for constancy of marginal cost and against the conventional theory of the firm as presented here and in other texts is J. Johnston, *Statistical Cost Analysis* (New York: McGraw-Hill, 1960), especially Chapters 5 and 6. His view is that many firms are monopolists.

[3] The idea was made explicit by George Stigler, "The Economics of Scale," *Journal of Law and Economics* 1 (October 1958): 54–71.

[4] The examples come from Paul Colinvaux, *Why Big Fierce Animals Are Rare: An Ecologist's Perspective* (Princeton, N.J.: Princeton University Press, 1978), pp. 58, 153.

not only is the upward curvature in fact observed when observation is possible, but it would have to be observed in a rational and finite-sized firm.

☐ *An Inelastic Supply of Inputs (Like a Downward-Sloping Demand) Can Also Limit It*
It is the shape of the cost curve, not the underlying production function, that matters for the firm. In particular, consider the following.

T or F: The production function of Bethlehem Steel might exhibit constant or increasing returns to scale, yet the resulting cost curve could have the normal shape if the supply curve of iron ore facing the firm were inelastic instead of perfectly elastic.

A: The reasoning is simply that as Bethlehem produces more, it buys more iron ore, which raises the price of the ore (if, as assumed, the ore is supplied inelastically to the firm). The rise in the price of the inputs can offset the advantage gained from increasing returns in needing less and less inputs per unit of output. Therefore, true. Throwing ore in with other inputs, the result is that shown in Figure 12.5.

The mathematics is simple and illuminating. Take the production and supply functions to be constant elasticity. Recalling for present use your earlier mastery of such things, you can write the production function as $Q = I^\alpha$ and the supply function for I as $I = w^\eta$. If the exponent α falls short of 1, the function exhibits diminishing returns to scale, if α equals 1 constant returns, and if α exceeds 1 increasing returns. Now the total cost is the input price, w, multiplied by the amount of input, I. That is, total cost $= wI$. The object is to transform this into an expression depending on output, Q (i.e., to transform it into a cost function). The object can be achieved by finding how w and I separately depend on Q and substituting. For example, by inverting the supply curve, one can see immediately that $w = I^{1/\eta}$. So the total cost will be (making the substitution for w) $I^{1/\eta}I$ or, collecting the exponents, $I^{1/\eta+1}$. The amount of input, I, however, depends on the amount of output. As later chapters will show in detail, the production function is not only a statement of how much output comes from a given input but also of how much input is required for a given output. Solving the production function for the required input gives $I = Q^{1/\alpha}$. The final step is to eliminate I from the cost function by substituting, to get total cost $= Q^{1/\alpha(1/\eta+1)}$, which is the expression desired.

The cost curve will thus have rising marginal cost if its elasticity with respect to Q, namely, the exponent $1/\alpha(1/\eta + 1)$, is greater than 1. If factor supplies are elastic, then η is very large, $1/\eta$ is very small, and the elasticity is simply $1/\alpha$, which is greater than 1 only if α is less than 1 (i.e., only if there are diminishing returns to scale). But if factor supplies are to some degree inelastic, then η is small, $1/\eta$ is significant, and the elasticity of the total cost curve depends on how significant it is. For example, were α as high as 1.5 (pronounced increasing returns to scale by the standards of most factual studies of the matter), then an elasticity of total input supply, η, of less than 2

Figure 12.5
Rising Costs of Bidding
Factors away from Other
Industries Can Offset
Increasing Returns in
Production

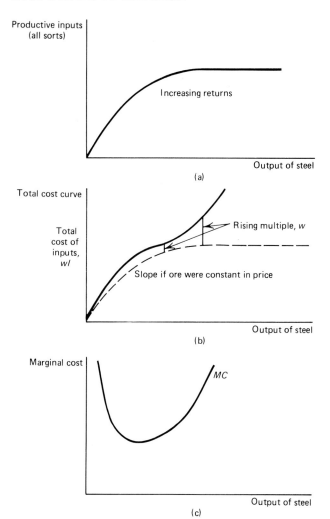

With increasing returns to scale, the marginal quantity of input needed to increase output may fall, but the increasing price of inputs on the market may still cause the marginal cost of output to rise.

would be necessary to keep the cost function well behaved. For example, if $\eta = 1$ (given $\alpha = 1.5$), the elasticity of the total cost function is

$$\frac{1}{\alpha}\left(\frac{1}{\eta}+1\right) = \frac{1}{1.5}\left(\frac{1}{1}+1\right)$$

$$= \left(\frac{2}{3}\right)2$$

$$= 1.33$$

which is an elasticity of cost with respect to output greater than 1, as required for good behavior.

□
***The Dual and the
Primal Problems***

In short, the <u>production function and the cost function are linked</u>, though one must know the character of the market for inputs before one can claim to know the link perfectly. The link is called <u>*duality*</u>, a thought so powerful in economics that in the higher reaches of abstraction in the field it dominates much thinking. The word comes from the jargon of *programming*, that is, the branch of applied mathematics that deals with maximizing something under many constraints. In the present context, the thought is that <u>the production function is the answer to one question</u>—what is the most quantity, Q, the firm can attain for a given input, I? And <u>the cost function is the answer to a related question</u>—what is the least cost, wI, the firm can attain for a given Q? And that the two questions are two sides of one question— what is the best thing the firm can do? They are *dual* to each other; that is, each is one of a pair. <u>The two solutions are solutions to the same problem, but one solution is to maximize and the other is to minimize</u>. In doing well an executive for General Motors can either start with a work force, a plant, and some raw materials and produce as many cars as possible or, equivalently, start with a certain number of cars and produce them with the given work force, plant, and raw materials as cheaply as possible. The two are not really two solutions, but the same, single solution looked at two ways. In other words, <u>maximizing output for a given input is the same as minimizing input</u> (and therefore input costs) <u>for a given output</u>; that is, Q/I, or the physical productivity of the inputs, is maximized when $w(I/Q)$, or the input cost per unit of output, is minimized. Fewer people per square mile means more square miles per person; more output of corn per person means fewer persons per bushel of corn. Elementary though it is, it is easy to get confused about the matter, and confusion about it is a reliable indicator of economic naïveté.

T or F: In a nonexpansive market managers will attempt to minimize costs rather than maximize output.

A: Taken literally, "minimizing costs" would occur at an output of zero, and "maximizing output" would occur at an output of infinity. Read more sympathetically, the assertion must refer to minimizing (input) costs *for a given output* and maximizing output *for a given input*. But these are merely alternative ways of expressing the same thing. Staying on the cost curve (minimizing costs) is identical to staying on the production function (maximizing output). Therefore, false or meaningless.

Similarly, consider the following.

T or F: The link between new farming methods and productivity is weak. The new methods *may* show up in higher output per unit of input (which is higher productivity) but alternatively may be used merely to pay higher wages, with no increase in output.

A: The second sentence is true, but it is false evidence for the first. The confusion is again between the amount produced and the efficiency with which it is produced. New, higher productivity methods will raise output per unit of input (which is what higher productivity means). They will therefore reduce input per unit of output. They will therefore permit higher pay for each unit of input; for less input is wanted per unit of sellable output. The argument illustrates the strength of the link between new methods and productivity, not its weakness.

The link is so very strong because it is so very obvious. <u>A firm must earn as much as it pays</u> (i.e., the price of its product times the quantity produced must equal the price per unit of inputs times the quantities of them used). The assertion that $PQ = wI$ implies, by the magic of elementary algebra, that $Q/I = w/p$. The new equation says that output per physical unit of input equals the price of the input divided by (or "deflated by") the price of the output. In other words, <u>there are two ways of measuring productivity, one with quantities and another—the price "dual" of the quantity "primal"</u> (*primal* means "the original problem")—<u>with prices.</u> The two are equal. The productivity of inputs is equal to their real price (i.e., their money price deflated by the price of output). The higher real wages, rents, profits, and so forth that Americans get compared with Ethiopians are not something apart from the higher physical productivity of the American economy but identical to it, because $Q/I = w/p$. The failure of incomes (which are input prices) to "keep up" with inflation (which is the output price) is not a consequence of an economic footrace but, rather, the necessary consequence of falling productivity unrelated to inflation, because $(w/p)^* = (Q/I)^*$. A similarity between a measure of productivity change based on quantities and one based on prices is not a happy accident but, rather, a necessary correspondence, because again $Q/I = w/p$.

Summary

Behind the marginal cost curve is the production function. Either diminishing returns to scale in the function or rising delivery costs or sufficiently inelastic supply curves of inputs can cause the marginal cost curve to slope upward. If it slopes downward, the firm will expand without limit, which suggests that it must slope upward. Somewhere in the constraints facing the firm, then, more gets you less.

The relationship between costs and production is one of *duality*. As the production function is the most output for a given input, so the cost function (the "dual" of the production function) is the least cost for a given output. The link between the two is the budget equation, $PQ = wI$, which is to say that revenues equal expenditures. The equation implies that $Q/I = w/p$, which is to say that physical productivity equals the real reward of the input.

QUESTIONS FOR SECTION 12.1

1. The McGouldrick Textile Mill of Manchester, New Hampshire is planned as a cube of height (and width and depth), *h*. Suppose that the construction and maintenance costs of the mill itself are proportional to the surface area of the mill, because the cost is determined by the extent of brick and glass ("Factory windows are always broken / Somebody's always throwing bricks.") Suppose too that the output, Q, of the mill is proportional to its cubic volume, because the larger the volume the more spindles, looms, and other producers of output can be crammed in. *True or false:* Total construction and maintenance costs will vary as $cQ^{2/3}$, where c is some constant; that is, marginal construction and maintenance costs will decline as planned output rises, two thirds being less than one. (Hint: Use the output equation to solve for h as a function Q; then substitute into the cost equation.)

2. A lone dealer in the London *Times* newspaper living at Isca at the end of the Fosse Way can get as many copies as he wants at 10 pence a copy (i.e., his marginal cost at Isca is constant). All his customers will pay only 15 pence a copy. At each mile marker north of Isca (the Fosse Way runs north from Isca to Lindum, you see, and is the only road), there are 1000 potential buyers of the *Times,* beginning at mile 1. Each mile of transport cost a quarter of a penny per copy. How many copies will he sell in this case? Draw a diagram illustrating the general case, with distance in miles along the horizontal axis (distance being equivalent to numbers of copies) and cost and selling price along the vertical.

True or False

3. If the production function for the airframe industry is characterized by constant returns to scale, the supply curve of the industry will be infinitely elastic in the long run.

4. If total costs $= cQ^\alpha$ and α is less than 1.0, then marginal cost is declining (the firm is experiencing increasing returns to scale).

12.2   Cost Curves in Use: The Long Run and the Short Run

□
The Production Function or Cost Curve Is the Best

That the production and cost curves measure the most output and the least cost implies that the firm can do worse. Indeed it can. It can take up positions anywhere in the upper area of either Figure 12.6(a) or (b), such as the point error, using excess inputs in amount ΔI to attain Q_0, which will therefore cost more than it should, by the amount ΔI multiplied by the cost of each unit of input ($\$W$).

A firm having full knowledge of its costs and managed by a genius would never be in error. Knowledge and genius, however, are expensive, more expensive for some firms than for others, with the result that actual firms depart more or less from the most output or the least cost. The departures from the total cost curve, shown as dots in the bottom panel, can be viewed either as mere errors or, more fruitfully, as the larger costs imposed by smaller amounts of inputs not explicitly measured. In either case the deviations make it difficult to find out what "the" cost curve is.

□
A Constrained Firm Does Worse than the Best

The key point is that real firms spend much of their time above "the" cost curve. The point can be put in the form of another one of those stunningly obvious but frequently misunderstood principles of economics: namely, adding constraints hurts. The principle was first stated

Figure 12.6
The Firm Can Do No
Better than the Production
(a) and Cost Curves (b),
but It Can Do Worse

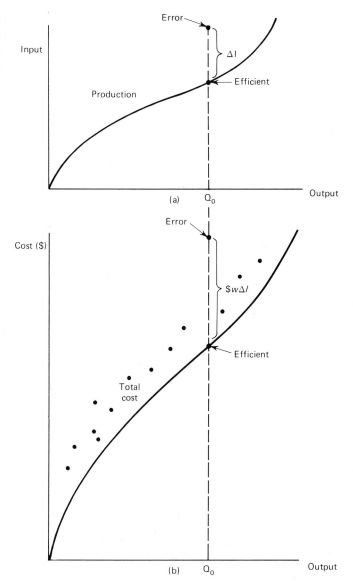

The production and cost functions show the least costly methods of production. If the profit-maximizing firm had full information, it would always choose points such as efficient. In practice, ignorance, which is costly to remove, makes the firm choose points like error.

in the chapter on utility functions. A firm constrained by the cost of finding better ones to use dull-normal managers will have higher costs than (will be hurt relative to) one free to use the best, just as a runner constrained to leap over hurdles while running 100 yards will have worse times than one free to run straight. The women's 100-meter freestyle record in swimming is never slower than the 100-meter back-stroke, since freestyle means that the swimmer could choose the back-stroke if it were the fastest way of covering 100 meters.

T or F: The costs of operating the World Trade Center building New York will be higher with the federal rule of 78°F in air conditioning than without it.

A: If constrained to shift from 72°F to 78°F, the building might save on energy costs (as a matter of fact, because existing equipment is designed to operate best at the old, low temperature, it might not) but will lose on other costs, such as the efficiency of the office workers who are using the building or the life expectancy of stored paper. The conclusion would be inevitable if the building were being operated at minimum cost before the federal rule was imposed, because if the higher 78°F temperature were the optimum, it would have been chosen anyway, in the absence of the federal rule. There-fore, true.

□
Constraints Put the Firm on the Short-Run Cost Curve

The most important class of examples of how firms can do worse and how constraints make them do so is that short-run costs are always above long-run costs. By *short run,* the economist always means "con-strained to use the equipment in place, that is, unwilling to adjust fully and immediately to a new scale of operation." Since the short run is a situation with more constraints than is the long run, it is clearly more costly than the long run. Constraints always hurt.

There are two reasons why a firm might suffer the constraints of the short run. The first is that, if a change in output is known to be short lived, the firm will not want to buy a long-lived piece of equip-ment to service it. For example, suppose (as was the case) that the output of skateboards was very large during the time that children were just discovering them, but fell to the replacement output as soon as every house in the land had a couple of skateboards in it. An intelli-gent firm wishing to cash in on the temporary boom would not buy specialized factories, retail outlets, and so forth suited to a long persis-tence of the boom output, because it knows the boom will not last. The specialized factories will last for 20 years. If the boom lasts as long, the per skateboard cost of the factories will be low. But if the boom lasts only two years, the cost per skateboard will be high. At such costs it may well be better to rent a factory than to buy, to get a factory suited to general use rather than one specialized in the produc-tion of skateboards, and to pay premiums to old workers to work over-time rather than to hire and train new ones. The first principle, then, is that one does not use a cannon to kill a fly.

The second reason why a firm might suffer the short run is that, even if the change in output is known to be permanent, it may be cheaper to adjust to it slowly. For example, if the college of the Univer-sity of Chicago decides to expand from 2500 to 3500 students, it will eventually want to have more housing, more classrooms, and more teachers to accommodate the increased number of students. But only "eventually." It will not immediately knock down the old buildings and rebuild them to better suit the higher scale; it will not immediately

Figure 12.7
Haste Makes Waste

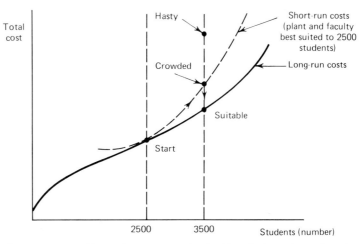

The university could pay the costs associated with point hasty for a short time to move quickly to the point suitable, or it could take longer to adjust while paying less at crowded. It chooses the less costly of the two alternatives.

---

hire new teachers. The costs of adjustment are high. Haste makes waste. It will, instead, house the students in rented hotels and hire visiting teachers on temporary assignment. These are expensive and inconvenient devices but cheaper than excess haste in adjusting. Only over the long run will it take advantage of the wearing out of buildings and the wider pool of good teachers available from a leisurely and thorough search to remake the plant and faculty to suit the higher scale. The long-run costs will be lower than the short-run costs, which are in turn lower than the hasty costs (see Figure 12.7).

A rational university wanting to increase its size will move from point start to crowded to suitable. The dashed short-run cost curve is exactly suitable only to the output of start. Everywhere else—at student numbers below as well as above 2500—it is higher than long-run cost. The second principle then is that haste makes waste.

The two principles are widely applicable. A sudden rise in the number of students in grade school should not inspire an immediate remaking of whole schools, even if the rise itself is permanent and especially if it is not. A rise in the demand for automobiles should inspire Ford to hire people on overtime at old plants before constructing new plants. And it applies to falls in output as well as to rises. A fall in attendance at Boston Red Sox baseball games should not inspire the management to tear down Fenway Park and build a new, smaller stadium at once. Firms spend some time on their short-run cost curves.

□
***Why Firms Choose
to Spend Time off the
Long-Run Curve***

Both principles would be false, however, if there was a frictionless secondhand market in university buildings, grade schools, auto plants, and baseball stadiums. Unless getting into and out of owning such things were expensive, the distinction between long- and short-run costs would be empty, because the firm would never be stuck with a short-run expedient.

T or F: A shirtmaker who owns easily sellable space on Seventh Avenue, rents his sewing machines, and buys labor by the week is never off his long-run cost curve.

A: He can resell all these things to the market at a moment's notice, repurchasing them at the next, with no significant cost of making and unmaking the deals. He will therefore never have to suffer the inconvenience of an unsuitable set of equipment. That is, true.

The distinction between the long- and short-run cost curve, then, is a crude way of allowing for the costs imposed by inconstancy of output, by ignorance of its duration, by haste in adjusting; in a word, the distinction allows for the cost of transacting. The costs of transacting are not given to the firm by God, for a firm has some choice of the set of transaction costs it will face. For example, it can choose either to rent or to buy equipment, such as sewing machines for shirtmaking. Renting has different sizes and types of transaction costs from ownership, and the balance of advantage of one over the other is not obvious. In particular, to mention an elementary point, owning one's machines does not make them costless.

T or F: Friedman, the sweatshop shirtmaker, who owns his sewing machines outright, has a cost advantage over Schwartz, who must pay rent on her machines.

A: One way of seeing the point is to note that Friedman had to borrow $500 (or whatever) per machine to become an owner and therefore must pay to the banker in interest on the borrowing an amount equal to the annual rental Schwartz pays to an owner. Another and deeper way is to note that the real "cost" of a machine to Friedman is what it could earn outside his own factory, which is precisely (in a rental market without transaction costs) the rental that Schwartz would pay. By either argument, false.

A firm must often make a choice between one or another short-run cost curve (i.e., between one or another set of transaction costs keeping the curve above the long-run curve). Stueland Electric in St. Joseph, Michigan, for example, must choose between arrangements such as owning outright its own trucks or supplies of cable that give the least cost when the firm is running at normal output and arrangements such as depending on a truck-renting firm in Baroda or a supplier of cable in South Bend that give higher costs at normal output but lower costs at very high or low outputs. If Stueland faces a predictable, stable demand, it will choose the inflexible but (perhaps) cheap arrangement of outright ownership. If it faces a highly variable demand, it will choose the flexible arrangement, for this will give the lowest cost over high and low outputs taken together. The choice is between the dashed total cost curve and the heavily emphasized total cost curve in the top panel of Figure 12.8. The bottom panel displays the same choice in terms of average cost (i.e., cost per unit), bearing in mind that, if one cost curve is higher than another in total cost for a given

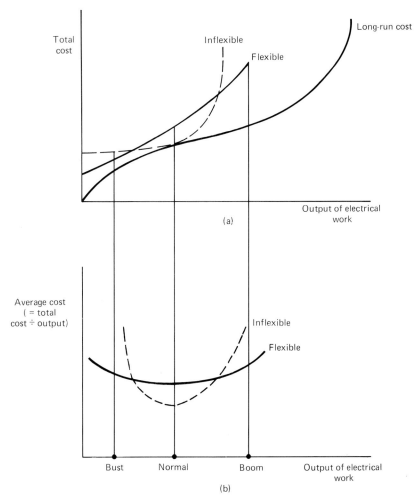

Flexible methods of production are less costly at very high or very low levels of output than are inflexible methods. If the demand facing the firm is sufficiently variable—if there is always a boom or a bust—the firm will choose flexible.

output, it must also be higher in average cost for that output. If the firm faces outputs such as boom and bust frequently enough, it will prefer the curve flexible to inflexible.

☐ The engine of analysis can at the end be thrown into reverse, deriving the long-run cost curve from the short instead of viewing the short-run cost curves as deviations from the long. For it is apparent that there are infinitely many short-run cost curves, some high, some low, some flexible, some inflexible. What is true of all of them is that the long-run cost curve is by definition below them and in fact consists of their combined lowest borders. Speaking technically, the long-run curve is the *envelope* of all the short-run curves. In mathematics a

The Long Run Is the Envelope of All the Short Runs

Figure 12.9
The Long-Run Cost Curve
Is the Envelope of All
Short-Run Curves in Terms
of Total (a) and Average
(b) Cost

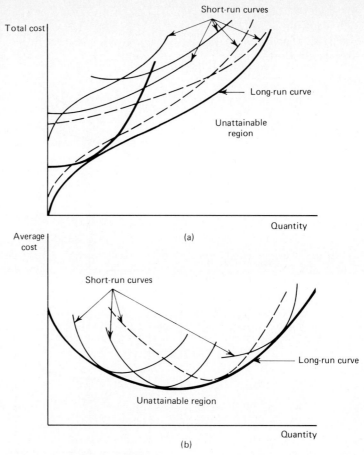

The long-run total and average cost curves are lower bounds, or envelopes, of all the points on the short-run curves.

curve that just touches all of a number of curves is known as the *envelope* of the curves, a term you can remember by thinking of the curve's enveloping (i.e., surrounding) the other curves. Evidently, the short-run cost curves are always above their envelope, since being always below is how the envelope is defined (see Figure 12.9). The diagram simply restates the opening theme of the section: the best that a firm can do is its long-run cost curve, but it can do worse.

Summary

The production function can be viewed as best practice, in which case the corresponding cost curve is lowest cost. Adding constraints hurts, a principle applicable in the present case to cost curves. When additional constraints drive firms off the lowest curve, the cost observed is obviously an imperfect estimate of the lowest cost. An important example of additional constraints are the transaction costs that force firms to operate along short-run cost curves. Firms do not fall blindly into such curves; on the contrary, they choose them, choosing, for example, a flexible plant that has lower costs calculated over episodes of boom and bust relative to an inflexible one that has low costs only if output is steady. In any event the long-run cost curve is the lowest attainable for a given (i.e., steady) output, which is to say that it is the envelope of all the short-run curves.

QUESTIONS FOR SECTION 12.2

1. You are Jan deVries, the fabulously wealthy owner of a fleet of oil tankers. As a common carrier you are required by law to accept any shipment of oil demanded of you; that is, you have no control over your output (contrary to the assumption in the last few chapters that output is the one thing a firm *can* control). Initially your output of oil shipped is old output, and you have chosen a collection of ships that minimizes the cost of producing old output (see Figure 12.10). Output and total cost are those that will persist into the indefinite future. You are on the old short-run cost curve.

**Figure 12.10
Transaction Cost Is a
Vertical Distance,
Placeable Anywhere**

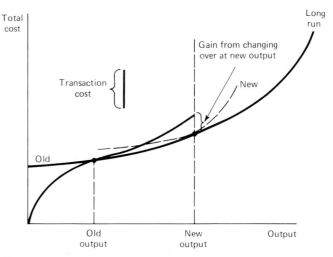

The vertical distance transaction cost tells the cost of using the market to change the method of production. The change shifts the firm from the old cost curve to the new. The firm that must increase output from old to new output will make the shift if the gain from changing over at new output is greater than transaction cost.

a. Look at the vertical distance called transaction costs: it is the cost (all costs that persist into the indefinite future) of shifting from the old to the (dashed) new short-run cost curve. Assume that it is the same length no matter where on the diagram it is moved. If output changes permanently to new output, will you find it worth your while to adjust your fleet to get the new cost curve?

b. Suppose, however, that the old fleet deteriorates a little each year, driving the old cost curve up. When will investment in an adjusted fleet take place?

c. Suppose that the new cost curve *falls* a little each year, reflecting the improvements in technology that permit a fleet built to embody the technology cheaper to operate. When will investment in an adjusted fleet take place?

d. Would you expect an industry with rapidly growing output, equipment that wore out quickly, and experiencing rapid technological change to have few or many occasions to invest in changing from one cost curve to another?

2. Marie and Brownie contemplate running an all-season skiing and camping resort near Montpelier, Vermont. They have two possible designs, one a general design that serves both for skiing in the winter and camping in the summer and the other a specialized design that makes skiing cheaper but camping more expensive. The costs expected into the indefinite future are as follows:

	Winter	Summer
Number of guests	10,000	5,000
Cost per guest, general	$10	$10
Cost per guest, special ski	$5	$30

Suppose that the number of guests is given (the common carrier assumption) and that it is invariant to the choice of design. What is the unit of time over which costs should be measured? Which design has the lowest cost?

True or False

3. Compulsory conservation of energy will save the nation's resources.

4. Since the long-run cost is the lowest-cost way of producing each output, the long-run cost curve runs through the minimum points of short-run costs curves.

12.3   Cost Curves in Use: Fixed and Variable Costs

☐

The Point of Maximum Profit Revisited

After so much attention to the domestic affairs of the firm, it is now time to return to its foreign affairs, that is, its decision of how much to produce for sale. The goal of making profit is served by two steps: first, plan how to produce any output at least cost; second, choose the output that maximizes the excess of revenues over costs. Lars Sandberg, a farmer in Ohio producing soybeans for sale to a market that will buy all he produces at a fixed dollar price, is in such a situation. His total cost has the usual stretched Z shape. His total revenue also has the usual shape, which is a straight line out of the origin because each additional ton brings him a fixed additional number of dollars (i.e., the total revenue curve has a constant slope). The top panel of Figure 12.11 shows what he does. He produces the output that makes the gap between the total revenue curve and the total cost curve as large as possible, because the gap is profit.

The bottom panel gives the usual correspondences between the totals on the top and the averages and marginals on the bottom. As usual, in the bottom panel the maximum profit point is at the output-equalizing marginal cost and price (marginal benefit), and as usual the amount

**Figure 12.11
The Gap Between
Revenue and Cost Is Profit**

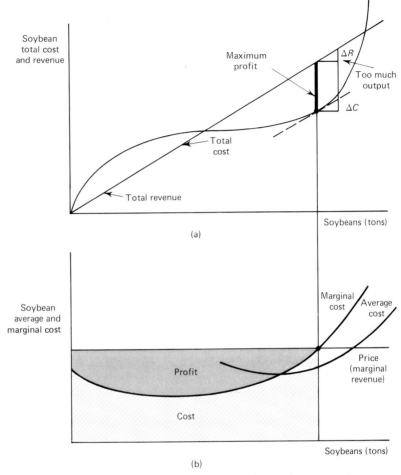

The firm maximizes profit by maximizing the vertical distance between total revenue and total cost. It does this by choosing the rate of output at which the slope of total revenue equals the slope of total cost, that is, at which marginal revenue equals marginal cost.

of profit is the area of revenue under the price line (equal here to the two shaded areas) minus the area of cost under the marginal cost curve (i.e., the heavily shaded area marked profit). The heavy line in the top panel is an alternative picture of the same profit. It will not come as a complete surprise that the maximum gap is at the output at which the slope of the total cost curve (look at the dashed tangent) is equal to the slope of the total revenue, because these slopes are exactly the marginal cost and the price, and by a well-known argument equalizing them brings bliss. You can overcome any residual surprise by translating the argument into the terms of the total cost diagram. At too much output, for example, total revenue has risen above what it is at maximum profit by the amount ΔR, but total cost has risen even farther, by ΔC. Clearly it will be better to move back to maximum profit.[5]

□

*Past Costs Are
Irrelevant*
The central message of the diagram—and of the last two chapters—is that in the pursuit of profit a rational firm is influenced by its costs. What costs? Future costs that can be altered by the amount of output.

> *Q:* A jeweler in Harper Court leaves the prices of her gold necklaces at their price when made even though the price of gold has since doubled. She says to an amazed and incredulous but grateful customer that "I make money even at the old prices." Does she?

> *A:* The "cost" relevant to a fully rational firm is not yesterday's outlay of money but the cost from the moment the sale is made into the future. To take an even more extreme case, if gold prices were going to triple tomorrow and if God had informed the jeweler, then it would be madness to make any sales today. Likewise in the present case: the true "cost" is the opportunity cost, that is, what the necklaces would bring now or later, at another time or place. A doubling of the price of gold sharply increases the cost (though by less than doubling, for the labor and capital in fabrication and in marketing would not double in price and are also part of the cost). Selling a necklace worth $70 for $50 is to incur on this account a $20 loss of opportunity, not a gain.

The point is that historical costs are not directly relevant to the forward-looking decisions of a rational firm. Historical costs are, as the vivid word in accounting has it, "sunk." The proverb is "let bygones be bygones"; that is, forget about the past and look to the future, for purposes of money-making if not of other sorts of wisdom. That Manhattan once cost $24.00 does not mean that for present purposes owners should care. If the owner of the land under the World Trade Center foolishly sells the land for $24.50 he cannot comfort himself by thinking "Well, at least I made some profit: once the whole island sold for less." Firms in regulated industries, to be sure, must often pay close attention to historical costs, because the accounting principles demanded by the regulations do. A regulated telephone company constrained to earn no more than 5% on the acquisition costs of its assets must calculate the acquisition costs historically, not at the cost in future that is relevant to their economic use. Furthermore, the past acquisition cost of even a nonregulated firm, such as the Evans Slipper factory, may be a useful estimate of its present cost of replacement if not much has happened since it was built to alter the cost of building or if what has happened is measurable. But these uses aside, historical

---

[5] First-year calculus reduces the matter to routine. Suppose that the cost function were some function $f(q)$, where q is the output chosen. Total revenue is of course pq, where p is the given prices. Profit is then revenue minus cost, $pq - f(q)$, and to find the condition for maximizing this profit function, one sets its first derivative with respect to the variable at choice q equal to zero. Well, its derivative is $p - f'(q)$, which when set equal to zero implies $p = f'(q)$, which is to say that the maximum gap of profit occurs when the slope of the total revenue function (in this case the slope is just p) is equal to the slope of the cost curve, $f'(q)$.

costs do not determine present and future costs and are therefore useless for measuring profit.

☐   A closely related point is that <u>fixed costs do not affect the output of the firm.</u> One of two distinct senses of *fixed costs* is "fixed and unavoid-able," which costs have as much effect on present and future decisions as do historical costs: none. Fixed costs in this sense, for example, are often identified with the repayment of debts incurred to invest in equipment. If you borrow $10,000,000 from your bank to invest in a ship, you must pay it back with interest. Suppose that the interest is 10% on the principal and that your schedule of paying back the principal is 5% of the $10,000,000 for each of the next 20 years. In each of the next 20 years, then, you will have to pay (10% + 5%)($10,000,000) = $150,000 to the bank.[6] You would be pleased to earn more than this amount from the ship, and surely you expected to when you made the investment, but whether or not you actually do so is irrelevant to your behavior during your tenure as a shipowner. Whatever you do, the bank each year presents you with a bill for $150,000. The bank could care less if you are still a shipping magnate or if business has been good. For your part, that you face a bill for $150,000 for the loan effects your business no differently than would a bill for $150,000 for something unrelated to your business, such as child support. The way in which you run the shipping business is unaffected by the burden of debt "on" it. The fixed and unavoidable cost has no effect on your business decisions—whether or not you keep the ship and how much a year you run it.

Q: British owners of old coal-powered (as distinct from oil-powered) ships after World War I earned enough in revenue to cover the captains, crew, supplies, fuel, and the like for operating the ships, but not enough to also cover the interest and repayment costs on the loans taken out before the war to buy the ships. *True or false:* The shipowners are probably acting irrationally when they bought the ships and were certainly acting irrationally when they continued to operate the ships despite the losses.

A: What matters to a judgment on the rationality of the initial investment is the *expectation* of future profits. The shipowners could well have made investments in 1910 in expectation of making money yet could find later that their expectation was mistaken, as it in fact was. And having made the initial mistake, the decision is bygone, irrelevant to the decision a ship-owner faces in 1930 of whether or not to keep the ship afloat. So long as the ship earns enough to pay all the *variable* costs (i.e., the costs that do vary with output), the rational decision is to carry on. Therefore, false.

---

[6] The important point here is the fixity of the payment, not the formula. The formula is wrong if you literally pay back all the money and do not borrow more to maintain the ship (which is wearing out, to choose a very convenient figure, at 5% a year), because the interest would be calculated on the remaining indebtedness in each year—for example, at 10 years only half the $10,000,000. The average indebtedness would in fact be half the principal. The halving can be assigned to the interest rate, giving (5% + 5%)($10,000,000) = $100,000 as the fixed annual payment.

Figure 12.12
A Fixed Tax per Firm (a)
Does Not Move Marginal
Cost (b)

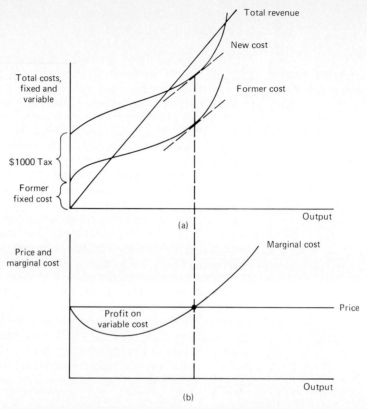

(a)

(b)

A tax that does not vary with output increases total costs by the same amount at all levels of output and does not change marginal cost. As long as the firm produces some output, the tax will have no effect on how much the firm produces.

Avoidable Fixed
Costs Determine
Whether or Not to
Produce Anything

Recall that there were two distinct senses of *fixed* costs. The second is fixed and *avoidable* if one closes down entirely. Payment on a loan used to open a restaurant is fixed and unavoidable even if the restaurant closes down; payment of a license to operate the restaurant is fixed (i.e., it does not vary with the output of the restaurant) but avoidable if it closes down and no longer begs permission of the sovereign power to exist. To look at it from the other side, there are two kinds of variable costs: costs that are zero when the output is zero and costs ("semivariable costs" in the accountant's lingo) that are *not* zero when the output is zero.[7] The significance of the distinction arises from problems of the following sort.

T or F: Since a tax of $1000 per firm imposed on the existence of firms does not affect marginal cost, it does not affect the output chosen by each

---

[7] The lingo comes from Sidney Davidson, James Schindler, Clyde Stickney, and Roman Weil, *Accounting: The Language of Business* (Glen Ridge, N.J.: Horton and Daughters, 1975).

firm (unlike a sales tax or an employment tax) and therefore does not affect the output of the industry.

A: The successive assertions travel from plain truth to probable error by small steps. The first assertion is plain truth and deserves a lot of talk and a diagram all to itself.

It is true that a tax of $1000 per firm does not affect marginal cost. The $1000 is a fixed cost, invariant with output given that some output is to be produced. The total cost (including here both fixed and variable cost) will move up by $1000 when the tax is imposed, thereby cutting profits by $1000. But because a uniform rise of $1000 in the cost curve does not alter its slope, the corresponding marginal cost is not moved (see Figure 12.12). That the shaded area of the profit on variable cost in the bottom diagram does not change after the tax even though the profit gap in the top diagram shrinks is due to its exact definition, now made explicit for the first time. It is profit on *variable* cost alone because it is calculated by subtracting from revenue the area of the costs under the marginal cost curve (i.e., all and only those costs that do vary with output).[8] Because the marginal cost does not move from its old position, the optimal output does not change. The economic common sense here is that the firm always wants to have as large a gap as possible between revenue and cost, whether the gap is big or small. The tax makes the gap smaller, and may even make it a loss, yet the firm still does as well as it can under the circumstances by setting marginal cost equal to marginal revenue. It is often said that low profits spur the firm on to greater effort and larger outputs; and it is also often said that they discourage the firm, causing less effort and smaller outputs. The middle ground claimed here, by contrast, says that the size of the profit earned has no effect whatever on the output chosen, given that some output is to be produced. The assertion is not self-evidently true, which is to say that it is a hypothesis about how people behave that might in some cases be proven false. In any event, it is the assumption made in the usual theory of the firm.

The later assertions in the question, however, do not follow from it. True, the $1000 tax per firm does not affect output *given* that some output is to be produced. But there's the rub. That some output is to be produced is not in the long run given but is a choice made by the firm. If the tax is so large that profits on variable costs are offset entirely, then the firm will close down. And in the long run all costs are variable; that is, all costs are avoidable. In the long run, then, the tax does affect output, for it affects whether or not the firm produces at all. Therefore it can affect the output

---

[8] Fixed cost, then, is a constant of integration in the calculus problem to find $\int_0^q MC(q)\,dq$, in which MC is the marginal cost function. Or, to look at it the other way, the total cost is variable cost (a function of q) plus fixed cost (a constant), meaning that marginal cost is the derivative of variable cost alone,

$$\frac{dTC}{dq} = \frac{d[VC(q) + FC]}{dq}$$

$$= \frac{dVC(q)}{dq}$$

since FC is a constant.

of the industry. As always, an extreme example helps. Suppose that the tax were $100,000 instead of $1000 and that it were imposed on each hot dog stand. Clearly, none would exist at such a high price of existence. To take the other extreme, suppose that the tax were $1. Clearly, the effect on the decision to exist as a hot dog stand would be trivial. The effect on the industry running hot dog stands is the more powerful the larger the effect on profit. In short, the answer is false: a $1000 tax *can* affect the output of the industry.

□

Average Cost Is Only Relevant to the Decision Whether to Produce at All

The logic of fixed and average costs, poorly suited for questions of what output should be, given that it is not zero, is well suited for questions of whether any output should be produced at all. For example, the investment in equipment that a firm makes is analogous to a tax, which profit over variable cost must cover in the long run if the firm is going to wish to embark on the investment. The analogy can be used to second-guess the decisions made by managers.[9]

Q: By the 1870s a reaping machine to replace hand harvesting of wheat and barley had been available for decades, yet in England (as contrasted to the United States) less than half the harvest was done by machine. It has been argued that this was a result of the small size of English farms, the high cost of machines, and the inconvenient nature of the English landscape (plowed for purposes of drainage into a "ridge-and-furrow" configuration, which made the cumbersome reaping machines less effective).

1. If a farmer bought a machine for 660 shillings on which he had to earn 12.7% a year to pay back the banker, what in shillings does the machine have to pay back every year to justify its purchase? If the labor saving on flat land *not* plowed into ridges and furrows were 3.3 shillings per acre harvested per year, what would be the lowest annual acreage harvested (the "threshold" acreage) at which a machine would become profitable?

2. The labor saving was lower on ridge-and-furrow land. Illustrate in a diagram of total cost against acres harvested per machine per year how the threshold acreage varies with the per acre labor saving. If the maximum annual capacity of a machine were 100 acres harvested, what is the minimum labor saving that will make the machine profitable?

3. If the labor saving on a ridge-and-furrow farm were 2 shillings an acre, what would you conclude about the rationality of *not* adopting the reaper in view of the fact that the wheat and barley acreage on a majority of English farms (mostly ridge-and-furrow) was less than 50 acres (with a good deal of variation around this average)?

4. How does this conclusion change if farmers can share a machine, if a market in machine time exists, if the size of farms can be altered, or if the percentage of a farm devoted to wheat and barley can be altered?

A: 1. The annual opportunity cost of the investment is 0.127(660) = 84 shillings. This is a fixed cost with respect to the number of acres harvested.

[9] The example is drawn from Paul A. David, "The Landscape and the Machine," in D. N. McCloskey, ed., *Essays on a Mature Economy* (London and Princeton, N.J.: Metheun and Princeton University Press, 1971), reprinted in David's book, *Technical Choice, Innovation and Economic Growth* (Cambridge: Cambridge University Press, 1975).

You pay it regardless. So if the machine saves 3.3 shillings an acre, you had better have at least $84/3.3 = 25$ acres to harvest with your machine.

2. The diagram is given in Figure 12.13. The minimum labor saving is simply $84 = 100(S)$, that is, $S = 0.84$.

3. The threshold acreage for 2 shillings an acre saving is $84/2 = 42$, so a good many farms in England harvested acreages below the threshold (for some harvested only, say, 20 acres). These farmers were not being irrational to ignore the charms of mechanized harvesting. One could build from these elements a full theory of the adoption of the reaper: as the benefits varied over time or as the size of farms varied, the percentage of the distribution of farm sizes that adopted the reaper would vary.

4. The conclusion of (3), however, changes radically if machines can be rented, loaned, or shared. Farmers could club together to buy a machine, for example, and harvest 100 acres with it each year, even if they have all pitiful 15-acre stands of wheat and barley. Or a farmer with a reaper on 70 acres could notice that his machine stood idle for the last week or so of the harvest and could rent it out to his reaperless neighbor. Or a company could be formed specializing in reaping. The threshold idea no longer has force, and the failure to adopt reapers remains a puzzle, as long as the labor saving on ridge-and-furrow land was more than 0.84 shillings an acre. Furthermore, the threshold could be changed if the size of farms or the percentage of a farm devoted to wheat and barley could be raised. The acreage to be harvested, in other words, is not given by God but is alterable, in which case it might be altered to take advantage of the machine.

Figure 12.13
The Economics of Lumpy Investments

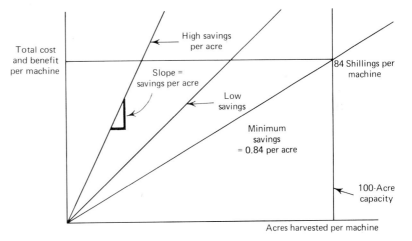

A farmer with at least 100 acres would break even on a harvesting machine if the savings per acre were 0.84 shillings. If the savings per acre were higher, the savings line would be steeper, the machine would be profitable for 100 or even fewer acres, and a profit-maximizing farmer would buy the machine.

Summary

A firm achieves the most profit by equalizing marginal revenue and marginal cost or (equivalently) finding as large a gap as possible between total revenue and total cost.[10] The total cost in question is future, variable cost, not past, fixed costs. Firms like all rational folk let bygones be bygones, do not cry over spilt milk, and look to the future. A tax levied in a lump or a machinery cost that can be avoided by refraining from any output, of course, is subject to choice by the firm. Costs of doing business do not affect marginal cost and therefore do not affect output if some is forthcoming. But if the cost imposed is too large, the firm will shut down entirely. The question—taken up in detail in Chapter 14—becomes whether or not profit on variable cost (such as the revenue over cost in a restaurant or the savings on labor cost in buying a machine) is large enough to offset the cost of licenses, buildings, or reaping machines. To be or not to be, that is the question.

PROBLEMS FOR SECTION 12.3

1. Label and explain two alternative and equal areas of profit in Figure 12.14.

Figure 12.14
Areas of Profit When
Costs Rise

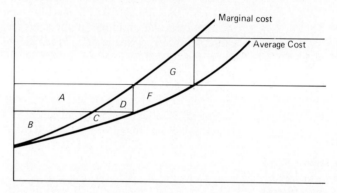

2. Do the same for Figure 12.15.

Figure 12.15
Areas of Profits When
Costs Fall Then Rise

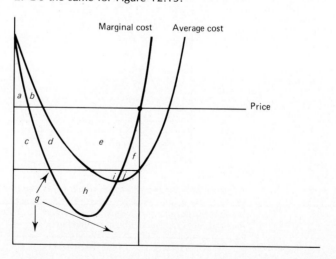

[10] It might as well be admitted here that the phrase "total cost" is ambiguous in economics. It sometimes means "all cost, including fixed and variable costs," but sometimes, as here, it means "cost in total, as distinct from marginal or average cost."

3. In the diagrams of total revenue drawn in the text, it is assumed that price (average revenue being the slope of a line from the origin out to the place on the total revenue curve) does not fall with larger quantities sold. If Saudi Arabia produces substantially more oil, however, the price *will* fall. Only oil at a lower price will find new demanders.

a. In such a situation, what is the shape of the total revenue curve?

b. Suppose that Saudi Arabia has the usual stretched Z for a total cost curve and faces the total revenue curve described in (a). Where would Saudi Arabia set its output to maximize profit? Would the resulting price be equal to marginal cost?

4. An Iowa City councilman argued that "We spent $30 million refurbishing the downtown: it would be silly not to build a highway now to make it easy for people to get to the downtown." Criticize.

13

Competitive Industry

13.1 Industry Supply with a Fixed Number of Firms and Costs Independent: Optimality and Upward Slope

☐
The Supply Curve of the Industry Adds up Marginal Cost

The theory of the typical consumer—of utility functions, budget lines, and all that—is useful in itself, but it is even more useful when the consumers are added up into market demand. Likewise, the theory of the typical firm—of production functions, cost curves, and all that— is useful in itself, but it is even more useful when the firms are added up into market supply.

The first step in the adding up is to notice that a firm need only be a price taker for its marginal cost curve to be its individual supply curve. If a brickmaking firm is such a small part of the whole supply of bricks that it cannot change the price by its own decisions on how much to produce, then it takes its demand curve as flat; that is, it takes the price of bricks as given and maximizes profit subject to the given price. Maximizing profit leads it to produce the output of bricks that brings marginal cost up to the marginal benefit (which is the price). In other words, for price taking the marginal cost is the firm's individual supply curve, as asserted. The next and final step is to the brick industry as a whole. In the same way as one adds up each person's demand curve horizontally when each takes price as given, one adds up each firm's supply curve of bricks to get the market supply. Many firms making bricks yield the total Chicago supply of bricks (see Figure 13.1).

☐
The Industry Produces the Best Output

The first of several lessons from this construction is the familiar one announced by Adam Smith in 1776 (Chapter 8) that profit maximizing leads to efficiency. One part of the meaning of "efficiency" made plain in the diagram is that the whole output is the socially correct size. Look at the shaded areas of profit for each firm. In the case portrayed, these are evidently maximized, subject to the condition that market supply equal market demand and that the firms believe themselves

288

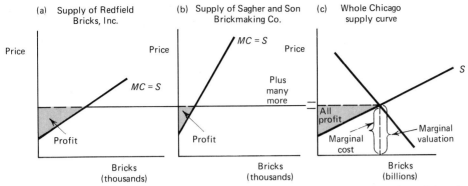

(a) Supply of Redfield Bricks, Inc.

(b) Supply of Sagher and Son Brickmaking Co.

(c) Whole Chicago supply curve

Figure 13.1
Add Curves of Marginal Costs to Get the Curve of Supply

The supply curves of price-taking firms are summed parallel to the quantity axis to give the industry supply curve. When each firm is at its optimum and the market is in equilibrium, the marginal cost of a unit supplied equals the marginal valuation of a unit consumed.

powerless individually to alter the price. No other output of Redfield, say, suits the firm better; no other gives higher profits. And because the industry as a whole must supply only the amount demanded, the marginal valuation (the height of the demand curve) in this happy equilibrium will be equal to the marginal opportunity cost (the height of the supply curve). To recall an earlier diagram of the argument (Figure 8.15), the scrambling for profit leads to the point of efficiency on the production possibility curve at which the slope of the curve is equal to the slope of the indifference curves. Without profits to guide them, capitalist firms would not produce the best output of bricks.

Q: A bumper sticker reads "People, Not Profits: Smash Capitalism." Comment.

A: The money-grubbing, selfish, penny-pinching, greedy, avaricious capitalists yield in their struggle with each other the highest income for the people, the correct output of bricks, the highest attainable point on society's opportunities. Private vice is public virtue. We the people are the capitalists, as owners or employees. We want the size of output to be efficient and can attain it by unleashing capitalism, at any rate if it works as the diagram alleges.

☐
Each Firm Produces the Best Output

Another part of "efficiency" is also plain in the diagram, namely, that the output is allocated among firms in such a way that it is produced at least cost. The cause is simple. Each firm faces the same price and therefore ends with the same marginal cost. The principle is that of equimarginality, as discussed in Chapter 11 for the allocation of students between two branches of the University of Maryland. In terms again of the diagram of an earlier chapter, the economy is brought to the production possibility curve, producing as many bricks for a given amount of all other goods as possible.

Q: Look at the diagram of the Redfield and Sagher brick firms. Suppose that the two companies make up the whole market supply. Suppose too that they take the price as given to them by the market. Use straight-line supply curves.

1. If the allocation of output between the two is as portrayed in the diagram, what is the *marginal* opportunity cost of bricks (i.e., the cost of the "last" brick) in terms of all other goods for each firm? What is the *total* (variable) opportunity cost (i.e., the amount of all other goods the society gives up to get the equilibrium amount of bricks)?

2. Now suppose Redfield Bricks, Inc. does not maximize profit but instead produces for any given price 10% less than its profit-maximizing output. Compared with the profit-maximizing case, what will happen to the industry supply curve? Suppose—merely to keep output the same as before to facilitate comparison—that the industry demand curve was perfectly inelastic. In equilibrium, what now is each firm's marginal cost? What is the industry's total cost of the output produced? How does it compare with the total cost when Redfield Bricks, Inc. does maximize profits?

A: 1. The marginal cost is the same for each firm, equal to the going market price. The total variable cost is the area under their marginal cost curves out to the quantities produced by each firm, the shaded areas in Figure 13.2 (ignore all the dashed lines for a moment).

2. With Redfield's supply swiveled back 10%, the whole Chicago supply swivels back by the same absolute amount (less relatively, of course, since Sagher is also part of the quantity supplied). So the market price will rise. At the higher price Sagher will be induced to make more bricks than in the profit-maximizing case. The price cannot rise enough, however, to leave Redfield too making more bricks. If it did both would be making more and the market output would rise, which is impossible with a higher price unless the demand curve has an upward slope, an absurdity. That is, Redfield necessarily makes fewer bricks than he did in the profit-maximizing equilibrium. Indeed, with the demand curve perfectly inelastic, the reduction in his output is precisely the same as the rise in Sagher's.

Now consider the costs. That Redfield ignores his true marginal cost does not mean it is not socially relevant. It is. The true marginal costs are now different, Redfield's being below Sagher's (look at the equilibria marked by the dashed lines). Since the principle of equimarginality is violated, one would expect costs to be needlessly high. One would be right. The total cost for the unchanging output rises by the emphasized area in the Sagher diagram marked rise and falls by the area in the Redfield diagram marked fall. The rise is clearly larger than the fall. The conclusion is that, if Redfield does not pursue profit larger than the fall, the total opportunity cost of producing the given output is higher. If the firms in an industry do not follow the rule of rational life, the society is pushed inside its production possibility curve, having to sacrifice for a given amount of bricks a larger amount of all other goods than necessary. A central planner could achieve the same allocation as do rational firms, but he would need the information they have. It is for these reasons that many socialist states embrace the profit motive, Yugoslavia being the most successful example. The state lets firms keep profits, adopting the capitalist system of profit maximization and the capitalist prices that give it meaning in order to achieve efficiency. Profits are good for you.

Figure 13.2
Failure to Be Greedy Puts the Society Below Its Production Possibility Curve

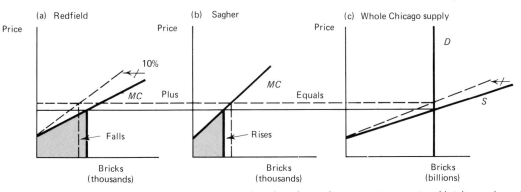

(a) Redfield   (b) Sagher   (c) Whole Chicago supply

If Redfield produces less than the profit-maximizing quantity of bricks, market price rises, Sagher expands output, and total industry costs increase because the marginal costs of production at Sagher and Redfield are no longer equal.

The Industry Supply Curve Slopes Upward

☐ Another general point that comes out of the construction of an industry supply curve from marginal cost curves is that the supply curve slopes upward. At the quantity a firm produces to maximize profits its marginal cost curve must be sloping upward, not downward.

T or F: If a firm's marginal cost curve is U shaped and if the given market price cuts across the U, then the upside cut is at the quantity of maximum profit, the downside cut at minimum profit.

A: True. The area under the price out to some output is the revenue from that output; the area under the marginal cost is the (variable) cost (see Figure 13.3).

The difference between the areas is profit. At the worst quantity, for example, revenue minus cost is $R - (R + L)$ or the top left area L, an area of loss, not profit. The loss is evidently greatest at worst. No firm would operate on the falling portion of its marginal cost. At best, however, revenue minus cost is the rectangle $I + (R + C)$ minus the area under the marginal cost $L + (R + C)$ or $I - L$, with the loss offsetting some of the gain. By the familiar argument, best is best. No rational firm would operate at a point such as worst. <u>Only the upward-sloping portion of the marginal cost, then, is the firm's supply curve</u>.

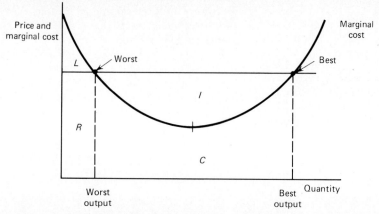

Points worst and best both satisfy the condition marginal revenue = marginal cost, but worst yields minimum profit (−*L*) and best yields maximum profit (*I* − *L*).

□

The Lower Portions
of the Marginal Cost
Curve Do Not Give
Enough Profit to Be
Relevant

In fact, only a portion of the portion is the supply curve, because the <u>price must be high enough to make the profits on variable cost positive</u>. A shoe factory facing such a low price for its shoes that it cannot pay even for its variable costs of labor and materials, not to speak of the fixed and in the short-run unavoidable costs of its buildings and machines, does better to close its doors entirely. The diagrammatic conditions are portrayed in Figure 13.4.

The lowest short-run supply price is the price that just equalizes the area of loss, *L*, with the area of surplus, *S*, giving zero profits. Another and exactly equivalent way to put it is to say that average

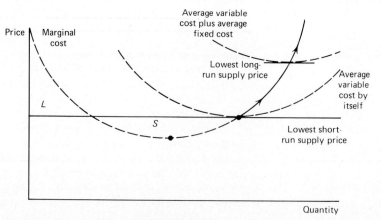

The firm will produce nothing unless price is at least equal to minimum average variable cost and, in the long run, will produce only if price is at least equal to minimum average total cost. The firm's short-run and long-run supply curves lie above these prices.

variable cost just equals the going price.[1] For a time the firm will be willing to supply along the portions of marginal cost with arrows. In the longer run the fixed cost of investment must be covered, which is to say that the area of surplus, S, must be large enough to offset not only L but also the fixed cost. Again, an equivalent way to put it is to say that average *total* cost just equals the price. In the long run, then, the supply curve is only the portion with a double-headed arrow.

In any event the supply curve of each firm slopes upward. Because it does the sum of them all does too. The industry's supply curve normally slopes upward, not downward.

Summary

The marginal cost curve of a competitive firm *is* its supply curve. Therefore the industry supply curve is the horizontal sum of all marginal cost curves, presuming that the costs of the firms are independent of each other and that the number of firms in the industry is fixed. The resulting equilibrium of demand and supply satisfies the rule of rational life, because the marginal valuation of, say, wheat is equal to the marginal cost from each farm. Wheat growing as a whole is at its efficient amount and the growing of wheat is allocated among farms in the most efficient way. A market organizes its affairs as though it were one rational individual or one perfectly knowledgeable planner, which is why the socialist governments of Eastern Europe use the market with such capitalistic enthusiasm.

The industry supply curve is upward sloping because each firm's supply curve is. And each firm's is because only the upward-sloping portion of its marginal cost curve is a rational place to be. In the short run, indeed, only the portion above average variable cost is rational and, in the long run, only the still more limited portion above average total (fixed and variable) cost. The cost curves of the firm, in short, have implications for the supply curve of the industry.

QUESTIONS FOR SECTION 13.1

1. "A cost-saving tactic that some hospitals embrace and others approach gingerly is plain old competing to raise occupancy rates. Mainly, of course, one hospital gains at another's expense. W. Daniel Barker, administrator at Crawford W. Long Hospital in Atlanta and chairman-elect of the American Hospital Association, says, 'I'm not sure competition does anything for the system. It's like drilling in someone else's oil field.' " If competition reduces the price of hospitals to customers, is it like drilling in someone else's oil field (fixed in amount)?

2. Suppose that you are the president of Progressive Pen, Inc., which has three branch plants run by Richard Craven, Samuel Farrington, and Robert Paul. The Craven plant has a total cost function cost $= 100 + (2/1000)(q^2)$, in which q is the output from the Craven plant and cost is expressed in dollars. Using calculus, the marginal cost from this plant is therefore

---

[1] It is "exactly equivalent" because one way subtracts from the same revenue the area under the marginal cost (which is variable cost) and the other subtracts the quantity multiplied by the average variable cost (which is also variable cost).

$$\frac{d\,\text{cost}}{dq} = \frac{d(100)}{dq} + d(2/1000)q^2$$

$$= 2(2/1000)q$$

$$= (4/1000)q$$

The Farrington plant has cost $= 200 + (2/1000)(q^2)$, the Paul plant cost $= 100 + (1/1000)(q^2)$. The branch plants send their output of pens to you and you in turn sell them in a competitive market at $1 per pen.

a. Without doing any algebra, what is the condition for the cheapest production of a given output of pens? Given the cheapest production, what is the condition for the profit-maximizing output of pens if pens sell for $1 each?

b. You could tell the branch plants how much to produce. What would you need to know to decide what to tell them? If you knew it, how much would you tell each to produce (do the algebra)?

c. Suppose that you did not have this knowledge but that the managers of the branch plants did. Suppose that you bring them together and say "Gentlemen, we are going to play a game. I am going to 'pay' you $1 for every pen you produce. Your job is to maximize 'profits' from each of your plants (handing the money over to me in the end, of course). Go ye forth and maximize." What outputs will this decentralized system yield?

d. What scarce resource does the decentralized, market-imitating system save?

3. a. What is the total profit earned by Progressive Pen, Inc. at its optimal output?

b. Review the appendix to Section 2.4 and its discussion of Lagrangean multipliers. Suppose that you make a mistake, telling the managers that $1.10 is the "shadow price" they face rather than the true market price of $1.00. What output will they produce? How much will it cost? (Do it a couple of times: it is easy to make an arithmetical error.) How much will it sell for? What, then, is the loss in profit if you make the mistake?

c. Describe a procedure for finding the correct shadow price (Lagrangean multiplier) when you do not know what it is but do know what profit is earned.

4. The median number of slaves per slave-holding farm in the South rose from 20.6 in 1850 to 23.0 in 1860. The distributions by size of holdings were as follows:

Number of Slaves per Holding	Percentage of All Slaves on Holdings of This Size		Increases or Decreases as a Percentage of 1850
	In 1850	In 1860	
1– 9	26.6%	25.6%	−3.8%
10– 19	22.8	21.6	−5.3
20– 49	29.0	27.6	−4.8
50– 99	13.1	14.9	+14.0
100–199	6.3	7.6	+21.0
200–299	1.3	1.4	+7.0
Over 300	0.9	1.0	+10.0
All sizes	100.0%	100.0%	

What were the unsuccessful sizes? The successful sizes? With this evidence, what curve of average total cost would you draw for 1850 over the range of sizes of slaves per holding? Were there economies of scale in slave owning? Formulate the general principle of survivorship as a test for economies of scale.

True or False

5. If individual brickmaking firms do not face a flat demand curve, then there is no individual or industry supply curve.

13.2 Industry Supply with a Fixed Number of Firms but Costs Interdependent: Externalities

□

Inelastic Supplies of Inputs Make the Supply Curve Even Steeper

The argument has so far supposed without comment that the cost curves of the firms are independent of each other and can therefore be added up without paradox. In certain simple and common cases this is true. The cost curves are truly independent whenever one firm can expand or contract without affecting in the slightest the costs of another firm. One producer of jet fuel can expand without raising costs to other producers; one producer of brass belt buckles can contract without lowering costs to others.

But even the cases in which it is false, also simple and common, in fact reinforce the argument that the industry supply curve slopes upward. The cases are those in which the individual firms all draw on a common resource or input supplied inelastically to the industry considered as a unit. If producers of all petroleum products expand (in contrast to the expansion of jet fuel alone, only one minor product among many), then the price of the input, oil, will rise, since it is supplied inelastically to the industry as a whole. If producers of all brass products expand, then the price of skilled brass founders will rise. One can look down the list of three-digit industries (i.e., very detailed industrial groups) and quite easily think of a specialized but important input supplied inelastically to each industry as a whole for each: for meat products, it is animals, cowboys, and skilled butchers; for dairy products, it is dairy equipment and experienced dairymen; for pulpmills, it is wood chips; for drugs, it is pharmaceutical chemists; for cut stone, it is stonecutters; for electrical lighting and wiring equipment, it is copper. By contrast, a single firm in these industries (or perhaps a single four-digit industry within the three-digit industry, like jet fuel within petroleum) faces itself an elastic supply of the inputs.

T or F: The elasticity of each firm's supply curve is normally greater than is the elasticity of the industry's supply curve.

A: The larger the share of total supply of an input (cowboys, copper) taken by an entity, the lower the elasticity of supply. The lower elasticity of supply facing all ranches if they expand together makes their supply curve less elastic than that of any one ranch if it expands in isolation. If all ranches at the same time expand output, each rancher will perceive the inelasticity of supply as an upward shift in his marginal cost curve (see Figure 13.5).

The dashed locus is a supply curve of a firm that can be added up with others to yield the industry curve. A firm would view such a curve as *the* supply curve if it correctly anticipated that all other firms would respond as it did to a change in price. If it believed itself to be brighter or luckier than the others, it would view the flatter curve as its supply, believing that no other firms would respond to the rise in price as it did. The dashed curve is in any event the single firm's share of the market supply, the curve along which the firms must in fact finish if they all rationally pursue profit. No other curve allows correctly for the impact of their combined outputs on the cost of inputs and thence on marginal cost. And it is less elastic. Therefore, true.

**Figure 13.5
The Industry Supply Is
Less Elastic Because It
Cannot So Easily Take
Specialized Factors away
from Other Uses**

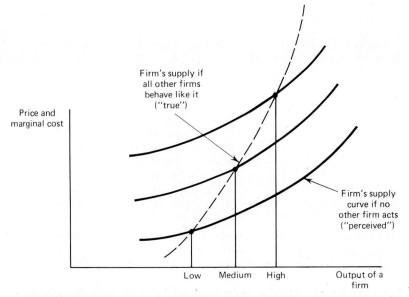

The perceived supply curve of a single firm, assuming that other firms will hold output constant, is more elastic than the true supply curve. The true supply curve reflects the fact that, if one firm increases output in response to an increase in demand, then other firms, experiencing a similar increase in demand, will also increase output. The other firms will bid up the price of inputs used by the industry more than would be the case if they held output constant.

☐

**Strangeness in the
Inputs Used Also
Makes the Supply
Curve Steeper**

Another way of demonstrating the tendency to rising supply price puts the tendency in economywide perspective.[2] When, say, the food industry expands, it draws away labor, land, capital, and materials from elsewhere in the economy to set them to work making food. A dollar's worth of food on the table does not use resources in the same propor-

[2] Joan Robinson, "Rising Supply Price," *Economica* n.s. 8 (February 1941): 1–8, reprinted in George Stigler and Kenneth Boulding, eds., for the American Economic Association, *Readings in Price Theory* (Homewood, Ill.: Irwin, 1952), especially pp. 236–237. See also Jacob Viner's "Supplementary Note (1950)" to his article in the same collection.

tions as does a dollar's worth from the rest of the economy. It uses more cooks, less paper, more land (to raise tomatoes), less capital, more flour, less steel. Evidently, then, the net result of shifting a dollar's worth of output from the rest of the economy to food is to reduce the demand for the things food uses little of, such as paper, capital, and steel, and to increase the demand for the things it uses much of, such as cooks, land, and flour. If supplies of these things are fixed, the relative price of paper, capital, and steel will fall and of cooks, land, and flour will rise. What rises is what food uses most of.

The argument looks different from the earlier one. But in fact it is merely a _general equilibrium_ (i.e., whole-economy) expression of the same _partial equilibrium_ (i.e., one-industry) point. The farther the food industry diverges from others in its use of, say, flour, the more rigid it is in its commitment to a particular combination of flour and other inputs. The larger the share of all flour it demands, the stronger will be the tendency to rising supply price. But these conditions are the same ones for making flour inelastic in supply and for making the inelasticity powerfully affect the elasticity of supply of food. The argument is at bottom the same. The _law of upward-sloping supply_ can be either built up from the theory of the firm as it was earlier in this chapter or deduced from lofty principles about the behavior of a whole economy, as here and in Section 8.4. The law holds true whether viewed from the factory floor up or from the central planning office down.

□
Economies of Industry Scale: Partial Equilibrium View

The exception to the law is the unusual case in which a rise in industry output lowers rather than raises the cost of an input. A rise in the output of cotton textiles, for example, might lower the cost of textile designers or humidifiers. It would do so only if these inputs had themselves downward-sloping instead of upward-sloping supply curves, perhaps because of strong economies of scale in the schooling of designers or the making of humidifiers. Such a happy event—a case of the more the merrier—is called a _pecuniary external economy of industry scale:_ "pecuniary" because it affects money costs of inputs instead of affecting the production function directly, "external" because it runs between firms instead of within one, "economy" because it is cost reducing (as opposed to a _diseconomy_, which is cost increasing), and "industry scale" because it arises from the rise in the industry's, not one firm's, output. If this external economy is strong enough, it can even offset the tendencies to diminishing returns and lead to a downward-sloping supply. Just as an upward-sloping supply curve of iron ore has the effect, as it were, of contaminating every product using iron with the upward slope, likewise a downward-sloping curve of, say, railroad engineering contaminates every product using railroad engineering (most notably, railroads themselves) with downward slope. In the extreme, the cost curve of each railway might fall rather than rise as the output of all railroads rose, and the locus could slope downward (see Figure 13.6).

Notice the demand curves in successive years 1985, 1986, and 1987. The outward march of the demand curve cheapens the product. By

**Figure 13.6
Powerful External
Economies of Industry
Scale**

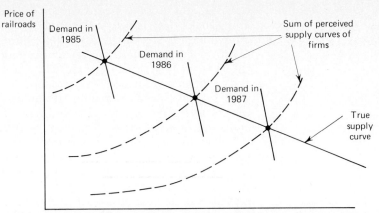

The true supply curve of a firm can be more elastic than the perceived supply curve, and can even be downward sloping, if there are sufficiently strong economies of scale in the production of one or more factors used by the industry. Then the price of factors is bid down, not up, by industry expansion.

demanding more railroads, one gets more and cheaper railroads. Ask, and it shall be given you. Society can pull itself up by its own bootstraps.

☐
***The Case for
Intervention in the
Presence of
Economies of Scale***

The analysis is popular. It is used, for example, to argue that the private, unsubsidized decision to invest in industries such as railroad engineering or railroads themselves will be too cautious, because it will not recognize the cheapening to be gotten from a larger scale of output. In the presence of economies of scale, it is said, the market is short-sighted: if it could see beyond the lumpy and large investment in a bigger railroad, it would catch sight of a promised land of riches; but it cannot (see Figure 13.7).

The railroad industry viewed as a collection of little firms each with rising cost has, one might argue, no private incentive to expand beyond *E:* that is what equilibrium means. But if it nonetheless did, or was ordered or induced to do so by the government, out to the quantity forced, something strange happens. To begin with, at the larger than equilibrium quantity forced, the cost of railroads would fall (not rise, as it will for ordinary industries and as each little firm here *believes* it will). Competition would assure that the lower cost was passed along to the customers, wheat producers, who would therefore themselves have a lower cost and supply curve, represented by the dashed line in the right-hand panel. At the lower cost of wheat, however, more would be demanded, which means in turn that more railroad services would be demanded. The result, which might have been anticipated by a farsighted railroad industry but is supposed here not to have been anticipated in fact, is that the demand for railroad services would move out, say, to the dashed line marked backward linkage demand. It could easily be the case, and is drawn here as though it were, that the new demand would more than justify (at induced) the government's enthusiasm for a forced output larger than private railroads wanted. Since

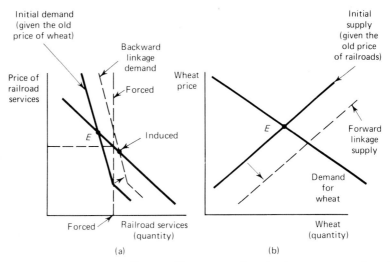

If the railroad industry, initially in equilibrium at *E*, is forced to increase output substantially, to a point such as forced, the lower price will shift out the demand for wheat, a complement of railroads, which in turn shifts out the demand for railroad services to induced.

---

the additional outputs of both railroads and agriculture equal or exceed in marginal valuation their marginal opportunity costs (measuring both along the after-forced curves), the government's plan raises national income. <u>In the presence of economies of scale and shortsightedness, voluntary exchange would not achieve the rise in income, yet compulsion would. Where the invisible hand of the market has failed, the mailed fist of the government has succeeded.</u>

Such external economies between industries, and the economies of scale within an industry that give rise to them, are considered to be among the major failures of *laissez-faire* capitalism, justifying proposals to supplement or replace it by subsidies or central planning.

☐
***Economies of
Industry Scale:
General Equilibrium
View***

In mathematical circles the situation is called <u>*nonconvexity*</u> because, as was seen in Section 8.3, economies of scale can lead to perverse, nonconvex bulges in the production possibility curve. The mischief this does is seen best by reverting again to the general equilibrium arguments. The marginal cost curve, which is the slope of the production possibility curve, is drawn in the top panel of Figure 13.8 as downward sloping in part of its range. Corresponding to this downward slope is in the bottom panel an inward bulge.

The demand curve is, as it says, along the production possibility curve (i.e., the slope of the utility functions along the curve), in the style of Section 8.3, which is why it does not move. Look at the three equilibrium points in the top panel. The point unstable is just that, because it is a minimum, not a maximum. To put the argument another way, the diagonal shading is all positions satisfactory to demanders, the vertical shading all positions satisfactory to suppliers. Only the cross-hatched areas are satisfactory to both, and only at their rightmost

**Figure 13.8
Economic Development
by Your Bootstraps: Told
in Terms of General
Equilibrium for Supply
and Demand (a) and
Production Possibilities
and Utility (b) Curves**

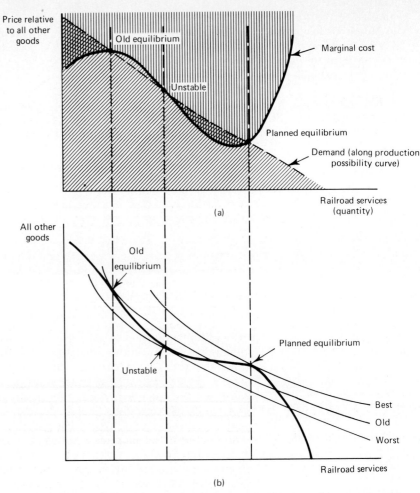

Old equilibrium and planned equilibrium are both stable, but planned is more desirable.

points are all mutually satisfactory deals exploited.[3] Old equilibrium and planned equilibrium are therefore stable, as is also made clear by looking at the corresponding points in the bottom panel. Both points are local maxima of social utility, in the sense that in their local neighborhood small moves to either side make society worse not better off. "In their local neighborhood" and "small moves" are the key phrases. Old equilibrium is on the con*cave*, not convex, portion of the production possibility curve, the best place *in a cave*. If business managers could see out of the cave, they would see that planned equilibrium is even better, the top of a hill. The utility of planned equilibrium is best, but unaided markets will fail to reach it. The failure is often

[3] Compare Chapter 10 on consumers' surplus and Milton Friedman, *Price Theory* (Chicago: Aldine, 1976), pp. 102–103.

said to be particularly serious in poor countries lacking infrastructure or social overhead capital in the form of railroads, schools, distribution networks, irrigation systems, telephones, and the like, such as America in 1837 or Eastern Europe in 1943 or Latin America in 1959.[4]

□

The Case Against Intervention

As a logical possibility, the main concern here, the argument has merit. It should be pointed out, however, that even on a logical level the notion that there is an obstacle to reaping economies of scale in railroads unless wheat first expands its demand for railroads has a flaw. It assumes that the market cannot see out of the cave. It assumes, as the economic historian responsible for one of the few serious factual inquiries into the matter put it, "not only the absence of perfect foresight, but virtual exclusion of foresight altogether."[5] It assumes that investors in railroads look fixedly at presently existing prices, not expected future prices, an assumption that ignores the forward-looking nature of economic rationality. But, to turn to the facts in the American case,

expectations do exist . . . and in the instance of American railroad investment [before the Civil War], they were typically optimistic. . . . The first annual report of the Norwich and Worcester Railroad [in 1837] . . . recognizes that "in regard to transportation of merchandise, etc., there is abundant reason to be satisfied that it will equal our highest anticipations, and *like all similar undertakings greatly increase the business upon its line."* . . . America before the Civil War thus did not suffer from a deficiency of railroad investment despite the private nature of its provision.[6]

Figure 13.7, in other words, is misleading in leaving out more farsighted behavior. The points E, with too small scale of both railroads and wheat, were not equilibria. One of the few factual studies of the matter suggests that the premise of nearsightedness may be false.

It remains to be seen whether the presumption in favor of central planning in the case of economies of scale will survive other factual studies. The theorizing thus far has been built on fragile foundations of fact. For example, the prior fact of the existence of economies of scale at the level of an industry is often supported by arguments such as the following.

T or F: Since industries that grow fast are commonly industries with falling prices, economies of scale at the level of industries are common, and rising

---

[4] The *locus classicus* for this view is Tibor Scitovsky, "Two Concepts of External Economies," *Journal of Political Economy* 17 (April 1954): 143–151, Section II, heading (b), which is an extension of P. N. Rosenstein-Rodan, "Problems of Industrialization in Eastern and South-Eastern Europe," *Economic Journal* 53 (June–September 1943): 202–211. The idea was extended further by Hollis B. Chenery, "The Interdependence of Investment Decisions," in M. Abramowitz et al., *The Allocation of Economic Resources* (Stanford, Calif.: Stanford University Press, 1959), pp. 82–110. The essays by Scitovsky and Chenery are reprinted in K. J. Arrow and T. Scitovsky, eds., for the American Economic Association, *Readings in Welfare Economics* (Homewood, Ill.: Irwin, 1969).

[5] Albert Fishlow, *American Railroads and the Transformation of the Ante-bellum Economy* (Cambridge, Mass.: Harvard University Press, 1965), p. 309.

[6] Ibid., pp. 309–310.

demand will cause prices to fall. (Hint: Suppose that the fall in prices were caused by cost curves' shifting downward.)

A: Taking the hint, if cost curves fall because of improvements tentatively assumed to be unrelated to industry scale (e.g., wider use of steam engines in nineteenth-century factories or of electric typewriters in twentieth-century offices), the lower price will cause the quantity demanded to increase. In other words, fast-growing industries such as the computer industry will have falling prices because falling prices of computation cause fast growth, not necessarily because fast growth causes falling prices. Therefore, false. Both directions of cause are possible (see Figure 13.9).

**Figure 13.9
The Evidence for
Economies of Scale Is
Inconclusive: Fast Growth
(Shifts in Demand) Causes
Falling Prices and
Economies of Scale (a)
Whereas Falling Prices
(Shifts in Supply) Cause
Fast Growth and No
Economies of Scale (b)**

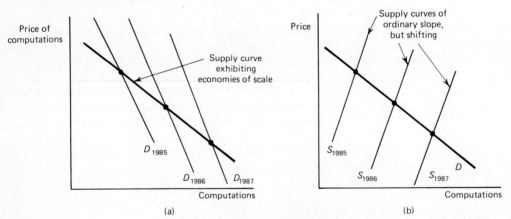

Price often declines in rapidly growing industries. This can be caused by economies of scale resulting in a downward-sloping supply curve or in technological progress that shifts the supply curve outward.

The three observed points in Figure 13.9 are the same in both cases, requiring one to bring other evidence to resolve the dispute in interpretation (another example of the "identification problem" mentioned in Section 6.1). The extent of rise required in the demand curve, for example, is often too large to fit known income elasticities and rises of income. In such a case one would find in favor of the second panel, rejecting economies of industry scale. The importance of economies of industry scale in the ruminations of English and American economists over the past 60 years should not be taken as an infallible measure of their importance in the world.

Summary

The cost curves of firms in an industry are not independent if some input is supplied inelastically to the industry as a whole. The expansion of all firms together will in such a case raise costs more than will a similar expansion in one firm. In other words the industry supply curve is less elastic than the individual marginal cost curves, the effect being more pronounced the more important is the inelastic input in costs. Normally, then, allowing for interdependence reinforces the conclusion that supply curves slope upward.

Pecuniary economies of industry scale is an exception. If the supply curve of an input into railroading slopes downward, not upward, it may transmit the downward slope to railroading itself. Downward slope spoils the optimality of the market. Since the reduction in costs is external to each firm, no firm takes account of the effect to its own expansion in reducing the cost of the input. Too little is produced, and there is room for government intervention to encourage balanced growth. Yet there is room for doubt that this leading objection to market capitalism is factually important.

QUESTIONS FOR SECTION 13.2

1. The argument for rising supply price on general equilibrium grounds assumes that the supplies of things food uses are fixed. Suppose that the things food uses *much* of are, on the contrary, available in perfectly elastic supply, whereas the things it use little of are fixed, as before. If demand shifts from all other goods to food, what will happen to the price of food *relative to all other goods*?

2. Since 1885 many observers of British railways have believed that coal cars in Britain are too small. Half the size of American cars, they are not owned by the railways themselves but by the coal mines. To make larger cars worthwhile would have taken large investment in loading equipment and sidings, and the railways (not the coal mines) owned the loading equipment and sidings. The division of ownership is similar to the case of pecuniary externalities. It is alleged to have the same result: the "interrelatedness" results in less than optimal investment, such as less than optimal investment in large coal cars.[7]

a. Supposing that the larger coal cars were in fact socially desirable, what could the railways do by way of buying up coal cars that would eliminate the "externality"?

b. Short of this, are there bribes by which the railway could induce the coal mines to replace old cars with new ones at the socially optimal time?

c. By 1947 both railways and coal mines in Britain had been seized by the state. Still supposing that the larger cars were desirable, would this nationalization solve the problem? What do you make of the fact that at present the coal cars are *still* small?

---

[7] Charles P. Kindleberger, *Economic Growth in France and Britain, 1851–1950* (Cambridge, Mass.: Harvard University Press, 1964), pp. 141–145.

True or False

3. Suppose there is an industry whose output fluctuates more over the business cycle than does a number we shall call *K*, defined as the fluctuation in national income multiplied by the income elasticity of demand for the product; the industry probably experiences economies of industry scale.

The Long-Run Supply Curve and the Principle of Entry

14.1 The Long-Run Supply Curve

☐
*The Mere Definition
of an Industry Can
Affect One's
Argument*

The analysis of the industry given so far starts to unravel if you ask insistently, "What is the industry?" For example, what is the industry in which a railway competes? The answer seems obvious: track and wheel, locomotives and cars, stations and tunnels, executives and porters. For purposes of a book on railway engineering or of a discussion of make-work rules by railway unions or of agitation in Congress for taxes on trucks this technological definition makes sense. In each case it is the technology that gives the feature in common. But for purposes of analyzing the market for the services of railways, the technological definition misses the point entirely. The Norfolk and Western Railroad and the Santa Fe Railroad do not supply substitutes: they are 2000 miles apart, supplying completely different customers. No single customer faces a mutually exclusive choice between shipping cattle from Norfolk to Roanoke by one railroad or from Santa Fe to Albuquerque by another. And looking at the matter from the railways' point of view, within a technologically defined "industry" the parts in different locations will have different interests.

Q: Like the airlines now, railways in the late nineteenth century divided into eastern and western companies at Chicago. There were a half-dozen companies from the East Coast to Chicago and about ten from Chicago westward. The Interstate Commerce Commission (ICC) was formed in 1887 to regulate this commerce, which it continues to do. The ICC says that it acts on behalf of the general public, but most economists and historians believe that it was in fact captured by the railways soon after its formation, if not actually created by them, and has been used since then to raise rather than lower rates. The simplest version of the "capture theory" ignores the geographical divisions within railways, arguing that the ICC is a simple conspiracy of all railways against the public.

1. Were the eastern and western companies in the same "industry"? How would a ton of wheat get from Iowa City to New York?

2. A ton of wheat cost $6 in 1890 to transport from Iowa City through Chicago to New York. All railways would clearly like to have seen the

rate be higher than $6. But given a $6 cost in total, why was it in the interest of eastern railroads to get the ICC to reduce western rates?

3. Not all goods transported to or from Iowa City came from or went to New York; some came from or went to Chicago. Why would this fact have made western (e.g., Iowan) customers of railways also enthusiastic about reducing western rates?

4. Restate the capture theory in a form that takes account of the two different industries making up "the" railroad industry.

A: 1. No. The two groups did not compete in the same market. They carried the same ton of wheat, but at different stages of its travels. A ton of wheat would travel on one of the western railroads (on the Rock Island as it happens) to Chicago and then to New York on one of the eastern railroads, say, the Pennsylvania Railway.

2. If the Pennsylvania could get the ICC to reduce rates on the Rock Island, the Pennsylvania would receive a larger share of the $6 total.

3. Since some of their business was not through to New York, the customers of the Rock Island would join the Pennsylvania in appealing for lower western rates. In fact they did, arguing that the high rates for the Iowa City to Chicago leg of a journey constituted unfair discrimination.

4. The ICC can be viewed in 1890 as a conspiracy of eastern railways allied with western customers against the western railways and eastern customers. It was not "the" railway industry against customers, but a blend.[1]

☐

How to Choose the Definition of an Industry Wisely: First, Substitutability

The trivial-looking task of defining the industry, then, is difficult and important. If one wants a workable definition of the industry in which railroads compete that means "all suppliers in the same market," then one must pick a single market such as the transport industry from Norfolk to Roanoke, including in it not only the Virginia Railroad and Norfolk and Western Railroad, but also the buses, trucks, autos, airplanes, barges, ships, and mule trains competing with the railroads over the route. If one defines the *personal transport industry* as "automobile-assembling companies, most of whose stockholders are Americans," then the automobile industry will appear to be nearly a monopoly, with four major companies, one much larger than the other three (General Motors, Ford, Chrysler, and American); if one recognizes that Toyota, Volkswagen, Honda, Mazda, Subaru, Fiat, Peugeot, Mercedes-Benz, Renault, and others compete with the Big Four in some markets and that at another remove public transport, motorcycles, bicycles, and shoe leather compete with them in others, it becomes less obvious that the people transport industry is a case of competition among the few, by which the few can rob their customers at will.

T or F: Since the U.S. Postal Service has a legal monopoly of first-class mail, people wishing to communicate between San Francisco and Los Angeles are at the mercy of the service.

---

[1] So argues David Haddock in an unpublished doctoral dissertation at the University of Chicago, 1978, entitled "The Regulation of Railroads by Commission."

A: False, if "at the mercy of" means "unable to find any alternative to." The industry is not the mail between the two cities but communication, with all the possibilities available of telephone, parcel post (e.g., United Parcel), telex, microwave, telegraph, radio, messenger, and personal travel.

The decision whether or not to include the telephone in the industry with the mail depends on the size of their cross elasticities of demand and on the demanders one wishes to emphasize. Cross elasticity, you recall, measures how sensitive telephone consumption is to the price of mail; that is, it measures *substitutability in consumption.* Business may well view a telephone call or a typed letter as close substitutes for many purposes; the courts, however, are required by law to do their official business by letter; and some lovers prefer the phone to the mail. The magnitude of cross elasticity one chooses will also vary from question to question. The only guide is consistency. If you bundle together the varied products of "the housing industry" for some question, you must admit a similar level of variety, and similar lowness in cross elasticities of demand, when asking a similar question about another part of the economy.

☐
How to Choose the Definition of an Industry Wisely: Second, Profitable Supply

The root definition of industry is "all firms that *can profitably supply* goods some group of consumers view as *close substitutes." Close substitutes*, it appears, is a feature of the utility functions of consumers. *'Can profitably supply,'* it will now be shown, is a feature of the cost curves of firms. The industry contains everyone who can make money at the going price, and at a higher going price more will enter.

Q: Tell what is wrong with the following argument used to explain the cheapening of cotton textiles in the early nineteenth century: "The expansion of demand for cotton textiles allowed each firm to expand, to spread fixed costs over a larger output, and therefore to lower prices."

A: Everything is wrong. To take the last point first. If the fixed costs were in fact fixed over such a long period, then they would not determine price, since fixed cost is no part of what does determine price, namely marginal cost. Furthermore, marginal cost for each firm must have been upward sloping, not downward sloping. If it were downward sloping, then each firm could have profited more by expanding at once, which is to say that the firms would not be in equilibrium at the earlier, small output. The argument needs at the least a supplement explaining why firms did not seize an opportunity for profit in front of their noses. Equilibrium and therefore an upward slope of marginal cost would imply in fact that expansion of the industry would have raised, not lowered, cost. The most important error, however, is the first, "the expansion of the industry allowed each firm to expand." This would be true only if the firms in the industry were unchangeable, that is, only if the expanded quantity had to be shared out among the existing firms. But in the long run it does not have to be shared. At the higher price from expanded demand, additional firms will enter (and at a lower price exit). The size of the whole industry does not fix the size of firms within it, only the number of firms. A permanent rise in the demand for cotton textiles increases the number (not the size) of firms, each of optimal size, just as a permanent rise in the attendance at Busch Stadium increases the number of ice cream vendors (not their daily capacity) and a permanent fall in the number of newspaper readers reduces the number of newspapers (not the circulation of each).

The long-run supply curve, in other words, includes potential entrants. The point is the same as that involved in defining the railroad industry, for in the business of transporting people from Boston to New York, the buses, airplanes, and autos are all potential or actual competitors with the New Haven Railroad. The correct supply curve of an industry (ignoring interdependence) adds up horizontally the supply curves of everyone who can at the various prices profitably supply the good.

□

The Meaning of Normal Profit

The remaining question is simply who can profitably supply the good, say, rental housing for students. The answer is anyone who can cover long-run total cost. The answer is straightforward, but it contains one piece of fancy footwork that should be noted. The definition of "cost" of rental housing for students includes of course all the costs of materials such as gas for heating and of labor such as janitors. Slightly less obviously, it includes the cost of capital, namely, the interest cost on the loan taken out to buy the apartment building, dormitory, hotel, or rooming house plus the annual cost of replacing the building as it wears out under the constant assault of late-night parties and the weather plus the expected annual capital loss from a fall in price of a building of given quality (or if a rise in price, minus the expected capital gain). Least obviously of all—and this is the fancy footwork— it includes the normal return to taking the bother, knowing the market, seeing the opportunity, assuming the risk. In a word, it includes the normal return to the entrepreneur.

The word *entrepreneur* is French, meaning "contractor" in the American sense of "building contractor," that is, someone who takes the considerable trouble of bringing together the carpenters, lumber, painters, and paint to remodel your house. The entrepreneuse, then, coordinates the other factors of production. Since she could hire a manager as one hires a janitor, it is not routine management that is her skill. Indeed, entrepreneurship could be defined as all inputs that cannot be hired. If she can buy insurance against some hazard in the business, for example, she is hiring "security," and only uninsurable risks remain with her. If she can hire scientists to do normal science, she is hiring new knowledge, and only unique discoveries come from her. The buck stops with her.

It is easy to point to entrepreneurs in this sense, for they are the heroes of our economic mythology: Eli Whitney, Thomas Edison, John D. Rockefeller, Andrew Carnegie, Henry Ford, Edwin (Polaroid) Land. It is much less easy to point to a line in the actual income statement of a real firm, or in the tax returns of the leaders of the firm, and say, "Ah, I see that the price of entrepreneurship has gone up this year." The income of an Edwin Land will include income as a normal research scientist and as a living advertisement for Polaroid, but mixed into it will be his income for the qualities of brains and energy that make him one of the company's entrepreneurs. The reason one needs a line for "entrepreneurship" in the hypothetical accounts of a firm is precisely because the brains and energy are scarce and have alternative employment. If entrepreneurship is not rewarded at Polaroid, it will leave to join Kodak or to join another industry entirely. The normal amount of entrepreneurship is rewarded at the normal rate and is included in normal costs. Building contractors are not earning "profits," really, when their price is above their costs of hired factors. Given the free entry to and exit from the industry, it is reasonable to suppose they are earning merely "normal profit," namely, the return to entrepreneurship necessary to keep it in the industry. The supply curve, in short, includes normal profit.

The Distribution of Entry Price Determines the Shape of the Supply Curve

The final step in constructing the supply curve allowing for entry is to add up the output produced at each price. When the expected, long-run price rises, more firms find that price exceeds their long-run average costs including normal profit. They enter and output jumps up. If all the potential entrants are clustered around one entry price, as they might well be if the skills required to enter the industry are widespread, then the resulting supply curve is at that price elastic (see Figure 14.1).

A case in point would be the restaurant industry. Because the skills of purchasing, cooking, and serving food are widespread (i.e., themselves elastically supplied), an increase in demand for ordinary restaurants evokes an increase in their number at roughly constant cost.

**Figure 14.1
An Industry That Anyone Can Enter Easily at the Same Price (a) Has a Flat Supply Curve (b)**

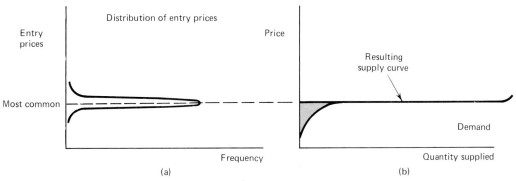

At the most common entry price, the quantity supplied will increase the most. If all the entry prices are clustered tightly around the most common entry price, then the increase in quantity supplied will be very large as price rises at little and the supply curve will be flat (elastic).

Almost all restaurants at the equilibrium of supply and demand would be earning virtually zero profits, because almost all would have entered (thus declaring their own point of zero profit) at or very slightly below the prevailing price. The supply curve for such an industry, with identical cost curves for all firms and no interdependence in the curves, is flat.

☐

Producers' Surplus Is Economic Rent Is Quasi-Rent Is Supernormal Profit

Notice in the diagram, however, the little shaded area. It is the sum of all the excess of the actual price over the minimum price necessary to bring forth various different supplies. In other words, some few of the firms are earning profit. The profit is called in this context *rent* or *economic rent* to distinguish it from a payment to a landlord (which may or may not be a true economic rent) or, if the profits are temporary, *quasi-rent*. It is larger when the entry prices are more varied.

Q: Suppose that there are only two kinds of oil land, Persian Gulf with a very low marginal cost curve and entry price and North Sea with a very high marginal cost curve and entry price. View the two as two firms, each of which (however) takes world price as given.

    1. If world demand for oil is such that the price is exactly at the Persian Gulf's entry price, what is the amount supplied? If the price fell 1 cent below the entry price in the long run, what would happen?

    2. If the price is above the Persian Gulf entry price but below the North Sea entry price, how is the amount of supply determined? Draw the diagram and show the rent earned at some price.

    3. If the price is slightly above the North Sea entry price, what happens? If it is still higher, what are the areas of rent?

    4. What, therefore, is the area above a supply curve, the area called producer's surplus in earlier chapters?

A: 1. If the price is at the Persian Gulf's entry price, the amount supplied is the amount on the Persian Gulf's curve of marginal cost at the entry price, that is, at the zero-profit (zero-rent) point. Evidently, then, rent is zero. If the price fell 1 cent below the entry price, the Persian Gulf would exit the oil industry, at least in the long run. World output of oil would jump down to nothing.

    2. Since the North Sea is still out of the picture, the supply curve when the price is between the two entry prices is simply the Persian Gulf's marginal cost curve. In Figure 14.2 it is the marginal cost curve between Persian Gulf entry and North Sea entry. The rent is the area behind the marginal cost curve, being all the profit in excess of zero profit (at Persian Gulf entry). If the price were 1 cent below North Sea entry, the Persian Gulf would supply out to that point and the rent would be the area old rent. The North Sea would be beyond the "margin of cultivation" (*margin* in this phrase means "edge" or "outer limit"). At some lower price the quantity supplied and the rent would be the lightly shaded area.

    3. If the price is slightly above the North Sea entry level, then the North Sea enters and quantity supplied jumps out. If it is still higher, the area of rent is new rent plus old rent.

    4. The area above a supply curve, it appears, *is* the sum of economic rents

earned in the industry, justifying the notion of producers' surplus used in earlier chapters. The supply curve in the right-hand panel has a scalloped shape because there are only two types of cost curves. If one generalized the argument to many types, ranging from Saudi Arabian through Venezuelan to North Sea oil, the scallops would look smoother and the supply curve more conventional. In any event the producers' surplus is the supernormal profit is the economic rent.[2]

Figure 14.2
An Industry That Few Can Enter at a Low Price Has a Steep Supply Curve and Much Rent

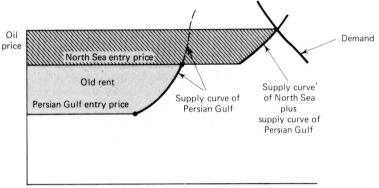

Because firms will enter only if it is profitable to do so, they will earn more than the minimum price at which they would enter. That is, they will be profitable. The profits—also called rents or quasi-rents or producers' surplus—are the area between the price they get and the price they would accept (their marginal cost curves).

The argument returns in the end to its beginning. The supply curve is the sum of each firm's marginal cost, with the condition that price be above the point of zero long-run profit. It is the condition of nonnegative rent that forces one's gaze outward from the existing firms toward all potential entrants. What one sees when one looks, as the next section will show, are the most typically economic pieces of reasoning.

Summary

The industry cannot for many purposes be defined as the existing firms or as the firms sharing a certain technology of supply. It must be defined as all potentially profitable firms sharing a set of consumers who view the products as substitutes. An industry such as American railroads or rental housing violates the definition by including too much in geography and too little in variety of product. The Boston and Maine Railroad does not share customers with

---

[2] By defining the rent as costs paid to the owners of the scarce resources earning them (such as very fertile oil land), one could eliminate the rent and declare all cost curves flat. Competition among owners of firms would result in their paying over to landlords all their "profits." This maneuvre, which protects the zero-profit condition of equilibrium from any conceivable criticism, is sometimes performed in theoretical works. It lacks point, for the rent is only known as what is left over from revenues when the other (opportunity) costs have been paid. Rent is a residual. To define it as a cost would merely encourage one to think that all cost curves are in fact flat when they have been made "flat" merely be definition.

the Chicago and Northwestern Railroad, but it does share customers with Eastern Airlines and the Maine Turnpike. Furthermore, an industry must include all firms, whether presently in existence or not, that can share the customers profitably. The existing firms grow and shrink in number (not necessarily in size) as the demand grows and shrinks. As the price rises above and falls below the point of minimum average total cost including normal profit, the firms enter or exit. When firms happen to have all the same entry price, the resulting supply curve is flat. When they do not have the same entry price the supply curve slopes upward, and the firms inside the margin (the edge) of cultivation earn economic rents.

QUESTIONS FOR SECTION 14.1

1. In explaining why British steel companies before World War I were slower than German or American companies to introduce large-scale plants, one historian wrote, "Great new plants could emerge in Germany and the States without other plants being stationary, let along shrinking or disappearing. . . . German and American markets had far larger and more expansive home markets."[3] Comment.

2. Overheard at a restaurant in Paris at the height of the battle of Verdun in 1916: "Do your know their latest demand? That the market [for arms] should be closed not only to middlemen, but to all businesses started since the war— yes, to all those manufacturers who were not operating in the same branch of industry before 1914!"[4] Supposing that the demand for arms were completely inelastic, would the closure reduce or raise the profits of arms manufacturers generally? Is closure an effective policy against profiteering on arms?

3. The attempt by the British after 1807 to stop the slave trade from Africa to the New World has been viewed by historians as noble but futile. The reason they believe it futile is that the main instrument of British policy in this matter was to use the Royal Navy to seize slave ships off the coast of Africa and to confiscate their cargoes (to free the slaves on the ships seized). Yet of the nearly 2 million slaves imported into the New World from 1811 to 1870, the Royal Navy intercepted only 160,000, or only 8%.

a. Is the smallness of this figure persuasive evidence of the futility of Britain's policy?

b. How would you go about estimating in a supply and demand diagram the true effect on the number of slaves imported? (Hint: Ask yourself how many slaves would have been imported in the absence of a chance of a ship's being seized.)[5]

4. The Bureau of Land Management rents public grazing land in the West to the same few ranchers year in and year out. The rent is low and secure—so low and secure that, when a ranch with public grazing rights is sold, the bureau

---

[3] D. L. Burn, *The Economic History of Steelmaking, 1867–1939* (Cambridge: Cambridge University Press, 1961), p. 240.

[4] Jules Romains, *Verdun*, trans. Gerard Hopkins (New York: Knopf, 1939), p. 384.

[5] The analysis is from J. Phillip LeVeen, "A Quantitative Analysis of the Impact of British Suppression Policies on the Volume of the Nineteenth-Century Atlantic Slave Trade," in Stanley Engerman and Eugene Genovese, eds., *Race and Slavery in the Western Hemisphere: Quantitative Studies* (Princeton, N.J.: Princeton University Press, 1975).

offers the same rights to the new owner. Despite this subsidy to the lucky ranchers, an inquiry by the National Association of Feedlot Operators into alleged excess profits in ranching found no difference in return between subsidized and unsubsidized ranches. Why?

5. One observes that steamboats on the Mississippi before the Civil War earned in any one year widely differing rates of return. *True or false:* This observation is inconsistent with an assumption that steamboating was competitive and had free entry.

6. A tariff is imposed on shoes into the United States. The shoe industry, composed of many small firms, has a constant-returns-to-scale production function. The tariff, therefore, will increase the size of the shoe industry, but not the rents to factors employed in it. *True or false:* In light of this fact, it is difficult to see why members of Congress from shoe-producing districts support such a tariff.

True or False

7. As the number of children in Philadelphia falls, the number of children per day care center will fall.

14.2 The Uses of Entry and Exit

☐

In the Long Run, Profits Are Normal

The idea that firms will enter at the smell of supernormal profit is among the half-dozen leading ideas in economics, ranking with the budget line, the utility function, the rule of rational life, equilibrium, the production function, and the one competing among many. If Americans suddenly develop a taste for carbonated water, the Perrier Company will suddenly become rich. But in the long run its riches will be dissipated by the entry of others, and the many new makers of carbonated water will earn only normal profits. If Chicagoans develop a distaste for living in the center of the city, the owners of property there will become poor. But in the long run their poverty will be alleviated by exit, and the few surviving landlords will earn normal profits. The assertion is that in the long run profits are normal, and in many shorter runs they are on their way to becoming normal. Notice that the assertion is not that super- or subnormal profits never happen. They do. That in the long run the weather is summer and that from December 22 onward it is on its way to becoming summer does not mean that winter is a mirage. But the tendency is nonetheless worth keeping in mind.

The principle of normal profits can be viewed a suggestion for analysis, like the suggestion in the analysis of supply and demand that one rivet one's attention on equilibrium or the suggestion in the analysis of a maximizing individual that one look for marginal costs and benefits. *A piece of economic analysis is not complete until everyone is earning only normal profits* or until the analyst has identified a reason why not.

T or F: If people have a great demand for diamonds, diamond sellers will earn much money.

A: If entry to diamond selling is free (i.e., not obstructed by law), then the sellers will earn only normal profits in the long run. The only doubt is whether the long run obtains. If the "great demand" is of long standing, then the entry of sellers seeking profit will already have taken place. Unless it is a recent development, the intensity of demand for a product (or its "essential-ness" or "basic-ness" or whatever) is irrelevant to its profitability. In short, false. To put the principle another way, whenever there is profit there should be doubt.

T or F: Since a patent on an invention makes the owner the only seller of it, the owner can charge much and therefore earn more than a normal return on investments in making inventions.

A: Apply doubt. If there were supernormal profits, then potential inventors would enter the inventing game until the return was normal. False.

☐
Normal Profits in Various "Industries"

The principle does not apply only to literal firms. A license to operate a taxicab in most cities is very expensive, a mere pittance at the city licensing office to be sure, but $30,000 in the open market because the city does not issue new licenses when the demand goes up. The actual drivers of the cab, therefore, are not usually the owner of the license, or even of the cab itself. They are college students, moonlighting firefighters, ambitious immigrants. The city sets the fares, raising them from time to time at the request of the owners. The owners are often able to recruit the drivers to the fare-raising cause.

T or F: Although they are sometimes tricked into supporting it, the drivers, as distinct from the owners, have no interest in a higher fare.

A: There is free entry to driving, as distinct from owning. The return to driving, therefore, is pegged to the return of the drivers in other occupations and cannot rise above it without attracting more drivers to, uh, drive it back down. Drivers get the average hard-working-but-unskilled wage no matter what the fare is, indeed, whether or not the cab industry exists. So, true.

A spectacular example of the principle of entry in action is entry to the industry of crime. The logic can be used to count the cost. The cost of crimes such as arson and vandalism that destroy property is straightforward, namely, the value of the property destroyed. A building burned down for fun or money is lost to the uses of society. But at first the cost of crimes such as burglary, robbery, fraud, extortion, counterfeiting, and blackmail that transfer property from one person to another appears quite different. After the theft, Al Capone and Bugsy Moran have the property instead of you, but society as a whole (which after all includes Capone and Moran) appears to have no fewer commodities. The value of goods stolen seems a mistaken estimate of the *social* cost.

Q: If there is entry to the theft industry, however, what relation would there be between the value of goods stolen and the value in alternative employment of the resources employed in theft? What, then, is a good way of estimating the social cost of theft (leaving aside police, locks, etc.)?

A: The zero-profit condition implies that crudely speaking the value of the burglar's time, the counterfeiter's engraving skills, the robber's boldness, and the con man's guile, as well as the value of the services supplied by related industries (fencing the stolen property, legal advice, and so forth) must equal the value of the loot. The equality is only "crudely" true because the loot is usually less valuable to the thieves than to the victims and because the theft industry might not always be in long-run equilibrium. In any case the skills and other resources used to reallocate property (i.e., in theft) are lost to the task of making more property. Crime does pay the individual criminal, but in this case does not pay society. The argument that theft is merely a transfer is true, but the value of the transfer is a reasonable estimate of another, social cost.[6]

The equality of revenue and cost, then, is the principle of entry, and is fundamental to thinking economically. It is also fundamental to thinking ecologically: a population of plants or animals grows into an ecological niche until the "profit" is zero, and no more entry is encouraged. So it is with human populations, which inspired economists at the birth of economics to formulate the subsistence theory of wages:

The natural price of labour is that price which is necessary to enable the labourers . . . to subsist and to perpetuate their race, without either increase or diminution. . . . The market price of labour may deviate from its natural price. . . . [But] when . . . by the encouragement which high wages give to the increase of population, the number of labourers is increased, wages again fall to their natural price. . . .[7]

□ The principle applies to politics as well.

Exit, Voice, and Loyalty: Normal Profits in Politics

Q: Laws, such as laws about jogging on the streets, are pure public goods, enjoyed by all if by any and supplied collectively. Among any fixed group of people, there will be disagreements over what laws are best, disagreements that simple majority voting, as we have seen, will not solve. Suppose, for example, that the cities of Wakefield and Reading are neighbors and have initially identical populations, *exactly* half who love jogging, half who detest

---

[6] The analysis is that of Gary Becker, "Crime and Punishment: An Economic Approach," *Journal of Political Economy* 76 (March–April 1968): 169–217, note 4. Destructive crime, such as arson, therefore, has a double cost: the goods or lives lost and the resources lost in plotting and executing the loss.

[7] David Ricardo, *On the Principles of Political Economy and Taxation,* first published in 1817 (Harmondsworth, England: Penguin, 1971), pp. 115–116. A tendency to entry and zero profits, however, is not its achievement. He discusses at length the possibility that "notwithstanding the tendency of wages to conform to their natural rate, their market rate may, in an improving society, for an indefinite period, be constantly above it" (p. 116).

it. Ordinances either to turn the public roads into jogging paths or to instruct the police to shoot joggers on sight are rejected in both communities. Jogging is tolerated but not encouraged. Now suppose that Francis McGrath of Wakefield converts from detestation to love of jogging, George Evans of Reading the other way.

    1. If people cannot move their residence from one city to another, what happens to the proposed ordinances and to the (new) minorities against whom the ordinances are directed?

    2. If the minorities can and do move to escape the oppression by a majority, what is the final composition and character of each town?

A: 1. Joggers are now a (bare) majority in Wakefield and vote to turn all roads into jogging paths, reducing the (bare) minority who detest jogging to ineffectual rage. Likewise, joggers are a bare minority in Reading and must dodge bullets if they venture out as they once did.

    2. Clearly the situation of (1) is not an equilibrium. There is still "profit" to be made by entry and exit. And this is the solution to the problem of providing a public good pleasing to all residents: change the residents. All the joggers will move to Wakefield and all the antijoggers to Reading. The initially identical towns become quite different.

The argument is called the *Tiebout effect*.[8] It asserts that people can vote about public goods with their feet, moving to communities having the bundle of public goods (schools, parks, police protection, jogging ordinances) they want. The problem that people disagree about the amounts of public goods to be provided is solved by moving the people. The result is a segregation by taste and income such as that which characterizes, say, American suburbs, some being rich and vulgar, others poor and refined, others poor and vulgar. It is a consequence of entry to and exit from political communities.[9]

If no one can enter, the existing firms continue to enjoy positive profits, as do citizens of the United States in view of the barriers to entering the country. If no one can exit, the existing firms can experience negative profits, as do citizens of the Soviet Union in view of the barriers to exiting the country. Effective barriers are in fact evidence that there is a profit or loss. Barriers to exit are essential for exploitation, which explains why governments such as the German Democratic Republic or South Africa, intent on forcing their subjects to do their will, erect barbed wire and guard towers at their borders.

T or F: If sharecroppers in the South after the Civil War were mobile, no single country store making loans to sharecroppers could exploit them.

---

[8] Charles Tiebout, "A Pure Theory of Local Expenditures," *Journal of Political Economy* 64 (October 1956): 416–424. An up-to-date discussion of this and related matters is Dennis C. Mueller, *Public Choice* (Cambridge: Cambridge University Press, 1979), Chapter 7.

[9] If exit is impossible, agitation ("voice") becomes the only remedy to an evil policy or evil times, as Albert O. Hirschman puts it in his brilliant and readable application of economic thinking to politics, *Exit, Voice, and Loyalty: Responses to Decline in Firms, Organizations and States* (Cambridge, Mass.: Harvard University Press, 1970).

A: The debt slave under such conditions could leave. The factual question is, "How mobile were the sharecroppers?" An answer to it determines the interpretation of the economic experience of black Americans after slavery. If the sharecroppers *were* mobile, they were not slaves. Therefore, true.[10]

☐

Exit to Avoid Economic Harm

Entry and exit mean that hurts and helps do not always stay where they are placed. The idea is *incidence*, that is, "on whom a burden ends up," which the next chapter will pursue in detail for the case of taxes. For the present, the lesson is to use the zero-profit condition.

Q: To encourage victims of price rigging to come forward, the federal law awards triple damages to the victims. The "victims" in the famous General Electric case of long ago were buyers of large-scale electric generators; the "damages" paid in triplicate to the existing buyers were the markups caused by the price rigging:

1. *True or false:* Because of exit, the firms driven out of business by the price rigging were not around to collect the damages.

2. *True or false:* Because of exit, the firms that survived the price rigging earned normal profits while it was going on, just as they had before.

3. *True or false:* Because of (2), only the ultimate consumers of electrical power, not the firms buying the generators, were hurt by the price rigging.

4. *True or false:* Because the damages paid were a windfall to the buyers, they enriched the owners of the buying firms but did not compensate the people really hurt (i.e., the ultimate consumers and the owners of the firms driven out of business).

5. *True or false:* Therefore, although it might be an efficient way of getting private companies to help the government pursue price riggers, the provision for triple damages has no basis in fairness.

A: The firms driven out were gone, and because their competition was gone the surviving firms could raise the price of electricity to cover the rigged price of electrical generators. That the surviving firms survived implies that their profits were unaffected by the conspiracy. The ultimate consumers, who could not exit, bore the burden in higher electricity prices. When the money damages were paid after the successful suit, the owners of the surviving firms kept the money, since the damages were a fixed (negative) cost that did not affect marginal cost or price. The price of generators was re-established at its competitive level, but the true victims were not compensated for past damages. The true victims were not compensated: that may be efficient, but it is not fair, and fairness is one purpose of the law. Therefore, true on all counts.

The problem looks to the past history of entry and exit; the next problem looks to the expected future history of entry and exit.

---

[10] Two contrasting views of the matter are Robert Higgs, *Competition and Coercion* (New York: Cambridge University Press, 1977); and Roger Ransom and Richard Sutch, *One Kind of Freedom* (New York: Cambridge University Press, 1977).

T or F: Because it will discourage new entry, a law preventing businesses from exiting from Ohio may, contrary to its intent, reduce the amount of business in Ohio.

A: The ability to move if a location proves mistaken is valuable. Businesses moving to Ohio will have to forego the possibility of leaving. Fewer will come under these terms. What Ohio gains by forcing old businesses to stay it may lose by failing to attract new businesses. Therefore, true.

If entry and exit does not protect you in the short run, it may do so in the long run.

T or F: Because a passenger is stuck in a cab once he gets into it, cab drivers would in the absence of regulation exploit passengers; the market in this case gives the passenger no protection.

A: This is the usual justification for regulation of cabs and other things (e.g., hotels). Were such behavior widespread—advertising $0.50 per ride, say, and then actually charging $5.00, backed up with physical threats—companies would form that based their appeal on a guaranteed fare. A roadside diner has the same incentive to serve bad food to nonrepeat customers; Howard Johnson's, Stuckey's, and the like have made fortunes guaranteeing a minimum (low) quality. So too would Reliable Cab, Inc. and No Rip-off Rented Cars, Inc. Therefore, false.

Comment

The argument is not that the market protects everyone all the time but, rather, that the market might in some cases be as effective a protector as regulation. Regulation is not perfect, either. As a Supreme Court justice once said, we must always remember that regulations are enforced by ordinary people, not by all-knowing saints. But we must also remember, as J. M. Keynes once said, that in the long run we are all dead. That fraud in cabs or restaurants will encourage nonfraudulent firms to enter in the long run is little comfort to the robbed passenger and poisoned eater in the short run. The argument for regulation is often that we cannot wait for the long run. And often it is persuasive.

□

Entry to Knowledge

The economist's presumption when she sees no entry is that entry is unprofitable. We are accustomed to complaining about the wretched apartments, the awful restaurants, and the crummy stores in our neighborhood. The economist counsels a mature reflection that after all what exists might possibly be the best that can be done, at least without someone else's subsidizing our apartments, restaurants, and stores. The reflection that opportunities for profit have already been seized is merely a presumption, not a law of nature. Sometimes it will be true that you could indeed make money opening a restaurant to compete with the overpriced hash houses in the town. If you could do so, then your complaint that no one else has done so deserves respect. But it is always worth asking the American question: "If you're so smart why aren't you rich?"

The question is serious. An economist who claims to see an unexploited opportunity for profit is supposing that business executives have not already seen it, entered it, exploited it, and therefore eliminated the profit in it. But it is the business of the executives, after all, to find opportunities for profit. To believe that economic theory or observation can see better what executives daily strain every nerve to see is arrogant. To announce the alleged sighting to the world without charging dearly for it is foolish. The plainest case in point is advice on investments. Your aunt hears that you are studying economics and asks you for advice on investing in the stock market. What do you reply? You reply that if you were so smart as to know which stocks to pick you would be rich; and anyway (if you do not particularly care for the aunt) you would not tell her. To tell other people is to spoil the opportunity, because those other people will drive up the present price of the "bargain" in stocks, making it a bad bargain. The reasoning should make you suspicious of cheap investment advice, such as the stock tips available for the price of a newspaper or for the price of tuning the television to "Wall Street Week." And even expensive investment advice is suspect.[11]

The if-you're-so-smart principle applies more widely. In fact, it is a profound limitation on knowledge of the economic future. You will hear economists and others making predictions about the coming boom or the coming fall in interest rates. You should ask whether such knowledge if it were true would create opportunities for profit. If Paul Samuelson's prediction of the coming fall in interest rates printed in his column in *Newsweek* were in fact true and not generally known, then he or you could make a fortune of immense size using it. Markets exist in which you and he could bet against other, less bright investors. That he is only well-to-do, not possessed of a fortune of immense size, and that the very announcement of the prediction eliminates the opportunity, by encouraging entry, should lead you to value his prediction at its price.[12]

☐

The Ultimate in the Logic of Entry and Exit: Rational Expectations

The implication is unsettling for any attempt to predict the economic future. The econometric forecasts sold to the government for making policy and to businesses for making money appear to be just like weather forecasts. If I am sure that it will rain tomorrow, I can make money buying up umbrellas today. It is not a meteorological principle, however, that people will enter until the weather forecast is worth only the cost of acquiring it. It *is* an economic principle. The very science that makes the economic forecast possible suggests that it is only worth its cost. And the mere announcement of the scientific finding changes the conditions on which the prediction was based. Cold fronts do not change their behavior when they hear the weather forecast; when they hear the economic forecast, people do. On both

---

[11] The case against security analysis—predicting which stocks will make money—is by now overwhelming, though the industry still prospers. See James H. Lorie and Mary T. Hamilton, *The Stock Market: Theories and Evidence* (Homewood, Ill.: Irwin, 1973).

[12] As Samuelson himself demonstrated mathematically in his "Proof That Properly Anticipated Prices Fluctuate Randomly," *Industrial Management Review* 6 (Spring 1965): 41–49.

counts the economic forecast should have built into itself the economics of how people acquire and use forecasts. This subtle and reflexive constraint on economic speculation, both intellectual and money-making speculation, is called *rational expectations.*[13] It is a version of the if-you're-so-smart principle, which is itself a version of the pervasive principle that entry drives profits to zero.

Summary

Profits draw business managers as flowers draw bees, with the result that in the long run profits are zero (or normal). An economist will do well to doubt any assertion that activity X earns super- or subnormal returns, correctly measured. The doubt will not always be warranted. Sometimes people do earn supernormal profits, do get to the gold first, do spot some undervalued stock. That they do, indeed, is the reason for the tendency toward normal profits, for their success attracts further entry. The principle of entry and exit is very widely applicable to businesses, to political communities, to economic regulation, to the stock market, and to every other situation in which movement can earn the mover profit. It appears and reappears throughout economics: as the zero-profit condition, as the condition that revenues equal cost, as the subsistence theory of populations, as the Tiebout effect, as the exploitation condition, as the principle of incidence, as the natural protector of consumers, as the if-you're-so-smart principle, as rational expectations.

QUESTIONS FOR SECTION 14.2

1. It has been observed that innovations in industrial or agricultural or any other sort of technique do not travel with lightning speed throughout an industry. When these innovations are very expensive (mechanical harvesters in nineteenth-century agriculture, computers in contemporary industry), as many innovations are in a relevant sense, and when firms vary in size within an industry, it is possible to develop a simple theory that accounts for this phenomenon (conceived by P. A. David of Stanford University), as follows.

a. Suppose that there is substantial variation in the size of firms before the innovation comes along. Suppose also that the adoption of the innovation reduces average cost by some fixed absolute amount at all scales of output and for all firms. Why, then, will larger firms be more likely to buy the innovation?

b. If we observe, as we often do, that small firms that do not adopt the innovation immediately do not disappear, what assumptions about entry into the industry are required to make the theory work? If the small firms were the more profitable ones, would this assumption be necessary?

---

[13] The most recent uses of the argument are in the mathematical theory of booms and busts, for example, Robert E. Lucas, Jr., "Econometric Policy Evaluation: A Critique," in Karl Brunner and Allan H. Meltzer, eds., *The Phillips Curve and Labor Markets* (Amsterdam: North-Holland, 1976). It was in fact anticipated in the writings of so-called "Austrian" economists, for example, Ludwig Von Mises, *Human Action: A Treatise of Economics* (New Haven, Conn.: Yale University Press, 1949), p. 867:

If the end of the boom could be calculated according to a formula, all businessmen would learn the date at the same time. Their endeavors to adjust their conduct of affairs to this information would immediately result in the appearance of all the phenomena of the depression. It would be too late for any of them to avoid being victimized. . . . What people expect from the economists is beyond the power of any mortal man.

c. What if the innovation could be rented out? What assumption about the costs of renting versus those of owning are required to make the theory work?

d. *Philosophical postscript:* Economies of scale at the level of individual firms are widely neglected by economists. Why?

2. In the middle of the nineteenth century, laws of incorporation were passed in England, France, and the United States that limited the liability of owners of companies in case of bankruptcy to the amount they had invested in the company (under the earlier law of partnership there was no such limit—any partner was liable for any debt of the company, no matter how large). The many opponents of the law argued that it shifted risk to, say, suppliers of a bankrupt company, who could not now be sure of collecting on all the credit they had extended to the company. *True or false:* Even if this were true, the suppliers would not be hurt.

3. Crême-de-la-Crême Canned Soup is usually tasty but it sometimes kills its eaters with botulism; its eaters, you may suppose, are fully aware of the probability of death. *True or false:* Unless the company selling the soup is made liable for the deaths, it will have no incentive to improve the soup (in healthfulness if not in taste).

4. Consumer groups want to prohibit the practice of "repricing," that is, marking up prices of products already on the shelves if a new shipment costs more. *True or false:* This will cause supermarkets to stock lower average amounts on their shelves and to raise prices.

5. *TV editorial:* [Wide shot of a carnival] The Jones Carnival arrived back in town yesterday. Before you send your child to it, you may wish to know of the shocking condition of the machinery [angle shot of dizzying ride, zoom in to tight shot of dirty machinery]. We tried to talk to the owner about the problem [shot of owner slamming a door in the face of the camera; distance shot of owner escaping out back door] but he refused. [Shot of earnest-looking executive of Channel 5.] We could find no state or local office responsible for carnival safety. It is a miracle that the injury rate is low; we should regulate the carnival business before our miracles run out [switch to Channel 5 logo, announcer's voice]: Channel 5 welcomes replies to its editorials.

What is your reply?

6. An economist working for the government shows you a statistical model he has developed of the housing market and makes the prediction with his model that the price of housing is going to climb 50% in the next year. Why do you not believe a word he says?

True or False

7. Since holders of MBAs now make a lot of money, you should go to business school.

8. Although the original owners of licenses to operate cabs in New York City have been enriched by the rise in value of a license to $50,000 each, any subsequent purchaser of a license makes only normal profit on his or her purchase.

9. A law preventing landlords from evicting nonpaying tenants will hurt the poor.

10. Since silver has doubled in price recently, it is a good investment, now.

15

Taxes

Taxes Add Constraints to Markets

☐ The preceding chapters have described the workings of supply and demand in the absence of any constraint but Adam's curse, namely, the cursed scarcity of resources and the cursed limitations of knowledge that constrain supply and the resulting scarcity of income that constrains demand. Many markets do operate in this comparatively unfettered way, and even when they do not, the fetters are for many questions unimportant. That the government by taxing cigarettes has added a constraint to the behavior of producers and consumers of cigarettes is no obstacle to predicting how a new report by the surgeon general or a new cigarette-making machine will change the price and quantity of cigarettes. Still, governmental constraints are common (whether lamentably or commendably common is a separate issue), they provide useful exercises in the theory of price, and their effects are of interest in their own right. Because the economic choice facing parliaments and princes is so often whether or how to constrain exchange, much economic thinking has grown up around such constraints. And the thinking, when fully grown, was found to apply to nongovernmental constraints as well.

Taxation is, aside from death, the most common constraint on exchange, and even in death the tax collector gets his due. It was said in 1820 and could be said again today that "the dying Englishman, pouring his medicine, which has paid seven per cent, into a spoon that has paid fifteen per cent, flings himself back upon his chintz bed, which has paid twenty-two per cent, and expires in the arms of an apothecary who has paid a license of a hundred pounds for the privilege of putting him to death."[1] The government intervenes between the apothecary and his customer, demanding a cut in the gains from their voluntary exchange. In the United States at present all levels of government—federal, state, and local—take together a cut of some 40% of national income and in some other countries, such as Britain and Denmark, their cut is higher. The effects of taxation are important.

[1] Sydney Smith, in the *Edinburgh Review* (1820), review of Seybeat's *Annals of the United States.*

Figure 15.1
Effect of a Tax on Gasoline

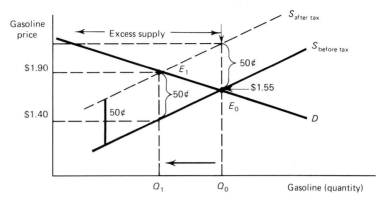

Imposing a tax creates an excess supply at Q_0. Quantity and price must fall to remove the excess supply.

A Tax Reduces the Amount of a Good

The first and obvious effect of a tax on spoons, chintz beds, or, to take a modern example, gasoline, is that it reduces the amounts of them consumed. A tax of $0.50 on every gallon of gasoline consumed will reduce the consumption of gasoline below what it would have been in the absence of the tax for the same reason that, by the operation of the law of demand, a rise in the price of crude oil, tank trucks, labor, or any other input into gasoline will reduce consumption. The government imposing the tax can be viewed as providing an input, namely, the right to operate a gasoline station on the sunny side of the local penitentiary wall. In return for this valuable right, the government requires payment of $0.50 on each gallon sold, increasing the cost at each quantity sold supplied by $0.50. Were the tax imposed on a market for gasoline originally in equilibrium at E_0 in Figure 15.1, the immediate effect would be to raise the price to $2.05.

At this high price, however, there would be excess supply—consumers do not wish to consume as much at $2.05 per gallon as they did at $1.55—and the new price including tax would fall until, by increasing demand and reducing supply, point E_1 is reached. In this new equilibrium output is lower and demanders pay more and suppliers receive less than before the tax put a wedge (of $0.50 in width) between the demand price and the supply price.

The First Fundamental Theorem of Taxation: A Tax Has Little Effect on Inelastic Goods

The amount of the fall in output caused by a tax depends on the elasticity of the demand and supply curves.

T or F: The less elastic is either the demand or the supply of gasoline, the less will a given tax reduce output.

A: True, as is apparent in Figure 15.2. In each the initial, pretax equilibrium is at the same point, and in each 50 cents has been added to the height of the supply curve. Look down a column for the effect a lower elasticity of supply and across a row for the effect of a lower elasticity of demand.

**Figure 15.2
The Less Elastic Are
Demand or Supply, the
Less Does a Tax Affect
Output**

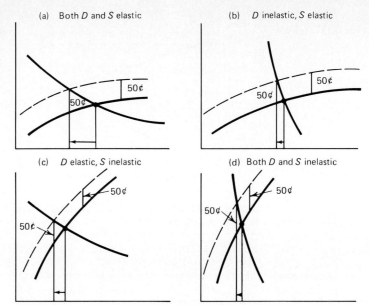

The price paid by demanders must rise and the price received by suppliers must fall, so that the tax can be paid. The less elastic demand or supply or both, the smaller the fall in quantity caused by these price changes. The curves are drawn as constant elasticity curves to make the assertion unambiguous.

In truth, the result is obvious without the diagrams. Taxes increase prices to demanders and reduce them to suppliers. If neither suppliers nor demanders change the amounts they wish to supply or demand very much when the prices they face change (which is what "less elastic" means), then it is evident that the tax will have little effect on the amounts.

You need information about both elasticities to answer such questions as the following.

T or F: If the elasticity of demand for automobiles is -2.0, an antipollution tax on their sale of 5% of their price will reduce the number of such automobiles consumed by 10%.

A: Only if the elasticity of supply of the automobiles were infinite (or, practically speaking, large) would the full 5% tax appear as a 5% rise in the price consumers face, reducing the quantity demanded by $(5)(2) = 10\%$. Otherwise some of the tax will stick to the auto companies or to owners of secondhand autos. Therefore, false. Inelastic suppliers or demanders pay taxes. The increase or decrease of the price from its pretax equilibrium measures on whom the burden falls.

But think before you jump.

T or F: A tax on the crops of blue-eyed soybean farmers over 47 years of age in northwest Iowa will fall chiefly on consumers of soybeans if the world demand curve for soybeans is highly inelastic.

A: False. It will fall chiefly on the blue-eyed farmers over 47 years of age in northwest Iowa, the point being that the demand curve facing them is very elastic indeed, regardless of the elasticity of the world's demand curve, because it is a residual from the demand of the world and the supply of farmers more popular with the taxing authorities. Not particular types of farmers but all farmers—blue-eyed or otherwise—face the world demand. A tax on the whole soybean crop would have the effect described, not a tax on one small part of the crop.

□
How to Sidestep the Question of How the Money from Taxes Is Used

The collecting of taxes, then, hurts somebody. But the collections from a new tax are not usually dumped into the sea. The government uses the command over resources acquired by taxation to redirect the resources toward palace guards, highways, diplomatic receptions, criminal courts, and other useful things. In other words, there is a spending

**Figure 15.3
Possible Repercussions of
a New Tax on Bread**

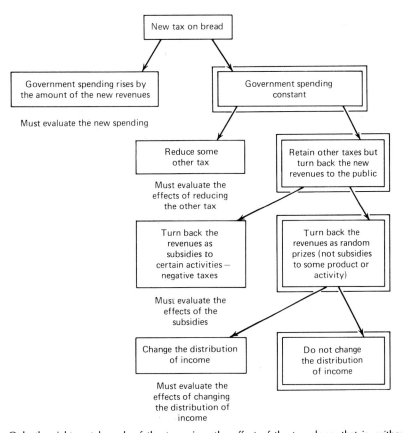

Only the rightmost branch of the tree gives the effect of the tax alone, that is, without the effects of the new spending or lowered taxes that the tax would bring.

as well as a taxing side to the interventions of governments in the market. And even on the taxing side by itself there are other taxes, which may or may not be changed when a new tax is introduced. These matters, however, are not the subject, and for clarity must be separated from the subject of a new tax in the same way that a household's decisions about what exactly to consume are separated from its decisions about what exactly to do to earn its income.

The way to accomplish the separation is to assume, solely for purposes of clear thinking, that the collections of a new tax on, say, bread are turned back to the public in a *neutral* way, that is, in a way that has itself no repercussions on the expenditures of government, the level of alternative taxes, or the size and distribution of income. It is not difficult to imagine nonneutral methods of turning back the collections of the tax on bread. They could be used to buy ammunition used to shoot half the population; or to eliminate a tax of $10 per gallon on gasoline that had stopped all travel by automobile; or to subsidize the output of hallucinogens, distributed free to soldiers at guided missile installations or to the president and his cabinet; or to increase the income of people with a very high income elasticity of demand for Latin poetry. The decision to do such things with the collections, desirable or undesirable as they may be, is distinct from the decision to impose the bread tax. The tree of possible treatments of a new tax is as shown in Figure 15.3.

The rightmost branch of the tree isolates the effect of the tax itself, leaving the examination of combinations of the new tax and changes in total expenditure, in other taxes or subsidies, and in the distribution of income for another day.

☐
The Second Fundamental Theorem of Taxation: A Tax Causes Deadweight Loss

Looking at a tax on bread this way might seem to assume away all the effects of the tax. What goes out of one pocket of the public in the form of a tax on bread goes back into another pocket in the form of a neutral turning back of the revenues from the tax. This is almost true, but not entirely. The fundamental truth about the effect of taxes can be put this way and demonstrated with consumers' and producers' surplus:

T or F: The sum of what suppliers and demanders lose from a tax is always at least as large as the revenue from the tax.

A: True. Consider the tax on bread, taking it to be a specific tax imposed on bakers as illustrated in Figure 15.4. The revenue from the tax is the area $A + B$, that is, the number of loaves of bread consumed after the tax multiplied by the rate of tax per loaf. Recall the notions of consumers' and producers' surplus. As a result of the tax and the reductions in quantities supplied and demanded that it induces, consumers lose consumers' surplus in the amount $A + X$ and suppliers lose producers' surplus in the amount $B + Y$. The sum of the two losses to the participants in the market for bread is therefore $(A + B) + (X + Y)$. The revenue portion of the loss, $A + B$, can be viewed as a transfer that makes someone else better off (whoever it is who gets the proceeds of the tax) even as it makes bread eaters and bakers worse off. In the absence of further knowledge—such as knowledge that bread eaters were on the whole malicious vandals whose destructive activities were fueled by bread—such reshuffling of income results in no net social loss. Alternatively, one could reach down into the lower right-hand corner of the tree of possible treatments of a tax and suppose that the revenues were in fact turned back to bread eaters and bakers each year, on April 15, say. In either case the portion $A + B$ is not socially burdensome. But no matter what the government did with the revenue, there would remain the shaded triangle, $X + Y$, in the diagram, a loss to bread eaters and bakers that cannot be made up by turning back to them the revenues from the tax. The triangle is the social hurt, the fall in national income, the "deadweight loss" from putting a wedge of taxation between the marginal cost of bread (the supply price), and its marginal valuation (the demand price).

Figure 15.4
The Social Loss from a Tax

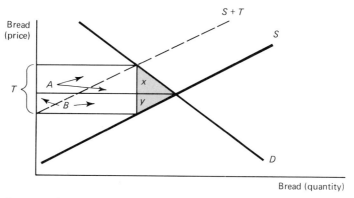

Consumers lose areas A and B when they pay taxes, but the government gains these areas because they collect the taxes. However, areas X and Y are lost to society because the exchanges that would have increased value-in-use by an amount equal to those areas do not take place.

☐ **Using the Identity Between the Change in Surplus and the Change in Income**

That there is indeed a deadweight loss from taxation can be made utterly clear by using the general equilibrium diagram of Chapter 8, interpreting the supply curve as the slope of the production possibility curve and the demand curve as the slope of successive indifference curves along the production possibility curve (see Figure 15.5).

At the after-tax equilibrium in the bottom panel, the slope of the indifference curve is greater than the slope of the production possibility curve, for a wedge (the tax) has been put between them. Look at the magnified view of the region around the after-tax equilibrium. At it an additional loaf of bread has a real opportunity cost in terms of other goods of σ. The tax adds the tax proceeds to this cost, resulting in a higher demand price, to which consumers respond. Indeed, the position of the after-tax equilibrium relative to the before-tax equilibrium is determined by holding tax proceeds constant at some level and sliding tentative choices of the after-tax equilibrium line about until a choice is found that satisfies, for one loaf of bread, the condition that the slope of the indifference curve equals the line plus the tax proceeds.

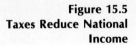

Figure 15.5
Taxes Reduce National Income

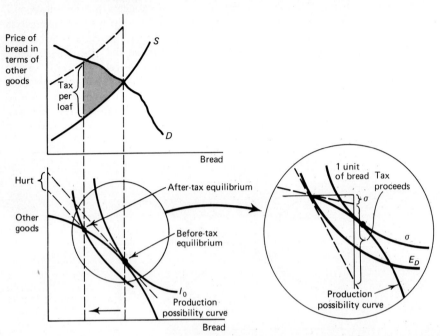

A tax changes the prices paid by demanders and received by suppliers. If these prices were originally at their socially optimal values, the tax will move society away from its optimum and leave it on a lower indifference curve, thus lowering national income as measured in terms of all other goods.

It is evident that pushing the economy to a position in which the slopes of the production possibility curve and the corresponding indifference curve are unequal is a bad thing. The before-tax equilibrium, after all, is on the highest attainable indifference curve. The badness can be measured as a loss in national income. Evaluated at the price (the slope) of the before-tax equilibrium, the national income in terms of other goods falls by the amount hurt on the vertical axis as a result of the tax. By the methods developed earlier for thinking about consumers' and producers' surpluses, the amount hurt can be shown to be equal to the shaded area in the top panel. Any disturbance to the blessed output of competitive equilibrium, in short, reduces national income.

☐ **The General Theory of Second Best**

Any disturbance? Not quite. The assertion is true if the only disturbance to competitive equilibrium in the economy is a tax on, say, food. But if there already exist taxes on other goods as well, a tax on food can *raise* national income. This startling proposition is an example of the logic of *second best,* so named by the British economist James

Figure 15.6
A Tax on All Other Goods
Is a Subsidy on Food

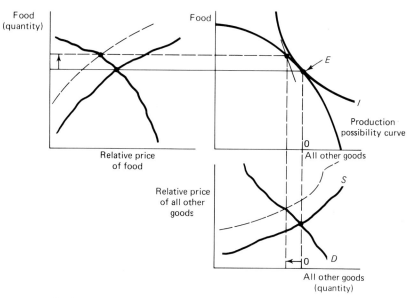

A tax on all other goods reduces the amount of them demanded and supplied. By the same token, however, it increases the amount demanded and supplied of food (the alternative to all other goods). The relative rise in one price constitutes a relative fall in the other price. A tax on all other goods, therefore, amounts to a subsidy on food. Imposing a tax on food (not shown in the diagram) would offset the subsidy and could well bring the society back to the correct equilibrium, *E*.

Meade and brought to the wide attention of the profession by Kelvin Lancaster and Richard Lipsey.[2] Suppose that there is initially a tax on other goods but not on food. The tax on other goods reduces national income by lowering the relative price of other goods that suppliers perceive and raising it to demanders, persuading them to produce and consume less than the optimal amount of other goods. Look at the two right-hand panels of Figure 15.6, where the effects of the tax on other goods are portrayed.

The important point to grasp is that the tax on other goods raises the price of other goods relative to food. If one views the tax as an imposition on suppliers (the result is the same if it is viewed as an imposition on demanders), then at each quantity of other goods supplied the relative supply price is raised by the amount of the tax. But this must mean that at each quantity supplied of the other good, food, the relative supply price of food is lowered (or, indifferently, the relative demand price is raised). That is, a tax on other goods amounts to a subsidy on food, by virtue of nothing more profound than the arithmetic of relative prices. To write out the arithmetic in full, if other goods sell at 2 tons of food per dozen of other goods before the tax, then food sells at 0.50 dozen of other goods per ton

[2] Kelvin Lancaster and R. G. Lipsey, "The General Theory of Second Best," *Review of Economic Studies* 24 (1956): 11–32.

of food; if the tax increases the price of other goods in equilibrium to 3 tons of food per dozen, then by that very fact food will sell for 0.33 dozen of other goods per ton. Food has essentially been subsidized to the extent of $0.50 - 0.33 = 0.17$ dozen other goods per ton. The subsidy is drawn in the demand and supply curves of food, in the upper left-hand panel of the diagram.

Now suppose that Congress contemplates imposing a tax on food as well. Will its economic advisors berate it for imposing still further losses of welfare on society? No, they will not, if the tax on food is enough to offset the tax on other goods, namely, a tax of 0.17 dozen other goods per ton of food. This tax will just offset the implicit subsidy on food provided by the previous tax on other goods and will re-establish the relative price of food and other goods (i.e., 0.50 dozen other goods per ton of food) that obtained before any taxes were imposed. Diagrammatically, such a tax would induce suppliers to operate along their initial supply curves and would bring the society to rest at the point it would have chosen in the absence of any taxes, E. The upshot of imposing a tax on food equal in percentage terms to the existing tax on other goods it to eliminate the distorting effects of all taxes. In short, the correct strategy for a society trying to do as well as it can given that it cannot attain the first-best position of no taxes at all is to achieve the second-best position attainable, and this may well involve imposing rather than eliminating taxes.

It might seem that we have here a formula for taxes with no costs in efficiency: impose an equal percentage tax of everything, for this will leave the true marginal costs and valuations of things undisturbed. If "everything" means just that, taxes not only on commodities that pass through markets but also those such as home handiwork, sleep, and the contemplation of sunsets that do not, then the formula is correct. If "everything" means, however, only marketed commodities, then it is false. The unspoken assumption in Figure 15.7 is that the categories food and other goods exhaust the uses to which scarce resources can be put, in which case a tax on both would offset each. But as a practical matter the tax collector cannot reach everything. If he taxes only marketed commodities, then the taxes on vacuum clean-

**Figure 15.7
Taxes on Marketed Goods
Alone Reduce Welfare**

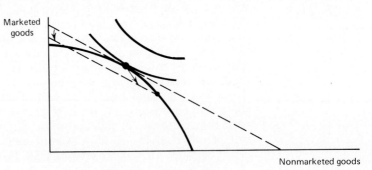

An equal percentage tax on all goods is nondistorting. However, an equal percentage tax that falls merely on market goods does distort.

ers, supermarket food, and psychoanalysis would amount to subsidies on unpaid housekeeping labor, backyard gardening, and transcendental meditation, and society would be pushed away from its optimal output of marketed and nonmarketed commodities.

The tax reduces income interpreted as all desirable but limited goods valued at their pretax relative prices; it reduces income interpreted as marketed output valued at its pretax price (on the vertical axis) even more. To put the matter another way, a tax on marketed goods shrinks the production possibility curve among marketed goods by inducing resources to move out of the market altogether. The second-best argument, then, is no warrant for supposing that an extension of taxation will always offset the evils of existing taxation.

☐
The Ideal Tax on
Efficiency Grounds
Is the Poll Tax

Aside from taxes on literally everything or taxes on goods inelastically supplied or demanded, the only tax without costs in efficiency is one that alters no incentive to do anything. No margin of substitution in production or consumption is to be undisturbed. The only way in which to accomplish this is to make the amount collected by the tax independent of decisions to produce or consume a little more of something. The tax, that is, must be a fixed cost.

Q: In the 1370s a poll tax (having nothing to do with elections: *pol* means "head" in Middle English) of so many shillings per head was imposed by the English king. So offensive did Englishmen find this tax that it contributed to the Peasant Revolt of 1381. *True or false:* Instead of rioting in the streets, pillaging manor houses, and presenting petitions to the king, Englishmen should have congratulated the king on hitting on a tax with no costs in efficiency.

A: True. Short of emigration or suicide, a head tax cannot be avoided by altering one's behavior. Therefore it does not change behavior, in particular the behavior of supplying or demanding goods.

☐
The Third
Fundamental
Theorem of
Taxation: A Tax
Falls Where It May,
Not Where It Is Put

The effect of taxation of gasoline on efficiency (the size of output, because the tax reduces it) and on equity (the distribution of the income between suppliers and demanders, because the tax changes it) depends, in short, on the size of the tax and the elasticities of supply and demand. Further, the effects depend *only* on these things; in particular, the efficiency and equity of a tax imposed on the exchange of gasoline for other goods does not depend on whether the tax is placed on suppliers or demanders.

T or F: A $0.50 tax per gallon of gasoline imposed on consumers at the pump will hurt consumers more than will a $0.50 tax imposed on producers at the refinery, because consumers pay the one, producers the other.

A: The consumer is hurt by a higher price. It does not matter to him or her whether the gasoline station owner supplies the stuff at $1.90 a gallon (having added the tax of $0.50 to its $1.40 cost) or supplies it at $1.40 cents, inviting the tax agent to swoop down to collect $0.50 more. $1.90 is $1.90 and is higher than the price to the consumer before the tax was imposed, say, $1.55 (higher than $1.40 because supply equals demand at a higher price). One can think of the tax as raising the supply price at every quantity by $0.50 because suppliers will want their normal return in addition to the tax. Alternatively, one can think of it as lowering the demand price at every quantity by $0.50 because demanders will value a gallon with a $0.50 tax $0.50 less than one without such a tax. It does not matter. Therefore, false. To put it another way, Figures 15.8(a) and (b) are equivalent ways of looking at the question of how a tax affects the market for gasoline.

**Figure 15.8
It Does Not Matter
Whether a Tax Is Placed
on Suppliers (a) or
Demanders (b)**

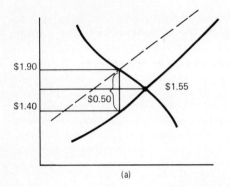
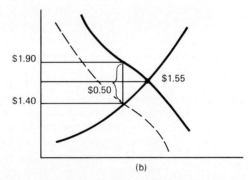

(a)   (b)

A tax can be viewed as shifting supply upward, demand downward, or as placing a wedge between demand price and supply price. In each case the result is the same: demanders pay $1.90, suppliers get $1.40, the tax collector gets $0.50. Whether the supply or demand curve is shifted does not matter because the economic effect is the same whether the tax collector takes the money from the demander's hand or from the supplier's.

To put it still another way, in the final position the new supply price plus the tax must equal the new demand price; which is the same as saying that the new supply price must equal the new demand price minus the tax.

This is all rather obvious, but the proposition that the legal location of a tax does not matter for its economic incidence is remarkably powerful; or perhaps one should say that the proposition is not understood remarkably often.

Q: The City of Chicago imposed some time ago an employment tax of so many dollars per month per employee in businesses over a certain size. Alderman Thomas Keane, defending the tax, asserted that the city's lawyers drafting the law had made very sure that it was a tax on employers, not employees. "The City of Chicago will never tax the working man," said Keane. Comment.

A: Well, no matter how skilled the city's lawyers, the tax does tax the working man. The tax increases the cost of employing labor, which one can view, indifferently, as a higher supply price for labor or a lower demand price. Like a tax on gasoline or food, the tax on employment will raise the cost of labor, hurting employers (and, by raising costs, hurt their customers), but it will also lower the wage paid, hurting the working man. The legal incidence of the tax—the people presented with the bill for the tax—is not the same as the economic incidence—the people made worse off by the tax.

A somewhat more subtle example of the same point arises in discussions of the corporate income tax. When state governments wish to increase taxes, the choice they face is often described as that between taxing people (with a sales or personal income tax) and taxing corporations. The contrast is imaginary. For one thing, corporations are people (if perhaps out-of-state people), not disembodied entities the taxation of which causes no personal pain. For another, the tax on corporate profits, which in the first instance might seem to fall on corporate stockholders, need not stay where it is put. The tax initially drives down the normal return to corporate ownership, inviting capital to leave the corporate sector or at any rate the corporate sector of the state imposing the tax. This in turn raises the relative price of goods produced in the corporate sector and reduces the wage (or employment) of resources employed in the corporate sector. The consumers and employees of General Motors Corporation and General Mills, Inc. pay some of the tax.

□
The Uses of Entry, Revisited

The third fundamental principle of taxation, like the first two, is a consequence of competitive equilibrium. In particular it is a consequence of the principle of entry. A tax or subsidy does not stay where it is put if putting it there creates profits above or below normal. The shifting of the incidence of the tax or subsidy does not stop until all profits are normal, which is to say that it does not stop until the marginal suppliers and demanders are back on their supply and demand curves. The argument applies in fact to much more than taxes.

T or F: Renters of apartments close to the University of Iowa get a valuable benefit from performances at the university by champion musicians or by champion basketball players and wrestlers.

A: If a renter did get the benefit, the renter would be earning, so to speak, supernormal profits. That is, by comparison with some renter far from the university paying the same price the renter nearby would get extra benefits, free. Such a situation is not an equilibrium. If it existed, people would shift from the sticks to Iowa City (in which metropolis the university is located), driving up rentals there and lowering them in the places they deserted. In other words, in equilibrium the renter near the university would pay more for the amenity of having the university close by. The amenity looks at first like a subsidy to renters in Iowa City, but in fact they pay for it in higher prices for apartments.

The beneficiaries of any new amenities in Iowa City are in fact the old owners of property, not the people who rent from them. The old property, especially the land itself close to the university, is supplied inelastically. Just as it would bear a tax on property (even if the tax were put legally on the renters instead of the landowners), so too the old property collects whatever element of subsidy to the neighborhood there is in the opening of a new theater or sports arena at the university. Reasoning of this sort is extremely important for all manner of questions of policy.

Q: The city fathers and mothers of Iowa City propose to run a highway through the west side of the city to make it easier for west-siders to get to the downtown. The downtown property owners claim that commuters into town will benefit. The near-west-side property owners over whom the highway will be built claim on the contrary that the only beneficiaries will be property owners, downtown and elsewhere. Who is right?

A: If the commuters into town in fact get any benefit in ease of travel, they will be willing to pay more for their houses and more for the goods they buy in the downtown. The resource that is inelastically supplied—land— benefits. Only to the degree that commuters also happen to be landowners will they benefit. The near-west-siders are right. On such logic are city govern- ments everywhere founded: landowners are in the long run the only people interested in effective schools, easy roads, and other amenities paid for by the city.

Summary

Taxes clog markets. A tax puts a wedge, to use another metaphor, between the buying and the selling price, raising one and lowering the other. If the taxed good is elastically demanded or supplied, the resulting change in price has a large effect on quantities. The inelastic supply or demand bears the burden of the tax disproportionately, being unable to move out from under it (to alter the metaphor once again): that is what "inelasticity" means—inflexi- bility. Society as a whole, however, cannot move out from beneath the burden of a lower than optimal output of the taxed good. The area of unsatisfied willingness to pay in excess of willingness to supply is the "deadweight loss" (still another metaphor, showing that scientific language is no less fanciful than literary language). The deadweight loss is indeed the fall in the nation's income caused by the imposition of a tax. But taxes do not always cause a net fall in income. If the tax offsets some implicit subsidy, for example, or if it offsets some other tendency to produce too much of a good, then, by the "theory of second best," the tax may be desirable. The only truly neutral tax is one that affects no incentive to do anything, whether the thing is mar- keted food or nonmarketed creative leisure. It is nearly impossible to imagine such a tax. Certainly no existing income or excise tax approaches it.

The clogging effects of taxes are not felt necessarily where they are placed by law. The notion that taxes and subsidies end up affecting people whom the law did not believe it was affecting is a good example of characteristically economic reasoning. And it is a good example of the principle of entry. Until all incentive to enter or exit is gone, the analysis of a tax or subsidy is not finished. When it is finished, it often turns out that all manner of benefit and burden have shifted in the night.

QUESTIONS FOR CHAPTER 15

1. a. Suppose that the United States consumes a small enough portion of the rest of the world's supply of shoes that changes in the demand of American consumers have little effect on the world price. Draw the supply curve of shoes facing the United States as it imports shoes from foreigners.

b. Suppose now that the United States produces some shoes. Draw a domestic supply curve on the diagram of (a). Draw the demand curve of Americans for shoes if the United States imports shoes as well as producing them. What determines the price of shoes in the United States? What is the quantity of imports?

c. Suppose that the American government, responding to the wishes of members of Congress from eastern Massachusetts, imposes a tariff of $$T$ per shoe imported. What happens to the foreign supply curve perceived by Americans after the tariff? What happens to the American price? to the American quantity supplied? to imports?

d. Identify the increase in producers' surplus to American producers of shoes and the decrease in consumers' surplus to American consumers of shoes. Identify the government's revenue from the tariff. Is this revenue a net loss to the United States?

d'. What, therefore, is the net loss to the United States of imposing the tariff?

2. In terms of the diagram in Question 1, what is the maximum amount that the beneficiaries of the tariff (the shoe producers and the taxpayers whose taxes are reduced by the revenue from the tariff) would be willing to pay to convince Congress to vote for the tariff? What is the maximum amount that consumers of shoes would be willing to pay for a vote against it? What do you conclude from the difference between these two amounts about the desirability of the tariff?

3. The United States is a major importer of cameras (chiefly from Japan and Germany). It consumes, in other words, a large share of the rest of the world's supply.

a. Draw the excess supply curve for cameras of the rest of the world and the excess demand curve of the United States in a diagram and identify the equilibrium point.

b. What happens to the equilibrium point when a tariff of $$T$ per camera is imposed?

c. What is the loss to American consumers of cameras? What is the gain to the American Treasury and thence to American taxpayers? Is the tariff ever desirable from the American point of view?

4. Suppose that Argentina, a small country in international trade, imposes a 10% tax on its exports, such as beef and wheat.

a. What will this export tax do to the Argentinian price of beef and wheat relative to the price of Argentinian imports, such as televisions and automobiles?

b. What will a 10% import tax do to the price of beef and wheat relative to televisions and automobiles?

c. If the value of imports is equal to the value of exports, what general assertion can you make about the effect of export taxes compared with import taxes?

5. Britain both produces and imports automobiles, taking a small percentage of foreign supply as its imports.

a. Show in a diagram the effects of a £100 import tariff on autos on government revenue, on imports, on rents to British producers, and on British consumers.

b. Show that a £100 tax on all autos consumed in Britain, whether foreign or British made, combined with a £100 subsidy to British manufacturers for every auto they make will have effects equivalent in every detail to the tariff.

c. Reflect briefly but cynically on the following facts. Britain and other Common Market countries are committed to free trade in autos among themselves. Yet Britain and other Common Market countries have large taxes on automobiles and large government subsidies to national auto manufacturers.

True or False

6. The social security plan is an excellent bargain for employees because their employer is required to contribute a dollar for every dollar the employees themselves pay into their retirement fund.

7. If bread is supplied perfectly inelastically, a tax on bread has no social cost.

8. If bread is demanded inelastically, a tax on bread has no social cost.

9. A once-for-all tax on stocks of paintings by Picasso has no effects on efficiency.

10. Subsidies are negative taxes. Since taxes reduce efficiency, a subsidy to shipbuilding will raise efficiency.

Competition for Property Rights

16.1 Competition for Supernormal Profits

The ingenuity of governments in constraining exchange is astonishing. In addition to ordinary taxes collected in money, the government, often with the enthusiastic approval of its citizens, imposes taxes and subsidies collected in goods, compulsory services, prohibitions, regulations, price controls, rationing, quotas, and constraints on entry.

☐ **Quotas**   Foreign trade is a good place to begin in exploring these fruits of the human imagination. An alternative to a tax on imports is a quota, a restriction on the physical amount per year of shoes from Italy or shirts from Hong Kong or autos from Japan permitted to enter the United States. In many ways the effects of a quota are the same as the effects of a tariff. If a quota on, say, shirts is to have any effect, the amount allowed to be imported must be less than the amount that would have been imported without the quota. In Figure 16.1, which shows the American excess demand for shirts, the constraint on the number of shirts imported must be to the left of equilibrium.

To the delight of the stockholders and workers at Hathaway and

Figure 16.1
Import Quotas Raise
Domestic Prices

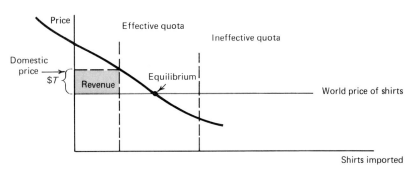

An effective quota causes price to rise by T, as does a tariff of T. The quota causes the transfer of area revenue from consumers to the owners of the quota rights; the tariff, from consumers to the government.

Arrow, the American price of shirts is raised from the world price to the domestic price, as though a tariff of $$T$ had been imposed on the importation of shirts. If the importation of shirts is not to become a mad scramble to import before the yearly quota is used up, however, the government must somehow allocate the right to import shirts. It could sell the licenses to import some number of shirts to the highest bidder, in which case the quota would have effects identical in all respects to an import tariff of height T in the diagram (namely, the import tariff that would restrain imports to the amount specified in the quota: 100,000 shirts per year, say). This is not the usual method the government chooses. More frequently, it bestows on certain lucky people the license to import, with the result that the revenues from the implicit "tariff" accrue to these people. This is the main difference between a tariff, under which the revenue goes to the government, and a quota, under which the revenue from being able to buy at the world price and sell at the higher domestic price goes to the fortunate holders of the right to import so many shirts, tons of butter, or barrels of oil.

☐
Licenses

A quota on foreign trade is merely a special case of restrictions on entry. Whenever governments—or, for that matter, gangster chieftains, local temperance societies, unions, professional societies, holders of patents, or hostile public opinion—restrict entry to the business of providing liquor by the drink or medical treatment or plumbing, they bestow on the lucky few who remain a prize. The prize is equivalent to the revenue from a tax, and the value of the license (which becomes apparent if it can be sold) is a measure of the size of the tax. Professional sports, for example, have long been exempted from the antitrust laws in the United States, with the result that owners of, say, baseball teams can enforce restrictions on entry. The right to operate a major league baseball team changes hands at prices of several million dollars.

☐
Price Controls

The enthusiasm with which governments impose price controls is usually a reflection of the enthusiasm with which people—or at any rate most of the people most of the time—call for price controls. Judging from their prevalence and persistence, few laws are more popular, for example, than the ones restricting interest rates to some figure below 8% or 18% or 80%—whatever figure is currently considered "usury." Eight centuries ago Christians in Europe were not permitted to loan money at all (needless to say, many Christians nonetheless did), and Jews and Moslems in Europe were permitted to loan it (to Christians) only at rates less than 42% per year. Rent controls, likewise, are perennially popular. Rents on some buildings in Paris have been frozen since World War I. Minimum wages are still another case in point, in this case a minimum rather than a maximum price. The periodic deliberations on its level find few members of Congress willing to vote against a rise.

Price controls are a search for a just price lower or higher than the one that demanders are willing to pay in view of suppliers' willingness to accept. The question that arises naturally is, if a ceiling on interest rates of 8% on mortgages in Illinois is better than the "usurious" rate of 10% at which the market would arrive without constraint, is not 4% or 0% still better? If rents in Paris at their level in 1915 are better than the "exorbitant" level they would reach without constraint, is not the level of 1789 or 1315 still better? If Congress can in fact improve the lot of workers by raising the minimum wage from $3 to $4 an hour, is not $10 or $100 an hour still better? The answer is made obvious by the extremes. The $100 an hour would prevent some mutually advantageous exchanges between the supplier and the demander of labor, namely, those numerous exchanges for which the labor was not worth $100 an hour. The loss from price controls, as from licenses or quotas or taxes, is a triangle of foresaken opportunities for exchange. Some particular person may be helped, but people as a whole are hurt.

☐
Completing the Analysis

But the argument that quotas and price controls stay where they are put and result merely in triangles of social loss (and rectangles of private gain) is incomplete. It is incomplete because it assumes that the citizens do whatever the government tells them to do. This is a pessimistic or an optimistic view of human nature depending on whether the government has told its citizens to hate foreigners or to love their neighbors, but it is at any rate questionable as description.

People in fact try to avoid the government's imposition or shift it to someone else or get for themselves the benefit it creates. An analysis of quotas or price controls that stops at full compliance is as incomplete as an analysis of the incidence of a tax that stops at its legal incidence, and for the same reason. A quota on auto imports or a license to operate a taxicab creates so to speak a social vacuum into which the air of self-interest rushes.

☐
The First Result: A Market for Rents Develops

The vacuum is the difference between the demand price and the supply price that a perfectly law-abiding and passive acceptance of the quota, control, license, or tax would bring. The first result is that there arises a market in the very right to buy low and sell high that a license to operate a cab, say, creates. Most cities restrict the number of cabs allowed to ply the streets for hire. The enforcement of the restriction has sometimes been given unwelcomed teeth by the owners and operators of licensed cabs. In London the attempt by "minicabs" to compete with the familiar black cabs was met with beatings, firebombings, and murder. The restrictions on entry reduces the supply of taxicab services, raises the price above the level to which open competition would drive it (cities also regulate the price of rides, but that is another story), and makes the right to own and operate a taxicab valuable. In many American cities the price of a cab license purchased from its previous owner is many thousands of dollars.

Q: Illinois restricts the number of liquor stores to a small number well below the number that would exist without the restriction. Describe how to derive the demand curve for licenses from the supply and demand curves of the industry.

A: The simplest assumption is that all liquor stores have identical cost curves, in which case the long-run supply curve of the industry (in the absence of restrictions) is flat at the point of minimum average cost. With the number limited to a small number, however, the supply curve of the industry beyond the point at which the small number of liquor stores are producing at minimum average cost is the horizontal sum of the liquor stores' long-run marginal cost curves, the solid upward-sloping curve in Figure 16.2.

At another number, say, even smaller, the supply curve is the dashed curve in the diagram, and the net revenues accruing to the owners of liquor licenses (who may or may not be the same people who operate the liquor stores) is different, area $P'e'N'c$ instead of $PeNc$. The various areas divided by the corresponding number of firms (and converted to a dollar sum that one would be willing to pay for such a stream of dollars by dividing by the prevailing interest rate) are the demand prices per license (see Figure 16.3). At the point competitive or beyond, of course, no one is willing to pay anything for a license, for only the competitive rate of return can be earned by using it.

The institution of licenses, in other words, creates a valuable right, the right to collect rents. People seek rents. The demand price for liquor licenses can be viewed as a demand price for restriction on entry,

**Figure 16.2
Restrictions on Entry
Result in Supernormal
Profits**

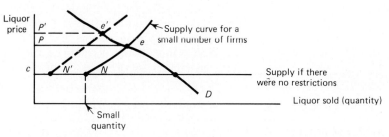

With entry limited to a small number of firms, at most a small quantity can be produced at minimum average cost. To produce more, existing firms must expand along their marginal cost curves, which are upward sloping. Therefore industry supply with entry restrictions is upward sloping and firms can earn profits.

**Figure 16.3
The Price per License at a
Small Number of Licenses
Is the Capitalized Value of
Net Revenues at a Small
Number**

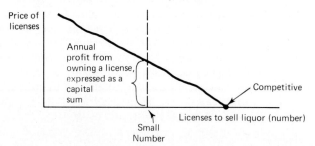

A license to operate a firm is worth an amount equal to the net present value of the firm's economic profits. This amount is smaller, the more firms are allowed to produce to satisfy a given demand.

payable as an illegal bribe to whatever public servant has liquor licenses within his or her gift.

T or F: The lower the salary of building inspectors in Chicago and the tighter the restrictions they are asked to enforce, the more common will be incidents of bribery of inspectors.

A: Other things must be assumed equal, such as the law of bribery, the wages of inspectors in alternative employment, and the prevailing standards of morality. The lower the salary, the lower the supply price of incidents; the tighter the restrictions, the higher the demand. In short, true.

☐

The Market's Evasions of Restrictions Encourage Efficiency

From the point of view efficiency alone, of course, evasion of a restrictive law and the associated bribery is not all bad. The restriction on unsafe electrical work, for example, might be argued to result in too few buildings; it may be better on balance to build many unsafe buildings than too few safe ones. Any evasion of the law would therefore result in an increase of efficiency, an increase in the number of mutually advantageous exchanges between builders and buyers of houses. That the building inspectors pocket part of the difference between the selling price and the buying price of housing created by the building code is a matter of the distribution of income, not its size. Petty and not so petty graft in government is in fact often defended on such grounds: it is said in Chicago and in many other places that no building could be built that adhered literally to every item in the building code.

And in less controversial cases the point is still plainer. Few economists think much of quotas on imports, for example, and view their evasion with indifference bordering on pleasure. That there is a market in the right to import under a quota, whether or not the market is fully legal, strikes the economist as a good thing, bringing the right into the hands that value it most. In this sense the restrictions bring no further evils than the welfare triangles of loss. That there develops a secondary market in the right to collect the rent does not affect its size, and any evasion of the restriction creating the rent reduces it.

☐

The Second Result: The Wastefulness of Nonmarket Competition

The second result of self-interest rushing into the vacuum created by restrictions, however, is less pleasing. Prohibited by law from buying a Japanese car at the low world price or even from offering a bribe in the secondary market to the customs officer in charge of enforcing the quota on cars, the self-interested person turns to other forms of competition. To the regular astonishment of legislators, lawyers, and journalists, if people are prevented from paying for objects of desire in money, they will attempt to pay in other coin—in theft, bribery, friendly persuasion, or queuing. A series of acts of Parliament limiting rent increases in Britain has encouraged "squatting," that is, the stealing of housing by occupying it when it is temporarily empty and trusting to the law's leniency and the law's delay to keep it for a while. Payments under the table (called "key money") to induce tenants of rent-controlled apartments in New York City to surrender them to a new one are commonplace. Rent control makes it costless for landlords to indulge their preferences for white, middle-class Protestants with no dogs or children: competing for housing with a pleasant, educated manner and the right color skin is the natural alternative when competing with money is outlawed and when the queue outside each apartment is, at the going price, long.

These adjustments to price control reduce national income, not only by the amount of the triangle of lost exchange but also by the amount wasted competing. The point is familiar from other contexts.

T or F: The value of the goods stolen plus the cost of police and locks to prevent stealing is a good estimate of the amount by which stealing reduces national income.

A: The question repeats an analysis given earlier. The cost of the police and locks is the obvious portion of the sum. The value of the goods stolen might seem at first irrelevant to the size (as distinct from the distribution) of national income: it is merely the amount transferred from legal owners to the thieves. But thieves will steal things to the point at which their reward in this profession (namely, the value of the goods stolen) is equal at the margin to their reward in an alternative profession, such as running a flower shop or lecturing on the economics of crime. In other words, the value of the goods stolen will equal the value of the flowers and lectures not provided to society when thieves embark on a life of crime. Therefore, true. National income is lower by this amount.

Even when applied to literal stealing, the point is widely useful. The Scottish highlander spends his days raising beef in order to transfer it to lowlanders in exchange for bread. An alternative way in which he can compete for the bread is to spend his days training for war in order to steal the bread from the lowlanders. The highlander by himself may well be indifferent between these two uses of his time, since both get him bread. In the one case, however, the time used results in a benefit to someone else (namely, beef to the lowlanders), while in the other, it does not. Scottish society as a whole is not indifferent between the two methods of establishing who eats the bread, the method using up resources to make beef to entice lowlanders into a voluntary exchange or the method using up the same resources to seize the bread. Scottish income will be higher (adding beef to the goods produced, for example) if competition is limited to voluntary exchange. One can in fact shed light on the economic development of Scotland from the sixteenth to the eighteenth centuries in just these terms.

☐

Waiting Time Is the Most Important Example of the Waste

Spending time waiting in a queue to buy bread is wasteful in the same way as is stealing and is a still more common method of competition alternative to money payment.

T or F: Time is money, it is said. Therefore it is equally efficient to allocate groceries by time (keeping the price of groceries low and letting people compete by offering more time in waiting lines for the underpriced groceries) as by money (raising the price and letting people compete by offering more money).

A: Waiting in line uses up resources (time in this case) in competing for the groceries without a corresponding benefit to someone (namely, owners of grocery stores). The resources are merely thrown away, with the most profligate line-stander getting the most goods. Therefore, false. Instead of shifting around more bargaining counters (money) at a low cost in waste motion, hours are used up in allocation itself, as distinct from making goods.

The cause of queuing is an inability to bid for the item with money. A selfish owner of a parking place, a loaf of bread, or a tennis court would always wish money to be given to him rather than time in a queue to be given to no one. That queues do form on roads, in supermarkets, or at tennis courts is testimony to the difficulty, natural or artificial, of raising the price on short notice to the extent necessary to eliminate the queue.

Queuing is usually defended on grounds of equity. People are more equally endowed with time than with money, it is argued, and therefore permitting a queue to form will be more equitable than will allowing a price to rise. This is sometimes true (although even if true not necessarily decisive), but it is also sometimes false. If one of the members of a wealthy household stays at home, then that household has more time to shop for groceries than does a poorer household in which both partners work. If companies provided chauffeured cars to their top executives (as British companies do), then the top executives (that is, their chauffeurs) will have more time to search for parking spaces than will less wealthy executives who must drive themselves. The point is that money can sometimes buy waiting time.

Here is another example of the waste from queuing, with a more quantitative flavor.

Q: A maximum price of 10 cents per loaf is imposed on bread. At the daily quantity supplied by bakers, when the price they receive is 10 cents (100 loaves), the demand price is 35 cents.

1. If consumers compete for the cheap bread by queuing, what is the *full* amount they pay for the bread (including the value they put on their queuing time)?

2. What is the full social loss from the price control on bread?

A: 1. The situation is as shown in Figure 16.4. Bakers produce the 100 loaves sold at 9 A.M. when the shops open each morning, for which consumers pay 10 cents per loaf, or area *B* ($10) in total. But they would be willing to pay 35 cents per loaf, and will. They will rise at dawn or before to join the queue outside the bakers' shops each day, paying in the end 10 cents per loaf in money and 25 cents (by their valuation) in time wasted waiting for 9 A.M. The consumer who does not value a loaf of bread as much as 35 cents will not join the queue (and will not get the bread). The customer who valued it more than 35 cents would be willing to join it still earlier. The queue will lengthen until the last person to bother joining it pays exactly 35 cents in total, the equilibrium price for a constrained supply of 100 loaves. The full amount that consumers pay is $A + B$ (= $25 + $10 = $35). Notice that if the demand curve has an elasticity of less than 1.0, they will pay *more* than they would pay at the unconstrained equilibrium.

2. The social loss is C, the usual triangular area, plus A ($25). Consumers have been induced by price controls to throw away resources valued at A (that they might throw away time for sleep or leisure rather than time at the factory is irrelevant: the hours are nonetheless scarce and desirable, a part of income measured correctly). The area A is the new element. For many analyses of the inefficiencies springing from constraints, it is much the largest.

Figure 16.4
Queuing Wastes
Resources in Addition to
the Triangle of Foregone
Exchange

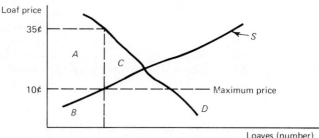

At a money price of 10 cents, not enough bread is supplied to satisfy demand. As a result, buyers who would be willing to pay more than 10 cents will try to bid up the price of bread. Since it is illegal to bid higher than 10 cents in money, they will try to find other means that do not involve money payments to suppliers. One is queuing, but no one collects payments made by waiting in line, and these payments (area *A*) are lost to society.

☐
Ration Coupons Can
Eliminate Queues

The only way to avoid the loss of queuing (or stealing or resource-using bribes or the like) is to make them pointless by defining clearly who has the right to exploit the price differential. Ration coupons do so by requiring a consumer to present along with the money a coupon entitling the purchaser to a certain number of loaves, the total number allotted to all consumers being the number of loaves supplied at the controlled price. Setting aside the possibility that people will devote resources such as queuing time to competing for the ration coupons themselves (they will), rationing eliminates queuing.

If the rationing device is to be effective, it must make it pointless to join a queue.

Q: During the Arab oil embargo a while back, a scheme known as the Oregon plan was widely adopted as a method for reducing queuing for price-controlled gasoline. Under the plan automobiles with odd-numbered license plates were allowed to buy gasoline only on odd-numbered days of the month and those with even-numbered plates only on even-numbered days. *True or false:* Setting aside the small placebo effect, which might reduce the time spent hitching to the pumps the autos of the nervous few who topped up their tanks every day (after the plan they would top them up every other day), the plan would have no effect on the length of queues.

A: Consumers would still value the gasoline supplied at more than its controlled price and would still be able to express this valuation by joining queues using up their time. If the equilibrium price for the restricted quantity was $1.80 a gallon and its controlled price $1.50 a gallon, $0.30 worth of time would have to be spent somehow—on odd-numbered days if the sages of the community so decree; or before 5 P.M. except on Sundays; or while dancing a jig—in order to reduce the quantity demanded to the lower quantity supplied. That is, true.

Ration coupons can eliminate the waste of queuing, but they must be freely exchangeable for money if they are not to result in a gratuitous social loss by allocating to the wrong hands the available bread or gasoline. The reasoning is familiar. Efficiency requires that all consumers have the same marginal rates of substitution for all pairs of goods, and this condition will be violated if coupons are not exchangeable. If the rich (or the red-haired or the fat) value a little of the rationed good more than the poor (or the black-haired or the thin), then the rich will be willing to buy a little of the coupons for the good from the poor at a price at least as high as the poor are willing to accept. Both will be better off.

Q: Suppose that gasoline, fixed at a price of $1.50 a gallon, is rationed by coupon (number of coupons = number of gallons forthcoming from suppliers at $1.50 a gallon) and that the marginal valuation of the quantity supplied at $1.50 is $1.80. If a ration coupon for a gallon of gasoline can be bought and sold, what will be its price? Does the initial distribution of coupons between sales representatives who drive 500 miles a week and old people who drive 1 mile a week matter for the outcome?

A: The coupons will sell for $0.30 each. Unless it is true that the marginal valuation of a gallon is equal to its opportunity cost from the point of view of consumers, the price of a coupon will change. That is, it must be true in equilibrium that $1.80 = $1.50 cents + the price of a coupon. The right-hand side of this equality is the opportunity cost of buying a gallon of gasoline, namely, its money price plus the money that can be gotten for a coupon. Therefore, a coupon sells for $0.30. To a first approximation the initial distribution of coupons does not matter. The old people will be enriched if all the coupons are given to them, as will sales representatives if all are given to them. Aside from the income effects on the price, therefore, the coupons—rights to buy a gallon at $1.50—are simply a commodity to be allocated to those who value it most.

Summary

Competing in ways other than offering money, then, can be wasteful. Giving bribes to police officers, expensive entertainment to members of regulatory commissions, key money to tenants in rent-controlled apartments, and money to people nearer to the front of a queue are not wasteful in this sense, for these gifts merely transfer money or goods from one person to another without using up resources to no one's benefit: they are the market, money competition thinly disguised. But time spent in queues, bullets used to hold up a bank, and accountants employed to evade income taxes are wasteful. The excess waste arises when people desire to enter an exchange but are unable to do so, that is, are unable to compete with money. The resulting gap between what people will pay and what the imported oil or illegal whiskey or rent-controlled apartment cost is supernormal profit to whoever can claim it. Competing for the privilege of supernormal profits—achieved by owning a patent, a loaf of bread priced below equilibrium, an import license, or untaxed moonshine liquor—can result in social waste well in excess of the usual triangular areas.

The waste from attempting to circumvent the market is not always on balance undesirable. Most would agree that using up resources in campaigning for the presidency is better than simply putting the presidency on the auction block. Using up resources in advertising Anacin or the Bible, it is said, transmits information about healing headaches or sin. People will compete regardless of whether the government has outlawed particular sorts of competition. Competing by exchange is in most cases the best sort and will therefore pop up. Political offices not for sale will be competed for by market transactions that closely approximate sale; building inspectors will be bribed; professional line-standers will offer their places for a price. The market is irrepressible, in two senses: first, that the problem of allocation it solves must somehow be accomplished, by nonexchange competition if not by exchange; and, second, that exchange, even if outlawed, has charms.

QUESTIONS FOR SECTION 16.1

1. The local government of London, in common with many other governments, wishes to reduce the volume of traffic in the center and does this by restricting parking. Instead of raising the metered price of parking spaces on the streets, it has decided to eliminate a good many of the parking spaces. Comment on the social cost of this decision.

2. The Polaroid Corporation owns over 1000 patents on various features of the Polaroid-Land and similar cameras that take instantly developed pictures.

a. Thinking of the marginal cost of Polaroid-Land cameras and the demand curve for them, describe what price Polaroid would charge to maximize its net revenues. Contrast this price and the resulting quantity sold to the equilibrium that would occur if Polaroid's patented knowledge were free for anyone to use.

b. Kodak is spending millions of dollars devising a substitute technology for instant pictures. Why? What is the social waste in this?

3. An alternative to allocating gasoline by queue during the oil embargo of 1974 was abandonment of price controls on gasoline. Most public figures were opposed to this alternative, and their opposition was given weight by the results of man-in-the-street surveys by journalists asking people what they would do if the price of gasoline rose. All answered, "Nothing. I need the amount of gasoline I'm consuming now." Suppose that the reduction in the supply of gasoline during the embargo was 25%, that the equilibrium price before the embargo and the controlled price after it was $0.50 a gallon, that consumers spent on average one hour waiting to buy 6 gallons at the controlled price, and that they valued their time on average at $1.80 an hour. Was the elasticity zero, as the man-in-the-street interviews implied? What was the elasticity? What do you think of determining an elasticity of demand by asking people what it is?

4. In the dear dead days of free international competition in oil, the United States had a system of import quotas for oil as a result of which oil inside the United States was a dollar a barrel more expensive than oil outside.

a. Supposing that the allocations of the right to import were distributed at random and that the recipients were able to buy and sell the rights after they were allocated, who were the gainers from the system and how much did they gain? Who were the losers?

b. What would happen if the total quota were the same as in (a) but were allocated to oil companies in proportion to the amount of domestic oil they raised and refined?

5. When the King Tutankhamen exhibit came to Chicago, the Field Museum charged only $3.00 for admission. Enormous lines developed at that price. The museum then offered queue tickets, like tickets at a bakery: if you got a ticket at 8 A.M. you could go about your business, such as touring elsewhere in Chicago, and come back to claim your place at, say, 3:00 P.M., when your place in the line was expected to be almost at the door. *True or false:* The giving of such tickets would not reduce the total value of the inconvenience caused by having to wait to get into the exhibit.

6. During much of the 1970s the U.S. government imposed a great many regulations on the oil industry at various points from well to filling station. By the late 1970s foreign oil was selling for much more than "old" domestic oil (i.e., oil from wells drilled long ago). There was a controversy about whether or not to remove the regulations, the assumption being that the price of oil products would rise to the foreign level if "old" wells were permitted to charge what the market would bear. *True or false:* In view of the absence of long lines at gasoline stations or other evidence of too low a price, the removal of the regulations could well be expected to have no effect at all on prices and might well be expected to reduce, not raise, them.

7. The price of cabs in New York is set by the Hack Bureau to be the same no matter what the time of day. During the day cab drivers in New York are courteous and accommodating, at least relative to what they become at night: spurning short rides, unaccommodating in manner, and unwilling to take people to Harlem. Why?

8. a. A government imposes a maximum price on gasoline and issues (marketable) coupons, each one of which bestows the right to buy 1 gallon. *True or false:* If the government issues coupons in a number exactly equal to the 100 gallons of gasoline forthcoming from suppliers at the maximum price, then the price of coupons will be equal to the demand price of 100 gallons minus the maximum price, and queues will vanish.

b. If the number of coupons is less than the 100 gallons, the money price and the quantity of gasoline sold will fall (coupons are necessary to buy gasoline) and the price of coupons will rise to the difference between the demand price and the supply price.

c. *True or false:* If the government in its generosity issues 1,000,000 one-gallon coupons, queues equal in length to those without coupons (but still a maximum price) will form.

9. *True or false:* Since an effective maximum price results in a queue, so will an effective minimum price.

16.2 Unassigned Property Rights and External Effects

□
Private Property with Zero Transactions Costs Eliminates Inefficiency

It will have occurred to the reader that a simpler way of curing wasteful competition brought on by price controls is to abandon the price controls. There is a more general way to look at this. When rights to use a resource are assigned unambiguously to someone, to sell the rights for what he or she can get for them, the resource will be used efficiently. This is *Adam Smith's generalization.* The generalization is in some cases wrong, doubtless. But an amusing sidelight on two centuries of attempts to dispute it is that a good many of the counterexamples put forward are in fact fine examples of the generalization in action. Consider, for example, the extreme case of controlled prices, that is, prices set by custom or convenience at zero.

T or F: The optimistic view that self-interest operating in an unconstrained market will lead a competitive industry to conserve its raw materials is plainly mistaken in the case of whaling. Whales are hunted and killed in larger numbers than the interests of the whaling industry as a whole would dictate. Indeed, they are in danger of extinction, taking with them into extinction the business of hunting them.

A: The facts are true enough, but the interpretation in the first sentence does not follow from them. The whales are overhunted because they are not owned by anyone and because the opportunity cost in terms of yet-to-be born whales of hunting them now, therefore, is zero. For the same reason alligators in Florida and buffalos on the Great Plains were overhunted before they were protected by law: no one owned them. Therefore, false. If whales were owned, the killing of them would have a price (collected by the owner), and the prospect of selling the right to kill them and their offspring in the future would lead their owners to conserve them. Conservationist organizations could if they wished bid for the whales in order to prevent them from being hunted at all.

The way in which whales and other denizens of the deep might come to be owned is indicated in the following question.

T or F: The selfish behavior of Peru and Iceland in extending their national fishing rights 200 miles out from their coasts is a great tragedy for a hungry world, for it will reduce the future supply of fish protein.

A: Before the extensions no one owned the fish, and the fish therefore were overfished. Now two governments own the fish. They have an incentive to conserve the breeding capacity of the fish by restricting fishing: by selling licenses to catch *N* tons, for example. In short, false. If it is owned, the resource will be better used, producing more not less fish.

In similar fashion the Santa Monica Freeway may be misused (i.e., made crowded, with queuing costs to drivers), Lake Erie may be misused (i.e., made dirty, with costs to swimmers), the peace of neighborhoods close to Kennedy Airport may be misused (i.e., made noisy, with costs to residents), and the air close to U.S. Steel's South Chicago Works may be misused (i.e., made polluted, with costs to breathers) if they are not owned. If a Mr. J. P. Morgan, for example, could charge admission to Lake Erie, then swimmers and fishermen could bid for the use of the lake against the operators of chemical plants and ore ships. If it is true that the lake is more valuable as a recreation spot than as a dump for chemicals and a fluid medium for ships, Lake Erie will be used for recreation. Lake Erie is in fact owned by the federal governments of Canada and the United States, by the Province of Ontario and the states of New York, Pennsylvania, Ohio, and Michigan, which has meant in effect that it has been owned by those who have polluted it most rapidly.

☐
An Externality Is One of the Inefficiencies Eliminated by Property

As was explained in Chapter 13, economists call such misuse of resources "neighborhood effects," "external effects," "nonpecuniary external diseconomies," or, for short, "externalities," the notion being that using Lake Erie for a chemical dump affects people external to the business of making and using chemicals, namely, swimmers, drinkers of water, and conservationists. Jones imposes a *pecuniary* externality on Smith merely by bidding more for a gallon of the lake than does Smith. No man is an island in an exchange economy. Each affects others, and should if the gallon is to be placed in the hands that value it most. It is the *nonpecuniary* nature of polluting Lake Erie that leads to misallocation, because swimmers and the rest have not been permitted to bid for the use of the water. They can "bid" only through political agitation and the state's compulsion. Another way of putting the matter is to say that, because of a failure to define property rights in the lake, the privately perceived opportunity cost of using it for a dump (namely, zero) is not equal to the social cost (namely, whatever swimmers and other potential users would be willing to pay).

☐
If Roads Are Owned, the Externalities of Congestion Are Eliminated

Congestion on freeways is a case in point.[1] When you join the Dan Ryan freeway at the Loop in Chicago already clogged with traffic at 5:00 P.M., you add another obstacle to every other car on the freeway. You join the queue, so to speak, in the middle, adding to the waiting time of all people behind you. Your external effect is small on each car, but large when summed over all cars. The trip from the Loop to 55th Street that took exactly 30 minutes without you, for example, might take 30 minutes and 0.10 second with you. But the additional 0.10 second is spread over, say, 6000 cars, making 600 seconds or 10

---

[1] The argument that follows is a translation of Frank H. Knight, "Some Fallacies in the Interpretation of Social Cost," *Quarterly Journal of Economics* 38 (August 1924): 582–606, reprinted in George Stigler and Kenneth Boulding, eds., *Readings in Price Theory* (Homewood, Ill.: Irwin, 1952), pp. 160–179, especially pp. 162–166.

minutes of additional travel time in total. When you decide to enter the freeway, you judge the cost to be roughly 30 minutes, as it in fact is by a selfish calculation. The social cost, however, is not 30 minutes but 40 minutes, that is, 30 minutes of private cost plus 10 minutes of externality—other peoples' costs. But you do not face other peoples' costs. You and each other individual person, therefore, will not make socially correct decisions.

In particular, if you could get home by side streets that were not subject to congestion but were poorer and slower roads than the mighty Dan Ryan (Cottage Grove Avenue, say), you would choose the Dan Ryan when your *private* costs were equal by both routes. Too many people (including you) would take the Dan Ryan, too many people, that is, in view of the high marginal *social* costs of another car's joining the freeway.

The situation can be made clear in a diagram of time cost measured against the number of trips initiated on the Dan Ryan (see Figure 16.5). The average time cost of a trip rises with more trips initiated: at 6 trips initiated from the Loop, each of the 6 cars could zoom home at great speed without fear of collision; at 6000 trips each car would have to drive slower and would take longer. Suppose that the time cost on the poor but numerous and uncongested alternatives to the Dan Ryan is 30 minutes for the standard trip from the Loop to 55th

**Figure 16.5
The Ownership of a Road
Eliminates the
Externalities of
Congestion on It**

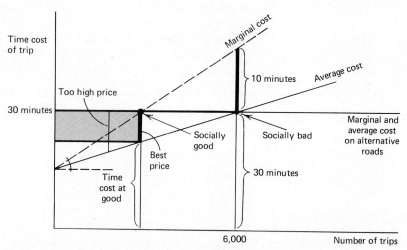

If the road is owned by no one, a driver contemplating entering it thinks only of the average cost he or she alone faces and does not take account of the increase in average cost the trip would impose on other drivers. In other words, drivers will enter the road until average cost equals the marginal cost on alternative routes, which is socially bad. If the road is owned by a profit-maximizing firm, or by a state authority that acts like a profit-maximizing firm, then there will be a toll on the road. The toll that maximizes revenue is the one that presents a driver contemplating entering the road with the full social marginal cost of his or her decision, arriving at socially good. The firm acts so to speak as a middleman between the marginal driver and the drivers already on the road, forcing the marginal driver to bid the full social cost of the road space that he or she contemplates taking. Congestion is a failure to apply markets.

Street, no matter how many trips there were (since this is what it means to say that they are "uncongested"). Rational drivers would join the Dan Ryan until point socially bad was reached.

By contrast, the correct allocation of traffic between the Dan Ryan and the uncongested alternatives is at socially good, where the marginal costs are equal. The reason this point is the correct one is that the curve of marginal cost on the Dan Ryan does indeed reflect all the costs of an additional car's joining the freeway. It is in fact the curve marginal to the average cost curve. That is, the horizontal shaded sliver of one additional second of average cost at 6000 trips is the same as the vertical shaded sliver of other peoples' total cost of an additional car (i.e., the marginal cost, as required). And if the marginal cost on the Dan Ryan were not set equal to 30 minutes, which is the marginal (and average) cost on the alternative roads, then by the usual argument something could be gained socially by shifting cars to different roads.

So, externalities of congestion lead to too much traffic on a freeway. The word "freeway," however, is the key. No one owns the space on the Dan Ryan. It is "free," in money if not in time. Consider the possibility, then, that it is the failure to define property rights in the road that leads to the congestion, not some inevitable feature of the technology of roads. It is intuitively plausible that bidding for road space among drivers would solve the problem of too much congestion. Bidding for road space is obviously impossible in a simple way. At least in an age before cheap computers, the transactions costs associated with such a property right are too high. But what of turnpikes, that is, of someone's literally owning the entire road and charging for admission to it?

Q: In Figure 16.5, which expresses price in terms of minutes, what price at most could a turnpike authority charge for the Dan Ryan at various different volumes of traffic? What is the profit-maximizing price? What are its welfare characteristics? (Hint: Guess the socially optimal price and then show that it is in fact the profit-maximizing one.)

A: The most that the turnpike authority could charge per trip in tolls would be the difference between the time cost on the Dan Ryan and the 30-minute time cost on the alternatives, a difference that varies down from a large number at zero trips to zero at 6000 trips. The vertical line marked too high price is one such price, one that does not lead to the maximum profit to the turnpike authority. The best price is the one that maximizes the shaded rectangle of profit because only at best price is what the authority loses on its previous sales by lowering the price a little (the short horizontal sliver) just equal to what it gains on new sales (the short vertical sliver). Such a point of balance in marginal gains and losses is clearly a maximum of profit. But it is also the best point from the social point of view. To be sure, the turnpike authority pockets the cash. But the authority is part of the society whose point of view is being taken. In the style of the last chapter, indeed, the authority could be defined simply as a device for putting the cash back into the pockets of the drivers through lump-sum transfers.

In short, selfish maximization of the profit from a property right in a highway leads to efficiency (yes, as though by an invisible hand). The negative externality is eliminated by bringing the market to life. Because you do not recognize the full marginal cost of setting out on a congested freeway, you enter it up to the socially bad point where your privately perceived cost of travel on the freeway is equal to the marginal cost on an alternative, uncongested route. A turnpike authority is led to charge the best price as the one that maximizes its net revenue. Happily, the best price is also the one that induces you to recognize to exactly the correct degree the costs you impose on others by adding to the congestion. Ownership of the road, in other words, leads to its socially correct use.

☐
External Economies

External effects need not be hurtful to cause misallocation of resources. If Smith gets pleasure from Jones's consumption of housing but is unable for some reason to express his pleasure by providing Jones with a housing subsidy, the amount of housing Jones consumes will be suboptimal. You can see the force of this by imagining that Jones is Smith's son-in-law. Another popular example of an external economy (as distinct from a diseconomy, which as you recall is a bad thing) is the relationship between the owner of an orchard and a nearby keeper of bees. The bees pollinate the orchard and the orchard provides the nectar for the honey. It is said, however, that the beneficial effect of more bees on the fruitfulness of the orchard is not captured in a payment to the beekeeper, with the result that he will keep too few bees; likewise, the orchard will be too small. The inability to specify, enforce, and sell property rights in the pollinating activities of bees and the nectar-producing activities of an orchard leads to suboptimal output of both. As it happens, this classic case of the inability of a market to operate is poorly chosen. In the State of Washington, for example, owners of orchards and bees do in fact pay each other for their services, exchanging them in elaborately worded and punctiliously enforced contracts.[2]

☐
Taxes as Substitutes for Property

Still, markets do sometimes fail; that is, sometimes it is too expensive to enforce and sell a property right. The Dan Ryan may be a case in point, although tolls could be imposed. A clearer case is noise pollution close to airports. What is to be done? Two extreme solutions are either to prohibit airplanes from flying anywhere or to permit them to fly anywhere. An extreme solution is not always inefficient. It is doubtless wise to prohibit active cases of cholera or smallpox from wandering where they will, imposing externalities on those with whom they come in contact. An alternative solution in the case of airplanes is to introduce quotas on the cause of the noise. Notice that the location of ears close to airports is as much a "cause" of the noise as are the engines of the airplanes. On these grounds one could justify ordinances (which in fact exist) to limit the building of houses close to airports. It is more usual to restrict airplanes to certain approach paths and

---

[2] See Steven N. S. Cheung, "The Fable of the Bees: An Economic Investigation," *Journal of Law and Economics* 16 (April 1973): 11–34.

times of day (as in Canada, where all airports close at 10 P.M.). These are quotas on the output of airlines, similar to those that ban automobiles from the centers of many British cities or that restrict the amounts of untreated sewage that may be dumped in many American waterways.

Most economists believe, however, that the better alternative is not to enforce quotas but to impose a tax on the airplanes in an amount that brings the marginal private cost of a landing into equality with the marginal social costs. A landing that takes place despite the tax, assuming that the tax reflects correctly the amount residents would be willing to pay to avoid the noise, is evidently worth more to the airline (i.e., its passengers) than it is worth to the people on whom the noise falls. By contrast, quotas would achieve this equality of marginal private and social cost crudely if at all—a party of economists willing to pay a large amount to escape from Toronto after 10 P.M. would not be able to do so. A tax on noise, as on air pollution by a steel mill or water pollution by a municipal sewerage department, would appear to result in the optimal amount of pollution.

□

Flaws in the Solution by Tax: The Coase Theorem

The argument seems attractive, but in its usual expression has a flaw. The tax usually contemplated is one equal to the damages to the ears of residents from the landing of the airplane. After all, this will present to the airline the full social cost of a landing. Suppose that the value of a landing at Kennedy Airport is $500 to the passengers, that a landing by an airplane without equipment to abate its noise causes $450 worth of damage to the residents (in other words, had they no other options they would pay $450 rather than tolerate the noise), and that the installation of abatement equipment on an airplane costs $400 per landing. If the state imposes a pollution tax of $450 per noisy landing (equal to the hurt from a noisy landing), the airline will install the abatement equipment, spending the $400 rather than sacrifice the $500 it can earn from a landing or pay the tax of $450 for the privilege of landing noisily. But suppose—this is the nub of the issue—that residents can avoid the $450 worth of hurt at a cost of only $200 per landing to themselves, the $200 being the cost of insulating their houses, say, or moving away. This would be the socially desirable event, at least in terms of efficiency. National income will be highest when airplanes land without abatement (saving the airlines and society the $400 opportunity cost of such equipment) and residents devote resources worth $200 in some other occupation to avoiding the noise. This is event 3 in Table 16.1.

Table 16.1
The Opportunity Costs of Landings and Nonlandings

Events	Output Foregone	
	By Airline	By Residents
1. Do not land	$500	0
2. Land, but airplane noise abated	400	0
3. Land, but residents' houses insulated	0	$200
4. Land, with no control of perceived noise by either airlines or residents	0	450

354 PRODUCTION AND MARKETS

It is assumed that the airline pays the tax only if noise is heard (i.e., only in event 4 in the table).

There are two possible outcomes. If, on the one hand, the costs of arranging deals between the airline and the residents are very low, then the airline faced with a $450 tax when noise is heard will be able to bribe the residents to insulate their houses (paying them, say, $201 to do so). The noise will not be heard and the airline will be absolved of the tax. In other words, if transactions costs are low, the exchange of rights will lead to event 3, the social optimum: Smith's generalization revisited. If, on the other hand, the costs of arranging deals are high, then the airline will not be able to bribe the residents and will be driven to install the abatement equipment at a social cost of $400—event 2. Setting the pollution tax at the value of the hurt from the pollution does *not* necessarily achieve the social optimum. This last proposition is known as the *Coase theorem:* in the presence of transaction costs the location of a pollution tax or of other liability for damages does matter for efficiency.[3]

Setting the Tax Correctly in View of Coase's Theorem

A number of insights follow from this analysis. Pollution taxes are usually not in fact arranged to cease when the nuisance ceases to be felt. In the present case, the airline might be required to pay $450 whether or not residents insulate their houses, giving the airline no incentive to bribe the residents into the social optimum. Further, were the tax set at the true opportunity cost of avoiding the noise—namely, $200—the social optimum would be reached, because the airline would land the planes without abatement equipment and the residents, facing $450 worth of peace and quiet sacrificed, would insulate their houses. But economists in pursuit of an equalization of marginal social costs and benefits have been prone to set the tax at the damage done.

T or F: In performing a cost-benefit analysis of a new steel mill, one must count as a social cost the damage to the health of the neighborhood from smoke pollution.

A: One must determine the least cost way of having steel and health (with due regard to the marginal valuation of each), which may well imply, for example, letting the smoke drive residents away from the mill. Therefore, false. This determination is a considerably more difficult one than simply measuring the damage from smoke (itself not simple).

Looking at the "Cause" of Pollution in the Light of Coase's Theorem

The most valuable insight of the Coase theorem, however, is the following: the technological, legal, or moral "cause" of some damaging externality is not necessarily the correct location for liability for the damages. The airline is usually viewed as causing the noise, but it has just been shown that placing the responsibility for compensating for the noise on the airline (instead of on the residents) may lead to an inefficient result. Of course, it may not (if noise abatement equipment is cheaper

[3] Ronald H. Coase, "The Problem of Social Cost," *Journal of Law and Economics* 3 (October 1960): 1–44, especially the last few pages.

than insulation). That jet engines produce noise, however, is irrelevant to determining on whom the liability for the noise should lie. That there are ears in the neighborhood of the engine is equally relevant to the issue, that is, not at all. A morally repulsive case will make the point clear.

T or F: On grounds of efficiency alone, it is unclear whether or not a drunken and reckless driver who injures a child should be held responsible for the crime.

A: Making the child responsible (i.e., demanding that the child avoid the car rather than that the car avoid the child) may result in a combination of consumed alcohol and surviving children superior to the one that would result from the opposite assignment of liability. Therefore, true. It might be desirable to excuse the person morally responsible. If this judgment seems appallingly amoral, that is because it is. Efficient arrangements are not necessarily moral, nor are moral arrangements necessarily efficient.

This is a case of high transaction costs. The child and the drunk cannot at the moment of the accident sit down to negotiate a price at which the child will agree not to run across the street in return for the drunk's undertaking not to drive the car on the sidewalk. Low transaction costs make the placement of liability inconsequential, for the same reasons that placing a tax on suppliers has the same result as placing the same tax on demanders. What is critical is a cash connection. For example, high wages for dangerous work (such as coal mining) serve the same function as placing the liability for accidents in the mine on the mine owner.

Q: The liability for accidents in coal mines can be placed on either the miner or the owner of the mine. That is, either the miner or the mine owner can be required to pay the hospital bill. *True or false:* If the owner of the mine is made liable for accidents, the owner will definitely spend more preventing them than if the miner is made liable.

A: The owner may, but may not. If the owner spends less on safety, the miner will demand (and get) higher pay, higher by the amount that it costs the miner to insure. Therefore, false.

And, to reiterate, the moral or legal position is irrelevant to the efficiency of the solution.

T or F: On grounds of efficiency, mine owners should be made liable for all accidents in their mines.

A: If the cash connection operates cheaply, it may not matter one way or the other. If it is expensive, making the owner liable may be inefficient. For example, miners may have more incentive to follow safety regulations if they themselves pay for accidents. In short, false.

Even in the presence of a cash connection, however, ambiguity in the placing of liability can itself lead to inefficiency.

Q: Until recently it has been nearly impossible to sue one's doctor for negligence (e.g., cutting off the wrong leg).

1. What would be the effect on the supply and demand curves for medical services if it became very easy to sue doctors for negligence? The liability for mistakes, in other words, would be fixed firmly on doctors. What would be the effect, if any, on the health of the nation?

2. Suppose instead that the legal rules of what constituted "negligence" were muddy, with liability not fixed firmly on either the patient or the doctor. What would be the effect on the nation's health and other income?

A: 1. The key point is that both the supply and the demand curve move. The supply curve moves backward if doctors are made liable because doctors must now be more careful (which is presumably more expensive than being careless) or must buy insurance to cover their mistakes. At the same time the demand curve moves outward because the probability of mistakes becomes smaller or the desirability of carrying insurance against doctors' mistakes becomes smaller. The shift in liability amounts to a shift in the location of a tax, and it is therefore unclear as to whether or not there will be any change in the quantity of health purchased (see Figure 16.6).

2. A muddy definition of liability may be worse than a clear definition. It is certainly worse for the income of the nation aside from health, because resources are devoted to adversary proceedings in the courts to establish liability in each case. And it may be worse for health, because the uncertainty of the result of these proceedings will lead both parties to insure, pushing back both the demand curve and the supply curve.

☐ **Why Property Rights Are as They Are**

The argument so far has concerned the welfare economics of property rights, that is, the goodness or badness flowing from the creation of property in whales, roads, clean air, safety, and other things. In the spirit of the tales of rent creation and dispersal in the last section, however, it is possible to imagine a positive economics of property

Figure 16.6
The Location of Liability May Not Matter If Transaction Costs Are Low

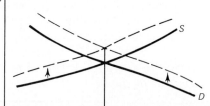

Making physicians liable for their mistakes causes physicians to add to the supply schedule an amount equal to the expected value of the compensation they must render patients. Patients add the same amount, which they expect to receive, to the demand schedule. In this case (which assumes that doctors and patients are risk neutral), both supply and demand schedules shift up by the same amount, and quantity, expected prices, or expected incomes are not affected.

rights, that is, an account of why in fact property comes to be created, whether desirable or undesirable in its consequences. The gist of the account, as imagined by economists over the last 20 years or so, is simply that property will be created when it is in someone's self-interest to do so. In most places no one objects if you pick up a small rock and carry it away. Although the rocks on my land are formally my property, it is not worth my while to define and enforce my property so stringently that alarms ring and lawyers come running whenever someone lifts a rock from my front lawn. If the small rock is a piece of petrified wood in the Petrified Forest, however, it is worth the while of the park rangers to erect threatening signs in an attempt to keep people from taking the forest away piece by piece. If the small rock is a gold nugget in the California gold rush, it was worth the while of the miners to define and enforce property rights in mining claims with great vigor, even in the absence of an outside government to do the enforcing.[4]

A piece of property, then, is not merely a thing but a social relation. Many things are not property, not "appropriated" (literally, "made one's own"). Air in Iowa City, for example, is not appropriated. It is in no one's self-interest to set up a stand selling bottled air (bottled pure oxygen is another matter, of course); nor is it in anyone's self-interest to engage in expensive legal suits over who is breathing whose air. In Los Angeles in the summertime, on the other hand, it may be worth the trouble to define and enforce rights to *clean* air.

Q: Most of the land in what is now the United States and Canada was not appropriated in the European sense before the Europeans came. The fact might be attributed to some peculiarity of native American culture, although the great variety in the culture makes the argument dubious. *True or false:* An economist, however, would find the low density of population of most places then a more persuasive explanation.

A: At low densities of population, the land is not worth much. It is not scarce. Therefore, it is not worth the trouble to define and enforce ownership in it. Therefore, true. Some of the social relations of the land *were* made explicit, namely, those that were valuable even with a low density of population, such as hunting rights over a certain range.

A particular physical thing, such as an acre of land, may have associated with it property rights at all stages of development, from full to none. And the rights in the same piece of land may be assigned to many different people. Land in so-called "open fields" in England eight centuries ago was owned for the most part by the peasant who worked it: the peasant had rights to the crops grown on it, for instance. But many rights to the piece of land were owned by others. The right to graze animals on the land after the crop was in, for example, was often assigned to the village herd, that is, to the rest of the village as

---

[4] John Umbeck, "The California Gold Rush: A Study of Emerging Property Rights," *Explorations in Economic History* 14 (July 1977): 197–226.

a whole. Particular neighbors, likewise, would have carefully defined rights to trespass at certain dates on the piece of land on their way to their own lands. The tangle of rights in the open field system was sorted out in the enclosure movement, especially in the fifteenth, seventeenth, and late eighteenth centuries. Essentially, all the rights to one piece of land were assigned to one owner, creating a more modern-looking bundle of property rights.[5]

With such arguments and observations, the science of property (that is, modern economics) turns its techniques onto the study of the origins of property itself. The American institutionalists and the German historical school could argue truly in the early years of this century that modern economics had no theory of the origins of property and could therefore not claim to understand the long sweep of economic development. The study of property rights may some day answer the charge.

Summary

Adam Smith's generalization asserts that, as a matter of logic, if everything is owned and if exchange is costless, then efficiency obtains. It will not matter in such a world where some right—or liability, the obverse of a right—is placed at the beginning of exchange. By its end (setting aside any effects through the distribution of income), the right will be found in the hands of the person who values it the most. Most "market failures" that have agitated economists are from this perspective not market failures at all, but failures to apply the market. If whales were owned, the argument avers, they would be hunted at the optimal rate, which may be zero. The argument applies to the externalities of smoke pollution as well, except that in this and many other similar cases the solution of creating a property right in clean air, or in whatever is being overused, is difficult.[6]

The obvious solution is to have the government impose a tax that will simulate .the result of a properly placed rights to air. Likewise, the government could bring charges against polluters or encourage citizens to being suit, placing the liability where it appears to belong—on the cause of the pollution, technologically speaking. But technologically speaking is not economically speaking. The obvious "cause" of pollution is not always the best place to put the liability or the tax burden. If the costs of making deals were low, the party that could most cheaply avoid the hurt from the pollution could be induced to do so. In such a case it would not matter for efficiency where the liability was placed. Even if it were placed incorrectly, Adam Smith's generalization would assure that it would find its way to the correct party. But if the costs of making deals are high—as they are, say, between a refinery and the neighborhood's being polluted by its smells—then Adam Smith's generalization does

---

[5] D. N. McCloskey, "The Persistence of English Common Fields" and "The Economics of Enclosure: A Market Analysis," in William N. Parker and Eric L. Jones, eds., *European Peasants and Their Markets: Essays in Agrarian Economic History* (Princeton, N.J.: Princeton University Press, 1975).

[6] Nonetheless, the Environmental Protection Agency has moved toward the goal of allowing free bidding for the air by proposing to create "pollution rights," which a polluting factory must buy from another, earlier factory if it is to set up its factory in the airshed.

not hold and Coase's theorem comes into play: if costs of making deals are high, then it does matter where a liability is placed.

All this is in aid of recognizing that clearly defined property rights underlie well-functioning markets. How the rights came to be defined clearly is an historical question, only recently taken up seriously by economists. The answer to the question that modern economics would like to give is that rights became clear when it was in someone's interest to make them clear. In particular, very scarce things, such as land in a heavily populated area, would give sufficient incentives to preserve it by creating and enforcing property rights. Historical research will determine whether the economists' theory is correct. It can only be remarked now that it fits with the rest of economic theory, such as the theory of rent seeking outlined in the previous section and the theory of the firm outlined in earlier chapters. It enlists the theory of self-interest to define the very object of self-interested desire.

QUESTIONS FOR SECTION 16.2

1. It is observed that the citizens of large industrial cities complain about air pollution more than do the citizens of isolated company towns, with a single mill. *True or false:* An explanation is that in the small company towns, facing a fixed price for their product and a fixed price of labor (laborers being mobile in and out of the town), the company has an incentive to adopt air pollution devices to the socially optimal degree.

2. National income would be higher if the iron ore of Minnesota were located next door to the coal of Pennsylvania or of southern Illinois; or if oranges grew in Times Square instead of Miami; or if, in general, production happened to be located close to consumption (or, equivalently, if transport costs were zero).

a. Exhibit the truth of this proposition.

b. Explain why "transport" costs of moving the right to use a cubic yard of clean air from one person to another, or moving capital from low- to high-valued uses, or moving risk-bearing from very risk-averse to less risk-averse people are all analogous to ordinary transport costs.

c. Each of the "transport" costs in (b) is called a "market failure": in order, an externality, an imperfection in the capital market, and a failure of the insurance market. The notion is that a market that "fails" warrants governmental intervention. In view of the analogy with transport costs, what do you think of the terminology of "market failure"? What is being assumed in the interventionist notion about the costs of governmental decision making and allocation?

True or False

3. California is beautiful and has a large number of magnificent public parks. Therefore, California is likely, from the strictly economic point of view, to be overpopulated.

4. If the people already on the Dan Ryan could bid against newcomers for the property right in the road, then the externality would be eliminated.

Part Five | MONOPOLY

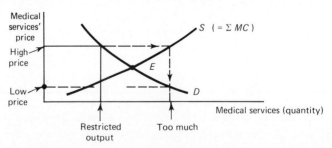

17

The Behavior of Monopoly

17.1 Monopoly: The Elements

*Monopolies Must
Restrict Output*

☐ Adam Smith observed that "people of the same trade seldom meet together, even for merriment and diversion, but the conversation ends in a conspiracy against the public, or in some contrivance to raise prices." His observation is not to be wondered at, because, as he observed elsewhere, "it is not from the benevolence of the butcher, the brewer, or the baker, that we expect our dinner, but from their regard to their own interest." Their own interest is to raise the prices, and if their mutual competition drives the price down to marginal cost, it is no wonder that their thoughts turn to raising the price by conspiracy or, a still better contrivance, by law.

A conspiracy, cartel, central selling agency, combination, corner, exclusive franchise, marketing board, pool, professional society, public utility, regulated industry, syndicate, trade association, trade union, trust, or monopoly can raise its price only by restricting the output supplied to demanders. If at a new high price the members of the European Coal and Steel Community or the American Medical Association (AMA) attempt to sell more than their customers wish to buy at that price, the price will fall (see Figure 17.1). Each member of the AMA, facing the high price for medical services and knowing that

**Figure 17.1
The AMA Must Restrict
Output to Raise the Price**

A monopoly cannot merely set a high price. Because it must stay on the demand curve of its customers (albeit finding the best possible place on the curve), it must set and enforce a low quantity to sustain the price.

his or her individual decision will not affect it, has an incentive to cut the price a little or, equivalently, to offer a larger quantity than the proper share of the restricted output. To be precise, summing each of these decisions, the members have an incentive (namely, the incentive of more profit for each cheater on the agreement) to offer the quantity too much. But if they do so, the price will fall, initially all the way to low price and eventually to the competitive point E.

To prevent such a distasteful result, the AMA as an organization must find some effective way to prevent individual doctors from cutting prices. One way is to restrict the number of doctors to a number that will wish to offer only restricted output, less than the competitive amount. This the AMA, with the help of state legislatures, has been able to do. Since the Flexner Report of 1910 (which recommended that the number of medical schools be cut) and subsequent enactments (that the AMA have charge of the cutting), the number of doctors relative to the population has fallen. The demand curve for medical care on the other hand has moved out: real income per head has more than doubled and medical care has a high income elasticity; subsidized medicine (e.g., Medicare) and medical insurance (e.g., Blue Cross) have moved the demand out still farther and made it less price elastic. The result is apparent in the incomes of doctors. From 1939 to 1959, for example, the average doctor's income grew two-and-a-third times faster than did the average manager's income and three-and-a-third times faster than did the average industrial employee's.[1]

Entry Must Be Blockaded

☐ Such are the rewards of monopoly. The key to the treasure is a limitation on entry. Without a way of punishing interlopers (such as shooting them, the method favored by monopolies of gangsters), or a patent (such as Polaroid had on the taking of instant photos), or a crushing natural advantage (such as an expensive railway line is said to have once it has been built), or a law (such as those enriching undertakers that require embalming of bodies whether or not they are to be cremated), monopolies cannot survive.

Q: Chicago Local 546 of the Amalgamated Meat Cutters & Butcher Workmen of North America limits membership in its union and compels supermarkets in Chicago to employ only its members. Until recently, furthermore, it prohibited its members from working after 6 P.M. (one could not buy freshly cut meat from union supermarkets in Chicago after 6 P.M.). *True or false:* The 6 P.M. restriction can be interpreted as an additional limitation on entry, raising the income of union members.

A: Without the 6 P.M. restriction, the union would not have full control over the number of hours its members supplied, for some members would be willing to work overtime or at unusual hours (e.g., at 6:01 P.M.). By restricting the total number of hours supplied to supermarkets, the union raises the wage that supermarkets are willing to pay for each hour. That is, true.

---

[1] L. E. Davis and D. C. North, *Institutional Change and American Economic Growth* (Cambridge: Cambridge University Press, 1971), pp. 204–208.

The key to monopoly, in other words, is stopping a buyer from buying elsewhere. If you buy first-class mail, you must buy it from the U.S. Postal Service. Each year postal inspectors in tan trench coats come around to investigate little children selling you Christmas card deliveries in the neighborhood. The service thus prevents you from buying service where you please. The AMA prevents you from buying doctoring where you please. The Amalgamated Meat Cutters union prevents you from buying meat cutting (and therefore meat) where you please.

Monopoly is, then, a restriction on the relation between a buyer and a seller. The analysis is similar and in some points identical to the analysis of taxes and other restrictions. The only difference is that the analysis of monopoly provides a theory of the origin of the restrictions and of the way in which they are exploited. The theory starts from the contrast to competition: if buyers and sellers can pair up in any way they wish, and if there are many buyers and sellers, then there is no monopoly. *Monopoly* means one seller (from the Greek, *monos,* meaning single, and *polein,* meaning to sell), the seller being the one—one company, one union, one trade association, one licensing body—from whom the buyer must buy. Similarly, *duopoly* means two sellers, *oligopoly* means few sellers, and, if you like this sort of thing, *polypoly* (rhymes with Tripoli) means many sellers (i.e., competition). Likewise on the buying side, a single buyer is a *monopsony:* the federal government is a monopsony in the buying of atomic bombs and the single coal mine in a remote village in West Virginia is a monopsony in the buying of labor.

T or F: The "reserve clause" in major league baseball before 1975 that required that the players bargain for their yearly contracts with their present owner alone (and not with other clubs) conferred monopsony power on the owner.

A: The owner was the sole buyer of their services as ball players. Other clubs could not bid for Carl Yastremski or George Scott if the 1967 Red Sox gave them low pay. The rules of the leagues restricted the pairing of buyer and seller, making the owner of the Red Sox the one buyer of the playing services of the Red Sox. The restriction was not slavery, because players had the option of leaving baseball entirely to become journalists or singers. Similarly, in general, monopoly or monopsony is not utter dependence; it is merely an advantage that one person has over another because luck, circumstance, or contrivance makes that person the exclusive buyer or seller. So, true.

☐
The Result Is Price Searching by the Monopolist

The exclusion of competitors creates a relationship between monopolist and victims quite different from the casual and anonymous relationship between buyer and seller in the grain pit of the Chicago Board of Trade or in the central food market of Hong Kong. No longer will competing suppliers rush in to fill the victim's plate at a price 1 cent above the competitive price. The monopolist is left alone with the victim. In this delicate situation, the question is, exactly how does the monopolist behave?

The monopolist's behavior is summarized in the phrase *price searching*. A single competitive firm among many is a price taker—taking its price as given by the market and making what it can of it. A monopolist, by contrast, faces not a price but an entire demand curve and is able therefore to search about for the best price to charge. Since the price that can be charged is fixed by the quantity that the firm offered, the analysis of a price searcher, like that of a price taker, can focus on the firm's choice of a quantity to offer. The rule of rational life is to bring the marginal cost of an activity into equality with its marginal benefit, to maximize the difference between benefit and cost. The marginal benefit (or marginal revenue) to a competitive, price-taking seller of wheat of selling one more metric ton of wheat is of course the current market price of $150 a ton. Thus, at 100 tons the marginal revenue of 1 more ton is the price; at 101 it is the price; at 102 it is the price (see Figure 17.2). The price does not fall when farmer Shlomowitz increases his output (since Shlomowitz is one of millions of farmers in the market), and each additional ton produces the market price in additional revenue to him.

But the marginal revenue to a monopolistic seller of telephone calls, postal services, photoreproduced copies, or exhibitions of the movie *Gone With the Wind* of selling one more call, stamp, copy, or exhibition is lower than the current price. Because the monopolist faces a demand curve rather than a given price, the one additional exhibition of *Gone With the Wind* (on national television, say) reduces what people are willing to pay the owner for "earlier" exhibitions (not earlier in time but earlier along the quantity axis and with higher marginal valuation). As the phrase goes, allowing another exhibition to some degree *spoils the market*. The loss of revenue on earlier exhibitions must be subtracted from the price the monopolist receives for the additional exhibition to get the net marginal revenue. The marginal revenue of one more exhibition is the going price minus the spoilage. The algebraic way of saying this, which will work wonders later, is that

Figure 17.2
The Marginal Revenue of
a Price Taker Is the Price

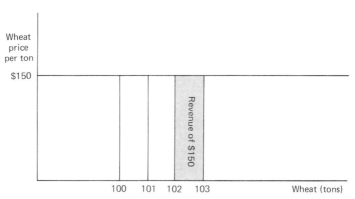

If a seller's share of the market is small enough, the seller can disregard any effect that his or her decisions have on the market price and act as if he or she faced a constant price.

Figure 17.3
The Marginal Revenue of
a Price Searcher Is Less
than the Price

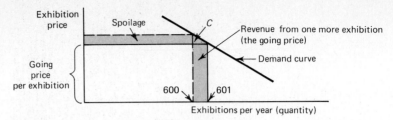

The monopolist collects the going price from the sale of the marginal unit but loses an amount equal to the fall in price caused by the sale times the entire market quantity (the spoilage). The monopolist's marginal revenue is thus less than the going price.

marginal revenue equals $P - Q\Delta P$. Read it out: it says price minus spoilage (as in Figure 17.3).

☐
The Algebra of
Marginal Revenue

If the words and diagrams do not convince you that the equation is true, then you deserve the following algebra. The meaning of marginal revenue is the new revenue minus the old revenue, these being the prices (new and old) multiplied by the quantities (new and old): $MR \equiv P_1Q_1 - P_0Q_0$. Another way of expressing this comes from replacing the new price and quantity with the old plus the change from old to new (or in the case of price, minus the change, because price falls): $MR = (P_0 - \Delta P)(Q_0 + \Delta Q) - P_0Q_0$. Multiplying out this expression leads to a simpler expression, by cancellation of the term P_0Q_0: $P_0Q_0 - Q_0\Delta P + P_0\Delta Q - \Delta P\Delta Q - P_0Q_0 = -Q_0\Delta P + P_0\Delta Q - \Delta P\Delta Q$. The last term, $\Delta P\Delta Q$, is very small when ΔP and ΔQ are small (it is the small triangle C in the diagram). So call it zero, approximately. The change in quantity, ΔQ, is one unit, 1.0, leaving the expression as $P_0 - Q_0\Delta P$. For small changes, it is not going to matter whether P_0 or P_1 or some intermediate going price appears in the equation, since all will be approximately the same. Likewise for Q_0. Therefore drop the subscripts, leaving $MR = P - Q\Delta P$. Q.E.D.

Now ask yourself the following.

Q: Is marginal revenue above or below the going price?

A: The equation of marginal revenue can be rearranged to say that marginal revenue plus spoilage is the demand price: $MR + Q\Delta P = P$. Marginal revenue falls short of price (by the amount of the spoilage). In other words, the marginal revenue curve is always somewhere below the demand curve.

☐
A Special Case:
Straight Lines

With a straight-line demand curve, the location of "somewhere" is simply described and makes straight-line demand curves especially simple for thinking about monopolies. It is the straight line (and its extension) from the point where the demand curve cuts the price axis to the point midway out to where the curve cuts the quantity axis (see Figure 17.4).[2] That the marginal revenue of a straight-line demand

---

[2] It is straightforward to show this with calculus. If the demand price is a linear function of the quantity—say, $P = \alpha - \beta Q$—then total revenue at any Q is $PQ =$

Figure 17.4
Marginal Revenue for
Straight-Line Demand
Curves

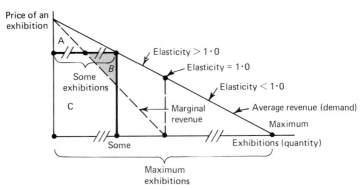

Marginal revenue bisects the quantity axis out to maximum and any line such as some exhibitions, which is parallel to the quantity axis. Total revenue = area under marginal revenue = $A + C = C + B$ = price × quantity.

curve intersects the quantity axis—that is, that marginal revenue is zero—at the midpoint is no surprise. At that quantity of exhibitions, the elasticity of the demand curve is 1.0; that is, total revenue remains constant as the quantity offered is changed a little. And to say that total revenue is constant is to say that marginal revenue is zero.

If the marginal revenue curve is a straight line that bisects the line maximum exhibitions, then it evidently also bisects the line some exhibitions (and similar horizontal lines), which implies that area A is equal to the shaded area B, since A and B are then identical triangles. This is a general feature of a curve marginal to another (as marginal revenue is marginal to average revenue, the demand). Because the marginal revenue is the change in revenue, the sum of all the changes from an output of zero to an output of some exhibitions in the diagram will give the total revenue: diagrammatically, the summing measures the area $A + C$ under the marginal revenue curve. The area under the marginal revenue curve, in other words, is total revenue. But so too is the average revenue (the demand price) multiplied by the quantity (i.e., area $C + B$). Since these have area C in common and both add to total revenue, area A must equal area B, as asserted.

☐
Straight Lines in the
Case of One Buyer

Similar reasoning applies to a monopsonist facing a straight-line supply curve, such as U.S. Steel might face for skilled blastfurnace operators in Gary, Indiana.

T or F: The marginal cost of labor for U.S. Steel's blastfurnaces is higher than its average cost.

A: Look at Figure 17.5. If U.S. Steel decides to increase its work force from old to new, it must pay a higher wage to get the increase and therefore

$(\alpha - \beta Q)Q = \alpha Q - \beta Q^2$. Marginal revenue, then, is $dPQ/dQ = \alpha - 2\beta Q$. The equation reveals that the marginal revenue curve is also linear, that the demand and marginal revenue curve have the same intercept on the price axis (i.e., α), and that the intercept of marginal revenue on the quantity axis $\frac{1}{2}(\alpha/\beta)$ is half the intercept of the demand curve α/β.

spoils the low wage it was able to pay before (unless it can discriminate, all workers—old as well as new—receive the higher wage). The marginal cost is the price (average cost) *plus* the spoilage. U.S. Steel's marginal cost of labor, therefore, exceeds its average cost of labor. Therefore, true: the marginal cost is higher. In the same spirit as the construction of a marginal revenue curve, the marginal cost curve is constructed by bisecting a line such as that out to old equilibrium or out to new. Likewise, area *A* equals the shaded area *B*. For the one buyer as for the one seller, then, the marginal and average price are not equal.

Figure 17.5
The Marginal and Average
Wage for a Monopsonist

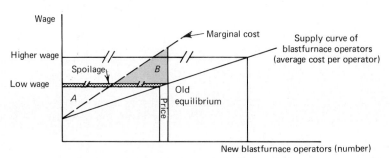

If the higher wage paid to attract an additional worker must be paid to each worker, the monopsonist's marginal cost is greater than the average wage.

□
The Point the
Monopolist Chooses
Without Costs

The marginal benefit of a monopolist selling movie exhibitions or bridge crossings is half of the rule of rational life. The other half, the marginal cost, involves no new principles (although see the next section for some exceptions). Bringing the two together yields the equilibrium of the monopolist.

The simplest case of monopoly is one with no marginal costs, such as a monopolist's holding all extant Impressionist paintings or a patent on the air brake or a bridge from Brooklyn to Manhattan. None of these has, at present, costs of producing one more unit.

Q: The New York Port Authority owns the Brooklyn Bridge. If it wishes to maximize revenue from the bridge and believes that the demand curve for crossings on the bridge are linear, what price will it charge?

A: Following the rule of rational life, it will charge the price that will cause the quantity of crossings to be such that marginal revenue equals marginal cost. Since marginal cost is zero, this quantity will be where marginal revenue is also zero, that is, where the marginal revenue line crosses the quantity axis, point best quantity in the top panel of Figure 17.6.

Notice that the revenue can be expressed either as the rectangle *C* + *B* (the price charged multiplied by the quantity demanded at that price) or as the triangle *A* + *C* (the sum of all marginal revenues out to best quantity, the area under the marginal revenue curve). The two are equal. Beyond best quantity, area *A* + *C* is diminished by

Figure 17.6
A Monopolist with No
Costs Arranges Marginal
Revenue to Be Zero:
Average Revenue Curve
(a) and Corresponding
Total Revenue Curve (b)

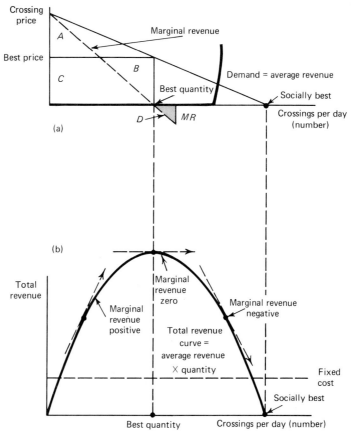

If costs are zero, maximizing net revenue is equivalent to maximizing total revenue. The monopolist chooses quantity such that marginal revenue at the quantity equals zero. The same argument can be represented in (b). The point of maximum revenue is evidently the same as the point of zero marginal revenue.

areas such as the shaded area D because marginal revenue is negative beyond best quantity. The condition that marginal cost equal marginal revenue has evidently had the desired result, namely, maximum revenue. A price that encouraged people to make more than best quantity of crossings would reduce total revenue, for this is what negative marginal revenue means.

In other words, a monopolist with no costs maximizes total revenue. By the usual reasoning, if the monopolist had only fixed costs (such as interest payments on the cost of constructing the bridge), the result would have been the same. The arguments are plainer in the bottom panel of the diagram, which gives the total revenue corresponding to each quantity. The point at which marginal revenue is zero is of course the peak of the hill. The presence of a fixed cost such as the dashed horizontal line would clearly not change the desirability of being at the peak. The peak would still represent maximum profit.

Monopoly Is Bad Because the Point Chosen Is Inefficient

☐ Figure 17.6 shows that the pursuit of profit by a monopolized industry, unlike a competitive industry, leads away from social happiness. The point of maximum profit for the bridge owner is best quantity. The point of socially best use of a bridge costing nothing to use a little more is socially best, where the marginal valuation of a crossing is equal to its true marginal cost, namely, zero. This argument in welfare economics is pursued at length in the chapters following, after the behavior of monopolies is explored more fully. In any event, it is not the profit or the arrogance of a monopolist that makes him socially obnoxious but the monopolist's desire to sell a smaller than socially best amount.

The Point the Monopolist Chooses with Costs, but Constant Costs

☐ The generalizations to a monopoly with costs are straightforward. For example, a government that taxes liquor can be viewed as a monopolist "buying" liquor from distillers at, say, a constant marginal cost and "selling" it to the drinking public at a higher price (in states such as Iowa or Vermont with state monopolies of the retailing of liquor the buying and selling is literal, not figurative). This is one of many examples of the monopoly model applied to subjects other than private monopoly. Governments are public monopolies, and when they pursue the maximum advantage from their position, the model applies. If the state of California agrees with John Stuart Mill that "taxation . . . of stimulants, up to the point which produces the largest amount of revenue . . . is not only admissable, but to be approved of,"[3] it will set the tax on liquor at tax. The price will be the tax plus marginal cost, and at that price only monopoly output will be demanded (see Figure 17.7).

By reducing the quantity demanded to monopoly output, the state has brought its marginal cost and marginal revenue into equality and has maximized the net revenue from the tax. The net revenue is either the rectangle $B + C$ (the tax per bottle multiplied by the number of bottles at monopoly output) or the triangle $A + C$ (the excess of marginal revenue over marginal cost on each successive bottle out to monopoly output, where the excess has fallen to zero).

The Case of Varying Costs

☐ The still more general case is a monopoly with varying (instead of constant) marginal costs. Under the National Recovery Administration (NRA) of the 1930s, for example, the federal government sought to aid recovery from the Great Depression by setting up monopolies. Through its trade association, an industry would submit a code of fair practices, and the approved code signed by the president had the force of law. Hundreds of such codes were approved in 1933 and 1934, covering industries from burlesque theatricals (Code 348) and dog food (Code 450) to cotton textiles and soft coal.[4] A code authority in, say, cotton textiles would increase or at least change cost by changing wages, hours, and working conditions, and the increase in cost would by itself reduce output. But the reduction came directly as well. By a 1933

[3] John Stuart Mill, *On Liberty*, first published in 1859 (New York: Dutton, 1910), p. 156.

[4] William E. Leuchtenburg, *Franklin D. Roosevelt and the New Deal, 1932–1940* (New York: Harper & Row, 1963), p. 68.

Figure 17.7
A State That Maximizes Its
Revenue from a Tax Acts
Like a Monopolist

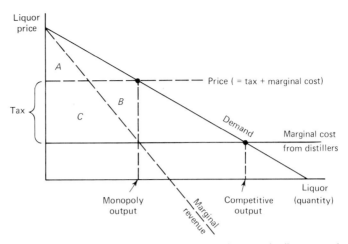

A state liquor store would buy liquor at marginal cost and sell it to people at a price that includes tax. Choosing a tax that caused output to fall to where marginal cost equals marginal revenue makes the net revenue from the tax, *A + C* or *C + B,* as large as possible. A private monopoly would act in the same way, replacing the word "tax" with the word "markup."

order the textile machinery in any factory was limited to two 40-hour shifts per week (and in 1934 to 30-hour shifts). To represent the situation, Figure 17.8 flips the usual order of panels, putting total revenue on top. Taking costs and the number of firms in the industry as unchanged, and supposing that the demand curve is linear, the goal of the industry acting as a monopoly can be viewed as moving from the point competitive to the point monopoly.

Monopoly, you see, gives higher profit to the cotton textile industry as a whole (the total profit gap is larger at monopoly than at competitive). Competitors sell too much for their own collective good. At competitive the marginal cost equals average revenue; at monopoly the marginal cost equals marginal revenue. And an equality of marginals is better for the industry. The equality is clearest in the bottom panel, but it holds true in the top as well. A move to lower output brings more profit to the industry than does the competitive point.

□ *A Monopoly*
Operates Only in the
Elastic Portion of
Its Demand

The top panel, incidentally, makes unforgettable a technical condition on the monopoly: a monopoly will never choose a price at which the demand curve is inelastic (elasticity less than 1.0). The demand curve is inelastic (recall: steep in slope, roughly) when a rise in quantity along it causes such a large fall in price that total revenue goes down instead of up. You can remember this by reflecting that a negative condition such as *in*elasticity is naturally associated with *falling* revenues. The neutral point is unit elasticity (elasticity equals 1.0), the peak of the hill in the top panel and the midpoint of the straight-line demand curve in the bottom. Since total cost is rising, it is obviously impossible for the monopoly to choose a point to the right, that is, on the downward slope of the hill, because it is impossible for something

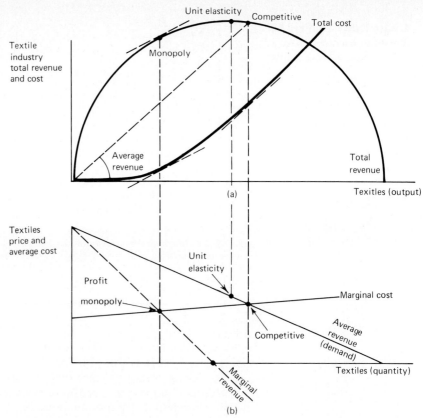

The monopoly's task in (a) is to find the line that makes revenue minus cost as large as possible. This it does where marginal revenue (the slope of total revenue) equals marginal cost (the slope of total cost). The equality is duplicated in (b). The geometry implies that the best output for the monopolist is always lower than the competitive output and is always lower than the point of unit elasticity.

with an upward slope (cost) to have the same slope as something with a downward slope (revenue to the right). So it chooses a point to the left. The demand curve at the point of equilibrium for a monopolist must be elastic (elasticity of demand greater than 1.0), as asserted.

Summary

Monopoly begins with a natural desire to earn more profit than is allowed under "cutthroat" or "ruinous" competition (as ersatz economics has it). More profit requires a higher price and a higher price requires a lower quantity. A successful monopolist restricts quantity, preventing others from supplying the customers. Because the monopolist prevents the customers from going to alternative suppliers, the monopolist faces the customers' demand curves, not a given market price. The monopolist's marginal revenue, therefore, is below the price, because additional output spoils the price on earlier output. To fit another unit of medical care or postal service into the demands of customers the price must fall—this applies to competition as well to monopoly. The difference is that the monopolist is one mind facing the demand instead of one among many and therefore recognizes the spoilage.

The analysis of a monopolist's behavior is especially simple with straight-line demand curves. A similar analysis applies to a monop*son*ist, a single buyer facing the supply curves of the victims. A mono*pol*ist with no costs, such as a bridge authority, will if rational set price (and therefore quantity) at the point of maximize revenue. A monopolist with costs, such as a state taxing liquor or an NRA code authority in cotton textiles, sets price or quantity at the point of maximize net revenue, that is, at the point at which marginal revenue and marginal cost are equal. These arguments hold in fact for all shapes of the curves involved. They lead to the central conclusions that monopoly output is lower than competitive output and that the profits from the output are higher.

QUESTIONS FOR SECTION 17.1

1. In 1784 the British import tariff on tea was 119% and 5 million pounds of it were imported. The accountant of the East India Company reckoned that no more than a third of the whole British consumption was imported legally, the rest being smuggled. He was apparently correct, for tea was inelastically demanded, and in 1785 after the reduction of the tariff to a mere 12.5%, the amount of legal tea imported increased to 16 million pounds. In light of the implied elasticity of the demand for *legal* tea, and using a straight-line "demand curve" (after smuggling), what was the revenue-maximizing tariff rate?

2. The telephone company is a monopoly. Suppose that an empirical study shows that the elasticity of demand it faces is −0.7. *True or false:* Something is wrong.

3. Professor Harberger calculates the welfare loss of monopoly in the American economy by assuming unit elasticities of demand in the monopolized industries. Professor Stigler argues that Professor Harberger's calculation is inconsistent because literal monopolists would not operate at such a point.

a. Briefly explain Professor Stigler's argument. Professor Harberger replies that the "monopolies" in question are not literally single sellers but, rather, a few. He points out that the elasticity of a whole industry's demand is therefore no measure of the firm's elasticity. The behavioral economics and the welfare economics are in this case quite consistent, says Professor Harberger.

b. Explain Professor Harberger's argument.

4. The racetracks in Illinois are scattered about, and therefore each has some monopoly power in its region. A state board assigns racing dates to each track each year, a process notorious for its corruption. *True or false:* No matter how many dates were already assigned to him or her, the owner of the track would always be willing to bribe the state officials to get additional dates.

5. Name all the areas in Figure 17.9 that equal the monopoly's net profits (putting the letters within each in alphabetical order).

Figure 17.9
The Areas of Monopoly
Profit

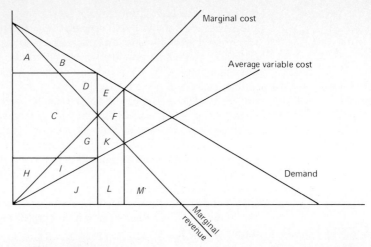

True or False

6. If the British government in 1784 were attempting to maximize its own revenues, it would act in setting an import tariff on tea as though it were a monopolist selling to its citizens, having a marginal cost equal to the world price of the tea.

7. A tax of t cents on an item selling initially in a monopolized market at $1 per unit will reduce the marginal revenue curve at the pretax output of the monopolist by more than will a tax of t%.

17.2 Applications of Simple Monopoly

☐
*The Monopoly's
Information
Problem*

The analysis of monopoly is an alternative to supply and demand, for supply and demand applies only to markets with price takers on both sides. Whenever one mind controls affairs on one side of a market, you can take it as probable that the analysis of monopoly applies, that is, that the point of maximum monopoly profit will be sought actively. It may not be found. Just as the equality of marginal cost and market price under competition is merely a tendency, which may be disturbed by ignorance or sloth, so too the equality of marginal cost and the market's marginal revenue under monopoly is merely a tendency. Even if they pursued profit single mindedly, neither a monopolist nor a competitor would know their price and cost perfectly, not to speak of such subtleties as the slope of the demand curve. In an auction market such as that for hogs (competitive) or fine art (monopolized), the price can vary hourly. In a list price market such as that for shoes at retail or steel at wholesale, the actual price received will depend on spoilage on the shelf, discounts for special customers (e.g., credit card customers or long-standing customers), and other things. Likewise, the costs of any enterprise are difficult to know with exactness. And even if the manager knew the prices and the costs exactly, she would have to search about for the point of maximum profit by trial and error. She would be lucky to find the point at which marginal cost exactly equals marginal revenue. As with all theories of rationality, the theory of monopoly is merely approximate.

☐
A Monopoly Does Not Have a Suppy Curve nor Does a Monopsony Have a Demand Curve

In any case, having located in one's mind the point of most profit toward which a monopoly tends, one can examine deflections. That is, one can perform comparative statics in the same spirit as watching the results in competitive markets of shifts in supply and demand or of impositions of price controls. The first lesson has been mentioned earlier, namely, that a monopoly faces a demand curve (of course) but does not itself have a supply surve. No single curve can tell how much quantity a monopolist will supply at various given prices, because the monopolist faces a whole given curve, not a given price. So it is with a monopsonist, too, a single buyer who faces a supply curve but does not have a demand curve.

Q: A new interstate highway brings a formerly isolated Vermont town, North-field, within easy commuting range of ten other towns, all of which, like this one, have one major employer. Nothing happens to the price of the Northfield Woolen Mill's product at the factory gate, yet both the number employed and the average wage paid by the company rise. *True or false:* Evidently the demand for labor by the company is perversely shaped, upward sloping: an increase in the potential labor supplied to the company (coming by the new highway) has increased, not decreased, the wage it is willing to pay.

A: The company was before the highway a monopsony in the buying of labor, employing less the better to pay less. The highway breaks its monopsony power, flattening out the supply curve of labor that it faces (shown in Figure 17.10). The demand curve (which is really the monopsonist's curve of marginal benefit from hiring labor) is unchanged and perfectly normal. Therefore, false. Before the highway the company, as a monopsonist, was not operating along its demand curve. So it jumped from being off to being on the curve and in the process traced out the two points old *E* and new *E*. A monopsonist does not have a demand curve, just as a monopolist does not have a supply curve.

Figure 17.10
A Monopsony Does Not Have a Demand Curve

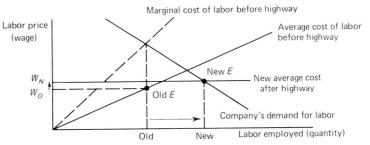

When the market for labor becomes competitive, the company's marginal cost of labor becomes the same as the wage rate, or new average cost. The company, originally at old *E*, increases employment, although the wage it must pay at old *E* has risen, because marginal cost around old *E* has fallen.

**Monopolies with
Price Limits Behave
Like Competitors**

□ A similar case for a monopolist with the usual, upward-sloping marginal cost curve is the following.

T or F: Placing a ceiling on the price a monopolistic stage coach service between Abilene and Dodge City can charge will reduce the amount the monopoly will produce: on each fare the monopoly will make less money and will therefore run fewer coaches.

A: Before the price ceiling is imposed, the monopoly charges old fare and finds that riders demand the old number of rides (or alternatively and equivalently, it offers the old number of rides and finds that riders are willing to pay old fare for each). After the ceiling is imposed, however, its demand curve at a price higher than the ceiling is no longer relevant. Up to the ceiling along its demand curve, nothing is changed, but at lower outputs, the ceiling *is* its demand curve (see Figure 17.11). To put it the other way, out to the quantity of controlled equilibrium of rides, its demand curve is now flat and its marginal revenue, therefore, is not below the price it gets (i.e., the ceiling) but equal to it. Beyond controlled equilibrium, after a leap downward, the marginal revenue is the portion of the old marginal revenue curve to the right of controlled equilibrium. In total, then, the monopoly's marginal revenue is the crossed line. There is nothing mysterious about the leap downward at controlled equilibrium. At that output an increase in output, for which consumers are only willing to pay something less than the former (ceiling) price, spoils the price, as before; at that output a decrease in output, however, does not enhance the price (as it did before), because the price is then limited by the ceiling and cannot be enhanced. At such a point the marginal revenue for an increase in output is radically different from the marginal revenue for a decrease. To answer the question, then, the monopolist facing the price ceiling produces where marginal cost goes through marginal revenue curve, in this case through the leap (or *discontinuity*). The monopolist produces the new number of rides and sells them at the ceiling price. Notice that the monopolist has been induced by the price ceiling to offer *more* rides. In general, then, the answer is false. If the price ceiling were set at competitive equilibrium, in fact, the self-interest of the monopoly would drive the monopolist to offer exactly the competitive output, where price is equal to marginal cost.

Another question with the same point—namely, that monopolies with artificially flattened demand curves produce an output closer to the competitive output—follows.

Q: The Organization of Petroleum Exporting Countries (OPEC) is a monopoly or more accurately a *cartel*, that is, a group of sellers acting together as a monopoly. Since 1974 it has been able to maintain a price of oil higher than the marginal cost of the least efficient producer, by restricting the supply. Suppose that the cartel price were $30 per barrel (by now it is higher). Senator Henry Jackson proposed once that a ceiling of $6 a barrel be placed on the price of oil in consuming countries (America in the first instance and also, he would hope, other countries) and that the resulting excess demand from the cheapness of oil be eliminated by rationing. Some economists, alternatively, have proposed that consuming countries impose import duties on OPEC oil, on a sliding scale: $24 a barrel when the domestic American price is $30, $23 when it is $29, and so on down to zero when it is $6. Show that either of these schemes (assuming perfect enforcement) could induce OPEC to increase the output of oil and reduce the price to $6.

A: Before the schemes are in place, OPEC, as a sensible monopolist, sells Q_0 at $30 a barrel. If the consuming countries hold the price they pay to OPEC at the ceiling, choking off the excess demand by imposing taxes of their own or by letting queues form at gas pumps, then OPEC faces the ceiling as its demand curve. Since further sales no longer spoil its (now low) price, OPEC will act like a competitive firm, selling out to Q_1 (see Figure 17.12).

The OPEC price will fall and the ceiling (or taxes) will become in the end unnecessary. And in the meantime the governments of the consuming countries instead of OPEC will earn the profits from the high price. Either the ceiling price or the sliding scale of import duty has the same effect, namely, to flatten out the demand curve facing OPEC at a price below the cartel price. No one is permitted to pay OPEC $30 a barrel (under Jackson's scheme no one pays $30, except in resources devoted to queuing or stealing; under the alternative scheme the government gets in tariff revenues the difference between OPEC's price and the domestic price that clears the market, a zero difference when OPEC increases output to the optimal extent). Faced with a flat demand curve at $6 a barrel, OPEC increases output to Q_1, for that is now its point of maximum net revenue. OPEC has been induced to behave as a price taker, because it faces, and must take, the price of $6 per barrel.

**Figure 17.11
Marginal Revenue for a
Monopolist Facing Price
Controls**

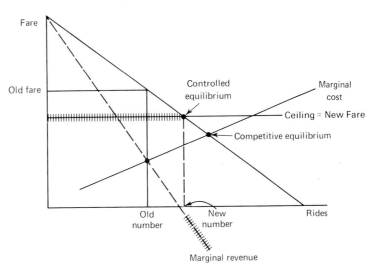

Price controls increase marginal revenue at the old number (though lowering total revenue), since price does not fall as output expands (i.e., price is no longer spoiled). Therefore the monopolist increases output when the ceiling is applied. A ceiling set at competitive equilibrium, in fact, would induce the monopolist to produce the competitive output.

Figure 17.12
How to Break a Cartel

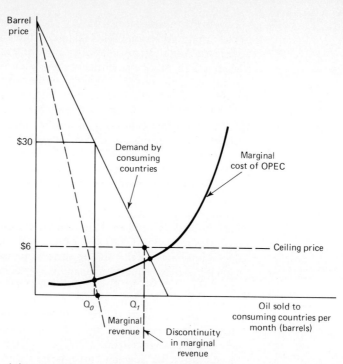

If the consuming countries hold the price they pay to OPEC at the ceiling, choking off the excess demand by imposing taxes of their own or by letting queues form at gas pumps, then OPEC faces the ceiling as its demand curve. Since further sales no longer spoil its (now low) price, OPEC will act like a competitive firm, selling out to Q_1. The OPEC price will fall, and the ceiling (or taxes) will become in the end unnecessary. And in the meantime, the governments of the consuming countries instead of OPEC will earn the profits from the high price.

Comment

The analysis is incomplete in one important respect, to be treated in more detail in Chapter 22. OPEC may well adopt the countervailing strategy of persisting in withholding oil even though it reduces its present new revenue by doing so, for it may believe that the consuming countries will not persist, if pressed, in their self-denying policy. In that case the outcome is a matter of pure bargaining, a matter, that is, of who is best able to convince the other party that he will indeed persist.

☐ In any case, the point here is to keep firmly in mind what marginal revenue (or, more broadly, marginal benefit) a monopolist faces.

The Rule of Rational Life Applies to Monopoly

Q: A monopoly selling iron ore merges with a monopoly that makes steel from iron ore. The new, *vertically integrated* monopoly will price ore sold to its steel mill in a competitive fashion, that is, at marginal cost. *True or false:* The merger, therefore, even though monopoly has increased its reach, produces more output.

A: The intuition is simple. It is obviously foolish to extract monopoly profits from oneself, which implies that the price of ore, formerly high (since the ore mine was a monopoly), will fall. The old monopoly price of ore was the marginal benefit that the consumer (the steel mill) got from buying a ton of ore: this is what a demand curve means. The price was above the marginal cost of producing ore: this is what a monopoly does. Now that the mill and the mine are one, the integrated firm will equalize marginal cost and benefit by lowering the price to marginal cost (for itself; not, of course, for outsiders). With lower costs of making steel, it will sell more. In short, true.

The marginal cost facing a monopoly deserves close attention as well.

Q: On any given day the supply of fish to the Billingsgate fishmarket is perfectly inelastic, because fish cannot be stored and within a day the daily supply of fish cannot be altered. The fishmongers undertake to sell any quantity supplied. The market closes on Sundays, any fish left over from the Saturday night being left to rot. One Saturday the fishmongers of Billingsgate form a cartel. *True or false:* On that Saturday the price of fish will rise above the competitive level and the quantity sold will fall (i.e., some fish will be left over to rot).

A: Not necessarily. Out to competitive output in Figure 17.13 the marginal cost of fish is zero, because once the day's fish are at the market, it costs no more to supply competitive output than to supply zero fish. At competitive output the marginal cost is infinite (or very high), because once the day's fish are at the market, at no price (or only at a very high price) can more fish than competitive output be supplied.

If the marginal revenue curve cuts the quantity axis at a point such as monopoly output, the price will rise and the quantity fall: the sale of fish that maximizes the revenue of the fishmongers (or whoever is conceived to be the owner of the fixed supply) is smaller than the extant fish. Fish will be left to rot. But if the marginal revenue curve cuts the vertical marginal cost curve, as does high marginal revenue, the price will not rise and the quantity will not fall: the sale of fish that maximizes revenue is the competitive sale. A simpler way in which to make the argument is to imagine a diagram of *total* revenue and to note that only if supply is beyond the peak of revenue will it be desirable to cut supply back.

Comment

For one Saturday the analysis is complete. For many Saturdays it is not. The supply is not inelastic in the long run. And even if it is—even if fishermen continue to supply the competitive output each Saturday regardless of the price—the cartel can be expected to reduce the sale, for a cartel is not worth forming (supposing that there are costs of organizing and enforcing it) unless it raises the income of its members. In other words, if you observe a cartel, you can presume that marginal revenue cuts the marginal cost curve at a quantity below the competitive quantity. This is another way of saying that a monopoly operates only in the elastic portion of its demand curve.

**Figure 17.13
A Monopoly May Let Fish
Spoil Before Letting Them
Spoil Their Price**

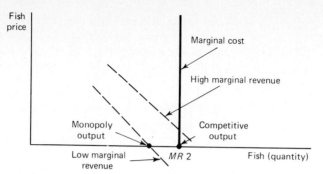

With supply fixed, a monopolist might sell on the same terms as a competitive industry. If marginal revenue cuts the vertical portion of marginal cost, the competitive price and quantity will prevail; otherwise, the monopolist will sell a smaller quantity at a higher price than will a competitive industry.

As is evident by now, the simplest model of how monopolies behave is widely applicable. For example, it applies to a problem in the theory of inflation.

T or F: Monopolists contribute to cost-push inflation by always passing on a higher share of a rise in costs than would a competitive industry.

A: Many members of the Council of Economic Advisors have believed it. The simplest counterexample (which is all that is required, because the assertion uses "always") is a flat, straight-line marginal cost curve and a straight-line demand curve, for, say steel (see Figure 17.14).

A competitive steel industry would respond to a rise from old to new marginal cost by raising the price of steel by the same amount. A monopolized steel industry would respond by raising it from old monopoly to new monopoly, which for straight-line demand and marginal cost curves (and marginal cost moving up in parallel) is always less, not more, than the competitive rise. Monopoly change is less than competitive change. Therefore, false.

**Figure 17.14
Monopolies Can Pass on
Lower Cost Rises than Can
Competitors**

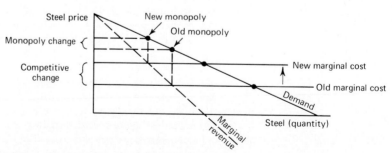

A rise in cost causes a smaller change in price if an industry is monopolistic than if it is competitive. This assumes that industry cost curves are the same in either case.

If My Grandmother Had Wheels, She Would Be a Tram: Comparing Monopoly and Competition

☐

Comparisons between monopoly and competition, however, are to be made gingerly. One is liable to fall into nonsense of the sort "If my grandmother had wheels, she would be a tram." The steel industry either is or is not a monopoly. Suppose that it is a monopoly. To imagine that it was not and to compare the hypothetical results with the actual is to step into a *counterfactual* world. The monopoly in the industry has, presumably, a cause, such as crushing advantages in marketing by one large company or a patent held by a few firms or a political atmosphere in which governments support cartels. One must, as it were, assume away the causes to contemplate alternative effects, the effects of a regime of competition rather than monopoly. This is acceptable if the causes themselves have only the effect of supporting the monopoly, but they might not. The marketing advantages of the dominant firm, for example, might reduce its costs; if they are eliminated (in order to perform the mental experiment without self-contradiction), the industry's costs may be higher. There is nothing inherently objectionable about counterfactuals, despite their alarming name. The innocent assertion that the demand curve for housing, say, has an elasticity of −0.5 involves a counterfactual. If the price were not what it is, but 10% higher, the quantity demanded would be 5% lower. But the point here, as elsewhere, is to avoid the sin of misusing the *ceteris paribus* clause, namely, holding constant what cannot by the nature of the question asked be held constant.

Another example of how the cost curves might be altered is the following.

Q: Suppose that the ironmaking industry, with a production function exhibiting constant returns to scale, is composed initially of 1000 identical firms. All inputs *except iron ore* are supplied to it perfectly elastically. The 1000 firms are now grouped into one cartel. What happens to the price of ore? What happens to the cost curve of the cartel by comparison with the cost curve of the competitive industry? In view of this, what do you think of the proposition "A cartel has lower output than does the corresponding competitive industry"?

A: The cartel faces the supply curves that the competitive industry as a whole faced. That is, the cartel faces an upward-sloping supply curve for ore. That is, the cartel is also a *monopsonist.* So the cartel will cut back its purchases of ore so that the *marginal* (not average, as before the cartel) factor cost of ore equals the marginal valuation of ore. This reduces the price of ore (the average factor cost) that the industry pays (the other factor prices being constant by virtue of their elastic supply). Therefore the cost curve of the industry falls. For example, consider an industry with constant factor shares for labor, capital, coal, ore, and so forth. The percentage change in factor prices is zero except for ore, and for ore it is negative. So the average of factor prices (weighted by their shares) falls and the cost curve falls. It is even possible for the cost curve to fall so much that the cartel produces more output.

In other words, "there are superior methods available to the monopolist which either are not available at all to a crowd of competitors or are not available to them so readily. . . . There are advantages . . . secured only on the monopoly level . . . because monopolization may increase the sphere of influence of the better, and decrease the sphere of influence of the inferior, brains, or because the monopoly enjoys a disproportionately higher financial standing." This element of the case for competition may fail completely because the monopoly prices are not necessarily higher or monopoly outputs smaller.[5]

☐
Natural Monopoly and Unnatural Competition

The advantages of the monopoly might be technological, which is the case of *natural monopoly*. The one railroad between Lynchburg and Danville, for example, might leave no economic room for the 100 others necessary to make each a competitive price taker. The relevant comparison between monopoly and competition is obscure. It would be silly to insist on replacing the monopoly by the 100 competitors, or even by 2. If 2 or many had to share a market best supplied by 1, the net social benefits might well be lower. The outcome depends on the counterfactual, that is, on what the alternative to the natural monopoly is imagined to be.

Q: Suppose that the alternative to a monopoly railroad between Lynchburg and Danville is transport by pack mule, which is supplied competitively both before and after the railroad, but at high cost. *True or false:* If the advantage of cheap transport by rail is inseparable from the existence of a monopoly providing it, then the coming of the railroad, even though it acts like a monopolist, is good for the consumers of transportation.

A: True. The price of transport by pack mule is the worst that consumers can do, since the pack mules stand ready to go if the price gets above their entry price. The monopoly price, therefore, must be below the old competitive price (the pack mule price), and consumers are better off (see Figure 17.15).

☐
Public Utilities as a Solution to Natural Monopoly

The monopolistic railroad does not, of course, produce the socially optimal output, where marginal valuation equals marginal cost. Regulation of the railroad as a public utility or as a government enterprise could bring it there, if the regulators were willing and able to perform the calculations. Electric utilities staffed by economic geniuses, such as Electricité de France, do exactly this, charging their customers the marginal cost and allowing the demands of the customers to pick off the point socially optimal. In the more common case the utility is compelled to price at average cost (including a normal return to capital). Consumers of the utility would be delighted with the low price at crude regulation, but the society as a whole is buying too much of a good thing. The social loss from crude regulation, in short, can be greater than that of monopoly.

[5] Joseph A. Schumpeter, *Capitalism, Socialism and Democracy*, first published in 1942 (New York: Harper Torchbook, 1962), p. 101.

Figure 17.15
Natural Monopoly Can Be
Good for You

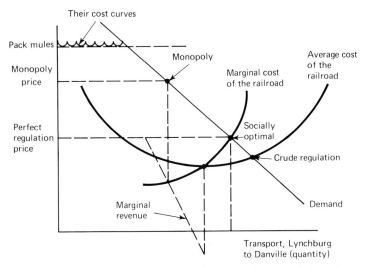

The one railway between two points may be a natural monopoly (i.e., the one firm that fits in the limited market) but may nonetheless be better than the alternative, even though the alternative (pack mules) is a competitive industry. Any price less than the old price is better. Further regulation of the natural monopoly may or may not improve matters further.

If My Grandmother
Had a Patent

☐ In any event, there is often no obvious competitive alternative to lend meaning to the assertion that "monopoly is worse than competition." Would my grandmother be better or worse off if she had wheels? The following is an example that ends with the same point, after applying the model of simple monopoly.

Q: A patented invention reduces the cost of making hand calculators. The owner of the patent can charge a royalty for each calculator that uses the invention. *True or false:* The invention will not reduce the price of calculators to consumers, because the optimal royalty per calculator from the point of view of the owner of the patent is a royalty just below the amount of cost reduction. The manufacturers will be willing to pay the royalty (just below) and the owner will make as much as possible.

A: False in general. The patent bestows a monopoly on the owner, similar to the state's monopoly in taxing liquor. Suppose that the preinvention marginal cost curve of calculators is flat, as is the postinvention marginal cost (see Figure 17.16).

Charging a royalty just below the amount of cost reduction will give the owner area *A + B*. But if at the old quantity the marginal revenue is greater than the new postinvention marginal cost, then a better royalty is the lower one, royalty, giving *B + C*. Such a royalty equalizes marginal cost and benefit, as though the owner of the patent bought the calculators manufactured with the new technology and sold them to consumers (compare the state's "buying" liquor at the pretax price and "selling" it at the posttax price to customers). And it results in a larger quantity of calculators sold at a lower price.

**Figure 17.16
Royalties on Patented
Inventions Are Not Always
So High That the Price of
the Product Stays the
Same**

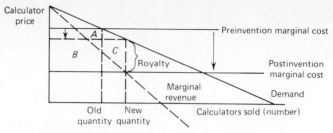

A monopolist will charge a lower price than will competitive suppliers if the monopolist's costs are much lower than theirs.

One can ask whether it is desirable to have such patents on invention at all.

T or F: Since price does not equal the marginal cost of production if the production process is patentable, patents should be eliminated.

A: One is free to imagine voiding the patent on hand calculators, leaving the industry pricing at postinvention marginal cost. This would seem to be the obvious alternative to contrast to the monopoly patent and is relevant when the patent expires (17 years under American law). But one is not free to imagine a world in which patents are regularly voided prematurely, or not granted in the first place, yet in which the same amount of knowledge about calculators is produced as in the actual world. The knowledge is produced because it is patentable. Therefore, false.

☐
The Moral

Monopoly, then, should not be diagnosed and treated as though it were one disease. A doctor who treats fever alone, disregarding its causes, does her patients wrong. Likewise, economists and lawyers who attack with the same analysis and policy all markets having the same ''structure'' (i.e., one seller or few) do their society wrong. An analogous case is slum clearance, the policy of all enlightened nations since Britain initiated it in the nineteenth century. Slums are bad relative to ideal communities, just as monopoly is bad relative to ideal marginal cost pricing. The instinct of the social engineer is to clear the slums (i.e., knock them down, possibly replacing them with clean buildings to a uniform plan). The result has been housing projects worse than the original slums. The enthusiasts for clearance have overlooked the possibility that the original slums might have been better than the actually available alternatives or that the slums had causes that might reassert themselves in more virulent form when the old community was disrupted. Analogous remarks can be made of monopoly. Sometimes even monopoly is better than the actually available alternatives. And it always has causes, differing from case to case, that must be brought into the cure.

Summary

The model of monopoly, then, is widely applicable. It applies to any situation in which one mind is facing an entire demand or supply curve instead of a given price. The question is, what is the monopolist's marginal revenue? Only changes in the monopolist's marginal revenue affect the optimal position as when imposing a lid on OPEC's price affects its marginal revenue and induces it to supply more oil. The assumption necessary for such exercises, however, is sometimes questionable: it is that the monopolist can be imagined to be transported to a world in which it is not a monopolist. If my grandmother had wheels, she might or might not be a tram; but she certainly would no longer be my grandmother. Facile comparisons between monopoly and competition are to be avoided, as are the policy prescriptions that go along with them. Monopolies are bad, surely—Chapter 19 will count their badness. But it is an error to try to eliminate their badness without understanding their causes, a point that applies to any issue of social policy.

QUESTIONS FOR SECTION 17.2

1. Imagine Britain in 1900 facing a downward-sloping demand curve for its loans to foreigners (the interest rate earned and paid is the price). Imagine, too, a marginal cost curve of the British in supplying such loans.
    a. What is the competitive equilibrium?
    b. Could Britain do better for itself if the British government restricted the amount supplied? Show the gain to the optimal tariff on exports of capital (loans to foreigners).

True or False

2. Because the company is a monopoly, a tax of t cents per kilowatt-hour of electricity sold by Consolidated Edison will fall on the company, not on its consumers.

3. If the city council sold the right to exercise a natural monopoly of a new trolley line in Chicago to the highest bidder, the problem of monopoly would be eliminated.

4. If the city council sold the right to exercise a natural monopoly of a new trolley line in Chicago to the company that promised to charge the lowest fares, the problem of monopoly would be eliminated.

5. If an electric utility has average costs that in the range of present demand always fall with increasing output, then marginal cost is below average cost at any output, and a policy of marginal cost pricing (to achieve the socially optimal output) will lose money.

18

Measuring Monopoly

Is Monopoly Common? The Debate and Its Importance

Monopolies, then, are different from competitive industries. An economist looking at an industry will wish to know with which case she is dealing. If she is looking at an entire economy she will want to know which case is typical of the whole. How will she know?

The economist will have a difficult time knowing from the testimony of other economists. The theory of monopoly was developed in the late nineteenth century to deal with allegedly rare cases of monopolies on salt, natural gas, mineral water, and falls of meteors. The economy was supposed to be on the whole competitive. Most economists still accept the competitive model as the best rough characterization of how the economy works.[1] Since the 1930s, however, many other economists have come to believe that the economy is on the whole monopolistic, pointing to the fewness of companies in autos, soap, steel, cereal, soft drinks, brewing, and elsewhere and to the restrictions on entry to unionized occupations, heavily advertised industries, and industries regulated by the government. Competition in this view is an exception today and was an exception historically, a brief interlude between an age of local monopoly in the eighteenth century and of national monopoly in the twentieth. A realistic model of the economy, these economists would say, must speak of monopoly capital and the balance of countervailing powers.

The dispute matters. True, many scientific propositions in economics survive transplantation to a world of monopolies. The law of demand would still hold, although no longer confronted by a simple law of supply. There would still be more than one way to skin a cat, although the right way would not in general be chosen. Comparative advantage would still be society's best guide to specialization, although market

---

[1] When 198 economists in the mid-1970s were asked to assess the statement that "The 'Corporate State,' as depicted by Galbraith, accurately describes the context and structure of the U.S. economy," half flatly disagreed and only a fifth agreed without provisions. Furthermore, 80% of the 25 economists employed as full professors at seven leading economics departments (as distinct from those at other universities, or in government or business) flatly disagreed, more so even than economists employed by the corporations themselves. J. R. Kearl, Clayne L. Pope, Gordon C. Whiting, and Larry T. Wimmer, "A Confusion of Economists?" *American Economic Review* 69 (May 1979): 28–37, especially pp. 30, 36.

prices would no longer be themselves a guide to comparative advantage. And so forth. But if monopoly were pervasive, there would be less reason to respect the pattern of output the economy produced. On the contrary, the pattern would be demonstrably wrong, and a case could be made to change it, perhaps even by using the coercive power of the state. It is said that if people buy General Motors cars because they have no alternative or if they work at a certain job because trade union rules have mandated it or if they invest in chemical and insurance companies because the owners are politically powerful, then interventions to restore competition in the car market or the job market or the investment market are not only acceptable but desirable. One's convictions about the prevalence of monopoly, in short, can affect one's politics.[2] And in any case they can affect one's economics.

Profit Is a Measure of Monopoly, Unless It Is Rent

The most obvious way of resolving the dispute is to look around the economy at the level of profit. Presumably monopolies make profits above normal. The industries with above-normal profit could be placed in the "monopoly" box, those with normal profits in the "competitive." You can see that the procedure would run into difficulties if all industries were in fact monopolies, for then it is unclear as to how any one monopoly would stand out as unusually profitable. Even supposing that the true situation is some monopoly contrasted to some competition, the level of profit is not a reliable guide, on many grounds. For one thing, the ordinary workings of a competitive economy make some nonmonopolists rich. The owner of a handsome face, a mellifluous voice, a charming air, and luck becomes a movie star without any intent or ability to engage in price searching. Fertile land, likewise, earns economic rent, even if its owners compete with each other in atomistic markets. Furthermore, the temporary quasi-rent to the entrepreneur who is first on the scene with polyurethane roller skates or a vaccine for tooth decay is the very way in which a competitive economy attracts entry to desirable activities. Yet a snapshot of the economy might easily mistake the quasi-rent for permanent monopoly rent. To be a monopoly rent, the excess payment above what is required to draw the resource from some alternative employment must be useless, serving to reward neither agility of response nor rare merit. Only some rents are monopoly rents.

For the Secondhand Owner of a Monopoly, the Profit Is a Cost

The monopoly elements in the rents are not easy to spot. Aside from the occasional governmental monopoly on salt or postal service, few monopolies are so arrogant as to have a line in their annual statements called "monopoly profit." Even without any desire to deceive, the profits from price searching are liable to be buried in accounting categories such as goodwill or salaries. They will look like normal costs instead of abnormal profits. For the person who buys the right to a monopoly

[2] Two important works along these lines in recent times are Paul A. Baran and Paul M. Sweezy, *Monopoly Capital* (New York: Monthly Review Press, 1966), and John Kenneth Galbraith, *The New Industrial State* (Boston: Houghton, 1967). Related writers in sociology and political science have attacked the notion analogous in the political sphere to competition that democratic pluralism is the way politics works. Compare C. Wright Mills, *The Power Elite* (New York: Oxford University Press, 1956).

from an earlier holder, indeed, the monopoly profits *are* normal costs. Because in the market for the monopoly right he competes with many others, the secondhand buyer of a patent on cellophane or a license to operate a cab in San Francisco earns only a normal return.

Q: Woody Fleisig buys the Chicago Bulls basketball team for $10 million and acquires thereby the rights to whatever he can earn from the services of a group of athletes after paying for their salaries, their equipment, and the rent on the stadium. Woody, in common with many other sportsman million-aires, proceeds to lose money, say, $5 million. *True or false:* This is evidence that professional basketball, far from being a closed monopoly (as some gloomy-minded economists sometimes argue), is competitive. After all, monopolies are profitable.

A: If professional basketball were competitive, in the sense of having free entry, the permission to enter (i.e., the franchise, the right for which Woody paid $10 million) would be valueless. The ownership of the residual income from the Chicago Bulls after paying salaries and so forth would be valueless, the taking of risk aside, because the right has no real social opportunity cost. The fact that Woody was willing to pay someone $10 million indicates that he expected that the value of the stream of returns to ownership was $10 million (after making the appropriate allowances for the value of any reductions in his income taxes that he might have anticipated from losing money on the property). That he did in fact lose money merely indicates either that he has a devilishly clever tax lawyer or that he had overly optimistic expectations about the future *rise* in the monopoly profit. Therefore, false. The person who earns the whole monopoly profit is the person who established the monopoly, not the one who later buys the rights to its profits, once established.

Indeed, the profits from monopoly can be buried so deeply in cost that literally no one earns above-normal returns. The principle here is the zero-profit condition and the jargon is *dissipation of rents.* Since monopoly rents are valuable, a monopolist is willing to spend valuable resources acquiring and defending them. The lawyers, accountants, chemists, economists, teachers, inspectors, and so forth hired to seek rents may well earn nothing above their value in alternative employment. Their employment in rent seeking is like standing in line, that is, a sheer waste of resources, benefiting no one. The monopoly rents can be dissipated entirely in wasted motion.

Medical education is a good example. The doctor in the emergency room who puts your finger sprained playing softball into a metal splint has been to college for four years, to medical school for another four, and to internship for one or two years. The expense of the four medical school years is very high, far above that for any other form of education. Large though the fees he charges are, the individual doctor may find himself earning only a normal return on this enormous investment and will therefore quite understandably resent being called a monopolist. That the athletic trainer with an eighth-grade education does a better job of fixing the sprain at a quarter of the cost, however, suggests that doctoring as a whole is indeed a monopoly, although one that throws away some of its monopoly rents on superfluous education.

☐
The Height of a Barrier to Entry Is a Measure of Monopoly, Unless It Is Advertising

The barrier to entry that the educational requirement of medicine erects is itself evidence of monopoly. So are other barriers to entry. Just as you might infer from locks, burglar alarms, and guard dogs that a house contained valuable jewels, so too you might infer from licenses, membership requirements, and patents that an industry contained valuable profits.

A case in point that has long been controversial in economics is advertising. Contrary to a widespread opinion, most advertising is merely informative, not argumentative. To be sure, the ring-around-the-collar ad on television is uniquely irritating and devoid of intellectual content, but in fact it is dwarfed in message time and dollars by the classified ads in the St. Louis *Post-Dispatch*, the billboard that tells you of a place to sleep on your trip to Montreal, or the radio jingle that informs you as a new denture wearer of the miracle of Dentu-Cream. Advertising executives will tell you that the industry's proverb is "you can bring a horse to water but you can't make him drink," and they can back up their modesty with stories of failed ad campaigns for failed products, such as Fruit Float or the Edsel.

Even admitting the informative nature of most advertising, however, the mere existence of advertising indicates something less than perfect price taking. In a trivial sense, even the sign on the grocery store is indicative of price searching by the store, because if it were literally a price taker it could sell all it wished at the going price and would have no incentive to spend money on increasing the amount it could sell. In a less trivial sense, large advertising budgets for soap and cigarettes indicate that the companies face downward-sloping demand curves and would like to move out their marginal revenue curves, a meaningless activity for a price taker, who has a flat marginal revenue. That the companies spend so much on advertising indicates that the demand curves are indeed moved out (or at least prevented from being moved in by the advertising of competitors), meaning that the large expense of advertising becomes a requirement of the trade, a barrier to entry. The significance of this line of reasoning, however, is much disputed. Some economists believe that the barrier is high and leads to large monopoly distortions; others do not. The evidence so far is ambiguous.[3]

☐
The Number of Firms Is a Measure of Monopoly, Unless There Is a Competitive Fringe

If the size of monopoly profits and the height of barriers to entry are difficult to measure, the number of competitors in an industry is easy. Count them. One or few implies monopoly; many implies competition. As was shown in the last chapter, however, the number of firms in an industry is always less than the number waiting on the fringe. The share of the market taken by the three largest auto firms,

---

[3] A view from the antiadvertising side is William S. Comanor and Thomas A. Wilson, "Advertising and Competition: A Survey," *Journal of Economic Literature* 17 (June 1979): 453–476; from the pro-advertising side, Harold Demsetz, "Accounting for Advertising as a Barrier to Entry," *Journal of Business* 52 (July 1979): 345–360.

say, may be very high but will result in little deviation from the competitive price if at a little above the going price five foreign firms will enter. A *concentration ratio* (the market share of the top *N* firms) looks like straightforward measures of monopoly power, but in fact it is made doubtful by the neglected fringe of potential entrants. Low concentration (many sellers) might show that monopoly does not exist—although what would one say about monopolies of doctors and plumbers?—but high concentration cannot show that monopolies do exist.

Elasticity of Demand Is a Measure of Monopoly Power

The very failures of concentration as a way of measuring monopoly, however, lead to another better measure, as follows. Whether or not the economist watching the monopolist does, one among few sellers of steel will know of both existing and potential entry and will allow for it. The entry will in fact increase effective elasticity of demand. The mathematics here is that of Chapter 7 on elasticities. There it was shown that the elasticity of demand facing one of the suppliers of steel, say, Inland Steel, rises as the elasticities of market demand and of supply from U.S. Steel, Bethlehem, and so forth become high and as Inland's share becomes small (the elasticity is defined here to be positive):

$$\epsilon_{In}^{D} = \frac{Q}{Q_{In}} (\epsilon^{D}) + \frac{Q_{others}}{Q_{In}} (\epsilon_{others}^{S})$$

Elasticity of demand facing Inland	=	inverse of Inland's market share	×	market elasticity of demand	+	ratio of others to Inland's output	×	elasticity of supply of others

There are four variables on the right-hand side. The presence of the fringe can be viewed as raising Q/Q_{In}, Q_{others}/Q_{In}, or ϵ_{others}^{S}, all of which raise the elasticity that Inland faces. The elasticity is a measure of Inland's monopoly power. If it is low, then Inland faces a sharply downward-sloping demand curve, approaching the condition of a literal single seller.[4] If it is high, then Inland faces a flat demand curve, approaching the condition of one perfect competitor among many.

Notice that in the present case it does not take a very large fringe, or a very small share, to make the elasticity very high. If the elasticity of demand overall were 1.5 and the elasticity of supply of others were 1.0, then an Inland share of 1 in 15 of every ton of steel produced would give an elasticity of

$$\epsilon_{In}^{D} = \frac{15}{1}(1.5) + \frac{14}{1}(1.0) = 36.5$$

The Fundamental Equation of Monopoly

But is 36.5 high or low? The way in which elasticity of demand affects a monopolist provides an answer and further justifies the elasticity as a measure of monopoly power. Most important, it makes it possible to measure the power without elaborate information on all the various

---

[4] The argument neglects the awareness that Inland will have of its effect on other steel makers and the awareness others will have of their effect on Inland. Chapter 21 takes up the matter.

elasticities of demand and supply. The marginal revenue of a monopolist, recall, is $MR = P - Q\Delta P/\Delta Q$. In equilibrium the monopolist arranges matters so that marginal cost equals this marginal revenue:

$$MC = P - \frac{\Delta P}{\Delta Q/Q}$$

It is one short step—dividing both sides by P—to a most useful idea:

The Fundamental Equation of Monopoly

$$\frac{MC}{P} = \frac{P}{P} - \frac{\Delta P/P}{\Delta Q/Q} = 1 - \frac{1}{\epsilon}$$

Ratio of marginal   inverse of the
cost to the price   = 1.0 − elasticity of demand
charged by a monopolist   facing the monopolist

If the elasticity is very, very high, say, the 1000 it might be for a seller in a large auction market competing against many hundreds of others, then the ratio of marginal cost to price is very near to 1.0—namely, $1.0 - 1/1000 = 0.999$—and marginal cost is virtually equal to price. If the elasticity is low, say the 1.5 it might be for the government acting on behalf of the steel industry to set quotas on steel that maximized the American steel industry's profits, then the ratio is well below 1.0—namely, $1.0 - 1/1.5 = 0.33$—and marginal cost is a fraction of price.[5] Ask the question again. Is 36.5 high or low? Well, it implies a ratio of marginal cost to price of $1.0 - 1/36.5 = 0.97$. A monopolist who knew the marginal cost to within plus or minus 3% would be an unusually discerning person. An economist who could second-guess her knowledge to within plus or minus double that figure would be a genius. In practical terms, then, 0.97 is indistinguishable from competition.

The Ratio of Marginal Cost to Price of Monopoly Is Not Impossible to Measure

In any event, the ratio of marginal cost to price provides an attractive measure of monopoly power.[6] Its attractions are two. First, because it is related to the elasticity, the ratio is a measure of the influence that the monopolist believes he has. In other words, it measures behavior. Second, because it is the ratio of the ideal price (marginal cost) to the actual, the ratio measures the hurt the monopolist's behavior imposes. In other words, it measures happiness. Detecting monopoly by measuring its profits or barriers to entry or numbers is inconclusive. Here is a conclusive measure: measure the ratio of marginal cost to price.

The fly in the ointment, of course, is that marginal cost is very difficult to measure. The total cost may rise in response to a rise in output in ways that the firm itself will find difficult to know, and

[5] Notice that the formula reflects the condition that elasticity must be greater than 1.0 for a monopolist. If ϵ were less, say, 0.5, then the implied ratio would be negative, $1.0 - 1/0.5 = -1.0$, which is ridiculous.

[6] Abba P. Lerner, "The Concept of Monopoly and the Measurement of Monopoly Power," *Review of Economic Studies* 1 (June 1934): 157–175.

the firm will have in any case no incentive to make whatever it does know public. The solution is to find a second market in which the monopolist firm is a competitor (i.e., facing an infinitely elastic demand), for it will in that market set its price equal to marginal cost, revealing its marginal cost. If a monopoly is temporary, such as a temporary coalition of gasoline stations in the neighborhood raising prices, then one may judge its marginal cost from the episodes of competitive pricing.[7]

An even better circumstance for self-revelation of marginal cost, however, is that of the monopolist selling in two markets, in one of which he is a competitor.

Q: The German steel cartel (monopoly) in 1890 supplied all the market in Germany (a tariff protected the German market from interlopers) and also exported to the world market. How would you measure the degree of its monopoly at home?

A: In the world market it takes price as given. Consequently, it will sell to the world until its marginal cost equals the world price. The marginal cost is common to production for either market, world or home—marginal cost is marginal cost no matter where the steel is sold. The world price divided by the German home price is therefore the degree of monopoly at home.

□   The argument is an extremely rich one.

**The Uses of the Case
of Elastic Foreign
Demand**

Q: Suppose that no foreigners may sell steel in Germany however high the price is there but that the Germany monopoly may sell steel abroad at the world price if it wished. *True or false:* If the Germany monopoly does sell abroad, then the price it sets at home will be rigid with respect to changes in costs of making steel.

A: True. That no foreigners may ever sell in Germany means that the Germany monopoly faces the whole German demand curve. That it may sell abroad means that the monopoly also faces a flat demand curve for exports. If it does sell abroad, it is evidently on a marginal cost curve like also go abroad instead of stay at home. The two marginal cost curves are to be viewed as alternatives, not the marginal cost of producing for the two different markets (on the contrary, the cost is supposed to be the same, from a common plant). Refer to Figure 18.1.

The also-go-abroad marginal cost intersects the total marginal revenue at most profit, the shaded area of profit being evidently maximized there. At such a point, marginal cost is equal to marginal revenue in both directions

---

[7] This way of implementing Lerner's measure of monopoly power first occurred to John T. Dunlop, "Price Flexibility and the 'Degree of Monopoly,'" *Quarterly Journal of Economics* 53 (August 1939): 522–534. It has been used to examine the competitiveness of the iron and steel industry in the nineteenth century, which had temporary monopolies, by Peter Temin, *Iron and Steel in Nineteenth-Century America* (Cambridge, Mass.: M.I.T. Press, 1964), p. 187; and D. N. McCloskey, *Economic Maturity and Entrepreneurial Decline: British Iron and Steel 1870–1913* (Cambridge, Mass.: Harvard University Press, 1973), pp. 24–28.

of sale, home and abroad. The rule of rational life permits no other conclusion. The marginal cost of a thing must be equal to the marginal benefit
in each of its uses if profit is to be maximized. The price at home is fixed
at lowest home price because at that price the marginal revenue abroad
(namely, the price abroad) equals the marginal revenue at home. Changes
in the position of the also-go-abroad marginal cost curve will over a wide
range (look at the arrows) have no effect at all on the best price to charge
at home. In other words, as asserted, the price will tend to be rigid.

Figure 18.1
Self-interest Puts a Floor
on the Marginal Revenue
of a Monopolist Able to
Sell in a Competitive
Market

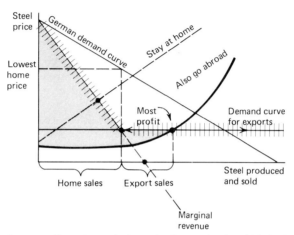

A monopolist at home facing a foreign market in which he is a competitor may sell in
both markets, at home and abroad. If the monopolist does, he is setting the marginal
cost of output equal to marginal revenue in both markets and therefore is setting them
equal to each other. Because the one marginal revenue is just the price the monopolist
faces, the foreign price drives the model. If it is too low (relative to marginal costs, such
as the high marginal costs of stay at home), no exports occur and the case is one of
simple monopoly.

A more general case introduces a useful fine point about monopoly
diagrams and says something about the limits on monopoly power.

Q: Suppose that in 1880 in Britain steel rails were made in Glasgow and Sheffield, 170 miles apart. Suppose that the Sheffield makers viewed the Glasgow
price in Glasgow as given: they believed themselves to have no monopoly
power in Glasgow. Likewise did the Glasgow makers in Sheffield. Suppose
finally that steel rails sold for 100 shillings a ton in Glasgow and could be
transported between the two cities for 5 shillings a ton.
   1. Within what limits must the price in Sheffield lie?
   2. Suppose that the Sheffield makers form themselves into a monopoly
at home. What is their curve of marginal revenue? What prices do they
charge at home for various curves of marginal cost?
   3. How many shillings is the lowest marginal cost that Sheffield will ever
produce at? How many shillings is the highest price? What therefore is the
lowest possible ratio of marginal cost to price? In view of the elasticity formula

for the ratio, what is the lowest possible elasticity of demand the Sheffield monopoly faces?

4. If transport cost to or from a market in which a monopoly is not a monopoly is $t\%$ of the foreign price, what is the most monopoly power that it can have?

A: 1. Clearly the Sheffield price must lie between 95 and 105 shillings, for at a price in Sheffield a little below 95 shillings the Sheffield makers do better to sell their rails in Glasgow and at a price a little above 105 shillings the Glasgow makers invade the Sheffield market (see Figure 18.2).

2. The marginal revenue curve needs to be constructed step by step. Start with highest marginal cost. In such a case the relevant marginal revenue is the 105 shillings set by imports from Glasgow. Now consider high marginal cost. The marginal revenue leaps down to the curve marginal to the Sheffield demand curve, as it did in the earlier problems on the stage coach and OPEC. To supply more than is demanded at imports cease is to force more on the market than will be bought at 105 shillings. The price must fall and must spoil the price on all previous amounts. Naturally, then, the marginal revenue beyond imports cease is much lower than it is before imports cease. Over a wide range of high marginal cost curves, the price is rigid at exactly 105 shillings, and the quantity supplied by Sheffield makers is the amount at imports cease. At low marginal cost the curve intersects the marginal revenue and it becomes worthwhile to supply more than the amount at imports cease. The price must therefore be a little lower. Finally, a lowest marginal cost Sheffield is such a cheap producer that it exports. But it never produces more for the home market in Sheffield than it does at exports begin. To produce more would drive marginal revenue at home below marginal revenue abroad (the export price), an irrational thing to do. The Sheffield price never gets below lowest price.

3. The lowest possible marginal cost is 95 shillings, by the argument just given. The highest possible price is 105 shillings, so the lowest ratio is $95/105 = 0.90$. The formula then becomes $0.90 = 1 - 1/\epsilon$. Solving for the elasticity of demand, ϵ, yields an ϵ of 10.

4. The most monopoly power is clearly twice the percentage transport cost. For many items such limits on monopoly power will be tight.

☐
The Rule of Rational Life for Two Markets: The Fundamental Equation of Discriminatory Monopoly

Knowledge of the elasticity a monopoly faces in one market, then, is enough to fix its marginal cost and to measure against market prices its monopoly power in all markets. If in one of the markets it faces an infinite elasticity of demand, the fixing of marginal cost is simple. It is whatever price the monopolist gets in that market. But even if it does not face infinite elasticity, the rule of rational life holds. The monopoly shifts outputs among the various markets in which it sells until marginal revenues in all markets are equal to each other and equal to the common marginal cost. Doing so will in general lead to unequal prices that cannot be explained by unequal costs, called *price discrimination*. For example, airlines charge lower prices for children than for adults, even though the marginal cost of providing a seat to Emily Redfield, who is 12 years old, is identical to that of providing

Figure 18.2
Imports and Exports Limit
Monopoly Power

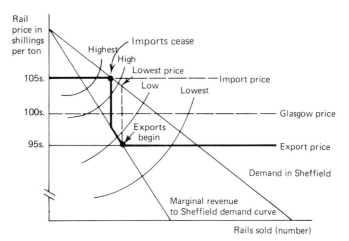

Extending the argument of Figure 18.1, the given import and export prices ("given" because the local monopolist of steel is merely local and is a negligible influence on world markets) set limits on the local monopoly. The local monopolist's marginal revenue is the emphasized jagged line, being equal to the import and export prices at the extremes. It is equal to the ordinary marginal revenue curve only over some range, and at the top of the range it makes a sudden leap up to the import price. The intersection of marginal cost (here given by several alternatives) determines the details of the monopoly's behavior.

---

one to the former Louise Bolduc, who is 37. The equation for the ratio of marginal cost to price for the child is as usual $MC/P_C = 1 - 1/\epsilon_C$, and likewise for the adult. Multiplying each by its price will give the equation for how price and elasticity, ϵ, must relate to marginal cost. In equilibrium, then, being equal to the common marginal cost implies the following:

The Fundamental Equation of Discriminatory Monopoly

$$P_C\left(1 - \frac{1}{\epsilon_C}\right) = P_A\left(1 - \frac{1}{\epsilon_A}\right)$$

| Price for the child | × | 1.0 − the inverse of the elasticity of demand for children | = | price for the adult | × | 1.0 − the inverse of the elasticity of demand for adults |

Children have a more elastic demand than do adults. The child's ride is usually not a business trip, for example, but a trip to Granny's that can easily be foregone. If the elasticity of demand by adults were, say, 1.5, the elasticity by children might be 3.0 or 4.0. Putting these values into the formula gives $P_C(\frac{2}{3}$ or $\frac{3}{4}) = P_A(\frac{1}{3})$. The adult, relatively inelastic market pays 2 (= $\frac{2}{3} \div \frac{1}{3}$) or 2.25 (= $\frac{3}{4} \div \frac{1}{3}$) times more for the same seat.

A useful diagram exhibiting a monopolist that sells in two (or in general many) markets draws the demand curves back to back, sharing a common price axis. If the marginal cost is constant, the diagram serves to determine how much is produced as well as how it is divided between the two markets. A railroad in 1920, for example, faced low-elasticity customers shipping general merchandise (freight such as clothing and farm machinery with high value relative to the shipping cost and few alternative shippers) and high-elasticity customers shipping bulk products (freight such as coal and wheat with low value relative to the shipping cost and many alternative shippers). It maximized profit by setting marginal cost per ton-mile, assumed to be the same for both, equal to marginal revenue in both markets (see Figure 18.3).

Figure 18.3
Why the Railroads
Charged More for Less

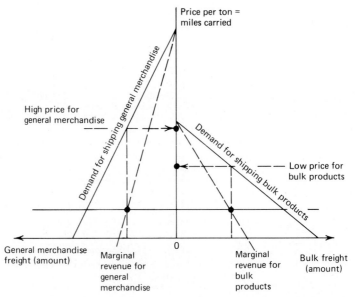

Before the coming of road trucking, the railroads faced two markets: one for bulk freight and one for general merchandise. The general merchandise, being of greater value per ton shipped, was able to bear high costs of shipping easily and, therefore, yielded an inelastic demand curve for transport. The railways charged the customers with inelastic demands higher prices.

The result was a high price for general merchandise and a low price for bulk products. The year 1920 is chosen because shortly thereafter long-distance trucking stole the general merchandise from the railroads, skimming the cream as it was called, which led to (successful) requests to bring trucking under the high-price rules of the Interstate Commerce Commission.

The general principle is that the inelastic demand pays a higher price, because it will stand still for the higher price.

Q: Marshall Fields, a department store in Chicago, offers to pay up to $30 for an old piece of luggage as a trade-in on the purchase of a new one. The old luggage is worthless to Marshall Fields, which throws it away once it has reduced the price to the buyer with old luggage by $30.

   1. What do you suppose the difference in elasticity of demand is between

a new buyer of luggage (newlyweds, say, with no old luggage) and an old buyer (who already has some serviceable but battered luggage)?

2. Now explain the $30 discount and other trade-ins involving goods with no secondhand value (refrigerators, televisions, etc.).

A: 1. The elasticity of demand for the new buyer is probably lower than is that of the old. The old buyer already has luggage, which competes with a possible purchase.

2. In other words, Marshall Field is price discriminating. It detects a high-elasticity buyer (to whom it charges a $30 lower price) by his ownership of old luggage. Likewise with trade-ins elsewhere. The old refrigerator in your house competes for the new, making you (unlike the first-time buyer) less willing to stand still for a high monopoly price.

☐
Price Discrimination Is Evidence of the Existence of Monopoly

Price discrimination, then, is evidence for the existence of monopoly power, serving even (as was shown earlier) to measure its degree if the elasticities are known. A doctor, for example, commonly charges lower prices for poor than for rich patients. Putting it so suggests that her motive is charitable. But putting it the other way, that the doctor charges higher prices for rich than for poor patients, suggests an alternative explanation: that she is able to price discriminate, charging a higher price to the presumably less elastic demanders with high incomes.[8]

T or F: Giving partial college scholarships that depend on the student's income is price discrimination.

A: True. The low-income student will not come to the college (read "buy the product") without a scholarship (read "without a lower price"). The student's elasticity of demand is higher. The same is true even of scholarships based entirely on "merit" (i.e., College Board scores or high school grades or, for that matter, unusual ability to stuff a large ball in a small basket while dressed in underwear and sneakers). People with such abilities have many colleges from which to choose; that is, they have a high elasticity of demand for the services of the University of Iowa. The economics of scholarships often puzzles observers. They wonder how it could be that a college can make more in tuition money by "spending" scholarship money. The answer is that the college is not in fact spending anything; it is merely offering discounts to students with especially elastic demand curves, in the style of a discriminating monopoly.

The exercise of discriminatory monopoly is impossible if the good can be resold. If the child could resell his airplane seat to an adult, if the new owner of luggage could resell to the old, if the poor patient could resell his medical care to a rich patient, or if a scholarship student could resell her place to a nonscholarship student, the two-price system would break down.

[8] See Reuben Kessel, "Price Discrimination in Medicine," *Journal of Law and Economics* 1 (October 1958): 20–53.

Q: Seen on Bronco Superfine Toilet Tissue: "Commercial Pack, Not for Resale to the Public." Why not?

A: Because with resale the Bronco Company could not charge two prices, a high one to retail customers at the grocery store and a low one to commercial customers with many alternatives available to them. In like fashion, makers of a plaster substance used in both taking casts of teeth and fixing walls put poison in the wall-fixing version. If by law, by poison, or by the personalized nature of the product resale is made impossible, then price discrimination is made possible.

□

Other Methods of Discrimination

The underlying reason a monopoly makes more profit by discriminating than by charging a uniform price is that freeing it of the constraint to charge a uniform price must make it better off. So it is with other pricing schemes. If the monopoly is free to impose ingenious tortures on the consumers, it can extract more money. By contrast, if it is a simple, single-price monopoly, it can only charge one price to all consumers and let them buy what they wish at the one price. If the monopoly has the power to go further, especially the power to stop consumers from reselling among each other, then it can present consumers with more complex deals that must make it still richer if, it in fact uses them. The more complex deals are all called "price discrimination," and all share with two-person price discrimination the feature that different consumers are treated differently.

The simplest complexity is an entry fee, Mafia "insurance" premium, membership fee, tribute payment, installation charge, or cover charge that varies with the person. Businesses, for example, are charged more for installation of telephones than are household customers. In the extreme such a charge can extract all the consumers' benefit from trade, by adjusting the fee to each consumer's consumers' surplus. The charge that the marginal consumer would accept, however, is of course zero, since he has by definition no consumer's surplus to extract. Therefore if the marginal consumer can trade with more eager customers, a variable fee cannot be sustained. If a club charges membership fees graduated by income, for example, the low-income members will sell their memberships (if they are transferable). No high-income member will in fact pay the high fee, since he will be able to more than compensate a low-income, low-fee member for giving up his membership. The variable fee will disintegrate into a single and simple monopoly.

A closely related scheme, often adopted by the same monopolists who charge discriminating fees, is to charge lower prices per unit to those who buy a lot. The offer of one box of Kleenex for $1.00, two for $1.50 is such a scheme in embryo. Electricity, for instance, is commonly sold according to a schedule of declining rates as more is purchased. The similarity between such *multipart pricing* and the discriminating fee is illustrated in Figure 18.4. The sock-it-to-them electricity monopoly can charge Lars Sandberg the shaded area as a fee and then sell him electricity at marginal cost.

Figure 18.4
A Pricing Schedule Can
Get a Monopolist More
than a Mere Price

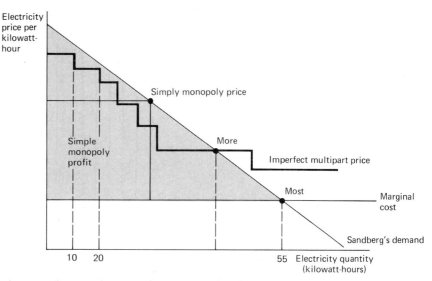

The rectangle is simple monopoly profit, namely, what the electric company could earn if it did not charge different prices for different portions of peoples' consumption. If it charged according to the step-function schedule, it could get more. And if it charged at prices along Sandberg's (and everyone else's) demand curve, it could get the most, the shaded area of consumer's surplus.

Alternatively, the monopoly can present Sandberg with the schedule called imperfect multipart price. The schedule charges him more for early amounts than for late. It induces him to buy out to more and yields more profit to the monopoly than does the simple monopoly price (which gives only the inscribed rectangle of simple money profit). With perfect knowledge the monopoly could arrange the perfect multipart price, namely, Sandberg's demand curve itself, selling him the last unit (55 kilowatt-hours) at marginal cost. The profit from such a scheme would be identical to the largest possible fee, scooping out all the consumer's surplus.

Another and better interpretation of multipart electricity pricing is not in fact that it charges less for Sandberg's last unit of consumption than for his first but that it simply charges Sandberg, as a residential consumer, less than Baack Bauxite Refining, which consumes vastly more electricity. The parts of the multipart price apply to different demand curves, not to different parts of one person's demand curve. The case is interpretable as the elementary one of two consumers with different elasticities. If high-volume consumers have higher elasticities (at the same price) than do low-volume consumers, then it will be rational for a monopoly that can prevent resale to charge the high-volume consumers less. That the monopoly expresses the price as a schedule is really irrelevant. It is in fact using volume as a meter to detect high-elasticity demanders, just as low age is used to detect high-elasticity demanders of airfares or movie seats.

The presence of quantity discounts, however, does not invariably indicate monopoly. After all, it is possible that large quantities are in fact cheaper per unit to sell, because fixed costs of ordering are spread over the larger volume. The high-income member of a club, likewise, might well be a more expensive member to serve, making for example more demands on the staff. In other words, a defense to a claim of price discrimination is always that the products sold at different prices to different consumers have in fact different costs. The defense will sometimes be persuasive.

The more general point is applicable to all the arguments. It is difficult to detect monopoly. Even discrimination among customers, the most public evidence of monopoly power, can sometimes be explained as a competitive result of differences in cost. No wonder, then, that the evidence on the prevalence of monopoly is not all in.

Summary

The question of whether the economy is predominantly monopolistic or competitive has been asked in a great variety of ways by economists over the past 50 years. The answer is important, affecting the enthusiasm with which one views market outcomes. The ways of measuring monopoly are many, but all are in some respect inconclusive. Profit above normal is one measure, but it is often confounded with normal rent or dissipated in seeking the monopoly. The height of barriers to entry is another measure of the profit, advertising being one example, and itself direct evidence that the advertiser is not a price taker. But the significance of the barrier is difficult to measure. The number of firms in the industry, a third possible measure of monopoly, is easy to measure but is irrelevant. The size of the fringe is what is relevant to the use of monopoly power. A fourth measure looks directly at the behavior of a monopoly, noting that it sets its price above marginal cost. The trick, then, is to measure marginal cost. Price discrimination between elastic and relatively inelastic demands is a good source of evidence on marginal cost, as when a monopoly charges its export customers less than its domestic consumers. The idea is a rich one, applicable to all manner of markets, from the steel cartel in Germany to the airlines in America. Price discrimination comes in many packages, all of which fall apart if the victims can resell the monopolized good. But such uses of the measure of monopoly are more successful than is their use to answer the original question of prevalence. The question remains unanswered. Is the modern economy predominantly competitive? We do not know.

QUESTIONS FOR CHAPTER 18

1. In the stock market the right to the future profits of a firm is priced. If George Marr and Co., Inc. is expected to earn, say, $1000 for the next 15 years and then to go broke, the total value of the company's stock (ignoring the lower value of distant earnings) will be 15 × $1000, that is, $15,000. *True or false:* If the stock market is functioning correctly, dividing income per year by the value of the stocks of firm will always give the competitive rate of return even if Marr and Co. is a monopoly.

2. The Justice Department accused Citibank and some other big U.S. banks in October 1978 of conspiring to make money by forcing down the price of the dollar. What one number characterizing the market for dollars would you want to have as an economist deciding whether or not the alleged conspiracy could have been effective? And what value would you like the number to take as an attorney for Citibank attempting to rebut the Justice Department's accusation?

3. In the text of the last section it was argued that the owner of a patent on a cost-reducing invention for hand calculators would not always charge all the cost reduction as a royalty; that is, the owner would sometimes charge a royalty that allowed price including the royalty to fall from its preinvention price. To find out when "not always" and "sometimes" occur, view the owner as a monopolist in the market for hand calculators, making calculators at some fixed marginal cost and selling them at a markup. Suppose that the older, more expensive technique was not available. According to the elasticity formula for monopolies, what would be the profit-maximizing markup? What is the markup if the older technique is available and the optimal markup is greater than the ratio of the old price to the new marginal cost? Try out some values for the elasticity and the old-new cost ratios. What do you conclude about the likelihood of passing cost savings on to consumers?

4. Consider the Sony Television Division selling televisions at home in Japan at a high monopoly price and in the United States at a low competitive price.
a. Draw Sony's entire marginal revenue curve.
b. Draw a U-shaped marginal cost curve that would induce Sony to sell some abroad. At the equilibrium point what is the total revenue (use the area under marginal revenue)? What is the total variable cost? What is total profit (net of variable cost, i.e., ignoring fixed cost)?
c. Sony is often accused of *dumping* in the United States. The definition of "dumping," however, varies. According to the model of a monopoly just developed, would Sony's behavior fit a definition that dumping is "charging a lower price to foreign than to home customers"? How about "charging a price to foreigners that is below marginal cost"?
d. Dumping is more usually defined as selling below *average* cost (whether average total or average variable cost), since average cost is easier to observe. Taking the extreme, would it ever be rational for Sony to price its televisions in the United States below average *variable* cost? That is, could Sony still be making money? Use U-shaped marginal and average cost curves and what you know about the necessary relations between average and marginal curves.

5. A local monopolist sells in two markets, home and abroad. At home Frederick Mallinson supplies 100% of the quantity consumed; abroad Mallinson sells 0.00000000001%. The price Mallinson charges at home is observed to be 50% above the price he gets abroad. *True or false:* Therefore the elasticity of the demand curve he faces at home is 3.0.

6. Alcohol refined from vegetable matter (e.g., corn) is commonly used as automobile fuel in Brazil. It is drinkable, being pure grain alcohol. The government, however, makes it poisonous by adding a little gasoline. Why?

7. A standard example of discriminatory monopoly is the case of International Business Machine a long time ago. As the case is usually described, IBM would not sell its large-scale electronic computers, only lease them at so much per month (the same for any user). It required that its customers buy computer cards from IBM, at a price above what a competitive firm selling cards would charge. The practice is alleged to have been a devilishly clever method of price discriminating (i.e., charging different prices to different customers). The customer who used his or her leased machine a lot would use also a lot of cards and would therefore pay a lot to IBM *per unit of computing service.* The customer who used it a little would pay a little per unit of computing service. The big user, the analysis goes, pays more than the little user, making the scheme a good example of price discrimination.

a. If the argument is put, as it has been so far, in terms of the price of a unit of computing services—say, one multiplication of two five-digit numbers—is it correct? That is, is the big user charged more per unit of computation?

b. How can one restate the argument in correct form? Suppose that the product on the horizontal axis is the number of computing machines instead of the number of computations? What is on the vertical axis? How much is a big user willing to pay compared with a little user?

True or False

8. That all the major coffee canners raised their prices at the same time and in the same amount is evidence of monopoly in the coffee canning industry.

9. The opening of an opportunity by a monopoly at home to sell abroad as a competitor will if anything raise the price at home.

10. Barbers charge less for children because it is less costly to cut the hair of children.

11. The practice of bringing out the hardback edition of a book well before an identical paperback is an example of price discrimination.

12. A discriminating monopolist will charge in each market the price that maximizes receipts in that market.

13. American Motor Company's offer to give back $200 of the price of small cars to buyers over the age of 65 reflects their concern for the aged.

14. Since it can be shown diagrammatically that straight-line demand curves with a common price at which the quantity demand is zero have at the same price the same elasticity, such demand curves should not be used in an analysis of price discrimination between two markets.

19

The Welfare Economics of Monopoly

*Monopoly May
Subsidize Some
Desirable Activity
(or May Not)*

☐ Monopoly has its defenders, chiefly the monopolists themselves. The most elementary and common defense of a monopoly is that it is good for some other social purpose. The postal service's monopoly of first-class mail is defended on the grounds that the service can thereby subsidize unprofitable customers, such as remote farmhouses. The United Automobile Workers' monopoly of labor sold to automakers is defended on the grounds that the union can thereby protect workers from arbitrary treatment and can in the end improve productivity. The government's monopoly of violence is defended on the grounds that the government can thereby supply the citizens with many valuable services, such as the construction of a new dam where none is wanted or the enforcement of monopoly prices for interstate furniture moving.

Q: Restricting entry to medical school (by restricting the number of places) is often defended on the grounds that it improves the average quality of doctors and therefore improves medical care. Even if the restriction does improve the quality of doctors, the argument is not decisive. Is it socially desirable that only the students with the greatest aptitude and affection for academic work be allowed into medical school? Compare a high-quality (and expensive) doctor with a high-quality (and expensive) automobile. Is the amount of transportation maximized by restricting entry?

A: What the apologists for the monopolists are forgetting is that the bright students attracted by the high monopoly rewards (coupled with imposing barriers to entry that make only very bright and hardworking students admittable to medical school) have alternative employment elsewhere, where the social benefit of I.Q. and energy might well be higher (ask yourself: does your local sawbones *really* need to have gotten straight A's in organic chemistry at Cal Tech?). And, of course, the quality of doctors being high does not imply that the quality of medical care, given its low quantity, is high. We could improve the quality of automobiles by requiring that everyone drive a Rolls-Royce, turning over to the Rolls-Royce company the task of certifying new entrants. The automobiles driven would be of high quality, to be sure, but there would be so few of them that the quality of transportation would fall.

403

One must always ask, in other words, whether a grant of a monopoly is the most efficient way to a social end. The standard case in point is the *infant industry tariff*, that is, a very high tax imposed on foreign goods to give a young industry at home a chance to grow up free of foreign competition. The high tariffs on cotton textiles and iron imported into the United States in the nineteenth century were commonly defended on such grounds: protect our monopoly for 10 (or 20 or 100) years, said the American industries, and we will eventually produce cotton cloth and iron rails even cheaper than the British. The argument is inconclusive. For one thing, the "eventual" low prices might not justify the many intervening years of high prices, especially if the lack of a foreign fringe makes it possible to sustain prices at home above even the high American cost. For another, there may be a more direct and less expensive way of teaching Americans to make cloth and rails as cheaply as the British. The government could subsidize research, set up a demonstration plant, or send technicians to Britain to study. In the nineteenth century such alternatives were politically unlikely, but in the twentieth century they are in fact taken by many developing countries. In the few instances in which the governments have been able to resist agitation to use tariffs to dull the stimulus of foreign competition, the countries have been made better off. They have gotten the industries they should, but by more efficient means than official monopolies.

□
Monopoly May Encourage Economic Progress (or May Not)

A closely related defense of monopoly is the one articulated in 1942 by Joseph Schumpeter, the great theorist and historian of industrial capitalism:

> The introduction of new methods of production and new commodities is hardly conceivable with perfect—and perfectly prompt—competition from the start. And this means that the bulk of what we call economic progress is incompatible with it. . . . In this respect, perfect competition is not only impossible but inferior, and has no title to being set up as a model of ideal efficiency.[1]

Monopoly like a patent protects the rewards of innovation from erosion by competition, giving more incentive to seek them. He admitted, however, that "it is certainly as conceivable that an all-pervading cartel system might sabotage all progress as it is that it might realize, with smaller social and private costs, all that perfect competition is supposed to realize."[2] From a theoretical point of view, in other words, it is unclear whether monopoly or competition is best for innovation. On the one hand the monopolist might reap the harvest of innovation; on the other the monopolist might have less incentive to plant the crop. In the static world of most economic theory the issue can hardly be joined, much less resolved.

[1] Joseph Schumpeter, *Capitalism, Socialism and Democracy*, 3rd ed. (New York: Harper Torchbook, 1962), pp. 105–106.
[2] Ibid., p. 91.

T or F: Because it is a monopolist in many markets and has no incentive to keep costs down, American Telephone & Telegraph Company has higher costs than would a competitive telephone industry.

A: Set aside the problem of if my grandmother had wheels. Lower costs translate into larger profits no matter what the state of competition. A dollar of additional value to AT&T stock is the same as a dollar of additional value to Corey Bell's local telephone service. Therefore, false. Only a misapplication of diminishing marginal utility would suggest that a monopoly swimming in profits would want them less than thirsty little competitors for your telephone business. Its monopoly might dull the vigor and raise the costs of the telephone company as a matter of fact. But as a matter of the simple logic of static economic theory, the result is not necessary.

Likewise, "planned obsolescence," a conspiracy against durable goods, is often attributed to monopolies. We have all heard (false) rumors that such-and-such a big company has kept the long-lived light bulb or the long-lived car off the market. But in fact the market form has little to do with the matter in logic.

Q: Alec Guinness was *The Man in the White Suit* (1951), who invented an indestructible and unsoilable fabric only to find that clothing manufacturers would not use it. To use it, they said, would ruin their business, which depends on the wearing out of old clothing. Would the fabric be used?

A: If the fabric lasted forever, it could sell at the value (allowing for changes in style) of the infinite series of ordinary pieces of clothing that it replaces. A monopoly of clothing manufacturers would be delighted to sell it at this price or in any event at the price that maximized profit. A competitive clothing industry would be forced to sell it at the lower price of its cost of production—forced, that is, by the attempts of each manufacturer to steal a march on the others. In either case the fabric would be used. That is, yes. The fabric would be used, contrary to the bit of ersatz economics in the manufacturers' argument.

The logic is not decisive, of course, for in such matters logic unassisted by fact is never decisive. The facts may be that monopoly does nonetheless have a good or bad effect on innovation. The logic implies only that the usual postulates of economic thinking do not lead to such a conclusion. In any particular case, the postulates may be to some extent wrong. If the executives and owners of the telephone company did in fact think of themselves as sheltered, then innovation would be retarded. If each clothing manufacturer did in fact think his own refusal to adopt the miracle fabric would stop its general use, then again innovation would be retarded. On the other hand, if each monopoly did in fact think of its monopoly profits as a fund of zero-interest money for investment in laboratories, then innovation would be advanced. Such irrationalities are possible. The point is merely that the usual theory of rationality cannot easily accommodate them.

□

**Monopoly Does
Produce Too Little
Output**

Whether or not the usual theory can show that monopoly retards progress in technique, it certainly can show that monopoly produces an
inefficient output from given techniques. An earlier section used supply
and demand curves to show this in the rough. The Edgeworth box
can now be dusted off and set working to show it in detail.

The Edgeworth box, you recall, represents an exchange of two goods
between two types of people. Suppose, for example, that the Organization of Petroleum Exporting Countries (OPEC) gives its oil in exchange
for the food of the Disorganization of Provender Exporters (DOPE).
The one mind of OPEC faces the many competing minds of DOPE.
OPEC maximizes its happiness in view of its effect on the world price
ratio between oil and food; each member of DOPE (and therefore the
entire group, since the members do not act together as a monopoly)
maximizes its happiness in view of a given, unalterable world price.
The constraint on OPEC's maximization is merely that it stay on
DOPE's offer curve. In other words, OPEC chooses the point monopoly
on DOPE's offer curve that puts OPEC on the best monopoly indifference curve (see Figure 19.1).

Notice that at monopoly the DOPE's offer curve is tangent to an
OPEC indifference curve (the curvature of the indifference curve makes
sense, you see, since OPEC's origin is in the lower left-hand corner).
Notice, too, that also at monopoly the definition of an offer curve
implies that the price line going through the point (and therefore
through rather than tangent to the offer curve) is tangent to a DOPE

**Figure 19.1
The First Astounding Fact:
The Exercise of Monopoly
Leaves a Region of
Unexploited Exchange**

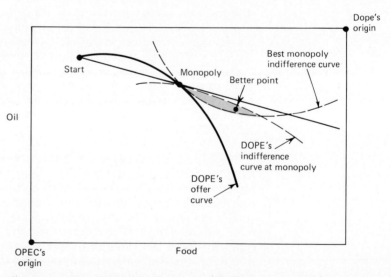

The exercise of monopoly power by one of the parties to an exchange of costs consists
of maximizing the monopolist's happiness subject to the constraint of the victim's offer
curve. Therefore, the monopolist's indifference curve at the monopoly point will be tangent
to the victim's offer curve. Therefore it will *not* be tangent to an indifference curve of
the victim. Therefore there will exist a lens shape of mutually advantageous exchange
unexploited. Note that the unexploited exchange is *mutually* beneficial. That is, even the
monopoly is made worse off than it could be.

indifference curve. That is, at monopoly the slopes of the two indifference curves are *not* equal. That is, at monopoly there is still a shaded lens or cigar shape of mutually advantageous exchange left to be taken. Monopoly is inefficient.

☐

Even the Monopolist Is Worse off

This is the first of three astounding facts about monopoly that the Edgeworth box makes plain. Monopoly leaves *even the monopoly* worse off than it could be if all opportunities for mutually advantageous exchange were taken. The monopoly is of course better off at the point monopoly than it would be if (like DOPE) it ignored its monopoly power and did not conspire to raise the price. But both the victim and the monopoly could be made even better off if they could somehow agree to seize the opportunity for more exchange, moving to a point within the cigar.

☐

Transaction Costs Are the Cause of Inefficiency

The second astounding fact is that the cause of single-price monopoly and its inefficiencies is merely the cost of making agreements. It was just said that "if the monopoly and its victims could somehow agree to seize the opportunity" all would be well. The agreement, however, is expensive to make and to enforce. For example, if OPEC wished to move from monopoly to a better point within the cigar, it would need to enforce an agreement to charge a lower price for the additional oil sold. Only the lower price would induce the victims to buy more. But to enforce the agreement, OPEC must be able to keep old oil (sold at the high price) distinct from new oil. Otherwise each member of OPEC will have an incentive to sell more old oil by calling it new, taking advantage of the high price and thereby spoiling it. And customers will have an incentive to buy only new oil, spoiling the market for old oil. All in all, the price discrimination necessary to get a better point is difficult and expensive to maintain.

A more extreme (and astounding) way of stating this second astounding fact is the following.

T or F: If the victims of OPEC would agree to pay tribute to OPEC in exchange for an agreement by OPEC to sell its oil competitively (i.e., along OPEC's own offer curve, instead of price searching along the victims' offer curve), both OPEC and its victims would be better off. (Hint: Note that tribute would shift the start point of initial endowment; imagine the two offer curves of the two parties coming out of the new start.)

A: True. After the tribute the heavily emphasized offer curves govern the behavior of OPEC and its victims. The size of the tribute, you see, can always be manipulated so that the equilibrium point price taking with tribute falls somewhere within the cigar shape coming out of monopoly. That is, the agreement results in an improvement for both parties over what they got at monopoly. The equilibrium, in fact, is a competitive equilibrium, on the contract curve. Only the costs of making the agreement prevent all goods (including oil) from being sold competitively (see Figure 19.2).

**Figure 19.2
The Second Astounding
Fact: Only Transactions
Costs Stand Between
Monopoly and
Competition**

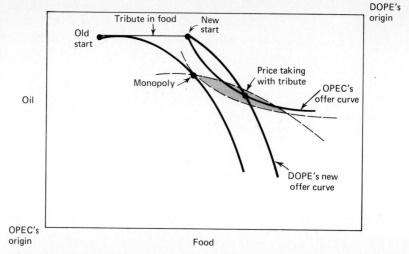

There always exists a bribe that the victim could pay the monopoly in return for an undertaking by it to pretend it is a competitor that would make both better off. The monopoly is made better off by the bribe, and the victims are made better off by the lower price. To be more precise, the bribe-and-marginal-cost-pricing scheme brings the little society into the lens-shaped area of mutually advantageous exchange coming out of the monopoly point. If arranged properly, the deal can get the society to an efficient point, from which there are no further lenses. But arranging deals properly is expensive. In other words, it is merely transactions costs that allow the inefficiencies of monopoly (or any other inefficiency) to persist.

☐
*Perfect Price
Discrimination Is
Efficient: Edgeworth
Box*

The third astounding fact is closely related. It is that the opposite extreme from price-taking competition, namely, multiprice monopoly, is (like price-taking competition) efficient. In other words only clumsy attempts to extract profit from victims are inefficient. Skillful attempts in fact arrive on the contract curve.

There are various ways of demonstrating this astounding fact, each way corresponding to a different set of monopolistic institutions. For example, in Figure 19.2 one can imagine that OPEC sets the tribute (or, in other contexts, the entry fee or membership fee) so high that at the competitive equilibrium the victims are no better off than they were at the start (see Figure 19.3). Such victimization is success in life for a monopoly. It can clearly extract no more than achieving the point where it is as well off as possible subject to the constraint that its victims, who can refuse to trade altogether if it comes to that, are no worse off than at start. But such a condition describes a point on the contract curve and is efficient. It may not be just or good. But it is efficient. Likewise, consider the following.

T or F: A trade union selling hours of labor in exchange for goods can arrive at the point of perfect discrimination by setting both the wage and the number of hours worked.

A: True. Look at Figure 19.3 of the third astounding fact. Imagine OPEC's origin to be the trade union's origin and imagine DOPE's origin to be the buyers'. The trade union starts with many hours of labor (measured along the oil axis) but little money (along the food axis). If it merely sets a monopoly price and lets the buyers choose how many hours they want, it will end up at the monopoly point. But if it also specifies the amount of hours to be bought and can enforce this specification, then it can achieve the dashed line of the deal that brings it to the point of perfect discrimination. Notice that the price per hour is lower than under simple monopoly but that the number of hours is larger. Notice, too, that the same point could be reached by charging the entry fee, installation charge, Mafia "insurance" premium, membership fee, tribute payment, or cover charge discussed in the last chapter.[3]

**Figure 19.3
The Third Astounding
Fact: Perfect
Discrimination Is Efficient**

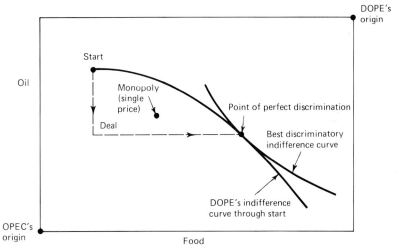

A perfectly discriminatory monopoly will be able to get to its best possible point, namely, that point at which the monopoly's own happiness is greatest and the happiness of its victims is at least no lower than it was to start. The deal the monopoly could arrange to achieve such a result would be an all-or-nothing offer that moved directly to the point of perfect discrimination. Alternatively, the monopoly could extract as much as possible (i.e., along the demand curve) from the first little bit of oil it sold, then as much as possible from the second, and so forth, arriving finally at the same point.

*Perfect
Discrimination Is
Efficient: Supply
and Demand*

☐ The argument can be translated into supply and demand. The simplest case is one in which the income effect on the consumption or retention of, say, electricity is zero for both buyers and sellers. The analytical purpose of the assumption is, as usual, to prevent supply and demand curves from moving about when there are changes in the distribution of income. In the top panel of Figure 19.4 the condition is exhibited by the vertically parallel indifference curves (drawn as dashed lines), yielding a vertical contract curve (drawn as the heavy line).

The curves of demand and marginal cost in the bottom panel remain the same under present assumptions no matter how the gains from

[3] Wassily Leontief, "The Pure Theory of the Guaranteed Annual Wage Contract," *Journal of Political Economy* 54 (February 1946): 76–79.

Figure 19.4
If the Income Effect Can
Be Ignored, Perfect
Competition and Perfect
Monopoly Have the Same
Equilibrium Point

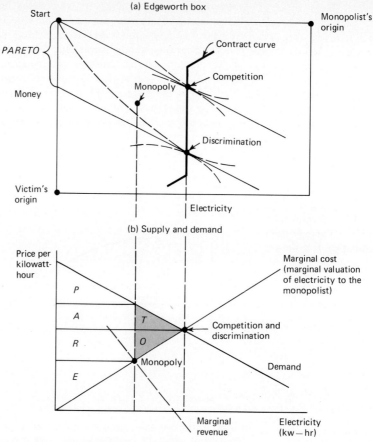

The exactions of a perfectly discriminatory monopoly are income to the consumers. If the demand for the product in question is unaffected by income, then perfect discrimination and perfect competition, both being points of marginal cost equal to marginal valuation, will overlap.

trade are divided between the monopolistic seller of electricity and its victims. Therefore one can compare the three possibilities without confusion. The points of competition and discrimination are in the diagram of supply and demand exactly the same. Perfect monopoly under these assumptions leads to the same point as perfect competition. The schemes of price discrimination that electricity companies in fact use may bring the society closer to an efficient outcome than would less subtle monopoly.

Q: 1. In the bottom panel, what is the area of competitive profit to the electricity company? Simple monopoly profit? Perfectly discriminating profit?

2. What is the sum of consumers' and producers' surplus under conditions of perfect competition, simple monopoly, and perfect discrimination? Therefore, what is the social loss from simple monopoly?

A: 1. A competitive electricity company, namely, one moving along its own offer curve (marginal cost curve), would earn the triangular area *ORE* in Figure 19.4. The simple monopoly, by restricting output and raising the price, could earn *ARE*, which will be larger than *ORE* if *A* is larger than zero. The perfectly discriminating monopoly, however, could earn all the gain from trade, namely, *PARETO* (in honor of Vilfredo Pareto, the Italian sociologist and economist who long ago systematized the idea of efficiency).

2. *PARETO* is the sum of producers' and consumers' surplus for both perfect competition and perfect discrimination. The distribution of income differs in the two cases, but its size is the same. The sum for simple monopoly, however, is only *PARE*. The shaded area *TO* is the social loss.

☐
Why the Efficiency Loss from Monopoly Appears to Be Small

There is nothing surprising here. Simple monopoly restricts output, sacrificing opportunities for trade. The sacrificed opportunities are the cost. If one knew the shapes of the curves involved, one could calculate the size of the loss. When calculated in this way the national loss from monopoly is usually small.

T or F: The percentage loss from monopoly is on the order of half the percentage reduction in output multiplied by the percentage difference between price and marginal cost.

A: True. The argument is familiar from earlier discussions of taxation and rent control. In Figure 19.5 the shaded area of monopoly losses is, geometrically speaking, half the emphasized rectangle. (Proof: Note that the demand and supply curves cut in half the two subrectangles above and below the dashed line.)

Figure 19.5
Why the Efficiency Loss from Monopoly Appears to Be Small

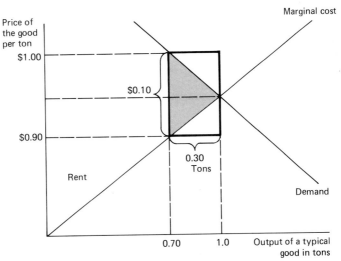

The loss from monopoly is a mere triangle in a world of rectangles. That makes it for a start half the size of the corresponding rectangle, as the diagram shows. Furthermore, the rectangle is small relative to the larger rectangles of revenue or cost when the elasticities of demand and supply take on reasonable values.

Take the (observed) monopoly price and the (unobserved) competitive output to be 1.0. Having fixed the scale, the marginal cost is therefore $1.0 \times$ marginal cost as a proportion of price (i.e., the measure of monopoly power developed earlier). And the monopoly output is $1.0 \times$ monopoly output as a percentage of competitive output. So the area of the rectangle is the product of the two. The typical marginal cost might be 90% of price. The typical elasticity of demand would be calculated by averaging the high elasticities facing the many competitive firms in the economy with the low elasticities facing the monopolistic firms. According to the fundamental equation of monopoly, if the typical ratio of marginal cost to price were 0.90, then the elasticity on average would be 10, a not unreasonable figure. If the corresponding fall in output were as much as 30%, then the size of the shaded area would be $\frac{1}{2}(0.30)(0.10) = \$0.015$. The whole national income earned in this typical industry is the price times the quantity, or ($1)(0.70 tons), or $0.70. In other words, the typical efficiency loss from monopoly is small, a mere $0.015/$0.700 = 2.1% of national income.

Arguments such as this persuade many economists that the efficiency losses from monopoly (or, indeed, from other distortions, such as excessive regulation of trucking or taxes on food) are small.

☐
Why Appearances Are Deceiving

The many economists, however, are mistaken. They are also mistaken, for the same reason, when they assert that discriminatory monopoly has no efficiency costs. The mistake is the familiar one of supposing that the competitive or monopolistic structure of markets does not itself have market causes, that it simply falls on the community like rain. The point is that monopoly of any sort earns supernormal returns. Therefore people will seek these returns. And in seeking them they may spend resources, wasting resources in addition to and quite possibly much larger than any little triangle of efficiency loss. That is, the seeking of monopolies is itself an industry, and it might well use up resources.[4]

The argument is identical to the argument about the waste from queuing. If seekers of a monopoly of import licenses for oil or offshore drilling leases simply bribe the relevant officials with cash, there is in the first instance no additional (deadweight) loss. But if to get the monopoly they hire lawyers, offices, restaurants, secretaries, and so forth, all employable elsewhere in the economy in some useful purposes, then additional loss is possible. It could be as high as the whole excess of marginal earnings of resources in the monopoly over their marginal cost, that is, as high as the whole amount of profit. In terms of Figure 19.5, the whole excess is $0.10 at the margin, or the rectangle of profit over rent, namely, ($0.10)($0.70), or $0.07 out of a total national income earned in the typical industry of $0.70. The 10% loss is in this extreme case almost five times the loss calculated as a triangle of open inefficiency.

[4] Gordon Tullock, "The Welfare Costs of Tariffs, Monopolies, and Theft," *Western Economic Journal* 5 (June 1967): 224–232; and Richard A. Posner, "The Welfare Costs of Monopoly and Regulation," *Journal of Political Economy* 83 (August 1975): 807–828.

Consider the following, which is a good example of the importance of viewing monopoly as behavior instead of a structure.

Q: Edwin Land was the first to invent an instant camera. He and his Polaroid Corporation continued to improve it, taking out over a thousand separate patents as they did so. Kodak wished to muscle in on this territory. To do so, however, it had to invent another sort of instant camera, different enough in its principles to avoid infringing the Polaroid patents. What was the social loss of Polaroid's monopoly? What single accessible figure would you want to have to measure it?

A: The social loss and the single figure is the entire, enormous cost of developing a new sort of instant camera. Little or nothing is gained socially by having two sorts. But the existence of a monopoly profit exploited by Polaroid gave the incentive to spend millions seeking it.

Summary

The defenses of monopoly are as varied as are the monopolists. The more subtle of the defenses are not easy to overcome: monopoly might indeed, for example, be a spur to invention. On a theoretical level all that can be said in reply is that it might not be, too. What can be said with confidence is that simple monopoly reduces output and, more deeply, that it leaves unexploited opportunities for exchange between the monopoly and its victims. Even the simple monopoly is worse off than it might be. Note the word "simple" in "simple monopoly." It means "single price" or "unable to discriminate by way of charging different prices to different consumers." By the same Edgeworth box that shows that simple monopoly is inefficient, one can show that perfectly discriminatory monopoly is efficient; that is, it arrives at a point with no unexploited opportunities for mutually advantageous exchange. The notion that discrimination tends to efficiency has some practical use. For example, it rebuts the natural but erroneous opinion that because monopoly is bad more and stronger monopoly must be worse. A multipart tariff for electricity may therefore be better than a single-price power company charging one, high, clumsy price to all. The main use of the notion, however, is theoretical. It alerts the economist once again, for example, to the great split between equity and efficiency in economic thinking. An inequitable society filled with fee takers may well be efficient, or an efficient society may be equitable, or any other pairing. And the logic of extreme monopoly reminds him that the inefficiency from less extreme monopoly comes from the transactions costs of making further deals between monopolist and victim. The amount of the inefficiencies (the triangle of social loss) is in a sense a measure of the transactions cost. More than they realize, perhaps, Marxists and other critics of capitalism are correct to view monopoly returns as a measure of the importance of friction in the system. The triangle turns out in fact to be small. But this does not end the argument between defenders and critics of the efficacy of markets. The triangle of social loss is a great underestimate of the whole social loss. The loss from the pursuit of monopoly profits, as distinct from the loss from exercising the monopoly power once attained, can be very large. Its size depends on how monopolies come to be monopolies, the subject of the next chapter.

QUESTIONS FOR CHAPTER 19

1. The large profits of major league baseball teams are often defended on the grounds that much of the profits, extracted from the players, go to pay for their training in the *minor* leagues (the major league subsidizes the minor leagues). Even if this is true, it is irrelevant to deciding whether or not to break up the monopsony power of the owners over the players. Compare the training of professional baseball players with that of professional tennis or golf or economics players.

2. Does a monopoly of razor blades have an incentive to make the life of the razor blades less than it could make it (free)? Consider what the consumer will be willing to pay for a blade that gives 10 shaves as against one that gives 20 shaves.

3. Macmillan brings out new editions of books such as *The Applied Theory of Price* very frequently, making earlier versions worthless in the secondhand market. *True or false:* This is obviously a case of planned obsolescence (i.e., making things wear out so that the maker can make more money).

4. In movie theaters only large candy bars are for sale. *True or false:* The practice is an example of setting both the price and the quantity of the victim of a discriminatory monopoly.

5. The medical profession is alleged to be a cartel. Supposing it to be a perfect one, illustrate the social loss from the cartel in the market for medical services, identifying separately the opportunity cost of the lost output and the willingness to pay for it. If a society found the loss disagreeable, what would be the obvious social policy for it to pursue? How much would doctors lose if this social policy were in fact pursued?

Having said this, suppose that this policy were impossible (because, say, doctors are too powerful politically to stand still for the loss of cartel profits or doctors are too highly esteemed for society to suffer their impoverishment without protest). Show that a subsidy by the state to the firms (usually individual doctors) producing medical services can, even in the presence of a cartel, yield the socially optimal output of medical services. Distinguish real opportunity cost from the marginal cost facing the cartel in this demonstration.

The point, as usual, is one of "second best." It is that when one is forced to accept conditions yielding a bad allocation of resources, adding another condition that would be bad in itself (subsidizing a firm, thus distorting its pattern of incentives) will sometimes make the situation better, not worse.

6. The text asserts that "if seekers of a monopoly . . . simply bribe the relevant officials with cash there is in the first instance no additional loss" from monopoly over the usual triangle of surplus lost.

a. Explain what is meant by the assertion.

b. Suppose that there is competition to become the "relevant officials" by studying law or buying advertising. In such a case is there excess loss?

c. Suppose now that potential officials can compete for high office only by offering themselves at lower pay. What happens to the loss?

7. Suppose that an American manufacturer of military tanks has a monopoly in the United States and is initially not permitted to export his product to other countries. Now suppose that he is permitted to export it (imports of foreign tanks are still not permitted) and suppose that he makes a small portion of the outside world's supply of tanks.

a. Compare his profits before and after he is permitted to export.

b. Compare American welfare before and after he is permitted to export.

c. What is the effect on profits and welfare of a technological change specific to the American manufacturer, both before and after exports are permitted?

8. The right to use a patented invention can be bought from the inventor in one of two ways: either with a fee paid each time the invention is used or with a lump sum. Thus, a new type of plastic could earn the inventor either $2.56 per ton produced (by you exclusively, perhaps, or by anyone else who contracts to work the patent) or a flat payment of $100,000 (again, with or without exclusivity), with no charge per ton. Both ways of licensing patents are in fact in use.

a. Explain why the fee per unit is worse than the lump sum on at least two grounds: the expense of enforcing the contract and the social waste of underusing knowledge.

b. Explain why an inventor might nonetheless wish to license by fee per unit if he or she did not know exactly how valuable the invention would be to its users. Ignore considerations of risk and insurance, but consider ignorance itself. Is the extra cost incurred by the fee per unit, according to (a), really inefficiency?

c. Inventions are commonly distinguished as product or process, for example, popular electronic calculators (a product sold to ultimate consumers) or a can-making machine (a process). And each of these can be novel or routine: a better vacuum tube is a routine process innovation; a transistor is a novel process innovation. These distinctions are not especially penetrating, memorable, or useful. But in accepting them for the moment, show that by the argument of (b) one would expect that routine process inventions would be licensed by lump sum and novel product inventions would be licensed by fee per unit. Factual note: one would be right, according to recent researches by S. N. S. Cheung of the University of Washington.

True or False

9. A good way in which to improve the welfare of society would be to subject monopolies to regulations limiting their rate of return to capital to some low figure.

10. Monopoly in one industry will create excess supply in another.

11. If one knew the elasticity of demand for medical services, the present price of those services, their present real opportunity cost at the margin, and the elasticity of this opportunity cost, then one could estimate the resources wasted by the presence of a medical monopoly in the United States.

Monopolistic Competition and the Economics of Location

20.1 Monopolistic Competition as Competition Among Local Monopolies

□
Who's in Charge Here?

The analysis of one seller takes as given the one mind in charge. The monopoly may have literally one mind, as does the monopolistic seller of a unique painting, or it may have many, as does the American Medical Association. But it behaves as though it had one. However it is organized, the industry maximizes its profits jointly, each participant surrendering to the common object of making as much as possible out of the customers any selfish advantage to be gotten by competition.

The question arises how an industry behaves when there is more than one mind in charge but fewer than the many minds of perfect competition. The answer to the question is the subject of this and the next chapters, the subject of a long and frustrating search in the dark by the economics profession. The answer is that there is no answer, only a number of partial answers, each more or less useful, none very satisfactory. Life is hard.

□
The Model Without Transport Costs

The demonstration works inward from either extreme: perfect competition (a very large number of sellers) or perfect monopoly (one seller). Take the very large number first.[1] Suppose that there are 150 sellers of groceries arranged every two miles along Route 66 through Oklahoma. Each has the usual array of cost curves, assumed to be the same for each. Suppose that the potential customers are scattered evenly along the highway and that each demands one bag of groceries a week regardless of the price that must be paid. The customer's demand curve, in other words, is perfectly inelastic. Inelastic though her demand is, however, the customer still wishes to pay the lowest price. If it costs this and other customers nothing to drive to each of the 150 stores, then each store would be forced to compete in the entire Oklahoma

---

[1] The exposition here follows that of Gordon Tullock in *Toward a Mathematics of Politics* (Ann Arbor: University of Michigan, 1967), Chapter V, "Single Peaks and Monopolistic Competition," especially in the matter of identifying transport models with monopolistic competition. Tullock's book is recommended.

market with every other store. The results would be the usual ones of competition: the price of a bag of groceries would almost exactly equal the marginal cost and the minimum long-run average cost of the bag at the stores. That is, the two features of competitive equilibrium would show themselves: first, marginal valuation would be equal to marginal opportunity cost; second, no one would be earning supernormal profits. Each firm would be operating at the minimum point of its average cost curve, supplying $\frac{1}{150}$ (or 0.0067) of the socially optimal output of groceries.

The Model with Transport Costs

☐ Optimality breaks down, however, if there are (as there are) costs of driving. The cost of driving to a store can and should be viewed as part of the price of the bag of groceries. Someone next to the store pays less in transport costs if not in the price at the store than someone two miles away. In other words, when there are transport costs, there are *local* monopolies, because the customers near David Haddock's store on Harvard Avenue in Tulsa do not have the option of visiting at the same low cost all the other stores along Route 66, such as those in Oklahoma City or Joplin (Missouri), each 100 miles away. Assuming that Haddock cannot distinguish between customers who have come merely from Yale Avenue a mile away and those who came all the way from Reed Park five miles down the highway, he cannot charge different prices to different customers in proportion to their willingness to pay. If he could, he would charge Esther Schultz, a customer from Yale Avenue, more, because such a close customer would be willing to pay over to Haddock as much as all her saving in transport cost in order to continue buying at such a convenient location for her as Harvard. Price discrimination is assumed to be impossible, leaving the storekeeper as a simple, single-price monopolist.

The Demand Curve Facing a Local Monopolist

☐ But a monopolist he is. The demand curve he faces is downward sloping. The slope depends on how his neighboring monopolists react to his activities. The simplest assumption is that in the short run they do not react at all. Remember this step in the argument: the assumption about what rivals do is the key.

Even under such a simple assumption, the derivation of the demand curve is somewhat involved. It goes as follows. Imagine Haddock sitting in his store at the corner of Harvard Avenue and Route 66, with a store competing with him two miles east (at Sheridan Road) and another two miles west (at Peoria Avenue). Obviously no one will bypass the Sheridan store, say, coming from far east to Haddock's store. Haddock's potential customers therefore are only the ones between Sheridan and Peoria, two miles east and west. A certain price at his store will attract a certain number of these customers in both directions. How many? The answer depends on what his two neighbors are doing. What they are doing can be summarized in their price at their stores, represented as the points Peoria price and Sheridan price in Figure 20.1.

The prices are taken to be the same in both places merely to shortcut some reasoning, reasoning that concludes that in the final equilibrium

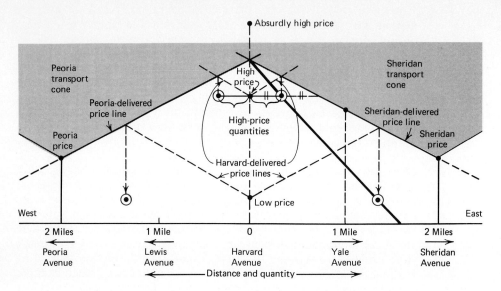

Figure 20.1
The Demand Curve Bisects the Angle of the Tent of Transport Costs

The quantity sold at Harvard Avenue depends on (1) the price charged at Harvard (such as low price); (2) the Harvard-delivered price line, which gives the total cost, including transport costs, to customers of Harvard; (3) the Sheridan- and Peoria-delivered price lines, which give price to customers of neighboring stores; (4) the density of customers along the road; and (5) the fact that customers choose the cheaper delivered price. The store at Harvard Avenue can sell to customers out to the point where the Harvard-delivered price line cuts, say, the Sheridan-delivered price line. The resulting demand curve is the heavy line equidistant from the Harvard axis and the Sheridan- (or Peoria-) delivered price line, on the suppositions that transport costs (the slopes of the lines) are equal and that the Sheridan price is given and fixed at the level it would attain in equilibrium.

there is no tendency for the prices to differ. The tent over the Harvard Avenue location is a result of adding transport costs on to the Peoria and Sheridan prices. It is a tent from Haddock's point of view, but from the Peoria or Sheridan point of view, it is a shaded *transport cone* balanced on each price. The sides are straight because the customers are supposed to be scattered evenly along the road, resulting in the same addition to sales for each additional mile. It gives the price to customers at various distances from the two stores including transport costs. The farther a customer is from, say, the Sheridan store, the more the customer must spend on transport to buy from it. Obviously a customer at, say, Yale Avenue would buy from the Sheridan store so long as it was the low-cost supplier. In other words, Haddock's price plus transport cost cannot be outside the tent formed by his competitors.

Now consider the problem of constructing the demand curve Haddock faces. A demand curve is a locus of combinations of prices charged at the store and of quantities demanded in the hinterlands. If Haddock charges absurdly high price in Figure 20.1, he will get no customers. Even customers across the street from his Harvard Avenue store will prefer to go to either the Peoria or the Sheridan store. But if he charges only high price, he gets all the customers out to where the dashed lines have the same slopes upward or downward as the tent, because it is assumed that the same cost of transport per mile is incurred by Haddock's customers as by others. The margin of Haddock's market is determined by the tent, because beyond the tent Haddock's price including the transport cost to the customer exceeds that of his competitor, and therefore the customers farther out go to his competitor instead. Since customers are distributed evenly along the highway in proportion to distance, the distance can be identified with quantities. At high price, then, Haddock sells the high-price quantities. Notice the equality of the horizontal lines (indicated by slashes). That they are equal can be seen by noting that their triangles are identical. The consequence is that, bisecting a horizontal line, the quantity purchased bisects the angle of the tent side and the tent pole (at Harvard). The argument is identical at other prices, such as low price. In short, the demand curve facing Haddock in either direction is constructed by linking up the circled points. The points themselves are halfway out to the tent sides. The emphasized line, for example, is the demand curve in the Sheridan direction.

Pause for a moment to note that the construction of the demand curve facing Haddock is in accord with common sense. If transport costs fell gradually, for instance, the tent would collapse gradually, until at last the tent sides and the demand curve converged on a flat limit at the price abroad. Local monopoly would decay, as it did to some degree with the spread of the automobile early in the century. On the other hand, if transport costs were very high, the tent would slope upward out of the pegs at Peoria and Sheridan more steeply, and the local monopolist would face a more inelastic demand curve. Services with high transport costs, such as elementary school education, have local monopolies. In the limit the local monopolist would be left entirely alone to exploit his local victims, transport costs forming a wall around the market.

☐
The Maximum of Profit for the Local Monopolist

Having found the demand, the completion of the theory of the local monopolist requires his costs to be set against the demand. Haddock's cost curve of bags of groceries is supposed to be of the usual U shape. It can be split into two halves to represent the simultaneous servicing of outputs in two directions, east and west. Haddock chooses his monopoly price as the one that maximizes the vertical distance between price and average cost multiplied by the horizontal distance of quantity, that is, the shaded area of profit in Figure 20.2. As usual, the point can also be shown (and is shown in the left-hand side) as that of equality in marginal cost and marginal revenue.

As the diagram is drawn, Haddock's choice of price is the same as everyone elses' (namely, the Peoria price and the Sheridan price). This is true in equilibrium. It reflects again the assumption of symmetry underlying the analysis, namely, that if all grocery stores are identical,

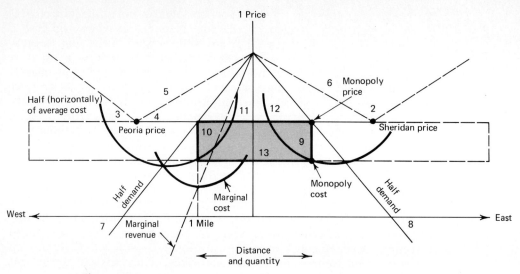

**Figure 20.2
Monopolistically
Competitive Equilibrium
When All Firms Are
Identical and Entry Is
Barred**

The numbers in the diagram are the sequence in which you should draw the lines. In full equilibrium with *N* identical and evenly spaced stores, each store chooses quantity such that marginal cost = marginal revenue, each store charges the same price, and by these policies stores evenly divide the territory between them. Notice that the equilibrium does *not* occur at the minimum point of the average cost curve and that the price does not equal marginal cost.

then each must in the end act in identical ways. The same diagram can serve therefore to represent any of the 150 stores from Joplin, Missouri to Erick, Oklahoma. Since each firm is motivated identically, each will be motivated to charge the same price in equilibrium and to get the same 1 mile of customers on either side. The equilibrium, in short, is an allocation of the entire 300 miles of Route 66 in Oklahoma into local monopolies covering 2 miles of customers each.

☐ *Q:* Is the equilibrium a long-run equilibrium?

***Entry Leads to the
Tangency Solution***

A: No, it is not. Supernormal profits are still being earned. In pursuit of the profits, more grocery stores will try to enter the industry, squeezing in beside the other stores. It would be unpleasant for Haddock if Ulen, for example, set up a store on Yale Avenue, at the very edge of Haddock's market. Haddock could make it less unpleasant by relocating in the long run away from Ulen, as Ulen's competitor on the other side could by relocating toward the east. The coming of Ulen would spread ripples of movement east and west, like parishioners shuffling over on a church bench as one more joins the row. The result in church is more people to a bench, that is, smaller spaces between each person. So, too, on Route 66. The neighboring stores are closer or more similar in some other dimension. The crucial point is that their

**Figure 20.3
Monopolistically
Competitive Equilibrium
When Entry Is Free**

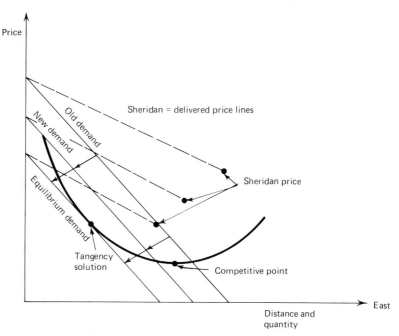

The economic profits earned at old demand induce entry. The more stores enter, the closer stores are to their neighbors, and the lower the delivered price line and demand curve each store faces. Entry continues until the demand curve facing each store falls to equilibrium demand, at which level no economic profits are earned.

closeness shifts inward the demand curve at any given price abroad facing Haddock, as from old demand to new demand in Figure 20.3. The diagram exhibits half of the two-sided figure used earlier.

The innermost curve, equilibrium demand, is just that, the only demand curve that leaves no supernormal profits to attract further entry. Its (negative) slope is, like the others, twice the cost of transportation (since the demand curves always bisect the tent side and pole). The grocery industry on Route 66 settles to rest.

The outcome is striking. If transport costs were zero, the industry would arrive at the competitive point on the bottom of the U curve of average cost, with each of a smaller number of grocery stores producing at a larger output and at the lowest possible cost (full capacity). But in the presence of transport costs, the industry ends at tangency solution, with a large number of Ma and Pa grocery stores producing at less than full capacity and at a high price. A theory that joins free entry to a monopoly with neighbors implies an equilibrium of profitless and inefficient little enterprises, like dry cleaners, local restaurants, corner drugstores, or gas stations.

Monopolistic Competition as Local Monopoly

The theory is called *monopolistic competition*. Invented by Edward Chamberlin in the 1920s, it has had a remarkable career of elaboration and criticism, if not of actual use.[2] "Its thesis is that both monopolistic and competitive forces combine in the determination of most prices, and therefore that a hybrid theory affords a more illuminating approach to the study of the price system than does a theory of perfected competition supplemented by a theory of monopoly." The theory is identical to the problem of the grocery stores on the road, except that distance in physical space is also interpretable as "distance" in "product space." Various breakfast cereals, for example, are more or less close to each other, Kellogg's Corn Flakes and Post Toasties being very close, perhaps indistinguishable in chemical content, whereas Corn Flakes and Ralston-Purina Corn Chex are farther apart and Corn Flakes and Nabisco Shredded Wheat still farther. A standard Ford is closer to a standard Chevrolet than it is to a Cadillac or a Honda.

The product, furthermore, is a variable at choice, not immutable. Firms can choose where to locate along the road or where to locate in product space. The emphasis on the product as well as on the price as a variable subject to economic choice is one of the lasting contributions of the theory of monopolistic competiton. It emphasized, too, that firms can create the image of differences in products as well as the reality. *Product differentiation* has come to be in economics another word for advertising. The firm in this view can create artificial distance between its products and its competitors, by persuading people that only at Burger King do you get it your way and only at Schlitz do they make a beer with gusto. What is distasteful about the result of monopolistic competition is the combination of the low output characteristic of monopoly with the proliferation of tiny, pointlessly differentiated firms characteristic of competition, all supported by advertising at the customer's expense.

The First Objection: Product Variety Is Not Bad

The spatial model suggests, however, that one must not be too quick to damn the differentiation of product. The differentiation along the road, after all, is real distance, expensive to traverse. If the differences are not wholly synthetic, then it is *not* desirable for there to be fewer grocery stores, each producing and pricing at the lowest point of its average cost curve. The consumers prefer a close store with a high price at the store to a far store with a low price. In other words, the

[2] Edward Chamberlin, *The Theory of Monopolistic Competition: A Re-orientation of the Theory of Value* (Cambridge, Mass.: Harvard University Press, 1933), especially Chapter V, submitted as a Ph.D. thesis at Harvard in 1927. The quotation is from the Preface to the first edition. Readers of Chamberlin will wonder where his famous *dd* and *DD* curves appear in the present exposition. The answer is that the demand curve here is Chamberlin's *dd* curve, that is, the curve drawn on the assumption that neighboring monopolists keep their prices constant no matter what Haddock does. The *dd* curve is the heart of Chamberlin's argument. The curve drawn on the other assumption, that neighboring monopolists match Haddock's prices, would be Chamberlin's *DD* curve. For given locations, it is simply a vertical line halfway between Haddock's place and the neighbor's place. The market always divides in half if Haddock's and the neighbor's price are the same. It is vertical because of the assumption here that each customer's demand curve is perfectly inelastic.

"lowest point of the average cost curve" is misdefined in the usual argument, because it ignores the unpleasant cost of travel (i.e., the pleasures of nearness). As Gordon Tullock has put the matter,

> Prices will never get down to the level of perfect competition. The customers can hardly complain about this since it arises out of an effort to please them. Their unwillingness to go long distances to take advantage of small differences in price gives the monopoly power. . . . [There is according to the traditional way of putting it overinvestment in stores. They] are not operating on the low point of their average cost curves, and . . . the prices are higher than would prevail if perfect competition reigned. [Such perfection], however, involves ignoring the preferences of the consumer, and hence is a most unusual type of optimum.[3]

The argument is identical to the one in the last chapter about natural monopoly: if the monopoly is natural, it may be good for you. If you yourself value a different product, product differentiation also may be good for you. The welfare economics of the theory of monopolistic competition is dubious.

The Second Objection: The Competitors Would Allow for Their Interactions

The behavior posited at the heart of the theory is also dubious. The heart of the theory is the combination of downward-sloping demand (characteristic of monopoly) with large numbers of firms *each of which can ignore its interaction with any one other firm* (characteristic of competition). If firms do not ignore their interactions, the taking of the neighboring prices as fixed for purposes of analysis will be false. But it is plain that Haddock and his near neighbor Ulen would in fact allow for, not ignore, their interactions. A decision by Haddock to alter his price would have powerful effects on Ulen, changing his behavior and in turn changing Haddock's, which would in turn change Ulen's, and so on into a hall of mirrors. The hall will be toured in the next chapter. At present it is enough to doubt Chamberlin's notion "that any adjustment of price or of 'product' by a single producer spreads its influence over so many of his competitors that the impact felt by any one is negligible and does not lead him to any readjustment of his own situation."[4] Along a literal road the notion is false: Haddock has necessarily two neighbors so close that their mutual effects are great. One may generalize the road to a space of many dimensions, but such a generalization would seem merely to multiply the number of close neighbors, multiplying the problem with them. Two analytical ploys are possible. If one multiplies the close neighbors enough, the price facing the monopoly in question becomes fixed by competition and the analysis reduces to perfect competition. If one pushes the neighbors farther away, to make the "impact felt by any one" truly "negligible," the group equilibrium is no longer important and the analysis reduces to perfect monopoly. The middle ground that Chamberlin attempted to occupy is a canyon.

---

[3] Tullock, *Mathematics of Politics*, pp. 68–69.
[4] Chamberlin, *Monopolistic Competition*, p. 83.

The Third Objection:
The Theory Has Not
Borne Fruit

The theory of monopolistic competition, then, has difficulties in the behavior it assumes as well as in the inferences about goodness or badness it draws. You will notice, furthermore, that the preceding pages have had no problems to solve. This is the third and most serious difficulty with the theory of monopolistic competition. Unlike perfect competition or monopoly, or even the oligopoly models to be discussed shortly, the theory has not been fruitful. It can be argued, and has been most vigorously by many economists, that monopolistic competition is a better description of many industries than is either monopoly or competition by itself. But along with the superiority of descriptive accuracy comes no striking proposition about how such industries behave that would make it worthwhile to develop a third thing between monopoly and competition. One might as well develop a model of "male-dominated competition," on the (true) argument that unfortunately males hold a disproportionate number of the positions of authority in the economy. The descriptive accuracy of the model would be greater than one that did not mention sex, but only in the single respect, since it seems unlikely (although on reflection perhaps not impossible) that the economy would behave much differently with more females in charge. The theory of male-dominated competition would probably not be fruitful in new and unexpected applications of economics. Neither has been the theory of monopolistic competition.[5]

Summary

The best way of representing the theory of monopolistic competition is to take literally its talk of "near" and "far" products. If the assumption about how each competitor believes the neighbors will react (namely, not at all) is true, then the model of grocery stores along a road yields a monopolistically competitive equilibrium. Too many grocery stores crowd onto the road, each protected in the profitless enjoyment of a local monopoly by the cost of transportation to another store and each producing too little at a high cost. The idea of the distance between different stores along a road can then be extended to "distance" between different products in the minds of consumers. The results are the same: firms that are too many, too little, too expensive.

The analogy with distance, however, suggests that product differentiation is not always artificial and pointless. After all, 125th Street *is* farther from downtown than is 42nd Street. Some people *do* prefer a big automobile with four-wheel drive and a vinyl roof to a small one with an airbag and a sun window. Furthermore, the assumption that a competitor believes that the neighbors will not react to his decisions is unreasonable. If the neighbors are close enough to matter, they are close enough to react, and the competitor in question will be intelligent enough to perceive that they will react. Finally, and most important, the theory has borne little fruit. It is a better description of the world than is perfect competition or perfect monopoly, but it is not a better instrument for scientific study.

[5] See R. Robinson, *Columbia Essays on Great Economists: Edward H. Chamberlin* (New York: Columbia University Press, 1971), for a more favorable view of the achievement.

20.2   The Theory of Location

☐
The Hotelling Model of Two-Party Competition for Votes

If the theory of monopolistic competition itself has not been fruitful, many of the devices developed to explore it have been. Above all, the idea of competition over space has been fruitful. A good example comes from a famous article by Harold Hotelling (1929), which was published independently of and before Chamberlin's book but which discusses the same "neglected fact that a market is commonly subdivided into regions within each of which one seller is in a quasi-monopolistic position" in which "a tiny increase in price by one seller will send only a few customers to the other."[6]

Q: Suppose that two soap stores called the Republican Party and the Democratic Party start at the right and left ends of a road called Political Spectrum Boulevard. They sell soap at the same, fixed price at the two stores. Because transport costs per mile are the same in all directions, the price the consumers pay rises from the price at the stores with distance from the stores. The consumers, who are distributed evenly along the road, have perfectly inelastic demands for soap (in the spirit of the grocery store problem). The two stores are assumed to have no costs, so that their profits are simply the number of miles of road they service multiplied by the price paid at the store.

1. Draw a diagram showing how the market for soap divides between the two stores when they are located at opposite extremes.

2. Suppose that the Democratic Party assumes that the Republican Party will not change its location if the Democratic Party moves a little. Show the incentive for the Democratic Party to move to the right.

3. Suppose the Republican Party makes the same assumption. Where will it move? Would it ever be desirable for it to stay sitting on the right extreme? Where will the sequence of moves end?

4. Can you imagine what feature of the American party system is explained by the model?

A: 1. The market divides where the delivered price of soap is equal from either store, namely, at the middle of the road in Figure 20.4. Consumers to the right go to the Republican Party, those to the left to the Democratic Party.

2. The incentive is that its sales will rise because the point of market division determined by the slope of transport costs will move right (as indicated by the dashed line). The Democratic Party will capture the additional market share. It will keep the profits to the left of its new location because those customers have nowhere to go.

3. But the Republican Party has exactly the same opportunity, and it will take it. Its incentive to do so is increased by the extermination that will come inevitably if it stays put on the right end of the road: the Democratic

[6] Harold Hotelling, "Stability in Competition," *Economic Journal* 39 (1929): 41–57, reprinted in G. J. Stigler and K. E. Boulding, eds., *Readings in Price Theory* (Homewood, Ill.: Irwin, 1952), pp. 468–470.

Party will march all the way to the right, seizing all the consumers. But since both parties do it, the moves cancel each other out, neither party gaining in the end. The parties end up sitting a bit to either side of middle of the road, having lost in the process nearly all their identity as left- and right-wing soap sellers.

4. As Hotelling put it,

> The competition for votes between the Republican and Democratic parties does not lead to a clear drawing of issues, an adoption of two strongly contrasted positions between which the voter may choose. Instead, each party strives to make its platform as much like the other's as possible. . . . Each candidate "pussyfoots," replies ambiguously to questions, refuses to take a definite stand in any controversy for fear of losing votes.[7]

**Figure 20.4
Why Parties Move to the
Middle in a Two-Party
System**

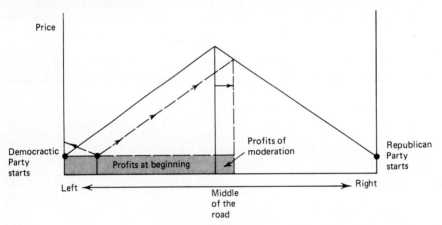

Each party sells to that part of the market that gets a lower delivered price from it than from its competitor. If parties start at the extremes, either party can increase its sales by moving toward the other.

□ The model is crude, but unlike the model of monopolistic competition that is its intellectual brother the attempts to improve it have yielded further fruit.

***Improvements on
the Simple Model
Are Persuasive***

T or F: With three political parties located in the beginning at the two extremes and the exact middle and constrained to stay in the same relative position, the two left- and right-wing parties will exterminate the middle.

A: The third, middle party has nowhere to go. Trapped between the other two moving in to poach votes, it ends up with no votes. Therefore, true: the two parties move in on the third.

[7] Hotelling, in Stigler and Boulding, eds., *Readings in Price Theory*, p. 482.

This happened in fact to the Liberal Party in Britain between the election of December 1910 and the election of October 1924. The Conservative Party on the right and the new Labour Party on the left crushed the Liberals by moving in on them. The final blow was the adoption in June 1924 of the policy of free trade by the leader of the Conservatives, the last of many examples of the other two parties' stealing Liberal positions and becoming thereby more similar. The Liberal Party lives on to the present, but as a mere shadow. For the same reason, middle-of-the-road third parties in the United States (if not, to be sure, in France and many other countries) have been short lived.

The assumption in the simple version of the Hotelling model that the only competition is by location, not by price, is also crude, but amendments of it also yield fruit.

Q: Imagine two stores located next to each other in Hotelling fashion at the middle of the road. They charge the same price at the store, each selling only in one direction (the left store to the left only, for instance). What happens if one of the stores lowers its at-store price below that of the other, and the other sticks to the high price? However stable it may be as a *location* equilibrium, is the Hotelling solution stable as a *price* equilibrium? View location as "the party's position on an ideological spectrum" and price as "the attractiveness of the major candidate." Now interpret the presidential election of 1952, in which the Republican Party triumphed by adopting Democratic positions on ideology (accepting the results of the New Deal) and getting a war hero (Eisenhower) to run as its candidate.

A: As a political scientist examining such models has put it, "if the difference in nearness for any given customer is negligible [as it is if the shops have placed themselves next door to each other], one of the competing shops will be able to get all the customers (and thus ruin the other) provided it can maintain its price just a shade below those of its rival. . . . The closer the parties become ideologically [i.e., in 'location'], the more people's votes are liable to turn on something other than ideology [i.e., on a 'price' such as the attractiveness of the candidate]."[8] The parties have no incentive to move away from a Hotelling equilibrium in location, but they do have an incentive to move away from it in price. Having set up shop next door to Democrats, the Republicans had only to shade their price (nominating General Eisenhower instead of ideologically purer but less personally attractive Senator Taft) to attract voters from the Democratic side of the spectrum.

☐
The Best Location   The locational models apply, of course, to problems of literal as well as figurative location.

---

[8] Brian Barry, *Sociologists, Economists, and Democracy* (Chicago: University of Chicago Press, 1978), p. 105. The page following contains the analysis of the 1952 election. Barry's Chapter V, "The Economic Theory of Democracy," is a penetrating summary and critique of such theories as Hotelling's and especially of the brilliant extension of his theories by Anthony Downs, *An Economic Theory of Democracy* (New York: Harper, 1957).

Q: You are organizing a conference with 50 invited participants drawn at intervals of 60 miles between each from a line across the United States 3000 miles long. You can locate the conference anywhere along the line. You pay the transport costs, which are constant and identical per mile traveled, and wish to minimize them. Where should you locate the conference?

A: Your instinct is correct in telling you that the midpoint is cheapest. The most elegant demonstration is to start with a location at the midpoint and show that movements away from it cause total transport cost to rise. The total transport cost can be approximated by (it is exact for an infinite number of participants) the area under the transport cone rising out of the location chosen. At the midpoint, for example, it is the area under the sloped lines in Figure 20.5.

A move from the midpoint at Kansas City to, say, Denver farther west will result in a larger area of loss on transport costs than gain. The shaded area is the excess loss. One can alter the assumptions slightly to favor one or another midwestern city. Kansas City is near the physical midpoint. St. Louis, however, is near the center of population. And Chicago is close to St. Louis and has more airline connections. In any case the minimization of transport costs leads to a midwest location.

Figure 20.5
All Conferences Should
Happen in the Midwest

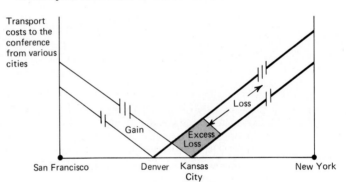

Transport costs to the conference from various cities

As the conference moves away from the central city, more attendees' costs rise (New York to Denver) than fall (Denver to San Francisco), so that total cost rises and a loss results.

The Isolated City

The earliest and most fruitful location argument in economics is that of Ricardo and, with more emphasis and detail, Johann H. von Thünen, in his book of 1826, *The Isolated State in Relation to the Economics of Land and of Nations*. It simply reverses the sense of the model of grocery stores. Instead of a store essentially sending goods out to customers along the line, farmers along the line send their goods into the central (isolated) city.

Q: Suppose that the price that citizens of the city of Rome are willing to pay for wheat is fixed; that is, their demand is elastic at some given price. Rome is the only consumer of wheat: in particular, farmers do not consume wheat. Suppose, too, that all roads lead to Rome and that shipping wheat along them costs some fixed amount per mile. Suppose that there is a limited amount of land available at each distance from Rome. Suppose, finally, as an unessential simplification, that wheat costs nothing to produce. In other words, the only difference between the price at Rome and the profit received by a farmer at a remote place such as Sutrium is the cost of transporting the grain from Sutrium to Rome. Draw a diagram showing the point along a road from Rome of zero profit in wheat growing. How much wheat is sent to Rome along the road?

A: The profit per bushel at any point is the price at Rome minus the cost of transporting the bushel from the point to Rome. The point of zero profit is where all the price is eaten up in transport costs. It is the margin of cultivation. If wheat produced per mile is a constant, then the amount sent to Rome is proportional to the distance from Rome to the margin of cultivation (see Figure 20.6).

Figure 20.6
The Margin of Cultivation
Is Determined by
Transport Cost

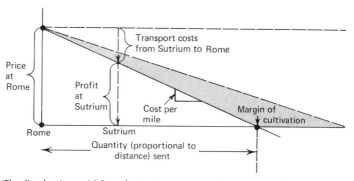

The fixed price paid for wheat at Rome goes either to pay for transport to Rome or as profits to wheat farmers. The extreme geographical limit of cultivation is the point at which transport costs equal price and profits are zero. A fall in transport costs shifts outward the margin of cultivation.

☐
Measuring the
Benefit of Cheaper
Transport to the
City

The idea that transport costs determine the profitability of cultivation is as powerful as it is simple.

T or F: If the cost of sending wheat to Rome is cheapened by the construction of a better road, then the profitability (rent) of land increases by the same amount as transport cost falls.

A: The transport cost swings out to, say, the dashed line in Figure 20.6. The profit at Sutrium and elsewhere rises as the transport cost falls, simply because everything left over from subtracting transport cost from the price at Rome is the profit. The margin of cultivation, naturally, moves out. The shaded area *is* the increase in rent. Therefore, true.

Similarly, consider the following.

Q: You are attempting to measure the social value of the Ohio canals constructed in the early nineteenth century. You do not have good information on the fall in the cost of transport after the construction of the canals.

You do, however, have good information on the rise in the rent of land around the canals. *True or false:* The rise in the rent is an estimate of the fall in the cost of transport.

A: The increase in an Ohio farmer's willingness to pay for land (i.e., its rent) equals the fall in transport, because every dollar of transport of his goods saved is a dollar in his pocket. The fall in transport cost is like a subsidy to the production of buckeyes and popcorn and other Ohioan things. The land in each location is supplied inelastically, with the result that the subsidy falls on owners of land.[9]

☐

Why Crops Around the City Fall into Zones: Bid Rent Curves

The same intellectual machinery can be turned to the question of what crops are grown where. Wool, for example, is grown in Northumberland or Montana, far from centers of population. Eggs, on the other hand, are grown close to where they are consumed. Why? One's instinct is to answer that wool is cheaper to transport than eggs, being more packable and less perishable. The instinct is useful but not complete. The complete answer views the crops as bidders for the land and asks what each crop is willing to pay.

Q: A certain crop yields Y tons per acre, sells for $\$P$ per ton at London, costs $\$T$ per ton to ship D miles, and costs $\$C$ per ton to raise. How much is it willing to pay at most for an acre located D miles from London?

A: An acre yields Y tons. Each of these Y tons would sell for P at London, from which must be subtracted the cost of raising, C, and the cost of transport, TD. The upshot is

$$\text{Willingness to pay for an acre} = Y(P - C - TD)$$

The crop with the highest willingness to pay at each distance, D, wins the land. The equation can be rewritten in a more illuminating form by multiplying and dividing by P:

$$YP \times \left[1 - \frac{C}{P} - \left(\frac{T}{P}\right)D \right]$$

Or in words,

$$
\begin{array}{l}
\text{Dollars of yield} \\
\text{per acre at} \\
\text{London prices}
\end{array}
\times
\left[
\begin{array}{l}
\text{raising costs} \\
\text{per ton as a} \\
1 - \text{fraction of} \\
\text{the price} \\
\text{at London}
\end{array}
-
\begin{array}{l}
\text{the product of} \\
\text{transport costs} \\
\text{of anything for} \\
\text{one mile per ton} \\
\text{as a fraction of} \\
\text{the price at London}
\end{array}
\begin{array}{l}
\text{distance} \\
\times \text{from London} \\
\text{in miles}
\end{array}
\right]
$$

---

[9] For further details see Roger Ransom, "Social Returns from Public Transport Investment: A Case Study of the Ohio Canals," *Journal of Political Economy* 78 (September 1970): 427–435.

The equation is called the *bid rent curve* for the crop, since it tells how much the crop will bid to rent land at various distances. One's instincts can be brought to bear on it. Obviously eggs, for example, have a higher dollar yield per acre at London prices than does wool, because you can fit

Figure 20.7
The Margin Between One Crop and Another Is the Point at Which Their Rental Bids Are the Same

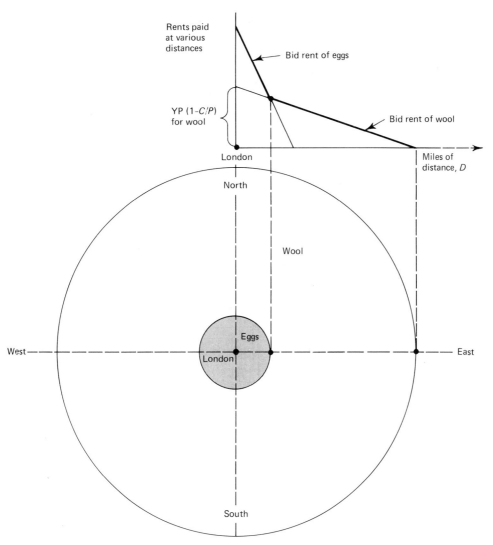

Eggs yield more profit per acre, excluding transport costs, than does wool but are more expensive to ship. Therefore eggs are produced nearer London and wool at a greater distance from London.

more hens producing valuable eggs on an acre than sheep producing wool. The transport costs per mile per ton for eggs, on the other hand, are obviously higher. In other words, the intercept for eggs is higher, but so too is the slope.

The results portrayed in Figure 20.7 are rings of cultivation around London, the division between rings being where one bid rent curve falls below another. Where the bid for wheat land exceeds that for egg land, as it does at such a distance that eggs cannot be delivered without excessive spoilage and breakage, the wheat ring begins. And so forth, out to the last ring of cheap goods cheap to transport.

□

*The Value of
Distance from a
Good or Bad Thing*

The emphasized, outermost line in the top panel is how much rent successful bidders will pay for the land at various distances from the center. Whenever greater distance costs more, it slopes downward, as here. The center can be a central business district to which people wish to commute daily, in which case the rings are rings of differing land use: very near the center, office buildings; a little farther out, high-rise apartment buildings willing to pay a great deal per acre; still farther out, low-rise apartments and tightly packed single-family houses; and in the outermost ring, suburbia, with low land rents (because no one will pay premium prices to be 20 miles from work) and accompanying large lots. The area under the bid rent curve is the rent of all land at various distances. Likewise, the value of other powerful amenities (a park, golf course, or lake) or disamenities (an airport, freeway, or dump) can be measured by the area under their bid rent curves).

Summary

The idea of "distance" between products is more fruitful when applied to literal distance. Hotelling's tale of stores along a road says much about the location of stores and about the location of political stores called parties. And once the diagram of rising cost with distance is developed, it says a great deal about location in general. It says, for example, that the midpoint of a road is the socially optimal location for a single store or a conference. It says, again, that remote locations are valued less than near ones, a simple idea that is the key to explaining the geography of production or to measuring the value of transport improvements or to planning parks or, a negative amenity, pollution.

QUESTIONS FOR SECTION 20.2

1. The Hotelling model of the location of two soap stores assumes that the demand curve for soap of each of the consumers scattered along the road is perfectly inelastic. *True or false:* If it is somewhat elastic, then the two stores will not locate exactly side by side because their moves toward the middle of the road will discourage consumers on the ends from consuming at all.

2. What is the political analogy to Question 1? Who is the "consumer"?

3. Imagine the road to be a circle rather than a line. Stores can locate anywhere along the circle. There is no end, for circles do not have ends. *True or false:*

The Hotelling equilibrium along a circular road is both stable and socially optimal.

4. At the beginning the nineteenth century a ton of iron made in England required 2 tons of iron ore and 8 tons of coal. By the end of the century it still required 2 tons of iron ore, but only 1.5 tons of coal. Where would ironmaking locate in the two periods relative to the (widely separated) deposits of coal and of iron ore?

5. The chief cost of visiting Yellowstone Park is the time spent getting there. Yellowstone is 4 hours from Butte, Montana, 11 hours from Spokane, Washington, and 17 hours from Seattle. *True or false:* If one knew the percentage of each city's population that visited Yellowstone in a year, one would have three points on the demand curve for visits per year (with price expressed in hours, which can be translated back into dollars at some wage rate per hour).

6. Using geometric methods (and given the simplifying assumptions in the text), show that the ratio of travel costs for a conference located at the end of the line of participants in New York to one located at the midpoint in Kansas City is 2.0. (Hint: Draw with some care to be accurate the transport cone out of the midpoint and the half cone out of the eastern endpoint. The areas under the cones are the costs, and if transport costs are constant, the edges of the cones are at the same angle to the line. Search the areas for similar triangles.)

True or False

7. If a third store joins the two already selling soap along the road in Question 1, the equilibrium is instable.

8. The Hotelling location for two firms is socially nonoptimal.

9. Land rents fall to zero as transport costs fall to zero.

21 Competition Among the Few

21.1 Simple Solutions: Bertrand and Cournot

Starting with Few Competitors

☐ The last chapter attempted to develop a satisfactory theory intermediate between competition and monopoly by beginning with competition (many sellers) and letting in elements of monopoly (downward-sloping demand curves). It failed, although the disappointment was softened by the many uses found for the bits and pieces of theory constructed along the way. The present chapter picks up the other end of the stick, beginning with monopoly and introducing some elements of competition. It proves to be the same disappointing stick. Again, however, the ideas prove useful in other directions. And the repeated experience of failure is a maturing one, as it often is, bringing us to accept the hard truth that there is in fact no good theory intermediate between monopoly and competition.

Cooperation as a Solution

☐ Begin with a John Hughes, a monopolist of mineral water in Mudlavia, Indiana, who has no costs. He sets his supply price—or, with equivalent results, the quantity supplied—at the profit-maximizing level, so that the marginal revenue on the mineral water is equal to its marginal cost (zero). The entire theory of *oligopoly* (few sellers) developed so far in economics can be summarized by imagining what happens if a new seller, Joel Mokyr, sets up shop beside Hughes. Two sellers is *duopoly*, the simplest case of oligopoly. If there is any reasonable prediction of how three or four or N sellers will behave, it should work for two.

One solution is cooperation, with Mokyr saying to Hughes, "Look, old buddy, we needn't quarrel: you just give me half your monopoly profits and we'll go on exploiting the customers to the optimal extent." Because the former monopoly price is the best that the industry can do, a cooperating pair of duopolists keep it. The problem with cooperation, however, is achieving and maintaining it. Hughes will naturally resent the upstart's demand for half the profits. And Mokyr might as well ask for 99% of the profits as for 50%. Although 50:50 might seem "fair," there is in fact no reason other than social convention for adopting it. Even if some division of the spoils is agreed, each

434

duopolist has an incentive later on to cheat on the agreement if he can. And if the cooperation somehow survives both the initial bargaining and the subsequent cheating, its very success will attract others, yielding a three-, four-, and five-firm industry, and so on, with each new entrant's dissipating the monopoly profit and complicating the already complicated agreement to cooperate.

☐

Market Sharing Leads to the Cooperative Solution

Though complicated and precarious, cooperation sometimes happens. And even when it is not explicit, it can occur.

T or F: If Hughes and Mokyr each believes that the other will in the end match both his price and his quantity, each will believe that he faces a demand curve that bisects the market demand, and each will set voluntarily the true monopoly price.

A: When Mokyr's price is the same as Hughes's consumers divide randomly (and equally) between them. When neither duopolist attempts to sell more than the other, this equality is undisturbed (see Figure 21.1). The one half of market demand is therefore each duopolist's demand curve when price and quantity are matched. The curve has the same elasticity at every price as does market demand, the simplest proof being that a constant elasticity demand such as $DP^{-\epsilon}$ continues to have the same elasticity, ϵ, when divided in half ($\frac{1}{2}DP^{-\epsilon}$ still has ϵ as an exponent). Therefore each duopolist acting as a monopolist along his market share demand curve has the incentive to set his price at the same markup over marginal cost as would a monopolist of the entire industry. An assumption of market sharing, in short, leads to the cooperative solution. Therefore, true. Because each duopolist is led by market sharing to act in the (monopolistic) interest of the two together, duopolists (or *N*-opolists, for that matter) setting up a monopolistic conspiracy often in fact specify that sales will be divided in fixed shares of the total. Each member of the market-sharing conspiracy has still an incentive to cheat, which can be policed by central selling, one office dividing up the market. The only remaining obstacle in the way of quiet enjoyment of the monopoly thus arranged is that such arrangements are against the law.

☐

Noncooperation: The Bertrand Solution or Price Competition

The alternatives to cooperation as a description of how the duopolists will behave are numerous. One is the price war of all against all, otherwise known as competition. That is, Mokyr could get all the market for mineral water by selling it for 1 cent below Hughes's old price. The assumption that Mokyr is making is that Hughes will not only not match his price but will not respond at all or will respond so slowly that Mokyr will make much money in the meantime. Notice that the assumption is in fact a correct one for a single firm among 100,000 to make, for it is literally true that the market (the 99,999 other firms) will not respond noticeably to the price cutting of one little firm unable to supply anything but a tiny share of the market. But 100,000 is very far from 2. If Hughes also is alert, he will respond, dropping his price 1 cent below the new price set by Mokyr and stealing back the entire market. In other words, since Mokyr is potentially a

**Figure 21.1
The Market Share Solution
Is the Same as Monopoly**

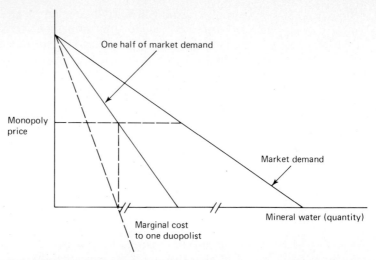

If duopolists divide the market, either by agreement or because one decides to imitate the other, market price and quantity will be the same as if the industry were a monopoly.

large part of the market, his initial shading of the price does have a noticeable effect on the other firms in the market—namely, a fall in Hughes's output from all the market demand to nothing—and does therefore evoke a response. The assumption that the other duopolist will keep his price fixed if one changes his price is in fact an irrational assumption for duopolists to make. If they nonetheless make it and persist in it despite all their unhappy experience to the contrary, the result will be a price war, eventually driving the price of mineral water down to marginal cost, namely, to zero. The analysis is known as the *Bertrand solution* to the oligopoly problem.

□
***Noncooperation:
The Cournot
Solution or
Quantity
Competition***

The other main solution to the oligopoly problem is the *Cournot solution.*[1] In the Bertrand solution each duopolist takes the other's price as given. In the Cournot solution he takes the other's quantity as given. The "given" amount is subtracted from the market demand to give the demand curve the duopolist believes he faces. The belief curve will be parallel to the market demand, because a constant amount is subtracted at every price. Having a demand curve before him, he will choose the best position along it as though he were alone. Whatever the duopolist believes he faces, however, he actually faces one half of market demand, his reality curve, because in equilibrium two indistinguishable duopolists must have the same price and output. Full equilibrium therefore requires that the point the duopolist chooses along his belief curve be sustainable, that is, be also a point along

[1] After A. A. Cournot (1801–1877), a French economist who proposed it in his *Researches on the Mathematical Principles of the Theory of Wealth*, first published in 1838, English trans. by Nathaniel Bacon (New York: Macmillan, 1897). The "Bertrand" of the other solution is Joseph, in *Journal des Savants* (September 1883), which is based on a misunderstanding of Cournot.

**Figure 21.2
The Cournot Solution
Bisects the Belief Curve**

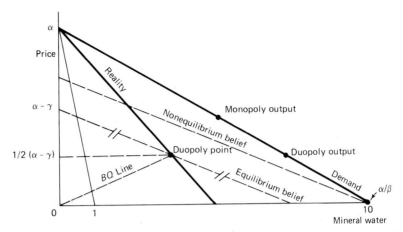

The Cournot duopolist constructs a belief curve on the assumption that the other duopolist's output will not change. In reality, however, the other duopolist, if he or she is also a Cournot duopolist, *will* react. The reality curve, by the symmetry argument, divides the market, and the only possible point of equilibrium is one that the duopolists choose on their belief curves, which is also on the reality curve. Since the midpoint of the belief curve is always chosen, the reality curve must bisect the belief curve.

his reality curve. For a straight-line demand curve and no costs, the condition is easily represented, because the duopolist's optimum is simply the midpoint of the belief curve, this being the point of maximum revenue (elasticity $= -1$ and no costs). That is, one shifts the belief curve (which is parallel to the whole demand curve) up and down the reality curve (which is the bisection of the demand curve) until the equilibrium belief is bisected, as is the bottom dashed line in Figure 21.2.

A number of results follow from the diagram. For one thing, the diagram permits an easy extension to 3-, 4-, . . ., N sellers. Look at the very steep reality curve close to the price axis, equal to a tenth share of the whole demand (when there are 10 sellers). The only dashed-line belief curve that will be bisected by such a steep reality curve is a very low one. That is, as numbers increase, the price resulting from Cournot behavior gets smaller, becoming finally the competitive price—here, zero. Furthermore with Cournot behavior an oligopoly falls neatly between a monopoly and a competitive industry.

☐
***The Algebra of
Cournot***

The algebra of the Cournot argument leads to a handy expression for output as a function of the parameters given to the firm. The derivation not using calculus simply replicates the geometry of Figure 21.2, as follows. Let the industry's demand curve be a straight line $P = \alpha - \beta Q$. Then the reality curve if there are N identical firms is $P = \alpha - N\beta Q$, which, as required, is a more steeply sloped line (by a factor of N) than the original demand curve and has the same intercept on the price axis. The belief curve, on the other hand, has a lower intercept and the same slope. Suppose for the moment, since we do not know at present what it is, that the intercept is lower by the amount γ.

The belief curve is therefore $P = \alpha - \gamma - \beta Q$. Finally, for the firm to feel it has maximized its profits, the price at equilibrium must be such that the belief curve is bisected. Looking at the matter from the price axis, therefore, the price must be $P = \frac{1}{2}(\alpha - \gamma)$. The bisecting condition is labeled in Figure 21.2. The equilibrium price and quantity must satisfy all three equations—the reality curve, the belief curve, and the bisecting condition.

1. $P = \alpha - N\beta Q$
2. $P = \alpha - \gamma - \beta Q$
3. $P = \dfrac{1}{2}(\alpha - \gamma)$

The problem is to use the three equations to solve for the three unknowns namely, P, Q, and γ. Use equation (3) to isolate γ and substitute the result into (2). The equations reduce, then, to

1. $P = \alpha - N\beta Q$, as before, and
2. $P = \alpha - (\alpha - 2P) - \beta Q$, by substitution

Collecting all the terms with P in the second equation on one side leads to $P = \beta Q$ (which is in fact a geometric condition interpretable in the diagram as collapsing the belief curve and the bisecting condition into one). Setting the two expressions for P equal to each other leads to

$$\beta Q = \alpha - N\beta Q$$

or, collecting terms in Q on one side, $N\beta Q + \beta Q = \alpha$ or $(N+1)\beta Q = \alpha$, or, solving for Q, $Q = [1/(N+1)](\alpha/\beta)$, which is the expression desired.

This is the quantity of each firm's output resulting from Cournot behavior. Since there are N firms, the whole output of the industry is $[N/(N+1)](\alpha/\beta)$. When the number of firms is very large, $N/(N+1)$ is very close to 1, and output is very close to the competitive, zero-cost output, namely, the output at the intercept of the demand curve along the quantity axis, α/β. When, at the other extreme, N is 1 the case is simple monopoly, and output is half $[1/(1+1) = \frac{1}{2}]$ the competitive output. The case of duopoly leads to an output equal to two thirds of the competitive output, triopoly to three fourths, and so forth.

☐
The Calculus of
Cournot

The calculus of the Cournot argument leads of course to the same result, but it is somewhat more transparent as economics. The output of the whole industry is the output from the single firm under examination, Q_i, plus the outputs from the $N-1$ other firms, each having output Q_j. The distinction in the subscripts is temporary. In a moment it will be acknowledged that all firms, being by assumption identical, will in the end produce identical outputs, that is, that $Q_i = Q_j$. The reason for the distinction initially is to capture the economic notion that the ith firm maximizes its profits assuming that the other $N-1$ firms will not change their output. The profit to be maximized is the ith firm's quantity times the market price (since there are no costs of the mineral water). The market price, in turn, depends on the whole output brought to market, which is $Q_i + (N - 1)Q_j$. For a straight-line demand curve with price intercept α and slope β, then, the profit is

$$Q_iP = Q_i\{\alpha - \beta[Q_i + (N-1)Q_j]\}$$

Multiplying this out and taking its derivative with respect to Q_i (that is, holding constant the Q_j) gives the following expression, to be set equal to zero to achieve maximum profit:

$$\alpha - 2\beta Q_i - \beta(N-1)Q_j = 0$$

The Q_j can be eliminated by now recognizing that $Q_i = Q_j$ in equilibrium and that $\alpha = Q_i\beta(2 + N - 1)$ or $Q_i = [1/(N+1)](\alpha/\beta)$, as in the algebraic derivation. Multiplying by N firms gives the equation for total output.

□
The Application of the Cournot Solution to the Analysis of Large Numbers of Sellers

All this is charming. For large N it is also reasonable. Indeed, the Cournot assumption (that others will keep their quantities constant) is one way of demonstrating the high elasticity (relative to that of the market demand) of the residual demand curve facing one competitor among many.

T or F: In the case of a straight-line demand curve and no costs, the elasticity of the belief curve in equilibrium is always 1.0.

A: True, because the firm will always choose the midpoint of the belief curve (where elasticity is 1.0), as the best it can do.

T or F: The elasticity of the market demand curve (the reality curve) in Cournot equilibrium is $1/N$. (Hint: Write out the expression for elasticity as $(P/Q)(\Delta Q/\Delta P)$, substitute $-1/\beta$, i.e., the slope of the demand curve, looking at the price as the horizontal axis, for $\Delta P/\Delta Q$, and the Cournot equilibrium values of P and Q in terms of N, and β for the P and Q.)

A: Taking the hint, fill in the expression for elasticity with $\Delta Q/\Delta P = -1/\beta$, $Q = [N/(N+1)](\alpha/\beta)$, and solving for P by substituting the expression for Q into the market demand curve

$$P = (\alpha - \beta Q) = \alpha - \left[\beta\left(\frac{N}{N+1}\right)\left(\frac{\alpha}{\beta}\right)\right] = \alpha\left[1 - \left(\frac{N}{N+1}\right)\right]$$

The result is

$$\frac{P}{Q}\left(\frac{\Delta Q}{\Delta P}\right) = \frac{[1 - (N/N+1)]}{\alpha/\beta(N/N+1)}\left(-\frac{1}{\beta}\right) = \frac{1}{N/N+1} - 1 = \frac{1}{N}$$

Therefore, true.

T or F: Therefore, the elasticity of the single firm's belief curve is N times the elasticity of the market demand.

A: Since 1 is N times $1/N$, true.

The proof in the three questions is in fact generalizable to any demand curve, whether straight line or not, and has already been given. The proof consists of the simple algebra of elasticities, as follows. If George Marr's firm faces other firms producing Q_0 and the whole market demand is Q, then evidently Marr faces a quantity demanded of $Q - Q_0$. Leaping to elasticities in the style of Chapter 7 his elasticity of demand is

$$\frac{Q}{Q - Q_0}(\epsilon^D) - \frac{Q_0}{Q - Q_0}(\epsilon^S)$$

where ϵ^D is the elasticity of demand of the market and ϵ^S is the elasticity of supply by the other suppliers. But the Cournot assumption is precisely that the elasticity of supply by the other suppliers is zero. Since ϵ^S is zero, the expression reduces to $[Q/(Q - Q_0)]\epsilon^D$. But Marr's company is a typical one among the N. So $Q - Q_0$ (which is Marr's output) is to Q as 1 is to N, which is to say that $Q/(Q - Q_0)$ may be replaced by $N/1$. The elasticity facing Marr is therefore N times the elasticity of demand; that is, it is $N\epsilon^D$. Were the number of firms 100 and the market elasticity 2, the elasticity facing one competitor would be 200 if he made a Cournot assumption.

□
The Application of the Cournot Solution to the Case of End-to-End Railroads and Other Matters

It is apparent, then, that Cournot and similar assumptions pop up in many different parts of economics. Here the Cournot assumption has popped up in the theory of the competitive firm facing large numbers of others. In the last chapter it popped up in the Hotelling analysis of political location, with each party's making the assumption that the other would not move. And the Bertrand assumption of given prices, a closely analogous assumption, underlies the theory of monopolistic competition. In simplicity and definiteness of result, it is clear that the Cournot assumption is hard to beat.

The best example is end-to-end railroads. Suppose that the trip of a ton of wheat grown in Scott City, Kansas and destined for bread in Philadelphia is broken into two legs, the first from Scott City to St. Louis on the Missouri Pacific Railroad and the second from St. Louis to Philadelphia on the Baltimore & Ohio. Consider the decision facing each railroad of what to charge the ton of wheat as freight. The number of such tons transported from Scott City all the way to Philadelphia depends of course on the combined prices for freight, not on how the combined price is divided up between the two railroads. Consumers of railroad services, then, do not care how the price is divided. The separate railroads, of course, do care, very much.

Q: Assume for simplicity that the two railroads have no costs, no competitors, and no other trade but the Scott City–Philadelphia one and assume that the demand for tons transported from Scott City to Philadelphia is a straight line.

   1. If the two railroads were merged into one company, what combined price would the company set? Draw the diagram exhibiting the setting.

   2. Suppose that the two railroads are separate and that each takes the other's *price* as given, unaffected by what the one railroad decides to do. Draw

the demand curve that the Baltimore & Ohio believes it faces if it believes that the Missouri Pacific's price for the Scott City–St. Louis leg of the journey is given. In view of the shape and position of this belief curve, what price will the Baltimore & Ohio charge on its leg?

3. Compare the answers to (1) and (2). Which situation—one big railroad or two end-to-end railroads—results in more profits for the railroad industry? Which results in lower prices for consumers? Does the breaking up of vertically integrated monopolies lead always to better outputs, socially speaking?

A: 1. The one big railroad would move to the true monopoly point in Figure 21.3, halfway down the heavy demand curve (since there are no costs).

2. The demand curve that the Baltimore & Ohio thinks it faces is the light line in the diagram, that is, the combined demand price minus a given amount charged by the railroad on the other leg of the journey. Notice the parallels with the Cournot assumption and its diagram: the combined price (like the combined quantity in the Cournot analysis) is fixed by the action of both parties, each party's taking the price (the quantity in Cournot) of the other as given and both having to match quantities (prices in Cournot). The parallelism is another example of the pervasive duality of price and quantity in economics.[2] In any case, the Baltimore & Ohio will choose the midpoint of its belief curve, giving a combined price of two minds.

3. Regardless of how exactly the railroads divide up the price of the two minds, it will be higher than the price of the true monopoly: this follows from the way in which the given price of the other pushes the demand curve facing the one railroad downward beneath the whole demand curve. The midpoint of the belief curve will always lie at a lower quantity than will the midpoint of the demand curve, since the demand curve is farther out. In consequence the combined profits of the two railroads, here equal to their revenues since costs have been assumed away, are less than the largest. Since a monopoly gets the largest profits, any divergence from the monopoly point reduces profits. The price, in short, is set too high from the industry's point of view. It is also set too high from the consumers' point of view. Any price is bad for consumers, and any price above zero for a costless good is bad for society as a whole. The higher the price, the worse, and the case of end-to-end companies leads to an even higher price than does a monopoly. The breaking up of a monopoly into parts that supply each other—as the Missouri Pacific supplies the Baltimore & Ohio with freight—is not always going to lead to better (larger) outputs.[3]

[2] Hugo Sonnenschein, "The Dual of Duopoly Is Complementary Monopoly; or Two of Cournot's Theories Are One," *Journal of Political Economy* 76 (March–April 1968): 316–318.

[3] The full solution to the end-to-end problem requires some assumption about what division of the price is an equilibrium division. That is, there has to be an analog to the assumption in the Cournot analysis of a duopoly that duopolists charging equal prices will receive each half the total quantity. Formally speaking, the analog is a line bisecting the demand price, in which case the entire diagram becomes an exact dual of the Cournot diagram, with price replacing quantity at every stage of the argument. But aside from its "fairness" a 50:50 division of the price has no persuasive claim to being an equilibrium. The end-to-end problem, therefore, cannot be solved quite so neatly as can its Cournot duopoly dual.

Figure 21.3
End-to-End Monopolies
Are the Dual of Cournot
Duopolies

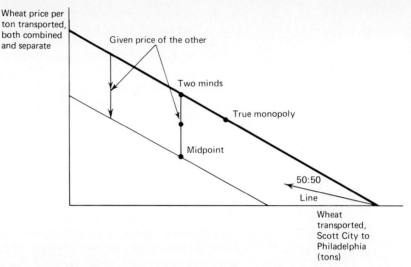

When price rather than quantity is the object of choice and belief, the Cournot analysis leads to a higher price (as it did to a higher quantity) under duopoly than under monopoly.

The end-to-end problem appears in many other forms. Cournot himself applied it to the making of brass out of zinc and copper. Since zinc and copper are used in fixed proportions, brass is analogous to the through journey from Scott City to Philadelphia, each leg of which is used also in fixed proportions. An integrated monopoly would result in a lower brass price, Cournot argued, than would a zinc firm separated from a copper firm. The Cournot assumption is clearly a useful one to begin an analysis.

But is it useful to end? We shall see.

Summary

The analysis of competition among the few can begin with monopoly (one seller) and work up toward many. The first step is duopoly (two sellers), which suffices to illustrate all the promise and problems. If duopolists cooperate, whether explicitly by contract or implicitly by assuming that each will take half the market, then duopoly reduces to monopoly. Any other assumption leads away from the monopoly solution. For instance, if the duopolists make the Bertrand assumption that the other will keep constant his price, the price will fall to the competitive level. For another instance, if the duopolists make the Cournot assumption that the other will keep constant his quantity, the quantity will rise toward the competitive level, stopping well short of it for two sellers and getting very close to it for some large number of sellers. For a large number of sellers, indeed, the Cournot solution provides one way of demonstrating the high elasticity of demand facing a single seller. For a small number of sellers the Cournot assumption provides a way of beginning the analysis: of Hotelling location, of monopolistic competition, of end-to-end monopolies. But all is not well in the small number case. Does the Cournot assumption make sense?

21.2 The Irrationality of Simple Solutions to the Problem of Fewness

The Inapplicability of the Cournot Solution to Rational People

☐ Were the number of firms small—say, two—Marr or Mokyr or any manager would be crazy to make a Cournot assumption. This fact rather spoils the prettiness of Cournotesque arguments. The manager is supposed to treat the actions of others as given, as part of the furniture. But the furniture moves when he tries to sit down. In fact, it moves *because* he tries to sit down. The problem is that when numbers get small it is no longer reasonable for a firm to believe that its own actions have a trivial impact on the other firms. On the contrary, to return to the mineral water duopoly, Mokyr's setting of quantity or price radically changes the environment that Hughes faces, and Hughes reacts. The point is that Mokyr would know that Hughes would react—contrary to the assumption that he is supposed, in the Cournot or Bertrand solution, to make. Mokyr would therefore be foolish to make the assumption that Hughes will keep his quantity or price unchanged. He would be doubly foolish to persist in the assumption after a couple of rounds of reaction from Hughes had shown him that Hughes *does* react. To assume foolish behavior in the science of rationality is at best aesthetically displeasing, at worst wrong.

In other words, the difficulty with the Cournot or Bertrand solution to the problem of competition among the few is that the few are by virtue of their very fewness placed in an environment of pure bargaining. Duopolists do depend on each other, and it would be foolish not to recognize the fact of mutual dependence. Interdependence recognized is bargaining. That is, the situation is similar to those early in Chapter 5 on exchange, in which West Germany trades pipes for gas from the Soviet Union or you trade money for a car from Dario Comi. To the extent that the transactions occur in isolation, the parties do not face prices given by the market and the outcome is unpredictable. Likewise, Hughes and Mokyr are in essence bargaining with each other as they set prices and quantities. The Cournot solution solves the difficulty of bargaining by assuming it away.

Pure Bargaining as the Game of Chicken

☐ An extreme case of the difficulty of analyzing pure bargaining is the game of chicken. This manly sport, alleged to have been popular among adolescent motorists in the 1950s, consisted of driving two cars at high speed on a collision course. The first to turn aside lost his honor. If neither turned aside both lost their lives. If Don Paterson, for instance, knows that Marvin McInnis will turn aside when the cars are 100 feet apart, Paterson can plan confidently to drive past the 100-foot mark—to say 80 feet—and win. But if McInnis knows that Paterson (thinks he) knows—and McInnis would know if he were fully rational, because it is his words and actions that give away the knowledge—then McInnis can stay on line until 60 feet and win. But if Paterson knows that McInnis knows that Paterson knows that McInnis will turn aside at 60, Paterson will by the same reasoning know to stay until 40 feet. And so forth. But zero feet is not the inevitable outcome, either, for both wish to avoid it. Bluff, a reputation for insanity, quickness of reflexes, understanding of the other party's psychology all play a part.

T or F: If McInnis chains himself to the car and locks the steering wheel irrevocably straight and tells Paterson that he has done so, McInnis will win.

A: True, so long as McInnis cannot be outflanked in turn. McInnis has removed the decision to chicken out from his own hands. A rational Paterson will not play a game of choice with a machine that has no choice but to go straight. On the other hand, Paterson could do the same to himself in his own car. The question would then be which competitor was sincere in his hell-bent plan. The competition simply rises to a higher plane, the trick being now to convince your adversary that you are *really* irrevocably committed to a straight course. Having done so, it then rises to a still higher plane. And so forth, on into the hall of mirrors of one intelligence trying to outsmart another.

The games of adults have a similar structure.

T or F: The United States should announce that it will bomb Moscow the next time the Soviet Union even shows up late to a diplomatic cocktail party, much less invades an ally of the United States.

A: Uncertain. If the Soviets believed that the United States was so touchy and violent that it would in fact carry out the threat, then Soviet insults of all sorts would cease forthwith. We would have persuaded the Soviets that "we mean business." On the other hand, it would be difficult to persuade them to the belief, and to do so might be perhaps unacceptably expensive in little wars (a mere 50,000 dead, say). And the same or offsetting strategies are open to the Soviets, who must be assumed to be at least as well informed as we are about the possibilities of international poker. For example, the Soviets can promise, and can attempt to convince us of the sincerity of their promise, to bomb New York and Iowa City if we bomb Moscow. To this we can reply that we will bomb Kiev and Odessa as well. And so on, back into the hall of mirrors. It is like the childish game of insults: "You're a silly head"; "So are *you*, twice over"; "Anything you say a thousand times over"; "Anything *you* say a million times over"; and on to exhaustion.

☐
The Arms Race Analyzed à la Cournot, and Why It Cannot Be So Analyzed

It is plain in a general way that the Cournot "solution" cuts short the chain artificially. For instance, the international arms race can be illuminated by its analogy to a duopoly problem under the Cournot assumption, but only as a very crude first step that must be followed by other steps. The 45° line in Figure 21.4 represents a condition of equal numbers of Soviet and American missiles. If Soviet strategists insist always on having more missiles than the Americans, then the Soviet reaction function would be everywhere above the 45° line. The existence of few American missiles, for instance, results in many Soviet

Figure 21.4
The Arms Race as a
Cournot Problem

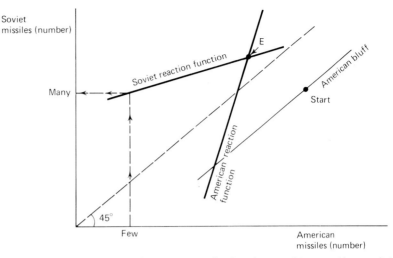

If the Soviets naïvely attempt to have more missiles than the United States, without realizing that the United States will continue to build more missiles if the Soviets do, then the arms race will never reach equilibrium unless the United States is content to have fewer missiles than the Soviets, or unless the United States can persuade the Soviets that they must accept inferiority or an unlimited arms race and induce the Soviets to change their reaction function so that they accept inferiority or equality.

missiles (follow the dashed arrow). The reaction functions, if fixed, embody a Cournot assumption, the Soviets assuming that American missiles will stay at few while the Soviets adjust their own missiles up to many. They never learn that the Americans also have a reaction function. And this is not the only problem.

T or F: If the United States is equally insistent on superiority, the arms race has no end.

A: If you draw in an American curve below the 45° line, you will see that there is no point of equilibrium. Therefore, true.

Still, the diagram seems usually to give a result.

T or F: As the American reaction function is drawn in the diagram, the arms race is stable at *E.*

A: True, as you can see by starting at, say, start and seeing how each party moves.

The fundamental trouble with such an analysis is that the Americans and Soviets would be irrational to react so predictably to the behavior of the other, just as a duopolist would be irrational to react so predictably to the outputs of the other. The reaction curves are themselves at choice. Suppose, for example, that America wished the equilibrium to be below the 45° line, with American superiority in numbers of missiles. Beginning at start, America could announce to the world that the light line through start was in fact how it would react. If the Soviets were buffaloed by the announcement, they would change their curve to allow it to intersect with the American bluff, since the Soviets no more wish to spend all their income on weapons (the ultimate in a runaway arms race) than do we. The American announcement is like McInnis's chaining his steering wheel straight ahead. But it has the same problem of outflanking: the Soviets can announce a similar, or even more belligerent, policy. We are back to bargaining.

☐
The Principle of Outsmarting

Anytime that it is possible to think of a better strategy, in short, the analysis is not finished. This *principle of outsmarting* in the analysis of game playing is the same as the principle of entry in the analysis of the firm. If the participants can still earn profits by intelligent entry, or by intelligent rethinking of their strategy in the game, it behooves the economist to imagine the consequences of entry or rethinking. If Hughes of mineral water fame, for example, acted like a Cournot duo-

**Figure 21.5
How a Cournot Duopolist
Can Be Outsmarted**

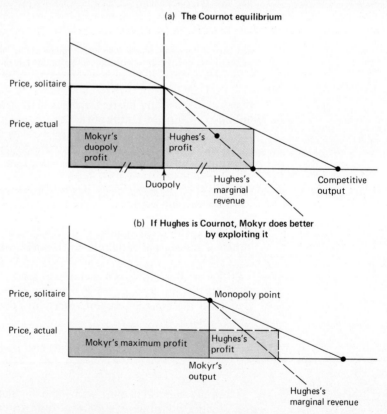

A Cournot duopolist always chooses a quantity that cuts the other duopolist's solitaire price and revenue in half. Knowing this, Mokyr can take advantage of Hughes by choosing a quantity that maximizes solitaire revenue. Mokyr chooses the monopoly output, thereby increasing his profits and reducing Hughes's.

polist, his competitor Mokyr could make more money by acting differently. The wise duopolist knows not merely the other's output (as the Cournot solution has it) but his policy. With such superior knowledge of his environment, Mokyr can obviously do at least as well as he can by stumbling about in Cournot fashion.

The point is easily demonstrated by giving first another (the third) representation of the Cournot argument (the other two, you recall, are the argument from bisection of the belief curve and the argument from the intersection of reaction curves). If Hughes takes Mokyr's output as given at, say, duopoly in the top panel of Figure 21.5, then Hughes will take the dashed line to be his own marginal revenue.

That is, Hughes foolishly thinks that his demand curve begins where Mokyr's present output leaves off. The situation illustrated in the top panel is in fact the Cournot duopoly solution. Each duopolist sells one third of the competitive output for a total of two thirds. Since both have the same output, Mokyr's profit (shaded) is the same as Hughes's. Notice also one geometric fact. Because the curves involved are here assumed to be straight and Hughes acts like a monopolist along what he thinks is his demand curve, the actual price is half the solitaire price that would occur if Mokyr produced the output in the absence of Hughes; therefore the area of Mokyr's profit is half the emphasized rectangle inscribed under the demand curve. So long as Hughes acts like a monopolist, Mokyr's profit will always be half of such an inscribed rectangle of total revenue.

Mokyr wishes to do better, and can if he exploits his understanding of Hughes's behavior. He gets half of an inscribed rectangle.

Q: What solitaire price (i.e., what output) should Mokyr choose in the bottom panel to make the best of the situation?

A: Mokyr should choose the output that maximizes the area of the rectangle inscribed at solitaire: if you get half of something, you want to make the something as large as possible. In the event Mokyr gets Mokyr's maximum profit, which is larger than Mokyr's duopoly profit, Hughes, of course, is hurt; and consumers, it happens, are helped, because output is closer to competitive.

To repeat, then, the Cournot and related solutions violate the principle of outsmarting, or of entry, because it is possible to think of a feasible way in which a Cournot duopolist could improve upon his or her situation. The principle of outsmarting is a principle of humility, in the following sense. Imagine that Hughes and Mokyr are selling mineral water before your eyes. If you really believe that their behavior is that of Cournot duopolists, it is easy for you, as a student of economics, to think of a way in which either person could do better. But something is wrong here. You or I—mere students of economics, mere outside observers, mere amateurs in selling mineral water—claim on the basis of learning about the theory of duopoly to be able to advise professionals in selling mineral water. The claim is arrogant. We claim to know better than people whose income depends on knowing as much as is worth knowing about how to sell mineral water. Indeed, the claim is antieconomic, for it asserts that the sellers of mineral water themselves have not bothered to spend the few hours of diagram shuffling (or of quiet thinking) that has as its reward an enormous increase in wealth. If we knew of such a profitable investment as outsmarting a Cournot duopolist, we should exploit it quietly. If we are so smart, in brief, we should be rich.

Q: If you could predict when the economy will turn around (moving from boom to bust or bust to boom) and could convince some bankers that your prediction was true, then you could make a very large amount of money by investing in ways that used the prediction. *True or false:* Therefore it must be false that you can predict when the economy will turn around.

A: According to the principle of outsmarting, an analysis is unfinished if it leaves open an opportunity for one of the parties to better his or her position. Well, you as the economic seer are one of the parties. Therefore, true. As was remarked in Chapter 14, which arrived at the same point, you should on this account be suspicious of government spokespeople or financial journalists who predict what the future will bring, if their predictions would allow someone to make money. And on the same account you should be suspicious of "solutions" to the oligopoly problem.[4]

21.3 Cartels and Game Theory as Solutions to the Oligopoly Problem

□
*Monopoly Itself Is
an Economic Good*

Useful as it is for beginning all manner of economic analyses, then, the Cournot and related assumptions do not lead to useful solutions to the original problem, namely, how will a group of firms behave that are neither perfectly numerous nor perfectly monopolistic? The Cournot assumption makes them out to be perfectly foolish. Perhaps it will prove more fruitful to imagine the results of assuming them to be perfectly wise.[5]

What is the best that a wise group of competing taxi firms can do? Obviously the best is to stop competing with each other for customers. That is, if there were no costs of collusion, the best that the taxi firms could do would be to collude to form a perfect taxi monopoly, dividing up the spoils among Yellow, Checker, and so forth in some agreeable way. The reason that collusion does not always happen is that it is expensive to enforce. Collusion among oligopolists, in other

[4] The first formal statement of the point in the context of prediction was John F. Muth, "Rational Expectations and the Theory of Price Movements," *Econometrica* 29 (July 1961): 315–335, reprinted in Arnold Zellner, ed., *Readings in Economic Statistics and Econometrics* (Boston: Little, Brown, 1968). Muth's article is difficult. It has spawned, with a considerable lag, a large literature in macroeconomics.

[5] Or so it seemed to George Stigler, who accomplished this reorientation of the analysis in his "A Theory of Oligopoly," *Journal of Political Economy* 72 (February 1964): 44–61, reprinted in his *The Organization of Industry* (Homewood, Ill.: Irwin, 1968), to which subsequent reference is made.

words, has a price, and the oligopolists will buy much or little of it, depending on whether the price is high or low. The cause of the price is that, like other laws for the mutual benefit of a group, an agreement to collude must be enforced, and police officers (literal or figurative) cost money. Industrial spies, lawyers, accountants, economists, and other worthy sorts might be employed to detect cheating on the agreement, but secret price cutting is usually possible to some degree, especially if the agreement is itself illegal—as such agreements are under the common law.

The reasons that resources must be spent to defend perfect collusion are apparent from two observations. The first is that a successful cheater on the agreement does better for himself than if he had cooperated with the agreement. A successful thief does better by cheating on the social agreement not to steal than if he were law abiding. A successful violator of the agreement by all taxi firms to charge a high price on a low volume does better than if he were agreement abiding. The second observation, however, is that, if all members of the agreement in fact cheat, then the agreement is a dead letter, and the thief (now living in a world of thieves) and the clever taxi company (now living in a competitive industry) are worse off than they would have been if they and their colleagues had cooperated. In a world of thieves and price cutters, it is foolish to continue to obey the old laws against stealing and price cutting.

☐

The Prisoner's Dilemma

The situation is known as the *prisoner's dilemma,* from the following tale. Michelle McAlpin and M. Morris, two members of a secret conspiracy against the government of the Soviet Union, are captured without warning one night and are placed in separate cells, unable to communicate with each other. The police offer McAlpin a deal. If she will defect from her pledge of comradeship with Morris and testify against him, she will be set free. If at the same time, however, Morris also defects from the pledge, both will be given heavy sentences at hard labor on the damning evidence that each gives of the other's nefarious activities. If McAlpin refuses to defect—that is, continues to cooperate with the pledge—and Morris defects, then McAlpin will be shot: she does not turn state's evidence and will therefore not make amends for her crimes against the state. If McAlpin cooperates and Morris does too, neither testifying against the other, then both are given light sentences, for even under the somewhat elastic constitutional limits on the Soviet state it needs at least some evidence to convict for heavy sentences.

The only way that you or the prisoners can keep matters straight is to draw up a little two-by-two table of options (see Figure 21.6). McAlpin's choice to defect or cooperate with Morris is given on the left, as the two rows; Morris's choice is given at the top as the two columns. The results of the interaction of his or her choice for McAlpin (upper left in each box) and Morris are given.

Looking at this table in her dreary prison cell, McAlpin faces a most distressing dilemma. No matter what her former comrade Morris does, McAlpin is selfishly better off if she defects, that is, if she turns state's

**Figure 21.6
In the Prisoner's Dilemma
It Is Best to Defect Under
Any Assumption About
What the Other Party Will
Do: Table of Payoffs to
McAlpin (her payoff =
upper left corner of each
rectangle)**

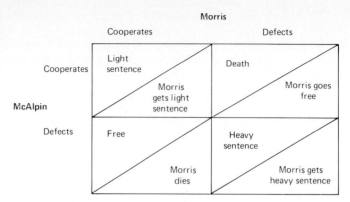

A prisoner's dilemma is a matrix of payoffs from cooperation and defection that make it always desirable to defect. No matter what Morris does, McAlpin will do best by choosing her defect option. For example, if Morris also defects, then McAlpin avoids death by choosing to defect as well.

evidence. Look at the table again. If Morris cooperates, McAlpin is presented with the first, Morris cooperates column. Since McAlpin obviously prefers being scot-free to getting a light sentence, she will (if selfishly motivated) choose to defect. On the other hand, if Morris defects, McAlpin is presented with the second, Morris defects column. Since she prefers a heavy sentence to death, she will again choose to defect. No matter what the other person does, then, a selfishly motivated McAlpin will defect. But the police offer the same deal to Morris, and he too has an incentive to defect no matter what the other does (his payoffs appear in the lower right-hand part of each rectangle). Both therefore defect. Both convict each other. Both end up with heavy prison sentences. By contrast, had they been able to keep faith, they would have received light sentences. The lower right-hand outcome is their equilibrium even though it is by no means the best for them.

□
***Cartels Pose the
Prisoner's Dilemma
to Their Members***

Although better than death, the equilibrium is of course worse than the light sentences that would result if both kept mum. If they were both devoted unselfishly to the cause and could each therefore be sure that the other would not defect, then both would cooperate, and the prisoner's dilemma would be avoided. It would also be avoided if they could communicate during the negotiations or could make legally binding contracts to cooperate or could punish the other in a subsequent play of the game for defecting on this play. All these have analogies in the case of a taxi cartel. If executives of the taxi companies simply believed that it was rotten behavior to cheat on the price agreement, they would be in effect devoted unselfishly to the cause. The cause would be stable. So too if they could take cheaters to court, as any cartel could in fact do under German law in the late nineteenth century and as taxi cartels in most American cities can do nowadays, or if they could punish defectors by fines or violence, the cartel would again be stable.

Figure 21.7
Any Cartel Faces a
Prisoner's Dilemma

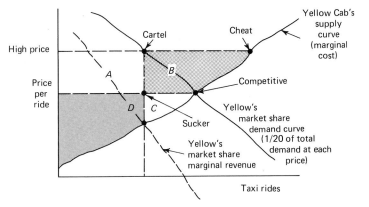

The cheater in a cartel agreement can get the high price of the cartel yet not pay the cost in sacrificed output: the cheater can produce all the way out to cheat, making much more profit (namely, areas *B* and *C* in addition to *A* and *D*). But when every person in the cartel thinks this way, as each will, the cartel is not effective, the price falls (since the market is glutted with output in excess of the output that would maintain the high cartel price), and each firm ends up at the competitive point. Only a sucker would continue to honor the agreement once the agreement was no longer effective.

The prisoner's dilemma highlights the forces pulling the cartel in the other direction, toward collapse. The analogy of the political prisoners to the taxi cartel is exact.

Q: The marginal cost curve of a typical member of a taxi cartel of 20 firms is drawn in Figure 21.7, together with the single firm's share of the market demand curve and the corresponding marginal revenue. Notice the four emphasized and named dots.

  1. What profit does Yellow make if it and all other companies cooperate in the cartel to set price and quantity at the cartel point?
  2. What profit does Yellow make if it is able to cheat, supposing that the other companies continue to cooperate with the cartel?
  3. What profit does it make if everyone including Yellow cheats?
  4. What profit does it make if everyone cheats but Yellow does not?

A: 1. Yellow gets the area *A* + *D* in profit, namely, the area that results from maximizing industry profit, setting output so that marginal cost equals marginal revenue.
   2. Yellow gets the high cartel price but does not suffer the low cartel quantity if it moves to point cheat. By shading its price a little, or by putting more than the allotted number of cabs on the street, it can do better than at cartel. It gets the whole area *A* + *B* + *C* + *D* in profit. In other words, the triangular area *B* + *C* is the incentive to cheat. Notice that it will be larger the larger is the elasticity of the marginal cost curve. That is, if it is very easy (cheap) for Yellow to expand its output, the incentive to do so will be great.
   3. If everyone cheats on the cartel, the equilibrium is of course competitive,

namely, the point of horizontal summation of the supply curves. The corresponding profit is $D + C$. Since C is less than A, each firm does worse under competition than under monopoly.

4. If everyone cheats except Yellow, Yellow arrives at point sucker: it loyally maintains the low cartel quantity but gets for its trouble only the competitive price (or only slightly above the competitive price, considering that its decision to keep a low output affects only one twentieth of the industry's output). The profit is only are a D.

Now, to complete the analogy with the prisoner's dilemma.

Q: Fill in the two-by-two table of results from Yellow's perspective for a game of cooperation or defection played between Yellow and all other taxi companies. Discuss the correspondence of each outcome to those in the prisoner's dilemma.

A: The table is given in Figure 21.8. Compare the table with the earlier diagram of the cartel and the earlier table of the prisoner's dilemma. The cartel cell corresponds to the light sentence, cheat to free, sucker to death, and heavy sentence to competition. The point is that the incentive to cheat lures the members of a cartel into a heavy sentence of competition.

Figure 21.8
The Table of Payoffs to Yellow Cab Is a Prisoner's Dilemma

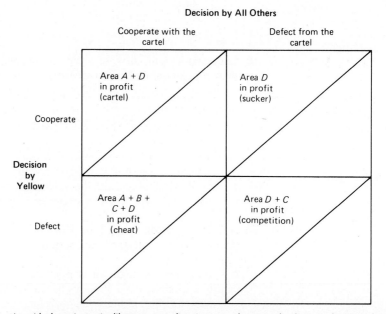

As with the prisoner's dilemma, one firm in a cartel tempts the firm to cheat on the cartel, regardless of whether the other members of the cartel decide to cheat or not. The result is to move the industry into the lower right-hand corner, that is, to universal defection. The heavy sentence of the prisoner's dilemma is, in the case of a collapsed cartel, the profits of competition, lower than the profits obtainable from a successful cartel.

The idea of the prisoner's dilemma is rich in applications. The most important application is to the leading question in political philosophy from Aristotle to the present, namely, the nature of the state. One economic analysis of a state such as the federal government of the United States, for example, is that it is a cartel, which can achieve benefits for its members that they would not be able to achieve individually. Like any cartel, however, its members have an incentive to cheat. That is, each citizen has a selfish incentive to take the benefits of citizenship, such as the provision of lighthouses, public roads, and, above all, protection from the predation of other states, but to pay none of the taxes. If taxes were not compulsory, most states would collapse. If it is thought that the services of the state are worth the trouble, therefore, taxes must be compulsory, and we would even wish them to be so. We would voluntarily agree to subject ourselves to the state's power to fine or imprison nonpayers. The state's prison overcomes the prisoner's dilemma.[6]

A large group lacking the power to imprison or in other ways discipline defectors faces great difficulties in collective action.

Q: You and 50 of your most intimate friends have clubbed together to buy a building in which to live communally. But as a poet said once, it takes a heap o' livin' to make a house a home. Yes (answered another poet), and a heap o' cookin', washin', cleanin', repairin', and above all, payin'. You hold a meetin' of the group on how to accomplish these things. "Let's not be authoritarian about it," says Betsy White at the meeting. "I think we can depend on everyone's public spirit and good sense to get these things done." What is your reply to Betsy?

A: "The problem, Betsy, is a classic prisoner's dilemma. Some people will be less public spirited than others and will take a free ride on the efforts of others. They will defect, getting their share of the benefits from the commune without doing their share of the work. With no rules to punish slackers, it will be rational for all to slack off. And in this tendency to collapse in the absence of rules, our commune will be following the lead of many a utopian community in history."

Another example is the following.

Q: "Bare-faced covetousness was the moving spirit of civilization from its first dawn to the present day; wealth, and again wealth, and for the third time wealth; wealth, not of society, but of the puny individual was its only and

---

[6] One alternative to the view that the state is a cartel that its citizens have joined voluntarily is that the state is a band of robbers into whose clutches its citizens have fallen. The analysis of the state reduces then to the economics of robbery instead of the economics of free exchange. On April 15 in the United States this view is surprisingly popular. On other dates it is taken seriously by anarchists (not bomb throwers, but *anarchos*, from the Greek, meaning "without a leader," that is, the notion that we can do quite well, thank you, without politicians endowed with special powers of compulsion).

final aim." In particular, "the bourgeoisie . . . has left remaining no other
nexus between man and man than naked self-interest." *True or False:* Even
if one believed these assertions by Karl Marx and Friedrich Engels to be
true, it would not follow from them that the bourgeoisie or any other class
would be motivated by covetousness or other self-interest to behave in its
class interest, because the cooperation required for class action suffers from
the prisoner's dilemma.

A: To quote Mancur Olson, from which the present analysis is drawn,

> If a person is in the bourgeois class, he may well want a government
> that represents his class. But it does not follow that it will be in his
> interest to work to see that such a government comes to power. If there
> is such a government he will benefit from its policies, whether or not
> he has supported it. . . . [O]ne individual bourgeois presumably will
> not be able to exercise a decisive influence on the choice of a government.
> So the *rational* thing for a member of the bourgeoisie to do is to ignore
> his *class* interests and to spend his energies on his *personal* interests.[7]

No bourgeois motivated solely by rational covetousness will bother to contribute his efforts to the common good. The point is identical to the one
on the irrationality of voting made earlier: no single vote matters for the
outcome, and therefore no person motivated solely by the desire to change
the outcome will bother to vote. Likewise, no single supplier bothers to
manipulate the amounts she supplies to change the price she gets, because
the output of no single small suppliers matters for the market price. Perfect
competition is a prisoner's dilemma into which, fortunately for society as
a whole, many firms are led, as though by an invisible hand.

The Prisoner's Dilemma Applies to Many Large Groups

The prisoner's dilemma—the incentive to free ride on the efforts of
others and the collapse of cooperation that such free riding brings—
is pervasive. A clear if trivial example is the cocktail party problem.

Q: People at a cocktail party want to be heard over the din of other people
who are talking. Everyone generally ends up shouting. Show that, if they
cooperated they could avoid shouting, but that the shouting is the equilibrium of a prisoner's dilemma.

A: The choices I alone have are to talk normally or to talk loudly. The results
of my choice and the choices of the group around me can be expressed in
terms of the distinctness with which I am heard by the person to whom I
am speaking relative to background noise. The results appear in Figure 21.9.
No matter what others do I will shout, because in each case I raise my
audibility. But everyone ("they") makes the same decision, with the result
that none of us is heard very well and all of us are hoarse leaving the
party.

[7] Mancur Olson, *The Logic of Collective Action: Public Goods and the Theory of Groups* (Cambridge, Mass: Harvard University Press, 1965), pp. 104–105; the Marx–Engels quotations appear on p. 104. Olson's book is brilliant and readable.

Figure 21.9
Why You Shout at Large
Cocktail Parties

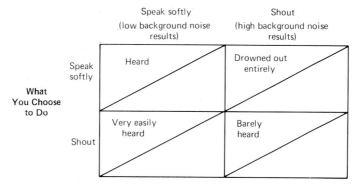

What the Others Choose to Do

	Speak softly (low background noise results)	Shout (high background noise results)
Speak softly	Heard	Drowned out entirely
Shout	Very easily heard	Barely heard

What You Choose to Do

Again, if you defect from the social agreement to speak softly, you will be better off (will be heard more easily) no matter what the rest of the party does. But everyone faces the same incentives, and the result is universal shouting.

Still another case is the annoying anxiety when you have to choose one of several lines to join at a college cashier's office, a grocery store, a bank, or an airline terminal: have I picked the fastest line? It is a corollary of Murphy's law that the line you join is always the slowest. In a very few colleges, a few grocery stores, some banks, and quite a few airline terminals, everyone is put into one common line, the person at the head of it being always the next to be served. The advantage of the system is that the variability of the waiting time is cut while the average time is unchanged, on the following reasoning. Contrary to Murphy's law, of course, the average time from arrival to service will in fact be the same whether there is a line in front of every server or a common line for everyone. In the many-line arrangement, the student or shopper or whoever with a complex and lengthy case to be served will choke up one line, significantly delaying the people behind her but not the people in other lines. In the single-line arrangement, however, the delay will be spread in a small amount over all the people waiting. With risk-averse people it will always be better to spread the cost of the unusually lengthy case over all the people than to burden more heavily the few who happen to have the misfortune to join a line at cage 12 or desk 5. Therefore, the one common line will always be best (ignoring administrative costs): same average, lower variability.

T or F: That such single common lines feeding into many servers never arise without compulsion (e.g., ropes and guards) shows that people are, contrary to economics, irrational.

A: The single common line without compulsion is the cooperative solution to a prisoner's dilemma. Anyone not at the head of the common line has an incentive to defect, jumping to the first unoccupied server, and even to join a server's line if it is relatively short. Because of the defections the cooperator who waits her turn in the common line never gets served. The common line breaks down or, rather, never forms in the first place. That is, the assertion is false. That a common line does not form shows that people are indeed rational, too rational for their own good.

☐ **Solutions to the Prisoner's Dilemma in Large Groups: Punishment**

Any solution to the prisoner's dilemma requires some system of punishment for defection. The guards in the bank can enforce cooperation with the single line by threatening embarrassment, emotional distress, or, ultimately, physical violence against those who do not follow the rule. The Internal Revenue Service can enforce cooperation with paying taxes for public goods by threatening fines or, ultimately, physical violence against those who do not pay. A cartel such as the American Medical Association can enforce cooperation with cartel policies thinly disguised as medical ethics by threatening to take away a doctor's license or his or her right to use a hospital. In some cases the cartel authority can offer rewards for cooperation rather than penalties for defection: the *Journal of the American Medical Association* comes only to members, as do other private goods such as malpractice insurance. Clearly, this amounts to the same thing as punishment, the threat being to cancel one's subscription or one's insurance if one does not cooperate.[8] The purpose of either device is to alter the payoff table facing any member.

Q: A union is being organized in the Lazonick Cotton Mill. Without the union the wages are $5.00 an hour; with full cooperation among the workers they would be $7.00 an hour. To be effective the union must collect $0.50 an hour in dues, leaving the cooperating (i.e., dues-paying) worker in a unionized mill with $6.50 an hour.

1. Write down the payoff table facing Gary Walton, an oppressed worker in Lazonick's mill, under the possibilities of cooperation or defection by him and by all others.

2. Suppose that the union can punish Walton for not paying his dues, by ruining his social life or his knees. Show the change a certain dollar value of ruined social life produces in Walton's payoff table. What now is the equilibrium of the game?

A: The answers to the two parts can be put into one table, with the penalty for defection worth, say, $2.00 per hour (see Figure 21.10). Without the penalty for defection the underlined figures are the payoffs, and Walton has the usual incentive to defect regardless of what all others do. But the penalty of $2.00 per hour changes the payoffs in the bottom row, changing his optimal strategy from defection to cooperation. For example, the (emphasized) payoff if he defects and others cooperate is reduced from $7.00 to $5.00 an hour, making defection a bad idea.

[8] Ibid., Chapter VI, "The 'By-Product' and 'Special Interest' Theories."

Figure 21.10
You Gotta Go Down and
Join the Union: The
Punishment-Reward
Solution to the Prisoner's
Dilemma

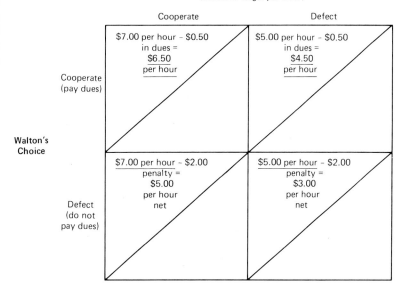

The Choice of All Others
(results in wages per hour)

	Cooperate	Defect
Cooperate (pay dues)	$7.00 per hour – $0.50 in dues = $6.50 per hour	$5.00 per hour – $0.50 in dues = $4.50 per hour
Defect (do not pay dues)	$7.00 per hour – $2.00 penalty = $5.00 per hour net	$5.00 per hour – $2.00 penalty = $3.00 per hour net

Walton's Choice

The ability to impose penalties for defection changes the matrix of payoffs that a single person faces and can change it enough to make it worth his or her while to cooperate rather than defect. On such arrangements are trade unions, political states, and many other social arrangements built.

Solutions to the
Prisoner's Dilemma
for Small Groups:
Shame and Self-
interest

Making defection a bad idea is the social glue of any group. For a very small group, however, there is often no need for explicit, formal penalties for defection. The shame of being caught shirking is enough. In fact, the smaller the group, the larger the chance of being caught and therefore being shamed or punished. One secret price cutter in a cartel of 50 firms limiting steel output is difficult to catch; one in a cartel of a few firms raising airfares between Boston and Washington is easy to catch. The one cartel will be unstable, the other stable. On such considerations of ease of detecting cheaters one can build a theory of oligopoly.[9]

If one single firm is so large a supplier to a market that the fate of the cartel hangs on its participation, then the crime of cheating brings its own punishment. No shame or fines or execution imposed by other members is necessary. The cartel is self-enforcing. The best example is the position of Saudi Arabia within the international oil cartel. Saudi Arabia produces such a large share of the world's supply of oil that its isolated decision of how much to produce significantly influences the world price of oil. If it produces little oil, the world supply is small and the price is high. If it produces much, the world supply is large and the price is low. That is, so large is its share that it faces by itself a downward-sloping demand curve. By comparison the other

[9] Stigler, *The Organization of Industry*, Chapter 5, pp. 39–63.

participants, such as Venezuela, Nigeria, and Iraq are tiny: they face the price Saudi Arabia arranges.

Q: What, then, does the payoff matrix to Saudi Arabia look like, interpreting "cooperation" as "restraining one's production of oil" and "defection" as "letting one's production rip, seizing the opportunity offered by the high price on a large instead of a restrained production"?

A: The payoff matrix is so to speak the opposite of the prisoner's dilemma (see Figure 21.11). No matter what the other countries do, Saudi Arabia finds that it is in its own interest to cooperate, that is, restrain its own production. So big is Saudi Arabia that the oil cartel's high price stands or falls as Saudi Arabia cooperates or defects. The situation is a common one. The United States is so important in world affairs that various collective undertakings—the United Nations, for example, or NATO—would fall apart if the United States did not support them. It is therefore in the self-interest of the United States to support them, even on unfavorable terms. A small country such as Sweden or France has the luxury of refusing to pay for collective undertakings in the sure knowledge that the United States will pay anyway. As Mancur Olson put it,

> Once a smaller member has the amount of the collective good he gets free from the largest member, he [sometimes] has more than he would have purchased for himself, and has no incentive to obtain any of the collective good at his own expense. In small groups with common interests there is accordingly *a surprising tendency for the "exploitation" of the great by the small.*[10]

☐

The Theory of Games

The prisoner's dilemma is a special case of a general *theory of games.*[11] The theory discusses the situation of intelligent people facing other intelligent people in games of tic-tac-toe, poker, chess, cartels, exchanges, collective bargaining, price wars, business mergers, politics, extortions, kidnappings, and wars. Invented in 1928 by the famous mathematician John von Neuman and brought to the attention of economists in 1944 by von Neumann and Oskar Morgenstern in their astonishing *Theory of Games and Economic Behavior,* the theory gave early promise of solving the problem of bargaining among small groups, such as oligopolists. Like monopolistic competition and other approaches to the problem, however, it has not fulfilled the promise. Yet cultivated for its own sake as a metaphor of social life, it must be judged a great intellectual success. At present its main use in general economics is in fact metaphorical. To say that the formation of a cartel is "just like" a prisoner's dilemma game or that a nuclear arms race between

[10] Olson, *The Logic of Collective Action,* p. 35 (italics in original).

[11] A brief idea of the theory can be gotten from William J. Baumol, *Economic Theory and Operations Analysis,* 4th ed. (Englewood Cliffs, N.J.: Prentice-Hall, 1977), Chapter 18. A more leisurely and thorough review is Morton D. Davis, *Game Theory: A Nontechnical Introduction* (New York: Basic Books, 1970). The original book of 1944 by von Neumann and Morgenstern mentioned in the text following (Princeton, N.J.: Princeton University Press, 1947) is highly technical on the whole, but also highly readable in places.

Figure 21.11
Little Members of a Cartel
Exploit the Big Members

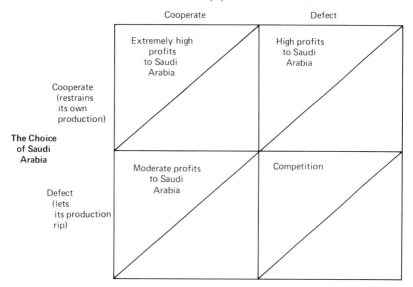

The Choice of Other, Smaller
OPEC Countries
(payoffs to Saudi Arabia)

Because the cartel will collapse without its participation, the big members of a cartel must abide by its rules no matter what the little members do. The little member can be irresponsible without suffering the consequences. The little member, therefore, exploits the big member.

the Soviet Union and the United States is "just like" a two-person negative-sum game is to state the essence of the situations with persuasive elegance.

The very notion that we are "playing games" with other people is enlightening. So, too, are the notions of the negative, positive, or zero sumness of the game. In a zero-sum game my loss *is* your gain, as in the neighborhood poker game or in the distributing of the gains from trade as viewed by medieval towns. Gary's winnings are John's losings; what Venice gained in the trade with the East in the Middle Ages Genoa lost, or so the Venetians and Genoese believed. It is apparent that any constant sum of spoils (or negative spoils, damages) will give the same results. That is, as long as Venice and Genoa are fighting over a fixed pie, it does not matter whether or not the total size of the pie is called zero (Venice gets what Genoa loses) or 100 (Venice gets 80, Genoa 20, both gaining over zero). The alternative to such a constant-sum game is a variable sum, in which the size of the pie to be divided does vary with how the players act. The sum of the payoffs from the arms race, for example, depends on which solutions are chosen. If the bombs are not used, each country loses only the cost of making the bombs; if they are used, each loses its entire population. A more cheerful example, and the focus of much attention in the theory, is exchange. Exchange is "positive sum"; that is, both parties gain or, at worst, do not lose. If two parties to bargaining over the exchange of steel pipes for natural gas fail to reach any agreement because they disagree over the price, the mutual benefit does not materialize. That is, the size of the pie in total varies with the bargaining strategies of the parties; the game is a variable-sum one. As one might expect, the variability introduces complications of threat and bluff that are not present in the simpler case. As was noted, the theory does not literally "solve" the problem of bargaining games. Game theory merely provides the economist with a rich harvest of metaphor: coalitions, the core (mutual benefit), imputations (the prices agreed to), side payments (bribes), maximin strategy (avoiding the worst that people or nature can do to you), saddle points (when such avoidance implies the same strategy for both players), mixed strategies (flipping coins to keep one's behavior from being predictable), and other wonders. It does not, alas, solve the oligopoly problem.

Summary

The theory of games is the ultimate response to the principle of outsmarting. In reaction to the unattractiveness of supposing oligopolists to be outsmarted easily, economists have developed in it a virtual theory of outsmarting. The goal of a set of competing oligopolists is ultimately to eliminate competition. They play a game of cooperation and defection that may or may not have monopoly as its outcome. The approach is more attractive to economists than are Cournotesque approaches because, as George Stigler put it,

> A satisfactory theory of oligopoly cannot begin with assumptions concerning the way in which each firm views its interdependence with its rivals. If we adhere to the traditional theory of profit-maximizing enterprises, then behavior is no longer something to be assumed but rather something to be deduced.[12]

As usual, however, the game theoretic approach to the theory of monopoly is more useful in applications by the way than in reaching a satisfactory theory of oligopoly. The uses of the prisoner's dilemma game alone justify the journey: the prisoner's dilemma is the very model of the social problem. Like a cocktail party or a line at a bank, a cartel is a little society facing the problem of defection from a mutually advantageous arrangement. The single member of an oil cartel ordered to cut back its output for the common good, like the single member of a state ordered to pay taxes for the common good, has an incentive to cheat, to receive the benefit of a high cartel price or a wealthy state without paying the price in lower output or higher taxes.

The society must either find ways to punish free riders or accept collapse. The history of numberless clubs, cartels, unions, and not a few states is written in the algebra of the prisoner's dilemma.

QUESTIONS FOR SECTION 21.3

1. If Morris and McAlpin mentioned in the text, faced the prospect of playing the game many times again after their first play (never mind how they would recover from the prison sentences imposed by the solution), would they behave

---

[12] Stigler, *The Organization of Industry*, p. 390.

in the same, uncooperative way? For example, if Morris defected in the first game, what would McAlpin do in the second and third game? Make the analogy with ordinary social games, such as giving the floor and one's attention in a conversation. If you do not permit others to speak and yawn and look away when they finally do, what will happen to you in the next playing of the conversation game?

2. Certain social customs are "mere conventions," that is, good because people agree on them. Driving on the right-hand side of the road is a good example: we could equally well all drive on the left-hand side, and if we were British we would, so long as we all did it. What is the payoff matrix for thee and me for driving on the right as against the left?

True or False

3. Since the money value of the hurt of the 10 million American consumers of automobiles from a protective tariff on automobiles is greater than the money value of the help to the four American producers of automobiles (or to 4 million stockholders represented by four companies), the proposal for a tariff will lose in the expensive political competition for votes in Congress.

4. A perfectly enforced cartel always earns more profits for the typical firm than does a competitive industry. That is, in terms of Figure 21.7, the area *A* is always bigger than area *C*.

5. That few people cast ballots, thereby endangering democracy for the gain of a half hour of leisure, is a prisoner's dilemma.

6. That a communal bowl of popcorn is eaten much faster than is a set of individual bowls is a prisoner's dilemma.

7. That a common property resource, such as the local public park, is overused and filthy from trash is a prisoner's dilemma.

8. The conventions of diplomacy whereby, for example, embassies are inviolable can be broken with impunity by little countries (e.g., Iran) but not by big countries (e.g., the Soviet Union, the United States).

Part Six

LABOR, CAPITAL, AND DISTRIBUTION

Marginal Productivity and the Demand for Labor: The Fundamentals

22.1 Labor as a Commodity

Factors of Production Are Owned by Households

☐ It is now time to close the economy—"close" meaning to finish the wheel of wealth. The wheel, you will recall, arrayed consumers on one side and firms on the other, as on the left-hand side of Figure 22.1. The top flows are the markets in the goods that have been the explicit subject of the analysis so far: corn, natural gas, housing, books, college education, and so forth. The bottom flow is the subject of the next two chapters, the market in the services of *factors of production* such as labor, land, and capital. The factors of production are those basic inputs from which all commodities can be thought of as flowing. Look at your pencil. True, it is made of wood: no factor of production there. But look a little harder. Where did the wood come from? Well, it came ultimately from land, labor, and capital—the land of a forest combined with the labor of the lumberjack and the capital of the sawmill operator cooperated to produce a piece of wood, fashioned at later stages into a wooden pencil. Analysis of this sort, in truth, finding in each commodity the "ultimate" factors of production that made it, is more persuasive than it has any right to be. After all, the sawmill's saw was itself produced by labor and land and capital; and the laborer is what he eats. Nothing is really "ultimate" or "basic." The wheel of wealth is indeed a wheel, with no beginning or end. Like salt or sugar, however, the story of basic factors of production is not bad if you do not take too much of it.

What comes out of the households on one side of the wheel as spending on commodities must come into the households on the other side as income. That is, what factors of production earn is income, the income that is spent on commodities. The way in which the households earn their income, in other words, is to sell their services—services of their labor or their land or their capital—in a market in which they are sellers and the firms are buyers. The market is called, then, the market for factors of production. It finishes the wheel and, as was just said, closes the model. In a sense, then, by this step the analysis of the economy is finished.

464

Figure 22.1
Factor Markets Complete
the Economy

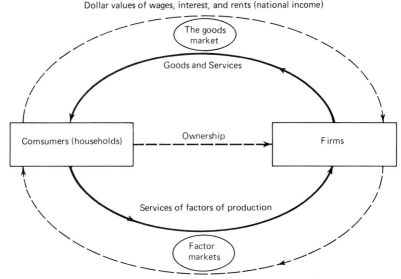

The solid lines represent the flow of goods and services from firms to consumers and the flow of factor services (labor, for instance) from consumers to firms. The dashed lines represent the money payments for these flows, the one being national product, the other national income. The next few chapters concern the lower, factor market.

The step is by now an easy and obvious one. Once you have become accustomed to viewing such noble things as doctor's services and college educations as mere "commodities," it comes as no shock to begin thinking of all sorts of, say, labor as objects of supply and demand. What is remarkable is that the mere realization that there is indeed a market for labor, and that like all markets it entails supply and demand, has so many consequences. It seems hardly fair that such a simple idea should be so powerful. For instance, the mere idea of closing the model of the economy is a great boon to anyone trying to measure the size of the economy.

T or F: The nation's output can be measured either by adding up the value of all goods and services sold to households or by adding up all the income earned by households.

A: As you will recall from your elementary course on macroeconomics, supposing that we set aside the nonhousehold parts of national income (e.g., government), true. What comes in must go out, somehow. The wheel of wealth provides therefore a check on income statistics calculated one way or the other (namely, the other way). If it proves difficult to get a good estimate of the value of housing services, food, clothing, and so forth produced, one can merely turn to measuring the value of labor, land, and capital used in the year to produce these housing services, food, clothing, and so forth.

☐
The Law of One Price
Applies to Labor
Markets

The wonders do not cease with national accounts. The mere idea that the factors of production sell in a market is a boon to anyone attempting to measure their rewards. If the market is functioning well and the cost of moving from one part of the market to another is not very great, then the price of all factors of production of a particular sort and quality must be the same. All land in a city must earn the same rent, once the special advantages of particularly favorable locations have been allowed for. All common laborers in the same country must earn the same wage. All machines of the same productivity must rent or sell for the same price. Factors of production, in other words, are to be treated like grains of wheat or tons of steel: as fungible.

T or F: The indexes of wages of building artisans in England over the past seven centuries are inadequate because they refer overwhelmingly to wages in southern England, especially in London and in a few cathedral towns.

A: More information is always better than less, to be sure. It would be nice, and a most suitable doctoral dissertation in economic history, to have wages from the North. But to suppose without further argument that a sample based on the South is wrong is to suppose that England as a whole did not constitute, roughly, a single market for labor. Perhaps it did not. But that it did not needs to be shown, not merely assumed without evidence. And if it was a single market, little is gained by further inquiry into regional wages—except perhaps to confirm the very oneness of the market or to detect some persistent superiority of one region's wages over another's due to differences in the cost of living, say, or climate.

☐
Equilibrium
Analysis Can Be
Used in Labor
Markets

The wonders never cease. The mere idea that factors of production are proper subjects of analysis of their supplies and demands is a boon to anyone thinking about their behavior. Chapter 26 will introduce the idea of the supply and demand for capital. The present and following chapters emphasize the supply and demand for labor, especially the demand. It is easy to imagine problems in the supply and demand for labor that are exactly analogous to one or another problem in the supply and demand for commodities: the ideas of elasticities and relative shifts and so forth transfer exactly. The simplest and most important transfer is the idea of modeling the markets with supply and demand curves, testing the validity of various verbal arguments about the market.

☐
A New Idea: Derived
Demand

Except for its subject, nothing so far is analytically new. Now turn to novel wonders. The substantive novelty in the analysis of the demand for labor can be summarized in the phrase *derived demand*. The demand for labor, it is pointed out, is largely a derived demand, that is, a demand not directly by consumers but by firms who will then use the labor to satisfy the demands of consumers. In fact, the only reason for the firms to buy the labor is to satisfy the demands of consumers. If a certain laborer cannot produce for the firm in consumer satisfaction enough to pay his or her wages, the firm simply does not hire the laborer. The demand for the laborer's services is derived from the demand for whatever the firm makes, such as popcorn, crackerjacks, or baseball .

Q: Pete Rose is a baseball player of high skill, a great pleaser of crowds, a star. *True or false:* Rose is, at $800,000 a year, overpaid by the Philadelphia Phillies.

A: If someone pays Rose such a sum with open eyes, that someone believes Rose will earn the club an amount equal to the sum or more. The owner of the Phillies is not (all claims to the contrary notwithstanding) in the business for his health. The payment was mutually advantageous or it would not have been made. The owner was willing to pay and therefore did not "overpay." The only meaning of "overpay" that would work here is one that objected to Rose's being paid so much "merely" for hitting, throwing, and catching a horsehide spheroid superbly well. But behind the willingness of the owner to pay Rose is the willingness of the fans to pay the owner. Would it make sense to object to 3 million separate deals between Pete Rose and his fans to put on an exhibition of his skills? No. The demand for Rose is a derived demand.

The point applies to all businesses and to "underpaying" as well as to "overpaying." Geoffrey Hellman wrote for the *New Yorker* magazine for a long time and had incessant quarrels with its editor, Harold Ross, about how little Ross paid a man of Hellman's seniority. Ross insisted that he paid what each piece of writing was worth:

You say that you have been here eighteen years and are not treated better than a good writer a couple of years out of college would be, so far as pay for individual articles is concerned. . . . My firm viewpoint is that we ought to pay what a piece is worth, regardless of age, race, color, creed, financial status or any other consideration. I don't know how, in an enterprise of this sort, one in my position can take into consideration anything beyond the actual value of the things.[1]

The point is that employers are not to be viewed as having tastes for employees in the way that consumers have tastes for apples or oranges. The steelworker makes steel that Bethlehem Steel proceeds to sell to automakers. It is not the steelworker that makes the owners of the company happy directly but, rather, the indirect profit from the worker's work. There will be cases that violate the point, of course. Otherwise it would not be much of a point. An important case in which the hired employee himself or herself does directly enter the utility function of the owner, instead of merely as an instrument for making money, is the case of discrimination in hiring, in favor of native-born citizens, say, or against blacks.

Q: If employers, to a varying degree, have a distaste for hiring black workers rather than white workers at the same wage, then a rise in the proportion

[1] Quoted in Brendan Gill, *Here at the New Yorker* (New York: Random House, 1975), p. 360.

of blacks to whites in a labor market will be accompanied by a fall in the relative wages of blacks.

A: As the proportion rises, the blacks must face more and more discriminatory employers. All blacks must be paid the same wages (assuming that blacks and whites are identical except for color), or else the low-wage person will undersell the high-wage one. So the black wage is determined by the wage differential that just compensates the most discriminatory employer hiring any black for hiring "the" marginal one. Therefore, true.[2]

Figure 22.2
The Economics of
Discrimination

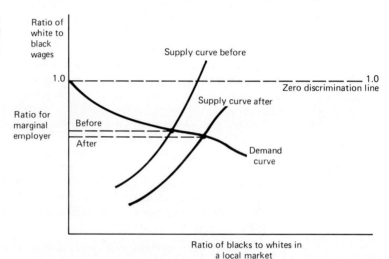

If there are few blacks in a labor market, then the least discriminatory employers will be able to hire them and in competing to hire them will keep their wages high. If the numbers increase, then more discriminatory employers will need to hire blacks, which they will only do if compensated by paying them lower wages than whites. For this reason the demand curve slopes downward. For the same reason a shift outward in the relative supply curve of blacks causes their wage to fall (it would not if blacks and whites were treated as identical by employers).

The relevant diagram appears in Figure 22.2. Notice that the number of firms with a given degree of discrimination is assumed constant—invariant, that is, to the wage paid. A perfectly functioning market would increase the elasticity of the curve, whatever its level, by driving out firms that discriminated a lot until all firms had the lowest discrimination (not necessarily zero) available among the class of potential employers. The point is that a firm that did not hire black workers—that indulged its taste—would pay more for labor than would a firm that took advantage of the lower wage for blacks. This applies across industries—relatively nondiscriminatory industries would have lower costs than they would in the absence of discrimination elsewhere. It

[2] See William Landes, "The Economics of Fair Employment Laws," *Journal of Political Economy* 76 (July–August 1968): 507–552, especially pp. 509–510; and Gary Becker, *The Economics of Discrimination*, 2nd ed. (Chicago: University of Chicago Press, 1971), pp. 5–85.

is said that the radical shifts in the racial composition of the work force in the New York garment trades is a result of this mechanism.

As useful as the exception is for analyzing some situations, it must be realized that it is indeed an exception. Most employers are cold blooded about hiring, within narrow limits. If a secretary does not do his job well, outside of Civil Service, he will lose his job. If he is obviously incapable of performing the job, he will not get it in the first place. If he is competent but demands special treatment of an expensive sort, again he will not get it. The discipline of the market stands ready to punish an employer who is anything but calculating in such matters. If he is the owner, he will be competed to bankruptcy by competitors who do watch carefully the value they get from the people they hire. If he is a hired manager he himself will be fired if he makes a habit of indulging his preference for white Anglo-Saxon Protestants as cooks when all the competition is using another sort of person that is easier and cheaper to hire. In short, it is a premise of the theory of the firm that employers normally do not indulge their own tastes: they hire to satisfy their customers' tastes.

The Law of Demand Applies to Labor as a Commodity

Although employers do not normally have pronounced tastes in employees, they do normally exhibit the behavior that consumers (with tastes) exhibit in the face of varying prices, namely, downward-sloping demand. The precise reasons for the convenient parallelism between the theory of the demand from household and the theory of demand from firms is the subject of later sections. The immediate common sense of the matter is compelling. At a high price for secretaries an insurance company will ration out the secretaries to its executives in small numbers. At a low price every suboffice of the company will have two or three. There are not, in other words, fixed and limited "slots" to be "created" (as in the piece of ersatz economics that military spending, say, will "create jobs"). The jobs to be done by the insurance company are unlimited. It could always use another person to organize the files just a little bit better, to handle claims just a little bit faster, and (above all) to collect premiums just a little more promptly. But doing these things a "little bit" more will not be worthwhile if the price of the person to do them is high. Only the most important secretarial tasks should get done if the person's price is high. For this reason, it will be rational for the company to be stingy with secretarial time when it is expensive and generous with it when it is cheap. That is, the company has a downward-sloping demand curve for secretaries. And so for other people hired.

By the usual argument, if the demand curve for each company slopes downward, then the demand curve for an entire industry probably slopes downward. And indeed as will be shown presently the demand curve slopes downward for the entire economy as well.

Uses of the Demand for Labor

That the demand for labor is a curve, not a point, is a tremendously important fact. It undermines, for example, all manner of manpower studies, projections, "needs," "supplies," and other products of the official imagination eager to find in its vision of the future a reason to act or not to act. "Demand for Nurses Outruns Supply" screams the headline. Why, the economist replies, do the wages of nurses not increase? "Shortage of Engineers Developing" screams another. But will not the consequent rise in wages provide the remedy? It is simply wrong to speak in terms of "the" supply or "the" demand of nurses or engineers as though each were a number, such as 1 million. The demand (and as Chapter 25 will show, the supply also) is dependent on the wage, the wage itself being determined inside the very market being discussed.

Q: Before the founding of the state of Israel, the administrators of the British Mandate in Palestine prohibited more than a certain number of Jews from immigrating. The number was increasingly lower than the number who wished to immigrate, with terrible consequences. One reason given for restricting immigration was that more than a small number would flood the labor market and result in unemployment. That is, the British believed that there were just so many slots in the economy: to pour more people into the given slots would be irresponsible and foolish. Comment.

A: The belief is another example of the tragedy of Palestine, in this case a tragedy complicated by mistaken economics. If jobs were slots, the British would have been right. But jobs are not slots. Jobs exist because at the going wage employers wish to hire people in that number. If there are more people, by the usual workings of supply and demand the wage will fall to induce employers to take up more of the workers. If more immigrants came the wage would fall. Perhaps this is what the British truly feared: impoverishment of the existing population. In the event, Israel came into existence, Jews poured into Israel in large numbers, and unemployment turned out to be in fact small and diminishing.

An example closer to home, if your home is the United States, is the minimum wage. According to the law most employers are not permitted to pay anyone less than some amount per hour.

Q: Use supply and demand curves to begin an analysis of the effects of the minimum wage, supposing for the present that the supply curve is perfectly inelastic.

A: Simply treat the labor market like any other, such as wheat. If the price of wheat is supported by law, then there will be "unemployed" wheat, that is, a surplus of wheat produced over what is consumed. Likewise with labor. If the wage is supported by law, then there will be a surplus of labor, unemployment. The hour that is worth $1.00 will not be used if an hour must by law be paid $4.00. As usual in economic arguments, the point is made clearer by going to an extreme. Suppose that the minimum were $50.00 an hour. In that case only doctors and master plumbers would have jobs. The rest of us would be prevented by the state from engaging in an exchange with our employer. I may be willing to work for $6.00 an hour; my employer may be willing to pay me the $6.00 for the hour; but the state forbids the deal. The victim of such interference may be forgiven for wondering at the state's claim to be forbidding the deal to protect the very worker who thereby loses the job. In any event, a worker whose value to the employer is less than the minimum wage per hour simply does not get employed. By contrast, if jobs were fixed slots, then the demand curve for workers would be inelastic, and the low-value worker would be hired. But if jobs are *not* fixed slots (and they are not), then the minimum wage forces the company up its demand curve and the low-value worker is not hired. The result in aggregate is as portrayed in Figure 22.3.

**Figure 22.3
The Minimum Wage
Causes Unemployment**

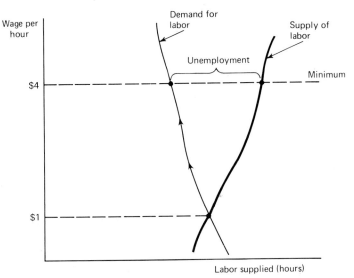

At a wage allowed to reach $1 an hour, the supply of labor equals the demand. If the wage is held at $4 an hour, however, the quantity supplied is higher and the quantity demanded is lower, leaving unemployment as indicated.

The usual example of the effect in action is unemployment among teenagers. Present company excepted, teenagers are on the whole less reliable, prompt, responsible, strong, and skilled than adult workers. They are therefore, by the logic of derived demand, less useful to, say, a manufacturing company. They are not worthless, but worth less. A minimum wage would therefore be expected to cause disproportionate unemployment among teenagers. It does.

Comment

The assertion that the minimum wage causes unemployment and especially that it causes it among teenagers is controversial. It is fair to say that most economists believe the assertion.[3] But some do not believe it, on various grounds. One line of counterargument is that the minimum wage encourages

[3] In J. R. Kearl, Clayne L. Pope, Gordon C. Whiting, and Larry T. Wimmer, "A Confusion of Economists," *American Economic Review* 69 (May 1979): 28–37, it was found that 68% of economists "generally agreed" with the proposition that "A minimum wage increases unemployment among young and unskilled workers," 22% agreed with some provisions (see the text following), and only 10% flatly disagreed.

businesses to improve the machinery, buildings, materials, and other things workers work with to justify the higher wage paid. It is argued that an unskilled worker pushing a broom is not as valuable as the same worker pushing a $1500 automatic broom-mop-waxer. There is an element of confusion in the argument, for it must be admitted that, if it were good for the economy to invest in such automatic equipment before the minimum wage, the economy might well have done so already; and if it were bad for the economy, it is strange to argue that the investment thus induced artificially by the minimum wage is a good thing. Another and more persuasive line of argument, which will be taken up again in Section 25.2, is that working conditions will adjust to offset the higher wages. A slow janitor at $2.00 an hour is no better bargain to the employer than a fast one at, say, $5.00. The company that hires the janitor will be willing to pay the higher price if it can specify that the janitors rush around at top speed. A faster pace of work or a greater degree of self-supervision or a higher standard of precision might all tend to compensate for the higher wage paid. This line of argument, however, has the same fault as the first. True as it may be, it does not necessarily justify the minimum wage, for the mix of wages and conditions that existed before the state intervened in exchange presumably had some desirable feature, or else they would already have been bargained away. In the end the argument in favor of the minimum wage must come down to a simple distaste for the result of exchange in the absence of intervention. The feeling is that we simply should not tolerate anyone in a job so undignified that it was worth only $2.00 an hour. Better that such people be supported by the rest of us, or even starve, than that they be required to work at such a job.

A less controversial example of the same point, familiar from Chapter 15, is the following.

T or F: That employers are required by law to pay half of the cost of social security taxes is irrelevant to the real burden of the tax.

A: The employers have a downward-sloping demand for labor. The demand price is what they are willing to pay for an additional hour of work in view of what the hour can earn for them in profits. But if their share of the tax is, say, 5% of the wages they pay, they will get 5% less profit, and their willingness to pay falls by 5%. The 5% imposed "on" employers results in a fall in the demand for labor by employers as a group. But the fall in demand results in a fall in the wage, as the intersection of supply and demand moves back down along the supply curve. Fewer workers are employed at a lower wage than before the tax was imposed "on" the employers. In short, true. The workers bear some of the burden. The 50:50 split of the tax between workers and employers is irrelevant for answering the question of who really bears the burden. What are relevant, as is always the case in such problems of supply and demand, are the elasticities of supply and demand and the total size of the tax, regardless of how it is apportioned legally among participants in the market.

Summary

The leading point is that firms have demand curves. That such an extension of the law of demand should have so many applications will come as no surprise. The law of demand would win a prize for the fact we all know with the most surprising consequences. On a formal level, the law of demand for firms serves to close the economy, giving households somewhere to earn the income that they spend in other markets on the products of firms. At a somewhat more substantive level, the result is that all the machinery of demand and supply curves applies to labor markets. The real surprises come from the proposition that firms buy labor in order to use it, not to admire it. That is, unlike the demand of households, the demand of firms for what they demand is "derived." The violation of this proposition gives a way of analyzing discrimination in the labor market. Its fulfilment gives a way of looking at all manner of ersatz economics that speaks of jobs as slots, such as the examination of labor "requirements" and the belief in the power of acts of Congress raising the wage to benefit working people. What remains is to understand the derivation of the firm's demand more deeply.

QUESTIONS FOR SECTION 22.1

1. One interpretation of the arrangements in early nineteenth-century England for aiding the poor (the so-called "old Poor Law") is that they applied money from taxing farmers to subsidizing the employment of poor people in the hire of the same farmers. The chief objections to the arrangement were two. First, it made the workers less dependent on the farmer for their income and more dependent on the state (in this case the local government of the village), thus undermining the respect of workers for their employers. Second, it reduced the effort of the workers, by enriching them. Decide which if any of these two propositions is correct by analyzing the old Poor Law in terms of the supply and demand for agricultural labor. Assume that the demand curve was unaffected by the tax (an argument can be made that it was not).

2. Private schools in Chicago often complain that the large increases in the wages of public school teachers increase the wages the private schools have to pay their teachers.

a. One conceivable method of hiring public school teachers in Chicago would be to announce a wage and to hire all qualified teachers who applied. If this were the method, would the complaint be true or false?

b. One interpretation of the actual method of hiring public school teachers is that the demand curve of the public schools is perfectly inelastic (they "need" N thousand), entry to employment is limited to N thousand (all being members of the teacher's union), the wage is held above the market clearing price, and increases in wages are granted in response to the political power and strike threats of the union. Under this interpretation is the complaint of the private schools true or false?

c. An alternative interpretation is that the union chooses a wage to demand this year, the public school system accepts the wage, but decides that at the higher wage it needs fewer teachers (average class sizes rise, teachers of calculus and football are dropped, etc.). Now is the complaint true?

3. Bumper sticker: "30 Hours Work for 40 Hours Pay Means More Jobs." Comment.

True or False

4. In Japan, workers cannot be fired once they have been hired, and therefore in Japan a minimum wage law would not cause unemployment.

5. Effective minimum wages in trucking increase the demand for truck-driving schools, which are good substitutes for on-the-job training.

22.2 Marginal Productivity as the Demand for Labor by the Firm

□
The Production Function Tells How Much Input Is Required for Profit- Maximizing Output

A deeper understanding of the demand for labor requires another use of that many-purpose idea, the production function. A lumber firm produces lumber to sell. The output of lumber, says the production function, is a function of the inputs of forests, tractors, and lumberjacks. Since the output depends on the input, the firm can be viewed either as choosing output (then looking around for the inputs to produce it) or as choosing inputs (then looking around for a place to sell the output). Clearly it does not matter which end of the stick one picks up. The following argument picks up the stick at the factor-of-produc- tion end, asking how the firm decides how much of various factors to demand to maximize profit. The problem is analogous, in other words, to the earlier characterization of the firm as deciding how much output to produce to maximize profit. One view suppresses some details in the firm's decision of how much to produce; the other suppresses some details in the firm's decision of how much labor and so forth to hire. The underlying problem—maximize profits—is the same.

If the lumber firm employs forest land, tractor capital, and lumberjack labor, it has three decisions to make that amount to the "single" deci- sion of how much lumber to produce and how (that is, with what recipe of inputs) to make it in order to make as much money as possible. Clearly it will make all three decisions about hiring the three factors of production in the best way it can; and equally clearly these three decisions are connected to each other. It simplifies the argument, how- ever, to ignore for the moment that the firm has three decisions and to concentrate on the hiring of one factor, which may be thought of as lumberjack labor or as inputs in general. In other words, take for the moment the inputs of other factors of production—forest land and labor—as fixed and given to the firm.

The upshot of the simplification is that output depends only on the amount of lumberjack input. That is, one can draw a diagram with output of wood on the vertical axis and inputs of lumberjack hours on the horizontal. The diagram, which appears in the top panel of Figure 22.4, is the diagram of the section on the cost curves of a firm but is here placed on its other side: instead of relating output to the inputs necessary (and thence to costs), it relates the inputs to

**Figure 22.4
The Demand Curve for
Labor Comes from the
Production Function and
the Going Price of Lumber**

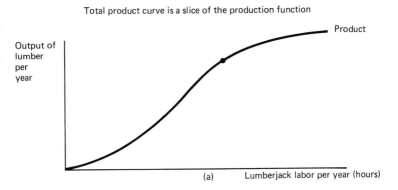

Total product curve is a slice of the production function

Output of lumber per year

Product

(a) Lumberjack labor per year (hours)

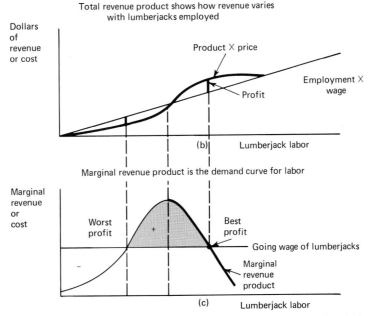

Total revenue product shows how revenue varies
with lumberjacks employed

Dollars of revenue or cost

Product × price

Profit

Employment × wage

(b) Lumberjack labor

Marginal revenue product is the demand curve for labor

Marginal revenue or cost

Worst profit

+

Best profit

Going wage of lumberjacks

Marginal revenue product

−

(c) Lumberjack labor

The top panel is a slice of the production function. The middle panel multiplies the slice by the price of lumber to get the total revenue product. The bottom panel is the slope of it to be set against the marginal cost of labor (the going wage) to maximize profit.

the output produced (and thence to revenue). You are by now familiar with the diagrammatic techniques that allow one to pass from panel to panel down the diagram. The top panel exhibits diminishing returns to employment of the lumberjacks. Notice how the curve becomes flat eventually, indicating that the employment of still more lumberjacks after a great many have been hired to work on one stretch of forest with a given set of tractors and power saws bears little fruit in additional lumber produced. And notice the upward curve at low numbers employed, indicating that at first each additional lumberjack bears great fruit in additional lumber produced.

The second panel merely multiplies the top one by the going price of lumber. The lumbering firm is supposed to be perfectly competitive in the market in which it sells lumber; that is, it is supposed to have no influence over the price it faces, which is to say that the price is indeed given. Naturally, multiplying the product curve by a price that does not vary as does the employment of lumberjacks (and therefore the output of the firm) is going to have the same characteristic S shape as the product curve does. The resulting curve is one of total revenue, because it is quantity produced multiplied by the price at which it is sold. One can then draw on the logic of marginal and average curves to infer what the curves in the bottom panel must look like. The curve is called the *marginal revenue product of labor.* The total revenue product is the middle panel, that is, the revenue produced from various different levels of employment of lumberjacks. The marginal revenue product is simply a plot of the slopes of the total revenue product. In accord with the S shape of the total product curve, it rises at first, reaches a maximum, then falls.

The emphasized portion of the marginal revenue curve is the downward-sloping portion. It is the firm's demand curve for labor, under the assumption ruling for the moment that other factors are fixed in amounts. The reason it is the demand curve may be seen by introducing a going wage for lumberjacks, say, $10 per hour and asking how much labor the firm will hire. The answer will be the demand curve, for that is what a demand curve is: the amount of X demanded at various different prices of X. The marginal revenue curve is evidently the marginal benefit to the firm from hiring an additional hour of labor (or at least it is if the firm does not, in the style of a racial discriminator, get pleasure or pain beyond profit from hiring the hour). The wage is the marginal cost. The rule of rational life suggests that the firm will do as well as it can by choosing the amount of hiring that brings the two into equality, namely, at the point best profit. The point *is* one of best profit. The area under the curve of marginal revenue product is the total revenue, because the curve is marginal to the total revenue curve. The area under the going wage is the total cost, because the wage multiplied by the amount hired is the labor cost, and the rest of the costs are by assumption fixed. It is obvious that the area between the marginal revenue and marginal cost reaches a maximum at best profit, the area marked with a plus offsetting the area marked with a minus. Any point on the rising portion of the marginal revenue product curve, such as worst profit, would be irrational. Therefore the demand curve is the falling portion.

☐
The Equation of Marginal Productivity

In the simplest case, in which the firm is a perfect competitor in both the lumber market and in the lumberjack market, the algebra corresponding to the diagrams takes on a particularly simple and revealing form. Call the amount that an extra lumberjack hour produces the *marginal physical product of labor,* or MPP_L. Call the (unchanging) price that the firm gets for each unit of the extra amount of lumber P. Call the wage, which is the cost of the extra hour, w. Then the profit the firm makes on the additional hour will be the price times the marginal physical product (often called the "value of the marginal product") minus the wage: hiring another hour causes the output and therefore the revenue and profit to go up by something, but it also causes the cost of production to go up by something. The "somethings" are the terms in the expression $(P \times MPP_L) - w$. The expression measures the increments to profit from hiring another hour. Evidently, the firm will make the most profit when no more profit is to be made by pushing hiring further. That is, profit will be at a maximum when $(P \times MPP_L) - w$ equals zero, or in other words when $P \times MPP_L = w$. When the wage equals the value of the marginal product, the firm stops hiring more labor.

The theory is called the *theory of marginal productivity*. It asserts that firms are willing to pay at most the dollar value of the marginal increment to product that the hiring of an additional lumberjack hour or machine or acre or lump of coal produces. Inputs are valued, in other words, not for their total product—not for how much lumber would be lost if all the hours of lumberjacks quit work—but for their marginal product—the lumber that would be lost if one alone quit work. Since one lumberjack hour is fungible with all others, all must receive this same marginal product. As the expression goes, the hourly wage of lumberjacks is *determined at the margin*. In this respect as in many others the theory of the demand for inputs is identical to the theory of the demand for products by consumers: the value of the marginal utility (the marginal valuation) determines the price at which a consumer will buy; the value of the marginal product determines the price at which a firm will buy. The argument is innocuous, even boring, until one realizes that alternative theories of value underlie the sentiments of the man in the street.

T or F: Garbage collectors should be paid $100,000, because the city would collapse in a stinking heap if the garbage collectors did not collect.

A: The total product, or the product taken away if all labor is taken away, does not determine economic value. It may determine moral value. That is, one may believe that such an argument implies that garbage collectors ought to be paid a lot, on moral grounds. But it does not determine observed economic value in a freely functioning marketplace. The marginal product of one extra garbage collector determines economic value, and this is at present well below $100,000. In short, false.

T or F: The price paid for water is no indication of its true value in use because the water makes the production of additional wealth possible. Thus a farmer may pay $8 for water for one acre of his land, yet the value of the crop grown on that land might be $100.

A: The $92 pays the other factors of production necessary to make the irrigation have more use than merely an expensive humidifying system. The marginal value product of the water is still $8, *its* marginal contribution. Therefore, false.

In a sense the firm is indifferent between hiring or not hiring the last worker or the last gallon of water or the last input of anything. The last worker is paid exactly what he or she contributes to revenue.

Q: Joe Namath (a famous football player) retires from the New York Jets (a famous football team) and begins to play for the Shreveport Steamer (another football team, *not* famous). The stock in the Shreveport Steamer rises in value and the stock in the New York Jets falls. Joe Namath was and is earning less than his marginal revenue product.

A: True. If he was earning his marginal revenue product, owners of either team (the stockholders) would be indifferent between keeping Namath or letting him go, because Namath's contribution to their profit would be zero (*he* would be receiving the contribution he made to the net revenues of the teams).

☐
Marginal Productivity Is a Theory of Distribution

In the manner of all marginal curves, the area under the curve of marginal product is the total product. The total revenue of the firm must be divided up in some way between labor and the other factors of production. If a lumber firm accords with the theory of marginal productivity, the division will be accomplished as shown in Figure 22.5.

The heavily outlined area is the total product. The rectangular area marked wL_E is just that: the wage multiplied by the amount of labor in equilibrium. Since it is the income to labor, the shaded triangular area must be the income to any other factors of production such as

**Figure 22.5
Marginal Productivity Is a
Theory of Distribution**

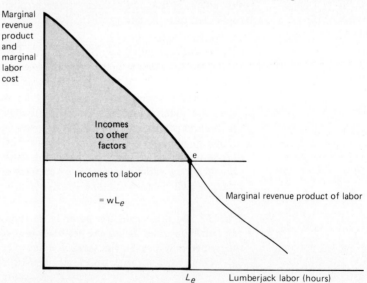

The whole trapezoidal area under the curve of marginal revenue product out to the equilibrium amount of labor is the total product. Subtracting out the rectangle of income to labor leaves the shaded triangle as the income of nonlabor factors. Marginal productivity, in other words, tells how income in total is divided up among those who make it.

land or capital. In other words, the theory of marginal productivity implies a particular distribution of the total product between labor and other factors.

☐

It Is a Theory of Profit

The triangular area is equivalent to consumer's surplus, the consumer in this case being the firm and the product being the labor hired. The other factors of production, such as land and capital, can be lumped together as fixed, owned factors, the reward to which the firm is trying to maximize. With such an interpretation, the triangular area becomes the profit. The interpretation is natural: just as consumer's surplus gives a measure of the total gains from trade to the consumer, so too profit (which is an analogous area) gives a measure of the total gains from trade to the firm. In view of the analogy, it is not surprising that the case in favor of free trade among firms involves the same diagram as the case for free trade among nations. Big firms such as Sears or General Motors, for instance, are often faced with the question of whether to buy an input (such as advertising or computing services) from the market (imports) or from one of their own subsidiaries (domestic supply). Since the subsidiaries earn profit for the mother firm, one might suppose that it would be desirable always to buy internally. But to suppose so would be to make the same mistake as in the false argument for keeping our business to ourselves as against trading with the Japanese. Clearly it is desirable for Sears to buy advertising from its own advertising division up to the point at which the rising marginal cost of the advertising reaches the price of advertising in the open market. Any further advertising, however, should be purchased in the open market, not taken from the now more expensive internal source.

Q: Draw the demand curve for advertising by Sears and the rising marginal cost for the Sears advertising subsidiary as more advertising is taken by Sears. Draw the market price of advertising (a horizontal line to Sears, assumed to be a small buyer of advertising). At what point should Sears start using outside advertising firms? At this point, what is the "profit" earned by Sears (i.e., the income earned by all factors other than advertising)? Make sure that you include the profit earned by Sears's own advertising division (viewing it as supplier's surplus). What would Sears's equilibrium amount of advertising and of "profit" be if Sears had a policy of making as much money as possible, but never using outside advertising? What would they be if Sears had a policy of making as much money as possible, but permitting itself to buy outside advertising?

A: Sears starts using outside advertising at the point start in Figure 22.6. The profit at that point is the area A, which is the consumer's surplus (so to speak) accruing to Sears as a buyer of advertising (from itself) plus the area B, which is the producer's surplus accruing to Sears as a seller of advertising (to itself). Sears's equilibrium point under the incorrect policy of forbidding outside advertising would be at autarky, with profits $A + B + C$. Sears could clearly do better by buying foreign advertising. The better equilibrium would be free trade, with more advertising bought and more profits (in

the amount of the shaded area, *D).* Notice that the question and the problem
is at bottom the same as an earlier one on the cost curves of American
Motors in making or buying crankshafts. The present problem concerns
the maximization of product; the earlier problem concerned the minimization
of cost. They are two sides of the same coin.

**Figure 22.6
The Maximization of Profit
Entails Seeking out the
Lowest-Cost Supplier**

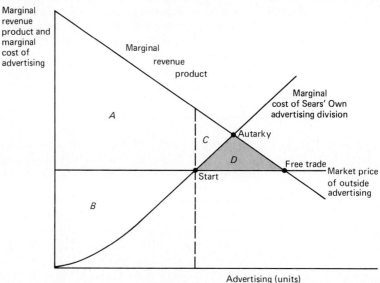

Like a nation considering whether to make its own automobiles or to buy them from the
Japanese, Sears does best by allowing itself to buy outside advertising services rather than
requiring that all its divisions buy advertising exclusively from Sears itself. The gain from
this cosmopolitan policy is the shaded area, *D.*

**And It Is a Theory of
National Income
Distribution**

The total product to be distributed to different factors can be the whole
national product as well. If other factors such as land and capital are
taken as fixed in amount, at least in the short run, then the marginal
product of the labor force of 1900 in producing American national
product in 1900 determines the prevailing wage (ignore the dashed
lines in Figure 22.7 for a moment).

The 1900 existing supply leads to the 1900 real wage. Notice that,
for economywide problems, it usually makes more sense to express
the equilibrium condition (and the diagram corresponding) as $w/p =
MPP_L$ instead of $w = P \times MPP_L$. In contrast to the situation of a
single firm, neither the money wage nor the money price of national
product is given from outside the nation. Only their ratio is determined
by marginal productivity. Notice too that the units work out correctly:
w/p is dollars per person divided by dollars per ton of product, which
reduces to physical tons per person, in keeping with the marginal physical product to which it is equal.

The diagram can be used to think about the effects of America's
policy in 1900 of free immigration (for healthy Europeans with ortho-

Figure 22.7
Free Trade in Labor Is
Good for Average
National Income

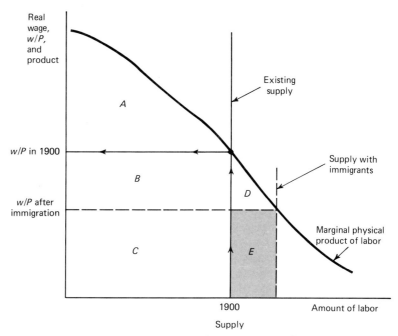

The increase from the existing supply of labor in 1900 to the supply with immigrants would cause the real wage to fall and the capitalists to be enriched at the expense of the workers in the amount of area *B*. The immigrants themselves receive area *E*. But area *D* accrues to former Americans, albeit American capitalists. Income of the former Americans increases by *D*.

dox political opinions). Between 1900 and 1910, 13.4 million people immigrated to the United States, a 15% increase in the population.

Q: 1. In Figure 22.7 identify the income earned by the existing supply of labor in 1900.

2. What is the whole national income? What is the income earned by nonlabor factors, such as capital and land?

3. Notice the supply with immigrants. How much do the immigrant laborers earn?

4. How does the coming of the immigrants affect the income earned by the laborers who were in America before immigration?

5. How does the coming of the immigrants affect the income earned by American capitalists and landlords?

6. What is the income earned after immigration by *all* former Americans (excluding what the immigrants themselves earned)—laborers, capitalists, and landlords together? Does immigration on the whole hurt or help nonimmigrant Americans?

A: 1. The income earned by labor in 1900 is area *B* + *C*.

2. The whole national income is *A* + *B* + *C*, which is to say that area *A* is earned by nonlabor factors.

3. The immigrants earn the lowered marginal product, getting in total the shaded area E for their trouble.

4. The coming of the immigrants lowers the marginal product of labor, effectively transferring the area B from former American workers to former American capitalists and landlords. It should be pointed out here that real wages did not in fact fall from 1900 to 1914, but rose sharply. Other things were happening, however. The thought experiment asks what the effect of immigration in isolation was.

5. To the delight of capitalists and landlords, their income grows by area B and by D (D being their earnings as capitalists and landlords on the hiring of immigrants).

6. In other words, the income of former Americans, once $A + B + C$, is after immigration $A + B + C + D$. It has risen by D. Immigration hurts the factor with which it competes (unskilled labor in the case in question), helps the other factors, and helps the other factors more, leaving a net gain to the whole of income.

Summary

The demand for labor by the profit-maximizing firm is related to the production function of the firm. To be precise, the demand curve is the marginal revenue product curve, derived from the total product curve. The theory is called marginal productivity and is closely analogous to the theory of marginal utility in consumption. In both, the amounts bought are determined by marginal, not total or average, valuation. The price of labor determines through the marginal revenue product curve the amount purchased by a firm; the amount of labor determines through the marginal physical product curve the real wage of labor. Both versions of the argument are widely applicable, to questions of the desirability of buying advertising from other firms, for example, or the desirability of buying citizens from other countries.

QUESTIONS FOR SECTION 22.2

1. It is said that in poor countries, especially in agriculture, the population is so large that labor is surplus, that people work at conventionally defined jobs, but that the marginal worker does not in fact add anything to income or that at best adds something less than what he or she is paid. In 1918–1919 India was struck by famine and, worse, by a flu epidemic that killed 5 million people. If the strong form of the surplus labor hypothesis is true (the marginal worker adds nothing), what would have happened to agricultural output? If the weak form is true (the marginal worker adds something, but less than his wage), what would have happened? In fact, agricultural output fell roughly by the amount of the wages paid to the workers killed. What do you conclude about the plausibility of the surplus labor hypothesis?

2. Suppose the production function in some industry is a Leontief or *fixed coefficient* function, namely, $Q =$ minimum of αL or βK, where L is the amount of labor, K the amount of capital, and α and β constants. What do the isoquants look like? For some given amount of K, what does the marginal product of labor look like?

True or False

3. If the total product curve did not bend downward (exhibiting diminishing marginal returns to additional inputs of labor, given other factors), then firms would specialize in hiring labor.

4. Since workers are paid their marginal product, shooting half of them would not affect the income of the rest of society.

23 | Marginal Productivity in Theory and in Use

23.1 Many Inputs, Constant Returns to Scale, and the Fundamental Theorem

□

Deciding on Many Inputs at Once Is a Problem in Simultaneous Equations

The relation between labor's marginal revenue product and its supply curve, then, determines how much labor a lumbering firm wants to hire. But of course similar considerations determine how much advertising or land or coal or machinery a firm wants to hire. One can view the firm as looking at the curves for each input and making a decision for each. The curves for each input are related to each other. The marginal product of lumberjack 100, for example, is obviously higher in a lumbering operation covering 10,000 rather than 10 acres, or having 12 caterpillar tractors rather than 1. The decisions to hire lumberjacks, forest land, and tractors should therefore be made simultaneously. But the analysis so far can simply be extended to three factors at once. The statement that the marginal revenue product for labor is related to the amounts of land and capital available amounts to saying that land and capital as well as labor appear in the algebraic expression for labor's marginal revenue product. The expression could take many forms, depending on the shape of the production function connecting output with the inputs of factors. The most general way of putting the matter is simply to note that MRP is some function of L, T (in French, *terre*, meaning land), and K. The marginal conditions are three:

1. $MRP_L(L, T, K) = w$

2. $MRP_T(L, T, K) = r$

3. $MRP_K(L, T, K) = iP$

in which each of the subscripts serves to specify a different mathematical form (in other words, MRP_L and MRP_T may be different forms, the one containing a squared T, for example, the other not). To each of these equations corresponds a marginal productivity diagram in which a marginal revenue product curve is set against a (flat) marginal factor cost curve. The w is the wage, r the rent (per acre, say), and iP is the annual cost of repaying the loan at $i\%$ per year on the P dollars necessary to buy a machine. The generalization of the procedure

484

of moving out to the point of equality of the marginal revenue product of labor and its price is to solve the three equations simultaneously.

☐

The Exhaustion of the Product

The extension of the argument to more than one factor brings up a problem that long bothered economists, namely, *problem of the exhaustion of the product.* The problem is that there does not appear to be any reason why satisfaction of the three equations by a firm would result in spending all and only the money that came in. A simplified farm, say, with two factors, land and labor, producing wheat and paying each acre and hour at its marginal product in wheat might over- or undercommit the wheat produced. The wheat crop per year might be 10,000 bushels, but the claims for rents and wages might be higher, 15,000 bushels; or the claims might be 7000, leaving 3000 unclaimed. A theory of distribution that left such large amounts undistributed would not be much of a theory.

☐

Production Functions That Overexhaust the Product

It is no trick at all to draw or to write down in algebraic form a production function for which rewarding factors by marginal products does not exactly exhaust the product. For example, suppose that wheat output, Q, were equal to TL, where T is the number of acres of land employed and L is the number of hours of labor employed. The equation appears to be perfectly ordinary and acceptable. Let us see, however, whether the output is just exhausted if labor and land are rewarded by marginal productivity. How much would output increase if one more hour of labor came to be employed? Well, with the production function being TL, the rate of increase of output is evidently T, the amount of acres: one can view the equation $Q = TL$ as a proportional equation in L, with the coefficient T being 100, for example, when 100 acres are in use; from $Q = 100L$ it is clear that each additional hour produces an output of 100. The marginal product of each hour is in this example therefore whatever T happens to be, which means that all the hours (L in amount) will earn in total TL if they are paid their original product. But TL is the whole output! There is nothing left to reward land (which indeed by the same argument itself demands the whole output for its reward).

Not every conceivable production function fails, however. For example, if $Q = T + L$, then rewarding land and labor by marginal product exhausts the product, neither more nor less. Output increases in this equation by 1 when L increases by one unit, since 1 (and not T as before) is the coefficient in front of L. The marginal product that each hour is paid will therefore be 1. In consequence the total payment to labor will be $1 \times L$ and to land $1 \times T$. Adding them up does indeed just equal the whole output, $Q = L + T$.

☐

Constant Returns to Scale Prevents Over- or Underexhaustion

The production functions that do not fail, it turns out, have one feature alone in common: they all exhibit constant returns to scale. Constant returns to scale, you will recall, is the tidy-sounding condition that when all inputs double the resulting output also exactly doubles— not triples or rises by 50%, but doubles. In the special case of an output produced by one output alone, it is easy to see why constant

**Figure 23.1
Constant Returns Exactly
Exhaust the Product: The
Case of One Input**

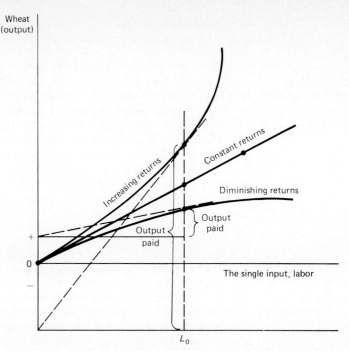

Since the marginal product is the slope of the total product curve, paying the only factor its marginal product would yield an output paid larger than the output made in the case of increasing returns and smaller in the case of diminishing returns.

returns would imply that the production function for wheat was a straight line through the origin, not increasing or diminishing returns in Figure 23.1.

Were the input at the level L_o, the low slope (i.e., the marginal product) along diminishing returns would imply that less than all the output would be paid out; along increasing returns the high slope would imply that more than all the output would be paid out. Only for constant returns is the output paid out equal to the output produced.

□
*Constant Returns in
the Two-Input Case*

In the more general case of two inputs, the idea of constant returns is captured geometrically by the following restriction. Imagine a production function rising out of the corner near the floor of your room, the right edge of the room near the floor being the labor axis, the left the land axis, and the corner of walls being the third axis, measuring output. The hill of production thus imagined could have any shape. But suppose that it has a shape that could be generated by sticking a rod through the zero point (the floor corner of the room) and rotating it through this zero point around the room in any way whatsoever. Every place through which the rod passed (one piece of the rod fixed at the origin always) would be the surface of the hill. The resulting surface exhibits constant returns to scale, as can be shown quite easily. Moving along any one position of the rod—going, say, from the floor corner to where your left thumbnail is now—the inputs of labor and land are increasing in some identical proportion (straight lines through the origin are lines of proportion). At the same time output is increasing by the same proportion. Therefore, as was to be shown, constant returns holds.

If you start the rod lying along the right floor edge of the room, rotating it in a smooth arc up toward the ceiling and then down to the left edge, the production function will have all the nice qualities known as "neoclassical"—output will be zero, for example, when any one of the inputs is zero (because the rod is on the floor—at zero output—when it is on either edge). Because the arc is smooth, the function will everywhere have well-behaved slopes (marginal products). Because the arc rises and then falls instead of snaking or jerking through the air, the isoquants, or contour lines on the hill of production, will have a normal shape, convex to the origin. Finally, to repeat, since the surface of the hill is made up of rays through the origin, the production function exhibits constant returns to scale.

It is not instantly obvious why constant returns as expressed in the geometric condition causes the product to be exhausted by rewards of marginal products. But it does suggest very strongly that the many-input case is analogous to the single-input case (in which it *is* obvious why the product is exactly exhausted: look at the diagram), the notion being that a moving rod is merely a generalization of a single ray through the origin.

□
The Algebra of Constant Returns

The corresponding algebra is necessary for later applications, and in fact exhaustion of the product is a theorem in this algebra. The theorem requires calculus (given in the appendix to this section), but the simple algebra at least makes precisely clear what is being asserted by exhaustion. A production function that is supposed to exhibit constant returns should have output doubling when all inputs do. For instance $Q = L + T$ does: if L and T are replaced by $2L$ and $2T$, the result is $2L + 2T = 2(L + T) = 2Q$, and as required output also doubles.

Q: Does $Q = LT$ exhibit constant returns?

A: Replacing L and T by $2L$ and $2T$ leads to $(2L)(2T) = 4(LT) = 4Q$, not $2Q$ as required. Therefore, the function exhibits increasing, not constant, returns to scale.

More generally, if some function F in $Q = F(L, T)$ exhibits constant returns, then multiplying all the inputs by some number λ will result in a rise in Q in the same proportion. That is, $F(\lambda L, \lambda T) = \lambda^1 Q$. The exponent of 1 on λ is meant to emphasize that such functions are *homogeneous of degree 1*, which is mathematical jargon for constant returns to scale. An exponent of 2 instead of 1 would indicate that the function exhibited increasing returns to scale, being homogeneous of a degree greater than 1 (namely, 2). A rough way of determining the degree of homogeneity is to treat all the different variables as the same, multiply them as indicated by the function, and examine the exponent on the resulting variable.

Q: Is $Q = LT$ homogeneous of degree 1?

A: If L and T were the same the equation would be L^2 (or T^2). The exponent 2 is not 1. Therefore, false.

☐
The Cobb–Douglas Production Function

The most famous example of a degree 1 homogeneous function is the *Cobb–Douglas production function*, named after an Amherst mathematics professor Cobb and a University of Chicago economics professor (later U.S. senator) Paul Douglas, who attempted in 1934 to fit it to the facts of the American economy 1919–1922.[1] The result was an equation such as $Q = AL^{3/4}K^{1/4}$, where A is a constant representing the height of the production function (that is, efficiency in the usual sense), L is the amount of labor, and K the amount of capital.

Q: Is the function homogeneous of degree 1?

A: If L and K were made identical, the equation would be $Q = AL^{3/4 + 1/4} = AL^1$, the exponent being 1 as required. Therefore, yes. The Cobb–Douglas function with exponents summing to 1 is homogeneous of degree 1.

Q: Does the more general version of the Cobb–Douglas production function, $Q = AL^{\alpha}K^{\beta}$, in which $\alpha + \beta$ do not necessarily sum to 1, always exhibit constant returns to scale?

A: The equation with K and L made identical would be $Q = AL^{\alpha+\beta}$, in which $\alpha + \beta$ need not be 1. Therefore, no, the function does not always exhibit constant returns to scale.

☐
Why Constant Returns and Marginal Productivity Exhaust the Product

The exhaustion of the product is assured by *Euler's theorem on homogeneous functions*, which essentially asserts directly that exhaustion is true for functions constructed of rays through the origin, that is, homogeneous of degree 1. A proof of Euler's theorem using calculus, which involves some mathematics important for later applications, is given in the appendix. A pretty geometrical proof goes as follows. Imagine a hill of production for Q as a function of K and L, $K(K, L)$ coming out of the corner of your room. For the moment it may be any shape, whether constant returns or not. Pick a point on the hill that is a particular pair of K' and L' and the corresponding Q'. Now imagine a plane tangent to the hill at the point. For reasons that will soon be clear, it is desirable to know the algebraic equation for the tangent plane. The equation can be built up by asking what happens to Q as one moves away from the initial amounts of capital and labor, K' and L'. What happens evidently depends on the slope of the hill in the K and L directions, that is, on the marginal products of K and L, for these are the slopes of the tangent plane. In other words, if Q is initially $F(K', L') = Q'$, then the value of Q at some other combinations of capital and labor, say, simply K and L, will be $Q = Q' +$

[1] Paul H. Douglas, *The Theory of Wages* (New York: Macmillan, 1934), especially Chapter V.

$(MP_K)(K - K') + (MP_L)(L - L')$. The equation says that the new output along the plane is the old output plus the difference in capital multiplied by the difference it makes (its marginal product), plus a similar expression for labor. The equation is the equation for the tangent plane at $Q' = F(K', L')$, telling how much Q is along the plane for various choices of K and L. Now insert the geometry of homogeneity of degree 1 (constant returns). Suppose that the production hill exhibited constant returns. Then, since the hill would be made up of rods through the origin, some tangent plane at the origin would be the *same* tangent plane as one at some point not at the origin. In the equation, then, suppose that the initial point were in fact taken to be at the origin, that is, $Q' = 0$, $K' = 0$, $L' = 0$. Making these substitutions in the equation leaves $Q = MP_K K + MPL$, which is, surprisingly, Euler's theorem. In short, one can construct a tangent plane going through the origin that applies to any other point one wishes, and because the plane is at the origin, it simplifies to Euler's theorem.

☐

How Can a Competitive Firm or a Varied Industry Have Constant Returns?

In short, if the production function exhibits constant returns to scale, then payment by marginal product just exhausts the product. But something is wrong. A firm that experienced constant returns, supposing that it faced elastic supplies of factors (i.e., fixed prices at which it could hire factors), would have a flat, not rising, marginal cost curve. And, as was shown in an earlier chapter on the firm, if a price-taking firm has a flat marginal cost curve, it will expand indefinitely (when the price of what it produces is greater than marginal cost) or contract to zero output (when the price is less than cost) or be indifferent among outputs (when the price is equal). None of these is very pleasing.

The response is something of a shell game, but it stiffles doubt. Suppose that all firms are identical but do not have production functions with constant returns everywhere. In full competitive equilibrium, however, each firm finds itself at the bottom of its average cost curve. If demand grows, another firm enters, keeping the supply price exactly at the minimum point of average cost. In other words, the whole industry has a cost curve that looks as if it came out of a constant returns production function. Indeed, at the precise point of competitive equilibrium, the average costs of each firm just exhaust its revenues (economic profits, or rents, are zero), suggesting the convenient fiction of thinking of each firm as being at the constant returns point of its individual production function. If the firms were not identical, some would be earning rents in equilibrium. But this deviation from a flat supply curve can be eliminated by assigning a name (*entrepreneurship*, say) to whatever it is about the firms that allows them to earn more profits. Their profits become, then, payments to the factor entrepreneurship, and voila! their underlying production functions are made to be identical and to exhibit constant returns. In other words, the argument moves from zero profits to constant returns, not in the other direction. Since profits are zero in competitive equilibrium, the product is just exhausted, and one can speak of "the" production function of either the firm or the industry as exhibiting constant returns.

The Fundamental Theorem of Marginal Productivity

□ Such flirting with tautology makes possible a useful tool, the *fundamental theorem* of *marginal productivity:* the share of costs actually paid to labor (or to capital or to whatever) in a competitive industry experiencing constant returns to scale is the elasticity of output with respect to labor (or capital or whatever). The proof goes as follows. For a competitive steel industry, say, the marginal value product of labor is simply the marginal physical product of labor multiplied by the going price of steel, since each company as a competitor believes that it will get the price (and not some marginal revenue lower than the price) if it expands output by one unit. According to the theory of marginal productivity, labor is hired up to the point where its wage, w, equals the marginal revenue product of labor, or, in this case, $w = P \times MPP_L$. The real wage, w/P, is therefore set equal to the rate of change of steel output with respect to labor inputs. Write out the equation in this form:

$$\frac{w}{p} = \frac{\Delta Q}{\Delta L} \ (= MPP_L)$$

Now multiply both sides by the workers used per ton of output (the inverse of output per worker):

$$\frac{L}{Q}\left(\frac{w}{P}\right) = \frac{L}{Q}\left(\frac{\Delta Q}{\Delta L}\right) = \frac{\Delta Q/Q}{\Delta L/L}$$

Notice the rewriting of the right-hand side. It is the elasticity of output with respect to the input labor. The left-hand side is the share of labor in total costs. That is,

$$\text{Share of labor} = \frac{wL}{PQ} = \frac{\Delta Q/Q}{\Delta L/L} = E_{Q(L)}$$
$$= \text{elasticity of output with respect to labor}$$

Uses of the Fundamental Theorem

□ Consider the following.

T or F: If the labor force in steel increased 10% and the share of labor in steel costs were 25%, output would increase 10%.

A: It would increase by the increase in the labor force multiplied by the elasticity of output with respect to labor. If steel is a constant returns industry, the companies can pay workers (and other inputs) the real value of their marginal product and survive. Therefore by the fundamental theorem of marginal productivity, the elasticity is 0.25 (one quarter) and the resulting increase is a quarter of 10%, (10%)(0.25) = 2.5%, not 10%. Therefore, false. Output increases less than any one input does if only that input is increasing. "Diminishing returns" applies to the application of more of one factor to fixed amounts of other factors, even if the production function exhibits *constant* returns *to scale* (i.e., to the application of more of every factor in the same proportion).

The reason that constant returns to scale is necessary for the fundamental theorem is that without it the payment of factors by marginal product will over- or undercommit the revenues available to pay costs, which means that the factors cannot really be paid their marginal products. The shares will have to be determined some other way. The shares resulting from this other way will not bear any relation to marginal product and therefore will not permit the algebra that led to the theorem.

The fundamental theorem is applicable to the output of an entire nation:

Q: It is often alleged that the United States is rich because of its land, rich in coal, oil, iron ore, and nutrients for plants. The share of land in American national income is well below 10%. How much would income fall if the riches of the land fell by 50%?

A: If the nation's production function can be thought of as exhibiting constant returns to scale, then the conditions of the fundamental theorem apply. Therefore, the fall would be $(50\%)(0.10) = 5\%$ at most. You should be suspicious of arguments that natural resources explain much of the differences in the wealth of nations.

Summary

The extension of marginal productivity to more than one factor of production is trivial. Instead of solving one equation, the firm solves—crudely, no doubt, and largely by rule of thumb—a set of simultaneous equations. But paying its marginal product to each factor does not always exactly use up the product, an embarrassing oversight in a theory of distribution. The one condition of the production function that assures exact exhaustion of the product is constant returns to scale, which amounts to the condition that the function be generated by pivoting a rod fixed at the origin. Constant returns can be reconciled with the diminishing returns necessary for equilibrium in the size of the firm by fixing attention on the long-run equilibrium at the minimum point of average cost and by introducing a background factor of production, entrepreneurship, units of which serve to define the firm. By these devices we are permitted to speak of an industry's production function exhibiting constant returns even if a firm's does not. And we are permitted to use the fundamental theorem of marginal productivity, namely, that an input's share in costs is the elasticity of output with respect to the input. An input with a small share is unimportant.

QUESTIONS FOR SECTION 23.1

1. Does the *constant elasticity of substitution production function,* $Q = (aK^{-\epsilon} + bL^{-\epsilon})^{-1/\epsilon}$, in which a, b, and ϵ are constants, exhibit constant returns to scale?

2. The differences around 1900 between the successes of German industry and the failures of British industry are often explained on grounds of differences in the quantity of entrepreneurship. Differences cannot have been very great, for only 30 years before it was British industry that was supposed to be superior in this regard. Suppose it is believed that in 1900 German entrepreneurs were effectively a third more numerous as British. Suppose, as appears to be the case, that the share of costs that could conceivably be attributed to entrepreneurship—as distinct from routine labor, capital, or land—was 10%. What is the greatest difference in output that can be explained by differences in entrepreneurship?

3. The elasticity of *output* with respect to the *quantity of an input* is the share of the input in cost. What is the elasticity of *cost* with respect to the *price* of the input? This is another example of duality.

4. In view of Question 3, if $Q = AL^\alpha K^{1-\alpha}$ is the Cobb–Douglas production function, what is the Cobb–Douglas cost function, which relates cost, c, to the prices of L (the wage, w) and of K (the rental rate, r)? Notice that output does not appear in it: it exhibits constant returns to scale.

True or False

5. In view of the fundamental theorem of marginal productivity, the coefficient α in the Cobb–Douglas production function, $Q = AL^\alpha K^{1-\alpha}$, is the share of labor in costs.

6. If the nation's output is produced by a Cobb–Douglas production function, then increases in the real wage of labor from increases in machinery per worker will not increase labor's share in national income.

7. The share of labor in the total costs of a nonprofit institution like a university is not the elasticity of output with respect to labor.

APPENDIX TO SECTION 23.1

The Proof of Euler's Theorem Using Calculus

Euler's theorem asserts that, for a first-degree homogeneous function, $K(MP_K) + L(MP_L) = Q$. The proof to follow calculates the marginal products, and from them shows that it is indeed true.

If F is homogeneous of degree 1 in K and L, then by definition $F(\lambda K, \lambda L) = \lambda Q$. Suppose you took λ to be $1/L$ (well, why not?). The result would be $F(K/L, L/L) = Q/L$, which says that the output per person, (Q/L), depends only on the *ratio* K/L, not on the absolute size of K or L separately. The result makes sense geometrically, since output per person is the slope relative to the L axis of a rod from the origin out to the point in question, and along any of the rods used to generate the production function the slope will of course not change, since a rod is a straight line no matter how you look at it. The whole output can therefore be written in a back-door manner as follows: $L(Q/L) = L[F(K/L, 1)] = Q$. Take the partial derivative of the middle expression for Q with respect to K alone to find the marginal product of K. The result is $\partial Q/\partial K = L(\partial F/\partial K)(1/L)$, by the function-of-a-function rule (K/L being the inside function, $F(\ )$ being the outside). The L's cancel, leaving $MP_K = \partial Q/\partial K = \partial F/\partial K$. That is, the marginal product of capital, as one might expect, is just the derivative of F.

In this way of putting it the F was a function of K/L alone, not K and L by themselves. So too, then, is its derivative. In consequence, for a production function homogeneous of degree 1, the marginal product of capital, $\partial Q/\partial K$, can be expressed as a function of K/L alone, not merely K and L separately. Only homogeneity of degree 1 allows one to draw a marginal product curve as a function of K/L alone, regardless of the absolute scale of the output.

What, then, is the other marginal product, MP_L? It is the partial derivative with respect to L of the total output expressed as $L[F(K/L, 1)]$, namely (by the derivative of a product rule),

$$MP_L = \frac{\partial}{\partial L}\left[L \times F\left(\frac{K}{L}, 1\right)\right] = F\left(\frac{K}{L}, 1\right) + LF_K\left(-\frac{K}{L^2}\right)$$

$$= F\left(\frac{K}{L}, 1\right) - F_K\left(\frac{K}{L}\right)$$

Notice that the derivative of F with respect to K appears in this because only the first, K, variable in F can change (the second, L, variable being equal to 1 all the time). The equation says that the marginal product of labor is output per person, $F(K/L, 1)$, minus the payment to capital, $F_K K$, per person (divided by L). Clearly this equation by itself is nearly Euler's theorem. In fact, if you multiply both sides by L, recognizing that F_K is indeed (by the earlier step) the marginal product of capital, the result is

$$L(MP_L) = L\left[F\left(\frac{K}{L}, 1\right)\right] - K(MP_K)$$

or, rearranging and noticing that L times the output per person is simply output,

$$Q = L(MP_L) + K(MP_K)$$

as required.

23.2 Changes in the Production Function

☐
***The Problem of
Detecting Different
Production
Functions***
The most fruitful use of the ideas of marginal productivity and the production function is in thinking about when they change. Our ancestors struggled with oxen and wooden ploughs to make wheat; we make ten bushels with the effort they expended on one. Steel before the 1850s was a luxury used in small quantities for sword blades; after the 1850s the cost of steel fell enough to make ploughs with it, and then ships and bridges. A computer that filled a building in 1950 can now be held in the palm of your hand and can be made for a thousandth of the cost. These are all cases of rising production functions, of getting more output for the same input of sweat and equipment and land.

It is often unclear whether two points are merely on different points of the same production function or truly on different production functions. For example, output per person was higher in America than in Britain around 1860. But it is an error to infer that American techniques were necessarily superior, because there are other factors of production besides labor to be brought into the accounting.

☐
***The Solution: The
Unit Isoquant***
A diagram with many uses will make the point. With constant returns to scale, the production function can be represented fully by one contour line, the contour line of a single unit of output (the unit isoquant), because 100 or 10,000 units are produced by scaling up the production of 1 unit.) If 10 laborers and 1 machine are used to produce 1 unit

of national income, 10,000 laborers and 1000 machines are used to produce 1000 units if production takes place without diminishing or increasing returns to scale. For example, if American national income were produced with labor and land in 1860, the American unit isoquant might be as pictured in Figure 23.2 (ignore the dashed lines for a moment).

With its abundant land relative to population in 1860, America might take up a position such as American point in the diagram, using the indicated (small) amount of labor and (large) amount of land to produce one unit of income. It might help make the argument more definite if you thought of income as bushels of wheat. Whether income or wheat, America takes up just one of many possible positions on the unit isoquant. The position it chooses is the one that its endowment of land and labor picks out, the slope of the tangent line being then the resulting price of labor relative to land. Alternatively, it can be thought of as the position that cost-minimizing industries are led to by the price of labor relative to land. At bad point for America, the same output would be produced, since the point is on the same isoquant as the American point, but at a higher cost, since a budget line with the correct slope would be farther out than at the American point.

As portrayed in the diagram, the British point is on the same production function. True, the British use radically different proportions of

**Figure 23.2
The Unit Isoquant
Captures All You Need to
Know About a Production
Function**

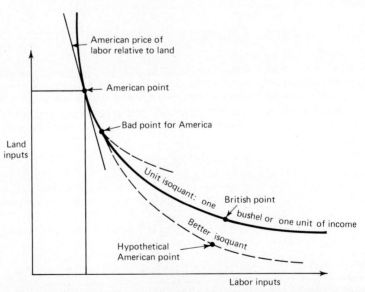

Under constant returns to scale, the ways in which 1 unit of the product can be produced with land and labor can stand for the ways in which 100 or 10,000 units can. The American higher output per person (i.e., lower amount of labor used to produce the one unit) is not necessarily indicative of technological backwardness in Britain. Britain might be at British point on the same isoquant, as it should be if it is endowed with relatively more labor and less land. Only if the Americans could if they wished operate along better isoquant are the British backward.

people and land to make wheat or housing or ships. But according to the diagram they have the same book of possible blueprints as the Americans. The production function, represented here by the shape of the unit isoquant, is a picture of what *can* be done, what is in the book of blueprints, not what *is* done. A "can" becomes an "is" only when firms are faced with the relevant factor prices picking out one blueprint. To recall an earlier discussion, there is more than one way to skin a cat.

Observe, however, that American output per person in the diagram is much higher than British, because American use of labor to produce the one unit of output is much smaller. British output per acre, of course, is much higher than is the American, on the same argument. America used labor sparsely and land generously, Britain the reverse. It is quite possible, and is the case if the production function is the solid isoquant, that the British higher output per acre in a sense offsets the lower output per person. Both countries are in such a case doing as well as they can. They are skinning cats differently because they have different endowments of factors and therefore pick different blueprints from the book, not because they have access to different books.

The alternative is the dashed better isoquant. It is better because it requires lower amounts of land and labor to produce the same amount, namely, one unit. If the American production function can be shown to be this dashed line, then the British were in 1860 definitely inferior. The higher output per acre does not make up for the lower output per person. If Americans with their superior book of blueprints faced British factor prices, the Americans would not, the argument says, go to the British point; they would go to the hypothetical American point on the better isoquant.

☐
How Much Better?

The question of whether American technology was superior to British in 1860 reduces, then, to the question of how much more output than one unit America could have produced with the resources used at the British point. In other words, such questions reduce to the question of how much higher one production function is over another. Think back to the hill of production coming out of the corner of your room. If the production function rises, each combination of, say, labor and capital marked off as a point on the floor produces more output measured by the height of the surface above the floor. The question is how to measure the height of the surface.

☐
Generalizing Average Product to All Inputs

The answer is to generalize the notion of output per person or output per acre into output per unit of all inputs, to move from partial productivity to total productivity. Nothing is lost by focusing on the rate of change (or difference) in productivity instead of on its level. A comparison of the level of productivity in steel making and in coal mining is meaningless because the steel and coal are in different units. Is a ton of coal less or more than a ton of steel? But a comparison of the rates of change of productivity is meaningful because rates of change are unitless. To reintroduce a well-worn piece of algebra from earlier chapters, then, the measure of productivity is the rate of change of output per unit of input, that is, signifying rates of change with asterisks, $(Q/I)^* = Q^* - I^*$.

The economics of the measure starts with the observation that under constant returns to scale a 10% rise in properly measured inputs to wheat growing will result in an exactly 10% increase in wheat. Suppose that the output of wheat actually grows 15%. Then the production function has risen 5%. The 10% rise in inputs explains only part of the rise in output, namely, two thirds of 15%, leaving 5% as the "rise in the production function" or "total factor productivity change" or, to be modest, "the residual," or, to be honest, "a measure of our ignorance." We do not know what caused the additional 5% increase. We call it productivity change.

☐

Using the Fundamental Theorem to Derive a Measure

The remaining question is how to give economic life to the notion of the rate of change of all inputs. The answer uses the fundamental theorem of marginal productivity. Crudely, a factor's share in cost is its importance among all inputs, and so its change should be weighted by its share in making up the rate of change of all inputs. Formally, the theorem says that in competitive equilibrium labor's share, S_L, is the elasticity of output with respect to labor inputs. If the elasticity is ϵ_L and the rate of change of labor in producing wheat is L^*, then $\epsilon_L L^* = S_L L^*$ will be the contribution of the rise in labor input alone to explaining the actual rise in output. The same holds for land. The whole rise in input is the sum of the contributions of labor and land, $S_L L^* + S_T T^* = I^*$, the rate of change of all inputs. If Q^* is the actual increase in output, then $S_L L^* + S_T T^*$ is so to speak the amount of that increase accounted for by the theory of marginal productivity, leaving the rate of change of output minus the rate of change of input, $Q^* - (S_L L^* + S_T T^*)$, as the residual measure of how much wheat productivity has risen.

☐

An Application to American Growth, 1800–1967

The idea is among the richest in economics. Here, for instance, are some statistics of American economic growth.[2]

	Growth Rate in Percent per Year in			
	Output	Land and Capital	Labor	Share of Labor
1800–1905	4.00%	4.00%	3.30%	0.55
1905–1967	3.25	2.20	0.71	0.55

Q: What was the rate of total factor productivity change in each period? Comment on the relative importance of capital accumulation and productivity change in explaining American growth per worker.

[2] Inferred with some difficulty from Moses Abramowitz and Paul A. David, "Reinterpreting Economic Growth: Parables and Realities," *American Economic Review* 63 (May 1973): 428–439, especially p. 431.

A: Applying the formula, in the 1800–1905 period $Q^* = 4.00$ and $S_{T,K}T^* + S_L L^* = 0.45(4.00) + 0.55(3.30) = 3.62$, leaving a residual of $4.00 - 3.62 =$ about 0.4% per year. Only a small part of growth was accounted for by invention, better education, and so forth: most was a matter of piling up land and machines. By contrast, in the later period the residual was $3.25 - 0.45(2.20) - 0.55(0.71) = 1.87\%$ per year, over four times its nineteenth-century value and a large share of growth in total. Not without reason, then, do historians speak of the first industrial revolution in terms of capital accumulation and the second industrial revolution in terms of science, education, and high technology.

☐

Another Derivation, with an Application to the Civil War

The measure of productivity change is sometimes called A^*, for reasons worth knowing. In 1957 Robert Solow showed that the measure is exact, or at any rate can be made exact to any desired degree, when the true production function before and after the change can be written as $AF(K, L)$.[3] The term A is the height of the function and $F(K, L)$ is some production function homogeneous of degree 1 in capital and labor. The point is that A stands outside F and simply multiplies it. No one factor is favored by the productivity change. The change is, as it is put, Hicks neutral. For instance, the Cobb–Douglas version would be $Q = AK^\alpha L^{1-\alpha}$. Although it is not necessary to do so, the constancy of the shares (K's share is α) makes it convenient to think of productivity calculations as following the adventures of A in such a Cobb–Douglas function.

Q: After the South had been defeated in the American Civil War and the slaves had been freed, agricultural output in the South fell by about a third. The supply of labor (formerly slave labor) also fell about a third, as did other important factors of production except land. Land, of course, did not fall. *True or false:* By translating these facts into the equation for the rate of change of A depending on the rate of change of land and of labor, labor standing for all nonland factors, one can assert that there was definitely a fall in the agricultural production function in the South, perhaps because the war damaged the South or because slavery, though morally repugnant, was productive.

A: Write down the formula for A^*, the rate of rise—or in this case possibly a fall—of the production function and see what the givens of the question say about it: $A^* = Q^* - S_T T^* - S_L L^*$. The Q^* and L^* were both -33%; the T^* was zero. So the formula reduces to $A^* = -33\% - S_L(-33\%) = (1 - S_L)(-33\%)$. That is, there was definitely a fall in the production function, because the 33% fall is multiplied by a positive number. If one minus the share of "labor" (i.e., all nonland inputs) were, say, 20%, the fall would be $(0.20)(33\%) = 6.6\%$. In short, true. In a sense the result is obvious. Output fell by a third, but inputs on the whole did not fall by a third, because the average of a zero fall in land and a one-third fall in nonland

---

[3] Robert M. Solow, "Technical Change and the Aggregate Production Function," *Review of Economics and Statistics* 39 (August 1957): 312–320; and Moses Abramowitz, "Resources and Output Trends in the United States Since 1870," *American Economic Review* 46 (May 1956): 5–23.

must be less than a third. Output, therefore, fell more than input. Productivity regressed, telling something about the changes wrought by the war.

☐
**The Price Dual
Measure of
Productivity
Change**

Productivity affects the ratio of prices as much as the ratio of quantities. Because it reduces the input required per unit of output, a rise in productivity will reduce the competitive price of the output relative to the prices of inputs. To put it another way, the measure of productivity change using quantities of inputs and outputs is a generalized average physical product, the rise in Q/I, where I is all inputs; the measure using prices is a generalized marginal physical product, the rise in P_I/P_Q (which in equilibrium is equal to the marginal physical product of I). To put it still another way, a cheapening of a product not explicable by a cheapening of its inputs is attributable to productivity change. The measure using prices is a dual to the primal using quantities.[4]

The proof is an exercise in the algebra of rates of change. In competitive equilibrium revenues equal costs:

$$PQ = wL + rK$$

Take the rate of change of both sides:

$$P^* + Q^* = \frac{wL}{PQ}(w^* + L^*) + \frac{rK}{PQ}(r^* + K^*)$$

Sorting out into price and quantity terms,

$$Q^* - S_L L^* - S_K K^* = -P^* + S_L w^* + S_K r^*$$

If constant returns to scale holds, then the left-hand side is a measure of productivity change. But then so too is the right-hand (price) side. The price measure is not merely an approximation to the quantity measure. If the data are collected consistently (so that L and Q are consistent with S_L, w, and P), the two are identical.

☐
**An Application to
Cotton Textiles,
1815–1859**

It is often more natural to use the price measure. A piece of cotton cloth that sold in England in the 1780s for 70 or 80 shillings was selling 70 years later for 5 shillings.

Q: In the second half of the period, 1815–1859, the price of cotton cloth fell at 3.5% per year, the price of raw cotton fell at 2.5% per year, and wages fell at 0.33% per year (1815–1859 was in fact a period of general deflation). Labor and raw cotton were each about half of the costs of cotton cloth.

1. What was the rate of rise of productivity?

2. A piece of cotton cloth cost about 28 shillings in 1815 and about 5 shillings in 1859. Had productivity change not occurred in cotton textiles, what would have been the price in 1859?

[4] The dual measure was invented, before the primal was, by an economic historian, G. T. Jones, in his *Increasing Returns* (Cambridge: Cambridge University Press, 1933). Since no one outside of British economic history read this book, it had to be reinvented by Dale Jorgenson in "The Embodiment Hypothesis," *Journal of Political Economy* 74 (February 1966), p. 3 n.; and by Jorgenson and Zvi Griliches in "The Explanation of Productivity Change," *Review of Economic Studies* 34 (July 1967): 249–283.

A: 1. The rate of productivity rise is $-P^* + S_c P_c^* + S_L w^* = -(-3.5\%) + 0.50(-2.5\%) + 0.50(-0.33\%) = 2.09\%$ per year. Two percent a year is very rapid productivity growth, most of it attributable in this period to the introduction of the power loom (a sum growing at 2% doubles in 35 years). As it happens, however, from 1780 to 1815 productivity change was even greater (about 3.5% per year), all attributable to advances in spinning (a sum growing at 3.5% doubles in 20 years).[5]

2. The rate of fall of the price of cloth would have been, looking at the calculation in (1), $0.50(-2.5\%) + 0.50(-0.33\%) = 1.41\%$ per year. You can look up an interest rate of 1.41% per year in tables or calculate it on your computer to find that a sum growing at 1.41% grows to 1.64 times its initial level, which is to say that the price would fall to 1/1.61 times its initial level. The price in 1859 would have been 0.61(28 shillings) = 17.09 shillings, nearly three and one half times its actual level of 5 shillings.

Why Productivity Change Occurs

☐ The measurement of productivity change is not a theory of why it happens. The measurement is typical of much applied price theory in that it measures something (technological advance) by looking away from it, asking what output would be in the absence of technological change if marginal productivity were a complete theory of why output changed. Likewise, one can measure changes in taste by asking what bundles consumers would reveal they preferred on the hypothesis that tastes did not change; one can measure the amount of irrationality of business managers in some industry by asking what techniques a perfectly rational manager would choose and comparing the ideal with the real.

It Might Be Viewed as Not Occurring

☐ An alternative intellectual strategy is to suppose that in fact marginal productivity *is* a complete theory and therefore that, if a measure of productivity change is anything other than zero, it is wrong. For if marginal productivity were the whole story of larger output, then all larger output would be attributable to larger input, not to some mysterious, noneconomic thing called "productivity change." The most radical expression of this view is the Griliches and Jorgenson work cited, which argues that invention itself is an economic activity expected to earn normal returns. True, the successful inventor of, say, the Bessemer process of steel making (by a remarkable coincidence named Sir Henry Bessemer) became rich and the price of steel fell to a fraction of its earlier price. But others had attempted a similar process unsuccessfully. Their investments yielding zero return must be added into the balance with Bessemer's yielding a high return. More generally, it can be argued that earlier investments in widespread literacy, in an orderly society of laws, in chemical education, and so forth contributed to Bessemer's success. On this view the cheapening of steel was not a free lunch dropping out of the sky, but the normal yield from investment.

[5] See Roderick Floud and D. N. McCloskey, eds., *The Economic History of Britain Since 1700*, Vol. I (Cambridge: Cambridge University Press, 1981), p. 110.

□
*The Cause of Biased
Technological
Change*

The view is attractive because it is economic, accepting scarcity and thinking about it. But it is little more than a speculative guide to research. Most attempts to think about the economics of changes in the production function have a speculative air. For instance, it is commonly argued that labor scarcity relative to land will result in a labor-saving bias in improvements of productivity. In other words, the unit isoquant will move inward more toward the labor axis than toward the land axis. The argument appears plausible on the surface, but it has flaws.

Q: A maker of rifles in America in 1850 faced a higher price of labor relative to materials and machines than did a British maker. *True or false:* Clearly, the American would want to save labor dollars more than materials dollars.

A: A dollar saved is a dollar earned, no matter which dollar. If inventive activity is free, every dollar to be saved would be saved. As expressed, therefore, false.

The argument can be rescued by getting down to the scarcity involved, the tinkering required to invent things. Suppose that, if the American maker devoted a month of tinkering to the matter, he could save two hours of labor per 100 rifles at 10 cents an hour. If he devoted a month to saving wood, he could save on each gun an eighth of a board-foot of hard wood at $10 per 1000 board-feet. The figures reduce to a labor savings of 20 cents per 100 rifles and a wood saving of

**Figure 23.3
If the Effort to Invent Is
Scarce, Then Expensive
Labor Does Lead to a
Labor-Saving Bias in
Technological Change**

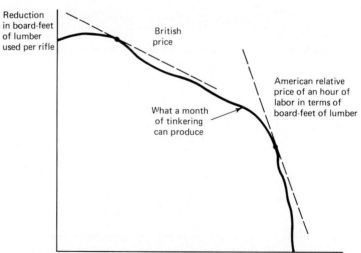

A given tinkerer can produce various different amounts of labor or wood savings in a month of tinkering. These can be arranged in the form of a production possibility curve. The correct amount of labor and wood to save can be picked off by the relative price line. The high relative price of labor in the United States, then, implies a labor-saving bias, that is, more labor saving than wood saving relative to what it is optimal to do in Britain.

12.5 cents per 100 rifles. That is, at 10 cents an hour for labor and $10 per 1000 board-feet of hardwood, and given the abilities of the tinkerer, it would be best for him to spend the month on labor saving. A British tinkerer with similar gifts but facing a higher price of wood relative to labor might well choose to spend it on wood saving. In other words, one can posit a production possibility curve of reductions per month of tinkering in labor and wood inputs against which is set a budget line embodying the relative prices of labor and wood (see Figure 23.3).

☐

The Problem of Spillovers

The amount of technological change, then, can be viewed as the return on investment and the direction of technological change as a result of relative factor prices. The trouble with applying the theory to America and Britain around 1860 is that technology even then was international. If a Yankee tinkerer developed a machine to save labor in rifle making, the machine would be available even to labor-rich Britain. Since after it was invented it would cost nothing to apply, the British industry would exhibit the same labor-saving bias as the American. America, too, would use Britain's wood-saving inventions. There might be a worldwide bias in technological change or a worldwide response of invention to profit, but the alleged differences between countries in their technologies (as distinct from their choice of position along a given technology) are not so easily explained economically.

☐

Knowledge Is Elusive as an Object of Economic Analysis

The difficulty with the economics of technological change is that it is the economics of knowledge. Though scarce, surely, knowledge is expensive to make private and like all externalities, therefore, is difficult to analyze. Knowledge spills over from American to British rifle makers and therefore is less likely to be produced in an optimal amount. Patents for inventions or copyrights for books attempt to internalize the externality. But they too run afoul of economic logic.

T or F: Since knowledge is costless once it is produced, the optimal price for the use of knowledge is not what the holder of the patent or copyright can extract but zero.

A: The use of knowledge does not have an opportunity cost. My use of the idea of transistors does not reduce the opportunity for you to use it. Knowledge is like national defense. Not only is it difficult to exclude another person from enjoying the plays of Shakespeare or the protection of the Navy, but to exclude another is inefficient. Therefore, true.

The problem is, of course, that transistors, national defense, and Shakespeare's plays are—or were—costly to produce. Once they are made, their use is costless, but they will not be made if no one pays the cost. The case is similar to that of the bridge. The marginal cost, and therefore the appropriate toll, is nearly zero, but the average cost is high. The social optimum requires that only marginal cost be charged for using the bridge of knowledge and that a charity or a state pay for its construction. For this reason universities depend on endowments and state funds to support their research. We would be sunk in barbarism if the charity of kings and the passion of scholars had not, quite irrationally, constructed knowledge for all to use.

Summary

The ideas of constant returns to scale and the fundamental theorem find use in measuring the rate at which the production function changes. The measure is a generalized average product, the change in output per unit of input. The rate of change of input is added into one number by factor shares, these being the elasticities of each factor. An identical measure, this time a generalized marginal product, can be derived using prices instead of quantities. Whether price dual or quantity primal, the result applies to all manner of issues, from productivity change in a single industry to the growth of a nation. To go beyond measurement to explanation, however, is difficult, because the economics of technological change is the economics of knowledge. Knowledge is the quintessential public good, and it is a wondrous thing that public goods are produced at all.

QUESTIONS FOR SECTION 23.2

1. During the 1870s, 1880s, and 1890s, Britain is said to have failed economically. In particular, British business managers are supposed to have been slow to adopt new technologies. The data of output, capital, and labor are as follows:

	GNP at 1900 Prices (millions)	Capital Stock (millions)	Labor Force (millions)
1870	1000	4320	13.06
1900	2040	6660	17.74

Assuming that the share of capital was 0.44 and that the share of labor was 0.52 (the rest, 0.04, was rent to land, but the rate of change of land can be assumed to be zero), what was total factor productivity change 1870–1900? If American productivity change in the same period was about 1.5% per year, how much of a British failure was there?

2. In 1348 (before the Black Death and subsequent plagues), the population of England and Wales was 4 million. By 1400 it had fallen to 2 million. Real wages had risen 40%, wages were always about half of national income, England and Wales were overwhelmingly agricultural countries, and no new land or capital was employed in agriculture over the half century. *True or false:* One can conclude from these facts that technological change was nil in England and Wales and that the fall in population by itself explains the rise in wages.

True or False

3. Without the assumption of constant returns to scale, the unit isoquant cannot be drawn.

4. In the diagram of the unit isoquant (Figure 23.2), the American point is revealed preferred at American prices to the British point, and likewise at British prices the British point is revealed preferred to the American.

5. The distance between two unit isoquants is subject to an index number ambiguity.

6. The rate of change of real wages is equal to the rate of change of output per person.

7. If productivity change occurred at the same rate in all industries, the relative prices of all goods would remain constant.

8. In the absence of well-enforced laws of patents internationally, a devotion to science in one country is irrational, at any rate if it is viewed merely as an investment in economic well-being.

9. If an invention (such as the cotton gin) raised the value of some asset (such as cotton land or slaves) and only the inventor knew about the invention before it was announced, then patents would be unnecessary to induce inventors to invent.

Misallocation and Monopoly in Factor Markets

24.1 Good and Bad Allocation

☐
Values of Marginal Product Are Equalized Across Industries

Marginal productivity is not at bottom a matter of engineering and production functions but one of sociology and markets. Thinking of it in engineering terms leads to error.

T or F: If the ratio of capital input to labor input is higher in the chemical industry than in the steel industry, then according to marginal productivity, the wages of labor in chemicals will be higher than in steel.

A: It is meaningless to say that the marginal physical product would be "higher" in the capital-intensive industry, because chemicals and steel are different products. What matters is the marginal *value* product (the price per ton multiplied by the tons per hour), which is not higher in chemicals merely because chemicals choose a capital-intensive point. It might fortuitously be higher, but if it were for an instant, the higher wage would attract workers out of steel and into chemicals until the values of the marginal products and therefore the wages became equal. If chemical workers do make more than steelworkers, it is because they are more valuable as workers in alternative occupations—better educated, say, or stronger—not because they work with more expensive machinery per person. The amount of machinery and land per person affects the marginal product of labor in the economy as a whole, but not in a single industry itself.

The principle applies generally. For instance, workers of a given quality in the computer industry, which did not exist before 1950 and has since then had faster productivity change than any other industry, earn the same amount (with some allowance for momentary disequilibrium) as do workers in the university industry, which has existed since 387 B.C. and has never experienced productivity change. It is a good thing, too. If the value of marginal product were different in the two industries, then something could be gained by shifting workers from the high- to the low-wage industry. Marginal productivity operates within a market, in which factors flow to their highest reward.

504

☐
Uses of the
Equalization of
Values of Marginal
Products

In the usual way of selfishness in economics, the pursuit of high rewards in a market maximizes national income. Suppose, for example, that the village of Vilyatpur in northern India experiences the green revolution, that is, the coming of dwarf varieties of wheat that can hold more grain on their short stalks than a normal plant. The revolution can be viewed as raising the curve of the value of marginal product for labor (and for land, capital, materials, and other things, but focus on labor).

Q: 1. If the number of laborers in Vilyatpur remains the same, what does the green revolution do to the wage and the village output? Draw a diagram of the value of the marginal product of labor before and after the revolution. Identify the area of increase in output, assuming that labor remains the same (refer to Figure 24.1).

2. If Vilyatpur faces an elastic supply of labor at the old equilibrium wage and if labor flows into the village in response to the initial rise in wages, what is the whole additional output in the village? How much is earned by labor on the one hand and by all other factors on the other?

3. How is output elsewhere in the economy affected by the inflow of labor to Vilyatpur? What therefore is the next social gain from the green revolution's coming to Vilyatpur and from allowing labor to flow into the village in response to it? Who gets all the gain, labor or the other, *in*elastically supplied factors, such as land?

A: 1. Clearly, the wage will rise, since the fixed labor is worth more. So too will output rise, productivity being higher. Labor's value of marginal product (which is the price of wheat multiplied by the marginal physical product of labor) rises because the marginal physical product has risen. At old amount of labor the output increases by the area A, since the output is now the area under the higher marginal product curve out to old amount.

2. The wage elsewhere is the elastic supply of labor. If labor flows into Vilyatpur, the new equilibrium will be at new equilibrium. Output is now the area under the higher marginal product curve out to new amount. That is, it is the collar area $A + D + E$. Labor (including the new labor) earns the rectangle $C + E$, namely, the unchanged wage multiplied by the new amount of labor. The nonlabor factors (call them land) earn what is left, the triangle $A + B + D$. Land earned B before; it earns $A + D$ more than B after.

3. The new labor earned E outside of Vilyatpur, which means that its marginal product was E. That is, output in the rest of the economy went down by the amount E when the labor moved to Vilyatpur. The whole higher output was just found to be $A + D + E$. The E part of this must be subtracted to avoid double counting, for it is not a net gain. The net gain therefore is the shaded area $A + D$. The area is the same as the rise in rents, that is, nonlabor incomes, supposing the nonlabor factors of production to be supplied inelastically, not elastically, to the village. The inelastically supplied factor gets all the gain because land is immobile, and therefore no more land can move to Vilyatpur to dissipate high rents. The result is a familiar one. Inelastic participants in a market pay a tax imposed on the market; urban landlords, not tenants, win from cleaner air; likewise, inelasti-

cally supplied factors earn the benefit or suffer the hurts of a change in agriculture.

Figure 24.1
The Rise in the Rents
Earned by Inelastically
Supplied Factors Is the
Rise in Social Product

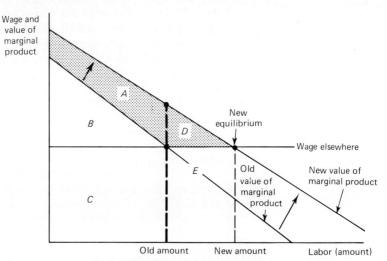

The whole rise in output from a technological change is the area $A + D + E$. But the area E represents the opportunity cost elsewhere of bringing additional laborers to this work. The net gain, therefore, is only $A + D$. If the other factors are fixed (as is land, for instance), then $A + D$ is also the increase in their reward. The fixed factors get all the social benefit in the first instance.

□
*A Failure of
Equalization Is
Inefficient*

Not allowing the labor to flow into Vilyatpur would prevent landlords from earning the benefit, but it would leave national income lower by the difference between the marginal valuation of labor in newly productive Vilyatpur and in the rest of the nation, namely, by the area D. The area is identical to the social loss from forbidding exchange in other contexts, such as housing or gasoline.

The general case in which Vilyatpur or whatever is not small in relation to the labor market it faces involves a diagram of many uses. Consider the allocation of the whole amount of labor in Iceland between two industries, fishing and all other industries.

Q: Draw a diagram with the whole amount of labor on the horizontal axis and the two curves of the value of marginal product facing each other, each with its origin at opposite ends of the line representing the amount of labor. What is the optimal allocation of labor? At the optimum what is Icelandic national income? If for some reason too much labor were allocated to fishing, what would be the lost income?

A: Following the instructions dutifully, the diagram (ignore the dashed line) appears in Figure 24.2. The optimal allocation of labor is the allocation best, in which the values of marginal products in the two industries are equal. Icelandic national income is the income earned in fishing plus the income earned in all other industries. That is, income is the entire M-shaped area under the two marginal product curves. It is evident that any movement away from best is going to result in less income. At bad, for example, the shaded area is lost to income. Fishing is pressed so far that the value of marginal product in fishing is well below that earned in all other industries. A transfer of labor into all other industries would capture the higher product, but the transfer does not occur.

Figure 24.2
The Lack of Ownership of the Sea, or Some Other Distortion, Causes Labor to Be Misallocated and Income to Fall

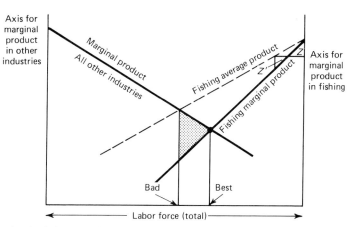

The shaded area is the loss from a bad allocation of the labor force relative to the best allocation. One way in which the bad allocation can come about, pictured here, is the overuse of the sea, the fisheries problem. The problem is that, if the sea is not owned by someone, no rents are charged for a scarce resource, and it is treated as free. Fishermen go to sea as long as the output per person (the average product of labor) is above the marginal product in other occupations. Too many go to sea, overfishing the fish and driving the marginal product down below its value elsewhere.

The Fisheries Problem Is the Failure to Charge Rent

One possible cause of overfishing is contained in the diagram. To be concrete, suppose that the other industry in Iceland is the farming of land. The situation appears symmetrical: Icelanders farm the land or farm the sea. But suppose further, as was the case before Iceland extended its territorial limits 200 miles into the ocean, that nobody owns the sea. No landlord can charge rent on the use of the sea, with the result that all the output goes to labor ("labor" here, as in the Vilyatpur problem, is meant to stand for all mobile factors). In other words, labor in farming earns only its marginal product, leaving a remainder to be earned by landlords, while labor in fishing earns its average product (output divided up among the people fishing), leaving no remainder. The fish in the sea are assumed here to be scarce (the average and marginal product of fishing does fall noticeably as Iceland fishes more), but because private property does not extend to them, the fish in the sea are not treated as though they are scarce. Unsurprisingly, misallocation is the result.

The result can be understood by looking closely at the diagram. The usual relation between average and marginal curves is portrayed up in the corner of the fishing curves by the equality of Z and Z'. If labor is paid its average product, clearly, all the product will go to labor—as is obvious from the algebra that $(Q/L)(L) = Q$. People (equipped with ships and nets) will keep entering fishing until the average product in fishing is equal to the marginal product in other industries. Such an allocation, however, is bad.

The case is known in economics as the *fisheries problem,* or the *common pool problem.*[1] The problem is that the fish are overfished if they are not owned and merely sit in a common pool for anyone who can catch them first. It has elements of the prisoner's dilemma. If Icelanders and other fishing nations could agree on quotas, the fish in the ocean would be treated as scarce. But each fisherman has an incentive to cheat on the agreement, with the result that all nations overfish.

☐
*Social
Arrangements, Not
Biology or
Engineering, Cause
the Problem*

Notice that it is not the biology that makes it a problem. That overfishing can interfere with the efficiency of breeding among the fish, say, and in the extreme make them extinct is just one cause among several for the marginal product to decline with much fishing. *Sic transit* many species, from the dodo to the Bengal tiger and the blue whale. But the problem of excessive "fishing" arises in exploiting minerals as well. The Ogallala Aquifer, for example, effectively a lake underlying much of the dry lands of Nebraska and neighboring states, is owned by no one. Anyone can take water out of it for the cost of drilling. As a consequence the water level is falling fast, it is said, and will fast finish irrigated agriculture in the Central Plains states. That the water is "nonrenewable" is not to the point, however much the word excites the engineering mind. Resources are to be used, not "conserved for our grandchildren." But the lack of ownership means that the water is being used too fast.

☐
*Taxation, Too,
Attenuates
Ownership and
Causes
Misallocation*

Any attenuation of ownership will cause a misallocation of resources. Taxation of wages in agriculture, for example, will reduce the incentive to apply labor to the land. The laborer will not own all the (marginal) fruits of his or her labor. The laborer will apply labor to the acre of land to the point at which the value of marginal product after taxes is equal to the wage in alternative, untaxed occupations before taxes. Too little labor will be applied to the acre.

☐
*Sharecropping as
Analogous to
Taxation*

One must, however, step with care. Consider the following important problem. The landlord of an acre of land, Hannah Gray, can profit from it in three alternative ways. She can hire Joe Reid as a laborer, supervising him in working the land directly; she can hire out the acre to Reid for a fixed amount per year, letting him keep for himself whatever he can grow in excess of the rent; or she can enter into a "sharecropping" agreement with Reid. Instead of getting wages or getting the excess over rent, under sharecropping Reid gets a share of the crop, the share being negotiated with the landlord. Suppose that

[1] Anthony Scott, "The Fishery: The Objectives of Sole Ownership," *Journal of Political Economy* 63 (April 1955): 116–124. Compare the earlier discussion of Frank Knight's case of the Dan Ryan Expressway and the city street.

the agreed share was 50:50. If Reid's seventieth hour applied to the cotton crop in picking time yields a marginal product of $3.00 worth of cotton, then Reid would keep only $1.50, giving the other half to Gray.

The situation looks very much like a tax on labor in agriculture. If the tax analogy is correct, then it follows that sharecropping will be a bad system, as bad as taxes, by discouraging Reid from working the cotton to the point where his full marginal product is equal to what he can earn per hour elsewhere.

Q: Draw the diagram for a 50% tax imposed on a declining marginal product of labor on a single acre. What net proceeds does the taxed laborer face? If his wage in alternative occupations is given, what amount of labor will be supply to the acre? What is the deadweight loss from the tax?

A: The tax cuts the curve of marginal product in half at every amount of labor (see Figure 24.3). The dashed line of after-tax marginal product is simply pivoted around the intersection of the before-tax marginal product on the horizontal axis (since half of zero is zero, the marginal product before and after the tax is the same only when the marginal product is zero). The taxed laborer faces the dashed share line. Reid will only supply labor out to bad, leaving the shaded area *D* as the deadweight loss from the tax. The cotton will get too little time, the acre will get too little profit, and the society will get too little cotton. Many people find sharecropping distasteful, and the tax analogy seems to support the distaste with analytic rigor.

☐
The Analogy Is False

Or so it seemed to many excellent economists for an embarrassingly long time. Looked at coolly, the facts were always a little disquieting. Sharecropping is used by lawyers and other business people to organize their own affairs. Strange. Sharecropping characterizes some rich agriculture, such as Iowa, as well as poor, such as India. Stranger. Sharecropped and rented land otherwise identical have identical outputs per acre, contrary to the implication of the tax model that output per acre would be lower under sharecropping. Stranger still. And sharecropping and renting (and owner occupation) coexist, sometimes with the same landlord renting one acre to Steven Cheung and letting out on shares another identical acre to Joe Reid. Strangest of all.

The diagram shows that the landlord will get the whole triangular area *A* + *B* + *D* in rent if she rents out the acre at a fixed rent, giving the tenant no incentive to hold back his labor. Likewise, it claims that the landlord under sharecropping gets only the area *A*, her share of the whole output *A* + *B* + *C*. An acre under sharecropping earns less than its value in alternative employment (namely, in renting) by the difference, *B* + *D*. The hours of the sharecropper's labor, on the other hand, earn more than their value in alternative employment by the area *B*, since he can earn *B* + *C* being a sharecropper part time and area *E* + *F* being employed elsewhere for the rest of his time, which is in total more than the rectangle *C* + *E* + *F* he earns if he rents. Something is wrong. All landlords would want to rent at

Figure 24.3
The Taxation Analysis of
Sharecropping Implies
That a Landlord Will Earn
Less than She Could Earn
by Renting out

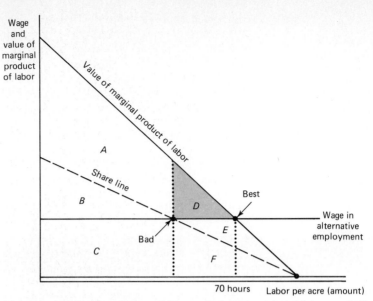

The sharecropper gets only part of his marginal product, drawn here as a half share. If he can move from best to bad, supplying less labor than would be socially desirable, he will. The landlord is hurt by the amount $D + E$ relative to what she could earn if she rented out the acre. The B accrues to the sharecropper as benefit; the D is simply lost to society. But will the landlord stand still for the move from best to bad?

a fixed rent and all laborers would want to enter a sharecropping agreement. The two systems could not coexist, but they do.

What is wrong with the tax analogy is that the landlord, unlike the tax collector, does not stand still for the withdrawal of Joe Reid's labor from the cotton field. She simply makes it a part of the sharecropping agreement that Reid must work out to best, regardless of whether his share of the $3 he makes putting in that hour equals his alternative wage. She is able to get away with such a requirement so long as Reid in following the requirement is even a cent better off than he would be in alternative employment as a renter with her, as a worker on someone else's acre, or as a worker outside of agriculture altogether. If renting and sharecropping coexist, the share line must swivel around until triangle B is equal to triangle E, that is, until what the landlord earns from sharecropping an acre, $A + D + E$, is equal to what she can earn from renting out an acre, $A + B + D$.

The upshot is that sharecropping and renting have identical outcomes. It is not the case that sharecropping is always the inferior system, or that one or the other party is exploited more under one system than under the other. As long as landlords can enforce the work clause of the agreement (and such clauses in fact exist in sharecropping agreements), the share will vary until both sides of the market are indifferent between the two. Why one is chosen over the other is unclear—perhaps one system has in some circumstances advantages of less riskiness or lower supervision costs than the other. But the gross differences that are implied by the tax analogy do not exist.[2]

☐
The Moral:
Efficiency Pops up

One must be wary, then, of claims of gross inefficiency in the allocation of resources. Someone is hurt if income is lower than it could be, giving the someone an incentive to remedy the inefficiency by evading the law or by creating the absent property right or by amending the faulty contract that gave rise to the inefficiency in the first place. The argument is no warrant for supposing that we live in the best of all possible worlds, but is ample warrant for supposing that tales of inefficiency are more complex than even economists believe them to be.

A good example is intellectual overfishing of the fisheries model. In one variant it is called "the tragedy of the commons," the tragedy being that grazing on the nonprivate land in English villages long ago is supposed to have resulted in overgrazing, like overfishing, and a tragic loss of output. The alleged history has been used as the archetype for ravaging of resources and the difficulty of cooperation. The history is wholly mythical, however, on two counts. For one thing, the land was private. Medieval villages knew property. For another, when it was threatened by overgrazing the village adopted rules called "stints" that prevented the inefficiency. To suppose that a village of 30 or 40 families would sit by and watch its grazing land be ruined by lack of private property or of public rules is ersatz economics in the guise of economic analysis.

Summary

If factor markets are functioning as they should, then workers of the same quality will receive the same wage, regardless of their location. The self-interest of the workers in seeking the highest pay will allocate the workers to their best employment until at the margin all products are equal. The factor market simulates the rule of rational life.

The argument can be used to answer the question of who benefits from an increase in agricultural productivity, or the question of how much is lost by putting too many fishermen in one ocean, or the question of whether sharecropping is a bad system in agriculture. The green revolution case illustrates the theorem in taxation that the inelastic party gets the benefit or bears the cost, the elastic parties having left for better climes. The fisheries case

---

[2] The modern position on sharecropping was first stated by Steven N. S. Cheung in *The Theory of Share Tenancy* (Chicago: University of Chicago Press, 1969), especially pp. 42–55. It was stated more explicitly in J. D. Reid, Jr., "Sharecropping and Agricultural Uncertainty," *Economic Development and Cultural Change* 24 (April 1976): 549–576. In truth, much of the modern position is contained in the two pages of Alfred Marshall's treatment, *Principles of Economics*, 8th ed. (London: Macmillan & Co., 1948), Book VI, Chapter X, Part 5, pp. 644–645: "His landlord has to spend much time and trouble, either of his own or of a paid agent, in keeping the tenant to his work. . . . If worked out thoroughly, it will result in the cultivation being carried just about as far and affording the landlord the same income as he would have on the English plan [i.e., fixed rent] for equally fertile and well-situated land equipped with the same capital, and in a place in which the normal ability and enterprise of candidates for farms is the same."

illustrates why scarce resources must be treated as scarce, that is, must be priced. The sharecropping case illustrates that one must look below the machinery of marginal productivity to the human incentives and market opportunities that drive it. An analysis that leaves some people worse off for no good reason is not much of an analysis. The economist should be as wary of inexplicable starvation as of the free lunch.

QUESTIONS FOR SECTION 24.1

1. The value of the marginal product of labor in Indian wheat growing is the marginal physical product times the price of wheat. The coming of the green revolution to Vilyatpur alone obviously does not much affect the whole supply of wheat and therefore does not affect the price. What happens to the analysis in the text if 50,000 Vilyatpurs adopt the green revolution? Who benefits?

2. In the eighteenth and earlier centuries England's ancient system of "open fields" was eliminated (enclosed). The impact was similar to the green revolution in type if not in magnitude: the marginal product of labor (and of land, but focus on labor) moved out. The enclosure movement was slow, affecting only a tiny portion of England's villages in any one year. The facts on output before and after enclosure are very poor. Rents of land, however, are easily available. *True or false:* The rise in the rent on a village enclosed in 1788 is equal to the rise in output attributable to enclosure.

3. Is it to the advantage of employers as a class to obstruct or assist the mobility of labor? One's instinct might be to answer "yes," but it is in fact more ambiguous. In answering the question, consider the following simple case. There are two regions with a given labor force to be distributed between the two. The only other factor of production is land, and it is immobile between the two regions. Employer-landlords own land everywhere (that is, each one has a portfolio of land in both regions). Initially, before mobility, there is a certain allocation of the labor force.

a. Set up the model in a diagram, assuming no labor mobility to start with. Identify the reward to labor as a whole and to land as a whole.

b. Construct an example with the sort of diagram you used in (a) of a case in which the introduction of mobility *increases* the reward to land as a whole and one in which it *decreases* it.

c. Can you make any general *ceteris paribus* statements about the conditions under which the total returns to land are more likely to rise than to fall when mobility is increased?

d. What mobility policy is in the interest of each individual employer-landlord if they own a portfolio of land concentrated in one region? Would concerted class action be likely in this case? What do you conclude about the fruitfulness of the model of class interests in explaining various obstructions to labor mobility (such as the Settlement Laws in England in the seventeenth through the early nineteenth centuries)?

4. The payment of a wage to cowboys equal to the wage the cowboys could earn elsewhere can be justified on the grounds that if it were lower cowboys would be overused (socially speaking) in herding cows. *True or false:* The payment of a pure rent to owners of cattle land in excess of what the owners could earn from the land in alternative employments (as garden plots, say) can be justified on the same grounds; that is, without the rent the cowboys would be overused.

5. Economists are fascinated by allocation and delight to find in misallocation corrected the cause of economic growth. Tariffs, taxes, racial discrimination, entrepreneurial sloth, and so forth put resources in the wrong places. But the loss of income—and therefore the gain of income from eliminating the misallocation—can be tiny even in what would seem to be favorable cases.

a. Suppose that the economy is divided into halves by tariffs, racial discrimination, linguistic prejudice, caste, distance, mountains, habit, or whatever. Each half has the production function $Q = cK^{0.5}$, where Q is the homogenous regional product and K is the region's capital stock (or labor force or whatever: the only essential point is that the other factors of production are held equal in the background, collapsed into the constant c assumed to be equal in both places). This particular production function is chosen partly because it represents reasonably well the usual facts and partly because it can be manipulated with the otherwise useless square root key on your calculator. The units of Q and K can be chosen such that c is 1.0—that is, when $K = 1.0$, Q also = 1.0. Let the total capital stock to be allocated between the two regions be 2.0 units. In view of the symmetry of this division of the economy, what do you suppose is the optimal allocation of the capital stock between the two regions? What is the corresponding *national* income? This is the maximum attainable income, isn't it?

b. If you have had calculus, you know that the marginal product of capital in a region will be $dQ/dK = (0.5)K^{0.5-1.0} = (0.5)K^{-0.5}$. If you have not had calculus, take this on faith. Now, a very large difference in factor rewards for mobile factors of production is a difference of 100%, that is, wages in one region twice what they are in another or interest rates in one social class twice what they are in another. It is a large difference because a lot of money can be made overcoming it. Migrants from Europe to the United States in the nineteenth century, for instance, doubled their incomes for their (considerable) trouble. In view of this, show that an allocation of 0.4 of the total capital stock of 2.0 units to one region and 1.6 to the other produces this degree of difference (twice) in the factor rewards. What is national income with such an allocation? How does it compare with the income attained under the correct allocation? Show that the correct allocation is in fact correct. If you were attempting to explain a doubling of national income over 50 years or so, would you put your intellectual faith in the power of reallocations to explain it?

6. Tithes were taxes on agricultural output for the support of the church, by tradition 10% of the value of output. By the eighteenth century they had existed unchanged for many centuries.

a. *True or false:* "No [eighteenth century] landlord could honestly believe that the [tithe] payments robbed them of any parts of the rents to which they were justly entitled."

b. *True or false:* "Nor could any tenant honestly complain that tithes increased the burden of his rent."

c. Does it follow from your answers to (a) and (b) that no one would have benefited from the elimination of tithes without compensation to the church?

d. "But the real practical grievance was . . . [that a tithe was] a charge which increased by good farming, or diminished by bad,—a tax on every additional outlay of money and labour,—a check upon enterprise and improvement." Discuss.

7. Alfred Marshall, the great English economist of the turn of the century, was chief among those who believed sharecropping to be analogous to a tax. Marshall's solution to the sharecropping problem is known to be incomplete, even wrong (although on the page after the incomplete solution Marshall himself completed it). Yet an economist studying sharecropping in northeastern Brazil (where the crop share is about 50%) applies Marshall's model without getting Marshall's results. That is, he develops a model in which landlords do *not* specify and enforce the amount of labor to be applied to an acre under sharecropping (i.e., the sharecroppers themselves decide), fits the model to the facts, and finds by simulation that sharecropping produces a socially optimal solution. In fitting the model to the facts, he alleges that the wage in alternative employment facing sharecroppers (after allowing for costs of search and travel) is only about half the wage paid by landlords to steady workers. Why does he get the result that sharecropping does not lead to inefficiency? What assumption in his model would you advise him to submit to creative self-doubt before he publishes a paper on his finding?

8. A worker in an agricultural community can either work for a fixed wage on the landlord's land or become a tenant on some of the land, paying a fixed rent. In the wage case the worker gets a low but stable income, because the worker bears none of the risk of variability in agricultural income; in the rental case the worker gets a high but variable income, bearing all the risk.

a. Draw the Edgeworth box for this situation, using total agricultural income and total variance as its dimensions. Locate the wage contract and the rental contract.

b. Under sharecropping the worker and landlord share whatever income there may be in some prearranged proportion (instead of one or the other taking a fixed income—a wage or rent—and leaving all the variability to the other). Place a typical sharecropping arrangement in the Edgeworth box. Why is it superior to either a wage or a rental contract alone?

c. Notice the word "alone" in the last sentence. If landlords and workers can engage in some wage work and some renting, together, what do you think of the common proposition that sharecropping has unique advantages in sharing the risks of agriculture?

True or False

9. The speed limit of 55 miles per hour will reduce the productivity of trucking labor but will not reduce its price.

10. A government policy for stopping inflation by prohibiting wage increases that are not matched by productivity increases in the industry will lead to inefficiency.

11. Cab drivers (keeping them distinct from owners of cabs and the artificially limited licences to operate them) are rational to support rises in fares.

12. In taking an examination it is desirable to work on a question until your marginal point product of a minute on the question is equal to the marginal point product on every other question.

13. A proportional tax on the rent of agricultural land (i.e., on its marginal product) will not reduce the incentive of the last acre to remain in use and will therefore not affect agricultural output.

24.2 Monopoly in Factor Markets

☐
Smallness Yields Optimality

The rule of rational life for a firm is to hire labor until the marginal cost of labor equals its marginal benefit. If the firm is small in all the markets it faces, then the rule reduces to hiring labor until the wage equals the value of the marginal product of labor (that is, the price of the product multiplied by the marginal physical product). Another hour of labor costs a wheat farm facing a large number of other demanders for the supply of labor the going wage. Another hour earns a farm facing a large number of other suppliers of the demand for wheat the amount of wheat the hour can produce multiplied by the going price of wheat. The smallness of firms in an industry has, as usual, pleasing consequences: the valuation that workers put on the last hour they supply (namely, the wage) is set equal to the valuation that consumers put on the product of the hour. If the last hour of bakers should become more valuable in some other use—if they should develop a passion for Latin, say, and would rather spend the hour studying the Latin use of the subjunctive in conditional sentences—then consumers would have to pay more for the bread produced in the hour and would reduce their consumption of it. The society would be induced to spend its hours where they were valued most, in studying more Latin and eating less bread.

☐
Bigness Spoils the Optimality

But of course all this is spoiled if the firm is large in one or more of the markets it faces. If General Motors has monopoly power in selling buses, it will recognize that selling another bus spoils the price and will therefore respond to a marginal revenue lower than price. In the hiring of labor to make the additional bus, therefore, it will view its benefits as the marginal revenue product (the additional revenue, allowing for spoilage, that another hour produces) not the value of marginal product (the additional revenue, *not* allowing for spoilage). Likewise, if General Motors has monopsony power in buying skilled bus designers, it will recognize that buying another hour spoils the wage. The marginal cost of hours is no longer equal to the average cost (namely, the wage) but is higher by the higher wages General Motors will have to pay to existing workers in the course of inducing another to join the company.

The upshot is that a firm with both monopoly and monopsony power sets the marginal revenue product (lower than the value of marginal product) equal to the marginal cost of labor (higher than the average cost). The diagram is as shown in Figure 24.4. The four possible equilibria are marked as perfect competition, monopsony only, monopoly only, and both monopoly and monopsony, this being a loosely reasoned diagram in which competitive and monopolistic situations can be compared directly.

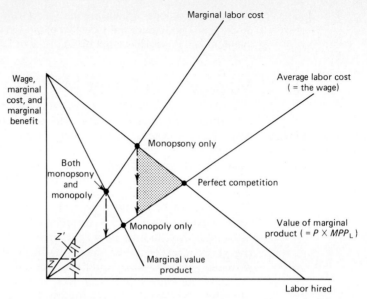

For a monopsonist in the labor market, the marginal cost of labor is higher than the average cost. For a monopolist in the product market, the marginal revenue product is below the value of marginal product. If the firm is one or the other or both, it buys labor only out to the point of monopoly only, monopsony only, or both monopsony and monopoly. The labor hired is less than at perfect competition and is less than desirable in view of the value of the last good produced and the value of the last hour given up to produce it. The shaded area is for example the income lost from monopsony only.

Note that the firm (or, when it is a monopoly, the industry) must always pay the average labor cost, or wage: it must remain on the supply curve of labor. The point of equilibrium marked monopsony only exists in the mind of the monopsonist, not in observed behavior in the labor market. It is analogous to the point of equality of marginal cost and marginal revenue for a monopolist. Just as the monopolist picks an observed point on the demand curve, so too here the monopsonist picks an observed point on the supply curve, indicated by the dashed arrow.

The equation mimicking the diagram is

$$\text{Marginal revenue product} = P(MPP_L)\left(1 - \frac{1}{E_Q^D}\right)$$

$$= w\left(1 + \frac{1}{E_L^s}\right)$$

$$= \text{marginal labor cost}$$

in which P is the price of the product, MPP_L the marginal physical product of labor, E_Q^D the elasticity of demand for the product, w the wage (or the average labor cost, itself dependent on how much labor is demanded), and E_L^s the elasticity of the average labor cost, that is, of the supply curve of labor. The appendix to this section gives a proof by calculus, but the equation is quite plausible without it. When the elasticity of demand for the product is very high, approaching perfect competition in the product market, $1/E_Q^D$ is very low and the left-hand side reduces to $P \times MPP_L$. When the elasticity of supply for labor is very high, approaching perfect competition in the factor market, the right-hand side reduces to w. In other words, under perfect competition the value of the marginal product of labor is set equal to the wage. Under monopoly or monopsony it is not.

□
Applications of Monopsony

The most prominent labor monopsony in the American economy is major league sports, which has long been given special exemption from the laws against monopoly the better to carry on one or another national pastime. The owners of the teams complain loudly when from time to time a new league springs up to share the monopsony and monopoly profits of the old. In 1973, for example, a new hockey league was competing for players against the old National Hockey League, resulting in a sharp rise in salaries for players. Sportswriters, swallowing as they invariably do the arguments of the owners of the few franchises in the old league, complained that the fans, not the owners, would pay for fancy salaries for Bobby Hull and other stars.

Q: Who pays the higher salaries resulting from more competition in the player market?

A: The new league breaks the monopsony power of the old owners, forcing them to treat the wage as their marginal cost of labor. The player market moves from both monopsony and monopoly to at worst monopoly only and at best perfect competition. More players will be hired by the leagues, new and old. More hockey will be played. The owners will no longer be able to exploit so well their monopoly in the market for professional hockey games. On this account, prices at the gate will go down, not up. The profits from a franchise will go down, transferring money from owners to players. Any monopoly profits of the franchise remain to be divided up between the owner and the players. The fans are unaffected. They pay a high price at the gate if supply is restricted, but they do not care whether the high price goes to the owner or the player. It is not Bobby Hull's salary that makes the price high but whatever monopoly in the sale of hockey survives the coming of new franchises.

Using the algebra of monopsony one can measure the monopsony power of owners of sports franchises. Before baseball players were liberated, they were paid only 20% of their marginal revenue product (and major stars were even more underpaid).[3]

T or F: The elasticity of supply that an owner faced was apparently only 0.25.

---

[3] Gerald W. Scully, "Pay and Performance in Major League Baseball," *American Economic Review* 64 (December 1974): 915–930.

A: The equilibrium condition for the owner is to set his hiring such that the marginal revenue product equals the wage times the value of $1 + 1/E_L^s$. If the marginal revenue product is taken to be 1.0, then the wage is 20% of it, or 0.20. Solve the equation

$$1 = 0.20\left(1 + \frac{1}{E_L^s}\right)$$

for E_L^s, the elasticity of supply of labor. The solution is

$$E_L^s = \frac{1}{1 - 0.20} - 1 = 0.25$$

Therefore, true.

☐
Discriminatory Monopsony

Monopsony in a labor market, like monopoly in a product market, can be discriminatory, even perfectly so. If it is, the social loss from the monopsony is lessened:

Q: Whaling was the chief occupation in New Bedford, Massachusetts in the early nineteenth century. Much whaling labor was highly skilled and the labor all lived in New Bedford. Suppose that the market for whaling labor was competitive initially.

1. *True or false:* If the owners of whaling ships in New Bedford band together to set up a central hiring hall, the employment of whaling labor will fall and the income of the owners will rise.

2. *True or false:* If the owners now charge to each laborer a personal fee for entrance to the hiring hall, their income will rise still further and employment will rise back to the competitive level.

A: 1. If the owners band together they will face the entire supply curve of labor and will therefore cut back their hiring to the point where the value of marginal product equals the marginal cost of labor (see Figure 24.5). Employment will indeed fall and the income of owners rise. Therefore, true.

2. If perfectly adjusted, the personal fee will extract all the benefit each person earns from exchange. No longer does the hiring of another worker increase the wage that must be paid to previous workers. Workers earn no economic rent. Their income does fall still farther and their employment rises. Employment rises until marginal benefit (the value of marginal product) equals marginal cost (which is now the wage necessary to induce one more hour of labor to supply itself, i.e., the wage along the supply curve, not the marginal cost of labor). As usual in such cases, the equilibrium for perfectly discriminatory monopsony is the same as the equilibrium for perfect competition. Discriminatory monopoly can achieve efficiency.

☐
Labor Monopoly

Thus far all the monopoly power has rested in the firm that hires the workers. A baseball firm faces both ways, selling tickets to fans and buying services from players, and its power in either market affects its behavior in the market for players. The players themselves, however, can also exercise monopoly power, at least if they can form a union and strike, as they did in the summer of 1981. The economics of monopoly applies in a straightforward way to unions and other restrictions on the supply of labor.

**Figure 24.5
Discriminatory
Monopsony Can Raise
Employment but Reduce
the Welfare of Workers**

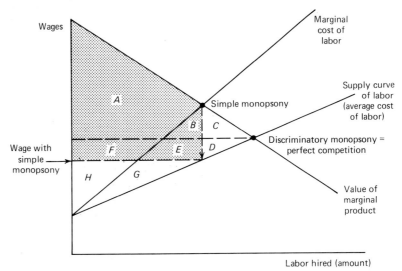

A competitive industry buying labor earns the triangular area $A + B + C$. If it forms itself into a monopsony, it will cut back its hiring to the level of simple monopoly, earning the larger shaded area. If it is able to discriminate perfectly, paying each person or hour exactly what is acceptable and nothing more, then clearly it will earn the entire triangular area between the demand curve and the supply curve (namely, all the lettered areas). Employment will increase.

A monopsonist such as the organization of baseball owners facing a monopolist such as the players' union is engaging in pure bargaining, about which little can be said. A strike or lockout is a failure to reach any bargain to exchange labor for money; the bargain struck will presumably make both sides better off than no bargain. Aside from such obvious points of terminology, the situation resists analysis. It is the oligopoly problem revisited, the problem of predicting behavior when two intelligent people bargain without competitive constraints. Only one-sided monopoly or monopsony is easy to analyze.

Labor monopoly has two peculiarities. First, like governmental monopoly such as the postal service in the 1980s and unlike enterprise monopoly such as the international steel rail cartel in the 1890s, labor monopoly is legal. Second, and more important for present purposes, it is a monopoly of a good used to make other goods. That is, labor has a derived demand. The power of a monopoly can be summarized in its elasticity of demand: the lower the elasticity, the more power has the monopolist to raise its price. The power of a labor monopoly to raise the wage, therefore, depends on the elasticity of the labor's derived demand.

☐

***The First Law of
Derived Demand:
The Elasticity of
Final Demand***

The reason that these obvious equivalences are important is that one can say a lot about the elasticity of derived demand, much more than about the elasticity of demand for most goods in final consumption. Consider for instance the demand for sailors, derived from the demand for the shipping services produced with sailors and with ships. One can make three assertions about how the elasticity of demand for sailors will depend on other things and therefore about how easily labor monopolies can extract high wages without a large fall of employment. The first two assertions can be made at once; the third must wait on their development.

First, the elasticity of demand for seamen will be lower the lower is the elasticity of demand for the things they make—shipping services. The reason is simple. A rise in the wages of sailors will raise costs, that is, the price of shipping services. If shipping services are demanded inelastically, the consequent rise in their price will increase the total revenue collected. The larger revenue will be available to pay higher wages to the same quantity of sailors. The derived demand will be inelastic. If sailors restrict entry to the National Maritime Union, say, their attempt thereby to raise wages will be more successful if the quantity demanded of shipping services is little affected by the high costs of sailors, that is, if the demand is inelastic.

The Second Law of Derived Demand: The Elasticity of Substitution

Second, the elasticity will be lower the lower is the ease with which more ships, the other factor of production, can be substituted for fewer sailors. If the same quantity of shipping services can be produced easily with somewhat smaller crews, maintaining and guarding the ships somewhat less well, then ships can substitute for sailors. On the other hand, if ships and sailors can be used only in rigidly fixed proportions, then sailors can raise their wages with impunity, safe in the knowledge that other factors cannot substitute for them.

The ease with which ships and sailors can substitute for each other in producing a given amount of shipping services is called the *elasticity of substitution*. The elasticity is the rate of rise of the physical capital-labor ratio induced along a given isoquant by a 1% rise in the price of labor relative to capital. If the recipe used of ships and sailors changes very little when sailors' wages rise relative to the price of ships, then evidently the isoquants reflect a rigid commitment to one recipe, and the elasticity is low. At the extreme, the isoquants are L shaped. At the other extreme, in which the slightest shift in the budget line faced by the firm causes the physical ratio of factor use to change radically, the isoquants are straight lines. A high elasticity of substitution is the same as high substitutability between factors, as odd- and even-numbered copies of the telephone book are perfect substitutes (indeed, the definition of elasticity of substitution can be used in consumption theory as well as in production theory).

To give the algebra, then, the elasticity of substitution, usually called σ, is $(K/L)^*/(w/r)^*$, in which asterisks signify rates of change, K and L are the quantities used along a given isoquant of capital and labor, and w and r are the prices (really, the marginal products) of labor and capital. Note the reversal of order of factors on top and bottom. The Leontief production function, $Q=$ minimum of $(\alpha L, \beta K)$, has an elasticity of substitution of zero. The linear function $Q = \alpha L + \beta K$ has an elasticity of infinity. The intermediate case is the Cobb–Douglas production function, $Q = cL^\alpha K^\beta$, which has an elasticity of 1.0, as can be seen in a few lines of algebra. Rewrite the definition of the elasticity of substitution, $\sigma = (K/L)*/(w/r)*$, as $(K* - L*)/(w* - r*)$, by virtue of the algebra of rates of change. If the elasticity is to be 1.0, the top and bottom of the fraction must be equal: $K* - L* = w* - r*$. Rearranging this gives $r* + K* = w* + L*$, which is, reversing the rule in the algebra of rates of change just mentioned, $(rK)* = (wL)*$. That is, if the elasticity of substitution is 1.0, the expenditure on capital rises or falls as does the expenditure on labor. That is, the shares of the two expenditures in total costs are constant. But the Cobb–Douglas production function is the production function with constant shares.

☐
Proof of the Substitution Effect

Figure 24.6 illustrates the effect of substitution. The shipping industry using sailor labor and ship capital might start at start with a low wage indicated by the low slope of the dashed line tangent to the 180-ton isoquant. The change to high wage will cause the equilibrium to move to only substitution, under the supposition that we wish to examine only the pure substitution effect.

The magnitude of the effect on the amount of labor—that is, the distance on the labor axis labeled substitution effect—comes from the following simple use of the fundamental equation of marginal pro-

**Figure 24.6
A Rise in Wages Causes an Income and a Substitution Effect on the Quantity Demand of Labor**

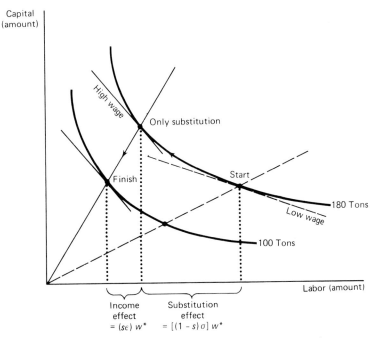

The substitution effect may be measured along a given isoquant, such as 180 tons and depends for its magnitude on how sharply curved the isoquant is, that is, on the extent of elasticity of substitution. The income effect arises from the rise in price and the fall, therefore, in demand for the final product that must follow a rise in wages. For a production function exhibiting constant returns to scale, it may be measured along a ray. The whole move from start to finish is split into an income and a substitution effect, in the style of consumer theory.

ductivity. According to the equation, the rate of change of output, Q^*, will be equal to the share of labor times its rate of change, that is, sL^*, plus the share of capital (which is one minus the share of labor) times its rate of change, that is, $(1-s)K^*$. But along an isoquant Q^* is zero, so the equation is $sL^* + (1-s)K^* = 0$. By the definition of the elasticity of substitution, σ, the rate of change of capital, K^*, is related to the rate of change of labor, wages, and rentals by $(K^* - L^*) = \sigma(w^* - r^*)$. Assume that the rental, r, is fixed by a perfectly elastic supply of capital (note this assumption, so that $r^* = 0$. Then the definition implies that $K^* = L^* + \sigma w^*$, which can be substituted into the first equation:

$$0 = sL^* + (1-s)K^*$$
$$= sL^* + (1-s)(L^* + \sigma w^*)$$
$$= L^* + \sigma w^* - s\sigma w^*$$

Rearranging this last yields

$$\frac{L^*}{w^*} = (1-s)\sigma$$

a pleasantly simple result. It says that the pure substitution effect, expressed as an elasticity of the demand for labor, is the elasticity of substitution multiplied by one minus the share of labor.

☐

Proof of the Income Effect

The pure substitution effect is not all that will happen, of course, if wages rise. The other, income effect involves the first truth given earlier about the elasticity of derived demand: that it is lower the lower is the elasticity of demand for the final product. The substitution effect supposes that factor proportions change and output does not as the wage rises. Suppose the opposite: that factor proportions stay the same but output is permitted to fall. As the wage rises by the amount w^*, the cost and price will of course rise by sw^*, that is, by a larger amount the larger is the share, s, of labor in costs. The rise in price will drive down the quantity demanded, the more so if the elasticity of demand is high, by the amount $sw^*\epsilon$, where ϵ is the elasticity of demand. Since factor proportions are taken as constant and since the argument applies only to conditions of constant returns to scale, the quantity demanded of labor must fall in the same proportion, at the rate $sw^*\epsilon$ if the wage rises at the rate w^*. The pure income effect, expressed as an elasticity, is evidently $s\epsilon$.

The total effect is the sum of the substitution and the income effect:

$$\frac{\text{The elasticity of derived demand for labor (given a perfectly elastic supply of capital)}}{} = (1-s)\sigma + s\epsilon$$

This is an elegant equation. It says that the elasticity of derived demand is a weighted average, that is, lies somewhere between the elasticity of substitution and the elasticity of final demand, the weights being relative shares.

T or F: The elasticity of demand for, say, plasterers, will be smaller if they are "only a small part of the expenses of production. . . . Since plasterer's wages are but a small part of the total expense of building a house, a rise of even 50 per cent in them would add but a very small percentage to the expenses of production of a house and would check demand but little."[4]

A: From the equation just derived, it is clear that the truth of the assertion depends on how σ stands relative to ϵ. If it is smaller, then the assertion is true. If σ is zero, for instance (as in fact the writer was assuming), then the substitution term drops out, and the lower is s the lower is the elasticity. But if σ is larger than ϵ, say, 1.0, where ϵ is 0.5, then a fall in s from, say, 0.5 to 0.25 will cause the elasticity to rise, not to fall; in the particular case from $(0.5)(1.0) + (0.5)(0.5) = 0.750$ to $(0.75)(1.0) + (0.25)(0.5) = 0.875$. (Notice that these are Cobb–Douglas assumptions: constant shares in costs and an elasticity of substitution of 1.0.) In general, then, false. It is important to be unimportant, so trivial a part of costs that employers readily accede to any extortion, only if, as J. R. Hicks put it, "the consumer can substitute more easily than the entrepreneur."

The Third Law of Derived Demand: The Supply Elasticity of Other Factors

☐ The third and final truth about the elasticity of derived demand for sailors producing shipping services with ships is that it will be lower the lower is the elasticity of supply of ships (or whatever is the other, nonlabor factor of production). If ships are hard to sell off quickly in response to a fall in the demand for them, then sailors can in the short run raise wages with impunity again, burdening shipowners with a lower return. If ships are easy to sell—that is, if their supply is elastic—then the owners will not, so to speak, stand still for the reduction in demand for them caused by the more expensive sailors. Their price will not fall and the sailors therefore will not get a higher share of the revenues from shipping services to take in higher wages.

The algebra just given took elasticity of supply of ships to be infinite—in the derivation of the elasticities the price of ships was taken to be constant. If instead the quantity of ships is taken to be constant, implying a zero rather than infinite elasticity of supply of the nonlabor factor, the expression for the *inverse* of the elasticity of derived demand turns out to be

$$\text{The inverse of the elasticity of derived demand for labor} = (1 - s)\frac{1}{\sigma} + s\left(\frac{1}{\epsilon}\right)$$
(given a zero elastic supply of capital)

The equation is beautifully symmetrical with the earlier one. The relation that holds among the elasticity of derived demand, the elasticity of substitution, and the elasticity of demand when the elasticity of

---

[4] Alfred Marshall, *Principles of Economics*, Book V, Chapter VI, Part 2, p. 385. The corrected analysis sketched here is due to J. R. Hicks in his *The Theory of Wages*, 2nd ed. (London: Macmillan & Co., 1968), Appendix III, pp. 242–246, and pp. 373–378.

supply of the nonlabor factor is infinite turns out to hold among the *inverses* of each elasticity when the elasticity of supply is zero. As was seen earlier, economics is filled with such relations of duality.

◻
Low and High Elasticities of Supply of Other Factors Represent the Short Run and the Long

Q: Suppose that in the short run the elasticity of supply of ships is zero, that in the long run it is infinite, that the production function is $Q = cL^{0.5}K^{0.5}$, and that the elasticity of demand is 0.5. What happens to the elasticity of demand for labor as the run lengthens?

A: The Cobb–Douglas form for the production function implies both that the share of labor, s, is constant at 0.5 and that the elasticity of substitution, σ, is 1.0. In the short run, then, the inverse of the elasticity of derived demand is

$$(1 - s)\frac{1}{\sigma} + s\left(\frac{1}{\epsilon}\right) = (0.5)\left(\frac{1}{1}\right) + (0.5)\left(\frac{1}{0.5}\right) = 1.5$$

implying an elasticity of $1/1.5 = 0.66$. In the long run the elasticity is $(1 - s)\sigma + s\epsilon = (0.5)(1.0) + (0.5)(0.5) = 0.75$. The elasticity rises from 0.66 to 0.75, illustrating the third truth about derived demand and confirming one's expectation that elasticities are larger in the long run than in the short.[5]

Another way of seeing the argument is an important argument in its own right:

T or F: The demand curve for a factor of production that holds constant the quantities of other factors of production is less elastic than is one that holds constant their prices.

A: If the quantities of other factors are held constant (as the physical plant of a factory might be in the short run), then an additional laborer is going to produce less than he or she would if the quantities were variable. That is, by a familiar principle, one does better with fewer constraints. The factory does better if it can vary the physical plant to suit a larger labor force than if it is stuck with the plant it had. In brief, true. The demand for labor is less elastic in the short run than in the long run. On the same grounds, as was argued in earlier chapters, the cost curve is lower in the long run than in the short, except at the precise point where the plant available in the short run happens to be exactly the plant wanted in the long run.

[5] The general formula for the elasticity of derived demand, given any value of the elasticity of supply of the nonlabor factor (call this elasticity η), is

$$\frac{\sigma(\epsilon + \eta) + s\eta(\epsilon - \sigma)}{\epsilon + \eta - s(\epsilon - \sigma)}$$

See Hicks, *Theory of Wages*, p. 244. For example, if in the problem in the text η were taken to be 1.0 (instead of the extremes of 0 or ∞), then the elasticity of derived demand would be

$$\frac{(1.0)(1.0 + 0.5) + (0.5)(1.0)(0.5 - 1.0)}{0.5 + 1.0 - (0.5)(0.5 - 1.0)} = 0.71$$

As it should, this falls between the extreme elasticities of 0.66 and 0.75.

Applications of Monopoly in Factor Markets: The Octopus Effect

☐ A monopolist tries to make as much money as possible. Cling to this truth in answering the following question.

Q: Suppose that the Teamsters hold a monopoly on truck-driving labor and suppose that they exercise the monopoly on behalf of their members, fixed in number. Consider a competitive trucking company, with downward-sloping demand for labor.

1. Where will the Teamsters set the wage to the company? What are the areas of profit to the Teamsters and nonlabor income to the company? By comparison with the wage and employment in the absence of the Teamsters, what is the social loss from the labor monopoly?

2. If the Teamsters owned the company, what wage would they set (now to themselves)? If they paid off the former owners of the nonlabor inputs, what would the Teamsters earn in additional profit?

3. Is there what might be called an *octopus effect*, that is, a tendency for a monopoly in a factor market to extend its tentacles forward into the product market?

A: 1. The diagram appears in Figure 24.7. The dashed line is the curve marginal to the company's demand-for-labor curve (it is emphatically *not* the marginal revenue product, which is in this competitive case identical to the value of marginal product). On behalf of their members the Teamster's charge the high monopoly wage, the wage that maximizes labor income. The excess of labor income over its value in alternative uses (given by the supply curve) is $C + D$, the conventional area of monopoly profit. The company earns in nonlabor income what remains from labor income, namely, the triangle $A + B$. The social loss from the monopoly is clearly the shaded area E.

2. The Teamsters need pay only $A + B$ to buy out the company. Once they own it they will set employment at the point competition, getting for their members the additional area of profit E. The merger of Teamsters and the company eliminates the social loss.

3. There *is* an octopus effect. If the labor monopoly merges with its victims, it becomes both the supplier and the demander. As a seller alone its interest was to maximize a trapezoidal area of monopoly profit, $C + D$. As both a seller and a buyer, its interest now is to maximize the entire triangular area of consumer's and producer's surplus, $A + B + C + D + E$. The point competition, of course, is where such a maximization takes place, although the income of labor is higher than it would be in competition. Labor unions—or any monopoly of an input, such as banks monopolizing inputs of funds—have an incentive to buy out the firms they sell to.

The octopus effect is a thinly disguised restatement of the proposition that monopoly is inefficient or is inefficient unless the monopoly is perfectly discriminatory. One can think of the labor monopoly as "discriminating against itself." Under monopoly there exist opportunities for mutually advantageous exchange between buyer and monopolist. The merging monopoly takes advantage of these. Everyone is made at least no worse off: the customers and the former owners of the firm are no worse off and labor is better off. More monopoly can be

**Figure 24.7
The Inefficiency of a Labor
Monopoly Is an Incentive
to Merge with Its Victims**

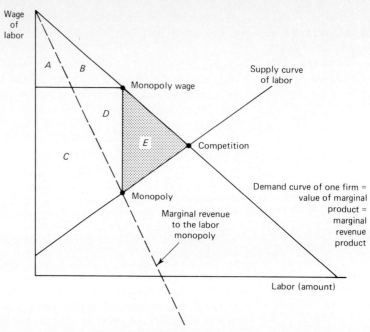

A monopoly facing a derived demand will move to the monopoly point, leaving the shaded area of unexploited opportunities for mutually advantageous exchange. But the monopoly can buy out the victims (for the amount $A + B$) and proceed to point competition. A monopoly in a factor market has an incentive to extend the tentacles of its power forward into its victims.

good for you, at any rate if you ignore the additional resources expended to pursue or protect the richer monopoly.

The octopus effect depends on some degree of substitutability in production. If the industry demands labor in fixed proportion to output, and has no leeway for substituting machines or material for people, then the labor monopoly can take its reward in the labor market or the output market indifferently. The monopoly will wish to send out a tentacle only if the exercise of monopoly in the labor market will cause an inefficiently small amount of labor to be hired there, a small amount because other factors have substituted for labor.

Summary

The failure of property rights is one source of misallocation in the factor market, as in any market. The exploitation of bigness is another. A big firm buying labor is a monopsony, a big firm selling it a monopoly. In the usual way of market power, either will lead to fewer exchanges of labor than is optimal.

A special case is the reduced exchange and higher wage of a labor monopoly. The labor monopoly will have more success in raising the wage the lower the elasticity of derived demand for labor. And the elasticity of derived demand will be lower the lower the elasticity of final demand, the lower the elasticity of substitution, and the lower the elasticity of supply of other factors of production. A monopoly of labor, or of any factor, is favored by stickiness in the world and by clots of habit. In the long run, when all things are adjustable, the elasticities are higher. The octopus effect is a use of these ideas: if the elasticity of substitution is anything but zero, the inefficiency from monopoly tempts the monopolist to take over his or her victims' affairs.

QUESTIONS FOR SECTION 24.2

1. What are all possible areas of profit in Figures 24.5 and 24.7?

2. League rules restrict the ability of professional athletes in baseball, basketball, football, and hockey to move to the team that will pay them the most. The owners defend the restrictions as necessary for equal competition among teams, equal competition being necessary to make the games close and worth paying to see. Without the restrictions, the owners say, the teams with the most money would buy up all the best players. Suppose that the New York Knicks already have five superstars (Sam Williamson, Gary Fethke, Tom Pogue, Bill Albrecht, and Sam Wu) and that the Chicago Bulls have none. The Knicks customarily beat the Bulls 130 to 80. Suppose that the acquisition of Albrecht by the Bulls would make the customary score 110 to 95, with occasional very close games. Who would pay more for Albrecht, the Bulls or the Knicks? Is the owners' argument sound?

3. The following question was devised by H. Gregg Lewis of Duke University and for many years of the University of Chicago, the inventor of modern labor economics. Suppose that coal mining is competitive, has constant returns to scale, is in long-run equilibrium, faces an elasticity of demand of 0.5, has an elasticity of substitution between labor and other factors of 1.5, faces perfectly elastic supplies of the other factors, and spends half its costs on labor. Calculate and explain the effect on the output of coal, the wage of miners, and the number of miners employed of each of the three following disturbances:
   a. An excise tax of 5% of the price of coal on each ton produced.
   b. A payroll tax of 10% on all labor employed.
   c. A minimum wage 10% above the initial level of wages.

4. If one confines attention to a single isoquant, output does not change and therefore the demand price does not change. In terms of the price dual, then, $P^* = sw^* + (1 - s)r^* = 0$. Using this equation and the definition of the elasticity of substitution, derive an expression for w^*/L^*, that is, for the inverse of the substitution term in the elasticity of demand for labor, when the quantity rather than the price of the nonlabor factor is fixed.

5. OPEC is a monopolist of oil. Suppose that there are no economies of scale at any stage of producing or using oil.
   a. If oil were used only for gasoline and were made into gasoline by a process using fixed proportions of other factors of production in refining, would OPEC care whether or not it integrated backward into owning all the world's oil refiners?
   b. If the same facts held as in (a) but gasoline were not being made with fixed proportions, would it care?
   c. If oil were used also for petrochemicals (other than gasoline), would it care?

6. Suppose that Tay Bridge Company has a monopoly on truck crossings from Perthshire to Fife; it has no costs (except for a negligible insurance payment, so invulnerable to disaster is it). Will it raise the monopoly profits of the bridge owners if the company integrates forward into trucking, that is, acquires control of the (competitive) trucking industry that uses the bridge? (Hint: Consider the demand for bridge passages derived from the demand and cost for truckloads crossing the Tay. Show the truth of your answer for the special case of a straight-line, but downward-sloping, demand curve for trucking services, a flat marginal cost of trucking, and as mentioned zero costs. Why is the result different from the case of the Teamsters in the text?)

True or False

7. The point monopsony only must entail a larger employment of labor than the point monopoly only.

8. The marginal revenue product is marginal to the value of marginal product as marginal revenue is to the demand curve.

9. The imposition of an effective minimum wage on a monopsonist will sometimes reduce the number of workers employed by a monopsonist.

10. Since the steel industry faces an inelastic supply of iron ore, Bethlehem Steel is a monopsonist.

11. A rise in demand for cotton would trap cotton producers in a cost cage as the price of labor in cotton rose.

12. If grape growing is a competitive industry with a Cobb–Douglas production function, a union of grape pickers cannot raise the total income earned by employed pickers.

13. If the elasticity of demand for housing is 2.0 and labor is half the cost of making a house, then the elasticity of demand for labor in the industry must be at least 1.0.

14. An iron ore monopoly merged with a steel monopoly will now sell ore to itself at a competitive price.

15. The victims have as much incentive to buy up the monopoly as the monopoly has to buy up the victims.

APPENDIX TO SECTION 24.2:

Proof of the Equation of Imperfect Competition in Factor Markets

The profit to be maximized, π, is revenue, PQ, minus cost, taken to be labor cost alone, wL. In the case of a large firm, the price, P, is a function of how much Q is produced, Q is a function of L hired, and w is a function of L hired. The expression to be maximized is therefore

$$\text{Profit is } \pi = P(Q)[Q(L)] - w(L)L$$

Taking the derivative with respect to L (since L is what is to be chosen) gives

$$\frac{d\pi}{dL} = p\left(\frac{dQ}{dL}\right) + Q\left(\frac{dP}{dQ}\right)\left(\frac{dQ}{dL}\right) - w - L\left(\frac{dw}{dL}\right) = 0$$

The expression can be rewritten in elasticity form. Factor out from the first two terms dQ/dL (the marginal physical product of labor, styled MPP_L) and notice that $Q(dP/dQ)$ lacks only division by P to be the inverse of the elasticity of demand. Likewise, multiplying and dividing the last two terms by w leads to a second term that is the inverse of the elasticity of supply of labor. The result is, defining all elasticities as positive numbers,

$$P\left(1 - \frac{1}{\epsilon_Q^D}\right)MPP_L = w\left(1 - \frac{1}{\epsilon_L^S}\right)$$

which is the expression in the text.

25

The Supply of Labor

25.1 The Leading Idea in Labor Supply: Compensating Differentials

☐
Equal Pay for Equal Unpleasantness

The labor and other factors demanded according to marginal productivity must also be supplied. They are supplied to any one job according to the *principle of compensating differentials.* Among the most useful of economic doctrines, the principle says simply that a person's pay in one job must equal his or her pay in another. More exactly, the *whole* pay, in happiness as well as money, of the *marginal* worker, just indifferent between the two jobs, must be equal in the two. If one's money pay is not equal, then one must be compensated by other differentials between the jobs, differentials in working conditions, say, or in the reliability of employment.

The principle is merely a condition of equilibrium: if it is violated the workers will move around until it is re-established. A professor of economics, for example, earns less than she could in business. If the difference is $15,000 a year she would have to "earn" $15,000 of differential pleasure as a professor, perhaps the pleasure of being largely her own boss or of associating with other people devoted to the life of the mind. If this were not so, she would change jobs.

The applications of the argument are limitless.

T or F: The introduction of workmen's compensation, under which employers pay all the costs of injuries on the job, will raise wages of college professors and file clerks relative to those of coal miners and trapeze artists.

A: Before the law the risky occupations earned a premium to compensate for the risk, a premium that will vanish with the coming of workmen's compensation. That is, true.

T or F: Legislation on safety in coal mines does not affect the welfare of miners.

A: The conclusion seems inescapable if workers are free to move into and out of coal mining. High wages compensated for risky mines. That is, true.

530

The natural tendency will be to resist such reasoning and to point out that in the bad old days not only were mines risky but wages were also low. The point is irrelevant. To be sure, people were poor long ago. Their poverty is their low income in total, money income plus the money value of working conditions. What matters for the question is the composition of the total. Legislation on safety makes the miners take their income, whether low or high, in safety rather than in money. Any other result would cause them to exit or enter mining. One can escape the conclusion only by arguing (as one might) that miners do not see their own best interest in safe mines.

Another surprising application of the idea of compensating differentials is the following.

T or F: A legal minimum wage may not cause unemployment (excess supply of labor) if working conditions can adjust (by increasing the intensity of an hour of work, say, or by reducing the employer's expenditure on safety devices on the job).

A: Again, entry and exit fixes the whole pay. A 16-year-old working at McDonald's can get $2.00 an hour (below the minimum) and a leisurely pace or $4.00 an hour (above the minimum) and a hectic pace. The hectic pace may well choke off what would otherwise be an excess supply of labor at the high wage. The worker may be indifferent between the two deals, as might the employer, leaving the society unharmed by the minimum wage, or harmed only a little.

☐
The Whole Pay Is Determined by Competition, Not by Its Composition

Bargaining over wages, then, cannot affect the welfare of workers unless the bargaining changes the amount of competition the workers face. The whole pay of miners will rise only if coal miners can extract a promise from owners to hire only workers at union wages and if the miners can restrict entry to the union. The whole pay of workers at McDonald's is not affected by air conditioning of the kitchens. The whole pay of college professors is not affected by a bargain to raise their money wages faster than supply and demand would warrant. Working conditions will adjust.

"Working conditions" include more than legal privileges. For example, theft from the company is part of the whole pay. The company will have to pay more in money wages if it does not allow a professor to use college stationery to write her mother, the waitress to eat the last piece of pie, or the longshoreman to steal television sets off the docks. The company can pay in money or it can pay in stationery, pie, and television sets.

T or F: The company has no incentive to prevent stealing if the value of the goods stolen is as high to the worker as to the company.

A: The money wage plus the value to the worker of the goods stolen is the whole wage, given by competition from the outside. Take the case of television sets stolen from the docks. The company will not care about the stealing if the longshoreman can sell the stolen television for the same price as the company would get, because he will then accept wages lower by exactly the value of the television set. The company does not care whether it pays $100 worth of wages or $100 worth of television sets. On the other hand it will care a lot if the longshoreman only gets $50 for the hot television set from his fence. The longshoreman will accept only $50 less wages, even though the company values the stolen television at $100. That is, true.

□
Ships and Chips

The history of the English Navy yards provides a spectacular case of the principle of compensating differentials in action:

Q: In the seventeenth and eighteenth centuries in the royal shipyards, where fighting ships were built, workers claimed the right to remove pieces of waste wood (called "chips") and sell them as lumber. Guards, floggings, and hangings failed to stop the practice, which ended only in the early nineteenth century, when mechanization took away the opportunities to create "waste" wood in cutting. Before mechanization only one sixth of the wood coming into the yard for ships went out as ships. The rest went out on the backs of workers, as chips.

1. *True or false:* The workers were made better off by being able to take and sell the chips (the chips sold for less than their cost to the Navy).

2. *True or false:* The coming of mechanization was therefore ruinous to the workers, another case of capitalism's robbing the workers of their dignity and self-determination.

3. *True or false:* Both the workers and the Navy would have been better off if workers had been paid exclusively in money and had been prevented from taking chips.

4. *True or false:* Nevertheless, the Navy could sustain no such mutually beneficial agreement to pay only in money if bad cutting (which produced chips on purpose) was difficult to detect.

5. *True or false:* If all scrap lumber could be burned by the Navy, no problem of chips would exist.

6. *True or false:* The official burners were bribable; the problem would return.

A: 1. No, the workers were not made better off by being able to take the chips. Competition fixed the whole pay of the workers. Taking the pay in chips meant merely that the money wage the Navy would need to pay was lower.

2. Therefore, no, the workers were not ruined by the coming of mechanization. Each worker quite properly viewed his own chips as a benefit to him, just as you would view part of your pay as a benefit. As people do, the workers did not understand that eliminating chips would raise their money wages, or at any rate the historian of the workers does not.

3. Yes, both the workers and the Navy would have been better off with money pay alone. The chips sold for less than they were worth to the Navy as ships. The wood was badly used, leaving a social gain from using it better to be shared out between the workers and the Navy. The Navy could get cheaper ships yet still pay the workers more in money alone than they earned in money and chips combined.

4. True, such a mutually beneficial agreement would be subject to free

riding, because each worker has an incentive to cheat and to take chips. The Navy in fact offered the workers an agreement, which they accepted. The agreement broke down when workers took not only the higher pay but also the chips.

5. Yes, if all chips were burned as soon as they were made, there would be no incentive to create them artificially for purposes of stealing and selling them. The utterly spiteful measure of burning up what is a valuable resource (the chips) would prevent another waste (creating the chips to order).

6. Yes, the official burners could be bribed to give up their chips. In fact the inspectors hired to prevent the theft of the chips in the first place were bribed to overlook the theft.

The principle of compensating differentials is a sharp tool. An extreme application of it is to the question of whether urbanization and industrialization made people better off.

T or F: If it is literally true that all differentials in pay are compensated by differences in the value of working conditions, then, despite the observed rise in money income during the Industrial Revolution, no increases in happiness came about from the movement of people from farms to factories.

A: True. The higher wages in the factory were not clear gain if they were merely compensation for bad working conditions. We wish to measure people's happiness, not their holdings of greenish portraits of George Washington (or King George). Conventional national income, which rose when people moved to factories, measures paper, not happiness.

□
The Indifference Curves for Equalizing Differentials

The theory of equalizing differentials can be put formally as a choice between two commodities, such as income earned as a professor and income earned as a pipefitter. The analogy with a person's consuming is exact. Instead of allocating money income between hamburgers and housing, the person allocates hours of time between pipefitting and professing. Just as each dollar buys a certain number of commodities, each hour earns a certain number of dollars to buy commodities, determining the budget line between the two fruits of the hours (see Figure 25.1).

People have feelings about how they would like to earn their daily bread, represented here by the solid indifference curve. If they did not care, the indifference curves would all be 45° lines like the one in the corner. The dashed budget line gives the terms of exchange between the two ways of using hours to earn. Just as money income is in consumer theory the scarcity behind the budget line, here the amount of hours is the scarcity. As drawn, an hour of professing is a much worse way of earning commodities than is an hour of pipefitting: professors earn less than pipefitters.

T or F: That Siebert, Nordquist, and Ichiishi do not usually do both pipefitting and professing implies that their indifference curves either intersect the axes or are straight lines.

A: They will do both if the indifference curves have the usual, convex shape and do not intersect the axes, because the equilibrium point will be interior, as in the diagram. Therefore, since we do not in fact observe people doing all sorts of jobs, indifference curves must have the shape that yields corner solutions. In other words, although people do not usually specialize in consuming food or housing, they do specialize in employment.

**Figure 25.1
The Formal Theory of
Compensating
Differentials**

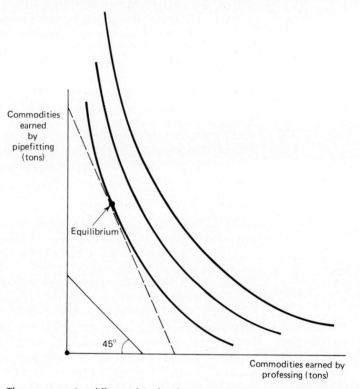

The compensating differential is the divergence from a 45° budget line required by the relative distaste that most people have for earning a dollar by pipefitting rather than by professing.

The diagram, therefore, best represents the whole market, not one person. You can read it as determining relative wages. The dashed line would be the relative wage if professors and pipefitters were demanded by the economy in fixed amounts given by the point equilibrium. Since most people are portrayed here as disliking pipefitting relative to professing, the pipefitters earn a compensating differential; that is, they earn more per hour.

Summary

For the marginal worker just indifferent between two jobs, the whole pay must be the same in both jobs. If working conditions are not the same, as they are not in coal mining and store clerking, the wage adjusts; if the wages are not the same, the working conditions adjust. This is the principle of compensating differentials. Entry and exit fix the whole pay, leaving the composition of the whole to vary. Therefore, safe miners will be miners with lower money pay; McDonald's workers with high pay will be workers with unsafe kitchens; dockers who steal television sets will be dockers with lower money pay or with unemployment if they insist on high money pay as well.

The theory can be put in the same way of the theory of consumption, showing how tastes for one as against another way of earning commodities determine the equilibrium differential between pay in different occupations. For a single person, the diagram shows how the given differential leads him or her to choose one occupation or the other. For a whole economy, the diagram shows how a given composition of demand leads to the differential pay.

QUESTIONS FOR SECTION 25.1

1. Liability for accidents in a plant is placed on the employer. *True or false:* The employer will spend no more in preventing accidents in his plant than he would if the liability (that is, the cost of hospital care, etc.) were placed on the employee.

2. Federal judges have more power and prestige than do most practicing lawyers. The salary of federal judges, however, is well below what a good practicing attorney can make. *True or false:* If the offer of judgeships is random with respect to ability, this implies that federal judges on average will be worse lawyers than practicing attorneys.

True or False

3. That a college professor earns less than NASCAR racers (whose average speed through life is 200 mph) is evidence of the perverted values of Americans.

4. You would expect bartenders to be worse off in countries where it is not customary to leave a tip on the counter.

5. The wage of garbage collectors is lower than that of engineers because their work is dirty and disgusting.

6. The choice among occupations is not affected by a proportional tax on money income.

7. An unemployment compensation law (in which all unemployed are eligible for benefits) would reduce the wage rate in depression-prone industries relative to that in safe industries.

8. A worker in a remote district who has to buy all his or her food at high prices in the company store is worse off than one in a big city who can spend his or her wages wherever the worker wants.

9. If the diagram illustrating the principle of compensating differentials would mix utility and budget lines if the axes were hours of work in the two jobs.

25.2   The Choice Between Work and Leisure

☐

The Shadow Wage of Leisure

In short, like many other theories in economics, the theory of labor supply is a theory of choice under scarcity. The scarcity is hours: "Life, Time's fool, must have a stop." The scarcity of hours requires not only a choice between two occupations but a choice between being occupied and being unoccupied. Being unoccupied is called conventionally *leisure*, but it is best to think of it as all uses of time other than working for wages. The "leisure" can be sitting in the sun or sleeping late. But it can also be raising four children or writing the great American novel, more demanding than most paid jobs. Leisure in the technical sense is not sloth but merely time not paid a wage.

The point is that the wage is the opportunity cost of whatever is produced at home—whether a happy family or merely a suntan. One can speak of a *shadow wage* as being the dollar value of what is produced at home, in which case a person's participation in the labor force depends on whether or not his or her shadow wage is higher than the available market wage.

T or F: As long as women are paid less than men, women will specialize more in housework.

A: You can assume that women are as skilled as or more skilled than men at housework (whether the skill is natural or acquired is not at issue). That is, their shadow wages in housework are the same or higher. But the opportunity cost of women's housework is less than men's if women earn less in the market. If anyone does it will be rational for a wife, not a husband, to stay home. Therefore, true.

The idea brightly illumines the domestic scene.

T or F: A narrowing of pay differentials between men and women will lead to more equal sharing of housework between husbands and wives.

A: By running the argument just given in reverse, true.

It is customary to exclude the value of housework from the national income. The custom arises from the difficulty of measuring shadow wages (except for the housewife who by jumping into and out of the market labor force exhibits indifference between wage work and housework: for her the market wage is the shadow wage). For the same reason the national accounts ignore most other nonmarket uses of time, such as most home vegetable gardens, much do-it-yourself home repair, all driving time in a car, and all leisure in the narrow sense. Measured income rises when people buy a tomato instead of growing it, hire a plumber instead of doing the work, buy a cab fare instead of driving it, and sell time instead of enjoying it.

That shadow wages are hard to measure is not much of an objection to including all the income of the nation in a measure of national income. All things are valued at their marginal values. The super house-wife with a high shadow wage earns so to speak a consumer's surplus from consuming housemaking, but so does a pizza lover with a total valuation of pizza higher than its price. The exclusion of consumer's surplus from national income is not a flaw if you believe that national income pretends only to measure the nation's budget constraint, not its happiness.

☐
The Theory of the Supply of Labor

The single supplier of labor faces a budget constraint in allocating his or her hours to leisure or to wage work, a budget constraint whose slope is the real wage (see Figure 25.2). The endowment point is 24 hours, where the dashed line begins. The units of its slope are dollars of wages per hour divided by dollars of price per ton of the commodity, which reduces as it should to tons per hour. Since leisure and commodities are goods, not bads, the indifference curves have the usual shape. The hours of work supplied by the worker in the figure are those left over from the 24 hours in a day after the worker has settled on, say, an equilibrium amount of leisure.

The apparatus is nothing but consumption theory with one commodity being leisure. The astonishing usefulness of the diagram will illustrate once again the astonishing usefulness of consumption theory. The first use is to undergird the supply curve of labor. As the wage varies, the equilibrium varies, from low wage through equilibrium to

**Figure 25.2
A Leisure-Commodity Choice Determines the Supply Curve of Labor**

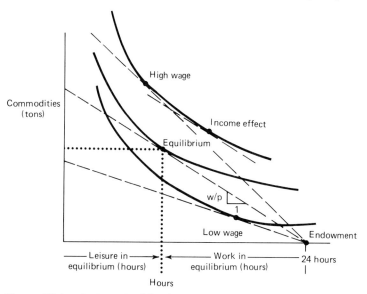

The equilibrium is determined by the tangency between an indifference curve and the dashed budget line coming out of the endowment of 24 hours of leisure. The amount of leisure chosen will leave some hours for work. As the person faces a steeper slope of the budget line (which is the money wage divided by the money price of commodities), his or her amount of work will increase, unless the income effect of the enrichment overcomes the substitution effect.

high wage. By the usual geometry, the rising hours of work could be plotted in a diagram below this one against the rising wage to give an upward-sloping supply curve of hours.

☐ But consider the following.

Backward-Bending Supply

T or F: Without violating any usual features of indifference curves, the point high wage can be to the right of equilibrium (implying fewer hours of work supplied at a higher wage).

A: Look at the point income effect. It represents what would have happened to the person's consumption of commodities and leisure had income gone up without a rise in wages. It represents, therefore, the pure income effect, without any substitution effect. If leisure is a normal good (as of course it is natural to assume it to be), then the hours of leisure increase as income does, leaving less time for work. The pure substitution effect of the cheapening of commodities relative to leisure is the move from the point income effect to the point high wage. You can see that the income effect depends on the curvature of the indifference curve—that is, on the elasticity of substitution between commodities and leisure. If stereos and McDonald's hamburgers were poor substitutes in consumption for flute practice and homemade bread, then the final high wage point could easily entail less, not more, labor supplied than the point equilibrium. The corresponding supply curve would show a portion that bent backward.

A single supplier, then, might not exhibit a conventional supply curve of labor. The singer Perry Como earns so much in one performance that he gives fewer performances than he gave before his reputation was established. But the proposition is much less likely to apply to all singers as a group, for the following reason.

T or F: A rise in real wages will increase the percentage of people who do some market work.

A: Before the wage goes up, some of the people who do not work are at a corner (the rest are around the corner, but will reach it at a higher wage). That is, they earn no wages (or no wages in singing), spending all their time at leisure (or in nonsinging jobs). The rise of wages has for them no income effect: they start by sliding up the same indifference curve as soon as they are induced to work at all. It is quite possible, and even likely, that the entry of new workers (or singers) will offset the growing reluctance of the old to give up more scarce leisure. At the least, the idea of a backward-bending supply curve looks much less attractive if one allows for new entrants to the labor force.

Consider the following, for instance.

Q: Suppose that Geoff McClelland, a Scottish highlander, is initially self-sufficient, producing oats by sacrificing some of the one other commodity that interests him, leisure. Describe briefly his position, assuming that McClelland has an initial endowment of 24 hours of leisure and the usual shape of the production possibility curve. Suppose that he is now presented with the opportunity to become a hired worker, working for constant hourly wages on a neighboring farm. What minimum wage will induce McClelland to abandon entirely self-sufficient farming? Suppose that the wage actually offered to him is exactly this minimum. Will his hours of leisure be larger than, smaller than, or equal to the hours under self-sufficiency?

A: McClelland's initial position is self-sufficient along his production possibility curve in Figure 25.3. The dashed line is the market wage just high enough to interest him. That is, it is the line just steep enough to touch the indifference curve through self-sufficient. Necessarily it touches it at a point such as enter, with less leisure than at self-sufficient. The tale is one of early industrialization: in the presence of diminishing returns to labor in subsistence agriculture, the first recruits to the factories chose to work long hours.

☐
Applications of Income Effects: Inheritances and Subsidies

Quite naturally, a larger endowment of commodities will reduce the amount of work that a person supplies. If Jeffrey Williamson receives a large inheritance, his endowment will move up off the leisure axis in Figure 25.4 to the point subsidy. The terms of the inheritance permit him to still earn a wage, but he earns it along the dashed line parallel to the original one. Since leisure is a normal good, he will always work less: other things equal, people rich from unearned income work less.

**Figure 25.3
Why Self-sufficient
Farmers Tempted into the
Factory Work Long Hours**

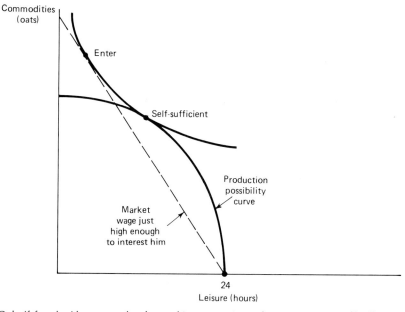

Only if faced with a wage that leaves him at a point such as enter can a self-sufficient farmer be tempted to abandon his production possibility curve. But at a point like enter he works more hours. Note that producing along the farmer's production possibility curve is assumed to be impossible to do at the same time that the farmer is a wage worker.

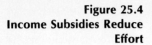

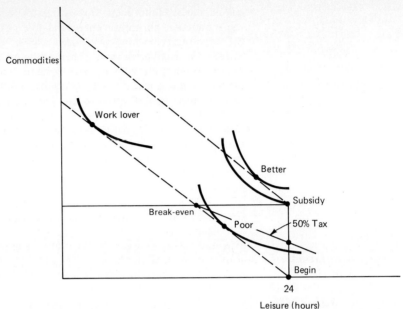

A gift of subsidy with no strings attached puts the poor on the higher dashed budget line. The poor will work less. A subsidy that requires the worker to abandon the work force or, what is equivalent, to give back a dollar of subsidy if he or she personally earns another dollar will cause the worker to work even less, unless he or she is a work lover. The negative income tax (here 50%) moderates the disincentive to work.

The argument and the diagram apply also to the poor. The subsidy point might then be a socially acceptable minimum of income. A straightforward subsidy in that amount will put some of the poor above the utility of the subsidy point, moving to point better at the expense of taxpayers. Such a poor person will work less (better is to the right of poor) but have more, because the poor person supplements the subsidy with earned income.

A clumsy mechanism for keeping the utility of the poor low but above the minimum is to specify that anyone who accepts the subsidy cannot earn any more. In early nineteenth-century England a subsidy without strings attached was called outdoor relief; with strings it was called indoor relief—that is, indoors in the so-called workhouse, which contrary to its name was a prison designed (by economists, regrettably) to prevent people from moving from the point subsidy to the point better by working for pay. The workhouse made the point subsidy less pleasant by setting the inmates to useless but difficult tasks and by separating the sexes, just as modern versions of such subsidies make it less pleasant by giving it through surly clerks, long lines, and inquisitorial social workers.

The effect of the workhouse or its modern equivalent is perverse, inducing many people who were willing to work to choose to do nothing but accept the point subsidy. The terms of the subsidy are that one cannot take it and also be in the labor market. The budget line is now the old dashed line augmented by the point subsidy (recall the analysis of free education early in the book). Whenever the point subsidy is on a higher indifference curve than some point on the old budget line, the recipient abandons the work line entirely. Only the work lover (or commodity lover) among the poor stays on the job, because for that person the point subsidy is on a lower indifference curve. The rest go on the dole full time.

> *T or F:* A scheme in which earned incomes below the level of the point subsidy were subsidized until they came up to subsidy would have the same effects on the incentive to work as the scheme in which the subsidy is an all-or-nothing offer.

> *A:* The subsidy would bring all incomes below subsidy up to the level of the horizontal solid line through the point subsidy. The worker would be faced with virtually the same budget line as the all-or-nothing offer. Only the point subsidy would be chosen by someone at poor because no one with a positive marginal valuation of leisure would take up a position on the horizontal line. In short, true. Unfortunately, at present many welfare programs have this feature.

☐
The Negative Income Tax

It is fruitful to look at the problem another way. If earned income is below the point subsidy, for each dollar a poor person earns the government takes away a dollar of subsidy. The scheme amounts to a tax on income, a tax with 100% marginal rates. The government taxes effort heavily and therefore the poor workers supply little of it. A partial solution to the problem is to let the poor keep some of the extra money they earn, reducing the tax rate. The diagram shows a tax rate of 50% on the poor, for example, the highest imposed on the earned incomes of the rich. As the tax gets lower, the line swings clockwise around the break-even point, giving less and less incentive to go on the dole, though also giving less and less of a dole. The desires of the society to encourage work and to maintain incomes above some minimum are inconsistent: to some degree one must be sacrificed to achieve the other.

The alternative policy is to subsidize the wage instead of income. That is, each hour of work offered is given a higher price, which brings in the substitution effect (increasing work) to do battle with the income effect (decreasing work). Aid to Dependent Children, public housing, social security, and Medicare are income subsidies; the minimum wage, summer jobs for inner-city youths, and protection of the auto industry are wage subsidies. Neither is ideal. Both distort the choice between work and leisure presented by the underlying scarcities in the economy, and therefore both cause misallocation. Both require taxes to pay for them, taxes that introduce their own distortions and inequities.

Summary

The theory of labor supply is the theory of the consumption of leisure, where "leisure" is "any activity that does not earn a wage and takes time from activities that do." If the shadow price of leisure is high relative to the market wage, labor is not supplied. Time is used at home.

All the usual features of consumption theory apply. For example, it is important to distinguish between the income effect and the substitution effect of a rise in wages. The income effect can make the corresponding supply curve of labor bend backward, perversely reducing the amount of labor supplied as the wage rises. It can, that is, but does not always do so: the entry of people out of leisure is a substitution effect alone, always working in the conventional direction. Like consumption theory in general, the theory of the consumption of leisure—the supply of labor—can be used to analyze changes in the budget line of the consumer imposed from outside. The chief case in point is a subsidy to the poor. If the subsidy is an income subsidy, the diagram shows that it reduces the amount of labor supplied; if it is a wage subsidy, it increases the amount supplied. In either case the theory casts a bright light on the perennial attempts to help the poor without altering their incentives to help themselves.

QUESTIONS FOR SECTION 25.2

1. In 1974 the average wage was $760 per month in the United States and $640 per month in Japan. Suppose (for simplicity) that women could earn this wage. Suppose further that in Japan most married women choose to stay at home and that in the United States most work in the market. *True or false:* The difference between the shadow wage at home in the two countries is less than the difference between the market wage; indeed, it may be that a housewife (whether or not that job is chosen) is more valuable in Japan than in the United States.

2. Examine the effect on the labor force participation of women of
a. increased subsidies for the construction of day care centers.
b. a subsidy per child given to married couples.
c. an increase in the income tax rate.
d. a stiffening of immigration rules for domestic help and other unskilled labor (warning: some women are unskilled, too).
e. the invention of the vacuum cleaner.
f. a reduction in the amount of discrimination against women.
g. a law forbidding women to work in dangerous industries.

3. How would you interpret the following facts:
a. The rate of labor force participation of married women is higher for the more educated.
b. In families with more children the rate of labor force participation of the mother is smaller.

4. Assuming that all suppliers of labor have the same indifference curves, rank the following from least to most work encouraging:
a. a gift of $10,000 per person.
b. a floor on income of $10,000 per person.
c. a proportional subsidy to the wage that equals $10,000 per person in equilibrium (that is, as actually paid).

5. A cheap pill is invented that makes four hours of sleep a night equivalent to the present eight hours. *True or false:* If leisure and commodities are normal goods, people will work longer hours and will be paid a lower wage per hour.

True or False

6. If household output is taken to be a measure of economic welfare, this measure would rise less rapidly during cyclical upswings and fall less rapidly during cyclical downswings than real national income as we currently define it.

7. You would expect that a "gold rush," in the form of panning for gold, occurred during the Great Depression of the 1930s.

8. By self-selection the wage that emigrants from Ireland to America get in America are likely to be higher than the wages their distant cousins could get in America if they, too, emigrated to America.

9. If the marginal valuation of leisure depends only on the amount of it consumed (and not on the amount of goods consumed as well) and if much unemployment in "normal" times consists of temporary layoffs—known to be temporary by both employees and employers—then unemployment insurance will increase the amount of measured unemployment.

10. At the point of backward bending in the supply of labor, the elasticity of demand for goods is 1.0. (Hint: Use the offer curve, not the supply curve or algebra.)

11. The amount of leisure might rise if the Scottish highlander of Figure 25.3 could work part time at home and part time in the factory, as if he might if the factory were not down in Glasgow but up in Inverness.

12. Taking H to be all hours available, H_W working hours, H_L leisure hours, P the price of the commodity, Q its quantity, and w the wage, the whole income is $wH = wH_W + wH_L = PQ + wH_L$.

13. In view of Question 12, if the income elasticity of demand for leisure hours is ϵ, then the income effect of a rise in w is $\epsilon(wH_L/wH)w^* = \epsilon(H_L/H)w^*$.

14. A negative income tax with a 100% marginal rate will induce some people above the subsidy level of commodity income to move to the subsidy point.

15. A proportional income tax reduces work supplied, even if the reduction in work supplied raises to some degree the wage of work in the market.

25.3   The Choice of Schemes of Payment

Explaining Budget Lines

☐ The various budget lines for helping the poor or taxing the rest are social experiments, not social events. That is, they are the result of explicit planning, not of the interaction of economic actors. Unless the economist can extend economics to the political reasons for the coming of Aid to Dependent Children or of the minimum wage or of the progressive income tax, the economist cannot say much about why such budget lines are as they are. The ambition of a political economy is a noble one, but far from achieved. On the other hand, the economist has readily at hand an explanation for the budget lines that businesses offer to their workers: they offer the budget line that makes them the most money. The one that makes them the most money depends on the character of the workers and the character of the competition for their services. The peculiarities of wage payments, in short, should be explicable in economic terms. The key to explaining them is to search for the mutual advantage in the peculiarity: because both workers and employers must agree on it, both must be made better off.

☐
Explaining Delayed Wages

Pensions, bonuses, stock options, and the like, for example, are budget lines with wages delayed, delayed in order to assure good behavior.

Q: In the seventeenth and eighteenth centuries, many American immigrants were indentured servants (in 1776 about a third of the white population were indentured servants or descendants of indentured servants). The terms were typically that the servant gave five or seven years of service and in exchange was awarded passage to the New World and subsistence while in service. Indentured servants could escape and would be more likely to do so the more experienced they were. At the end of their term, however, they received a grant of land or a cash bonus. Why?

A: To keep them to the terms of their agreement. A servant who escaped received no land or cash at the end of the indenture term. The greater the total pay piled up at the end of the term, the less likely would the servant be to escape. But the passage to the New World (chiefly to the Chesapeake Bay region, incidentally) was a very expensive and early payment to the servant: some decided therefore to escape anyway, though less than would have without the bonus.

☐
Overtime

Overtime pay is another important example of how the wage offer itself is an object of choice between worker and employer. Alan Nagel, who works as a cook, gets $8 an hour up to 40 hours a week and $12 for every hour above 40.

T or F: By having such a two-part system, the restaurant gives Nigel less wages in total for the same work than it would have to give if it paid the same amount for all hours.

A: Nagel chooses the point overtime along the solid two-part budget line in Figure 25.5.

Look at the point straight time, which is on the same indifference curve as overtime. Since the dashed budget line tangent to straight time must have less slope than at overtime (which has a $12 slope), the point straight time must be to the right of overtime. The entire offer curve for straight time must therefore be above or to the right of overtime. If Nagel's employer wants to get the same work out of him as at overtime, he will have to move up the offer curve. But such points involve more pay to Nagel, that is, a higher value along the commodity axis. If the restaurant pays straight time only, it will have to pay Nagel more. In short, true.

Schemes of two-part pay are schemes of price discrimination, and

**Figure 25.5
Overtime Pay Gets the
Employer the Same
Amount of Labor for Less
Cost**

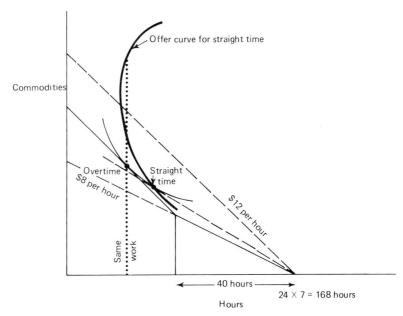

a firm can do better if it can discriminate. The question remains why some other restaurant does not offer Nagel the one-part scheme (straight time) that he prefers. The answer must be that the other restaurant would in fact offer less pay to Nagel in total, for some reason connected with the pay scheme. The discrimination does not actually make Nagel worse off than he could be working for another restaurant, only worse off than he would be if the same restaurant would pay straight time.

**Pay by Time versus
Pay by the Piece**

☐ The alternative to paying people by time put in is to pay them by the piece, that is, by how much they put out. The choice between the two provides the last, best example of the uses of the commodity-leisure diagram. It is generally believed that one will work harder if on a piece rate than on time pay, the argument being that a piece rate gives an incentive to put in the last ounce of effort. If you recognize the parallel to the fallacious argument that a renter is more energetic than a sharecropper, you will suspect that the argument is incomplete. It is.

Suppose that Arcadius Kahan works in an eighteenth-century Russian ironworks. To keep the same axes as before, suppose that it is impossible to withdraw effort from an hour but that it is possible to withdraw hours (the analysis could be framed in terms of effort instead of hours, with similar conclusions). His shirking if he is paid by the day takes the form of cheating on the number of hours he puts in: he agreed to put in 12 hours a day, but can secretly withdraw some of the hours. If he is paid by the piece, on the other hand, his input of hours is automatically confirmed, because each hour results in, say, a ton of iron and he is paid by the ton. It would seem that the piece rate is always superior from the employer's point of view.

Not so. As a first approximation both employer and employee are indifferent between the two systems (unsurprisingly, since both exist, sometimes side by side). The reason becomes clear when the two deals are made explicit. Under a piece rate in making iron, the employer presents Arcadius with a schedule of payments and lets him choose the output. In Figure 25.6, he moves along the dashed piece rate (remember: the "piece" here is just an hour) to bribe.

Under a salary (or time) rate the employer presents Arcadius with the output desired and with his total pay (determined by market competition) and tells Arcadius that he will get fired if he does not perform. In general the negative prospect of being fired works just as well as the positive prospect of earning an extra ruble for the extra hour. Both systems end at the point bribe.

Some minor advantage, not a gross difference in efficiency, explains why one system is in fact adopted over the other. For example, the option of threatening to fire a worker may be more advantageous to the employer if the worker has large costs of searching for a new job—though as usual one must handle such an asymmetrical argument gingerly, because one party to a mutual agreement cannot impose unfavorable conditions on another. The ability of each worker to choose his or her output may be inconvenient to a coordinated enterprise, such as an assembly line or an office. Such places will give salaries, while places that sew collars on shirts will give piece rates. The cost of monitoring output may be high—as in an office, again, while it is low if one has merely to count sewn collars—in which case the more or less vague threat of firing can inspire self-monitoring by the worker personally. And so forth. The possibilities are many. The main point is that the reward of a schedule of piece rates is symmetrical with

**Figure 25.6
Piece Rates Are
Symmetrical to Time Rates
as Rewards Are to
Punishment**

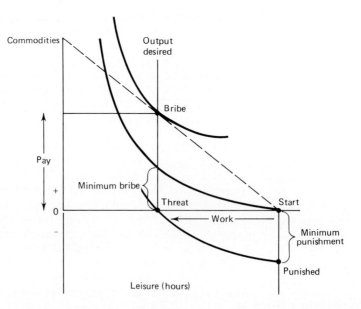

the threat in an agreement for a salary and can achieve the same result. Similar remarks apply to the schemes for worker participation, profit sharing, cooperatives, and so forth: more conventional arrangements can and do mimic their results.

☐   The symmetry runs deep.

Bribery versus Punishment

Q: If an employer has the power to hide Arcadius from other job offers, what in Figure 25.6 is the minimum bribe he can offer to get Arcadius to produce the output desired? If the employer's power over Arcadius is still greater, so that he can take from Arcadius as well as give to him, taking off his hide with a knout if he has nothing else to be taken, what is the minimum punishment the employer can inflict sufficient to get Arcadius to produce the output desired? If punishing Arcadius, like rewarding him, is expensive, how would the lord (for with such powers that is what he is) treat the serf?

A: Look at the diagram. The analysis is identical to that of alternative taxes and subsidies. The indifference curve through the threat point defines how much of a punishment from start is necessary to induce Arcadius to prefer the point threat to the point punished. The lord gets the work he wants. But likewise he could get it by bribery, the minimum bribe being the one of perfect wage discrimination. The lord can choose the carrot or the stick. If punishment is expensive (in overseers to give it or in resentment and sabotage once it is given) then bribery may be better, even for a lord of serfs. The power to inflict punishment does not imply that punishment will always be chosen. The matter is one of economic, and moral, choice.

The government's monopoly of violence puts it in the position of lord of its citizens. Therefore, it too faces a choice between punishment and bribery. For example, in getting soldiers to defend our vital interests in Addis Ababa or Alicante or Antigua, the government can choose to hire soldiers with a wage high enough to get volunteers or it can choose to draft them with jail sentences high enough to get compliance. Gangsters face the same choice: they can get what they want by offering you a good price or by making an offer you can't refuse, namely, to dump you in the river if you do not give it. In competitive markets, by contrast, the range of methods of competing is narrowed to mutually advantageous exchange.

Summary

Budget lines do not come down from God, or from the Office of Management and Budget. They come from the behavior of people, people employing and people employed. The deal that employer and worker make must be mutually advantageous. Thus, a bonus at the end induces indentured servants to stay until the end of their term, reducing the hiring costs of the employer. Higher pay per hour induces workers to work more for less pay than a one-price system would, but most offer some compensating advantage. Piece rates appear at first to extract more work than pay by the hour, but the threat of dismissal contradicts the appearance. The extreme use of the principle of mutual advantage is slavery: here the principle still holds, except that the slave has and keeps zero advantage. Punishments and rewards are symmetric ways of dealing with slaves, or with citizens. The choice between them, too, is economic.

QUESTIONS FOR SECTION 25.3

1. Leisure is a good, work a bad. Redraw the analysis of piece rates versus time rates in a commodity-worktime diagram.

2. Give a diagrammatic interpretation of the following argument: "In the professions of law, medicine and the like, it is the reputation of enjoying a large practice which attracts new clients. Thus a successful barrister or physician generally labours more severely as his success increases." (Hint: Is the budget line as described straight?)

3. Molly McClelland is paid $2.00 per hour for the first eight hours that she gives up from her daily leisure. She is paid $3.00 per hour for any additional hours that she chooses to give up to get more income. When she can choose the number of hours to be worked, she works ten hours per day. *True or false:* Therefore, if a single price of $2.20 per hour is paid for all the hours, and she can choose, she will surely choose to work less than ten hours.

4. The harvest work on each of many quite different fields in a medieval village could be done at the best time for each field "if each landholder enlisted the help of other peasants. . . . [But] each individual would spend much of his time working for his neighbors rather than for himself, and all the problems associated with working for others would significantly reduce the effective input of labor." Comment. The writer offers no evidence on how "significantly" the effective input would be reduced. Is an estimate necessary for his conclusion?

5. In preindustrial societies, such as northwestern Europe in the seventeenth century, the pace of work was slow and many days of the year were holidays. During industrialization, the pace of work quickened and the number of holidays declined; that is, the supply of labor hours increased. This increase has been explained in terms of rising supplies of energy (calories, say) making it possible for laborers to supply more effort.

a. If the total amount of energy, E, is unaffected by the wage, w, or consumption of goods, C,—that is, if it is exogenously given—and if an hour of leisure, H_1, requires e_1 units of energy and an hour of work, H_w, acquiring the consumption good, C, by working at a wage of w requires e_w units of energy, write down the energy constraint below which a worker must operate in C,H_1 space. In other words, write down the inequality connecting C and H_1 (consumption and hours of leisure) in terms of e_1, e_w, and w. What is the slope (i.e., what is $\Delta C/\Delta H_1$ for a given endowment of energy)?

b. Write down the market-wage constraint, that is, the trade-off between C and H_1 when the worker can purchase C by giving up H_1 at the rate w. What is its slope? Plot both contraints on a graph of C against H_1. What do you conclude about the relative slopes of the two constraints if work requires more units of energy than does leisure? Show the attainable combination of C and H_1. If both constraints are binding in equilibrium, where does a worker end up?

c. If wages remain constant and the energy constraint is always binding, what will happen to the supply of labor, H_w, if the amount of energy, E, increases? It is this effect that was mentioned earlier: more energy changes the amount of labor supplied. Does it matter if w increases at the same time E does?

d. Now suppose that energy is determined by the amount of C by the relation $E = aC$. Write down the new energy constraint. What is the new $\Delta C/\Delta H_1$ (the slope of the constraint in C, H_1 space)? Why does $(a) \times (w)$ have to be greater than e_w? What, therefore, is the sign of the slope of the new energy constraint?

e. Graph the new energy constraint in the C, H_1 plane. Include the wage constraint and graph the attainable area. Show how it changes when w increases. If the energy constraint is always binding, what will happen to the supply of labor, H_w? Does the introduction of an energy constraint, even if binding only at low wages (low w), increase or reduce the likelihood that effort will rise when w rises? (Hint: Look at the situation when the energy constraint is binding at low wages and ask whether eliminating the energy constraint would raise or lower the H_w supplied.)

f. What do you conclude about the plausibility of the theory outlined in parts (a)–(c)?

True or False

6. A draft is better than a volunteer army because it is cheaper. (Hint: To whom?)

7. A tax on all wages will decrease the labor supplied by less than a tax with the same yield to the Treasury on overtime pay alone.

26

Capital's Supply and Demand

26.1 The Interest Rate

A dollar tomorrow is not worth as much as a dollar today, because there is a positive rate of interest (the next section discusses the reasons in turn for the positive rate of interest). Because you can earn interest, you will always choose the dollar now if offered a choice between a dollar now and a dollar—*without* interest—a year from now. You could put the dollar now in a bank to earn interest at, say, 10%. The $1.00 would become $1.10 a year from now, bettering the dollar-for-a-dollar deal by $0.10. To enter a deal that earns less than $1.10 later for each $1.00 given up now is to forego interest.

The point is one of opportunity cost. The cost of interest foregone is faced whether or not it comes as a monthly bill with a demand to pay.

Q: Improvements on late-eighteenth-century English farms were financed largely out of profits from farming, not from borrowing. *True or false:* Therefore the rate of interest on borrowing (roughly equal to interest on lending) was not a relevant cost to the farmers when deciding to invest.

A: Whether or not the money came from borrowing, the interest rate measures what the funds could have earned in lending, a use other than investment in farms. When the interest rate is i, the opportunity cost of a fund of $P_K K$ (being, say, the cost of K feet of fences times the price per foot) is $i(P_K K)$. That is, false. Sources of funds are fungible, and the interest rate was relevant. When it was low, farmers would face a bad alternative to investing in the farm and would invest; when it was high, they would face a good alternative and would not invest.

The Full Equation for the Cost of Capital

The annual opportunity cost of investing in a machine, building, or other long-lived thing is in fact a little more than merely the interest foregone, though all the additions to a full accounting are interest like in being rates per year. The question is, what is lost each year by spending $P_K K$ on K machines? The interest $i P_K K$ is lost. But so too is lost the wearing out or obsolesence of the machines: if these take place like evaporation of water, at a steady percentage rate of δ per year on the remaining value, then the whole "depreciation" is $\delta P_K K$. Finally, even if it did not wear out, the machine might increase or decrease in price over a year: if the rate of change of P_K is P_K^*, then the "capital gain" is $(P_K^* P_K K)$ per year, which offsets other costs if it is positive. The whole cost of capital is therefore $(i + \delta - P^*)P_K K$, the term $(i + \delta - P^*)P_K$ often being called the rental rate of capital, abbreviated r. That is, one could rent the machine from a competitive firm at r if r covered in a year the year's opportunity cost of interest plus evaporation of the amount of the machine minus the rise in value of a nonevaporated machine.

T or F: Since the interest rate was higher in the United States than in Britain during the nineteenth century, an investment would have to be more productive in the United States to justify doing it.

A: The cost of capital includes more than the interest rate alone. In the United States depreciation might have been lower (it was not), capital gains larger (they were), or the price of capital goods, P_K, smaller (it may or may not have been). Although the assertion is true other things equal, it may not have been true unconditionally.

☐
Uses of the Idea of Opportunity Cost

A project over the next year or the next month must earn, then, at least the rental rate on the capital invested. Holding some wheat in storage after the harvest in the Middle Ages is such a project. The earnings from it is its rise in price, the price becoming higher every month until the next harvest by the monthly opportunity cost of the money tied up in wheat. As usual, the argument is simply an equilibrium condition. If the price were not expected to rise from November 15 to December 15 enough to compensate wheat storers for the rental rate on the money invested for a month, the storers would remove some wheat from storage on November 15 and sell it. The sale would drive down the price on November 15 and, by reducing the store available to sell, drive up the price on December 15. The price curve could continue to tilt until the slope just equaled the rental rate, at which point further removals from storage would stop. A similar story from the other direction assures that a slope that was excessive would fall to the rental rate as well. Consider, then, the following.

Q: In England during the thirteenth and fourteenth centuries, 1075 pairs of prices of wheat in the same year and in the same village show an average increase of 2.7% per month. What was the rental rate per year? If depreciation (rotting) was 10% per year, what was the interest rate per year on safe loans in the Middle Ages?

A: The rate must be compounded at least each month to get the relevant figure. It is $1.027^{12} - 1 = 37.7\%$. Since the full rental rate (capital gains are not relevant here) is $i + \delta$, the interest rate, i, was $37.7\% - 10.0\% = 27.7\%$. By the sixteenth or seventeenth centuries, in contrast, it had fallen to 10%, a great change in the environment for investment.

☐

The Real versus the Nominal Rate of Interest

The interest rates over 25% in the Middle Ages do not look high when compared with recent experience, rates 20% or higher for the prime customers of banks as recently as 1981. The high interest rates in the late 1970s and early 1980s, however, reflected inflation of prices in general, not the real rate. If prices in general are going up at 15% per year, the price of a sausage machine, say, will rise 15% in the year, reflecting the rising price of sausages and machines. A borrower can borrow $100 to buy a sausage machine paying back $115 in a year simple from the inflation. On the other side, a lender getting only 15% on his money is only just keeping up with inflation. Lenders will require more than 15%. And if the project of buying and using a sausage machine has real productivity, it can earn something real above mere inflation. If the prevailing real something is 4 or 5% (as it is in developed economies nowadays, in contrast to over 25% five centuries ago), then the "nominal" interest rate will be 20%: 5% "real" interest plus a 15% allowance for inflation.

T or F: When countries such as Israel, Chile, and Brazil have annual inflation rates over 100%, you can expect to see interest rates there over 100%.

A: A 105% interest rate in an economy with a 100% inflation is really only a 5% interest rate. That is, the goods you get back by investing goods in some project are only 5% greater, not 105%. Therefore, true. Your inducement to save and invest is the real rate, not the nominal rate. You give up present satisfaction for a future yield in the expectation of earning the 5% real rate.

☐

The Ubiquity of Interest Rates

The interest rate on invested capital pervades a society, no less than does the wage of labor. The price of a future dollar in terms of a present dollar affects any choice to hold assets from the present into the future. For example, it pervaded the market for animals in the Middle Ages, confirming the astonishingly high interest rates revealed in the wheat market. Like holding wheat, the project of holding a flock of sheep for a year must repay the opportunity cost of the money invested in it.

Q: On one of the Bishop of Winchester's estates in the thirteenth century the flock was worth £56 (about 22 person-years' worth of sheep, to give an idea of the size of the enterprise); the sheep required little in the way of care and produced £25.4 of wool, pelts, cheese, and lambs per year. What is the implied interest rate?

A: If costs of caring for the sheep could actually be neglected, then it would be 25.4/56 = 45% per year. In truth, there were some few costs, so 45% is somewhat too high an estimate. But it accords with the finding of high interest rates in the Middle Ages.

☐

The Far Future Is Worth Less

Waiting for an investment to bear fruit, then, has an opportunity cost. For an asset not subject to depreciation and not expected to gain in capital value, the cost is the interest you would get if you lent the money. To put it the other way, in an economy with 10% interest you would be willing to pay only $0.91 for the privilege of getting $1.00 a year from now: $(1.10)($0.91) = 1.00.

Such downward valuation of future income in the presence of an interest rate is called *discounting*. Many bonds, for example, are sold as promises to pay a $1000 on a certain date, say, a year from now. The bonds sell now at a discount below their *face* or *par* value ($1000), namely, at a discount just sufficient to earn anyone who holds them for a year the going interest rate. This is a condition of equilibrium in the market, not a conscious plan; arbitrageurs would rush in or out if the price were lower or higher. At 10% simple (i.e., uncompounded) interest, for instance, the one-year bond would sell for P in the equation $(1.10)P = 1000, or $909.09. As the date of *maturity* approaches, the price will rise. For instance, if maturity is only half a year away the price will be halfway from $909.09 to $1000. On the other hand, the farther away the date of maturity, the lower the price of the bond, because the price has to be low enough to earn many years' worth of interest.

T or F: If the interest rate is 10%, a project that will yield $1000 five years from now will sell now for only $620.92.

A: There are five years' worth of 10% interest to be covered by the eventual rise of the price from P to $1000. Therefore, using compounding between years but not within them, P is the solution of $(1.10)(1.10)(1.10)(1.10)$ $(1.10)P = 1000. Your calculator reduces this to $(1.6105)P = 1000, or $P = 620.92. Therefore, true. A more sophisticated calculator can measure the daily compounding, which is in fact closer to how such prices are calculated. The correct price is a little lower, P in $(1 + 0.10/365)^{5(365)}P = 1000 or $606.60.

The wider point arising out of discounting is that very distant payoffs in economies with very high interest rates are not worth having. We are urged to save oil "for our grandchildren." The policy is dubious. For one thing, our grandchildren may invent ways of doing without oil entirely—uncertainty about the state of technology or tastes in the far future is another, separate reason for discounting it. For another, our grandchildren are very likely to be richer than we are, which means that the policy transfers oil from the poor to the rich. For still another—and the central point here— at 10% interest a dollar of benefit for a grandchild 50 years from now is worth now only P in $(1.10)^{50}P = 1, or less than one cent. To put it the other way, we would have to value each dollar's worth of pleasure by our grandchildren at over 100 times our own (117.4 times our own to be exact) to want to save oil for them. Even at 5% interest we would have to value them over ten times our own, a figure that does not accord with the actual behavior of even the most loving grandparents toward their grandchildren.

□

The Algebra of Valuing Distant Returns

The central idea is *present value*. The right to a stream of income in the future from any asset, such as a State of Iowa bond or a piece of land at Melrose Avenue and Grand Avenue Court, has a price today. The price today can be no more or less than the sum of money now that could earn the stream of income if invested in a bank at the going rate of interest. This sum is the present value of the stream. For example, suppose that a voyage to the Orient begun today will earn $1000 a year from now. If the interest rate is 10% the present value of the $1000 is, as you have come to expect, $1000 ÷ (1 + 0.10) = $909.09. The right to collect the $1000 earnings from the voyage could not sell for more than $909.09 and, if it was quite certain that the $1000 would be forthcoming, nobody but a fool would sell it for less.

The formula being used here (and earlier) is obviously $P = R_1/(1 + i)$, where P is the present value, R_1 is the principal plus yield coming all at once one year from now, and i is the interest rate that could be earned on the sum P used to buy the stream. That is, $(1 + i)P = R_1$: the sum P invested for a year gives back itself plus iP at the end of the year. The formula will prove important in the next section.

☐

The Perpetuity and Its Uses

The formula more important in this section is the present value of a stream of annual returns of $1000 lasting forever. In such a situation there is no repayment of the principal—or, if you wish, it is postponed until the end of time. The return is the net return, above principal. The present value of the stream is $P = R/i$, where R with no subscript is the annual return repeated into the indefinite future. You can see that the formula is true by rearranging it as $iP = R$: if a sum P is invested forever at an annual interest rate i, the owner gets iP—call it R—in return on each New Year's Day forever. Using the formula, then, the present value of $1000 forever if the interest rate is 10% on $10,000.

T or F: A fall in the real rate of interest will increase the value of china plates relative to paper plates.

A: One can pretend that china plates survive forever, paper plates 1 year. The pretense is not too misleading: 20 years, as will be shown in a moment, is nearly forever at high interest rates; an equivalent stack of paper plates might well sit in a pantry for two years before being used up. In any case, the present value of the china is the use (one meal), R, divided by the interest rate, i; the present value of the paper is $R/(1 + i)$. The price of china relative to paper is therefore $(R/i) ÷ (R/1 + i) = (1 + i)/i$. If i is 5%, for instance, a china plate sells for 21 times a paper plate of comparable beauty and usefulness—which does not in fact seem to be far from the truth. If i fell to 3% the ratio would rise to 34.33. That is, true. A fall in the interest rate favors the use of relatively durable things relative to flimsy things.

It will now be clearer what the chapter on the firm meant by saying that the firm seeks to maximize its value. Its value is its present value, that is, what the price would be of the right to collect the profits of the firm forever.

T or F: Since capitalists are mortal but forests (if properly managed) are immortal, capitalism will lead to premature cutting of forests.

A: The reasoning suggests that Gary Walton the capitalist would not care about returns after his death. But Walton can at any time sell his ownership in the forest for the amount R/i, where R is the annual return from proper management, even if Death is at his side. He cuts off the future R's and reduces now the value of his forestry firm if he adopts "short-run maximizing." In truth, what is best for the short run is what is best for the long, namely, maximizing the present value of the forest. Therefore, false. Capitalism is not shortsighted. Quite the contrary: a socialist country that for doctrinal reasons did not permit the taking of interest would be the shortsighted one, for there would be no way for future events to affect present incentives through present values.

☐

The Annuity and Its Uses

The formula R/i gives the price of a perpetuity, a stream of income R per year forever. The formula for any stream of income R_1 in the first year, R_2 in the second, and so on for N years, is

$$P = \frac{R_1}{1+i} + \frac{R_2}{(1+i)^2} + \frac{R_3}{(1+i)^3} + \cdots + \frac{R_N}{(1+i)^N}$$

This is the general discounting formula. The squared, cubed, and higher-order terms reflect the increasing force of compound interest at more and more distant dates. A special and especially useful case is an annuity, in which all the R's are equal, say, R unsubscripted. The annuity formula can be written more neatly as

$$P = \frac{R}{i}\left[1 - \frac{1}{(1+i)^N}\right]$$

which is worth memorizing, so useful is it. Notice what it says: the present value of an annuity is some fraction of the value of the same amount in perpetuity, the fraction being closer to 1.00 the longer is the number of years and the higher is the interest rate. At $N = 20$ years and $i = 10\%$, for instance, the fraction is 0.85; at $i = 20\%$ it is 0.97.

The formula is in fact just a neater way of writing the previous formula, as can be seen by writing out the first couple of terms. For $N = 1$, the formula is

$$P = \frac{R}{i}\left(1 - \frac{1}{1+i}\right) = \frac{R}{i}\left(\frac{1+i}{1+i} - \frac{1}{1+i}\right) = \frac{R}{1+i}$$

which is the formula for discounting one period. For $N = 2$, it is

$$P = \frac{R}{i}\left[1 - \frac{1}{(1+i)^2}\right] = \frac{R}{i}\left[\frac{(1+i)^2}{(1+i)^2} - \frac{1}{(1+i)^2}\right]$$

$$= \frac{R}{i}\left[\frac{1+2i+i^2-1}{(1+i)^2}\right] = \frac{R}{i}\left[\frac{i(2+i)}{(1+i)^2}\right]$$

$$= R\left[\frac{2+i}{(1+i)^2}\right] = R\left[\frac{(1+i)+1}{(1+i)(1+i)}\right]$$

$$= R\left[\frac{(1+i)}{(1+i)(1+i)} + \frac{1}{(1+i)^2}\right] = R\left[\frac{1}{1+i} + \frac{1}{(1+i)^2}\right]$$

Even more tedious algebra shows that it is indeed the annuity formula for $N = 3$ and so on.

The formula has many uses, for example, in illuminating the tragically important subject of slavery.

Q: 1. Slavery was abolished in Brazil in 1888. In the 30 or so years before abolition one could rent a 25-year-old slave for a year in Rio for 330 mil reis, which must therefore have been the annual earnings from a slave. If the rate of return on investments having the same risk were 25% and if a slave lived forever (effectively they did: the life expectancy of a 25-year-old slave was about 20 years more, and with such high interest rates this is "forever"), what would be the price of a slave?

2. As far as their owner is concerned, slaves "die" when they are freed. What do you make of the following pattern of slave prices for 25-year-olds in Rio in the 1880s?

1880:	1223	1883:	589	1886:	54
1881:	1700	1884:	700	1887:	24
1882:	1128	1885:	543	1888:	0

A: 1. Apply the perpetuity formula: $330/0.25 = 1320$ would be the price. Notice that this is roughly the price in 1880–1882 (the 1700 of 1881 reflects perhaps temporary optimism about the future value of slaves, from a sudden rise in the price of their output—in this case, coffee).

2. Evidently people anticipated abolition, expecting it to come in the near future by 1883. Slaves continue to earn their annual rental regardless of whether or not they are going to be freed next year. So the price is the capital value of an annuity of 330 mil reis per year, R, for N years at an interest rate, i, of 25%. Using the formula for an annuity,

$$P = \frac{R}{i}\left[1 - \frac{1}{(1+i)^N}\right]$$

(in continuous compounding it is

$$P = \frac{R}{i}(1 - e^{-iN})$$

which gives virtually the same results), in 1883 the expected life of slavery was the solution of N in

$$589 = \frac{330}{0.25}\left(1 - \frac{1}{1.25^N}\right)$$

You can solve this by experimenting with N's until you get about the right one. Or you can draw on college algebra and use logarithms. That is,

$$N = \frac{\ln[R/(R - iP)]}{\ln(1+i)}$$

or

$$N = \frac{\ln 330/[330 - (0.25)(589)]}{\ln 1.25} = \frac{0.59}{0.22} = 2.65 \text{ years}$$

In 1884 their pessimism decreased—$N = 0.76/0.22 = 3.43$—but they predicted abolition with accuracy. What is striking about these results is that there was no legal announcement that 1888 would bring abolition.[1]

☐
The Price of an Asset Contains an Estimate of Its Future Income

The problem shows well that the price of any asset embodies expectations about the future. Expected returns, as it is said, are *capitalized* into the value of the asset earning them, that is, made into a capital sum that can be bought and sold today. Someone with special foresight could make money by anticipating the future better, forming a more accurate estimate of the value of the asset. The money-making is limited, however, by the principle of entry and exit and its brother, the American question ("If you're so smart, why aren't you rich?"). The corollary here is that public information is already capitalized into the value of the asset.

Q: The price of stock in O'Grada Irish Creamery Ltd. falls as a result of a report announcing poor prospects for sales of Irish cream. *True or false:* The price fall makes the stock a bargain: you can make much money if you buy it.

A: False. The price is low now because the future for the company looks bleak. That is, the market has already capitalized the knowledge of reduced prospects into the price, making the knowledge useless as a profit maker for someone who hears about it late. Holding the stock will now earn only a normal return—as should be expected from only normal knowledge of what the future will bring.

The point is that it is usually foolish to believe that one has access to information superior to that already capitalized into the price. In particular, it is exceptionally foolish to believe that one can profit much from a study of the pattern of movement of the price itself. A successful study would be a money-making machine of unlimited scope. There is usually little reason to believe that you are the first to seek and to find such a treasure.

T or F: Hog prices move up and down in a regular three-year cycle.

A: Suppose they did. Then Paul David, the hog farmer, could make money selling at the peak. But he would have to believe, contrary to fact, that he had more information than did other hog farmers, such as Robert Fogel. The three-year cycle is there for all to see. All would act on it, eliminating it. The only rational expectation is that such cheap machines for making unlimited amounts of money do not in fact exist.

Summary

To wait for a return without interest is to forego the interest. The cost of investing in a machine or other asset is the interest foregone, with depreciation

[1] Pedro de Mello, "The Effect of the Abolition Movement on the Market for Slaves in Brazil, 1871–1888," in Robert William Fogel and Stanley L. Engerman, *Without Consent or Contract: Technical Papers on Slavery* (New York: W. W. Norton, forthcoming).

subtracted and capital gains added. For example, stored wheat is an asset, which must have earned for its holders the interest rate plus the depreciation of the grain. The interest rate involved is a real one, corrected for the rate of inflation.

If the real rate is high, then, a distant prospect is worth little, flimsy things are worth nearly as much as durable things, and economic behavior is short-sighted, though properly so. Whether high or low the price of an asset—a bond or a business or a slave—embodies an opinion about the future, capturable in precise equations for discounted value. Only abnormal knowledge of the future can earn an abnormal return.

QUESTIONS FOR SECTION 26.1

1. The period of the French Wars (1793–1815 with interruptions) witnessed a large number of "enclosures" (expensive projects of agricultural improvement) in England. Yet interest rates rose up from 4% before the wars to $5\frac{1}{2}$% during them, leading some historians to doubt that interest rates had much to do with the decision to enclose. The rate of inflation rose from zero before to $2\frac{1}{2}$% during the wars. Are the historians' doubts well founded?

2. Why were American railways flimsy and British railways not in the nineteenth century?

3. Slave prices in the United States rose during the 1850s. Did slaveowners anticipate emancipation?

4. Most emancipation of slaves in the North was gradual, freeing not the slaves but the children of slaves and often freeing the children only after some long period of "apprenticeship" (28 years of age in the Pennsylvania law of 1780, for instance). The owner of a female slave owned her children. Explain, in view of interest rates of 5 to 10%, why you are not surprised to learn that such emancipation cost slaveowners only a few percent of the value of their slaves.

5. News item, *The New York Times,* December 2, 1973, under the headline "Australia Again Bars Export of Her Prized Merino Rams": "The Australian Merino is considered the top wool-producer in the world as result of more than a century of intensive selective breeding. In the current situation, with exports allowed, a fine stud Merino may sell for more than $10,000 and some have brought many times that sum in auctions. Merino-raisers oppose export of the studs in the belief that increasing the number abroad would undercut the Australian wool market. Some experts dispute this, however." As an expert in economic analysis, if not in sheep raising, dispute this. In particular, would it be reasonable for specialized Merino *raisers* to oppose exports?

True or False

6. Since modern corporations finance much of their investment from their own earnings, not from issues of bonds, the interest rate is irrelevant to their decisions.

7. The cost of capital is the same in Lahore and in Cleveland when the interest rates are equal.

26.2 Supply and Demand Curves

☐

***Some Capital
Controversies***

The theory of interest is a theory of demand for capital, where "capital" is the mass of long-lived and reproducible implements of production such as ships, roads, machines, educations, and houses. Materials, such as coal and cloth, are implements but are short lived. Laborers are not implements because they own themselves. Land is not reproducible. An investor in capital wants to know what its rate of return will be, in order to choose whether to invest in it or to save the trouble and invest in a bond. The rate of return expresses the marginal productivity of capital. Just as a laborer should be hired to dig a ditch if his marginal product in that activity is greater than his wage (which is his marginal product elsewhere), so too a machine should be built if its marginal product is greater than its opportunity cost. You can draw a demand curve for capital as you draw one for labor.

Among the most controversial assertions in economic thinking is the assertion that capital has a demand curve like other things and that the interest rate is related to its price. The violence of the controversy suggests that something more than mere logic or fact is involved. What is involved is a metaphor describing the economy, and economists have not learned to argue quietly about metaphors. Without ways of arguing about the accuracy or aptness of a metaphor, the economist has been reduced to the primitive conviction that those who do not see that his or her metaphor for "capital" is just like the economy is surely a fool and probably a villain.

The simplest possible metaphor is elaborated here. You are warned to rely on it as one would on the assertion that the age from 1300 to 1600 was a "rebirth" or that the orbit of the moon around the earth is an "ellipse" or that a Grecian urn is an "unravish'd bride of quietness, a foster-child of silence and slow time." Fortunately, less hinges on the literal truth of the capital metaphor than on the truth of these.

☐

A Seminal Diagram

The metaphor is contained in the definition of the axes of a diagram of present grain plotted against future grain shown in Figure 26.1. You will be asked in a moment to believe that the axes can represent all consumption possibilities for the economy in the present and future. In the meantime, the story of grain is entirely cogent. The curve that looks like a production possibility curve is just that: present grain can be put back into the ground as seed to yield more grain next year. Notice in particular that the investment of seed yields diminishing returns. The seed can be viewed as capital, K, in a production function relating output next year, Q_{t+1}, to inputs of capital and labor, L_t, this year: $Q_{t+1} = F(L_t, K_t)$. If one were portraying the whole economy, L_t would be fixed by population, and returns might diminish both with respect to capital and with respect to scale; if portraying one small sector, L_t would be varied optimally to match the rise in K_t, and only

Figure 26.1
The Interest Rate Brings
the Marginal Product of
Capital into Equality with
the Value of Future
Relative to Present
Consumption

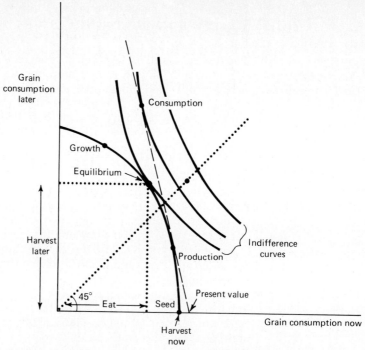

A society organizing its present and future consumption as well as it can will pick point equilibrium, where the slope of the production possibility curve (the marginal product of capital) is equal to the slope of the future/present indifference curve (the rate of time discount). An individual with the same objective can move outside the production possibility curve by trading along the dashed line of market borrowing and lending.

diminishing returns to scale could produce the bulge in the curve. In any event the slope of the curve is the marginal product of capital: it is the change in output caused by diverting some present consumption to investment in seed capital. It is in the same units as the interest rate plus 1: if the marginal bushel in seed now yields 1.15 bushels later, the return is 15%.

The other curves are of course indifference curves between present and future consumption. Their slope is impatience, known as the rate of time discount or time preference. If Ginalie Swaim's bushel now were just as good for her as her bushel later, she would exhibit zero time preference; her rate of time discount, which is the slope of the curve, would be 1.00. If on the other hand she required 1.10 bushels later to offset a loss of 1.00 bushels now, her rate of time preference (also analogous to an interest rate) would be 10% and the time discount would be 1.10.

If Swaim faced a marginal product of capital of 1.15 and a time discount of 1.10, she would want to invest more in seed. As she did so the marginal product would fall and the time discount rise, until at equilibrium they were equal. At equilibrium she has maximized her utility. In the usual fashion, it would be easy to draw below the present diagram a pair of supply and demand curves that were the slopes of the two curves and that intersected at their own equilibrium. The supply of and demand for capital would be equal at some slope, measured in units of 1 plus the interest rate. The standard theory of interest says essentially this: that the tastes for present as against future goods interact with the technology of producing future goods from present goods to determine the price of future goods in terms of present goods, namely, the rate of interest.

☐ **The Seeds of Growth Theory**

The point equilibrium has been arranged to also illustrate the core of the standard theory of economic growth. Notice that the vertical distance harvest later happens to be equal to harvest now. If the harvest now did not reproduce itself in the future, the economy would contract. The production possibility curve between later and much later would start with a lower harvest, that is, with a lower income available for consumption (eating) or investment (seeding). On the other hand, if the harvest later exceeded the harvest now, as it does at the point growth, the economy would enlarge in each period. The enlargement contains the seeds (as it were) of its own demise. As the production possibility curves move outward, the growth point moves closer to equilibrium, reaching it sometime in the future. The capital stock stops growing, and income stops rising, a condition known as the steady state.

☐ **Borrowing and Lending at Market Interest Rates**

The economy as a whole must of course stay on its production possibility curve. But a single person can trade outside it, just as a single country can exchange wine for cloth. If the interest rate is high enough, for instance, the person will be able to produce at point production, putting a little seed into the ground and loaning a lot of it at the high interest rate (which will be someone else's rate of time discount or marginal product of seed). Swaim will be able to have the combination consumption of grain eating now and grain available for eating later. If the interest rate were lower than the slope at equilibrium, she would be on the borrowing instead of the lending side: she would invest much seed herself in the ground, borrowing along the line of market interest to get back to a point of higher consumption now and lower later. The bankers would give her a grub stake.

☐ **Uses of the Idea of Capital: Theoretical Points**

If you accept the diagram as a metaphor of society, then it finishes the tale of the distribution of income by marginal product. Taste and technology determine the interest rate and how fast capital grows; the interest rate (plus depreciation) multiplied by the price of capital goods (grain here: otherwise, buildings, machines, education) determines the rental on capital. In short, markets determine the incomes of capitalists as well as of laborers and landlords.

The uncontroversial use of the idea is simply as a convenient summary of scarcity over time: you must, alas, abstain a little from consumption now if you wish to consume anything later; and the amount of abstention, if you are wise, maximizes the present value of your plan of production. Look back again at the diagram. The point production is the best possible in a world with an interest rate equal to the slope of the dashed line minus 1. Notice the point at which the dashed line cuts the horizontal axis. It is the present value of the production plan. Choosing any other production plan would get lower present value, because a line through the plan and parallel to the dashed line would intersect the horizontal axis at a smaller value.

Notice that the borrowing and lending line separates the decision of how to invest from the decision of how to consume. The proposition is known as the *separation theorem;* all it says is that a given slope to the market line determines the production point and also determines the consumption point; the two decisions are independent of each other. Michael Edelstein the farmer makes his decision of how much to invest in seed, machinery, and storage bins by choosing the investment (i.e., production) plan that maximizes the present value of his farm at the going interest rate. Having done this he has maximized his wealth—"wealth" being the present value of all one's prospects and assets. He can then move along the market line of borrowing and lending out to wherever he is happiest. If the capital market (i.e., the borrowing and lending market) were so poorly developed that he did not have access to a dashed line, he would be forced back into producing in each year exactly what he consumes, just as a country burdened by tariffs or transport costs is forced back into autarky. The utility gain from the capital market is the move from the point equilibrium to the point consumption.

☐ The rule of maximizing present value applies to all business decisions.

The Rule of Investment: Maximize Net Present Value

T or F: Because it pays back in one year rather than in two, a project costing $1000 now and yielding $2000 and zero in the next two years is better at a 10% interest rate than another project costing $1000 now and yielding $500 and $1700.

A: Calculate the present value of the returns. The first project has a present value of $R_1/(1 + i) = \$2000/1.10 = \$1818$. The second has a present value of $R_1/(1 + i) + R_2/(1 + i)^2 = \$500/1.10 + \$1700/(1.10)(1.10) = \$455 + \$1405 = \$1860$. That is, false. The businesswoman who chooses the second project gets higher wealth than from the first, by $\$1860 - \$1818 = \$42$, enough for a decent business dinner for one in New York City. The general point is that the criterion of payback, though commonly used, is irrelevant.

The wise businesswoman will in fact do both projects if they are not mutually exclusive, because both increase her wealth. Both cost only $1000 now but give present values now of $1818 and $1860. Good deals. The argument can be taken further. She should do all projects that have a net present value greater than their present cost, or, to put it another way, she should do all projects that add to her wealth.

A somewhat backhanded way of satisfying the criterion is to find the interest rate, i, that brings the present value of the stream of benefits into equality with the present value of the stream of costs. The rate is called the *internal rate of return*. For example, for the second project it is the i that solves

$$\text{Present value of costs} = \$1000 = \frac{\$500}{(1+i)} + \frac{\$1700}{(1+i)^2}$$

$$= \text{present value of benefits}$$

The procedure for solving a quadratic equation learned in high school and since forgotten says that you first put the equation in standard form, $1000i^2 + 1500i - 1200 = 0$, then apply the forgotten formula to find that $i = -62\%$. When you have recovered from your surprise that an apparently desirable project has a large negative rate of return, you will remember that quadratic equations have two roots. The other is 112%. You will leave the exercise satisfied that a project earning 112% is worth doing when the opportunity cost of the funds is 10%, but a little wary of a technique so heavy in algebra that you cannot do it and so wide open to absurd results. Your wariness is justified: stick to present values.

The most engaging use of the economics of investment is to understand investment in human skills, for example, your own.

T or F: Since their present incomes are low, college students are poor.

A: Their present value—their wealth—is high, higher than that of many people of similar age who cannot go to college and higher even than most older people who did not go. The students are at present investing, but that their consumption now is low now does not mean that it will be low later; quite the contrary. Therefore, false.

T or F: In view of the question just answered, low tuitions at state universities are subsidies of the rich (the students) by the poor (the taxpayers).

A: True.[2]

Someone getting an education or learning skills as an apprentice or running 15 minutes three times a week is investing, investing in human capital. The very idea has been fruitful.

T or F: If education is painful, one will buy less of it than will maximize one's wealth.

A: The whole demand curve for years of education is the vertical sum of the marginal valuation of it as investment and the marginal valuation of it

---

[2] See Armen Alchian, "The Economic and Social Impact of Free Tuition," *New Individualist Review* 5 (Winter 1968): 42–52, reprinted in his *Economic Forces at Work* (Indianapolis, Ind.: Liberty Press, 1977), highly recommended.

as consumption. A given rising curve of opportunity cost for each successive year intersects with the summed curves at a number of years lower than the years that would maximize wealth (namely, the years implied by the marginal valuation of investment alone).

Another example of this sort of reasoning is:

T or F: It will never pay an employer to pay for the training of workers if after completing the training the workers can move to another employer.

A: If the training is specific to this one employer, it is trivially false. Telling your employees the location of the bathrooms in your plant does not raise their value to other employers. If the training is general and *does* make the employee more valuable to other employers, the employee will recognize this. The employee will be willing to work for a wage lower than his or her current marginal product in the plant in which he or she is acquiring the education. In other words, the employer is acting as a schoolmaster and is paid for this service the difference between the employee's current marginal product and the (lower) wage paid. That is, false.

The metaphor of investment in human capital is itself derived from the metaphor of capital. But it, like capital, is a powerful one.

Summary

The idea of capital contains many puzzles, none of which have been discussed here. The image of capital accumulation as an investment of seed avoids the puzzles and keeps what is worthwhile in the story. What is most worthwhile is the notion that future consumption requires a sacrifice of some present consumption, that is, savings and investment. The best way of making the sacrifice is the way that maximizes the present value of production, for this way enlarges most the opportunities for consumption. A market line of borrowing and lending separates the decision of how to consume from the decision of how to produce. Any capitalist will do well to maximize present value, which is to say to maximize wealth. And workers can be seen as capitalists of labor, unable to sell their capitalized value (even voluntary slavery is illegal) but able nonetheless to augment it by investment and to borrow on its promise. The theory of labor and of capital are at bottom united.

QUESTIONS FOR SECTION 26.2

1. Prove diagrammatically that the growth process described in the text converges to a point of tangency such as the point equilibrium. (Hint: Use a compass to plot each successive harvest later back onto the harvest now axis, starting a new production possibility curve; use roughly parallel production possibility and indifference curves.)

2. The European Common Market announces a temporary one-month experiment in free trade for meat; this announcement increases the price of meat in Argentina and increases the quantity sold. Next month it makes the free trade permanent, to last by law for at least 15 years; *this* announcement further increases the price of meat in Argentina but *de*creases this year's quantity sold. What is happening?

True or False

3. If the rate of interest at which Paul Uselding can borrow is sufficiently above the rate at which he can lend, he will stay at the autarkic equilibrium.

4. If Eric Jones expects his future income to be larger than his present income, Jones will always save.

5. That human capital cannot be sold, or even partially precommitted at a far future date, will lead to underinvestment in it.

6. It can be argued that the exemption for students in college from the (now defunct) military draft in the United States would in the long run help those who did not go to college by changing the distribution of income.

7. If today or at any time in the next ten years you can make an investment of $1000 that will yield a return of $2718.52 ten years from now (in 1885), then you will make the investment now rather than later only if the interest rate is below 10%.

□ *Index*